Pages listed are first occurrences.

Topography of a bird

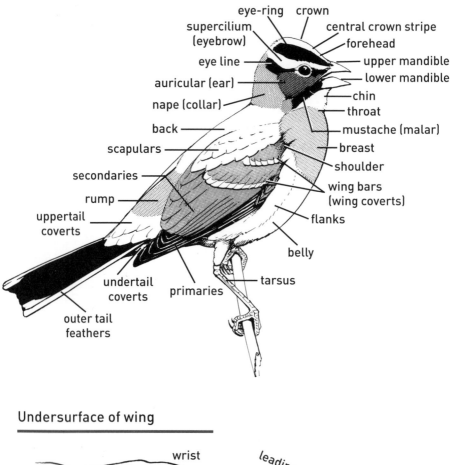

- eye-ring
- crown
- supercilium (eyebrow)
- central crown stripe
- forehead
- eye line
- upper mandible
- auricular (ear)
- lower mandible
- nape (collar)
- chin
- back
- throat
- scapulars
- mustache (malar)
- secondaries
- breast
- rump
- shoulder
- uppertail coverts
- wing bars (wing coverts)
- flanks
- belly
- undertail coverts
- primaries
- tarsus
- outer tail feathers

Undersurface of wing

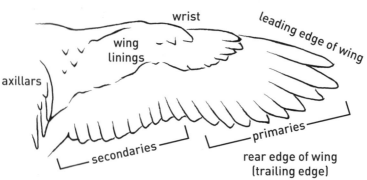

- wrist
- leading edge of wing
- wing linings
- axillars
- secondaries
- primaries
- rear edge of wing (trailing edge)

On the upper surface of the secondaries, some waterfowl have a bright-colored patch, called a *speculum*.

PETERSON FIELD GUIDE TO

BIRDS OF
NORTH AMERICA

PETERSON FIELD GUIDE TO
BIRDS OF NORTH AMERICA

SECOND EDITION

Roger Tory Peterson

WITH CONTRIBUTIONS FROM

Michael DiGiorgio

Paul Lehman

Peter Pyle

Larry Rosche

HOUGHTON MIFFLIN HARCOURT
BOSTON   NEW YORK   2020

For information about permission to reproduce selections from this book,
write to trade.permissions@hmhco.com or to Permissions, Houghton Mifflin Harcourt
Publishing Company, 3 Park Avenue, 19th Floor, New York, New York 10016.

hmhbooks.com

PETERSON FIELD GUIDES and PETERSON FIELD GUIDE SERIES
are registered trademarks of Houghton Mifflin Harcourt Publishing Company.

Library of Congress Cataloging-in-Publication Data

Names: Peterson, Roger Tory, 1908–1996, author.
Title: Peterson field guide to birds of North America / Roger Tory Peterson;
with contributions from Michael DiGiorgio, Paul Lehman, Peter Pyle, Larry Rosche.
Description: Second edition. | Boston : Houghton Mifflin Harcourt, 2019.
Series: Peterson field guides | Includes index.
Identifiers: LCCN 2019041657 (print) | LCCN 2019041658 (ebook)
ISBN 9781328771445 | ISBN 9781328771469 (ebook)
Subjects: LCSH: Birds—North America—Identification.
Classification: LCC QL681 .P455 2019 (print) | LCC QL681 (ebook) | DDC
598.097—dc23
LC record available at https://lccn.loc.gov/2019041657
LC ebook record available at https://lccn.loc.gov/2019041658

Book design by Eugenie S. Delaney

Printed in China

SCP 10 9 8 7 6 5 4 3 2 1

ROGER TORY PETERSON INSTITUTE
OF NATURAL HISTORY

*Continuing the work of Roger Tory Peterson
through Art, Education, and Conservation*

In 1984, the Roger Tory Peterson Institute of Natural History (RTPI) was founded in Peterson's hometown of Jamestown, New York, as an educational institution charged by Peterson with preserving his lifetime body of work and making it available to the world for educational purposes.

RTPI is the only official institutional steward of Roger Tory Peterson's body of work and his enduring legacy. It is our mission to foster understanding, appreciation, and protection of the natural world. By providing people with opportunities to engage in nature-focused art, education, and conservation projects, we promote the study of natural history and its connections to human health and economic prosperity.

Art—Using Art to Inspire Appreciation of Nature

The RTPI Archives contains the largest collection of Peterson's art in the world—iconic images that continue to inspire an awareness of and appreciation for nature.

Education—Explaining the Importance of Studying Natural History

We need to study, firsthand, the workings of the natural world and its importance to human life. Local surroundings can provide an engaging context for the study of natural history and its relationship to other disciplines such as math, science, and language. Environmental literacy is everybody's responsibility—not just experts and special interests.

Conservation—Sustaining and Restoring the Natural World

RTPI works to inspire people to choose action over inaction, and engages in meaningful conservation research and actions that transcend political and other boundaries. Our goal is to increase awareness and understanding of the natural connections between species, habitats, and people—connections that are critical to effective conservation.

For more information, and to support RTPI, please visit rtpi.org.

CONTENTS

PETERSON FIELD GUIDE TO

BIRDS OF
NORTH AMERICA

What Are Its Field Marks?

Some birds can be identified by color alone, but most birds are not that easy. The most important aids are what we call field marks, which are, in effect, the "trademarks of nature." Note whether the breast is spotted as in a thrush (1), streaked as in a thrasher (2), or plain as in a cuckoo (3).

Tail Pattern

Does the tail have a "flash pattern" — a white tip as in the Eastern Kingbird (1), white patches in the outer corners as in the Eastern and Spotted Towhees (2), or white sides as in the juncos (3)?

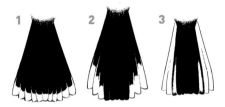

Rump Patch

Does it have a light rump like a Cliff Swallow (1) or flicker (2)? Northern Harrier, Yellow-rumped Warbler, and several shorebirds also have distinctive rump patches.

Eye Stripes and Eye-ring

Does the bird have a stripe above, through, or below the eye, or a combination of these stripes? Does it have a striped crown? A ring around the eye, or "spectacles"? A "mustache" stripe? These details are important in many small songbirds.

Wing Bars

Do the wings have light wing bars or not? Their presence or absence is important in recognizing many warblers, vireos, and flycatchers. Wing bars may be single or double, bold or obscure.

Wing Pattern

The basic wing pattern of ducks (shown below), shorebirds, and other water birds is very important. Notice whether the wings have patches (1) or stripes (2), are solidly colored (3), or have contrasting black tips.

Bird Songs and Calls

Using sounds to identify birds can be just as useful as using visual clues. In fact, in many situations, birds are much more readily identified by sound than by sight. The species accounts here include a brief entry on voice, with interpretations of these songs and calls, in an attempt to give birders some handle on the vocalizations they hear. Authors of bird books have attempted, with varying success, to fit songs and calls into syllables, words, and phrases. Musical notations, comparative descriptions, and even ingenious systems of symbols have also been employed. To supplement this verbal interpretation, there are recording collections available for nearly every region of the world and for individual groups of birds. The Peterson *Birding by Ear* CDs provide a step-by-step method for learning how to develop your listening and identification skills. Preparation in advance for particular species or groups greatly enhances your ability to identify them. Some birders do a majority of their birding by ear, and there is no substitute for actual sounds — for getting out into the field, tracking down the songster, and committing the song to memory. However, an audio library is a wonderful resource to return home to when attempting to identify a bird heard in the field. Many such collections can now be taken into the field on mobile devices. *Caution:* When using recordings to attract hard-to-see species, limit the number of playbacks, and do not use them on threatened species or in heavily birded areas.

Bird Nests

The more time you spend in the field becoming familiar with bird behavior, the more skilled you'll become at finding bird nests. It is as exciting to keep a bird nest list as it is to keep a life list. Remember, if you happen to find a nest during the breeding season, leave the site as undisturbed as possible. Back away, and do not touch the nest, eggs, or young birds. Often squirrels, raccoons, several other mammals, crows, jays, grackles, and cowbirds are more than happy to have you "point out" a nest and will raid it if you disrupt the site or call attention to it. Many people find juvenile birds that have just left the nest and may appear to be alone. Usually they are not lost but are under the watchful eye of a parent bird and are best left in place rather than scooped up and taken to a foreign environment. In the winter, nest hunting can be great fun and has little impact, as most nests will never be used again. They are easy to see once the foliage is gone, and it can be a challenge to attempt to identify the maker.

Conservation

Birds undeniably contribute to our pleasure and quality of life. But they also are sensitive indicators of the environment, a sort of "ecological litmus paper," and hence more meaningful than just chickadees and cardinals that brighten the suburban garden, grouse and ducks that fill the sportsman's bag, or rare warblers and shorebirds that excite the field birder. The observation and recording of bird populations over time lead inevitably to environmental awareness and can signal impending changes. In this edition we have indicated the status of species or populations as threatened or endangered according to the current U.S. Endangered Species List. This is especially critical in Hawaii, where 31 species are listed as Endangered, several of which are likely already extinct.

Please help the cause of wildlife conservation and education by contributing to or taking part in the work of the following organizations: American Bird Conservancy (abcbirds.org), American Birding Association (www.aba.org), BirdLife International (www.birdlife.org), Cornell Laboratory of Ornithology (www.birds.cornell.edu), Defenders of Wildlife (www.defenders.org), Ducks Unlimited (www.ducks.org), National Audubon Society (www.audubon.org), National Wildlife Federation (www.nwf.org), The Nature Conservancy (www.nature.org), Partners in Flight (www.partnersinflight.org), Roger Tory Peterson Institute of Natural History (www.rtpi.org), Hawaii Audubon Society (www.hawaiiaudubon.org), Hawaii Conservation Alliance (www.hawaiiconservation.org), and World Wildlife Fund (www.wwf.org), as well as your local land trust and natural heritage program and your local Audubon and ornithological societies and bird clubs. These and so many other groups are on the forefront of bird conservation and merit your support.

The Maps and Ranges of Birds

The ranges of many species have changed markedly over the past 50 or more years. Some species are expanding because of protection given them, changing habitats, bird feeding, or other factors. Other avian species have diminished alarmingly and may have been extirpated from major parts of their range. The primary culprit here has been habitat loss, although other factors, such as increased competition, predation from other species, and (in Hawaii) avian diseases, may sometimes be involved. Many bird species will face challenges from impending changes in our climate. Species that are in serious decline in North America run the gamut, from Ivory Gull to Lesser Prairie-Chicken and Loggerhead Shrike to Bewick's Wren, Rusty Blackbird, and Red Knot, to Oahu Elepaio, Akikiki, and Maui Parrotbill in Hawaii.

Successful introductions of some species, such as Trumpeter Swan and Eurasian Collared-Dove, have resulted in self-sustaining, growing populations (the latter was either introduced to the Bahamas or flew over from Africa, then dispersed throughout the U.S. and Canada on its own). And a good number of additional vagrant species — out-of-range visitors from faraway lands — continue to be found (such as a Red-footed Falcon in Massachusetts, Rufous-necked Wood-Rail in New Mexico, Chatham Albatross in California, and Chinese Sparrowhawk in Hawaii). Some species that were formerly thought to occur only exceptionally have, over the past several decades, become much more regular or widespread visitors (such as Cave Swallow and Lesser Black-backed Gull) and sometimes even become local breeders (such as Clay-colored Thrush). Such changes in status can be the result of actual population increases or may also reflect better observer coverage and advances in field identification skills.

The maps in this book are approximate, giving the general outlines of the range of each species. Within these broad outlines may be many gaps — areas ecologically unsuitable for the species. A Marsh Wren must have a marsh, a Ruffed Grouse a woodland or a forest. Certain species may be extremely local or sporadic for reasons that may or may not be clear. As noted above, some birds are extending their ranges, a few explosively while others are declining or even disappearing from large areas where they were formerly found. Winter ranges are often not as well-defined as breeding ranges. A species may exist at a very low density near the northern limits of its winter range, surviving through December in mild seasons but often succumbing to or moving south to avoid the bitter conditions of January and February. Varying weather conditions and food supplies from year to year may result in substantial variations in winter bird populations.

The maps are specific only for the area covered by this field guide. The Mallard, for example, is found over a large part of the globe. The map shows only its range in North America and, where appropriate, Hawaii. Species found regularly in both North America and Hawaii may have range maps for each area.

The maps are based on data culled from many publications (particularly from monographs detailing the status and distribution of a state or province's avifauna, as well as from breeding bird atlases), from such journals as *North American Birds,* and from communication with many state and provincial experts throughout North America and Hawaii.

Range maps don't depict how abundant a particular species is within its range. The following list defines terms of abundance used throughout the book. The definitions presume you're in the habitat and season in which a species would occur, but note that this in itself can vary throughout the continent.

COMMON: Always or almost always encountered daily, usually in moderate to large numbers.

FAIRLY COMMON: Usually encountered daily, generally not in large numbers.

UNCOMMON: Occurs in small numbers and may be missed on a substantial number of days.

SCARCE: Present only in small numbers or difficult to find within its normal range.

RARE OR VERY RARE: Annual or probably annual in small numbers but still largely within its normal range.

CASUAL: Beyond its normal range; occurs at somewhat regular intervals but usually less frequently than annually.

ACCIDENTAL VAGRANT: Beyond its normal range; one record or a very few records.

LOCAL: Limited geographic range within the U.S. and Canada.

ENDEMIC: Found only in the described region; here most often used for Hawaiian species.

INTRODUCED OR EXOTIC: Not native; population derived from deliberately released or escaped individuals. These terms can be used for species that are present in limited numbers and may or may not be breeding, or for well-established species such as House Sparrow and European Starling.

UNESTABLISHED EXOTIC: Nonnative releasee or escapee that does not have a naturalized breeding population, though some may be breeding in very localized areas.

Habitats

Gaining a familiarity with a wide range of habitats will greatly enhance your overall knowledge of the birds in a specific region, increase your skills, and add to your enjoyment of birding. It is unlikely you will ever see a meadowlark in an oak woodland or a Wood Thrush in a meadow. Birders know this, and if they want to go out to run up a large day list, they do not remain in one habitat but shift from site to site based on time and species diversity for a given type of habitat.

A few birds do invade habitats other than their own at times, especially on migration. A warbler that spends the summer in the boreal forests of Canada might be seen, on its journey through the southern U.S., in a palm, or in coastal scrub. In cities, migrating birds often have to make the best of it, like the American Woodcock found one morning on the window ledge of a New York City office. Strong weather patterns can also alter where a bird happens to appear. Hurricanes, for example, can be a disaster for many species. As these violent storms sweep over the ocean, the eye can often "vacuum" up oceanic species that seek shelter in its calmness. Upon reaching land, these normally offshore species are faced with an entirely strange habitat and account for sightings such as a Yellow-nosed Albatross heading up the Hudson River, a White-tailed Tropicbird in downtown Boston, and numbers of storm-petrels on inland reservoirs in the desert Southwest.

Most species, however, are quite predictable for the major portion of their lives, and for the birder who has learned where to look, the rewards are great.

To start, familiarize yourself with individual habitat types. Become familiar with the dominant plant types that are indicators—for example, oak-beech woods, cactus desert, grass-shrub meadows, native Hawaiian cloud forest, salt- or freshwater wetlands and marine microhabitats at sea—and keep accurate records of what species you find in each. In a short time you will have a working knowledge of the predominant species in each habitat, and this will help you with identification by allowing you to anticipate what might be found there.

The seasonal movements of birds at your sites will provide an overview of migrant species that come through at a given time and will be a reference point for future visits during these migration periods. A forest dotted with migrant warblers in spring may revert to relative quiet accented by the repetitive calls of a Red-eyed Vireo or the drawn-out call of a Western Wood-Pewee in midsummer.

Be sure not to overlook cities and towns, where well-adapted species can be found. Peregrine Falcons have shown remarkable adaptability, nesting on strategic ledges in the "walled canyons" of many cities. The fertile grounds for hunting Rock Pigeons and European Starlings seem to suit this raptor quite well.

Ecotones are edges where two habitat types interface—a forest and a shrub meadow, for example. As this is not a gradual change, ecotones offer habitat for species from both of the adjoining areas and are therefore rich in bird life.

The changes in habitat over the years will also affect your favorite birding areas. Fields turn to shrubby lots and then woodlands. Bobwhite, Savannah Sparrows, and meadowlarks may move on, but Indigo or Lazuli Buntings and Field or Lincoln's Sparrows establish themselves. This dynamic is normal in the natural world. However, humankind's alterations to this process have had a great impact. Forest fragmentation is an example. Land development has affected numerous species. Sudden disruptions have a more drastic effect than slow changes, which allow for adaptation. As we have divided up habitat with roadways, range lands, and agricultural fields, we have created a greater edge effect, and this has allowed Brown-headed Cowbirds to penetrate into forest areas where they would not have ventured in the past. They now parasitize many more species than before, and such parasitization has led to marked declines in total numbers of many species. Forest fragmentation has also affected the success rate of nestling fledging by increasing the access of some predators and by altering prime habitat requirements for obtaining food to raise young.

Some species are obligates to a specific habitat type, and searching these areas greatly improves your chances of finding such birds. These include Golden-crowned Kinglet nesting in coniferous woodlands and Kirtland's Warbler in Michigan, which breeds only in jack pine woodlands of a specific height. Even in migration, many species remain faithful to selected habitats, such as waterthrushes along watercourses. Running or dripping water has proven to be an important attractant for migrating land birds, and in areas where fresh water is scarce, a water drip can be a gold mine for migrant warblers and other passerines.

Subspecies and Geographic Variation

Many species of birds inhabit wide geographic areas. The Song Sparrow (*Melospiza melodia*), for example, breeds throughout North America, from Mexico north into Alaska and from California to Newfoundland. In such a wide-ranging species, there are geographic subsets within the population that show distinct plumage patterns and/or song variants. When these reach a point when individuals are recognizably different from nearby populations, they may formally be designated as subspecies by attaching a third, subspecific name to the scientific name of the species. Thus, the pale Song Sparrow of the southwestern deserts of North America is called *Melospiza melodia saltonis,* to distinguish that form from up to 25 other subspecies found throughout North America. The Song Sparrow ranks among the most geographically variable of North American birds.

Often subspecific groups are so distinct that they can be easily recognized in the field by bird watchers. Good examples of this are subspecies within Dark-eyed Junco *(Junco hyemalis)*. With 12 subspecies, at least 5 subspecies groups are easily discerned: the "Oregon," "Pink-sided," "White-winged," "Slate-colored," and "Gray-headed" Juncos (p. 376). For the birder, identification of subspecies can add greater challenges to birding and, when documented, valuable information, especially when subspecies are reclassified to full species status. Such has been the case, for example, with the splitting of Solitary Vireo *(Vireo solitarius)* into Blue-headed (retaining *V. solitarius)*, Cassin's *(V. cassinii)*, and Plumbeous *(V. plumbeus)* Vireos (p. 322). Field studies of Sage Grouse *(Centrocercus urophasianus)* leading to the separation of Greater Sage-Grouse *(C. urophasianus)* and the rare and threatened Gunnison Sage-Grouse *(C. minimus)* prove how valuable these studies of subspecific populations can be. The differences between Bicknell's Thrush *(Catharus bicknelli)* and Gray-cheeked Thrush *(C. minimus)* illustrate how subtle field marks can be between species and why they had once been considered subspecies. The shifting of this line between subspecies and species is ongoing. Recording data on location and numbers can prove helpful in completing a picture of a species' and subspecies' distribution.

In this edition, distinct subspecies that are easily recognized, such as those of Yellow-rumped Warbler *(Setophaga coronata)* and Dark-eyed Junco *(J. hyemalis)*, are represented. When in the field, challenge yourself to discern the subspecies. It will increase your visual and listening skills and add a new level of understanding and enjoyment of birds.

Similarly, the ages and sexes of birds can be identified to various degrees in many species, and being able to accurately determine age/sex groups can add fulfillment to your birding experience. It can also be important in assessing the degree to which less common species are reproducing. In this new edition, we have made an effort to point out every identifiable age/sex classification of each species, illustrating many of them. We have also refined and standardized our terminology, replacing such imprecise terms as "immature" with specific age groupings (such as juvenile, adult, first-year, second-winter, etc.) and, for plumages, we have replaced the labels "breeding" and "nonbreeding" with "spring/summer" and "fall/winter," respectively, to better align with age classifications and because plumage state does not directly equate to breeding state.

PLATES

GEESE, SWANS, and DUCKS Family Anatidae

Web-footed waterfowl. **RANGE:** Worldwide.

GEESE

Large, gregarious waterfowl; heavier bodied, longer necked than ducks; bills thick at base. Noisy in flight; some fly in lines or V formations. Sexes similar. Geese are more terrestrial than ducks, often grazing. **FOOD:** Grasses, seeds, waste grain, aquatic plants; eelgrass (Brant); shellfish (Emperor Goose).

GREATER WHITE-FRONTED GOOSE Fairly common
Anser albifrons (see also p. 22)

25–31 in. (65–80 cm). Gray-brown with *pink to orangish-pink* bill. *Adult:* Has *white patch on front of face* and sparse to heavy *black bars* on belly. The only other N. American goose with yellow or orange feet is Emperor Goose. *First-year:* Dusky with dull pinkish bill; gradually acquires white at bill base and black on belly. **VOICE:** High-pitched tootling, *kah-lah-a-luk*, in chorus. **SIMILAR SPECIES:** In East, see Pink-footed Goose (p. 50) and may also be confused with domestic Graylag Goose (p. 50). **HABITAT:** Marshes, prairies, agricultural fields, lakes, bays; in summer, tundra.

EMPEROR GOOSE *Anser canagicus* (see also p. 22) Scarce, local

26 in. (66 cm). Alaskan. *Adult:* A small blue-gray goose, scaled with black and white; identified by its *white head and hindneck.* Throat *black* (not white as in dark-morph Snow and Ross's Geese). Golden or *orange legs. Juvenile:* Has dark head and bill; quickly becomes white in first fall. **HABITAT:** In summer, tundra; in winter, rocky shores, mudflats, seaweed.

SNOW GOOSE *Anser caerulescens* (see also p. 22) Locally very common

White morph: 25–33 in. (64–84 cm). *White* with *black primaries.* Head sometimes rust-stained from feeding in muddy or iron-rich waters. Bill pink with black "lips." Feet pink. Base of bill curves back slightly toward eye. *Juvenile and first-winter:* Pale gray; dark bill and legs. Dark morph ("Blue Goose"): 25–30 in. (64–76 cm). Suggests Emperor Goose, but has *white throat, dark "lips,"* and *lacks scaly pattern.* Intermediates with white morph of Snow observed rarely. *Juvenile and first-winter:* Similar to young Greater White-fronted Goose, but blacker, feet and bill *dark.* **VOICE:** Loud, nasal, double-noted *houck-houck,* in chorus. **SIMILAR SPECIES:** Ross's Goose. **HABITAT:** Marshes, grain fields, ponds, bays; in summer, tundra.

ROSS'S GOOSE *Anser rossii* (see also p. 22) Locally fairly common

23 in. (58 cm). Like a small Snow Goose, but neck shorter, head rounder (steeper forehead). Bill has *gray-blue or purple-blue base,* stubbier (with *vertical border* between base and facial feathering), *lacking distinctive "grinning black lips"* and with warts at bill base (can be difficult to see). *Juvenile and first-winter:* Whiter than young Snow Goose. Rare dark morph has more extensively dark neck, whiter wing patches and abdomen than "Blue" Snow Goose; hybrids with Snow Goose occur. **VOICE:** Higher than Snow's, suggesting Cackling Goose. **SIMILAR SPECIES:** Snow Goose. **HABITAT:** Same as Snow Goose; often together. Rare vagrant to E. Coast.

GEESE

juvenile/
first-winter

GREATER WHITE-
FRONTED GOOSE

adult

adult

adult

juvenile

EMPEROR
GOOSE

adult

adult

adult

juvenile/
first-fall

adult

SNOW GOOSE
dark morph
("Blue" Goose)

dark morph
(rare)

adult

ROSS'S GOOSE

juvenile/
first-winter

adult

Snow

intergrade
between
dark
and white
morphs

SNOW
GOOSE

white
morph

Ross's

Snow

adult

BRANT *Branta bernicla* (see also p. 22)　　　　　Locally common

24–26 in. (59–66 cm). A small black-necked goose. Has white vent and undertail, conspicuous when it upends, whitish flanks, and band of white on neck. *First-year:* shows smaller neck patch and thin white wing bars. Travels in large irregular flocks. Eastern subspecies, "Pale-bellied" Brant (*B. b. hrota;* casual vagrant to W. Coast), has *light belly, less contrasty flanks,* and usually *two separated neck patches.* Pacific Coast subspecies, "Black" Brant (*B. b. nigricans;* casual vagrant to E. Coast), has dark belly and more complete white band across foreneck. **VOICE:** Throaty *cr-r-r-ruk* or *krr-onk, krrr-onk.* **SIMILAR SPECIES:** Foreparts of Canada and Cackling Geese not black to waterline, and those species have large white face patch. Brant is more strictly coastal. **HABITAT:** Salt bays, estuaries; in summer, tundra. Rare to scarce migrant or vagrant inland.

BARNACLE GOOSE *Branta leucopsis*　　　　　Accidental vagrant

26–27 in. (66–69 cm). Similar in size to Brant. Has white sides and black chest to waterline, strongly contrasting with white belly. Note *white face* encircling eye. Back distinctly barred. Ages similar. **VOICE:** Like Snow Goose, but higher-pitched, doglike barks. **SIMILAR SPECIES:** Canada and Cackling Geese with brown (not gray) bodies, lack barring, have dark faces. Brant has all-dark head. **RANGE:** Casual winter visitor from Greenland and Europe to Atlantic Coast; accidental vagrant farther west. Some reports likely represent escapees. **HABITAT:** Ponds, lakes; grazes in fields.

CACKLING GOOSE *Branta hutchinsii*　　　　　Locally fairly common

23–32 in. (58–81 cm). Recently elevated to full-species rank separate from larger Canada Goose, this species includes the variably sized smaller subspecies *hutchinsii* ("Richardson's"), *taverneri* ("Taverner's"), *minima* ("Ridgway's"; see p. 412), and *leucopareia* ("Aleutian"). Like Canada Goose, shows variable breast color and neck collar. Ages similar. **VOICE:** High, cackling *yel-lik.* **SIMILAR SPECIES:** Told from Canada by smaller size, shorter neck, smaller, rounder head, stubbier bill, and higher-pitched voice. Distinctions between larger Cacklings (such as Taverner's) and smaller Canadas (such as Lesser) can be subtle. **HABITAT:** Lakes, marshes, fields; in summer, tundra. Individuals will sometimes occur with larger Canadas and are usually noticeably smaller and shorter necked.

CANADA GOOSE *Branta canadensis* (see also p. 22)　　　　　Common

30–43 in. (76–109 cm). The most widespread goose in N. America. Note black head and neck, or "stocking," that contrasts with pale breast and *white chin strap.* Ages similar. Flocks travel in strings or in Vs, "honking" loudly. Substantial variation in size and neck length exists among populations: subspecies *canadensis* and *moffitti* ("Greater"), *occidentalis* ("Dusky"), and *parvipes* ("Lesser") split from smaller Cackling Goose. **VOICE:** Deep, musical honking or barking, *ka-ronk* or *ka-lunk.* Lesser Canada Geese have higher-pitched calls but not as high as Cackling's. **SIMILAR SPECIES:** Cackling Goose. **HABITAT:** Lakes, ponds, bays, marshes, fields. Resident in many areas, frequenting parks, lawns, golf courses.

EGYPTIAN GOOSE *Alopochen aegyptiaca*　　　　　Local, exotic

25–29 in. (63–73 cm). Native to Africa, introduced and spreading rapidly in s. FL and e. TX. Small stocky goose, largely grayish to tan with variable *rufous eye patch and lower back;* large *white wing patch;* blackish green speculum. Bill pink with black tip and nostril; legs pink. *Juvenile and first-winter:* Duller than adult, head mostly brown with white around bill. **VOICE:** A sharp, repeated *caow-caow-caow.* **RANGE:** Locally common and spreading in se. FL (Martin to Miami-Dade Counties) and around Houston, TX; escapees and incipient populations in other states. **HABITAT:** Ponds, city lakes, coastal wetlands, golf courses.

GEESE

juvenile/
first-winter

Pacific

Pacific

adult

BRANT

"Pale-bellied"
(Atlantic)

adults

"Black"
(Pacific)

BARNACLE
GOOSE

"Richardson's"

"Aleutian"

CACKLING
GOOSE

"Lesser"

"Dusky"

CANADA
GOOSE

"Greater"

adult

EGYPTIAN GOOSE

SWANS

Huge, all-white swimmers; larger and longer necked than geese. Juveniles and first-winter birds are pale gray-brown. Sexes alike. Swans migrate in lines or Vs. Feed by immersing head and neck or by "tipping up." **FOOD:** Aquatic plants, seeds.

MUTE SWAN *Cygnus olor*   Fairly common, local, introduced
60 in. (152 cm). Introduced from Europe. This graceful ornamental park swan often swims with an S curve in neck; wings often arched over back with ornamental feathers extended. *Black-knobbed orange bill* tilts downward. *Juvenile and first-winter:* Usually dingy, with dull pinkish bill, lacking knob. **VOICE:** Hissing and wheezing sounds. **SIMILAR SPECIES:** Tundra and Trumpeter Swans have straighter necks, blacker bills. **HABITAT:** Ponds, fresh and salt; coastal lagoons, salt bays.

TUNDRA SWAN   Uncommon to locally common
Cygnus columbianus (see also p. 22)
52–53 in. (132–135 cm); wingspan 6–7 ft. (183–213 cm). Our most widespread native swan. Often heard long before seen. All-white plumage and long neck. Bill *black*, usually with *small yellow basal spot*. Eurasian subspecies *bewickii* ("Bewick's" Swan), casual from AK to CA, has *much more yellow on bill* above nostrils. *Juvenile:* Dingy, with pinkish bill variably dark at base and tip; quickly becomes whiter during first year. **VOICE:** Mellow, high-pitched cooing: *woo-ho, woo-woo, woo-ho.* **SIMILAR SPECIES:** Trumpeter and Mute Swans. **HABITAT:** Lakes, marshes, large rivers, bays, estuaries, grain fields; in summer, tundra.

TRUMPETER SWAN *Cygnus buccinator*   Uncommon
58–60 in. (147–152 cm). Larger than Tundra Swan, with longer, heavier, *all-black bill*, which has *straight ridge.* Black on lores wider, *embracing eyes* and lacking yellow spot. Bill base forms *V* shape (rather than U shape) on forehead. *Juvenile and first-year:* Keeps dusky body color later into first spring than Tundra. **VOICE:** *Deeper, more nasal calls* than Tundra Swan, often described as buglelike. **HABITAT:** Lakes, ponds; in winter, also marshes, grain fields. Scarce east and south of normal range.

WHISTLING-DUCKS

These somewhat gooselike ducks with long legs and erect necks are placed in a different subfamily than geese and ducks. Ages and sexes similar. They are named for their high-pitched calls. Gregarious. **FOOD:** Seeds of aquatic plants and grasses.

BLACK-BELLIED WHISTLING-DUCK   Uncommon to locally common
Dendrocygna autumnalis
21 in. (53 cm). A gooselike duck with long pink legs. Rusty with *black belly*, gray face, bright *coral red* bill. Broad *white patch* along forewing, visible in flight. Thrusts head and feet down when landing. Frequently perches in trees. **VOICE:** High-pitched squealing whistle. **HABITAT:** Ponds, freshwater marshes. Casual vagrant well north of breeding range.

FULVOUS WHISTLING-DUCK *Dendrocygna bicolor* (see also p. 44) Uncommon
20 in. (51 cm). Note *tawny body, dark back, pale side stripes.* Flies with neck slightly drooped and feet trailing, showing *black underwings, white band* on rump. **VOICE:** Squealing slurred whistle, *ka-whee-oo.* **SIMILAR SPECIES:** See female Northern Pintail. **HABITAT:** Freshwater marshes, ponds, irrigated land, rice fields. Active at dusk and night. Seldom perches in trees. Casual vagrant well north of breeding range.

SWANS AND WHISTLING-DUCKS

juvenile

adult

TUNDRA SWAN

juvenile/first-winter

adult

MUTE SWAN

adult

MUTE SWAN

adult

TUNDRA SWAN

juvenile

TRUMPETER SWAN

adult

FULVOUS WHISTLING-DUCK

Black-Bellied Whistling-Duck

Fulvous Whistling-Duck

BLACK-BELLIED WHISTLING-DUCK

GEESE and SWANS in FLIGHT

CANADA GOOSE *Branta canadensis*   p. 18
Large, slow wingbeats. Cackling Goose (p. 18) smaller, more Brantlike, faster wingbeats.

BRANT *Branta bernicla*   p. 18
Small; black head and neck, white stern.

GREATER WHITE-FRONTED GOOSE *Anser albifrons*   p. 16
Adult: Gray-brown neck, black bars or splotches on belly.
Juvenile and first-winter: Dusky, with light bill and feet.

EMPEROR GOOSE *Anser canagicus*   p. 16
Gray with white head, black throat, white tail.

TUNDRA SWAN *Cygnus columbianus*   p. 20
Very long neck. *Adult:* Plumage entirely white. Trumpeter Swan (p. 20) similar, larger.

SNOW GOOSE (WHITE MORPH) *Anser caerulescens*   p. 16
Adult: White with black primaries. Juvenile and first-winter grayer.

SNOW GOOSE (DARK MORPH, "BLUE" GOOSE) *Anser caerulescens*   p. 16
Adult: Dark body, white head.
Juvenile and first-winter: Dusky, with dark bill and feet.

ROSS'S GOOSE *Anser rossii*   p. 16
Smaller, slightly shorter necked and shorter billed than Snow Goose. Juvenile and first-winter grayer. Rare dark morph blacker than larger "Blue" Goose.

Many geese and swans fly in line or V formation.

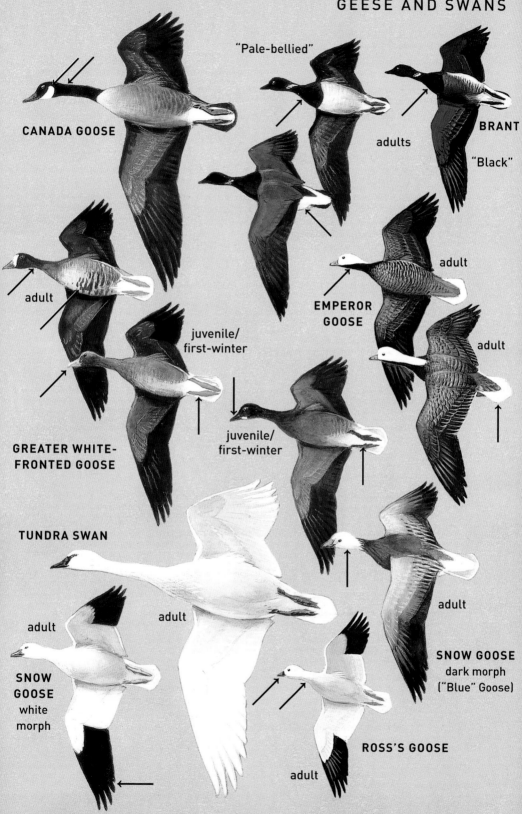

GEESE AND SWANS

CANADA GOOSE

"Pale-bellied"

BRANT

adults

"Black"

GREATER WHITE-
FRONTED GOOSE

adult

juvenile/
first-winter

EMPEROR
GOOSE

adult

juvenile/
first-winter

adult

adult

TUNDRA SWAN

adult

adult

adult

SNOW
GOOSE
white
morph

adult

ROSS'S GOOSE

adult

SNOW GOOSE
dark morph
("Blue" Goose)

DABBLING DUCKS

Feed by dabbling and upending; sometimes feed on land. Take flight directly into air. Most species have an iridescent "speculum" on secondaries from above. Adult males brighter than females in most species; in midsummer, males molt into drab "eclipse" (alternate) plumage, usually resembling females. Juvenile males also resemble females but gain colorful plumage in first fall. **FOOD:** Aquatic plants, seeds, grass, waste grain, small aquatic life, insects.

MUSCOVY DUCK *Cairina moschata* Scarce, local

Male 32 in. (81 cm); female 28 in. (66 cm). Black, gooselike duck with large white wing patch and underwing coverts. *Male:* Bare, knobby, red face. *Female:* Duller, has reduced facial knobs. *Juvenile and first-winter:* Head and neck brown, bill marked dark, facial knobs absent or reduced. Flight slow, heavy. **VOICE:** Usually silent. Occasionally utters a soft quack or a hiss when threatened. **SIMILAR SPECIES:** Widespread domestic Muscovy Ducks have varying amounts of white in plumage. **RANGE:** Native of tropical America (Mex. to n. Argentina). Recent colonizer of lower Rio Grande Valley, TX. Feral populations established in FL and near Brownsville, TX. **HABITAT:** Freshwater ponds and backwaters; wooded river corridors of Rio Grande in TX.

WOOD DUCK *Aix sponsa* (see also p. 42) Fairly common

18–19 in. (45–49 cm). Highly colored; often perches in trees. Speculum steely blue and purple. In flight, white belly contrasts with dark breast and wings. Note also the long, almost square, dark tail; short neck; and squat, large-headed look in flight. *Male:* Striking face pattern, sweptback crest, red coloration to bill, and rainbow iridescence unique. Juvenile and eclipse male are more like female but have reddish bill and muted head pattern. *Female:* Dull-colored; note dark crested head, gray bill, and *white eye patch*; similar female Mandarin Duck (p. 50) has smaller bill, lacks blue speculum, has whiter, less-patterned underwing. **VOICE:** Male, hissing *jeeeeeeb*, with rising inflection. Female, a loud, rising squeal, *oo-eek*, and sharp *crrek, crrek*. **HABITAT:** Wooded swamps, rivers, ponds, marshes.

EURASIAN WIGEON *Mareca penelope* Rare

19–20 in. (48–51 cm). *Male:* Note *red-brown* head, *buff* crown. A *gray-sided* wigeon with rufous-pinkish breast. May have weak suggestion of green patch behind eye. *Female:* Very similar to female American Wigeon, but head is less grayish, brown, or reddish brown. A good field mark in flight is grayish (not white) axillars, or wingpits. **VOICE:** Male, a long whistle, *wheeee-oo.* Female, a purr or quack. **HABITAT:** Same as American Wigeon, with which it is usually found. Rare winter visitor to coasts; casual vagrant inland.

AMERICAN WIGEON *Mareca americana* (see also p. 42) Fairly common

19–20 in. (48–51 cm). Speculum green. In flight, recognized by *large white patch on forewing.* When swimming, rides high, picking at water like a coot. Often grazes on land. *Male:* Warm brownish; head pale gray with green eye patch. Note *white crown* (nicknamed "Baldpate" by hunters). *Female:* Brown; gray head and neck; whitish belly and forewing. **VOICE:** Male, a two-part whistled *whee whew.* Female, *qua-ack.* **SIMILAR SPECIES:** See Eurasian Wigeon. Squarish head and small bluish bill separate wigeon from other ducks. Distinguish from female Gadwall and Northern Pintail by whitish patch on forewing. Pale blue wing patch of shovelers and some teals can appear whitish, but these have longer head shapes and bills. **HABITAT:** Marshes, lakes, bays, fields, grass.

DABBLING DUCKS AND MUSCOVY DUCK

adults

domestic variation

MUSCOVY DUCK

female

male in eclipse (summer)

male

WOOD DUCK

female

male

EURASIAN WIGEON

female

male

AMERICAN WIGEON

SILHOUETTES OF DUCKS ON LAND

dabbling ducks (dabblers)

sea and bay ducks (divers)

mergansers (divers)

Ruddy Duck (diver)

whistling-ducks (dabblers)

GADWALL *Mareca strepera* (see also p. 42) Fairly common

19–20 in. (48–51 cm). In flight, upperwing dark, speculum black, white, and dark ruddy. *Male:* Gray body with brown head and *black rump, white inner speculum* on rear edge of wing. When swimming, often shows as a white square patch near flank. Belly white, feet yellow, bill dark. *Female:* Brown, mottled, with *white inner speculum,* yellow feet, orange sides on gray bill. **VOICE:** Male, a low, reedy *bek;* a whistling call. Female, a nasal quack. **SIMILAR SPECIES:** Female told from female Mallard by steeper forehead, wing pattern, more nasal call. **HABITAT:** Lakes, ponds, marshes.

AMERICAN BLACK DUCK *Anas rubripes* (see also p. 44) Fairly common

22–23 in. (55–58 cm). A dusky duck, darker than female Mallard. In flight, shows flashing *white underwing linings.* Sooty brown with paler head, violet speculum with only thin white trailing edge; feet red or brown. Sexes similar except for bill (yellow in male, dull green in female); females and first-year males with duller speculum. Hybridizes extensively with Mallard. **VOICE:** Male, a low croak. Female quacks like female Mallard. **SIMILAR SPECIES:** Mallard, Mottled Duck. **HABITAT:** Marshes, bays, estuaries, ponds, rivers, lakes. Casual vagrant to West, accidentally to CA.

MOTTLED DUCK *Anas fulvigula* Fairly common

22–23 in. (55–58 cm). Like a pale brownish version of American Black Duck. Note tan head, unstreaked buffy throat, and unmarked yellow bill with *dark spot at base of bill* at gape. Speculum bluish green with narrow white tips. Sexes similar although female has duller bill and speculum and less black at base of bill. Female Mallard paler and with more black on bill and broader white border to speculum. **VOICE:** Very similar to Mallard's. **SIMILAR SPECIES:** American Black Duck, Mallard. **HABITAT:** Marshes, ponds. Casual vagrant north of breeding range.

MALLARD *Anas platyrhynchos* (see also p. 44) Common

22–23 in. (55–59 cm). Speculum greenish blue to blue with broad white tips. *Male:* Note uncrested *glossy green head* and *white neck ring,* grayish body, chestnut chest, white tail, yellowish bill, orange feet. *Female:* Mottled brown with *whitish tail.* Dark bill with orange patches, feet orange. In flight, shows white bars on both sides of blue speculum. In subspecies *diazi* ("Mexican" Mallard) of se. AZ to sw. TX, both sexes similar to female Mallard but have *grayish brown* instead of whitish tail; white bars on speculum narrower; bill colors by sex as in Mallard. **VOICE:** Male, *yeeb;* a low *kwek.* Female, boisterous quacking. **SIMILAR SPECIES:** Female Gadwall, American Black Duck. **HABITAT:** Marshes, wooded swamps, grain fields, ponds, rivers, lakes, bays, city parks.

NORTHERN PINTAIL *Anas acuta* (see also p. 42) Fairly common

Male 25–26 in. (63–66 cm); female 20–21 in. (51–54 cm). Speculum brownish with pale tips. *Male:* Slender, slim-necked, white-breasted, with long, *needle-pointed tail.* A conspicuous *white point* runs onto side of dark head. *Female:* Variably mottled grayish brown to cinnamon brown; note rather pointed tail, slender neck, *gray bill.* In flight both sexes have a *single light border* on rear edge of speculum. **VOICE:** Male, a double-toned whistle: *prrip, prrip;* wheezy notes. Female, a low quack. **SIMILAR SPECIES:** Female has thinner and longer neck and bill than those of other dabbling ducks. **HABITAT:** Marshes, prairies, ponds, lakes, salt bays.

DABBLING DUCKS

dabbling ducks tip up

female

male

GADWALL

dabbling ducks spring directly from the water

female

male

female

AMERICAN BLACK DUCK

MOTTLED DUCK

"MEXICAN" MALLARD
male (female similar)

female

male

MALLARD

NORTHERN PINTAIL

female

male

BLUE-WINGED TEAL   *Spatula discors* (see also p. 42)   Fairly common

15–16 in. (38–41 cm). A medium-small dabbling duck; speculum green. *Male:* Note *white facial crescent* and large *chalky blue* patch on *forewing*. Molting males hold eclipse plumage later in year than other dabbling ducks and resemble females. *Female, juvenile, and first-winter male:* Mottled brown; dark eye line; partial eye-ring; pale loral spot; blue on forewing duller. **VOICE:** Male, quiet whistled peeping notes. Female, a high quack. **SIMILAR SPECIES:** Cinnamon and Green-winged Teal. **HABITAT:** Ponds, marshes, mudflats, flooded fields.

CINNAMON TEAL   *Spatula cyanoptera*   Fairly common

16–17 in. (41–43 cm). *Male:* A small, *dark chestnut* duck with large chalky blue patch on forewing. Adult has *red eye*, which it retains in eclipse plumage. *Female, juvenile, and first-winter male:* Very similar to female Blue-winged but tawnier; bill slightly larger (more shoveler-like), face pattern duller. In flight suggests Blue-winged Teal. Beware juvenile Cinnamon can be more similar to female Blue-winged, with slightly smaller bill and sometimes somewhat bolder face pattern than adult female Cinnamon. **VOICE:** Like Blue-winged. **HABITAT:** Marshes, freshwater ponds, flooded fields. Very rare vagrant to East, casually to coast.

NORTHERN SHOVELER   *Spatula clypeata* (see also p. 42)   Fairly common

18–19 in. (46–49 cm). The long *spoon-shaped bill* gives a front-heavy look distinctive among puddle ducks. When swimming, it sits low, with bill angled toward or in water; often strains water. Speculum green. *Male: Rufous* belly and sides; *white breast;* pale blue patch on forewing; orange feet; dark bill. *Juvenile and female:* Brown. Note large, spatulate, dusky orange bill, blue-gray forewing patch, white tail, orange feet. *First-winter male:* Variable between female and male; can have dark head with white crescent in front of bill. **VOICE:** Male, a soft *thup-thup.* Female, short quacks. **SIMILAR SPECIES:** Cinnamon Teal. **HABITAT:** Marshes, ponds, sloughs; in winter, also salt bays.

GREEN-WINGED TEAL   *Anas crecca* (see also p. 42)   Common

14–15 in. (36–39 cm). Our smallest puddle duck; flies in tight flocks. Green-wingeds lack light wing patches (speculum *deep green*). *Male:* Small, compact, gray with brown head (a green head patch shows in sunlight). On swimming birds note *butter-colored streak* near tail and, on common N. American subspecies *(carolinensis), vertical white mark* near shoulder. Uncommon (w. AK) to rare Eurasian subspecies, also known as "Common Teal" (subspecies *crecca*), shows *longitudinal* (not vertical) white stripe above wing, bolder buffy borders to eye patch. Intergrades are encountered. *Female:* A nondescript, small speckled duck with *green* speculum, pale undertail coverts; subspecies not distinguishable. **VOICE:** Male, a high, froglike *dreep.* Female, a sharp quack. **SIMILAR SPECIES:** Female Blue-winged and Cinnamon Teal slightly larger and larger-billed, have light blue wing patches; in flight, males have dark belly whereas Green-winged has white belly, broader dark border to underwing. **HABITAT:** Marshes, rivers, bays, mudflats, flooded fields.

TEAL

male

female

BLUE-WINGED TEAL

male

female

CINNAMON TEAL

female

male

NORTHERN SHOVELER

male

GREEN-WINGED TEAL

Eurasian

female

male

female

American

CANVASBACK *Aythya valisineria* (see also p. 48)   Uncommon
21–22 in. (53–56 cm). A large duck with *long, sloping head profile. Adult male:* Very white, with *chestnut red* head sloping into *long blackish* bill. Red eye, black chest. *Female, juvenile, and first-year male:* Pale grayish brown; pale rust on head and neck. In winter, often form mixed flocks with Redheads, scaup. **VOICE:** Courting male gives cooing notes; female, a raspy *krrrr*, etc. **SIMILAR SPECIES:** Redhead grayer on body, lacks sloping forehead and bill. **HABITAT:** Lakes, salt bays, estuaries; in summer, freshwater marshes and lakes.

REDHEAD *Aythya americana* (see also p. 48)   Uncommon
19–20 in. (48–51 cm). *Adult male:* Gray; black chest and *round rufous head;* bill bluish with black tip. *Female, juvenile, and first-year male:* Brown overall; *diffuse light patch* near bill. Both sexes have indistinct *gray* wing stripe. **VOICE:** Courting male a harsh catlike *meow* and deep purr; female, soft *krrr* notes. **SIMILAR SPECIES:** Male Canvasback. See female Ring-necked Duck, scaup. **HABITAT:** Lakes, salt bays, estuaries; in summer, freshwater marshes and ponds.

RING-NECKED DUCK *Aythya collaris* (see also p. 48)   Fairly common
17–17½ in. (43–46 cm). *Adult male:* Like a scaup but with *black back* and less distinct *gray* wing stripe in flight. *Vertical white mark* before wing; bill with white ring. *Female, juvenile, and first-year male:* Similar to female Lesser Scaup but with *indistinct* light face patch, darker eye, *white eye-ring,* grayer wing stripe, and *pale ring on bill.* **VOICE:** Courting male a low-pitched whistle; female, a quacking growl: *arrp-arrp-arrp.* **SIMILAR SPECIES:** Told from female Redhead by peaked head, darker crown, grayer face. **HABITAT:** Wooded lakes, ponds; in winter, also rivers, bays.

LESSER SCAUP *Aythya affinis* (see also p. 48)   Fairly common to common
16½–17 in. (42–44 cm). Scaup (both species) have a broad white stripe in wing, shorter (more confined to secondaries) in Lesser. *Adult male:* On water, black at both ends, whitish or pale gray in middle. Bill *blue;* head has "peaked" shape, often glossed dull purple. Flanks and back very finely barred. *Female, juvenile, and first-year male:* Dark brown, usually with clean-cut white patch near bill. **VOICE:** Courting male, a soft whistle; female, a loud *scaup;* also purring notes. **SIMILAR SPECIES:** Greater Scaup, Ring-necked Duck, Redhead. Tufted Duck (p. 50) usually has wispy crest; female darker, more often lacks white at base of bill. **HABITAT:** Lakes, bays, reservoirs; in summer, marsh and taiga ponds. Tends to inhabit fresher-water less-marine habitats than Greater Scaup.

GREATER SCAUP *Aythya marila* (see also p. 48)   Common
18–18½ in. (46–48 cm). Very similar to Lesser Scaup, but slightly larger, with more gently rounded head, bill slightly wider with larger black tip (nail), and *white wing stripe longer,* extending onto primaries. *Adult male:* Head often glossed dull green rather than dull purple, but use this with caution. *Female, juvenile, and first-year male* (not shown): Averages a larger white patch at base of bill and sometimes shows pale ear crescent, which Lesser typically lacks. **VOICE:** Courting male, soft, wheezy whistles; female, a raspy *scaup-scaup.* **SIMILAR SPECIES:** Lesser Scaup, Ring-necked Duck, Redhead, Tufted Duck (p. 50). **HABITAT:** Lakes, bays, estuaries, nearshore ocean waters; in summer, tundra and taiga ponds. Scarce migrant or vagrant in interior West.

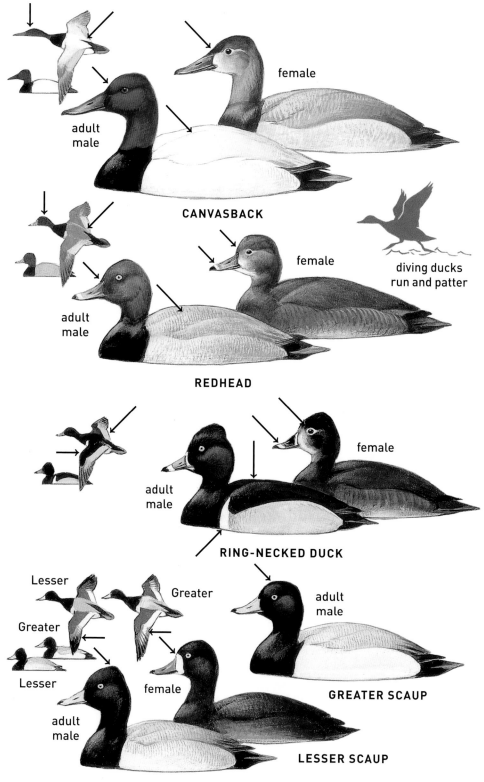

DIVING DUCKS

adult male

female

CANVASBACK

diving ducks run and patter

adult male

female

REDHEAD

adult male

female

RING-NECKED DUCK

Lesser

Greater

Greater

Lesser

adult male

female

adult male

GREATER SCAUP

adult male

LESSER SCAUP

DIVING DUCKS

Also called "sea ducks" or "bay ducks," but many are found on lakes and rivers and breed in marshes. All dive; legs close to tail. In taking wing, these heavy ducks must patter across surface of water to get airborne. Adult sexes differ but juvenile and first-winter males are femalelike. **FOOD:** Small aquatic animals and plants. Seagoing species eat mostly mollusks and crustaceans. Labrador Duck (*Camptorhynchus labradorius*), see plate 9, p. 35, formerly bred in ne. Canada, wintered to NJ; became extinct around 1878.

EIDERS

Eiders are seldom seen ashore apart from breeding. They usually mass in flocks off shoals and rocky coasts and often fly in line formations. Adult males are colorful and show white wing patches in flight; females are brown. Eclipse males in late summer resemble females but have bill colors and upperwing patterns of males. **FOOD:** Mostly mollusks, crustaceans.

SPECTACLED EIDER *Somateria fischeri*   Rare, local, threatened
21–22 in. (53–56 cm). *Adult male:* Boldly patterned head; black below, white above, suggesting male Common Eider, but head largely pale green, with large *white "goggles"* narrowly trimmed with black. *Female, juvenile, and first-winter male:* Brown and barred like other female and young male eiders, but with pale *ghost image of goggles.* Feathering at base of bill extends far down upper mandible. **VOICE:** Mostly silent. Both sexes give calls similar to Common Eider's, but softer. **SIMILAR SPECIES:** Female Common Eider larger, shows broad pale eyebrow, lacks goggles. See King Eider. **HABITAT:** In summer, Arctic coasts, tundra ponds; in winter, breaks in pack ice.

KING EIDER *Somateria spectabilis* (see also p. 46)   Rare to uncommon
22 in. (56 cm). *Adult male:* A stocky sea duck; on water, foreparts appear white, rear parts black; crown and nape powder blue. Note protruding *orange bill-shield. Female, juvenile, and first-winter male:* Warm brown; weak pale eye-ring and thin stripe curving behind and down from eye, flanks barred with crescent-shaped marks. Note facial profile. *First-spring male:* Dusky brown with light breast; bill becomes orange. Second-year male intermediate in plumage and bill characters. **VOICE:** Courting male, a low crooning phrase. Female, grunting croaks. **SIMILAR SPECIES:** Common Eider larger, with flatter head profile, longer bill-lobe before eye; adult male has *white* back, female evenly barred flanks. First-spring male King Eider has darker head and lacks white shoulder stripe of first-spring Common. In flight, note position of white patches in male versus White-winged Scoter. **HABITAT:** Rocky coasts, ocean. Nests on tundra. Casual vagrant well south of winter range; accidental inland.

COMMON EIDER *Somateria mollissima* (see also p. 46)   Fairly common
24–25 in. (61–64 cm). This bulky, thick-necked duck is oceanic, living in flocks near shoals. Flight sluggish and low; flocks usually in a line. *Adult male:* This and Spectacled Eider are only ducks in N. America with *black belly and white back.* Forewing and back white; head white with black crown, greenish nape. *Female, juvenile, and first-winter male:* Large, brown, *closely barred, with pale eyebrow;* long, flat profile. *First-spring male:* Dusky or chocolate with white breast and collar; white areas come in irregularly through second year; bill slowly becomes brighter yellow. **VOICE:** Male, a moaning *ow-ooo-urr.* Female, a grating *kor-r-r.* **SIMILAR SPECIES:** See King Eider. Female scoters smaller, lack heavy dark barring of female eiders. **HABITAT:** Rocky coasts, shoals; in summer, also islands, tundra. Casual vagrant well south of winter ranges and accidental inland.

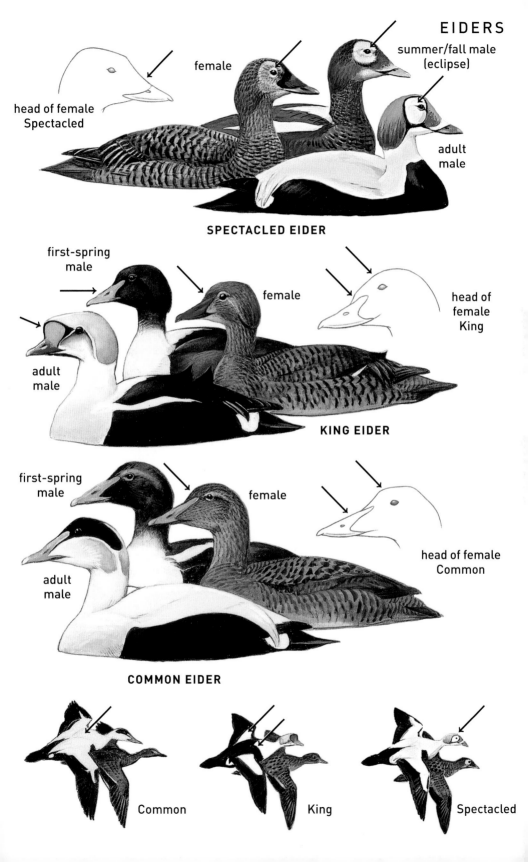

EIDERS

head of female Spectacled

female

summer/fall male (eclipse)

adult male

SPECTACLED EIDER

first-spring male

female

head of female King

adult male

KING EIDER

first-spring male

female

head of female Common

adult male

COMMON EIDER

Common

King

Spectacled

STELLER'S EIDER *Polysticta stelleri*   Scarce, local. threatened

17 in. (43 cm). Unlike other eiders in shape, bill. *Adult male:* Black and white, with *yellow-buff underparts, white head,* black throat, and green bump on back of head. Note *round black spot* on side of breast. As in other eiders, white forewing is conspicuous in flight. *Female, juvenile, and first-winter male:* Dark brown, mottled, with pale eye-ring; distinguished from other eiders by much smaller size and *shape of its small head and blue-gray bill.* Purple speculum bordered in white, visible at short range, suggests a female Mallard. First-spring and second-year male increasingly develops adult malelike plumage. **VOICE:** Usually silent. Male's crooning note resembles Common Eider's but is quieter. Female has a low growl. **SIMILAR SPECIES:** Other eiders, Long-tailed Duck. **HABITAT:** Coasts, ocean. Vagrant south of winter ranges.

HARLEQUIN DUCK *Histrionicus histrionicus* (see also p. 46)   Uncommon

16–17 in. (41–44 cm). A smallish dark duck. *Adult male:* Spectacularly patterned, slaty with chestnut sides and elaborate white patches and spots. In flight, has stubby shape of a goldeneye but appears uniformly dark. *Female:* A small dusky duck with three round white spots on each side of head; no wing patch. *First-year male:* Intermediate between male and female; eclipse male also female-like but can be tinged bluish and shows white in wing coverts and tertials. **VOICE:** Usually silent. Male, a squeak; also *gwa gwa gwa.* Female, *ek-ek-ek-ek.* **SIMILAR SPECIES:** Female Bufflehead has white wing patch and only one white facial patch. Female scoters larger, with larger bills. **HABITAT:** Turbulent mountain streams in summer; rocky coastal waters in winter. Casual to accidental vagrant inland and well to south of range.

LONG-TAILED DUCK   Fairly common in East, rare in West, threatened
Clangula hyemalis (see also p. 46)

Male 21–22 in. (53–56 cm); female 16 in. (41 cm). A small duck except for long tail in adult male. The only sea duck combining much *white on body and unpatterned dark wings.* It flies in bunched, irregular flocks, rocking side to side as it flies. *Fall/winter male:* Note needlelike tail, pied pattern, dark cheek. *Spring/summer male:* Dark with white flanks and belly. Note white eye patch, pink on bill. *Fall/winter female:* Dark unpatterned wings, white face with dark cheek spot, lacks long tail feathers. *Spring/summer female:* Similar but darker. Lacks pink on bill. *Juveniles and first-winter males:* Femalelike but duller. Much individual variation in plumages. **VOICE:** Talkative; a musical *ow-owdle-ow* or *owl-omelet.* **SIMILAR SPECIES:** Bufflehead. In flight, sometimes confused with alcids because of dark underwings and rapid wingbeats. **HABITAT:** Ocean, harbors, large lakes; in summer, tundra pools and lakes. Widespread but rare winter visitor or vagrant inland across N. America and well south of range.

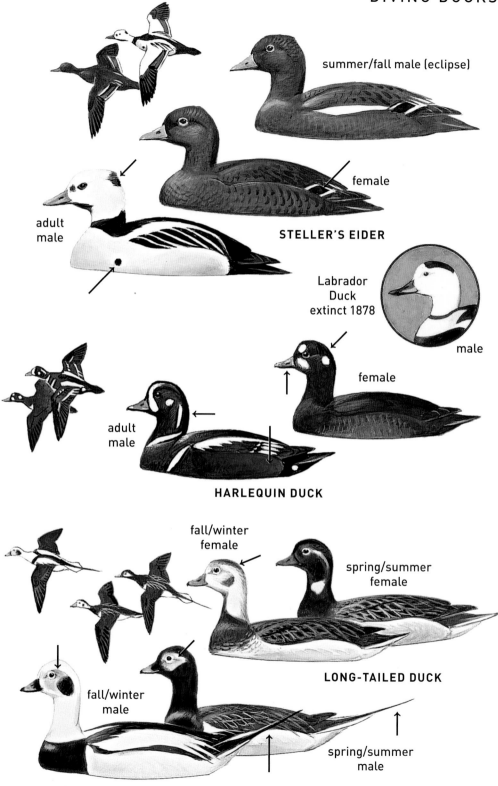

DIVING DUCKS

summer/fall male (eclipse)

female

adult male

STELLER'S EIDER

Labrador Duck extinct 1878

male

female

adult male

HARLEQUIN DUCK

fall/winter female

spring/summer female

LONG-TAILED DUCK

fall/winter male

spring/summer male

SCOTERS

Scoters are heavy, blackish ducks seen in large flocks along ocean coasts. They often fly in thin line formation. They are usually in flocks, either single species or mixed, so look them over carefully. Scoters are usually silent but during courtship and mating may utter low whistles, croaks, or grunting noises; wings whistle in flight. **FOOD:** Mainly mollusks, crustaceans.

WHITE-WINGED SCOTER
Melanitta deglandi (see also p. 46)

Uncommon to fairly common

21 in. (53 cm). White-winged is the largest of the three scoters; bill is feathered to nostril. On water, white wing patch is often barely visible or fully concealed (wait for bird to flap or fly). *Adult male:* Black, with a "teardrop" of white near eye; bill orange with black basal knob. *Female and juvenile male:* Sooty brown, with white wing patch and two light oval patches on face (sometimes obscure; patches more pronounced on young birds). First-year male gradually becomes blackish; bill becomes orange, swollen; underparts bleached white in both sexes of all three scoters. Stejneger's Scoter *(M. stejnegeri)*, very rare in w. AK, has hornlike knob at base of bill. **VOICE:** Usually silent. **SIMILAR SPECIES:** Other scoters. **HABITAT:** Salt bays, ocean; in summer, lakes. Rare winter visitor or vagrant to interior states.

SURF SCOTER
Melanitta perspicillata (see also p. 46)

Fairly common to common

19–20 in. (48–51 cm). Medium-sized, the most common scoter on both N. American coasts. *Adult male:* Black, with bold *white patches* on crown and nape. Heavy, sloping bill patterned with orange, black, and white. *Female and juvenile male:* Dusky brown; dark crown; two light spots on each side of head (sometimes obscure; more evident on young birds), one mostly vertical, the other more horizontal. First-year male gradually becomes blackish; bill becomes orange, swollen. **VOICE:** Usually silent. A low croak; grunting sounds. **SIMILAR SPECIES:** Female White-winged Scoter slightly larger overall, has more extensive feathering on bill, more horizontal, oval face patches, and white wing patch (may not show until bird flaps). Black Scoter has rounder head profile (more like Redhead, whereas Surf Scoter more like Canvasback), lacks feathering on bill, and has silvery underside to flight feathers; female has entirely pale cheeks. **HABITAT:** Ocean, salt bays; in summer, lakes. Rare winter visitor or vagrant to interior states.

BLACK SCOTER *Melanitta americana* (see also p. 46)

Rare to fairly common

18½–19 in. (47–48 cm). The smallest scoter. Bill upturned and not as bulbous as in other scoters. *Adult male:* An all-black sea duck. Bright *orange-yellow knob* on bill ("butter nose") is diagnostic. In flight, underwing shows two-toned effect (silvery gray and black), more pronounced than in other two scoters. *Female and juvenile male:* Sooty; *entirely light cheeks* contrast with dark cap. First-year male gradually becomes blackish, especially in head; bill becomes yellow, swollen. **VOICE:** Usually silent. Male, melodious cooing notes. Female, growls. **SIMILAR SPECIES:** First-spring male Surf Scoter may appear all black above, lack white head patch, and have variable orange coloration to mandible, but note higher-sloping bill with developing black round spot at base. Female and juvenile scoters of other two species have smaller light spots on side of head, not entirely pale cheeks. Female Black Scoter may suggest fall/winter male Ruddy Duck but is larger and found primarily in marine habitats; Ruddy is in primarily fresh water. **HABITAT:** Seacoasts, bays; in summer, tundra and taiga ponds. Very rare winter visitor or vagrant to interior states.

scoters can fly in V formation or in loose clumps

SCOTERS

Surf

Black

White-winged

adult male

female

first-winter/ spring male

WHITE-WINGED SCOTER

adult male

female

first-winter/ spring male

SURF SCOTER

first-winter/ spring male

adult male

female

BLACK SCOTER

diving ducks (sea ducks and bay ducks) raft on water, skitter when taking wing

COMMON GOLDENEYE *Bucephala clangula* (see also p. 48) Fairly common

18½–19 in. (47–49 cm). *Adult male:* Note large, *round white spot* before eye. White looking, with black back and blocky, green-glossed head that appears black at a distance. In flight, short-necked; wings whistle or "sing," shows large white patches. *Female, juvenile, and first-year male:* Gray, with white collar and dark brown head; wings have large square white patches that may show on closed wing. Bill black in males, with some yellow in winter/spring females. **VOICE:** Courting male has harsh nasal double note, suggesting *pee-ik* of Common Nighthawk. Female, a harsh *gaak.* **SIMILAR SPECIES:** Barrow's Goldeneye. Male scaup have black chest. Male Common Merganser long, low, with different bill. **HABITAT:** Forested lakes, rivers; in winter, also open lakes, salt bays, seacoasts.

BARROW'S GOLDENEYE *Bucephala islandica* Scarce to uncommon

18 in. (46 cm). Similar to Common Goldeneye, but bill shorter and "cuter." *Adult male:* Note *white facial crescent,* blacker above; head often glossed with *purple* (not green); nape blockier; shows dark *"spur"* on shoulder toward waterline, less white in back and wings. *Female and first-year male:* Similar to female Common but head slightly darker, with steeper forehead and suggestion of blocky nape, less white in wing. Besides being smaller, bill can become *entirely yellow,* often a good field mark but subject to seasonal change. Female Common Goldeneye often has band of yellow on bill, rarely all yellow. **VOICE:** Usually silent. Courting male, a grunting *kuk, kuk.* Female near nest, a soft *coo-coo-coo.* Wings of both species whistle in flight. **SIMILAR SPECIES:** Common Goldeneye, Bufflehead. **HABITAT:** Wooded lakes, ponds; in winter, lakes and rivers, protected coastal waters. Rare winter visitor or vagrant to most interior areas; accidental to TX.

BUFFLEHEAD *Bucephala albeola* (see also p. 48) Common

13½–14 in. (34–36 cm). Small. *Adult male:* Mostly white with black back; blocky head with *large, bonnetlike white patch.* In flight, shows large white wing patches. *Female and first-year male:* Dark and compact, with *white cheek spot,* small bill, smaller wing patch. **VOICE:** Male, in display, a hoarse rolling note. Female, a harsh *ec-ec-ec.* **SIMILAR SPECIES:** Male Hooded Merganser has spikelike bill, brown sides. See female Black Scoter, fall/winter male Ruddy Duck, Long-tailed Duck. **HABITAT:** Lakes, ponds, rivers; in winter, also salt bays.

STIFF-TAILED DUCKS

Small, chunky divers, nearly helpless on land. Spiky tail. Adult sexes not alike. **FOOD:** Aquatic life, insects, water plants.

RUDDY DUCK *Oxyura jamaicensis* (see also p. 48) Fairly common

15 in. (38 cm). Small, chubby; note *white cheek* and dark cap. Often cocks tail upward. Flight "buzzy." Can barely walk on land. *Spring/summer male:* Vivid rusty red with white cheek, black cap, large and strikingly *blue* bill. *Fall/winter male:* Gray with *white cheek,* dull blue or gray bill. *Female and juvenile male:* Similar to fall/winter male, but duskier cheek crossed by dark line. **VOICE:** Courting male, a sputtering *chick-ik-ik-ik-k-k-k-kurrrr,* accompanied by head bobbing. **SIMILAR SPECIES:** Female Bufflehead, Black Scoter; see female Masked Duck (rare, p. 50). **HABITAT:** Freshwater marshes, ponds, lakes; in winter, also salt bays, harbors.

COMMON GOLDENEYE

adult male

female

BARROW'S GOLDENEYE

adult male

winter/spring female

summer/fall female

BUFFLEHEAD

adult male

female

RUDDY DUCK

spring/summer male

fall/winter male

female

MERGANSERS

Long-lined, slender-bodied diving ducks with spikelike bill, saw-edged mandibles. Most species have a crest. In flight, bill, head, outstretched neck, and body are on a horizontal axis. Adult sexes not alike; first-year and eclipse males resemble female. **FOOD:** Chiefly fish.

COMMON MERGANSER *Mergus merganser* (see also p. 44)　　　Fairly common

24–25 in. (62–64 cm). In flight, singles, pairs, or lines of these slender ducks follow the winding courses of rivers. Whiteness of adult male and merganser shape (bill, outstretched neck, head, and body held horizontally) identify this species. *Adult male:* Note long whitish body, black back, green-black head; primarily white upperwing. Bill and feet red; breast can be tinged rosy peach. *Female and first-year male:* Gray with crested rufous head contrasting with white chin and clean white chest; wing patch on trailing edge. First-spring males can show dark green in face. **VOICE:** Male, in display, low staccato croaks. Female, a guttural *karrr*. **SIMILAR SPECIES:** Female Red-breasted Merganser very similar to female Common. Note distinct cut-off of rusty head and neck from breast in Common; this is diffuse in Red-breasted. Female mergansers might suggest male Canvasback or Redhead, but those have black chest, no crest, different bill profiles. **HABITAT:** Wooded lakes, ponds, rivers; in winter, open lakes, rivers, rarely coastal bays.

RED-BREASTED MERGANSER *Mergus serrator* (see also p. 44)　　　Common

22½–23 in. (56–58 cm). *Adult male:* Rakish; black head glossed with green and *crested;* breast at waterline dark rusty; *wide white collar* between head and breast; bill and feet red. *Female and first-year male:* Gray, with crested, dull rusty head that *blends* into color of neck; red bill and feet. First-spring male can molt in dark green feathers in face and black feathers in back. **VOICE:** Usually silent. Male, a hoarse croak. Female, *karrr*. **SIMILAR SPECIES:** Male Common Merganser whiter, without collar and breast-band effect; lacks shaggy crest. See Common Merganser for female. Common's bill slightly thicker at base. **HABITAT:** Woodland and coastal lakes, open water; in winter, also bays, tidal channels, nearshore ocean waters.

HOODED MERGANSER　　　Uncommon to fairly common
Lophodytes cucullatus (see also p. 44)

17–18 in. (43–46 cm). *Male:* Note vertical *fan-shaped white crest,* which may be raised or lowered. Breast white, with two black bars on each side. Upperwing has white patch; *flanks rusty brown. Female and first-winter male:* Recognized as a merganser by silhouette and spikelike bill; known as this species by its small size, dusky look, and *dark head, bill, and chest.* Note loose *tawny crest.* First-spring male can molt in black and white feathers in head and breast. **VOICE:** In display, low grunting or croaking notes. **SIMILAR SPECIES:** Male Bufflehead smaller and chubbier, with *white* sides. Other female mergansers larger and *grayer,* with rufous head, reddish bill. In flight, wing patch and silhouette separate female Hooded Merganser from female Wood Duck. **HABITAT:** Wooded lakes, ponds, rivers; in winter, also tidal channels, protected bays. Rare in Southwest.

MERGANSERS

mergansers fly with bill, head, body, and tail on the same horizontal axis

saw-edged mandibles of merganser

female

adult male

COMMON MERGANSER

female

adult male

RED-BREASTED MERGANSER

adult males

crest down

crest up

first-winter male

female

HOODED MERGANSER

Common

Red-breasted

Hooded

FLIGHT PATTERNS of DABBLING DUCKS

Note: Only males are described below. Although females are unlike the males in body plumage, their wing patterns are quite similar. The names in parentheses are common nicknames used by hunters.

NORTHERN PINTAIL ("SPRIG") *Anas acuta*   p. 26
From below: Needle tail, white breast, thin neck.
Above: Needle tail, neck stripe, single thin white border on speculum.

WOOD DUCK ("WOODY") *Aix sponsa*   p. 24
From below: White belly, dusky wings, long square tail.
Above: Stocky; long dark tail, white border on dark wing.

AMERICAN WIGEON ("BALDPATE") *Mareca americana*   p. 24
From below: White belly, pointed dark tail.
Above: Large white shoulder patch.

NORTHERN SHOVELER ("SPOONBILL") *Spatula clypeata*   p. 28
From below: Dark belly, white breast, white tail, spoon bill.
Above: Large pale bluish shoulder patch, spoon bill.

GADWALL ("GRAYDUCK") *Mareca strepera*   p. 26
From below: White belly, white underwing, square white patch on rear edge of wing.
Above: White patch on rear edge of wing.

GREEN-WINGED TEAL ("ROCKET") *Anas crecca*   p. 28
From below: Small; light belly, dark head, broad dark borders to underwing.
Above: Small, dark-winged; green speculum.

BLUE-WINGED TEAL ("WHITEFACE") *Spatula discors*   p. 28
From below: Small; dark belly, narrow dark borders to underwing.
Above: Small; large chalky blue shoulder patch.
Note: Cinnamon Teal *(S. cyanoptera)* shows similar wing pattern to Blue-winged Teal.

upper wing of a dabbling duck showing the iridescent speculum (secondaries)

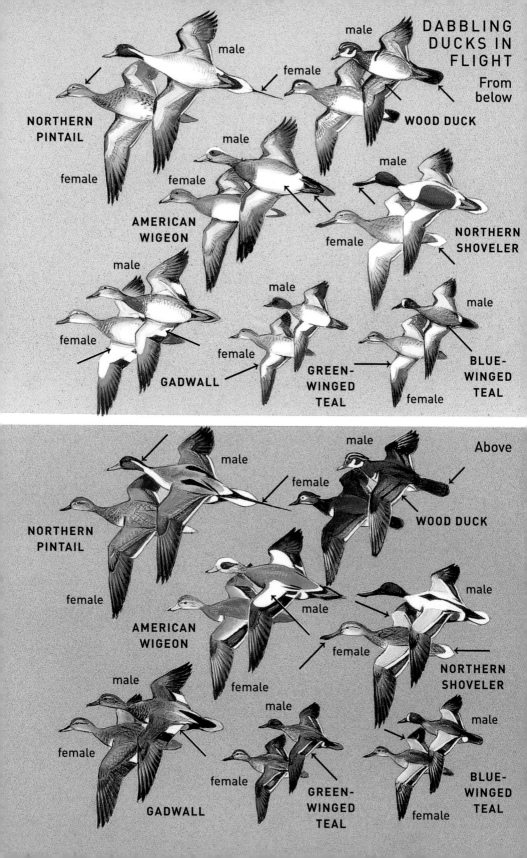

DABBLING DUCKS IN FLIGHT

From below

NORTHERN PINTAIL — male, female

WOOD DUCK — male, female

AMERICAN WIGEON — male, female

NORTHERN SHOVELER — male, female

GADWALL — male, female

GREEN-WINGED TEAL — male, female

BLUE-WINGED TEAL — male, female

Above

NORTHERN PINTAIL — male, female

WOOD DUCK — male

AMERICAN WIGEON — male, female

NORTHERN SHOVELER — male, female

GADWALL — male, female

GREEN-WINGED TEAL — male, female

BLUE-WINGED TEAL — male, female

FLIGHT PATTERNS of
DABBLING DUCKS and MERGANSERS

Note: Only males are described below. Although most females are unlike the males, their wing patterns are quite similar. Mergansers have a distinctive flight silhouette. The names in parentheses are common nicknames used by hunters.

MALLARD ("GREENHEAD") *Anas platyrhynchos*   p. 26
From below: Dark chest, light belly, white neck ring, white tail.
Above: Dark head, neck ring, two white borders on bluish speculum.

AMERICAN BLACK DUCK ("REDLEG") *Anas rubripes*   p. 26
From below: Dark body, white underwing linings.
Above: Dark body, paler head, purplish speculum lacks forward border.

FULVOUS WHISTLING-DUCK *Dendrocygna bicolor*   p. 20
From below: Tawny, with blackish underwing linings.
Above: Dark, unpatterned wings; white band on rump.

COMMON MERGANSER ("SAWBILL") *Mergus merganser*   p. 40
From below: Merganser shape; outstretched neck, dark head, white body, white underwing linings.
Above: Merganser shape; white chest, large white wing patches.

RED-BREASTED MERGANSER ("SHELDRAKE") *Mergus serrator*   p. 40
From below: Merganser shape; outstretched neck; dark chest band, white collar.
Above: Merganser shape; dark chest, large white wing patches.

HOODED MERGANSER ("HOODIE") *Lophodytes cucullatus*   p. 40
From below: Merganser shape; dusky underwing linings.
Above: Merganser shape; small white wing patches.

DABBLING DUCKS AND MERGANSERS IN FLIGHT

From below

MALLARD
male
female

AMERICAN BLACK DUCK

FULVOUS WHISTLING-DUCK

male
female
COMMON MERGANSER

male
female
RED-BREASTED MERGANSER

mergansers fly on a horizontal axis

male
female
HOODED MERGANSER

Above

MALLARD
male
female

AMERICAN BLACK DUCK

FULVOUS WHISTLING-DUCK

male
female
COMMON MERGANSER

male
female
RED-BREASTED MERGANSER

male
female
HOODED MERGANSER

FLIGHT PATTERNS of DIVING DUCKS

Note: Only adult males are described below. The names in parentheses are common nicknames used by hunters.

LONG-TAILED DUCK ("KAKAWI") *Clangula hyemalis*   p. 34
From below: Dark unpatterned wings, white belly.
Above: Dark unpatterned wings, much white on body.

HARLEQUIN DUCK ("BLUEDUCK") *Histrionicus histrionicus*   p. 34
From below: Solid dark below, white head spots, small bill.
Above: Dark with white marks, small bill, long tail.

SURF SCOTER ("SKUNKHEAD") *Melanitta perspicillata*   p. 36
From below: Black body, white head patches (not readily visible from below), sloping forehead.
Above: Black body, white head patches, sloping forehead.

BLACK SCOTER ("BUTTERBILL") *Melanitta americana*   p. 36
From below: Black plumage, paler flight feathers, rounded forehead.
Above: All-dark plumage. Body slightly smaller and pudgier than Surf Scoter's, rounded forehead.

WHITE-WINGED SCOTER ("WHITEWING") *Melanitta deglandi*   p. 36
From below: Black body, white wing patches.
Above: Black body, white wing patches.

COMMON EIDER ("IDAH") *Somateria mollissima*   p. 32
Above: White back, white forewing, black belly.

KING EIDER ("KING") *Somateria spectabilis*   p. 32
Above: Whitish foreparts, black rear parts.

DIVING DUCKS IN FLIGHT

From below

HARLEQUIN DUCK — male, female

LONG-TAILED DUCK — male, female

SURF SCOTER — male, female

BLACK SCOTER — male, female

WHITE-WINGED SCOTER — male, female

Above

LONG-TAILED DUCK — male, female

HARLEQUIN DUCK — male, female

COMMON EIDER — male, female

KING EIDER — male

BLACK SCOTER — male, female

SURF SCOTER — male, female

WHITE-WINGED SCOTER — male, female

FLIGHT PATTERNS of DIVING DUCKS, etc.

Note: Only adult males are described below. The first five all have a black chest. The names in parentheses are common nicknames used by hunters.

CANVASBACK ("CANNIE") *Aythya valisineria*   p. 30
From below: Black chest, long profile.
Above: White back, long profile. Lacks contrasty wing stripe of next four species.

REDHEAD ("POCHARD") *Aythya americana*   p. 30
From below: Black chest, roundish rufous head.
Above: Gray back, broad gray wing stripe.

RING-NECKED DUCK ("BLACKJACK") *Aythya collaris*   p. 30
From below: Not safe to tell from scaup from below; gray wing stripe sometimes evident.
Above: Black back, broad gray wing stripe.

GREATER SCAUP ("BROADBILL") *Aythya marila*   p. 30
From below: Black chest, white stripe showing through wing.
Above: Broad white wing stripe (extending onto primaries).

LESSER SCAUP ("BLUEBILL") *Aythya affinis*   p. 30
Above: Wing stripe shorter than in Greater Scaup.

COMMON GOLDENEYE ("WHISTLER") *Bucephala clangula*   p. 38
From below: Dark underwing linings, white wing patches, rounded dark head.
Above: Large white square wing patch, short neck, dark head.

RUDDY DUCK ("STIFFTAIL") *Oxyura jamaicensis*   p. 38
From below: Stubby; white face, dark chest, long tail.
Above: Small; dark with white cheeks, long tail.

BUFFLEHEAD ("BUTTERBALL") *Bucephala albeola*   p. 38
From below: Like a small goldeneye; note head patch.
Above: Small; large wing patches, white head patch.

Silhouettes of Ducks on Land

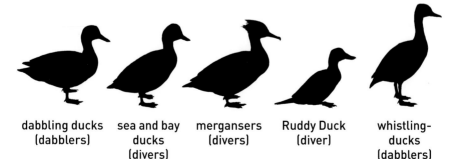

| dabbling ducks (dabblers) | sea and bay ducks (divers) | mergansers (divers) | Ruddy Duck (diver) | whistling-ducks (dabblers) |

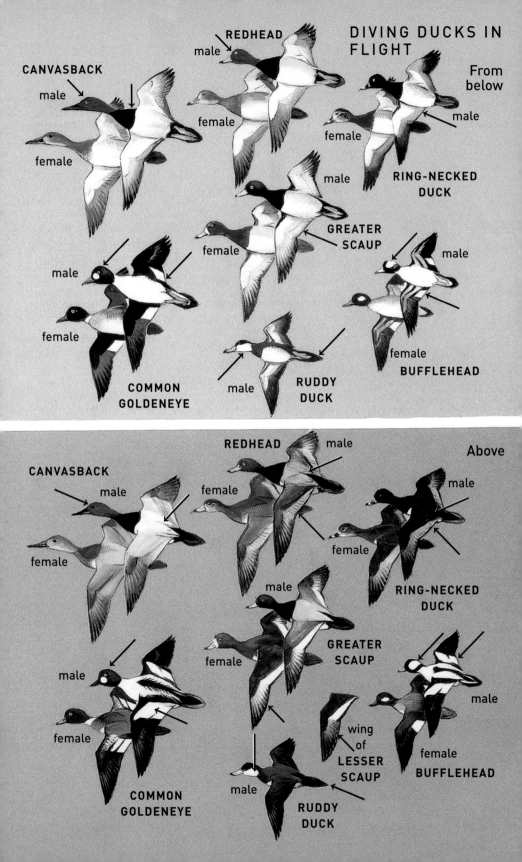

DIVING DUCKS IN FLIGHT

From below

CANVASBACK
male
female

REDHEAD
male
female

RING-NECKED DUCK
male
female

GREATER SCAUP
male
female

COMMON GOLDENEYE
male
female

RUDDY DUCK
male

BUFFLEHEAD
male
female

Above

CANVASBACK
male
female

REDHEAD
male
female

RING-NECKED DUCK
male
female

GREATER SCAUP
male
female

wing of **LESSER SCAUP**

COMMON GOLDENEYE
male
female

RUDDY DUCK
male

BUFFLEHEAD
male
female

VAGRANT WATERFOWL

PINK-FOOTED GOOSE *Anser brachyrhynchus*   Scarce vagrant

25–30 in. (65–75 cm). Slightly smaller than Greater White-fronted Goose, head entirely brown, bill mostly dark, tail whiter. **RANGE:** Very rare but increasingly being observed in ne. Canada and New England in winter; accidental farther west. Usually found with Canada Geese.

GARGANEY *Spatula querquedula*   Very rare vagrant

15–16 in. (38–41 cm). *Male:* Broad white eyebrow stripe, silvery shoulder patch (in flight). *Female:* Bolder face pattern than Blue-winged and Cinnamon Teal, grayer (less blue) upperwing patch, dark legs, and white borders on speculum. **RANGE:** Very rare visitor from Eurasia to w. Aleutians; casual elsewhere in N. America, primarily along coasts.

MASKED DUCK *Nomonyx dominicus*   Very rare vagrant

13–13½ in. (33–34 cm). *Male:* Rusty body with black face and blue bill. *Female:* Buffy with black crown and two distinct face stripes, heavily barred back. **SIMILAR SPECIES:** Female Ruddy Duck has just one face stripe. **RANGE:** Very rare and irregular visitor to TX and FL. **HABITAT:** Ponds and marshes with dense vegetation. Often hidden.

TUFTED DUCK *Aythya fuligula*   Rare vagrant

16½–17 in. (41–43 cm). *Adult male:* Differs from male scaup and Ring-necked Duck by conspicuous wispy crest; note also black back, white sides, white wing stripe. *Female, juvenile, and first-year male:* Resembles female scaup but develops small tuft, broad band at bill tip, lacks eye-ring and ring on bill of Ring-necked. May or may not have white at base of bill. **RANGE:** Regular visitor from Eurasia to NL, w. AK; very rare along coasts and in Great Lakes; casual elsewhere inland. **HABITAT:** Sheltered ponds, bays, reservoirs. Usually with scaup.

SMEW *Mergellus albellus*   Accidental vagrant

16 in. (41 cm). Smaller and shorter-billed than other mergansers. *Adult male:* Very white, with black eye patch, black-and-white crest and wings. *Female, juvenile, and first-year male:* Small and gray, with white cheeks, chestnut cap. **RANGE:** Rare but regular spring visitor from Asia to w. AK; accidental elsewhere. Some birds might be escapees.

COMMON SHELDUCK *Tadorna tadorna*   Very rare vagrant

23–26 in. (58–67 cm). Plumage unmistakable (male and female similar). Increasing records in ne. Canada and U.S. now regarded as vagrants.

UNESTABLISHED EXOTIC WATERFOWL

CHINESE GOOSE *Anser cygnoides*   Exotic

WHITE-CHEEKED PINTAIL *Anas bahamensis*   Provenance in question

(W. Indies) 17 in. (43 cm). Occasional reports from s. FL may include vagrants.

GRAYLAG GOOSE *Anser anser*   Exotic

30–35 in. (75–90 cm). Common domestic species. One shipboard vagrant off NL.

BAR-HEADED GOOSE *Anser indicus*   Exotic

MANDARIN DUCK *Aix galericulata*   Exotic

RUDDY SHELDUCK *Tadorna ferruginea*   Provenance in question

24–26 in. (61–67 cm). Record of six birds in NU probably of vagrants.

VAGRANT WATERFOWL

PINK-FOOTED GOOSE

adult

female

male

GARGANEY

MASKED DUCK

female

adult male

adult male

female

TUFTED DUCK

adult female

female

male

SMEW

COMMON SHELDUCK

UNESTABLISHED EXOTICS

CHINESE GOOSE

EGYPTIAN GOOSE

WHITE-CHEEKED PINTAIL

male

BAR-HEADED GOOSE

GRAYLAG GOOSE

female

male

MANDARIN DUCK

RUDDY SHELDUCK

adult male

CORMORANTS Family Phalacrocoracidae

Large blackish waterbirds that often stand erect on rocks, posts, or dead limbs; may rest with wings spread out to dry. Breeding adults may have colorful facial skin, throat pouch, and eyes. Bill slender, hook-tipped. Sexes alike. Cormorants swim low like loons, but with bill tilted up at an angle. They often fly in lines or Vs, somewhat in the manner of geese. Silent except for occasional low grunts at nesting colonies. **FOOD:** Fish, crustaceans. **RANGE:** Nearly worldwide.

BRANDT'S CORMORANT *Phalacrocorax penicillatus*   Common
34 in. (86–89 cm). *Adult:* Similar in size to Double-crested Cormorant but has dark chin (*blue* when breeding), shorter tail, longer bill, and flies without marked kink in neck. *Buff throat patch* behind pouch. *First-year:* Underparts extensively brown, becoming bleached by spring; buff throat. **SIMILAR SPECIES:** Other cormorants, loons. First-year Double-crested has yellow in bill, face, and throat pouch, paler breast; Pelagic and Red-faced show darker brown more limited to breast. **HABITAT:** Ocean, coasts, rocky islets; nests colonially on flats of offshore islets.

PELAGIC CORMORANT *Phalacrocorax pelagicus*   Fairly common
26–29 in. (66–73 cm). *Adult:* Noticeably smaller and plumage more iridescent greenish or purplish than other Pacific cormorants, with more *slender neck* (no kinks in flight), longish tail, small head, and smaller, *thinner bill.* In late winter through midsummer it has double crest and *white patch* on flanks. Throat pouch and part of face dull red, obvious only at close range. *First-year:* Deep brown on chest, brownish black elsewhere, darkest on back. **SIMILAR SPECIES:** Other cormorants, loons. **HABITAT:** Ocean, coasts, rocky islets, sounds. Despite name, seldom seen far from shore. Breeds on cliff faces.

RED-FACED CORMORANT *Phalacrocorax urile*   Uncommon, local
30–31 in. (76–79 cm). *Adult:* Note *bright red* face (extending to forehead and behind eye). Throat pouch *bluish; bill mostly pale.* Has white flank patches in spring/summer. Pelagic Cormorant is slightly smaller, has duller red pouch, restricted dull red on face, and thinner, all-dark bill. *First-year:* Differs from Pelagic in having thicker, mostly pale bill; pinkish facial skin. **SIMILAR SPECIES:** Other cormorants, loons. **HABITAT:** Ocean, coasts; nests on sea cliffs.

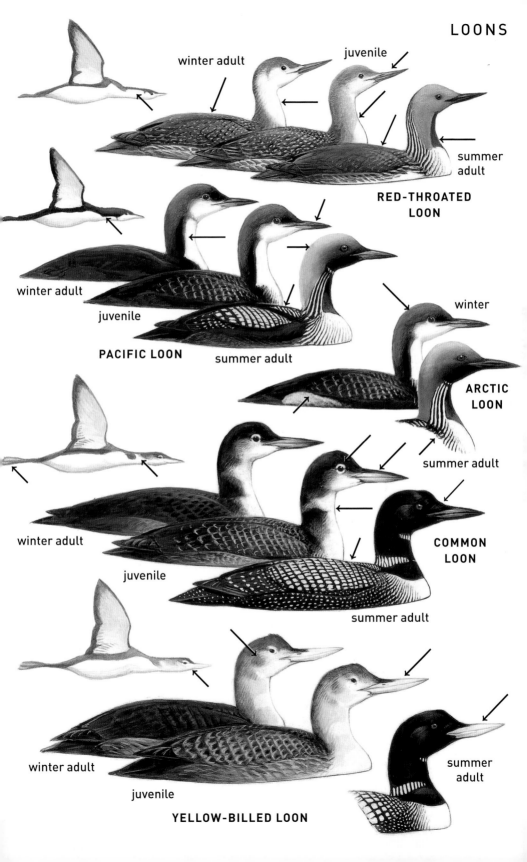

LOONS

winter adult

juvenile

summer
adult

**RED-THROATED
LOON**

winter adult

juvenile

summer adult

PACIFIC LOON

winter

**ARCTIC
LOON**

summer adult

winter adult

juvenile

summer adult

**COMMON
LOON**

summer adult

winter adult

juvenile

summer
adult

YELLOW-BILLED LOON

GREBES Family Podicipedidae

Somewhat ducklike divers with thin necks and bills; tailless look. Most have white wing patches, pointed bills. Sexes alike. Juvenile has striped head. May dive from surface or sink. Flight labored. **FOOD:** Small fish, other aquatic life. **RANGE:** Worldwide.

PIED-BILLED GREBE *Podilymbus podiceps* Fairly common

13–13½ in. (33–34 cm). Note "chickenlike" bill, puffy white undertail. No wing patch. *Spring/summer: Black throat patch* and *ring* around pale bill. *Fall/winter:* Lacks black bill markings. *Juvenile:* Striped on head. Male's bill thicker than female's. **VOICE:** Song *kuk-kuk-cow-cow-cow-cowp-cowp-cowp,* whinny, sharp *kwah.* **HABITAT:** Ponds, lakes, salt bays and estuaries.

HORNED GREBE *Podiceps auritus* Fairly common

13½–14 in. (34–36 cm). *Spring/summer: Golden ear patch* and *chestnut neck. Fall/winter:* Black cap *clean-cut to eye level;* white foreneck, thin straight bill. **VOICE:** Loud *gamp,* trills. **SIMILAR SPECIES:** Molting birds may be confused with Eared Grebe, but note flatter crown, pale lores, straighter, pale-tipped bill. Red-necked Grebe larger, bill with yellow. **HABITAT:** Lakes, ponds, coastal waters.

EARED GREBE *Podiceps nigricollis* Common

12½–13 in. (32–33 cm). Note peaked crown, skinny neck, slightly upturned, all-dark bill. Often floats high in water. Gregarious. *Spring/summer: Wispy golden ear tufts, black neck. Fall/winter:* Dark cap extends *below eye,* neck often dusky. **SIMILAR SPECIES:** Horned Grebe. **VOICE:** Musical *poo-ee-chk,* froglike *poo-eep* or *krreep.* **HABITAT:** Prairie lakes, ponds; in winter, also open lakes, coastal bays and estuaries; in late summer and fall congregates in high numbers at salt lakes. Rare vagrant to much of East.

RED-NECKED GREBE *Podiceps grisegena* Uncommon

18–19 in. (46–49 cm). A largish grebe. *Spring/summer:* Long *rufous neck, white cheek,* black cap. *Fall/winter:* Grayish brown; white crescent on face; variable *yellowish* base of bill. In flight, double wing patch. *First-fall/winter:* Paler, face pattern less distinct. **VOICE:** Loud braying on breeding grounds. **SIMILAR SPECIES:** Loons, Red-breasted Merganser. **HABITAT:** Lakes, ponds; in winter, prefers salt water, estuaries, sometimes large lakes. Rare inland.

LEAST GREBE *Tachybaptus dominicus* Uncommon, local

9½ in. (24 cm). Smaller, darker than Pied-billed Grebe, with white wing patches (usually concealed), puffy undertail coverts, slender *black bill, golden eyes.* **VOICE:** A chattering whinny. **HABITAT:** Ponds, marshes, and lake edges. Accidental vagrant to CA.

WESTERN GREBE *Aechmophorus occidentalis* Common

25 in. (64 cm). A large slate-and-white grebe with long neck. Bill long, greenish yellow with dark ridge. Black of cap extends *below eye.* **VOICE:** Loud, reedy *crik-crik,* often heard on nonbreeding grounds. **SIMILAR SPECIES:** Clark's Grebe, Red-throated Loon. **HABITAT:** Rushy lakes, sloughs; in winter, large lakes, bays, coasts. Rare vagrant to Midwest, casual to E. Coast.

CLARK'S GREBE *Aechmophorus clarkii* Fairly common

25 in. (64 cm). Bill *orange-yellow.* Dark eye *surrounded by white* (may be pale gray in first-year and winter plumages). Back and flanks slightly paler than Western's, and gray on nape slightly narrower. Downy young are white, not gray. **VOICE:** Single-noted *creet* or *criik.* **HABITAT:** Scarcer than Western in ocean waters during winter. Very rare vagrant to Midwest, accidental to E. Coast.

GREBES

PIED-BILLED GREBE

lobed foot of grebe

fall/winter male

spring/summer female

spring/ summer male

juvenile

downy young

fall/winter variant

HORNED GREBE

bill of Horned

fall/winter

fall/winter variant

fall/ winter

spring/ summer

bill of Eared

EARED GREBE

spring/ summer

first fall/winter

fall/ winter adult

spring/ summer adult

RED-NECKED GREBE

fall/winter

spring/ summer

LEAST GREBE

male display

WESTERN GREBE

CLARK'S GREBE

AUKS, MURRES, and PUFFINS Family Alcidae

The northern counterparts of penguins, but alcids are smaller and can fly, beating their small narrow wings in a whir, often veering. They have short necks and pointed, stubby, or deep and laterally compressed bills. Alcids swim and dive expertly. Most species nest on sea cliffs or in burrows, often in crowded colonies, and virtually all winter on open ocean. Mostly silent away from breeding grounds. Sexes alike. **FOOD:** Fish, squid, krill, zooplankton. **RANGE:** N. Atlantic, N. Pacific, and Arctic Oceans. Great Auk (*Pinguinus impennis*) formerly bred on rocky islets of ne. Canada and the N. Atlantic; became extinct around the late 1840s.

RAZORBILL *Alca torda* Uncommon

17 in. (43 cm). Size of a small duck. *Adult:* Black above and white below; characterized by rather heavy head, thick neck, and flat bill crossed midway by a white mark; male's bill deeper than female's. On water, cocked-up pointed tail is often characteristic. Complete black head in spring/summer replaced by white face and throat in fall/winter. *First-year:* Shows smaller bill, retains white face through first spring/summer; bill develops to adult-sized in second year. **VOICE:** Deep guttural growls; juvenile gives piercing whistle. **SIMILAR SPECIES:** Fall/winter face pattern suggests Common Murre. Bill of first-year Razorbill may recall that of a murre but is stubbier and more rounded. See also Long-tailed Duck. **HABITAT:** Nests on rocky offshore islands; forages in coastal waters; winters primarily in open ocean.

THICK-BILLED MURRE *Uria lomvia* Scarce

18 in. (46 cm). Similar to Common Murre, but a bit *blacker above.* Bill slightly shorter, thicker, with *whitish line along gape.* Overall a bit stockier. *Spring/summer adult:* Head and face black, white of foreneck forms inverted V. *Fall/winter adult and first-year:* Face whitish with dark on head extending *well below eye;* no dark line through white ear coverts as in most Common Murres. White bill mark often less evident. Bill also much smaller, shorter, during first year. **VOICE:** Guttural calls and moans, hence the name "murre." Juvenile gives loud whistles. **SIMILAR SPECIES:** Common Murre. **HABITAT:** Nests on coastal cliff ledges. Spends fall/winter season on offshore ocean waters.

COMMON MURRE *Uria aalge* Fairly common West, uncommon East

17–17½ in. (43–45 cm). Size of a small duck, with slender, pointed bill. *Spring/summer adult:* Head, neck, back, and wings dark, *tinged brownish;* underparts, underwing linings, and line on rear edge of wing white. *Dusky markings on flanks on some birds. Fall/winter adult and first-year:* Similar, but throat and cheeks white. *Black mark extends from eye to cheek* in most birds (see also Razorbill) but note some birds off CA retain mostly dark heads in winter. Murres often raft on water, fly in lines, stand erect on sea cliffs. Chicks in Pacific may be mistaken for murrelets but accompany adults (fathers) until mostly grown. Bridled morph occurs regularly in N. Atlantic and AK. **VOICE:** Similar to Thick-billed Murre's. **SIMILAR SPECIES:** Thick-billed Murre, Razorbill, Long-tailed Duck. **HABITAT:** Same as Thick-billed Murre, but regularly seen from shore throughout year along Pacific Coast.

ALCIDS (AUKS)

first-year

spring/summer
adult

fall/winter
adult

RAZORBILL

COMMON

spring/
summer
adults

fall/winter

THICK-BILLED MURRE

COMMON
MURRE

fall/winter

chick

COMMON

THICK-BILLED

bridled
morph

RAZORBILL

spring/
summer
adults

Great Auk
extinct 1844

DOVEKIE *Alle alle* — Scarce

8–8¼ in. (20–21 cm). A very small alcid (by far the smallest in East), about the size of European Starling. Chubby and seemingly neckless, with very stubby bill. In flight, flocks bunch tightly, starlinglike. *Adult:* Contrasting alcid pattern—black above, white below. Black-hooded in spring/summer, white-chested in fall/winter. *First-year:* Similar to fall/winter adult, including through first summer, but bill smaller; primaries browner. **VOICE:** Shrill chatter. Noisy on nesting grounds. **SIMILAR SPECIES:** AK, fall/winter Marbled Murrelet similar but more slender, bill thinner; white stripes on sides of back more distinct. Parakeet Auklet larger with larger reddish bill, less clean-cut, lacks white in back. Fall/winter Least Auklet much smaller. **HABITAT:** Nests in high Arctic on coastal cliffs. Winters at sea in N. Atlantic.

BLACK GUILLEMOT *Cepphus grylle* — Fairly common

12½–13½ in. (32–34 cm). *Spring/summer adult:* Midsized black bird with large white wing patch, bright red feet, and pointed bill. Inside of mouth red. *Fall/winter:* Pale with whitish underparts and barred back. Wings black with white patch as in summer. *First-year:* Darker above than fall/winter adult, with dingier, mottled wing patch; plumage remains mostly white through first summer. **VOICE:** Wheezy or hissing *peeee;* very high pitched. **SIMILAR SPECIES:** No other Atlantic alcid has white wing patch (although others have a narrow line of white on trailing edge of wing). White-winged Scoter much larger and chunkier, black through fall/winter, wing patch positioned at rear of wing. In nw. AK, compare with Pigeon Guillemot. Black Guillemot's white wing patch lacks dark bar; underwing linings *white* with thin dark border (at least half dusky in Pigeon). Fall/winter and juvenile Black Guillemots average whiter than similar-plumaged Pigeon Guillemots, have paler underwing in flight, slightly shorter bill. **HABITAT:** Inshore ocean waters; breeds in small groups or singly in holes in ground or under rocks on rocky shores, islands. Less pelagic than other Atlantic alcids. Accidental vagrant inland.

ATLANTIC PUFFIN *Fratercula arctica* — Uncommon

12–13 in. (30–33 cm). Colorful triangular bill is most striking feature of this chunky "Sea Parrot." On the wing, it is a stubby, short-necked, thick-headed bird with buzzy flight. No white border on wing. *Spring/summer adult:* Upperparts black, underbody white, cheeks pale gray; triangular bill bluish bordered yellow basally, broadly tipped with red. Feet bright orange. *Fall/winter adult:* Cheeks darker gray; bill smaller (summer bill shield sheds), duller, but still obviously a puffin. *First-year:* Bill much smaller, mostly dark, but both mandibles well curved. Chunky shape and gray cheeks (kept through first summer) are unmistakably those of a puffin. Second-year shows bill in between first-year and adult. **VOICE:** Usually silent. When nesting, a low, growling *ow* or *arr.* **SIMILAR SPECIES:** First-years may be mistaken for first-year Razorbill, but note gray cheeks, all-dark underwing. Horned Puffin very similar in winter but bill shape differs; malar area, throat, and neck have broader black band; ranges do not currently overlap but vagrants to opposite coasts might be expected with melting polar cap. **HABITAT:** Very rarely seen from shore except near breeding colonies on rocky islands.

ATLANTIC ALCIDS (AUKS)

spring/summer adult

fall/winter

DOVEKIE

fall/winter

spring/summer adult

spring/summer adult

fall/winter

spring/summer adult

BLACK GUILLEMOT

spring/summer adult

juvenile

spring/summer adult

ATLANTIC PUFFIN

fall/winter adult

breeding adults

Black Guillemot spring/summer

Atlantic Puffin

Dovekie spring/summer

TUFTED PUFFIN *Fratercula cirrhata* — Uncommon

15–16 in. (38–40 cm). A stocky, black seabird with large head and bill. *Spring/summer adult:* Blackish, with *massive, triangular, orange-red* bill; white face; and *long, curved, ivory yellow ear tufts.* Feet orange. *Fall/winter adult:* White face and ear tufts much reduced (a trace of dull buffy-yellowish); duller orange-red bill, smaller and not as triangular as in summer because of shedding of outer bill plate. *First-year:* Body brownish black with broad brown swath behind eye, belly pale grayish; bill smaller, with no red; lacks white face and head plumes during first summer. Three years generally required to reach full adult appearance. **VOICE:** Throaty growling in nesting colony; silent at sea. **SIMILAR SPECIES:** First-year Rhinoceros Auklet. First-year Horned Puffin has gray face, contrasting distinctly with black neck and throat (contrast is lower on breast and less distinct in Tufted Puffin). **HABITAT:** Same as Horned Puffin.

HORNED PUFFIN *Fratercula corniculata* — Fairly common, local

15 in. (38 cm). A puffin with *clear white underparts* and broad black collar. Feet bright orange. *Spring/summer adult:* Cheeks *white,* with small, dark erectile horn above each eye. Bill massive, *triangular,* laterally flat; *yellow with red tip.* *Fall/winter adult:* Cheeks dusky; bill duller, blackish with orange tip. *First-year:* Resembles fall/winter adult with dusky cheeks, but bill smaller and darker; keeps dusky cheeks through first summer. **VOICE:** Low, growling *arr.* **SIMILAR SPECIES:** First-year Atlantic Puffin. **HABITAT:** Nests on rocky ocean cliffs. Forages in offshore waters.

PIGEON GUILLEMOT *Cepphus columba* — Fairly common

13½ in. (34 cm). *Spring/summer adult:* A medium-sized, black, pigeonlike waterbird, with large *white wing patches* (subdivided by variable black bar or wedge), *red feet,* pointed black bill, orange-red mouth lining, and mostly dark or dirty underwing. *Fall/winter adult:* Pale gray to whitish with dusky eye patch and back; wings with large white patches as in summer. *Juvenile and first-year:* Similar to fall/winter adult, but head darker, white wing patches mottled; underparts and flanks more heavily marked gray; remains in this plumage through first summer. **VOICE:** Feeble wheezy or hissing whistle, *peeeeee.* **SIMILAR SPECIES:** Young juveniles can be confused with Marbled and other murrelets but have longer neck, rounder head, and dark reddish mouth lining and feet. See Black Guillemot. **HABITAT:** Inshore ocean waters; less pelagic than most other alcids.

RHINOCEROS AUKLET *Cerorhinca monocerata* — Fairly common

15 in. (38 cm). A dark stubby seabird with a blocky wedge-shaped head. *Spring/summer adult* (plumage acquired in late winter): *White mustache* and narrow *white plume* above and behind eye, *short erect horn* at base of yellowish bill. *Fall/winter adult:* Note size and *uniform dark color with paler lower vent.* White plumes shorter, horn absent. *First-year:* Similar to fall/winter adult, with smaller, darker bill. **VOICE:** Wide array of barks, growls, groans. **SIMILAR SPECIES:** First-year Tufted Puffin. Cassin's Auklet smaller, rounder headed. Parakeet Auklet has longer eye stripe originating at rear of eye, red bill, whiter below. **HABITAT:** Nests colonially in burrows on islands. Found in both nearshore and offshore ocean waters.

PACIFIC ALCIDS

TUFTED PUFFIN

venile

fall/
winter
adult

spring/summer adult

Black Guillemot
(p. 62)
for comparison

juvenile

fall/winter adult

spring/
summer
adult

HORNED PUFFIN

juvenile

fall/
winter

**PIGEON
GUILLEMOT**

fall/
winter

spring/summer
adult

Horned
Puffin

**RHINOCEROS
AUKLET**

spring/
summer
adult

Tufted
Puffin

Tufted Puffin
breeding

Horned Puffin
breeding

Horned Puffin
breeding

Rhinoceros
Auklet

breeding

LONG-BILLED MURRELET *Brachyramphus perdix*   Casual vagrant

10–11 in. (25–28 cm). *Spring/summer adult:* Paler brown than Marbled Murrelet; *white to whitish throat. Fall/winter and first-year:* Like Marbled, but *lacks white collar* and shows two small pale *oval patches* on nape. In all plumages, dark crown contrasting with white face in straighter line than in Marbled Murrelet, bill longer, head more wedge-shaped. **RANGE AND HABITAT:** Casual visitor from Asia to W. Coast, accidentally far inland all the way to Atlantic Coast. Declining.

MARBLED MURRELET *Brachyramphus marmoratus*   Uncommon, endangered

9¾–10 in. (24–25 cm). *Spring/summer adult: Dark brown; heavily mottled* on underparts. The only alcid south of AK so colored (in AK, see Kittlitz's Murrelet). *Fall/winter and first-year:* Small and squat, dark above and white below, with *white stripe on scapulars,* white collar. **VOICE:** Sharp *keer, keer* or lower *kee*. **SIMILAR SPECIES:** Fall/winter Pigeon Guillemot larger, with white patch on wing. See Long-billed Murrelet. **HABITAT:** Coastal ocean waters, bays. Breeds short distance inland, mainly high on limbs of mossy old-growth conifers if available.

KITTLITZ'S MURRELET   Scarce, local, endangered
Brachyramphus brevirostris

9¼–9½ in. (23–24 cm). *Spring/summer adult:* Buffy or tan overall, *mottled and freckled with white* above, giving a pale look. *Fall/winter and first-year:* Similar to Marbled Murrelet, but *white on face surrounds eyes.* White outer tail feathers in all plumages. **SIMILAR SPECIES:** Marbled Murrelet, fall/winter Pigeon Guillemot. **HABITAT:** Glacial waters; nests on barren slopes above timberline.

SCRIPPS'S MURRELET *Synthliboramphus scrippsi*   Uncommon, local

9½–9¾ in. (24–25 cm). Formerly lumped with Guadalupe Murrelet as "Xantus's Murrelet." A small alcid, contrastingly sooty black above, white below. Suggests a miniature murre. Ages and sexes similar. **VOICE:** High-pitched twittering at colonies; occasionally heard at sea. **SIMILAR SPECIES:** Pure white underwings distinguish Scripps's and Guadalupe Murrelets from Craveri's Murrelet. Guadalupe Murrelet has white above eye in all plumages. **HABITAT:** Breeds in rocky crevices of offshore islands; disperses to open ocean, typically far from shore.

GUADALUPE MURRELET   Scarce, local, threatened
Synthliboramphus hypoleucus

9½–9¾ in. (24–25 cm). Very similar to Scripps's Murrelet, but with distinctive white arc above eye. **RANGE AND HABITAT:** Breeds on islands off Baja CA, a rare late-summer and fall visitor north to BC, often farther offshore (in warmer water) than Scripps's Murrelet.

CRAVERI'S MURRELET *Synthliboramphus craveri*   Rare, local, threatened

9¼–9½ in. (23–24 cm). Very similar to Scripps's Murrelet, but slightly browner, with *dark partial collar* extending down sides of breast, slight black chin (below bill), and *dusky* (not white) underwing linings. Bill very slightly longer and head shape slightly more rounded. **RANGE AND HABITAT:** Breeds on offshore islands, ranges far at sea. Disperses irregularly north to our area in summer and fall, often during warmer-ocean years.

ANCIENT MURRELET *Synthliboramphus antiquus*   Scarce

10 in. (25 cm). In all plumages, *gray back contrasts with black cap. Spring/summer adult:* Note sharply cut *black throat patch* and *white stripe over eye.* Bill yellow. *Fall/winter and first-year:* Throat mottled dusky (juvenile's not dark); weaker head stripe. **VOICE:** Songbirdlike trills at colonies; occasionally heard at sea. **SIMILAR SPECIES:** Other similarly sized alcids lack back/crown contrast. **HABITAT:** Breeds on rocky and debris-strewn slopes. Acccidental vagrant inland as far as Atlantic Coast.

MURRELETS

LONG-BILLED
MURRELET

fall/winter

flying birds
in winter

MARBLED
MURRELET

fall/winter

spring/
summer
adults

spring/
summer

KITTLITZ'S
MURRELET

fall/winter

GUADALUPE
MURRELET

spring/summer

SCRIPPS'S
MURRELET

CRAVERI'S
MURRELET

fall/
winter

spring/
summer adult

ANCIENT
MURRELET

spring/
summer

CRESTED AUKLET *Aethia cristatella* Fairly common, local

9½–10½ in. (24–27 cm). A droll auklet of the Bering Sea. *Spring/summer adult:* Completely slate gray, darker on back; thin white plume behind eye. Stubby bill is *bright orange* and a curious crest *curls forward* over bill. In fall/winter adult, orange gape on bill is lost and crest is shorter. *First-year:* Paler gray overall, with dark bill; juvenile can lack white head stripe and plume. VOICE: Doglike bark in nesting colony. SIMILAR SPECIES: Whiskered and Cassin's Auklets. HABITAT: Nests on remote islands and coastal areas of Bering Sea. Forages in open ocean.

WHISKERED AUKLET *Aethia pygmaea* Scarce, local

7¾–8 in. (20 cm). Similar to slightly larger Crested Auklet, but in addition to curled black plume on forehead, spring/summer adult has *three thin white plumes* (whiskers) on each side of face. In fall/winter and first-year plumages, plumes are shorter. Juvenile can lack head plumes. At all times flying birds show *paler lower belly and undertail coverts* (can be inconspicuous on sitting birds). HABITAT: Tidal rips, rocky coasts.

PARAKEET AUKLET *Aethia psittacula* Uncommon, local

10 in. (25 cm). A medium-sized alcid with *stubby, red bill* (like colorful bill of a parakeet) and whitish underparts. *Spring/summer adult:* Entire head black, with thin white plume behind eye. *Fall/winter and first-year:* Mostly whitish underneath, and bill has less red. Juvenile can lack white head stripe. VOICE: At nesting colony, a high whinny. SIMILAR SPECIES: Crested Auklet entirely dark. Least Auklet much smaller. Rhinoceros Auklet in winter larger, bill longer and not reddish, thin streak originates above eye, less white below. At sea, can look similar to smaller Cassin's Auklet but head plume is usually present, whiter underneath, including undertail coverts. HABITAT: Offshore occurs singly or in small loose groups (not in flocks like other small alcids); nests in scattered pairs or in colonies on sea cliffs and rubble slopes.

LEAST AUKLET *Aethia pusilla* Fairly common, local

6–6¼ in. (15–16 cm). The tiniest alcid; chubby, neckless. Black above, white below. In flight, a whirring ping-pong ball. *Spring/summer adult:* Has dark band across upper breast. *Fall/winter and first-year:* White below, lacks plumes. Tiny size and small stubby bill separate it from other alcids except Dovekie. VOICE: High-pitched chattering in colony. SIMILAR SPECIES: Dovekie is much larger. HABITAT: Nests on remote rocky islands in colonies with other auklets. Forages in open ocean.

CASSIN'S AUKLET *Ptychoramphus aleuticus* Fairly common

9 in. (23 cm). A small stubby seabird; entirely dark gray except for white crescent above eye, white iris (darker in juvenile and first-year), and white belly; note pale spot at base of lower mandible. VOICE: In nesting colony, a series of ringing wheezy *kueek-kueek* notes; silent at sea. SIMILAR SPECIES: In winter, all other small alcids in its range have much more white. See Rhinoceros and Parakeet Auklets. HABITAT: Nests in island burrows and crevices. Forages for krill in open ocean.

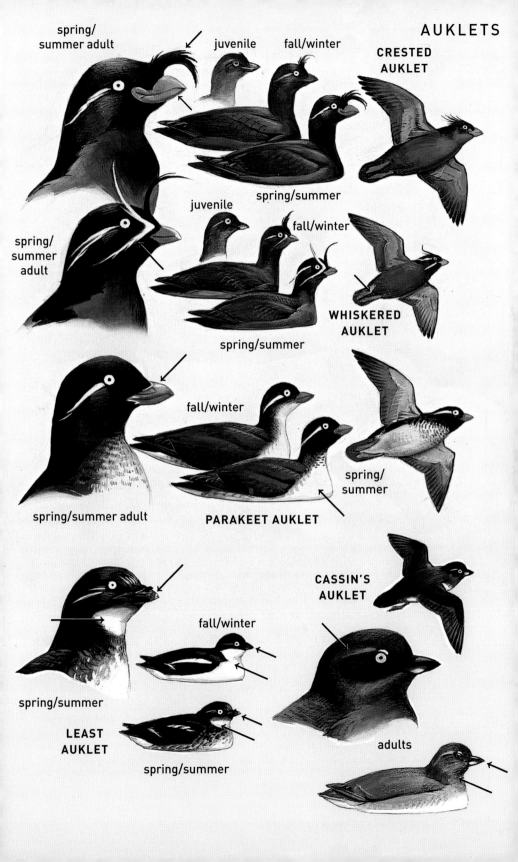

AUKLETS

CRESTED AUKLET

spring/summer adult

juvenile

fall/winter

spring/summer

WHISKERED AUKLET

spring/summer adult

juvenile

fall/winter

spring/summer

PARAKEET AUKLET

spring/summer adult

fall/winter

spring/summer

CASSIN'S AUKLET

LEAST AUKLET

spring/summer

fall/winter

spring/summer

adults

SHEARWATERS and PETRELS Family Procellariidae

Somewhat gull-like birds of open sea that glide low over waves. They often bank, or arc, up and down like a roller coaster, particularly in strong winds; in calm weather they typically are found sitting on water or flying with several flaps and then a glide. Wings narrower than those of gulls. These, along with albatrosses and storm-petrels, have tubelike external nostrils on bill and are thus called "tubenoses." Ages and sexes similar. Largely silent at sea (most apt to call at feeding frenzies) but noisy at breeding colonies. **FOOD:** Fish, squid, crustaceans, ship refuse. **RANGE:** Oceans of world. Most species rarely or never seen from our mainland shores.

NORTHERN FULMAR *Fulmarus glacialis*   Uncommon to fairly common

18½–19 in. (47–49 cm). A shearwater-like seabird but stockier with larger head, shorter, rounder wings; flies like shearwater but aspect more horizontal, with quicker wingbeats, less gliding. Note rounded forehead; *stubby, yellowish/pinkish tubenose bill* with variable dark band; longish tail. Primaries show a *pale flash or patch.* Leg color pinkish to bluish. Comes in dark and light color morphs, each variable and with some intermediates. *Light morph:* Gull-like in plumage, some whiter; white wing patches distinct. *Dark morph* (more common in Pacific): Uniformly smoky gray, wings have reduced whitish patches. First-spring birds can become quite worn and disheveled. **VOICE:** Hoarse, grunting *ag-ag-ag-arrr* or *ek-ek-ek-ek-ek.* **SIMILAR SPECIES:** At a distance, more rounded head and wings, flight style, and stubby yellowish bill distinguish light morph from gulls and dark morph from browner (less gray) Sooty, Short-tailed, and Flesh-footed Shearwaters. **HABITAT:** Open ocean; breeds colonially on sea cliffs.

MURPHY'S PETREL *Pterodroma ultima*   Rare

15½–16 in. (40–41 cm). A dark brownish petrel, with bluish sheen when fresh; *underwing primaries pale with dark crescent,* faint dark M across back and wings, and *pale throat, extending around bill.* Flight in windy conditions quick and darting. **SIMILAR SPECIES:** Sooty Shearwater, dark-morph Northern Fulmar. Accidental Great-winged Petrel (*Pterodroma macroptera;* not illustrated) larger and stockier, bill stouter, more white on face. **RANGE:** Breeds in sw. Pacific; rare but regular offshore visitor, mostly in spring.

COOK'S PETREL *Pterodroma cookii*   Rare, threatened

10½–11 in. (27–28 cm). *Dark M across gray back and upperwing and gleaming white* underwings suggest much larger Buller's Shearwater, but note Cook's paler head with black ear patch and light sides of tail. Flight in windy conditions quick and darting. **SIMILAR SPECIES:** Accidental Stejneger's Petrel (*Pterodroma longirostris;* not illustrated) similar but bill slightly smaller, crown dark gray to black. **RANGE:** Nests off New Zealand; occurs rarely and irregularly off W. Coast, primarily in summer and fall.

MOTTLED PETREL *Pterodroma inexpectata*   Rare

14 in. (36 cm). *Dark M across back and upperwing and contrasting dark belly* and *heavy diagonal black bar* across underwing. **RANGE:** Nests in New Zealand; regular summer visitor to deep offshore AK waters, very rare though probably somewhat regular south to well off CA, mostly in late fall and winter.

HAWAIIAN PETREL *Pterodroma sandwichensis*   Rare, endangered

17–18 in. (43–46 cm). Larger and longer-winged than other petrels off W. Coast; blackish to brownish upperparts with slightly darker M; *black hoodlike cap* with broad *white patch around bill;* broad dark diagonal *underwing carpal bars.* **RANGE:** Breeds in HI (see p. 414), rare but increasingly observed well off CA and OR, primarily in summer and early fall.

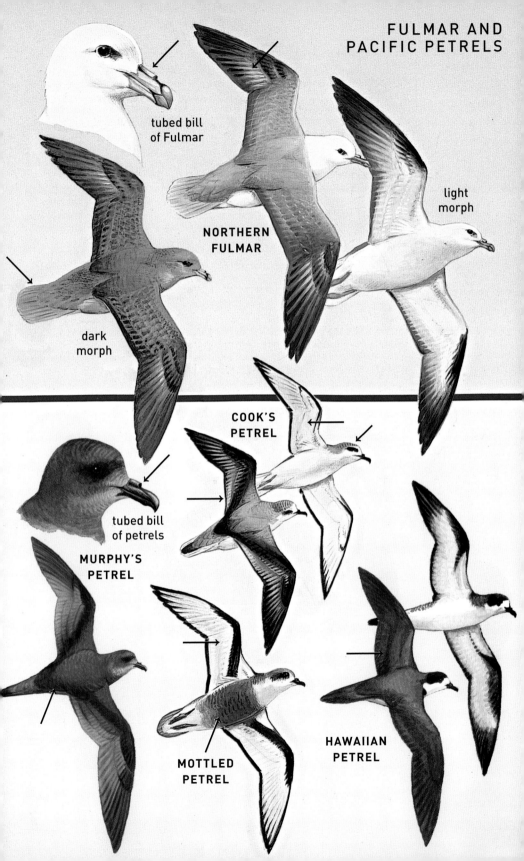

FULMAR AND PACIFIC PETRELS

tubed bill
of Fulmar

NORTHERN FULMAR

light morph

dark morph

tubed bill
of petrels

MURPHY'S PETREL

COOK'S PETREL

MOTTLED PETREL

HAWAIIAN PETREL

BLACK-CAPPED PETREL *Pterodroma hasitata*   Scarce, endangered

16 in. (41 cm). Larger than Audubon's and Manx Shearwaters; looks quite similar to Great Shearwater but has thicker bill and characteristic crook-winged shape and flight style of petrels. Note also black cap, white forehead, variable white collar, *white rump* patch extending to tail. **RANGE:** Rarely seen outside Gulf Stream. Nests on Hispanola and Cuba. Casual vagrant inland after hurricanes.

BERMUDA PETREL *Pterodroma cahow*   Casual, endangered

15 in. (38 cm). Also known as "Cahow." One of the world's rarest seabirds. Differs from Black-capped Petrel by *smudgy gray* rump, absence of white collar, smaller size and bill. **RANGE:** Breeds only on certain small islets off ne. end of Bermuda, where it comes and goes at night. Sightings may become more regular in Gulf Stream off NC coast as protection efforts in Bermuda enhance population size.

TRINDADE PETREL *Pterodroma arminjoniana*   Rare

15½–16 in. (40–41 cm). Known as "Herald Petrel" until recently split from that counterpart Pacific species. Dark, intermediate, and pale morphs. Most N. American records are dark, differing from Sooty Shearwater by *dark* underwing linings, longer tail, and slower wingbeat. Light area at primary base suggests a jaeger. Light morph typically has dark head, white breast and belly, and more prominent white wing patches. Feet and legs black. **RANGE:** Reported annually in small numbers in Gulf Stream off NC coast from May to Sept. Nests in tropical S. Hemisphere. Accidental vagrant inland after hurricanes.

FEA'S PETREL *Pterodroma feae*   Very rare

14–15 in. (36–38 cm). Brownish gray above, with M pattern across upperwings. Distinguished from Black-capped Petrel by less contrasty pale *gray rump and tail,* pale gray cowl on head, and *dark underwing.* **RANGE:** Breeds on islands off W. Africa. A rare but regular spring and summer visitor to Gulf Stream waters off Cape Hatteras, NC; casual elsewhere.

ATLANTIC
PETRELS

BLACK-CAPPED
PETREL

BERMUDA
PETREL

dark
morph

TRINDADE
PETREL

light
morph

FEA'S
PETREL

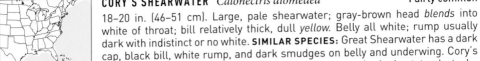

CORY'S SHEARWATER *Calonectris diomedea* **Fairly common**

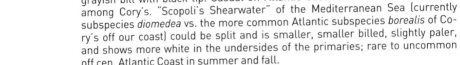

18–20 in. (46–51 cm). Large, pale shearwater; gray-brown head *blends* into white of throat; bill relatively thick, dull *yellow*. Belly all white; rump usually dark with indistinct or no white. **SIMILAR SPECIES:** Great Shearwater has a dark cap, black bill, white rump, and dark smudges on belly and underwing. Cory's has more pronounced bend to wing than Great, and wingbeat tends to be slightly slower. Cape Verde Shearwater (*C. edwardsii*; not shown), formerly considered a subspecies of Cory's, is smaller, darker above, and has a thinner dark grayish bill with black tip. Casual off Atlantic Coast but should be looked for among Cory's. "Scopoli's Shearwater" of the Mediterranean Sea (currently subspecies *diomedea* vs. the more common Atlantic subspecies *borealis* of Cory's off our coast) could be split and is smaller, smaller billed, slightly paler, and shows more white in the undersides of the primaries; rare to uncommon off cen. Atlantic Coast in summer and fall.

GREAT SHEARWATER *Ardenna gravis* **Fairly common**

19 in. (48 cm). A large shearwater, dark above and white below, rising above waves on stiff wings off Atlantic Coast, is likely to be this or Cory's Shearwater. Great Shearwater has dark cap separated by a light band across nape. Note also white rump patch and dark smudges on belly and underwing. **SIMILAR SPECIES:** Cory's Shearwater. **RANGE:** Casual vagrant inland after hurricanes.

SOOTY SHEARWATER **Common in Pacific, uncommon in Atlantic**
Ardenna grisea

17–18 in. (43–46 cm). Often seen in massive flocks in summer in Pacific, regularly close to shore. Looks all dark at a distance; rises over and arcs above waves on narrow, rigid wings. Note *whitish linings* on underwings. Flight rapid and directed, usually low along water surface, often following each other in long pathways during migration. **SIMILAR SPECIES:** Dark jaegers (white in primaries, fly differently), Short-tailed and Flesh-footed Shearwaters, dark-morph Northern Fulmar. **RANGE:** Breeds in S. Hemisphere, undertakes extensive migrations into N. Pacific (see also p. 418) and Atlantic, where it molts.

MANX SHEARWATER *Puffinus puffinus* **Uncommon**

13½ in. (34 cm). A small black-and-white shearwater; half the bulk of Great Shearwater; shows complete *white undertail* coverts and can have white flank patches on either side of rump. Note dark cap extends below eye; white extends upward from neck behind ear coverts. **SIMILAR SPECIES:** See Audubon's Shearwater. Wingbeat quicker than in Great or Cory's Shearwater. In Pacific, rare Manx is similar to Black-vented Shearwater but is blacker above, with white rather than dark undertail coverts and vent, and more contrasting and whiter face.

AUDUBON'S SHEARWATER *Puffinus lherminieri* **Fairly common**

12 in. (30 cm). A very small shearwater, similar to Manx Shearwater but with slightly browner upperparts, *dark undertail*. Wings slightly shorter, *tail longer*. Often has *white markings* around eye. **HABITAT:** Prefers warmer water than Manx Shearwater.

ATLANTIC SHEARWATERS

CORY'S
SHEARWATER

GREAT
SHEARWATER

Cory's

Great

SOOTY
SHEARWATER

Manx

MANX
SHEARWATER

AUDUBON'S
SHEARWATER

SHORT-TAILED SHEARWATER *Ardenna tenuirostris* Uncommon

16–17 in. (40–43 cm). Very similar to Sooty Shearwater; best distinguished by *shorter bill, steeper forehead,* and *variably smoky gray* underwing linings, slightly smaller size and narrower wings, more rapid wingbeats. May have contrasty pale throat. Sooty has variably whiter underwing linings, often with dark marks (usually lacking in Short-tailed). **RANGE:** Common in Alaskan waters in summer and early fall; found only in small numbers and mostly between late fall and late winter off Pacific Coast to south.

FLESH-FOOTED SHEARWATER *Ardenna carneipes* Rare

18–19 in. (43–45 cm). This dark-bodied shearwater is a rare but regular visitor, mostly in fall. *Larger* than Sooty Shearwater; flight more sluggish. Distinguished by *pale pink bill* (with dark tip), *pinkish feet,* dark underwing linings (some slightly paler flight feathers). **SIMILAR SPECIES:** Dark-morph Northern Fulmar, Sooty Shearwater. Rare darker Pink-footed Shearwater similar in size, shape, and bill, but plumage grayer (less brown), underparts and underwing lining usually mixed with whitish, very rarely entirely dark.

PINK-FOOTED SHEARWATER *Ardenna creatopus* Fairly common

19½ in. (50 cm). Two fairly common shearwaters with *mostly white underparts* are regularly found off W. Coast: Pink-footed and Black-vented. Pink-footed is larger than common Sooty Shearwater, has dark-tipped pinkish bill and slower wingbeats. Black-vented is much *smaller* than Pink-footed, has all-dark bill, and wingbeats faster with little arcing. Underparts and underwing variably dusky, in darkest cases approaching all-gray (considered "dark morph" by some). **SIMILAR SPECIES:** Buller's Shearwater; see Flesh-footed Shearwater.

BLACK-VENTED SHEARWATER *Puffinus opisthomelas* Fairly common, local

13½–14 in. (34–36 cm). A small shearwater, dark brown above and whitish below with dusky breast sides, dark undertail coverts, dark cap extending below eye. Small size, contrasting *dark-and-white* pattern, and rapid wingbeats with short glides are distinctive among common Pacific Coast shearwaters. Less contrasting than Manx Shearwater, and rarely shows white patches on sides of rump. Often seen in flocks from shore, mostly in fall and winter. **SIMILAR SPECIES:** Manx and Pink-footed Shearwaters.

BULLER'S SHEARWATER *Ardenna bulleri* Uncommon, irregular, threatened

16 in. (41 cm). A very white-bellied shearwater. Separated from other white-bellied shearwaters by distinct *dark M* pattern on back and wings; more buoyant flight, underparts *gleaming white.* Cap dark. Tail wedge-shaped. Feet pale, but variable. Occurs in fall (primarily late July through Oct.) in variable numbers from year to year. **SIMILAR SPECIES:** Pink-footed Shearwater is larger with *dingier* underwings, more *uniform* upperparts, more *blended* face pattern.

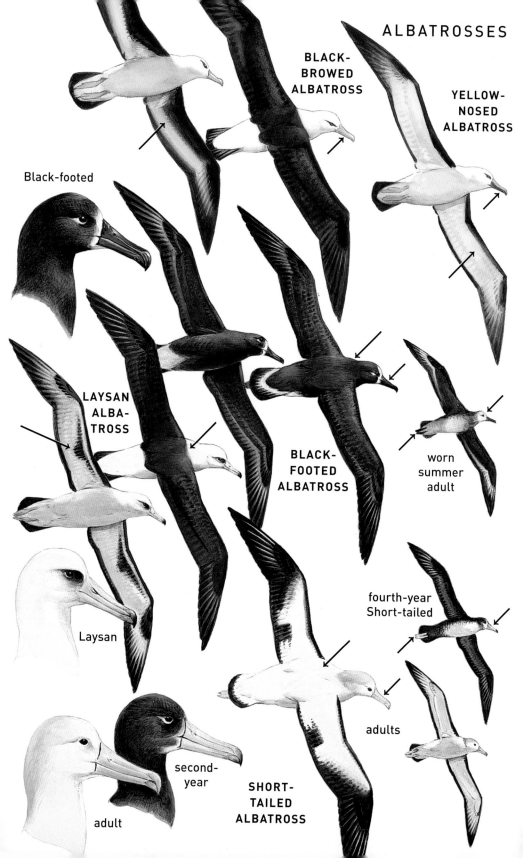

ALBATROSSES

BLACK-BROWED ALBATROSS

YELLOW-NOSED ALBATROSS

Black-footed

LAYSAN ALBA-TROSS

BLACK-FOOTED ALBATROSS

worn summer adult

Laysan

fourth-year Short-tailed

adults

adult

second-year

SHORT-TAILED ALBATROSS

STORM-PETRELS Families Oceanitidae and Hydrobatidae

Small seabirds that flutter or bound over open ocean. They nest colonially on islands, returning to burrows at night. Nostrils in a fused tube over top of bill. Usually silent at sea, calling occasionally at feeding frenzies; vocal at breeding colonies. **FOOD:** Plankton, crustaceans, small fish. **RANGE:** All oceans except Arctic. Family Oceanitidae (White-faced and Wilson's Storm-Petrels here) recently split from Hydrobatidae; the former have longer legs used to kick or patter upon water while foraging.

WHITE-FACED STORM-PETREL *Pelagodroma marina*   Casual

7½ in. (19 cm). A medium-large storm-petrel with white head and underparts, two-toned underwing, dark eye patch. Very long legs. Bounds "kangaroo style" over water on stiff flat wings. **RANGE:** Se. Atlantic, sw. Pacific, Indian Ocean. Rare Aug.–Sept. off Atlantic Coast from MA to NC, usually far offshore.

WILSON'S STORM-PETREL *Oceanites oceanicus*   Common

7¼–7½ in. (18–19 cm). A medium-small storm-petrel with somewhat triangular wings and *white uppertail-covert* (often called "rump") *patch that wraps around sides;* tail slightly rounded or square-cut, *not forked.* Feet yellow-webbed (hard to see), show *beyond tail* in flight. Direct flight, with short glides, pausing to flutter over water. **SIMILAR SPECIES:** Leach's and Band-rumped Storm-Petrels. **HABITAT:** Open ocean. Often follows ships (Leach's does not). May rarely be seen from shore. Casual vagrant inland in East after hurricanes.

LEACH'S STORM-PETREL *Hydrobates leucorhous*   Uncommon

8 in. (20 cm). Note obscurely divided (double-oval) *white uppertail-covert patch* and forked tail. Pale bar on upperwing often reaches leading edge. In flight, bounds about erratically, suggesting a nighthawk. Breeds in N. Atlantic and Pacific. *Does not consistently follow ships.* "Dark-rumped" birds nesting in Mex. and fall visitors off s. CA can lack or have reduced white in uppertail coverts. **VOICE:** At night on breeding grounds, nasal chattering notes and long crooning trills. **SIMILAR SPECIES:** Wilson's Storm-Petrel; Band-rumped Storm-Petrel; Black and Ashy Storm-Petrels similar to "dark-rumped" Leach's. See Townsend's Storm-Petrel. Wedge-rumped Storm-Petrel (*Oceanodroma tethys*), a scarce vagrant from Mex. waters to CA and AZ, is smaller, has white uppertail coverts that extend to tail or nearly so.

TOWNSEND'S STORM-PETREL *Hydrobates socorroensis*   Scarce

7 in. (17–18 cm). Recently split from Leach's Storm-Petrel and very similar. Slightly smaller and darker in appearance, with shorter and less-forked tail. Uppertail-covert patch often less divided and contrasting more with dark plumage than in Leach's, but beware individuals with darker uppertail coverts as well. **SIMILAR SPECIES:** Leach's Storm-Petrel. **RANGE:** Breeds on Guadalupe I. off Mex.; scarce (perhaps uncommon) visitor well off s. CA in summer/early fall.

BAND-RUMPED STORM-PETREL *Hydrobates castro*   Scarce

8½–9 in. (21–23 cm). A "white-rumped" storm-petrel, larger than Wilson's, similar to Leach's. Feet do not project beyond *squarish* tail. Uppertail-covert band more clean-cut than Leach's, less extensive to undertail region than Wilson's; bases to outer rectrices white. A stiff-winged flier, with short glides, reminiscent of a shearwater. **RANGE:** Casual vagrant inland in East after hurricanes. Uncommon breeder in HI (p. 418) and accidental vagrant to CA.

EUROPEAN STORM-PETREL *Hydrobates pelagicus*   Casual vagrant

6 in. (15 cm). Smaller than Wilson's Storm-Petrel; shorter legs, which do not extend beyond square tail. Yellow on feet, not on webs. Has whitish underwing patch. **RANGE:** Nests in ne. Atlantic and Mediterranean. Casual off NC, NS.

STORM-PETRELS

WHITE-FACED STORM-PETREL

WILSON'S STORM-PETREL

LEACH'S STORM-PETREL

BAND-RUMPED STORM-PETREL

TOWNSEND'S STORM-PETREL

EUROPEAN STORM-PETREL

WHITE-RUMPED STORM-PETRELS

Wilson's

Leach's and Townsend's

Band-rumped

European

FORK-TAILED STORM-PETREL *Hydrobates furcatus* Uncommon

8½ in. (22 cm). *Pale gray* overall, with contrasting *slaty underwing linings;* all of our other Pacific storm-petrels are blackish overall. Dark eye patch; faint dark bar across upperwing; forked tail. Observed in irregular numbers at sea; sometimes close to shore off CA, when birds can "wreck" and occur coastally, during storms or due to lack of food resources.

LEAST STORM-PETREL *Hydrobates microsoma* Rare, local

5¾ in. (15 cm). A late-summer and fall visitor in variable numbers. Small. Our only storm-petrel with *very short rounded or wedge-shaped* tail. Flight similar to Black Storm-Petrel but much smaller. **SIMILAR SPECIES:** Ashy Storm-Petrel is larger and grayer with notched or forked tail, paler underwing, and quicker, shallower wingbeats. Beware molting Ashies, which can resemble Least more in tail shape and flight style.

ASHY STORM-PETREL *Hydrobates homochroa* Uncommon, endangered

8 in. (20 cm). Separated from Black and "dark-rumped" Leach's Storm-Petrels by slightly smaller size, shorter wings, more direct flight (shallower wingbeats, lower to water). At close range, plumage looks more ashy colored; underwings and rump have *pale cast.* **RANGE:** Feeds far offshore but aggregates into large molting flocks in Aug.–Sept. in specific localities of cen. and n. CA, where they're most easily observed.

BLACK STORM-PETREL *Hydrobates melania* Fairly common

9 in. (23 cm). The largest all-black storm-petrel found off CA, primarily in fall. Forked tail. Larger than Ashy Storm-Petrel, with longer wings and *more languid flight.* Separated from "dark-rumped" Leach's Storm-Petrel by larger overall size, slower wingbeats, and more direct flight; Leach's tends to be farther offshore than Black. Irregular in our area; numbers tend to be higher and occurrence more northerly during warm-ocean events. Accidental vagrant inland in West after hurricanes.

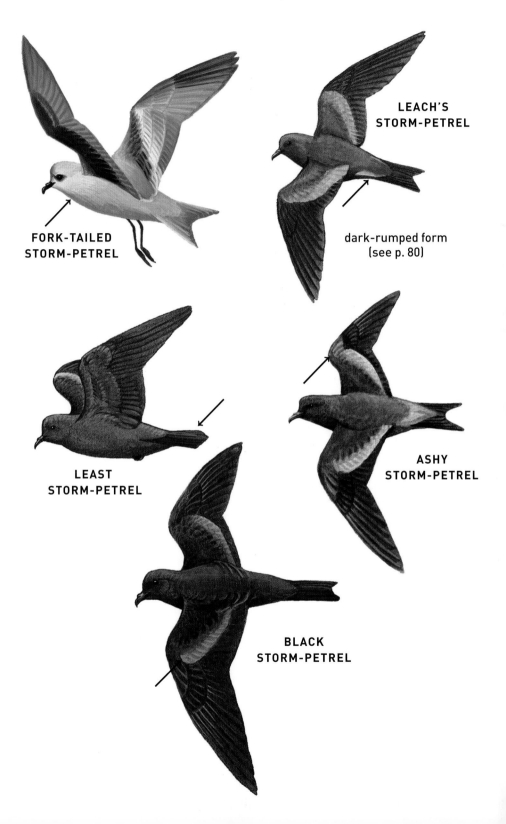

LEACH'S
STORM-PETREL

FORK-TAILED
STORM-PETREL

dark-rumped form
(see p. 80)

LEAST
STORM-PETREL

ASHY
STORM-PETREL

BLACK
STORM-PETREL

TROPICBIRDS Family Phaethontidae

These seabirds resemble (but are unrelated to) large terns with two greatly elongated central tail feathers (adults) and stouter, slightly decurved bills. Tropicbirds fly with shallow wingbeats, rarely glide, and swim with tail held clear of water. Sexes alike. Largely silent at sea. **FOOD:** Squid, fish, crustaceans. **RANGE:** Tropical oceans.

WHITE-TAILED TROPICBIRD *Phaethon lepturus*   Rare
15 in. (38 cm), adults to 30 in. (76 cm) with tail-streamers. *Adult:* Distinguished from other tropicbirds by its *diagonal black bar* across each wing. Note two extremely long white central tail feathers. Bill yellow (Pacific) to orange-red (Atlantic). *Juvenile:* Lacks tail-streamers; from other juvenile tropicbirds by *white*, not black, primary coverts, *coarsely* barred with black above; bill grayish olive with black tip. **VOICE:** Harsh ternlike scream. Also *tik-et, tik-et.* **SIMILAR SPECIES:** Red-billed Tropicbird. **RANGE:** Rare in N. American waters, common breeder in HI (p. 420).

RED-BILLED TROPICBIRD *Phaethon aethereus*   Rare
18 in. (45 cm), adults to 37 in. (94 cm) with tail-streamers. *Adult:* A slender white seabird with *two extremely long white central tail feathers, heavy red bill,* black patch through cheek, extensive black in primaries and primary coverts, and *finely barred back.* Juvenile lacks long tail; back more heavily barred, bill grayish yellow to dull orangish. **SIMILAR SPECIES:** Juvenile White-tailed Tropicbird is slightly smaller and smaller-billed; has more coarsely barred back than juvenile Red-billed, duller, more olive-based bill, and less black on wing, including white (not black) primary coverts.

RED-TAILED TROPICBIRD *Phaethon rubricauda*   Casual
18 in. (46 cm), adults to 37 in. (94 cm) with tail-streamers. Slightly slower wingbeats than other tropicbirds. *Adult:* Whiter above than other two tropicbirds; tail-streamers *red.* Juvenile lacks tail-streamers, thinly barred on back, bill dusky. **SIMILAR SPECIES:** Juveniles of other two tropicbirds more coarsely barred above, bills not black. **RANGE:** Nests in tropical and subtropical Pacific, including HI (p. 420). Rare to uncommon, regular visitor far off CA coast.

FRIGATEBIRDS Family Fregatidae

Primarily black tropical seabirds with extremely long wings (greater span in relation to body weight than that of any other bird). Bill long, hooked; tail deeply forked. Frigatebirds normally do not swim. **FOOD:** Fish, jellyfish, squid, other seabird chicks. Food snatched from water or ground in flight, scavenged, or pirated from other seabirds. **RANGE:** Pantropical oceans.

MAGNIFICENT FRIGATEBIRD *Fregata magnificens* Uncommon to scarce, local
36–46 in. (91–117 cm); wingspan 7–8 ft. (215–245 cm). A large, mostly black seabird with extremely long angled wings and *scissorlike* tail (often folded in a *point*). Soars with extreme ease. Bill long, hooked; orbital skin bluish. *Male:* All black, with *red throat pouch* (inflated like a balloon in display). *Female:* White breast, dark head. *Juvenile:* Head and breast white. Most birds seen in w. U.S. are juveniles. Can take up to ten years to develop adult plumages. **VOICE:** Voiceless at sea. A gargling whinny during display. **SIMILAR SPECIES:** Great Frigatebird of w. Mex and HI (see p. 420) is accidental vagrant off CA and elsewhere. Lesser Frigatebird *(F. ariel),* accidental across N. America, is smaller; adult has white spur on axillars; female has red orbital skin; juvenile has russet head. **RANGE:** Uncommon in FL; scarce and declining off CA; accidental to scarce vagrant away from coast. **HABITAT:** Tropical oceans; coastal habitats; breeds in mangroves.

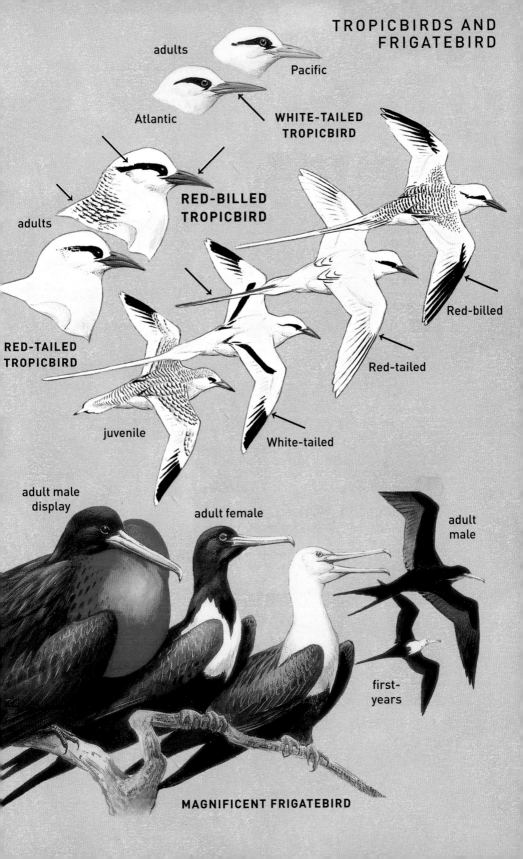

TROPICBIRDS AND FRIGATEBIRD

adults

Pacific

Atlantic

WHITE-TAILED TROPICBIRD

RED-BILLED TROPICBIRD

Red-billed

adults

RED-TAILED TROPICBIRD

Red-tailed

juvenile

White-tailed

adult male display

adult female

adult male

first-years

MAGNIFICENT FRIGATEBIRD

GANNETS and BOOBIES Family Sulidae

Seabirds with large, pointed bills and pointed tails, making them appear tapered at both ends. Larger and longer necked than most gulls. Sexes largely alike. Boobies sit on buoys, rocks; fish by plunging from air like Brown Pelicans. Mostly silent at sea, except when at feeding frenzies. **FOOD:** Fish, squid. **RANGE:** Gannets live in cold seas (N. Atlantic, S. Africa, Australia), boobies in tropical seas. All nest colonially on islands.

BLUE-FOOTED BOOBY *Sula nebouxii*   Casual

32–33 in. (81–83 cm). *Adult:* White body; whitish head; *light patches on upper back and rump;* dark-mottled back and wings, the underwing mostly dark with white axillaries ("armpits"); *blue feet. Juvenile:* Has darker head and neck, slowly becomes stippled with white by a year of age. **SIMILAR SPECIES:** First-year Masked and Brown Boobies. Adult male Brown Booby in w. Mex. also has pale head, grayish bill, but back entirely dark. **RANGE:** Rare to casual vagrant inland in West, especially Salton Sea.

BROWN BOOBY *Sula leucogaster*   Scarce, local

29–30 in. (74–76 cm). *Adult:* Chocolate brown with *white belly in clean-cut contrast to dark breast.* White underwing linings contrast with dark flight feathers. Feet yellowish. Male of w. Mex. subspecies *brewsteri* ("Brewster's Booby") white around head (varies to largely white headed) and has paler breast and grayer bill (vs. yellower in other subspecies). *Juvenile:* Underparts mostly dark, with little or no contrast between breast and belly; bill grayish. *Second-year:* White lower breast and belly mottled brown. Fairly common breeder in HI (p. 420). **SIMILAR SPECIES:** First-year Northern Gannet lacks clean-cut breast contrast; shows some white patches or mottling above; feet dark (not yellowish). First-year Red-footed Booby (which has dark tail) more buffy overall with dark underwing; has blackish bill that becomes tinged pinkish then lilac at base; feet pinkish to pale reddish. First-year Masked Booby resembles adult Brown Booby, but brown head meets white underparts higher on breast, near lower throat, and is usually set off from back by white nape collar. Blue-footed Booby has weaker contrast below, shows whitish patches on upper back and rump. **RANGE:** Rare to casual vagrant inland in West, especially Salton Sea.

RED-FOOTED BOOBY *Sula sula*   Casual vagrant

27–28 in. (69–71 cm). The smallest booby. *Adult:* Feet *bright red,* tail *white.* Two color morphs. *White morph:* Gannetlike; white, with black tip and trailing edge of wing (as in Masked Booby but tertials white), tail white. *Dark morph:* Brown back and wings, paler head; white tail and belly; in flight, *underwing dark,* thin dark trailing edge on upperwing. *Juvenile:* Brownish overall with *dark underwing,* blackish bill that becomes pink with dark tip by second year, pink feet that become red by second year. **SIMILAR SPECIES:** Juvenile Brown Booby is darker overall than juvenile Red-footed; has a more conical and paler grayish bill, yellowish feet. **RANGE:** Nests in Tropics, including commonly in HI (p. 420). Very rare, mostly young birds, at Dry Tortugas, FL; casual elsewhere in FL and along W. Coast.

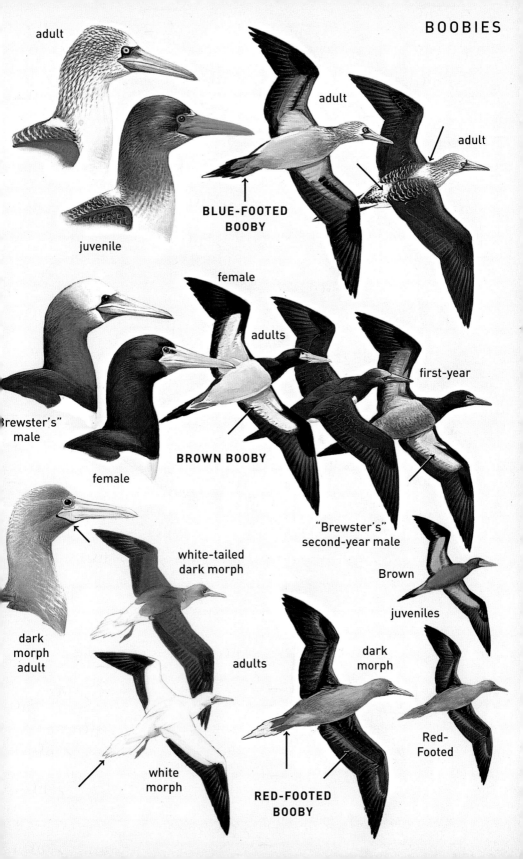

adult

juvenile

adult

adult

BLUE-FOOTED BOOBY

female

adults

first-year

"Brewster's" male

female

BROWN BOOBY

"Brewster's" second-year male

dark morph adult

white-tailed dark morph

Brown

juveniles

adults

dark morph

white morph

Red-Footed

RED-FOOTED BOOBY

NORTHERN GANNET *Morus bassanus* Common

37–38 in. (94–97 cm). A goose-sized seabird that soars over ocean and plunges headlong for fish. Migrates in long lines. Much larger than Herring Gull, with pointed tail, longer neck, larger bill (often pointed toward water). *Adult:* White with extensive black primaries. *Juvenile:* Dusky, but note "pointed-at-both-ends" shape. *Second- and third-year:* Look piebald in transition from juvenile to adult. **VOICE:** In colony, a low barking *arrah.* **SIMILAR SPECIES:** Boobies. In windy conditions, gannets in flight may arc up and down, suggesting a large tubenose such as an albatross. **HABITAT:** Ocean, but seen regularly from shore. Breeds colonially on sea cliffs. Scarce winter vagrant to Great Lakes; accidental inland and to CA.

MASKED BOOBY *Sula dactylatra* Scarce, local

31–32 in. (79–81 cm). *Adult:* White; smaller than Northern Gannet, with *black tail* and black along entire *rear edge of wing.* Yellowish to greenish yellow bill; dark bluish facial skin; feet olive to slate. Mostly white underwing. *Juvenile:* Variably mottled with dark on upperwing and head, white hind collar. **VOICE:** Usually silent. In nesting colony, a variety of whistles, grunts, bill-rattling. **SIMILAR SPECIES:** Other boobies, first-year Northern Gannet. Nazca Booby *(S. granti),* casual but increasing vagrant to CA and HI, similar but bill orangish in adult, becomes horn colored or tinged orange at base with deep yellow tip during first year. **RANGE:** Uncommon breeder in HI (p. 420).

PELICANS Family Pelecanidae

Huge waterbirds with long flat bills and great throat pouches (flat when deflated). Neck long, body robust. Sexes alike. Flocks fly in lines, Vs, or kettles, alternating several flaps with a glide. In flight, head is hunched back on nape, the long bill resting on breast. Pelicans swim buoyantly. **FOOD:** Mainly fish, crustaceans. **RANGE:** N. and S. America, Africa, s. Eurasia, E. Indies, Australia.

AMERICAN WHITE PELICAN *Pelecanus erythrorhynchos* Common

62 in. (157 cm). Huge; wingspan 8–9½ ft. (244–290 cm). White, with black primaries and a great orange-yellow bill and throat pouch. Adult in breeding condition has keratinous appendage or "centerboard" on ridge of bill that develops in spring, drops off in fall. *First-year:* Dusky wash on head, neck; dark mottling to upperwing coverts; second-year birds intermediate. This pelican does not plunge from air like Brown Pelican but scoops up fish while swimming, often working in groups. Flocks often circle high in air on thermals. **VOICE:** In colony, a low groan. Young utter whining grunts. **SIMILAR SPECIES:** Swans have no black in wings. Wood Stork and Whooping Crane fly with neck and long legs extended. Snow Goose much smaller; noisy. **HABITAT:** Lakes, marshes, estuaries. Rare vagrant to Southeast and Gulf coasts; casual to Northeast.

BROWN PELICAN *Pelecanus occidentalis* Common

48–50 in. (122–127 cm); wingspan 6½ ft. (198 cm). An unmistakable, ponderous dark waterbird. *Adult:* Much white and buff on head and front of neck. Dark chestnut brown on back of neck and reddish throat when breeding. *First-year:* Duskier brown overall, with dark head, paler underparts; second-year intermediate. Large size, head and bill shape, and powerful slow flight (a few flaps and a glide) indicate pelican; dark color and habit of *plunging bill-first* distinctive to this species. Lines or broken Vs of pelicans glide low over water, wingtips almost touching. **VOICE:** Adults silent (rarely a low croak). Nestlings squeal. **HABITAT:** Salt bays, beaches, ocean; more rarely inland lakes. Perches on posts, piers, rocks, buoys, beaches. Casual to accidental vagrant inland across N. America.

GANNET, BOOBY, AND PELICANS

adult

juvenile

adult

diving

second/
third-year

NORTHERN GANNET

MASKED BOOBY

spring/
summer
adult

adults

juvenile

adult

NAZCA BOOBY

adults

first-year

AMERICAN WHITE PELICAN

fall/winter
adult

spring/
summer
adults

BROWN PELICAN

juvenile

SKUAS and JAEGERS Family Stercorariidae

Falconlike seabirds that harass gulls, terns, and shearwaters, forcing them to disgorge or drop their food. Light, intermediate, and dark morphs exist in at least two species; all have flash of white in primaries. Adult jaegers have two projecting central tail feathers, which differ in shape and length among the species and ages. In juveniles and molting birds these feathers can be shorter or lacking, or sometimes blunter-tipped than in adults. Separating jaegers in most plumages can be very difficult. Skuas are larger, powerful birds that lack elongated tail feathers and are broader winged. Sexes alike. **FOOD:** In Arctic, lemmings, eggs, young birds. At sea, food taken from other birds or from water. **RANGE:** Seas worldwide, breeding in subpolar regions. In N. America, all five species occur as rare to accidental vagrants inland.

SOUTH POLAR SKUA
Stercorarius maccormicki

Scarce in East, uncommon in West

21 in. (53 cm). Skuas are near the size of a large gull, but stockier, with deep-chested, hunchbacked look. Dark, with short, slightly wedge-shaped tail and *conspicuous white wing patch at base of primaries visible on both upperwing and underwing.* South Polar Skua is slightly slimmer in build and bill, is colder and grayer brown, and averages a *paler nape* than Great Skua. *Adult:* Has *pale head and underparts* contrasting with darker wings; older adults can be much paler than shown. *Juvenile and first-year:* Darker and more uniform, similar to but often with a paler nape than like-aged Great Skuas. **SIMILAR SPECIES:** Great Skua; dark jaegers (particularly Pomarine Jaeger) may lack elongated tail feathers, but skuas larger, their wings wider, and they have more striking white wing patches. **HABITAT:** In our area, open ocean; rarely seen from or close to shore.

GREAT SKUA *Stercorarius skua*

Scarce

22–23 in. (56–58 cm). Note conspicuous white wing patch visible on both upper- and underwing. Near size of large gull, but stockier. Flight strong and swift; harasses other seabirds. *Adult:* Dark brown with rusty and streaked upperparts and short, slightly wedge-shaped tail. *Juvenile and first-year:* Darker brown, less rusty, and with fewer streaks; found only at sea post-fledging. **SIMILAR SPECIES:** Dark jaegers may lack distinctive tail-feather extensions. However, skuas' wings wider, less falconlike, white wing patches more striking both above and below, and flight more powerful. Very much like South Polar Skua but averages larger and heavier-billed. Note *warmer brown color, dark cap,* often *less distinct pale nape,* and more *streaked appearance* to upperparts. **VOICE:** Soft, nasal *kare, kare* on breeding grounds. **HABITAT:** Rocky islands in subarctic regions for breeding; otherwise, open ocean, seldom close to shore.

SKUAS AND JAEGERS

SOUTH POLAR
SKUA

adult

first-year

GREAT
SKUA

tail shape
of skua

Parasitic
Jaeger

Long-tailed
Jaeger

Pomarine
Jaeger

first-year and molting
jaegers, minus the long
tail points, are often
best distinguishable by
size and build

Great
Skua

Pomarine
Jaeger

Parasitic
Jaeger

Jaegers
in flight
p. 93

Long-tailed
Jaeger

PARASITIC JAEGER
Uncommon (East) to fairly common (West)

Stercorarius parasiticus

17–19 in. (44–49 cm). This is the jaeger most frequently seen from shore. Flies with strong, falconlike wing strokes. Smaller and less chesty than Pomarine Jaeger; larger and with a longer bill than Long-tailed Jaeger. Typically chases larger terns and medium-sized gulls. Like other jaegers, it shows variable white wing-flash. *Spring/summer adult:* Dark crown and pale underparts (light morph) to completely dark brown (dark morph). Sharp central tail feathers project up to 3½ in. (9 cm). Shows small *pale spot* above base of bill. *Juvenile and first-year:* Juvenile jaegers are highly variable in body plumage and have heavy barring, especially on underwing. Juvenile Parasitic often with *more distinct white patch on upperwing;* dark morph is usually *warmer brown* than other juvenile jaegers. Up close, look for streaked head and pale-edged primary tips, along with size and structural differences. Second-years of all three jaeger species retain partial barring on underwing and elsewhere. Winter adult (not seen in our area) can lack dark crown and has barring on back and flanks. **SIMILAR SPECIES:** Pomarine and Long-tailed Jaegers; along Pacific Coast, Heermann's Gull, which can occasionally show white wing patches and also sometimes harasses terns, small gulls. **HABITAT:** Primarily ocean, regularly seen from shore; in summer, tundra.

POMARINE JAEGER
Uncommon (East) to fairly common (West)

Stercorarius pomarinus

19–21 in. (48–53 cm). Like Parasitic Jaeger, but slightly heavier with more gull-like flight style. Typically chases larger gulls, shearwaters. *Adult: Broad and twisted* central tail feathers are blunt-tipped and project 2–7 in. (5–18 cm); bill heavy and *pink-based.* In light morph, dark cap extends *farther* down sides of head and near bill base; breast-band *darker* and more barred than in Parasitic. Dark morph averages sootier than dark-morph Parasitic. *Juvenile:* Plumage variable, but compared with juvenile Parasitic it lacks warm tones, and very short central tail feathers are blunt-tipped. Look for white-based primary coverts creating *double white flash* on underwing. Second-year and adult-winter plumages as described under Parasitic Jaeger. **SIMILAR SPECIES:** Plumages of Pomarine and Parasitic Jaegers are so variable that they are often best distinguished by structural features and behavior. Large molting Pomarine Jaegers can resemble skuas but bills are more slender, white wing flashes not as extensive, especially from above. **HABITAT:** Open ocean, seen from shore in small numbers; in summer, tundra.

LONG-TAILED JAEGER
Scarce (East) to fairly common (West)

Stercorarius longicaudus

17–22 in. (44–56 cm). The smallest, slimmest jaeger with buoyant, ternlike flight style, and small short bill. Typically chases smaller terns and gulls. *Adult:* Plumage less variable than that of other jaegers, virtually all being light morph. Paler and grayer above, with distinctly *two-toned upperwing* in flight; *long attenuated tail-streamers* project 8–15 in. (20–38 cm); black cap neat and *sharply defined; no breast-band;* almost *no white in wings. Juvenile:* Varies from light to dark morph. All have very *limited white on upperwing* (two or three primary shafts), *stubby bill,* and longer, blunter-tipped central tail feathers than Parasitic Jaeger. White patch on underwing variable but often smaller than in juvenile Parasitic Jaeger. Light-morph juvenile has distinctively *pale grayish head and breast* and extensively *white belly.* Dark morph cold gray-brown and often with pale nape and *pale lower breast patch.* **HABITAT:** Open ocean; tundra in summer. Most pelagic of the jaegers; seldom if ever seen from shore.

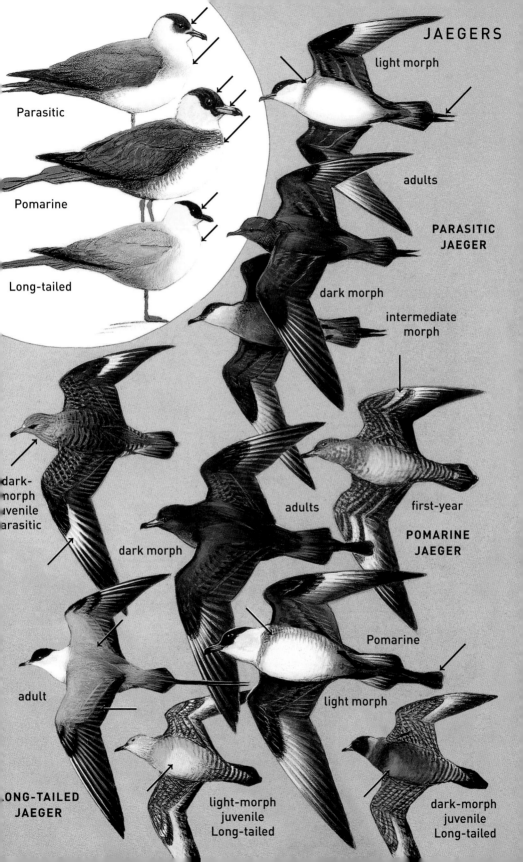

JAEGERS

light morph

adults

Parasitic

Pomarine

Long-tailed

PARASITIC
JAEGER

dark morph

intermediate
morph

dark-
morph
juvenile
Parasitic

adults

dark morph

first-year

POMARINE
JAEGER

Pomarine

adult

light morph

LONG-TAILED
JAEGER

light-morph
juvenile
Long-tailed

dark-morph
juvenile
Long-tailed

GULLS Family Laridae

Long-winged swimming birds with superb flight. Most are more robust, wider winged, and longer legged than terns, and most have larger and slightly hooked bills. Tails square or rounded (terns usually have forked tail). Gulls seldom dive (most terns hover, then plunge headfirst). **FOOD:** Omnivorous; marine life, plant and animal food, refuse, carrion. **RANGE:** Nearly worldwide.

AGING GULLS

It is often important to determine the age of a gull before identifying it. Knowing what a gull looks like in both its adult and first-year plumages is helpful in placing the bird to species in its intermediate (second- and third-year) stages. Sequence of plumages in gulls can be divided into three groups based on the age at which "adult" plumage is reached. Generally, this equates to the size of the gull, but note that maturation of plumage in all species is variable, with some individuals reaching full adult plumage a year before or after that described below. Most (but not all) gulls also have differing plumages in fall/winter and spring/summer, which become more distinct in each successive age class. When learning gulls, it is helpful to first focus on the size and structure of easier-to-identify adults, then consider size and structure of younger birds.

SEQUENCE OF PLUMAGES IN SMALL GULLS

In the top panel of the opposite page, the Bonaparte's Gull illustrates the transition of plumages directly from first-year to adult, usually without a very distinctive second-year plumage. Species in this category include Bonaparte's, Black-headed, Little, Ross's, Sabine's, and Ivory Gulls, and Red-legged Kittiwake. Adult Bonaparte's is also an example of a gull that has a distinctive spring/summer plumage for breeding.

SEQUENCE OF PLUMAGES IN MEDIUM-SIZED GULLS

In the middle panel of the opposite page, the Ring-billed Gull illustrates the transition of plumages from first-year to adult, with a distinctive second-year plumage that then generally transitions into adult. Species in this category include Ring-billed, Laughing, Franklin's, and Mew Gulls, and Black-legged Kittiwake. Of these, Laughing and Franklin's Gulls have distinctive spring/summer plumages in their second year and as adults, whereas in the others, winter plumages have slight dusky streaks to the head, lost for breeding.

SEQUENCE OF PLUMAGES IN LARGE GULLS

In the bottom panel of the opposite page, the Herring Gull illustrates the transition of plumages from first-year to adult, including distinctive second- and third-year plumages. Species in this category include California, Herring, Lesser Black-backed, Great Black-backed, Slaty-backed, Western, Yellow-footed, Glaucous-winged, Glaucous, and Iceland Gulls. Plumages tend to be similar between winter and summer, although some species have streaking on the head in winter, which is lost in summer, and the Yellow-footed Gull has a more-advanced second-summer plumage than other large gull species. The medium-sized Heermann's Gull is also a four-year species, and the only one of these with distinct fall/winter and spring/summer plumages as adults.

Caution: There is extensive variation within species (particularly the second- and third-year plumages), resulting from several factors, including dimorphism (males are larger than females) and variation in molt extents and timing, as well as plumage wear and bleaching. In addition, hybridization is a regular phenomenon among most large species, especially along the Pacific Coast (commonly between Glaucous-winged and Western, Herring, and Glaucous Gulls, and between Glaucous and Herring Gulls). Even expert birders leave some gulls unidentified.

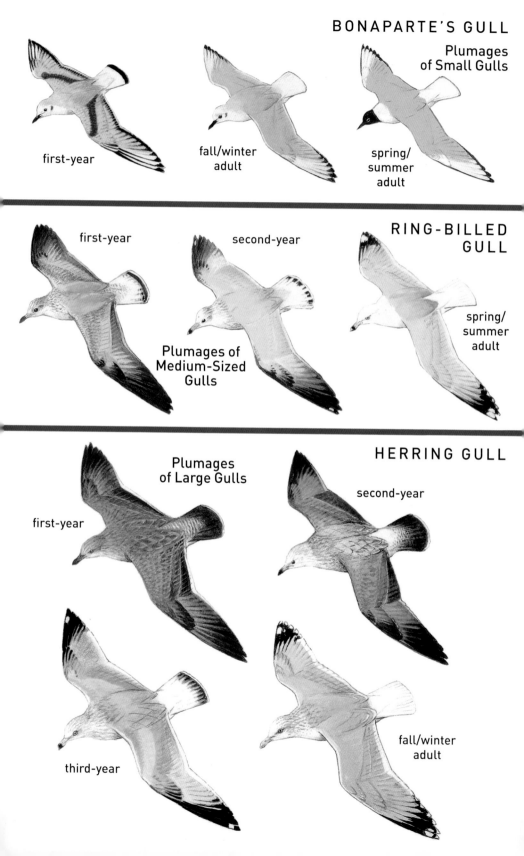

BONAPARTE'S GULL

Plumages
of Small Gulls

first-year

fall/winter
adult

spring/
summer
adult

RING-BILLED GULL

first-year

second-year

Plumages of
Medium-Sized
Gulls

spring/
summer
adult

HERRING GULL

Plumages
of Large Gulls

first-year

second-year

third-year

fall/winter
adult

LAUGHING GULL *Leucophaeus atricilla* Common

16–16½ in. (41–42 cm). A medium-small coastal gull named for its call. *Adult: Dark mantle blends into black wingtips.* Head *black* in spring/summer plumage; pale in fall/winter plumage with dark gray smudge across eye and nape. Bill longish, often with slight droop to tip; reddish when breeding, mostly dark when not breeding. *Juvenile and first-winter:* See p. 104. **VOICE:** Nasal *ha-a* and strident laugh, *ha-ha-ha-ha-ha-haah-haah-haah*, etc. **SIMILAR SPECIES:** Franklin's Gull is slightly smaller, shorter billed, and has broader white eye-arcs, and *different wingtip pattern.* **HABITAT:** Salt marshes, coastlines, parks, farm fields. Rare inland in East and north along Pacific Coast; accidental elsewhere in West.

FRANKLIN'S GULL *Leucophaeus pipixcan* Fairly common

14½–15 in. (37–38 cm). *Adult:* Note *white band* near wingtip, separating black from gray. In spring/summer plumage, head black; breast often has rosy bloom; bill red. In fall/winter plumage, head paler but with dark cheeks and nape forming partial hood; bill mostly dark. *First-year:* See p. 104. **VOICE:** Shrill *kuk-kuk-kuk;* also mewing, laughing cries. **SIMILAR SPECIES:** Laughing Gull. **HABITAT:** Prairies, inland marshes, lakes; in winter, coasts, primarily in S. America. Scarce migrant along Pacific Coast and casual vagrant to E. Coast.

SABINE'S GULL *Xema sabini* Fairly common off W. Coast, rare in East

13½–14 in. (34–36 cm). A small, *ternlike* gull with slightly *forked tail. Adult:* Note *bold upperwing pattern* of black outer primaries and *triangular white wing patch.* Bill black with *yellow tip;* legs dark. In winter plumage, a dusky wash. *Juvenile:* See p. 104. **VOICE:** Various grating or buzzy ternlike calls, given mostly on breeding grounds. **SIMILAR SPECIES:** Bonaparte's and Laughing Gulls, Black-legged Kittiwake. **HABITAT:** Ocean; nests on tundra pools. Rare to casual vagrant inland throughout N. America.

BLACK-HEADED GULL Scarce vagrant in West, uncommon in East
Chroicocephalus ridibundus

15¾–16 in. (40–41 cm). This Eurasian species regularly visits coastal e. N. America; accidental in West. *Adult:* Similar in pattern to Bonaparte's Gull and often associates with it or with Ring-billed Gull. Slightly larger than Bonaparte's; mantle slightly paler; shows much *blackish gray on underside of primaries;* bill *dark red,* not black. In fall/winter plumage, loses dark brown hood and has black ear spot. *First-year:* See p. 104. **VOICE:** Harsh *kerr.* **HABITAT:** Same as Little and Bonaparte's Gulls; also beaches, lawns.

BONAPARTE'S GULL Fairly common in West, common in East
Chroicocephalus philadelphia

13–13½ in. (33–34 cm). A petite, almost ternlike gull. *Adult:* Note *wedge of white* on *fore edge* of wing. Legs red to pinkish; bill small, black. In spring/summer plumage, head blackish. In fall/winter plumage, head whitish with *black ear spot. First-year:* See p. 104. Also see Sequence of Plumages in Small Gulls, p. 94. **VOICE:** Nasal, grating *cheeer* or *cherr.* Some calls ternlike. **SIMILAR SPECIES:** Franklin's, Black-headed, and Little Gulls. **HABITAT:** Ocean, bays, lakes, sewage-treatment ponds; in summer, muskeg.

LITTLE GULL *Hydrocoloeus minutus* Scarce vagrant in West, rare in East

11 in. (28 cm). This rare visitor is the smallest gull; usually associates with Bonaparte's Gull. *Adult:* Note *blackish undersurface of rather rounded wing* and absence of black above. Legs red. In spring/summer plumage, head black, bill dark red, breast may be washed rosy. In fall/winter plumage, head *dark-capped, black ear spot,* bill black. *First-year:* See p. 104. **VOICE:** Series of one- or two-syllable *key* notes. **SIMILAR SPECIES:** Bonaparte's Gull. **HABITAT:** Lakes, rivers, bays, coastal waters, sewage-treatment ponds; often with Bonaparte's Gulls.

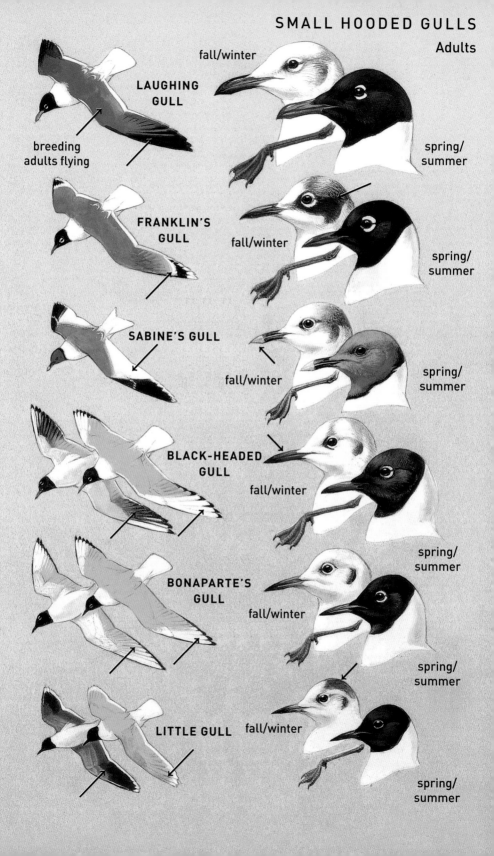

SMALL HOODED GULLS
Adults

LAUGHING GULL

fall/winter

breeding adults flying

spring/summer

FRANKLIN'S GULL

fall/winter

spring/summer

SABINE'S GULL

fall/winter

spring/summer

BLACK-HEADED GULL

fall/winter

spring/summer

BONAPARTE'S GULL

fall/winter

spring/summer

LITTLE GULL

fall/winter

spring/summer

HEERMANN'S GULL *Larus heermanni*   Common

19 in. (48 cm). The easiest gull in West to identify. *In all plumages, has black legs and feet.* Adult: Has *dark gray body, black tail* with thin white tip, *red bill with black tip.* White head in winter/spring becomes gray in summer/fall. A few birds have white patches on upperwing. *First- and second-years:* See p. 104. **VOICE:** Whining *whee-ee;* also a repeated *cow-auk.* **SIMILAR SPECIES:** May be confused with jaegers because of habit of chasing other birds for food, dark plumage, and occasional white wing patches; in chases, more buoyant flight and behavior eventually betrays Heermann's as a gull rather than a jaeger. **HABITAT:** Ocean and immediate coastlines. Accidental vagrant inland and to East.

CALIFORNIA GULL *Larus californicus*   Common

21–21½ in. (53–55 cm). *Adult:* Resembles smaller Ring-billed Gull (both may have yellow or yellowish green legs) or larger Herring Gull, but note darker mantle and *darker eye,* bill with both red and black spots. Wings proportionally long. Has more white in wingtips than Ring-billed. In fall/winter plumage, head streaked or mottled brownish, dark spot on bill may extend to upper mandible, bill and legs slightly duller, the latter often grayish green. *First- and second-years:* See p. 106. **VOICE:** Like Herring Gull's but higher, more hoarse. High-pitched *keeer* in flight. **HABITAT:** Ocean and coasts, lakes, farms, dumps, urban centers. Casual vagrant to E. and Gulf Coasts.

RING-BILLED GULL *Larus delawarensis*   Common

17–17½ in. (43–45 cm). Similar to Herring Gull, but smaller, more buoyant, and dovelike. A medium-small and somewhat delicate gull. *Adult:* Shows *pale eye* and *light gray mantle* (similar to Herring but paler than California and Mew); *legs yellow or greenish yellow* (may be duller in fall/winter). Note complete *black ring* encircling bill. In fall/winter plumage, shows some fine dark streaking on head and bill and legs become duller. *First-year:* See p. 104. Also see Sequence of Plumages in Medium-sized Gulls, p. 94. **VOICE:** Higher pitched than Herring Gull's. **SIMILAR SPECIES:** Mew Gull has smaller bill that lacks bold blackish ring, darker mantle, dark eye, and, in fall/winter plumage, more extensive dark mottling on head and neck. Also see first-year Mew Gull. **HABITAT:** Lakes, bays, coasts, piers, dumps, plowed fields, sewage outlets, shopping malls, fast-food restaurants; rarer on open ocean than other gulls.

MEW GULL *Larus canus*   Common

16–17 in. (41–44 cm). *Adult:* Slightly smaller than Ring-billed Gull, with more greenish yellow legs and dainty, short, *unmarked greenish-yellow bill.* (Birds in full breeding condition have yellow bill and legs.) *Darkish eye. Mantle medium gray, noticeably darker than Ring-billed's.* Mew shows larger white "mirrors" in its black wingtips than either California or Ring-billed Gull. In fall/winter head is streaked and bill is duller. *First-year:* See p. 104. **VOICE:** Low, mewing *queeu* or *meeu.* Also *hiyah-hiyah-hiyah,* etc., higher than voice of other gulls. **SIMILAR SPECIES:** First-year Ring-billed Gull; adult Black-legged Kittiwake. **HABITAT:** In winter, ocean, coastlines, parks, dumps, wet fields, tidal rivers; in summer, lakes, taiga, tundra. Casual vagrant well inland and along E. Coast.

BLACK-LEGGED KITTIWAKE *Rissa tridactyla*   Uncommon

16–17 in. (41–43 cm). A small, buoyant oceanic gull. *Adult:* Wingtips lack white spots, *solid black,* almost *straight across,* as if dipped in ink. Bill slightly curved, without angle to lower mandible of other gulls; pale yellow, unmarked. Legs and feet *black. Eyes dark.* Fall/winter plumage (not shown) similar but rear nape has dusky band. *First-year:* See p. 104. **VOICE:** At nesting colony, a raucous *kaka-week* or *kitti-waak.* **SIMILAR SPECIES:** Mew, Ring-billed, and Sabine's Gulls; in w. AK, Red-legged Kittiwake (p. 110). **HABITAT:** Chiefly oceanic; rarely on beaches, casual inland. Nests on sea cliffs. Rare to casual vagrant inland throughout N. America.

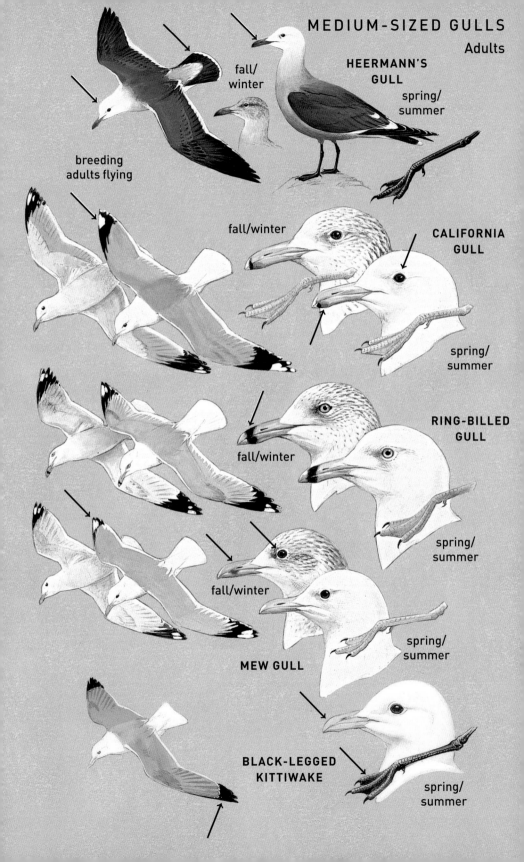

MEDIUM-SIZED GULLS
Adults

fall/winter

HEERMANN'S GULL

spring/summer

breeding adults flying

fall/winter

CALIFORNIA GULL

spring/summer

fall/winter

RING-BILLED GULL

spring/summer

fall/winter

spring/summer

spring/summer

MEW GULL

BLACK-LEGGED KITTIWAKE

spring/summer

HERRING GULL *Larus argentatus*   Common in East, fairly common in West

24–25 in. (61–64 cm). A widespread (though less numerous and more coastal in West than in East), fairly large gull. Regularly hybridizes with Glaucous-winged Gull in AK. *Adult: Pale gray* mantle, *pinkish* legs, *pale eye.* Outer primaries contastingly *black* with moderately extensive white spots or "mirrors." Bill yellow with red spot on lower mandible. In fall/winter plumage, head and neck streaked or mottled with brownish; bill and legs duller. *First- and second-years:* See p. 106. Also see Sequence of Plumages in Large Gulls, p. 94. **VOICE:** A loud *hiyak . . . hiyak . . . hyiah-hyak* or *yuk-yuk-yuk-yuk-yuckle-yuckle.* Mewing squeals. Anxiety call *gah-gah-gah.* **SIMILAR SPECIES:** "Thayer's" (Iceland) and California Gulls. Adult of latter darker mantled, has dark eye, greenish yellow legs; first-years can be similar (see p. 106). **HABITAT:** Ocean, coasts, bays, beaches, lakes, dams, piers, farmland, dumps.

GLAUCOUS-WINGED GULL *Larus glaucescens*   Common

25–26 in. (63–66 cm). *Adult:* A *very large pinkish-legged* gull, with large bill, pale gray mantle, and *medium gray* primaries. Head streaked grayish and bill duller in fall/winter. *First- and second-years:* See p. 108. Hybridizes extensively with Western Gull where their ranges overlap in Pacific Northwest (see p. 102), and with Herring and Glaucous Gulls in AK. **VOICE:** Low *kak-kak-kak;* a low *wow;* a high *keer, keer.* **SIMILAR SPECIES:** Adult Glaucous Gull has whitish primaries, thinner bill, paler eye. See also Western, "Thayer's" (Iceland), and Herring Gulls. **HABITAT:** Ocean, coastlines, parks, dumps, lakeshores. Rare vagrant in the interior West (hybrids with Herring Gull?); accidental vagrant to E. Coast.

GLAUCOUS GULL *Larus hyperboreus*   Uncommon

27–28 in. (68–72 cm). A large, chalky white gull with pinkish legs. *Adult:* Note "frosty" wingtips. Has pale gray mantle and *unmarked white outer primaries.* Light eye. Head slightly streaked and bill duller in fall/winter. *First- and second-years:* See p. 108. **VOICE:** Much like Herring Gull's. **SIMILAR SPECIES:** Iceland Gull is smaller; bill also smaller, head rounder, and wings proportionately longer (extending well beyond tail when sitting). Spring/summer adult Iceland has narrow red eye-ring (Glaucous has yellow), but this is hard to see. See also Glaucous-winged Gull. **HABITAT:** Mainly coastal; a few inland at large lakes and dumps. Rare inland and casual vagrant well south of normal winter range.

ICELAND GULL *Larus glaucoides*   Uncommon

22–24 in. (56–61 cm). Eastern N. American "Kumlien's" Gull *(kumlieni)* is a pale, ghostly gull, slightly smaller than Herring Gull. *Adult:* Mantle pale gray; primaries, which extend *well beyond tail,* are whitish with gray or dark markings, variable in hue, with large white "mirrors" (not black with white mirrors as in Herring Gull). Western "Thayer's" Gull (subspecies *thayeri*), formerly a separate species, is slightly larger and larger billed than Kumlien's and has blacker primary tips like Herring Gull. Has a darker eye, a smaller bill (often tinged greenish in winter), a thinner trailing edge of black on grayish underside of primaries, and more-extensive white mirrors than other adult W. Coast gulls. Variation in wingtip pattern between Kumlien's and Thayer's breeding in the high Arctic may be nearly continuous. *First- and second-years:* See p. 108. **VOICE:** Similar to Herring Gull but higher pitched; rarely heard away from breeding grounds. **SIMILAR SPECIES:** Glaucous Gull similar to Kumlien's but has larger bill, shorter primary extension. Herring Gull larger and has paler back and eye than Thayer's. First-year Glaucous-winged Gull can be very similar to first-year Thayer's (see p. 108). **RANGE:** Iceland Gull rare inland across N. America; Kumlien's a scarce vagrant to W. Coast and Thayer's a scarce vagrant to E. Coast. **HABITAT:** Ocean, coastlines, freshwater outflows, dumps.

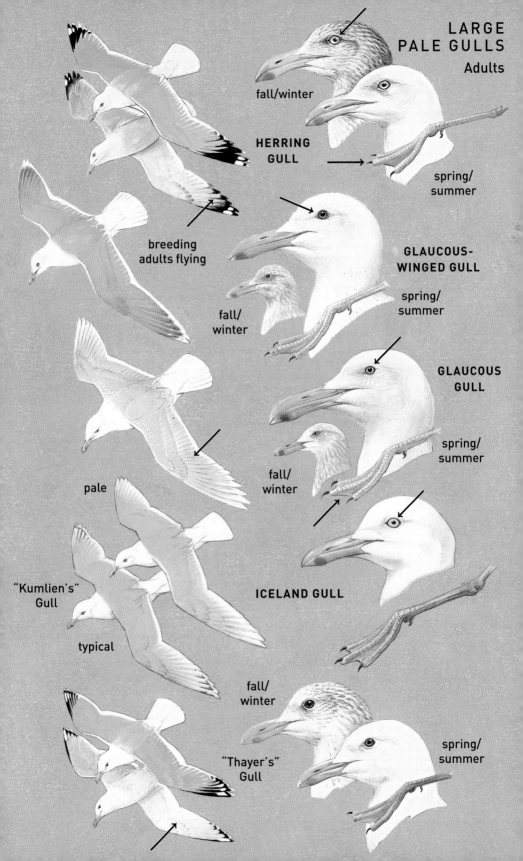

LARGE
PALE GULLS
Adults

fall/winter

HERRING
GULL

spring/
summer

breeding
adults flying

GLAUCOUS-
WINGED GULL

fall/
winter

spring/
summer

GLAUCOUS
GULL

spring/
summer

fall/
winter

pale

"Kumlien's"
Gull

ICELAND GULL

typical

fall/
winter

"Thayer's"
Gull

spring/
summer

WESTERN GULL *Larus occidentalis* Locally common

25–26 in. (64–66 cm). A large, large-billed gull. *Adult:* Note *very dark* back and wings *(mantle)* contrasting with snowy underparts. Legs and feet dull pinkish. Northern subspecies (cen. CA to WA) has paler mantle, but it is still noticeably darker than that of California Gull. Southern subspecies *(wymani)* is blacker backed. From below, dark primaries and secondaries contrast with white wing lining more than in other gulls. *First- and second-years:* See p. 106. *Note:* There is extensive and near-continuous hybridization with Glaucous-winged Gull where their breeding ranges overlap (notably in the Olympic Peninsula, WA, south to CA and sometimes inland in winter). Hybrids have intermediate mantle and wingtip coloration (see p. 106). **VOICE:** Guttural *kuk kuk kuk;* also *whee whee whee* and *ki-aa.* **SIMILAR SPECIES:** Glaucous-winged, Herring, and California Gulls. Back and wingtips of hybrid Western × Glaucous-winged Gulls not as contrasting and note also the much larger and stouter bills. **HABITAT:** Offshore and coastal waters, beaches, piers, city waterfronts, parks, lower reaches of tidal rivers. Casual to accidental vagrant well inland and to E. Coast.

SLATY-BACKED GULL *Larus schistisagus* Scarce, local

25–26 in. (64–67 cm). A dark-backed Asian gull. *Adult:* Similar to Western Gull, but with paler "staring" eye, deeper pinkish feet, more *extensive head markings* in fall/winter plumage. White subterminal tongues form *thin white bar* crossing dark outer primaries. *First-year:* Similar to Herring Gull but dumpier, legs darker purplish, bill stout and black, inner primaries not as pale. *Second- and third-years:* Follow plumage and bill color changes of Kelp Gull as shown on p. 110 but legs dark pink; eye paler than in similar-aged Western Gull. **SIMILAR SPECIES:** Siberian subspecies of Herring Gull *(vegae),* also found in w. AK, is darker mantled than N. American subspecies. **RANGE:** Regular visitor to w. AK, rare vagrant to CA, casual vagrant across much of the rest of N. America. **HABITAT:** Seacoasts, beaches, dumps.

YELLOW-FOOTED GULL *Larus livens* Fairly common, local

27 in. (69 cm). In the U.S., found regularly only at Salton Sea, CA. *Adult:* This large gull closely resembles Western Gull, but adult has *yellow* (not pinkish) legs and feet and slightly thicker bill. *First-, second-, and third-years:* Similar to equivalent plumages in Western Gull (p. 106) but second-summer plumage more adultlike. Attain yellow legs and feet by second winter. **VOICE:** Deeper than Western's. **HABITAT:** Same as Western Gull. Accidental along CA coast.

GREAT BLACK-BACKED GULL *Larus marinus* Common

29–30 in. (73–76 cm). Largest gull in the world, with broad wings and heavy body and bill. *Adult:* Black back and wings, snow-white underparts, no head streaking in winter. Legs and feet *pale* pinkish. *First- and second-years:* See p. 106. **VOICE:** Harsh deep seal-like *kyow* or *owk.* **SIMILAR SPECIES:** Lesser Black-backed and Slaty-backed Gulls. **HABITAT:** Mainly coastal waters, estuaries, dumps; a few well inland on large lakes and rivers. Rare vagrant to West, accidental to W. Coast.

LESSER BLACK-BACKED GULL *Larus fuscus* Scarce to uncommon

21–22½ in. (53–57 cm). Similar to Great Black-backed Gull but smaller (usually smaller than Herring Gull) and slimmer, with longer wings and smaller, slimmer bill. Distinguished by yellowish (not pink) legs and slate gray (not black) mantle. Extensive head and neck streaking or mottling in fall/winter plumage. Pale eye. Oblong red spot on bill. *First- and second-years:* See p. 106. **VOICE:** Harsh *kyah.* **SIMILAR SPECIES:** Great Black-backed Gull, Slaty-backed Gull. **HABITAT:** Same as Herring Gull. Rare vagrant inland across N. America; scarce vagrant to W. Coast.

LARGE DARK GULLS
Dark-backed Adults

WESTERN GULL

Southern

Northern

SLATY-BACKED GULL

spring/summer

YELLOW-FOOTED GULL

Great Black-backed Gull

LESSER BLACK-BACKED GULL

among the gulls on this plate, only Slaty-backed and Lesser Black-backed show heavy head streaking in fall/winter

GREAT BLACK-BACKED GULL

FIRST-YEAR and SECOND-YEAR GULLS

First-year and second-year gulls of many species are more difficult to identify than adults. They are usually darkest the first year, lighter and more adultlike the second and third years (see p. 94). Body and bill size and structure are useful for identification. Expect intermediate and successive plumage stages to those shown here.

LAUGHING GULL *Leucophaeus atricilla* Adult, p. 96

Most reach adult plumage by third year. *Juvenile:* Brownish, black tail, white rump, *broad white* trailing edge of wing. *First-year:* Neck and back smudged with gray. *Second-year:* Similar to fall/winter adult but wing tips darker, some black in tail.

FRANKLIN'S GULL *Leucophaeus pipixcan* Adult, p. 96

Most reach adult plumage by third year. *First-year and Second-year:* Similar to Laughing, but *smaller with smaller bill, more extensive blackish half-hood, incomplete tail band,* paler underside to primaries. *Second-year:* Close to second-year Laughing but with blackish half-hood, pale underside to primaries.

BLACK-HEADED GULL *Chroicocephalus ridibundus* Adult, p. 96

Most reach adult plumage by second year. *First-year:* Similar to first-year Bonaparte's but slightly larger; bill longer, redder; *sooty underwing.*

BONAPARTE'S GULL *Chroicocephalus philadelphia* Adult, p. 96

Most reach adult plumage by second year. *First-year:* Note dark ear spot, narrow black tail band, neat dark trailing edge to wings, and white in outer primaries. Pale underwing. See also Sequence of Plumages in Small Gulls, p. 94.

LITTLE GULL *Hydrocoloeus minutus* Adult, p. 96

Most reach adult plumage by second year. *First-year:* Smaller than Bonaparte's Gull, with *bolder black-and-white M pattern* across back and wings, *dusky cap.*

SABINE'S GULL *Xema sabini* Adult, p. 96

Most reach adult plumage by second year. *Juvenile:* Has adult's bold *triangular wing pattern* but back brown, scaled white. *First-spring:* Black hood partial.

HEERMANN'S GULL *Larus heermanni* Adult, p. 98

Most reach adult plumage by fourth year. *Juvenile: Dark chocolate* with pale-fringed feathers. *First-year and Second-year:* Plumage becomes grayer with broader white tips to secondaries and tail. *Black legs and feet,* salmon to reddish bill, tipped black.

BLACK-LEGGED KITTIWAKE *Rissa tridactyla* Adult, p. 98

Most reach adult plumage by third year. *First-year: Dark bar on nape, black M across back and wings;* tail may seem notched. White trailing edge to wings. *Second-year:* Like adult with more black to upperwing.

MEW GULL *Larus canus* Adult, p. 98

Most reach adult plumage by third year. *First-year:* Smaller than Ring-billed and darker overall, with shorter, slimmer bill, rounder head, browner primaries, darker tail and uppertail coverts. *Second-year:* See second-year Ring-billed; some third-year Mews may be identified as in other large gulls.

RING-BILLED GULL *Larus delawarensis* Adult, p. 98

Most reach adult plumage by third year. *First-year: Bicolored (pinkish-based) bill, pale gray back.* Well-defined subterminal tail band; contrasty wing pattern. *Second-year:* Like adult but upperwing has more brown and black and tail has some black. See also Sequence of Plumages in Medium-sized Gulls, p. 94.

SMALL AND MEDIUM-SIZED GULLS
First- and Second-Years

juvenile

first-winter

juvenile

Laughing Gull

first-winter

LAUGHING GULL

first-year

FRANKLIN'S GULL

Franklin's Gull

first-year

BONAPARTE'S GULL

first-year

first-year

BLACK-HEADED GULL

first-year

LITTLE GULL

first-year

SABINE'S GULL

juvenile

first-year

HEERMANN'S GULL

first-year

second-year

first-year

BLACK-LEGGED KITTIWAKE

first-year

first-year

MEW GULL

RING-BILLED GULL

FIRST-YEAR, SECOND-YEAR, and THIRD-YEAR LARGE DARK GULLS

WESTERN GULL *Larus occidentalis*　　　　Adult, p. 102

Most reach adult plumage by fourth year. First-year Western is very dark; larger, larger-billed, and sootier brown than most California and Herring Gulls and lacks pale inner primaries of latter. Back and wing-covert fringing not as patterned as in first-year California Gull and bill entirely black. *Second-year:* Similar to first-year but not as patterned, gains some gray upperpart feathers by spring; bill black with dull and messy pinkish base. *Third-year:* Resembles adult but upperwing has some brown and more blackish to tip; bill has dusky ring or smudge; tail has some black. Hybridizes extensively with Glaucous-winged Gull; first-year hybrid shown.

CALIFORNIA GULL *Larus californicus*　　　　Adult, p. 98

Most reach adult plumage by fourth year. *First-year:* Like Herring Gull, but more slender, with slimmer and always distinctly bicolored bill. Upperparts have distinct paler checkering, and wing lacks pale area on inner primaries. *Second-year:* Legs and bill base often dull gray-green. Somewhat similar to first-winter Ring-billed Gull, but larger, darker, retains dark eye, and tail mostly dark rather than with only a dark subterminal band. *Third-year:* Like adult but more black in wingtips, some black usually in tail, black of bill more extensive, sometimes forming ring (but red spot also present). In larger gulls, females have smaller bills and rounder heads than males, as shown here. Casual vagrant to East, accidental to E. Coast.

LESSER BLACK-BACKED GULL *Larus fuscus*　　　　Adult, p. 102

Most reach adult plumage by fourth year. Smaller, slimmer than Herring Gull. *First-year:* Like miniature first-year Great Black-backed but with broader tail band, much darker wings and back, more heavily streaked breast. Colder brown than Herring with white tail base, paler head and underparts, darker wings; black bill. *Second- and third-years:* Follow plumages and bill colors of other large gulls except some are more adultlike in second spring/summer.

HERRING GULL *Larus argentatus*　　　　Adult, p. 100

Most reach adult plumage by fourth year. *First-year:* Extremely variable; combine body and bill structure with plumage to identify. Brownish overall, with brownish-black wingtips and dark brown tail; only all-brown gull commonly seen in the East. Often shows much mottling or checkering on upperwing coverts and rump. *Pale area on inner primaries visible in flight.* Bill all dark in juvenile, becoming paler at base during first or second year (variable). *Second- and third-years:* Head and underparts variably become whiter; eye paler; back pale gray; rump white; bill pink then yellow, dark-tipped. See Sequence of Plumages in Large Gulls, p. 94.

GREAT BLACK-BACKED GULL *Larus marinus*　　　　Adult, p. 102

Most reach adult plumage by fourth or fifth year. *First-year:* Larger and more salt-and-pepper patterned than first-year Herring Gulls; more contrast, becoming whiter on head, rump, and underparts. Bill entirely black. *Second-year:* Similar to first-year but mantle becomes blacker during winter, up to completely black by second spring; bill becomes paler at base and often tipped yellow. *Third-year and some fourth-years:* Adultlike but secondaries and wing coverts (sometimes mantle) brownish or washed brown; wingtips darker, with smaller white mirrors; tail with black; bill variably black and yellowish.

LARGE DARK GULLS

First-Years and Second-Years

second-year

first-year

juvenile

WESTERN GULL

second-year

first-year Glaucous-winged x Western Gull

second-year

California Gull

CALIFORNIA GULL

first-year

second-year

variation in first-years

male

LESSER BLACK-BACKED GULL

first-year

first-year

HERRING GULL

female

GREAT BLACK-BACKED GULL

first-year

second-year

FIRST-YEAR and
SECOND-YEAR LARGE PALE GULLS

ICELAND GULL *Larus glaucoides*   Adult, p. 100

Most reach adult plumage by fourth year. For Thayer's subspecies, first-year is tan-brown and checkered; similar to juvenile Herring Gull but lighter; primaries paler, usually *light tan-brown* (not brownish black) *with pale edges to tips; bill entirely or almost entirely blackish, more petite; underside of primaries pale.* Often has dark smudge through eye. Usually smaller and darker-winged than first-year female Glaucous-winged but can be rather similar. *Second-year:* Paler and grayer; primaries gray-brown with darker outer webs. Plumages of Kumlien's subspecies similar to Glaucous Gull's, but size and structure differ as in adults (p. 100); bill of most first-year Iceland Gulls mostly dark, only very rarely as sharply demarcated as in Glaucous. Most birds have at least a hint of a tail band as well as some dark in outer primaries, both lacking in Glaucous. *Third-year:* In both subspecies, similar to adults but tail and bill usually have some dusky; white mirrors to outer primaries smaller.

GLAUCOUS GULL *Larus hyperboreus*   Adult, p. 100

Most reach adult plumage by fourth year. *First-year:* Recognized by its large size, pale tan when fresh, becoming white by late winter; primaries white with small black marks when fresh. Brownish barring on undertail coverts and mottling in wing coverts and tail. Bill *pale pinkish* with *sharply demarcated* dark tip. *Second-year:* Pale gray back and pale eye acquired; first- and second-year plumages often become nearly pure white through bleaching by spring. *Third-year:* Like adult but bill usually retains a dark tip or smudge.

GLAUCOUS-WINGED GULL *Larus glaucescens*   Adult, p. 100

Most reach adult plumage by fourth year. Variable. Size of or larger than Herring Gull, and with similar sequence of plumages (see p. 106), but primaries are close to same tone as rest of wing, not markedly darker as in Western and Herring Gulls, or paler or translucent as in Glaucous Gull. Hybrids with Western or Herring Gulls have intermediate-colored primaries. *First-year:* Can vary from checkered to muddy olive-gray in plumage. Smaller first-year females can be difficult to separate from first-year Thayer's but bill is usually larger. Worn first- and second-year Glaucous-wingeds in spring and summer may appear very white, but lack clean-cut two-toned bill of similar-aged Glaucous Gulls. Hybridizes extensively with Western Gull; see p. 106.

LARGE PALE GULLS

First-Years, Second-Years, and Third-Years

ICELAND GULL
"Thayer's"

second-year

first-year

first-year

second-year

first-year

"KUMLIEN'S" GULL

third-year

GLAUCOUS GULL

second- or third-year

Glaucous Gull first-year

"Kumlien's" Gull first-year

second-year

first-year

second-year

first-year

GLAUCOUS-WINGED GULL

RARE GULLS

BLACK-TAILED GULL *Larus crassirostris*　　　　Casual vagrant
18–18½ in. (46–47 cm). Size and shape of California Gull, with slightly longer bill. Adult has red tip to black-banded bill, slate gray mantle, and wide black subterminal band on tail. First-year very dark with bright pink-based bill. **RANGE:** Casual visitor from e. Asia, with widely scattered accidental records across much of N. America.

YELLOW-LEGGED GULL *Larus michahellis*　　　　Casual vagrant
24–24½ in. (61–63 cm). Native of s. Europe; very similar to Herring Gull but bill slightly stouter, adult's mantle slightly *darker gray,* and head flatter and only *finely streaked on crown* in fall/winter. *Yellow legs* of adult usually distinctive; occasional Herring Gulls can have yellowish tones to legs in early spring. **RANGE:** Casual visitor to NL and Atlantic Coast.

KELP GULL *Larus dominicanus*　　　　Vary rare vagrant
22–25 in. (56–64 cm). A black-backed, stocky gull of S. America that has reached the Caribbean and Gulf Coast as vagrants (accidental elsewhere throughout N. America); small numbers bred or hybridized with Herring Gulls during the 1990s in L.A. *Adult:* Black back, reduced mirrors to primaries (typically a *square patch on outermost primary only*), bill very stout, *legs bright greenish yellow.* Younger plumages and bill colors parallel those of other large dark-backed gulls. **SIMILAR SPECIES:** Lesser Black-backed Gull has similar plumages but is usually smaller, more slender, and has slimmer bill; juvenile and first-year Kelp Gulls have darker legs, blacker base to tail in flight.

RED-LEGGED KITTIWAKE　　　　Uncommon, very local, threatened
Rissa brevirostris
15 in. (38 cm). *Adult:* Similar to Black-legged Kittiwake but smaller, with *darker gray mantle* (noticeable when both species together); *shorter bill and rounder head* give it a more dovelike look; legs *bright red.* Wing pattern similar, although white trailing edge broader; *darkish gray underwing. First-year:* Wing and tail pattern similar to Sabine's Gull but back paler gray. Legs dull red. **VOICE:** High-pitched *tuu-WEE* near nesting colony. **HABITAT:** Open ocean, where it often forages at night. Nests in colonies on steep, rocky ocean cliffs. Accidental winter vagrant to CA.

ROSS'S GULL *Rhodostethia rosea*　　　　Very rare
13–13½ in. (33–35 cm). A rare Arctic gull of drift ice. Note *wedge-shaped tail, medium gray underwing linings,* and *small black bill. Spring/summer:* Rosy blush on underparts, *fine black collar. Fall/winter:* Less rosy, lacks black collar. *First-year:* Similar in pattern to first-year Black-legged Kittiwake or Little Gull, but intermediate in size and note longer *wedge-shaped tail* with black tip and *gray linings of underwing;* lacks dark nape of young kittiwake. **HABITAT:** Arctic waters, tundra in summer. Vagrant well south of normal winter range.

IVORY GULL *Pagophila eburnea*　　　　Very rare
17 in. (43 cm). A declining species of Arctic pack ice; those that wander south of normal range are usually first-years. Bill dark greenish with yellow tip. *Adult:* Small, all-white gull with black legs. Pigeonlike in size and head shape; wings long, flight ternlike. *First-year:* White, with dark *smudge on face, black spots* above, wing and tail feathers tipped black. **HABITAT:** Open Arctic waters near pack ice; vagrants well south of normal winter range found on coasts, lakes.

RARE GULLS

KELP GULL

juvenile

second-year

third-year
spring/summer
adult

YELLOW-
LEGGED GULL

BLACK-
TAILED
GULL

fall/winter
adult

spring/
summer
adult

spring/
summer
adult

RED-LEGGED
KITTIWAKE

fall/winter

spring/summer
adult

fall/winter

spring/
summer
adult

spring/
summer
adult

first-year

ROSS'S
GULL

adult

first-year

IVORY GULL

TERNS Subfamily Sterninae

Graceful waterbirds, more streamlined than gulls; wings more pointed, tail usually forked. Bill sharply pointed, often tilted toward water when bird is flying. Most terns are whitish with black cap; in fall/winter plumage, black crown replaced by white forehead and black masks through eyes, often connecting around nape. Sexes alike. Terns often hover and plunge headfirst for fish. Normally do not swim, as gulls do. **FOOD:** Small fish, marine life, large insects. **RANGE:** Almost worldwide.

FORSTER'S TERN *Sterna forsteri*   Common

14½ in. (37 cm). Very similar to Common Tern, but paler; adults have frosty wingtips (paler than rest of wing; darker in Common, although variable in both species depending on molt and wear), with more orange tone to thicker bill. Whitish below in all plumages, lacking gray wash of spring/summer Common. Tail grayer. Fall/winter adult and first-year have isolated *black mask;* first-year has slightly darker gray carpal (shoulder) bar, not as dark as in Common. See also Arctic Tern. Juvenile has upperpart fringing washed cinnamon; wing coverts tipped dark; tail short, forked. **VOICE:** Harsh, nasal *za-a-ap* and nasal *kyarr.* **HABITAT:** Fresh and salt marshes, lakes, bays, beaches, nests in marshes.

COMMON TERN *Sterna hirundo*   Uncommon in West to common in East

14 in. (36 cm). A graceful, black-capped, slim bird with deeply forked tail. *Spring/summer adult:* Pearl gray mantle and black cap; bill red with black tip; feet orange-red. Similar to Forster's and Arctic Terns, but *dark wedge on upperwing primaries.* *Grayer below* than Forster's, bill and legs smaller than in Forster's, larger than in Arctic. *Fall/winter adult and first-year:* Cap, nape, and bill blackish. *Dark shoulder bar. Juvenile:* Upperparts washed brownish; wing coverts tipped dark. Asian subspecies *(longipennis),* a very rare visitor in w. AK, darker, with *black bill* in spring/summer plumage and *blackish legs and feet.* **VOICE:** Drawling *kee-arr* (downward inflection); also *kik-kik-kik;* a quick *kirri-kirri.* **HABITAT:** Lakes, ocean, bays, marshes, beaches; nests colonially on sandy beaches and small islands. Rare inland in West.

ARCTIC TERN *Sterna paradisaea*   Uncommon

15 in. (38 cm). A pelagic (seagoing) tern when away from nesting grounds. Similar to Common Tern, but bill and neck shorter, head rounder. *Legs shorter.* Bill smaller. From below, note *translucent* effect of primaries and *narrow* black trailing edge; from above, secondaries pale. *Spring/summer adult:* Bill usually *blood red* to tip, uniform pale gray upperwing, extensive wash of *gray below,* setting off white cheeks. *Fall/winter and juvenile:* Like Common, but black on head slightly more extensive, shoulder bar somewhat *weaker, secondaries whitish,* and same structural differences noted above. **VOICE:** *Kee-yak,* similar to Common Tern's cry, but less slurred, higher. A high *keer-keer* is characteristic. **HABITAT:** Open ocean; in summer, taiga lakes, tundra; rare vagrant on coasts and casual inland.

ROSEATE TERN *Sterna dougallii*   Scarce, local

15½ in. (39 cm). Similar to Common Tern, but much paler overall, with longer tail points. *At rest, tail extends well beyond wingtips.* In spring and summer, *thin, long black bill sets it apart from similar terns,* all of which have reddish bill at that time of year. When breeding, Roseate may acquire rosy blush to breast and varying amounts of red at base of bill; *shallower wingbeats* and *different call* also separate it from Common. *Adult winter, first-year, and juvenile:* Similar to respective Common Terns but back of juvenile has pattern of coarse black crescents (can be darker than shown); forehead darker. **VOICE:** Rasping *ka-a-ak;* a soft two-syllable *chu-ick* or *chiv-ick.* **HABITAT:** Salt bays, estuaries, ocean. Northeastern U.S. populations endangered, FL populations threatened.

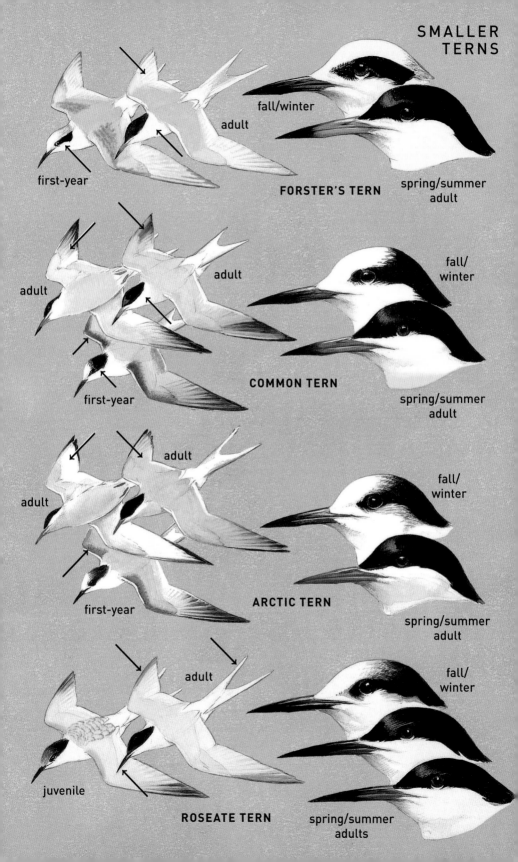

SMALLER
TERNS

first-year

adult

fall/winter

spring/summer
adult

FORSTER'S TERN

adult

adult

first-year

fall/
winter

COMMON TERN

spring/summer
adult

adult

adult

first-year

fall/
winter

ARCTIC TERN

spring/summer
adult

adult

juvenile

fall/
winter

ROSEATE TERN

spring/summer
adults

SANDWICH TERN *Thalasseus sandvicensis*　　Fairly common

15–15½ in. (38–40 cm). Larger than Common Tern. Note *long black bill with yellow tip* "as though dipped in mustard." Outer primaries variably dark from above, tipped dusky from below. Legs black. *Adult:* All-black cap in spring/summer plumage, white forehead in fall/winter plumage; feathers on back of crown elongated, forming crest. *First-year:* Like winter adult, tertials with dark centers, cap mostly white in spring/summer. *Juvenile:* Upperpart feathers tipped black; bill can be mostly black or mostly yellow. **VOICE:** Grating *kirr-ick* (higher than Gull-billed Tern's *kay-weck*). **SIMILAR SPECIES:** Gull-billed Tern has stout black bill. **HABITAT:** Coastal waters, jetties, beaches. Often seen with Royal Tern. Scarce vagrant inland after hurricanes in East; accidental vagrant along W. Coast.

ELEGANT TERN *Thalasseus elegans*　　Locally common

17 in. (43 cm). Smaller and slimmer than Royal Tern. Bill orange or orange-yellow, proportionately *longer, more slender,* and slightly droopier than deeper orange bill of Royal. In spring/summer, Elegant's black crown extends farther down nape. In fall/winter and first-year plumages, dark of head *includes eye.* *First-year:* Like winter adult, tertials with dark centers, cap mostly white, and outer primaries darker in spring/summer. *Juvenile:* Upperpart feathers fringed dusky; bill yellow to pale orange. Note head pattern of juvenile can be similar to Royal Tern. Following breeding, juveniles follow adults north along W. Coast. **VOICE:** Nasal *karrik* or *kerr-rik.* **SIMILAR SPECIES:** Royal and Caspian Terns. **HABITAT:** Ocean, coasts, beaches, salt bays. Accidental vagrant inland and to E. and Gulf Coasts.

ROYAL TERN *Thalasseus maximus*　　Common

20 in. (51 cm). A large tern, slimmer than Caspian, with medium-large *orange* bill (Caspian's bill heavier, redder, and has dark mark near tip, Elegant's bill much thinner, proportionately longer, and paler orange or yellow-orange). Tail forked. Although some Royal Terns in spring have solid black crown, for most of year they have *much white on forehead,* black crown feathers forming a crest. In fall/winter plumage, black feathers behind eye usually *do not encompass eye* as they do in fall/winter Elegant Tern. Dusky upperside and *pale underside to primaries,* opposite of Caspian. *First-year:* Like winter adult, tertials with dark centers, cap mostly white, and outer primaries darker in spring/summer. *Juvenile:* Upperpart feathers have neat black crescents; wing coverts streaked black. **VOICE:** Sonorous *karr-rik,* mellower (slower and lower-pitched) than Elegant or Sandwich; also *kaak* or *kak.* **SIMILAR SPECIES:** Caspian and Elegant Terns. **HABITAT:** Ocean, coasts, beaches, salt bays (accidental vagrant inland). More closely tied to coastal waters than Caspian, which is regular inland.

CASPIAN TERN *Hydroprogne caspia*　　Uncommon

21 in. (53 cm). Large size and *stout reddish bill with small dark mark near tip* set Caspian apart from all other terns. Tail of Caspian *shorter;* head and bill larger, crest shorter and less shaggy. Royal's forehead is usually *clear white* in adult fall/winter plumage, whereas Caspian has *gray-streaked* forehead. Caspian shows obvious *grayish black on undersurface of primaries, but pale upper surface.* *First-year:* Rare in our area but cap like winter adult's. *Juvenile:* Upperpart feathers boldly marked gray and black; wing coverts have dusky markings. **VOICE:** Raspy, low *kraa-uh* or *karr,* also repeated *kak;* juvenile gives whistled *wheee-oo.* **SIMILAR SPECIES:** Royal and Elegant Terns. Caspian ranges inland, Royal usually does not. **HABITAT:** Large lakes, rivers, coastal waters, beaches, bays.

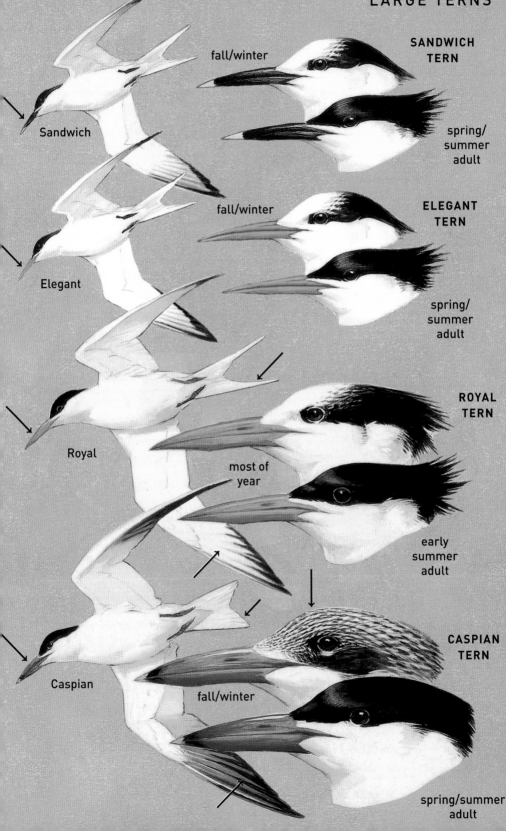

LARGE TERNS

fall/winter

Sandwich

SANDWICH
TERN

spring/
summer
adult

fall/winter

Elegant

ELEGANT
TERN

spring/
summer
adult

Royal

ROYAL
TERN

most of
year

early
summer
adult

Caspian

CASPIAN
TERN

fall/winter

spring/summer
adult

GULL-BILLED TERN *Gelochelidon nilotica* Uncommon

14 in. (36 cm). Note *stout black bill*. Stockier and paler than Common Tern; tail much less forked; feet *black*. In fall/winter plumage, head white with smudgy dark ear patch, pale dusky on nape; suggests a small gull with notched tail. *First-year:* Similar to fall/winter adult; carpal bar dusky; crown mostly pale in spring/summer. *Juvenile:* Pale; crown and upperparts washed pale brown; wing coverts grayish. This tern plucks food from water's surface and often hawks for insects over marshes and fields, swooping (rarely diving) after prey. **VOICE:** *Kay-weck, kay-weck;* also a throaty, rasping *za-za-za.* **SIMILAR SPECIES:** Sandwich Tern, Forster's Tern in winter, small gulls. **HABITAT:** Marshes, fields, coastal bays. Accidental vagrant inland.

LEAST TERN *Sternula antillarum* Locally common

9 in. (23 cm). A *very small* tern, with rapid wingbeats (quicker than other terns). *Spring/summer adult:* Dark-tipped *yellow bill, yellow legs and feet* (in fall, all birds may have dark bill, but feet still show dull yellow), and *white forehead*. Long black wedge on outer wing. *First-year:* Dark bill, dark cheek and nape, dusky crown, dark carpal (shoulder) bar, duller legs. *Juvenile:* Upperpart feathers and wing coverts streaked dusky and fringed brownish cinnamon. **VOICE:** Sharp, repeated *kit;* a harsh, squealing *zree-eek* or *k-zeek;* also a rapid *kitti-kitti-kitti.* **SIMILAR SPECIES:** Forster's Tern is much bigger. **HABITAT:** Beaches, bays, ponds, large rivers, sandbars. Populations breeding in CA (subspecies *browni*) and those of *antillarum* in the Mississippi R. drainage endangered. Rare to casual vagrant inland throughout U.S.

ALEUTIAN TERN *Onychoprion aleuticus* Scarce, local

13½–14 in. (34–36 cm). A gray-backed tern of Alaskan coastal waters. Told from Common and Arctic Terns by its *blackish bill and legs, clean-cut white forehead, dark bar along underside of secondaries.* *Spring/summer adult:* Pale gray underparts and medium-gray mantle contrast with white tail. *Fall/winter adult and first-year:* Not seen in our area; underparts white; cap whitish, dark carpal upperwing mark in first year. *Juvenile:* Upperpart feathers and wing coverts largely brown to rusty brown; legs orangey red. **VOICE:** Three-syllable whistle, suggesting a shorebird or House Sparrow. **HABITAT:** Open ocean; summers/ nests along AK coast on islands, sandbars.

BLACK TERN *Chlidonias niger* Uncommon

9½–9¾ in. (24–25 cm). A black-bodied tern in summer. Short tail only slightly forked. *Spring/summer adult:* Head and underparts (except undertail coverts) black; back, wings, and tail dark gray; underwing linings whitish. *Fall/winter adult:* By midsummer, molting birds are mottled, with black largely replaced by white. Note pied head, with dark smudge from crown to ear coverts and on sides of breast. *First-year:* Similar to winter adult but with stronger blackish shoulder bar; body and head remain at least partly white through first summer. *Juvenile:* Similar to first-year but with upperpart feathers fringed brown. **VOICE:** Sharp *kik, keek,* or *klea.* **SIMILAR SPECIES:** White-winged Tern. **HABITAT:** Freshwater marshes, lakes; in migration, also coastal waters, including open ocean.

WHITE-WINGED TERN *Chlidonias leucopterus* Scarce vagrant

9¼–9½ in. (23–24 cm). *Spring/summer:* Underwing lining black, upperwing mostly white, tail paler. *Fall/winter and first-year:* Paler than Black Tern; lacks dark mark on sides of upper breast. **RANGE:** Vagrant from Eurasia. Widespread sightings in East; accidental in West and HI.

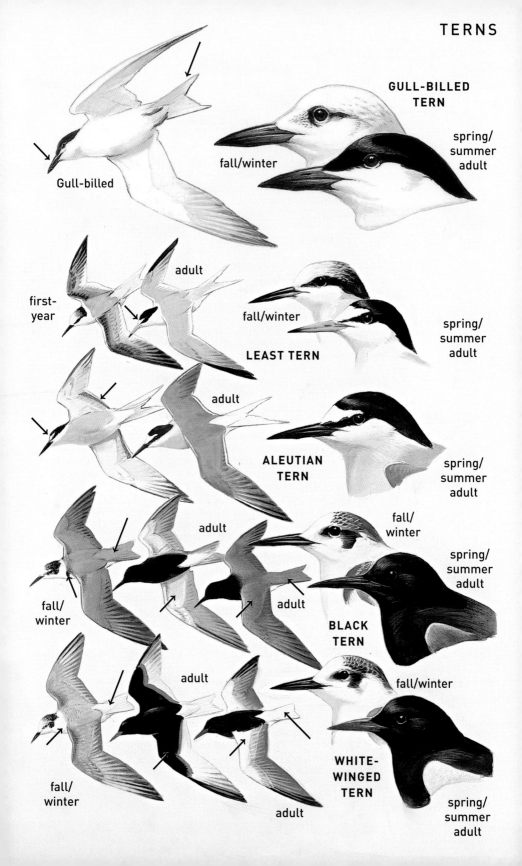

TERNS

GULL-BILLED TERN

Gull-billed

fall/winter

spring/
summer
adult

LEAST TERN

first-
year

adult

adult

fall/winter

spring/
summer
adult

ALEUTIAN TERN

adult

adult

spring/
summer
adult

BLACK TERN

adult

fall/
winter

adult

adult

fall/
winter

spring/
summer
adult

WHITE-WINGED TERN

fall/
winter

adult

adult

fall/winter

spring/
summer
adult

BROWN NODDY *Anous stolidus* Uncommon, local

15–15½ in. (38–40 cm). A brown tern with *whitish cap.* Long, wedge-shaped tail. First-year has duller cap. **VOICE:** Ripping *karrrrk* or *arrrrowk;* a harsh *eye-ak.* **SIMILAR SPECIES:** Black Noddy occurs occasionally with Brown Noddies at Dry Tortugas, FL. Scarce vagrant along E. Coast after hurricanes. **HABITAT:** Warm ocean waters. Fairly common breeding species in HI (p. 426).

BLACK NODDY *Anous minutus* Very rare visitor

13½ in. (34 cm). A rare but almost annual spring visitor to Dry Tortugas, FL, and casual visitor to TX. Slightly smaller and sootier colored than Brown Noddy, with thinner and proportionately *longer bill,* shorter forked tail, and more extensive and *sharply defined white cap.* Most birds seen in U.S. are one-year-olds, which show worn, brownish wings and less sharp cap. **VOICE:** Variety of chatters, croaks, and bill rattles. **SIMILAR SPECIES:** Brown Noddy. **HABITAT:** Tropical islands. Fairly common breeding species in HI (p. 426).

SOOTY TERN *Onychoprion fuscatus* Uncommon, local

16 in. (41 cm). *Adult:* A cleanly patterned tern, black above and white below. Cheeks and patch on forehead white; bill and feet black. *Juvenile:* Dark brown; back spotted with white; underwing lining and vent grayish; note forked tail. Fall/winter adult and first-year have whitish nape. Can occur farther north and inland after hurricanes. **VOICE:** Nasal *wide-a-wake* or *wacky-wack.* **SIMILAR SPECIES:** Bridled Tern. Juvenile somewhat similar to spring/summer Black Tern but larger, upperpart feathers tipped white; underwing and vent darker (grayish, not white). **HABITAT:** Warm ocean waters. Common breeding species in HI (p. 426). Rare vagrant in East inland and to Northeast coast after hurricanes; accidental vagrant to CA.

BRIDLED TERN *Onychoprion anaethetus* Uncommon, local

15 in. (38 cm). A tern of warm oceans and, after hurricanes, farther north and occasionally inland. Adult resembles Sooty Tern, but back brownish, not blackish; *note whitish collar separating black cap from back;* white forehead patch extends noticeably behind eye (in Sooty, to above eye). Sooty also has more limited white in tail and more contrasting black-and-white underwing lining. Juvenile and first-year have whiter head; upperparts barred white. **VOICE:** Mostly silent; sometimes gives a soft, nasal *wheeep.* **SIMILAR SPECIES:** Sooty Tern. **HABITAT:** Warm ocean waters, usually well offshore. Rare vagrant in East inland and to Northeast coast after hurricanes; accidental vagrant to CA.

SKIMMERS Subfamily Rynchopinae

Slim, short-legged relatives of gulls and terns. Scissorlike red bill; lower mandible longer than upper. **FOOD:** Small fish, crustaceans. **RANGE:** Coasts, ponds, marshes, beaches, rivers of warmer parts of world.

BLACK SKIMMER *Rynchops niger* Locally common

18–18½ in. (46–47 cm). More slender than a gull, with very long wings. Skims low, with stiff wingbeats, dipping lower mandible in water, snapping shut when it comes in contact with a food item. (Forages mostly at night.) *Adult:* Black above (nape becomes white in fall/winter); white face and underparts. Bright red bill (tipped with black) is long and flat vertically; *lower mandible juts up to a third beyond upper.* Reddish legs. *Juvenile:* Upperpart feathers paler brown and broadly fringed with whitish, bill smaller, bill and legs duller. *First-year:* Retains white-fringed outer wing coverts, nape whitish in spring/summer. **VOICE:** Soft, short, barking notes. Also *kaup, kaup.* **HABITAT:** Bays, marshes, beaches, protected ocean waters. Accidental vagrant inland.

Black Tern
(p. 116)

fall/winter for
comparison

BROWN NODDY

BLACK
NODDY

juvenile

SOOTY TERN

Sooty Tern

adult

BRIDLED
TERN

adult

juvenile

adult

BLACK SKIMMER

adult

SHOREBIRDS

Many shorebirds (or "waders," as they are called in the Old World) are real puzzlers to the novice, and to many experienced birders as well! There are a dozen plovers in our area, and nearly 60 sandpipers and their allies. Many species have up to five different plumages: spring/summer adult (Apr.–Sept.), winter adult and first-winter (Oct.–Mar.), first-summer (Apr.–Sept.), and juvenile (July–Sept.). Being able to properly age many species is an important part of correctly identifying them. Noting size, shape, and feeding style is also a critical part of the identification process.

Plovers are usually more compact and thicker necked than most sandpipers, with a pigeonlike bill and larger eyes. They run in short starts and stops.

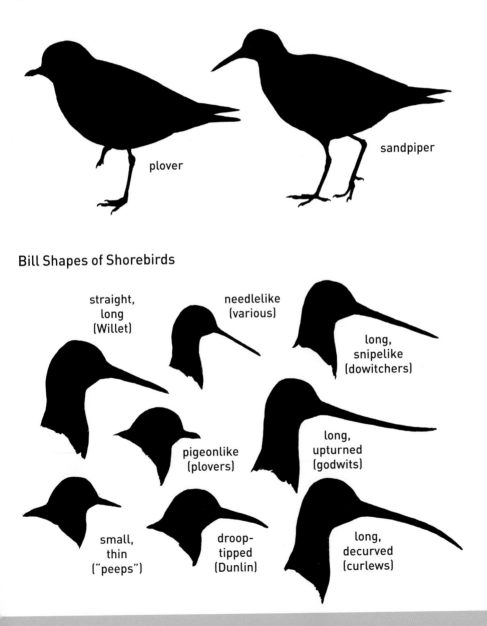

plover

sandpiper

Bill Shapes of Shorebirds

straight, long (Willet)

needlelike (various)

long, snipelike (dowitchers)

pigeonlike (plovers)

long, upturned (godwits)

small, thin ("peeps")

droop-tipped (Dunlin)

long, decurved (curlews)

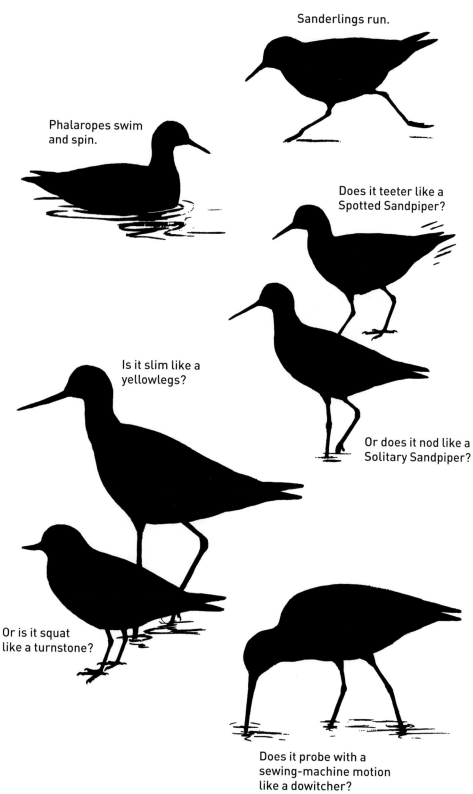

Sanderlings run.

Phalaropes swim and spin.

Does it teeter like a Spotted Sandpiper?

Is it slim like a yellowlegs?

Or does it nod like a Solitary Sandpiper?

Or is it squat like a turnstone?

Does it probe with a sewing-machine motion like a dowitcher?

PLOVERS Family Charadriidae

Largely nonwading birds, more compactly built and thicker necked than most sandpipers, with shorter, pigeonlike bills and larger eyes. Call notes are distinctive and assist identification. Unlike most sandpipers, plovers run in short starts and stops, often on dry mud and in fields. Sexes alike or differ slightly. **FOOD:** Small marine life, insects, some vegetable matter. **RANGE:** Nearly worldwide.

BLACK-BELLIED PLOVER *Pluvialis squatarola* (see also p. 146) Common

11½ in. (29 cm). A large plover, recognized as one by stocky shape, hunched posture, and short, pigeonlike bill. *Spring/summer adult:* Has *black face and breast* (duller and mottled white in female) and pale speckled back. *Fall/winter adult, first-winter, and juvenile:* Look tan-gray to grayish white (juvenile scalier backed). *First-spring/summer:* Variable between winter and summer. In any plumage, note *black wingpits* and white rump and tail in flight. **VOICE:** Plaintive slurred whistle, *tlee-oo-eee* or *whee-er-eee* (middle note lower). **SIMILAR SPECIES:** American and Pacific Golden-Plovers slightly smaller and slimmer, smaller billed, buffier or more golden on at least some feathering, have more distinct supercilium, and *lack pattern of white in wings and tail.* **HABITAT:** Mudflats, marshes, beaches, rocks, short-grass habitats; in summer, tundra. Uncommon to rare inland across N. America.

AMERICAN GOLDEN-PLOVER *Pluvialis dominica* (see also p. 146) Uncommon

10¼–10½ in. (26–27 cm). Size of Killdeer. Shows distinct wingtip extension, the primaries extending well beyond tail tip when standing. *Spring/summer adult and first-summer:* Dark, spangled above with *whitish and pale yellow spots;* underparts black (slightly mottled white in female). *Broad white stripe* runs over eye and down sides of neck and breast. *Winter adult and first-winter:* Gray-brown, darker above than below, with distinct pale supercilium, dark crown. *Juvenile:* Similar to winter plumages but back slightly brighter golden, more scaled. **VOICE:** Whistled *queedle* or *que-e-a* (dropping at end). **SIMILAR SPECIES:** Black-bellied Plover, Pacific Golden-Plover. See European Golden-Plover (p. 154). **HABITAT:** Prairies, mudflats, shores, short-grass pastures, sod farms; in summer, tundra. Rare vagrant to W. Coast.

PACIFIC GOLDEN-PLOVER *Pluvialis fulva* (see also p. 146) Uncommon, local

10–10¼ in. (25–26 cm). Very similar to American Golden-Plover but wingtip extension beyond tail tip shorter. *Spring/summer adult:* White neck stripe *extends down to flanks* and there is more white on undertail coverts (but molting adult American Golden-Plovers may have this look). Golden spangles on back brighter. Bill slightly larger and legs slightly longer. *Winter adult and first-winter:* Slightly more golden above than American. *Juvenile:* Substantially *more golden* above than American and with golden buff on face and breast. *First-spring/summer:* Variable between winter and summer. See also juvenile Eurasian Dotterel (p. 154). **VOICE:** Whistled *chu-wee* or *chu-wee-dle.* **HABITAT:** Same as American, though typically breeds in lower, wetter tundra. Common in HI (p. 428). Accidental vagrant well inland.

MOUNTAIN PLOVER *Charadrius montanus* Scarce, local

9 in. (23 cm). *Spring/summer adult and first-summer:* White forehead and face, black forecrown and loral stripe, and brownish rufous back. *Winter adult and first-winter:* May be told from golden-plovers by tan-brown back devoid of mottling and by pale tan, unmarked breast; juvenile (not shown) is scalier-backed. Has pale blue-gray legs, light wing stripe, and dark tail band. **VOICE:** Low whistle, variable. **SIMILAR SPECIES:** Black-bellied Plover, golden-plovers, Buff-breasted Sandpiper. **HABITAT:** Plowed fields, short-grass plains, dry sod farms. Casual vagrant well east of range; accidental to E. Coast.

PLOVERS

fall/winter

fall/winter

spring/
summer
adult

juvenile

BLACK-BELLIED
PLOVER

juveniles

fall/winter

juveniles

spring/
summer
adult

AMERICAN
GOLDEN-PLOVER

fall/winter

spring/
summer
adult

PACIFIC
GOLDEN-PLOVER

fall/winter

MOUNTAIN
PLOVER

spring/summer

COMMON RINGED PLOVER *Charadrius hiaticula*   Rare, local

7½ in. (19 cm). A largely Eurasian breeding species, very similar to Semi-palmated Plover; best distinguished by *voice*. Slightly longer bill, darker cheeks. Lacks obvious orbital ring. Spring/summer adult male has slightly bolder supercilium, wider breast-band. In all birds there is less-extensive basal webbing between toes. **VOICE:** Softer, more minor *poo-eep* or *too-li*. **RANGE:** Breeds in e. Canadian Arctic and in w. AK; winters in Old World. Casual or accidental vagrant elsewhere in N. America. **HABITAT:** Same as Semipalmated Plover.

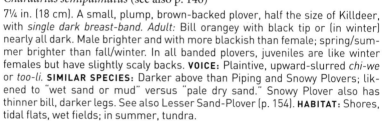

SEMIPALMATED PLOVER   Common
Charadrius semipalmatus (see also p. 146)

7¼ in. (18 cm). A small, plump, brown-backed plover, half the size of Killdeer, with *single dark breast-band*. *Adult:* Bill orangey with black tip or (in winter) nearly all dark. Male brighter and with more blackish than female; spring/summer brighter than fall/winter. In all banded plovers, juveniles are like winter females but have slightly scaly backs. **VOICE:** Plaintive, upward-slurred *chi-we* or *too-li*. **SIMILAR SPECIES:** Darker above than Piping and Snowy Plovers; likened to "wet sand or mud" versus "pale dry sand." Snowy Plover also has thinner bill, darker legs. See also Lesser Sand-Plover (p. 154). **HABITAT:** Shores, tidal flats, wet fields; in summer, tundra.

PIPING PLOVER *Charadrius melodus* (see also p. 146) **Uncommon, threatened**

7¼ in. (18 cm). Quite pallid in color, like dry sand. Legs yellow or orange. *Spring/summer male:* Bill has yellow-orange base, black tip; black band on upper breast can be complete or incomplete. *Female and juvenile:* Black on collar less distinct or lacking, bill dark. Note tail pattern. **VOICE:** Plaintive whistle: *peep-lo* (first note higher). **SIMILAR SPECIES:** Snowy and Semipalmated Plovers. **HABITAT:** Sandy beaches, dry mudflats; in summer, also lakeshores and river islands. Midwestern populations considered endangered, others threatened. Rare in interior East; accidental vagrant to W. Coast.

SNOWY PLOVER *Charadrius nivosus* (see also p. 146)   Uncommon

6¼–6½ in. (16–17 cm). A pale flatter-headed plover of beaches and alkaline flats. Note *slim black bill,* dark (sometimes pale) legs. Male has *dark ear patch,* paler and better-marked in summer than winter. *Female and juvenile:* Duller, lack black in plumage in winter. **VOICE:** Musical whistle, *pe-wee-ah* or *o-wee-ah;* also a low *prit*. **SIMILAR SPECIES:** Juvenile and winter Piping Plovers may also have dark (though stubbier) bill, but they are rounder headed, have brighter orange legs, and *paler rump* and uppertail coverts in flight. **HABITAT:** Beaches, sandy flats, alkaline lakeshores. W. Coast populations (subspecies *nivosus*) threatened. Casual to accidental vagrant well north in West and in East away from Gulf Coast.

WILSON'S PLOVER *Charadrius wilsonia* (see also p. 146)   Uncommon

7¾–8 in. (19–20 cm). Larger than Semipalmated Plover, with *wider breast-band* and longer, *heavier black bill*. Legs pinkish gray. Male has black breast-band in summer; female and first-year male browner. **VOICE:** Emphatic whistled *whit!* or *wheet!* **HABITAT:** Open beaches, tidal flats, sandy islands. Casual vagrant to Midwestern states and CA.

KILLDEER *Charadrius vociferus* (see also p. 146)   Common

10½ in. (27 cm). The common, noisy plover of farm country and ball fields. Note *two black breast-bands* (chick has only one band and might be confused with Wilson's Plover). Shows *rusty orange rump*, longish tail, white wing stripe. Sexes similar. **VOICE:** Noisy, often heard at night, a loud, insistent *kill-deeah*, repeated. Also a plaintive *dee-ee* (rising), *dee-dee-dee*, etc., and a low trill. **SIMILAR SPECIES:** Other banded plovers smaller, have single breast-band. **HABITAT:** Fields, airports, lawns, riverbanks, mudflats, shores.

BANDED PLOVERS

spring/
summer
adult male

COMMON
RINGED
PLOVER

fall/winter

SEMIPALMATED
PLOVER

spring/
summer
adult male

spring/
summer
adult male

fall/winter

SNOWY
PLOVER

spring/
summer
adult male,
breast-band
may be
unbroken

PIPING PLOVER

spring/summer
adult male

adult

first-year
female

WILSON'S
PLOVER

KILLDEER

spring/summer
adult

chick

adult and
first-year

Common Ringed

adult males

Piping

Killdeer

Snowy

Wilson's

Semipalmated

OYSTERCATCHERS Family Haematopodidae

Large shorebirds with long, laterally flattened, chisel-tipped, red bills. Sexes alike. **FOOD:** Mollusks, crabs, marine worms. **RANGE:** Widespread on coasts of world; inland in some areas of Europe and Asia.

AMERICAN OYSTERCATCHER *Haematopus palliatus*   Fairly common
17½–18½ in. (44–47 cm). A very noisy, thickset, black-headed shorebird with dark back, white belly, and large white wing and tail patches. Outstanding feature is large straight red bill, flattened laterally. Legs pale pink. *Juvenile and first-year:* Bill dark-tipped. **VOICE:** Piercing *wheep!* or *kleep!;* a loud *pic, pic, pic.* **SIMILAR SPECIES:** Differs from Black Oystercatcher in having *white belly,* browner upperparts, white wing stripe and rump patch. Subspecies found in nw. Mex. *(frazari)* and casually to s. CA, somewhat less clean-cut than birds in e. N. America; can have some dark mottling on upper breast and flanks. Also, hybrids between the two oystercatcher species occur in s. CA, which have more extensive dark mottling on underparts and rump. **HABITAT:** Coastal beaches, tidal flats. Accidental vagrant inland, as far west as ID.

BLACK OYSTERCATCHER *Haematopus bachmani*   Fairly common
17–17½ in. (43–44 cm). A large, heavily built, blackish shorebird with straight *orange-red bill,* flattened laterally. Thickish legs are pale pinkish. *Juvenile and first-year:* Bill dark-tipped. **VOICE:** Piercing, sharply repeated, whistled *wheer!* or *kleer!,* often repeated excitedly or in series. **SIMILAR SPECIES:** American Oystercatcher. Second-year Heermann's Gull can resemble Black Oystercatcher when asleep with bill tucked, but has black legs and feet. **HABITAT:** Rocky coasts, sea islets.

STILTS and AVOCETS Family Recurvirostridae

Slim waders with very long legs and very slender bills (bent upward in avocets). Sexes fairly similar. **FOOD:** Insects, crustaceans, other aquatic life. **RANGE:** N., Cen., and S. America, Africa, s. Eurasia, Australia, Pacific region.

BLACK-NECKED STILT *Himantopus mexicanus*   Fairly common
14 in. (36 cm). A large, extremely slim wader; black above (female and juvenile have browner backs), white below. Note *extremely long dark-pinkish legs,* needlelike bill. In flight, black *unpatterned* wings contrast strikingly with white rump, tail, and underparts. **VOICE:** Sharp yipping: *kyip, kyip, kyip.* **SIMILAR SPECIES:** Fall/winter American Avocet. **HABITAT:** Marshes, mudflats, pools, shallow lakes (fresh and alkaline), flooded fields. Resident subspecies occurs in HI (p. 432). Rare vagrant north of range and to E. Coast.

AMERICAN AVOCET *Recurvirostra americana*   Fairly common
18 in. (46 cm). A large, slim shorebird with very slender, *upturned bill,* more upturned in female. This and striking white-and-black pattern make this bird unique. In spring/summer plumage, head and neck pinkish tan or orangey buff; in fall/winter plumage, this color replaced by pale gray. Avocets feed with scythelike sweep of head and bill. **VOICE:** Sharp *wheek* or *kleet,* excitedly repeated. **HABITAT:** Mudflats, shallow lakes, marshes, prairie ponds. Rare vagrant to E. Coast.

OYSTERCATCHERS, STILT, AND AVOCET

BLACK OYSTERCATCHER

AMERICAN OYSTERCATCHER

BLACK-NECKED STILT

spring/summer

spring/summer

fall/winter

AMERICAN AVOCET

SANDPIPERS, PHALAROPES, and ALLIES
Family Scolopacidae

Small to large shorebirds. Bills more slender than those of plovers. Sexes mostly similar, except in phalaropes. **FOOD:** Insects, crustaceans, mollusks, worms, etc. **RANGE:** Cosmopolitan.

HUDSONIAN GODWIT *Limosa haemastica* (see also p. 148)   Scarce

15–15½ in. (38–39 cm). Rather large size and long, *slightly upturned* bill mark this wader as a godwit; *blackish underwing linings* proclaim this species. Black tail *ringed broadly with white. Spring/summer:* Male ruddy-breasted, female duller. *Fall/winter:* Both sexes gray-backed, pale-breasted; juvenile with more patterned scaly back; first-spring/summer birds not regularly found in our area. **VOICE:** *Tawit!* (or *godwit!*); higher pitched than Marbled Godwit's call. **SIMILAR SPECIES:** Bar-tailed and Black-tailed Godwits (see p. 156). **HABITAT:** Mudflats, prairie pools; in summer, marshy taiga and tundra. Rare inland in East and scarce vagrant to W. Coast.

MARBLED GODWIT   Common (West) to uncommon (East)
Limosa fedoa (see also p. 148)

17½–18½ in. (44–46 cm). Rich, mottled *buff-brown* color identifies this species. Underwing linings *cinnamon.* Spring/summer adults have more barring underneath than fall/winter birds and juveniles. **VOICE:** Accented *kerwhit!* (*godwit!*); also *raddica, raddica.* **SIMILAR SPECIES:** When head tucked in, difficult to tell from Long-billed Curlew except slightly smaller and thinner, leg color blackish (more blue-gray in the curlew), supercilium averages more distinct. See Bar-tailed Godwit (p. 156). Hudsonian Godwit has white on wings and tail, blackish underwing linings. **HABITAT:** Prairies, pools, shores, mudflats, beaches. Rare migrant or vagrant inland in East.

LONG-BILLED CURLEW   Fairly common
Numenius americanus (see also p. 148)

22–24 in. (55–60 cm). Note *very long, sickle-shaped bill* (4–8½ in.; 10–21 cm). Larger than Whimbrel and warmer colored overall; lacks distinct dark crown stripes. From below has *cinnamon underwing linings.* Ages and sexes rather similar; female larger with longer bill. **VOICE:** Loud *cur-lee* (rising inflection) or *curlew;* rapid, whistled *kli-li-li-li;* on breeding a longer drawn-out *curleeeeeeeeuuu.* **SIMILAR SPECIES:** See Marbled Godwit. Whimbrel is smaller, grayer (lacks cinnamon tones), and has shorter and blacker bill. **HABITAT:** High plains, rangeland; in winter, cultivated land, mudflats, beaches, salt marshes. Rare to casual migrant or winter vagrant to E. Coast.

WHIMBREL *Numenius phaeopus* (see also p. 148)   Fairly common

17–18 in. (43–46 cm). A large gray-brown shorebird with long *decurved bill.* Much grayer brown than Long-billed Curlew; bill shorter (2¾–4 in.; 7–10 cm); crown *striped;* in flight, uppersurface to outer two primaries has distinct white shafts. Ages and sexes similar through year. Vagrant Eurasian subspecies (*phaeopus* and *variegatus*) have white wedges up lower backs (p. 156) vs. dark in N. American *hudsonicus.* **VOICE:** Five to seven short, rapid whistles: *chee-chee-chee-chee-chee-chee.* **SIMILAR SPECIES:** Long-billed Curlew, Eskimo Curlew (p. 156). In AK and HI, see also Bristle-thighed Curlew (pp. 156 and 428). **HABITAT:** Mudflats, beaches, marshes, pastures, short-grass habitats; in summer, tundra. Uncommon to rare inland.

LARGE SANDPIPERS

spring/summer

fall/winter

fall/winter

HUDSONIAN GODWIT

spring/
summer male

MARBLED
GODWIT

LONG-BILLED
CURLEW

WHIMBREL

WANDERING TATTLER *Tringa incana* Uncommon

11 in. (28 cm). Recognized from other rock-inhabiting shorebirds by *lack of pattern in flight.* Solid lead gray above; light line over eye, dark line through it. Legs yellowish. Bobs and teeters like Spotted Sandpiper. *Spring/summer:* Underparts *barred. Fall/winter:* Gray-chested, with no barring. *Juvenile:* Like fall/winter but scaly above. **VOICE:** Clear, distinctive *wheedle-deedle-dee,* less sharp than Greater Yellowlegs, and all on same pitch. **SIMILAR SPECIES:** Willet much larger, with very different wing pattern. In w. AK, see Gray-tailed Tattler (p. 158). **HABITAT:** Rocky coasts, pebbly beaches, more rarely mudflats and sandy beaches. Nests near mountain streams above timberline. Common in HI in winter (p. 428). Accidental vagrant in N. America away from Pacific coast.

SURFBIRD *Calidris virgata* Uncommon

10 in. (25 cm). A stocky, dark sandpiper of wave-washed rocks. Note conspicuous *white rump and tail,* the latter *tipped with broad black band;* legs *yellowish.* Bill short, yellow at base. *Spring/summer:* Heavily streaked and spotted with blackish above and below; orangey scapulars. *Fall/winter and juvenile:* Gray above (juvenile slightly scaly) and across breast. **VOICE:** Sharp *pee-weet* or *key-a-weet.* **SIMILAR SPECIES:** Rock Sandpiper smaller and slimmer, with longer, slimmer bill, different tail pattern. Black Turnstone smaller, darker, has slimmer bill, white stripe up back, and reddish brown legs. **HABITAT:** Rocky coasts; nests on mountain tundra. Accidental vagrant inland and to E. Coast.

ROCK SANDPIPER *Calidris ptilocnemis* Uncommon

8¾–9¼ in. (22–24 cm). *Spring/summer:* Suggests a Dunlin, with rusty back, black splotch on breast (but Dunlin redder, with black splotch lower down, black legs). *Fall/winter:* Slaty, with white belly, white wing stripe. Legs dull yellow or greenish. Resident Pribilof Is. subspecies *(ptilocnemis)* slightly larger and paler than other subspecies *(couesi* and *tschuktschorum,* the latter wintering to n. CA). **VOICE:** Flickerlike *du-du-du.* When breeding, a trill. **SIMILAR SPECIES:** Its rock-feeding associates, Black Turnstone and Surfbird, are plumper, have shorter bills, and have broad *white band* across base of tail. Purple Sandpiper of Atlantic Coast and a rare vagrant to w. N. America can be very similar but usually has brighter orange legs and bill base, wing stripe slightly less extensive; in summer, rufous edging to back feathers broken (solid in Rock Sandpiper). **HABITAT:** Rocky shores; nests on mossy tundra.

PURPLE SANDPIPER *Calidris maritima* (see also p. 152) Uncommon

9 in. (23 cm). Stocky, dark sandpipers on rocks, jetties, or breakwaters along our n. Atlantic Coast in winter are likely to be this hardy species. *Fall/winter:* Slate gray with white belly. At close range, note short yellow-orange legs, dull orangish base of bill, and white eye-ring. *Spring/summer:* Much browner, more heavily streaked above and below with purplish sheen to some back feathers. **VOICE:** Low, scratchy *weet-wit* or *twit.* **SIMILAR SPECIES:** Fall/winter Dunlin, also found roosting on jetties, has plain brown back and breast, black bill and legs. See Rock Sandpiper. **HABITAT:** Wave-washed rocks, jetties, rarely sandy shoreline. Often quite tame. In summer, coastal tundra. Casual vagrant inland in East and to Gulf Coast; accidental vagrant to West.

ROCK-LOVING
SHOREBIRDS

WANDERING
TATTLER

spring/
summer

fall/
winter

SURFBIRD

spring/summer

fall/
winter

ROCK
SANDPIPER

spring/
summer

fall/
winter

spring/
summer

PURPLE
SANDPIPER

fall/
winter

RUDDY TURNSTONE *Arenaria interpres* (see also p. 146)   **Fairly common**

9½ in. (24 cm). A squat, robust, *orange-legged* shorebird, with *harlequin pattern*. *Spring/summer:* With russet back and curious face and breast pattern, bird is unique, but in flight it is even more striking. *Fall/winter and juvenile:* Duller, but retains body feathers and striking upperpart and wing patterns. **VOICE:** Staccato *tuk-a-tuk* or *kut-a-kut;* also a single *kewk.* **SIMILAR SPECIES:** Black Turnstone. **HABITAT:** Beaches, mudflats, rocky shores, jetties; in summer, tundra. Uncommon to rare inland. Declining along Pacific Coast but common in winter in HI (p. 428).

BLACK TURNSTONE   **Fairly common**
Arenaria melanocephala (see also p. 146)

9¼ in. (23 cm). Flight pattern similar to Ruddy Turnstone's but face and breast blacker. In spring/summer, has oval white spot before eye, and white speckling; winter birds and juveniles duller, browner. Legs darkish. **VOICE:** Rattling call, higher and longer than that of Ruddy Turnstone. **SIMILAR SPECIES:** Winter and juvenile Ruddy Turnstones have brighter legs, more white in faces, browner backs, and more rounded and defined breast patches not fully meeting in center. See also Surfbird. **HABITAT:** Strictly coastal (accidental vagrant inland in West). Rocky shores, surf-pounded islets, occasionally sandy beaches and mudflats. Nests on coastal tundra.

RED KNOT   *Calidris canutus* (see also p. 152)   **Uncommon**

10½ in. (27 cm). Larger than Sanderling. Stocky, with medium-length straight bill and short legs. *Spring/summer:* Face and underparts *pale robin red;* back mottled with black, gray, and russet. *Fall/winter:* A dumpy wader with washed-out gray look and mottled flanks; medium bill, pale rump in flight, greenish legs. *Juvenile:* Has *pale feather edgings* above and pale buff wash on breast. **VOICE:** A low, mellow *tooit-wit* or *wah-quoit;* also a short, low *tchrrt.* **SIMILAR SPECIES:** Dowitchers. Great Knot (p. 160). **HABITAT:** Tidal flats, sandy beaches, shores; tundra when breeding. Populations breeding in Canadian Arctic and migrating through East (subspecies *rufa*) considered threatened. Uncommon to rare inland.

SANDERLING   *Calidris alba* (see also p. 152)   **Common**

8 in. (20 cm). A plump, active sandpiper of outer beaches, where it chases retreating waves like wind-up toys. Note bold *white wing stripe* in flight. *Spring/ summer:* Bright rusty about head, back, and breast (male averages brighter than female). *Fall/winter:* The palest sandpiper; snowy white underparts, plain pale gray back, *black shoulders.* *Juvenile:* Has salt-and-pepper pattern on back and breast sides. **VOICE:** Short *kip* or *quit.* **SIMILAR SPECIES:** Western Sandpiper, Red-necked Stint (p. 158). **HABITAT:** Beaches, mudflats, lakeshores; when nesting, stony tundra. Uncommon to rare inland. Common in winter in HI (p. 428).

DUNLIN   *Calidris alpina* (see also p. 152)   **Common**

8½–8¾ in. (22–23 cm). Larger than a peep (p. 134), with *longish, droop-tipped bill.* Black legs. *Spring/summer: Rusty red above,* with *black patch on belly. Fall/ winter:* Unpatterned gray or gray-brown above, with *grayish wash across breast. Juvenile* (this plumage rarely seen away from nesting areas): Rusty above, with buffy breast and suggestion of belly patch. **VOICE:** Nasal, rasping *cheezp* or *treezp.* **SIMILAR SPECIES:** Winter Sanderling and (smaller) Western Sandpiper have clean white breast; Sanderling also paler above and has straighter bill. See also Rock Sandpiper, Purple Sandpiper, Curlew Sandpiper (p. 160). **HABITAT:** Tidal flats, beaches, muddy pools; in summer, moist tundra.

SANDPIPERS

fall/winter

fall/winter

spring/
summer
male

RUDDY
TURNSTONE

BLACK
TURNSTONE

spring/
summer

fall/winter

fall/winter

juvenile

spring/
summer

RED KNOT

juvenile

SANDERLING

spring/
summer

fall/winter

juvenile

fall/winter

DUNLIN

spring/
summer

PEEPS

Collectively, the three common small sandpipers of N. America are nicknamed "peeps" (other slightly larger *Calidris* sandpipers also referred to sometimes as "peeps"). In Old World, similar small peeps are called "stints."

LEAST SANDPIPER *Calidris minutilla* (see also p. 152)   Common

6 in. (15 cm). Distinguished from the other two common peeps by its slightly smaller size, *browner* upperparts and breast, and *yellowish or greenish* — not blackish — legs (but which might appear dark if caked in mud). *Bill slighter, finer, and slightly drooped at tip.* Adult: Mostly brownish with some rufous and black in back (spring/summer) or brownish gray (fall/winter). Juvenile: Much brighter, with extensive rufous on upperparts and buff wash across breast. VOICE: Thin *krreet, kree-eet.* SIMILAR SPECIES: Western and Semipalmated Sandpipers have blackish legs, thicker-based bill, paler upperparts, and different voice; whitish breast in fall/winter plumage. See also Temminck's and Long-toed Stints (p. 158). HABITAT: Mudflats, marshes, rain pools, shores, flooded fields; in summer, taiga wetlands.

SEMIPALMATED SANDPIPER   Scarce (West) to common (East)
Calidris pusilla (see also p. 152)

6¼ in. (16 cm). A small black-legged peep with a *straight*, somewhat *bulbous-tipped bill* of short length (female's bill longer than male's). *Spring/summer:* Gray-brown above, many birds with a tinge of russet to cheeks and back; dark streaks on breast. *Fall/winter:* Uniformly plain gray across upperparts (rarely seen in our area). *Juvenile:* Breast washed with buff and with fine streaks on sides; scaly upperpart pattern rather uniform, with pale feather edges tinged buff (sometimes reddish) when fresh. VOICE: Call *chit* or *chirt* (lacks *ee* sound of Least and Western Sandpipers). SIMILAR SPECIES: Typical Western Sandpiper (especially female) has *longer bill, slightly drooped* at tip. Spring/summer Western more rufous above, more heavily streaked below, particularly on flanks. Juvenile Western has rusty scapulars forming a diagonal bar on grayer back and slightly paler face. Not all birds distinguishable in winter plumages. Least Sandpiper smaller, browner, and thinner billed; has *yellowish or greenish* legs; in fall/winter plumage, has darker breast. See also Red-necked and Little Stints (p. 158). HABITAT: Mudflats, marshes, shores, beaches; in summer, tundra. Scarce vagrant to W. Coast.

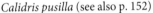

WESTERN SANDPIPER *Calidris mauri*   Common (West) to uncommon (East)

6½ in. (17 cm). Very similar to Semipalmated Sandpiper. Legs black. Bill averages thicker at base and *longer* than Semipalmated's and *droops near tip.* Male peeps have shorter bills than females and thus male Westerns may be particularly difficult to separate from female Semipalmateds. *Spring/summer: Heavily spotted* on breast and flanks; *rusty scapulars, crown, and ear patch.* Fall/winter: Gray or gray-brown above, unmarked whitish below. Juvenile: Buffy wash on breast; scaly upperparts, like juvenile Semipalmated but with distinct rusty scapular bar. VOICE: Distinct high-pitched *jeet* or *cheet,* unlike lower, soft *chirt* of Semipalmated. SIMILAR SPECIES: Semipalmated and Least Sandpipers, Dunlin. Because of their shorter bill, many male Westerns may be particularly difficult to separate from female Semipalmateds; see also voice. Semipalmated rarely winters in our area, but Western regularly does. HABITAT: Shores, beaches, mudflats, marshes; in summer, tundra.

SMALL "PEEP" SANDPIPERS

fall/winter

juvenile

LEAST SANDPIPER

spring/summer

fall/winter

juvenile

spring/summer

SEMIPALMATED SANDPIPER

fall/winter female

juvenile male

WESTERN SANDPIPER

spring/summer female

Least

Semipalmated

Western

WHITE-RUMPED SANDPIPER *Calidris fuscicollis* (see also p. 152)   Uncommon

7½ in. (19 cm). Larger than Semipalmated Sandpiper, smaller than Pectoral Sandpiper. The only peep with completely *white rump*. At rest, this long-winged bird has *tapered* look, with *wingtips extending well beyond tail*. Distinct pale supercilium. *Spring/summer:* Some rusty on crown, face, back. *Dark streaks and chevrons on sides extend to flanks.* Base of lower mandible bright reddish orange. *Juvenile:* Spangled upperparts scalloped rufous and white; fine streaks to buff-washed breast; bold white eyebrow. Winter birds are grayer and plainer; not seen in our area. **VOICE:** High, thin, mouselike *jeet*, like two flint pebbles scraping. **SIMILAR SPECIES:** Long wings and very attenuated look shared only by Baird's Sandpiper among other peeps, but Baird's buffer brown overall, has scalier back, and dark center to rump, lacks bold supercilium and dark streaks on flanks, and has much lower-pitched call. **HABITAT:** Prairie pools, shores, mudflats, marshes; in summer, tundra. Rare to E. Coast; scarce vagrant to W. Coast.

BAIRD'S SANDPIPER *Calidris bairdii* (see also p. 152)   Uncommon

7½ in. (19 cm). Larger than Semipalmated and Western Sandpiper, with more *long-winged, tapered look* (wings extend ½ in., 1 cm, beyond tail tip). Legs *black*. *Spring/summer:* Grayish white upperparts with black centers to back feathers; white throat; black breast streaking heaviest to sides. *Juvenile:* Head and breast washed *buff*, throat and breast finely streaked; back feathers with *dark centers and rich buff to buff-orange fringing* creating highly *scaled* appearance. *Fall/winter:* Browner and duller than juvenile; not found in our area. **VOICE:** Call a low *kreep* or *kree*; a rolling trill. **SIMILAR SPECIES:** White-rumped and Pectoral Sandpipers. Buff-breasted Sandpiper buffer below, without streaks, and has *yellow* (not *black*) legs. **HABITAT:** Pond margins, grassy mudflats, shores, upper beaches; in summer, tundra. Scarce migrant or vagrant to E. and W. Coasts.

PECTORAL SANDPIPER *Calidris melanotos* (see also p. 150)   Fairly common

8¼–8¾ in. (21–23 cm). Medium sized (but variable; male larger than female); plump-bodied but neck longer than in smaller peeps. Note that heavy breast streaks end rather *abruptly*, like a bib. Dark back with two white stripes. Wing stripe faint or lacking; crown variably rusty. Legs usually dull yellowish. Bill may be pale yellow-brown at base. On breeding grounds, males display by expanding breast, exposing black-based feathers. Juvenile similar to adult but brighter rufous present on upperparts and crown, buffer wash on breast under streaking. **VOICE:** Low, reedy *churrt* or *trrip, trrip*. **SIMILAR SPECIES:** Sharp-tailed Sandpiper (p. 160). Baird's and Least Sandpipers smaller, usually lack sharp breast-band; legs of Baird's black. **HABITAT:** In migration, prairie pools, sod farms, muddy shores, fresh and tidal marshes; in summer, tundra. Rare in interior West.

Basic Flight of Sandpipers

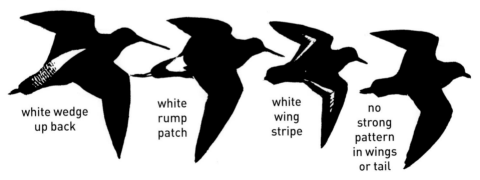

white wedge up back

white rump patch

white wing stripe

no strong pattern in wings or tail

juvenile

WHITE-RUMPED
SANDPIPER

spring/
summer

juvenile

spring/
summer

BAIRD'S
SANDPIPER

breeding
male

juvenile

spring/
summer

PECTORAL
SANDPIPER

SPOTTED SANDPIPER *Actitis macularius* (see also p. 152) **Fairly common**

7½ in. (19 cm). The most widespread sandpiper along shores of small freshwater lakes and streams. Usually solitary. Teeters rear body up and down nervously. Note moderately *long tail*. *Spring/summer:* Note *round breast spots*. *Fall/winter and juvenile:* No spots; brown above, with white line over eye (juvenile lightly scaled above). Dusky smudge enclosing white wedge near shoulder is a good aid. Flight distinctive: wings beat in a *shallow arc*, giving a stiff, bowed appearance. Wing stripe prominent above and below. **VOICE:** Clear *peet* or *peet-weet!* or *peet-weet-weet-weet-weet*. **SIMILAR SPECIES:** Solitary Sandpiper; see Common Sandpiper (p. 158). **HABITAT:** Pebbly shores, ponds, streamsides, marshes; in winter, also seashores, rock jetties.

STILT SANDPIPER **Uncommon**
Calidris himantopus (see also pp. 142 and 150)

8½ in. (22 cm). A tall sandpiper with slight *droop* to tip of bill, legs long and greenish yellow. Feeds like a dowitcher (sewing-machine motion) but *tilts tail up* more than a dowitcher while probing. *Spring/summer:* Heavily marked below with *transverse bars*; back brown with black mottling. Note *rusty cheek patch*. *Fall/winter:* Yellowlegs-like but unmarked gray above, dark-winged and *white-rumped;* note also more *greenish legs* and *white eyebrow. Juvenile:* Brownish-buff wash to breast; upperpart feathers brown with even pale edgings. **VOICE:** Single *whu* (like Lesser Yellowlegs but lower, hoarser). **SIMILAR SPECIES:** Yellowlegs. Dowitchers pudgier, have longer, yellowish-based, less drooped bills, and in flight show white wedge up back. In winter, Wilson's Phalarope very similar in plumage (see pp. 144 and 150) and structure but has different feeding posture and behavior, shorter legs, straighter bill. See also Curlew Sandpiper (p. 160). **HABITAT:** Shallow pools, mudflats, marshes; in summer, tundra. Rare along W. Coast; casual inland in West.

BUFF-BREASTED SANDPIPER *Calidris subruficollis* (see also p. 150) **Scarce**

8¼ in. (21 cm). No other small shorebird is as rich *buffy* below (paling to whitish on undertail coverts). A docile, buffy bird, with erect stance, small head, short bill, and yellowish legs. Dark eye stands out on plain face. In flight or in "display," buff body plumage contrasts with underwing, which is *white* with marbled tip and distinct dark crescent at base of primaries. Ages and sexes similar through year. **VOICE:** Low, trilled *pr-r-r-reet*. Sharp *tik*. **SIMILAR SPECIES:** Baird's, Pectoral, and Upland Sandpipers. Juvenile Ruff (p. 160). **HABITAT:** Dry dirt, sand, and short-grass habitats, including drying lakeshores, pastures, sod farms; in summer, drier tundra ridges. Rare inland in East; scarce vagrant to W. Coast.

UPLAND SANDPIPER *Bartramia longicauda* (see also p. 150) **Uncommon**

12 in. (30–31 cm). A "pigeon-headed" brown sandpiper; larger than Killdeer. Short bill, *small head,* shoe-button eye, thin neck, and *long tail* are helpful points. Often perches with erect posture on fenceposts and poles; on alighting, holds wings elevated. Ages and sexes similar through year. **VOICE:** Mellow, whistled *kip-ip-ip-ip,* often heard at night. Song a weird windy whistle: *whoooleeeeee, wheeloooooooooo.* **SIMILAR SPECIES:** Buff-breasted Sandpiper is smaller, richer buff and unmarked below. See also Eskimo and Little Curlews (p. 156). **HABITAT:** Grassy prairies, open meadows, fields, airports, sod farms. Scarce vagrant to W. Coast.

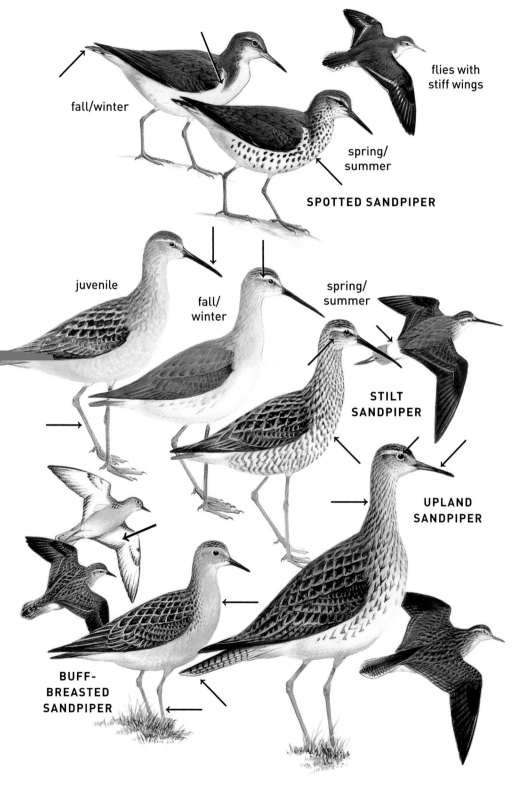

SANDPIPERS

flies with
stiff wings

fall/winter

spring/
summer

SPOTTED SANDPIPER

juvenile

fall/
winter

spring/
summer

**STILT
SANDPIPER**

**UPLAND
SANDPIPER**

**BUFF-
BREASTED
SANDPIPER**

AMERICAN WOODCOCK

Fairly common but secretive

Scolopax minor (see also p. 150)

11 in. (28 cm). A woodland-loving shorebird. Near size of Northern Bobwhite, with extremely long bill and large bulging eyes placed high on head. Rotund, almost neckless, with leaflike brown camouflage pattern, broadly barred crown. When flushed, produces whistling sound with wings. Ages and sexes similar through year. **VOICE:** At dusk in spring, a nasal *beezp* (suggesting nighthawk). Aerial "song" a chipping trill made by wings as bird ascends, changing to a bubbling twittering on descent. **HABITAT:** Wet thickets, moist woods, brushy swamps. Spring courtship by male is a crepuscular display ("sky dance") high over semiopen fields, pastures. Accidental vagrant to West, as far as CA.

WILSON'S SNIPE *Gallinago delicata* (see also p. 150)

Fairly common

10¼–10½ in. (26–27 cm). A tight-sitting bog, marsh, and wet-field prober; on nesting grounds may be seen standing on posts. Note *extremely long bill*. Brown, with *buff stripes on back* and a *striped head*. Ages and sexes similar through year. When flushed, flies off in *zigzag*, showing *short rusty orange tail*. **VOICE:** When flushed, a rasping *scaip*. Song a measured *chip-a, chip-a, chip-a*, etc. In high aerial display, a winnowing *huhuhuhuhuhuhu*. **SIMILAR SPECIES:** Dowitchers. See Common Snipe (p. 160). **HABITAT:** Marshes, bogs, ditches, wet fields and meadows.

SHORT-BILLED DOWITCHER *Limnodromus griseus* (see also p. 152)   Common

11–11¼ in. (27–28 cm). A snipelike bird of open mudflats. Note long bill, sewing-machine feeding motion, and, in flight, *long white wedge up back*. *Spring/summer:* Underparts rich rusty with some barring on flanks. Eastern subspecies *(griseus)* duller and paler below than cen. *(hendersoni)* and w. *(caurinus)* subspecies, although there is much variation. *Fall/winter:* Gray. *Juvenile:* Brighter upperparts, buff wash to neck and breast; *patterned tertial feathers* (fringes broken orange and black) an important distinction from juvenile Long-billed. **VOICE:** Staccato, muted *tu-tu-tu*; pitch of Lesser Yellowlegs. **SIMILAR SPECIES:** Bill length overlaps with that of Long-billed Dowitcher (by about 50 percent) but can be used with caution, especially when assessing variation among groups of birds; shorter bill also results in more angled back when feeding, on average. In fall/winter plumage, differences in call notes and habitat are usually the best way to distinguish the dowitchers; see also Stilt Sandpiper, Red Knot. **HABITAT:** More frequent on large tidal mudflats than Long-billed Dowitcher. In summer, taiga and tundra. Migrates earlier in fall than Long-billed. Uncommon to rare inland.

LONG-BILLED DOWITCHER

Common

Limnodromus scolopaceus (see also p. 152)

11½ in. (29 cm). When feeding, shows more round-bodied profile than Short-billed; dark tail bars average wider; bill averages longer (see Short-billed Dowitcher). *Spring/summer:* Underparts *evenly bright rusty to lower belly* (white or very pale lower belly in most Short-billed Dowitchers), with dark spotting on neck and barring on sides. Dark bars on tail broader, giving tail a darker look. *Fall/winter:* Averages darker than Short-billed with smoother gray breast and darker centers to scapulars. *Juvenile: Gray tertials with unpatterned solid pale fringe;* Short-billed has *internal rusty markings* similar to "tiger barring." **VOICE:** Single sharp, high *keek,* occasionally given in twos or threes but differs in quality from Short-billed call. **SIMILAR SPECIES:** The two dowitcher species are most easily separated by voice, along with plumage, bill length, habitat. **HABITAT:** Shallow pools, marshes, mudflats during migration; when breeding, tundra. More partial to fresh water than Short-billed, especially in winter, but some overlap.

SNIPELIKE WADERS

AMERICAN
WOODCOCK

SHORT-
BILLED
DOWITCHER

winnowing
display
flight

WILSON'S
SNIPE

juvenile

eastern
spring/
summer

fall/winter

snipe

Short-
billed

western
spring/
summer

probing

juvenile

fall/
winter

spring/
summer

LONG-BILLED
DOWITCHER

Long-
billed

probing

WILLET
Common (West) to fairly common (East)

Tringa semipalmata (see also p. 148)

15–16 in. (38–41 cm). Stockier than Greater Yellowlegs; has grayer look, heavier bill, blue-gray legs. In flight, note *striking black-and-white wing pattern.* At rest, this large wader is rather nondescript: gray above, mottled or barred below in spring/summer, unmarked in fall/winter. *Juvenile:* Browner above with light buff spots and bars. **VOICE:** Musical, repetitious *pill-will-willet* (in breeding season); a loud *kay-ee* (second note lower). Also a rapidly repeated *kip-kip-kip,* etc. In flight, *kree-ree-ree.* **SIMILAR SPECIES:** Greater Yellowlegs; Wandering Tattler (which is much smaller). **HABITAT:** Marshes, wet meadows, mudflats, beaches. Uncommon to rare inland, away from breeding range.

GREATER YELLOWLEGS *Tringa melanoleuca* (see also p. 150) **Common**

14 in. (36 cm). Note *bright yellow legs* (shared with next species). A slim gray sandpiper; back checkered with gray, black, and white. Often teeters body. In flight, appears *dark-winged* (no stripe), with *whitish rump and tail.* Bill long, *slightly upturned, paler at base.* Spring/summer adults blacker above, more barred on breast; fall/winter birds grayer above, whiter below; juveniles pale brownish gray, evenly scaled above. **VOICE:** Three-note strident whistle, *dear! dear! dear!* or *teer-teer-turr* with emphasis on first note. **SIMILAR SPECIES:** Lesser Yellowlegs, Willet; Common Greenshank and Spotted Redshank (p. 154). **HABITAT:** Marshes, mudflats, streams, ponds, flooded fields; in summer, wooded muskeg, spruce bogs.

LESSER YELLOWLEGS
Fairly common (West) to uncommon (East)

Tringa flavipes (see also p. 150)

10½ in. (27 cm). Like Greater Yellowlegs, but smaller (obvious when both species are together). Lesser's shorter, slimmer, all-dark bill is *straight* and about *equal to length of head;* Greater's appears slightly uptilted, paler based, and longer than bird's head. Readily separated by voice. Age and seasonal differences similar to Greater. **VOICE:** *Yew* or *yu-yu* (usually one or two notes); less forceful than usual three-syllable call of Greater. **SIMILAR SPECIES:** Solitary and Stilt Sandpipers, Wilson's Phalarope. Both yellowlegs species may swim briefly, like a phalarope. **HABITAT:** Marshes, mudflats, ponds, flooded fields; in summer, open, moist boreal woods and taiga. Uncommon along Pacific Coast.

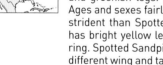

SOLITARY SANDPIPER
Scarce (West) to uncommon (East)

Tringa solitaria (see also p. 150)

8½ in. (22 cm). Note *dark wings* and conspicuous *white sides of tail* (crossed by bold black bars). A dark-backed sandpiper, whitish below, with *light eye-ring* and greenish legs. Nods like a yellowlegs. Usually alone, seldom in groups. Ages and sexes fairly similar. **VOICE:** *Peet!* or *peet-weet-weet!* (higher and more strident than Spotted Sandpiper's call). **SIMILAR SPECIES:** Lesser Yellowlegs has bright yellow legs, white (not dark) rump, is paler above, lacks bold eye-ring. Spotted Sandpiper teeters, tail (not head) has white wedge at breast-side, different wing and tail patterns. See Wood Sandpiper (p. 154). **HABITAT:** Streamsides, wooded swamps and ponds, ditches, freshwater marshes. Rare west of breeding range and along Pacific Coast.

STILT SANDPIPER *Calidris himantopus* **See p. 138**

Fall/winter: Long yellow-green legs, slight droop to bill, white rump; distinct light supercilium.

WILSON'S PHALAROPE *Phalaropus tricolor* **See p. 144**

Fall/winter: Straight needle bill, clear white underparts, pale gray back, dull yellow legs.

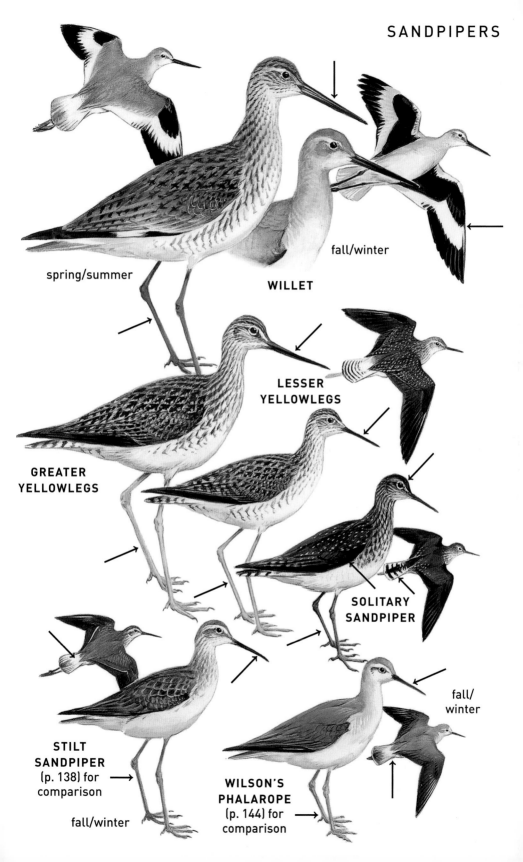

spring/summer

fall/winter

WILLET

**LESSER
YELLOWLEGS**

**GREATER
YELLOWLEGS**

**SOLITARY
SANDPIPER**

**STILT
SANDPIPER**
(p. 138) for
comparison

fall/winter

**WILSON'S
PHALAROPE**
(p. 144) for
comparison

fall/
winter

PHALAROPES

Shorebirds with lobed toes; more at home wading or swimming than on land. When feeding, phalaropes often spin like tops, rapidly dabbling at disturbed water for plankton, brine shrimp, and other marine invertebrates, mosquito larvae, and insects. Female slightly larger and, in spring/summer when breeding, more colorful than male. **RANGE:** Two of the three species are circumpolar; whereas Wilson's breeds in N. American interior, winters in S. America.

WILSON'S PHALAROPE   Fairly common
Phalaropus tricolor (see also pp. 142 and 150)

9¼ in. (23½ cm). This trim phalarope is plain-winged (no stripe), with white rump. In addition to spinning in water, may also feed by dashing about on shorelines. *Spring/summer:* Female unique, with *broad black face and neck stripe blending into cinnamon.* Male duller, with just a wash of cinnamon on sides of neck and white spot on hindneck. *Fall/winter:* Suggests Stilt Sandpiper or Lesser Yellowlegs (plain wings, white rump), but whiter below, with no breast streaking; bill *needlelike;* legs greenish or straw colored. *Juvenile:* Has buffy and brown pattern above, buffy wash on breast. **VOICE:** Low nasal *wurk;* also *check, check, check.* **SIMILAR SPECIES:** Other two phalaropes have white wing stripe, dark central tail, and bolder dark patch through eye. See also yellowlegs and Stilt Sandpiper (p. 138), which may swim for brief periods of time. **HABITAT:** Shallow lakes, freshwater marshes, pools, shores, mudflats; in late summer and fall, also large salt lakes (such as Mono Lake, CA, and Great Salt Lake, UT) and marshes. Rare vagrant to E. Coast.

RED-NECKED PHALAROPE   Common offshore, scarce inland
Phalaropus lobatus (see also p. 152)

7¾ in. (20 cm). A shorebird out to sea is most likely a phalarope, although Red-necked is not as pelagic as Red Phalarope. Note dark patch through eye and needlelike black bill. *Spring/summer:* Female gray above, with *rufous chestnut on neck,* white throat and eyebrow. Male duller, but similar in pattern. *Fall/winter:* Both sexes gray above with whitish streaks, white below; rare in our area in this plumage. *Juvenile:* Has distinct buff stripes on back. **VOICE:** Sharp *kit* or *whit,* similar to call of Sanderling. **SIMILAR SPECIES:** Red Phalarope. **HABITAT:** In migration, nearshore ocean, bays, ponds; in summer, tundra; in winter coastal ocean and estuaries (mostly south of the U.S.). Uncommon to rare inland.

RED PHALAROPE   Uncommon offshore, very rare onshore
Phalaropus fulicarius (see also p. 152)

8¼–8½ in. (21–22 cm). Seagoing habits and buoyant swimming (like a tiny gull) distinguish this as a phalarope. *Spring/summer:* Female has deep *reddish underparts, white face,* and mostly yellow bill. Male duller. *Fall/winter:* Both sexes plain gray above, white below; in flight suggest Sanderling, but with *dark patch* through eye. Bill mostly dark with yellow base. *Juvenile:* Has peach-buff wash on neck. **VOICE:** *Whit* or *kit,* higher than Red-necked Phalarope's call. **SIMILAR SPECIES:** Red-necked Phalarope slightly smaller and daintier (less stout), has more needlelike bill; juvenile darker gray above with thin pale back stripes. Slightly thicker bill of Red Phalarope has small yellowish base, visible at closer range. In our area, most or all phalaropes observed in winter are Reds. **HABITAT:** More strictly pelagic (less coastal) than Red-necked in migration and winter; along Pacific Coast, sometimes "wrecks" (irruptions of weak or starving birds) to coastal water bodies following winter storms. In summer, tundra. Casual to accidental vagrant inland.

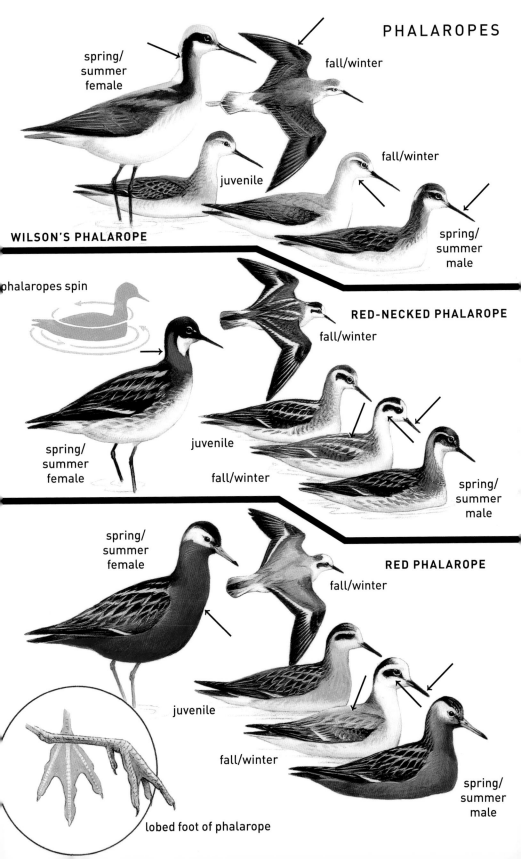

PHALAROPES

spring/
summer
female

fall/winter

juvenile

fall/winter

spring/
summer
male

WILSON'S PHALAROPE

phalaropes spin

RED-NECKED PHALAROPE

fall/winter

spring/
summer
female

juvenile

fall/winter

fall/winter

spring/
summer
male

spring/
summer
female

RED PHALAROPE

fall/winter

juvenile

fall/winter

spring/
summer
male

lobed foot of phalarope

PLOVERS and TURNSTONE in FLIGHT

Learning their distinctive flight calls can substantially help with identification.

PIPING PLOVER *Charadrius melodus*   p. 124
Pale sand color above, wide black tail spot, whitish rump.
Call a plaintive whistle, *peep-lo* (first note higher).

SNOWY PLOVER *Charadrius nivosus*   p. 124
Pale sand color above; tail with dark center, white sides; rump not white.
Call a musical whistle, *pe-wee-ah* or *o-wee-ah*.

SEMIPALMATED PLOVER *Charadrius semipalmatus*   p. 124
Mud brown above; dark tail with white borders.
Call a plaintive upward-slurred *chi-we* or *too-li*.

WILSON'S PLOVER *Charadrius wilsonia*   p. 124
Similar in pattern to Semipalmated; larger with big bill.
Call an emphatic whistled *whit!* or *wheet!*

KILLDEER *Charadrius vociferus*   p. 124
Tawny orange rump, longish tail.
Noisy; a loud *kill-deeah* or *killdeer*; also *dee-dee-dee*, etc.

BLACK-BELLIED PLOVER *Pluvialis squatarola*   p. 122
Spring/summer adult: Black below, silvery white above, white undertail coverts.
Fall/winter, juvenile, and some first-summer birds: Pale grayish above and below.
Year-round: Black wingpits, white in wing, white rump and tail base.
Call a plaintive slurred whistle, *tlee-oo-eee* or *whee-er-ee*.

AMERICAN GOLDEN-PLOVER *Pluvialis dominica*   p. 122
Spring/summer adult: Black below, black undertail coverts.
Fall/winter, juvenile, and some first-summer birds: Speckled brown and buff
above, grayish below.
Year-round: Underwing grayer than Black-bellied Plover's; no black in wingpits.
Call a querulous whistled *queedle* or *que-e-a*.

PACIFIC GOLDEN-PLOVER *Pluvialis fulva* (not shown)   p. 122
Like American, but spring/summer birds have narrower and longer white stripe
down sides and some white along flanks and undertail; fall/winter birds and
juveniles more gold-washed on upperparts and face; wings shorter proportionally.
Call a loud, whistled *chu-whee* or *chu-wee-dle*.

RUDDY TURNSTONE *Arenaria interpres*   p. 132
Harlequin pattern in face distinctive; bold white upperpart patterns.
Call a low, chuckling *tuk-a-tuk* or *kut-a-kut*.

BLACK TURNSTONE *Arenaria melanocephala* (not shown)   p. 132
Similar to Ruddy but blacker, including head and breast.
Call a short series of rattling notes.

SNIPELIKE WADERS AND
SANDPIPERS IN FLIGHT

WILSON'S SNIPE

AMERICAN
WOODCOCK

SOLITARY SANDPIPER

GREATER YELLOWLEGS

LESSER
YELLOWLEGS

WILSON'S
PHALAROPE
fall/winter

STILT
SANDPIPER
fall/winter

UPLAND SANDPIPER

BUFF-BREASTED
SANDPIPER

PECTORAL
SANDPIPER

SANDPIPERS and PHALAROPES in FLIGHT

DOWITCHERS *Limnodromus* spp.   p. 140
Long bill, long wedge of white up back. Flight call of Short-billed Dowitcher a staccato mellow *tu-tu-tu;* that of Long-billed Dowitcher a single sharp *keek*, often given in twos or threes but not repeatedly or consistently (unlike Short-billed).

DUNLIN *Calidris alpina*   p. 132
Fall/winter: Slightly larger than peeps, darker than Sanderling. Flight call a nasal rasping *cheezp* or *treezp*.

RED KNOT *Calidris canutus*   p. 132
Fall/winter: Washed-out gray look, pale rump. Flight call a low *knut*.

PURPLE SANDPIPER *Calidris maritima*   p. 130
Slaty color. Rock Sandpiper (p. 130; not shown) similar but often not quite as dark; averages slightly broader wing stripe. Flight call a low *weet-wit* or *twit*.

WHITE-RUMPED SANDPIPER *Calidris fuscicollis*   p. 136
White rump; only smallish peep so marked, but beware partial or poor views of other peeps, all of which have mostly white rumps with narrow dark stripe. Flight call a mouselike squeak, *jeet*.

CURLEW SANDPIPER *Calidris ferruginea*   p. 160
Fall/winter: Suggests Dunlin, but rump white.

RUFF *Calidris pugnax*   p. 160
If seen well, oval white patch on each side of dark tail distinctive. Usually silent.

SPOTTED SANDPIPER *Actitis macularius*   p. 138
Shallow wing stroke gives stiff, bowed effect; longish tail. Flight call a clear *peet* or *peet-weet*.

SANDERLING *Calidris alba*   p. 132
The most contrasting wing stripe of any small shorebird. Flight call a sharp metallic *kip* or *quit*.

RED PHALAROPE *Phalaropus fulicarius*   p. 144
Fall/winter: Paler above and plumper than Red-necked Phalarope; bill slightly thicker, yellow based.

RED-NECKED PHALAROPE *Phalaropus lobatus*   p. 144
Fall/winter: Sanderling-like, but with dark eye patch, long black needlelike bill. Flight call (both Red-necked and Red Phalaropes) a sharp *kit* or *whit*.

LEAST SANDPIPER *Calidris minutilla*   p. 134
Very small, brown with short wings and tail; faint wing stripe. Flight call a thin *krreet, krreet*.

SEMIPALMATED SANDPIPER *Calidris pusilla*   p. 134
Grayer than Least Sandpiper. Western Sandpiper (p. 134; not shown) similar but bill longer. Flight call a soft *chit* or *chirt* (lacks *ee* sound of Least); call of Western a more-strident *jeet* than Least's.

BAIRD'S SANDPIPER *Calidris bairdii*   p. 136
Larger and longer winged than above two. Size and shape of White-rumped Sandpiper, but rump dark. Flight call a low, raspy *kreep* or *kree*.

SANDPIPERS AND PHALAROPES IN FLIGHT

SHORT-BILLED DOWITCHER

Long-billed has similar pattern

All in fall/winter plumage

DUNLIN

RED KNOT

PURPLE SANDPIPER

WHITE-RUMPED SANDPIPER

CURLEW SANDPIPER

female

RUFF

SPOTTED SANDPIPER

SANDERLING

RED PHALAROPE

RED-NECKED PHALAROPE

LEAST SANDPIPER

SEMIPALMATED SANDPIPER

BAIRD'S SANDPIPER

RARE SHOREBIRDS from EURASIA

NORTHERN LAPWING *Vanellus vanellus*   Casual vagrant
12–12½ in. (30–32 cm). A distinctive round-winged plover with unique long wispy crest. **RANGE:** Casual European vagrant, mostly in late fall and early winter, from Atlantic Canada south to Mid-Atlantic states; accidental farther south and west. **HABITAT:** Farmland, marshes, mudflats.

LESSER SAND-PLOVER *Charadrius mongolus*   Rare migrant and vagrant
7½ in. (19 cm). Asian. Slightly larger and larger-billed than Semipalmated Plover. *Spring/summer:* Very distinctive, with *broad rufous breast-band.* Female duller. *Fall/winter and juvenile:* Breast-band gray-brown; no white collar. **VOICE:** Calls include a ploverlike whistle and a rolling trill. **RANGE:** Rare but regular migrant to Aleutians and Bering Sea islands. Casual vagrant from mainland AK to CA, accidental farther east and in HI.

EUROPEAN GOLDEN-PLOVER *Pluvialis apricaria*   Casual vagrant
11 in. (28 cm). Very similar to American and Pacific Golden-Plovers but shows *white* underwings. Spring/summer adult has white along flanks and undertail like Pacific but is larger-bodied, smaller-billed. **VOICE:** Melodic drawn-out whistle. **RANGE:** Rare spring vagrant to NL, accidental elsewhere in N. America.

EURASIAN DOTTEREL *Charadrius morinellus*   Casual vagrant
8¼–8½ in. (21–22 cm). Narrow white stripe crossing midbreast identifies this dark plover. Broad *white eyebrow stripes* join in V on nape. **VOICE:** Repeated piping, *titi-ri-titi-ri,* running into a trill. **RANGE:** Very rare Asian visitor to w. AK, casual vagrant along Pacific Coast to CA and in HI. A few pairs may breed locally in montane tundra of nw. AK.

SPOTTED REDSHANK *Tringa erythropus*   Casual vagrant
12½ in. (32 cm). A slender, long-legged, long-billed shorebird. *Spring/summer: Sooty black,* with small white speckles on back and wings, making bird appear a trifle paler above. Long legs *dark red;* long black bill *reddish basally,* has *slight droop at tip. Fall/winter and juvenile:* Gray and somewhat yellowlegs-like, but legs *orange-red,* bill *orange-red* basally. In flight, shows *long white wedge* on back, white underwing. **VOICE:** Sharp, whistled *tcheet,* with rising inflection. **RANGE:** Casual spring and fall visitor; records widely scattered.

COMMON GREENSHANK *Tringa nebularia*   Casual vagrant
13½ in. (34 cm). Slightly larger than Greater Yellowlegs, legs *dull greenish* (not bright yellow). Wedgelike white rump patch runs up back, as in a dowitcher. **VOICE:** Ringing, whistled *tew tew tew,* similar to Greater Yellowlegs. **RANGE:** Eurasian species; annual visitor on w. AK islands, accidental elsewhere.

WOOD SANDPIPER *Tringa glareola*   Very rare vagrant
8 in. (20 cm). Shape of Solitary Sandpiper, but has pale (not dark) underwings. Pale supercilium. Upperparts slightly paler and browner, *heavily spotted* with pale buff. Rump patch *white* (Solitary has dark rump). Legs dull yellow. Overall, looks very short in rear. **VOICE:** Distinctive, sharp, high *chew-chew-chew* or *chiff-chiff-chiff.* **RANGE:** Regular migrant on Aleutians and Bering Sea islands, accidental elsewhere in N. America and in HI.

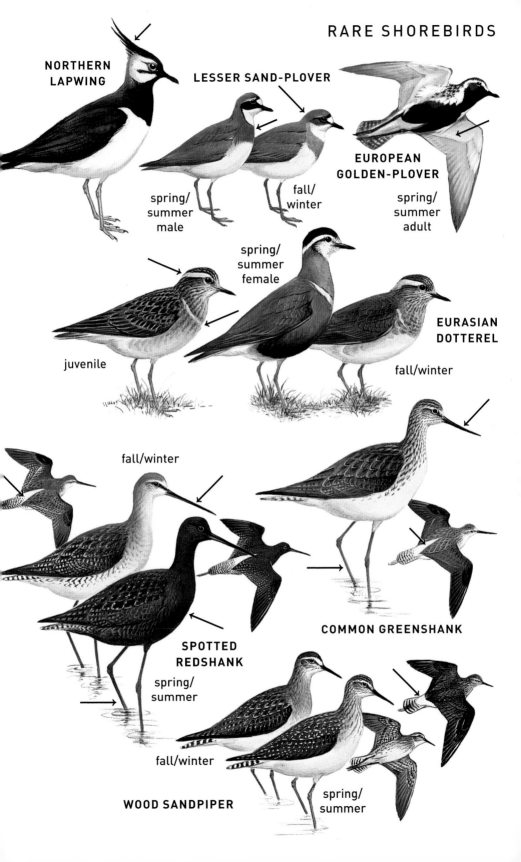

RARE SHOREBIRDS

NORTHERN
LAPWING

LESSER SAND-PLOVER

spring/
summer
male

fall/
winter

EUROPEAN
GOLDEN-PLOVER

spring/
summer
adult

spring/
summer
female

EURASIAN
DOTTEREL

juvenile

fall/winter

fall/winter

COMMON GREENSHANK

SPOTTED
REDSHANK

spring/
summer

fall/winter

spring/
summer

WOOD SANDPIPER

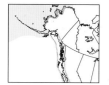

BAR-TAILED GODWIT *Limosa lapponica*   Rare, local
16–17 in. (41–44 cm). A smaller godwit than Marbled and Hudsonian; bill straighter; legs shorter; underwing plumage distinctive. Alaskan birds (subspecies *baueri*) have *mottled rump* and *whitish tail* crossed by narrow dark bars. European birds *(lapponica)* have whiter, more boldly barred rump. *Spring/summer adult:* Male rich *reddish orange*, particularly on head and underparts. Female duller. *Fall/winter and first-year:* Both sexes grayish above, white below, underwing whitish with few markings. *Juvenile:* Underparts washed buffy, back with neat buff-and-black pattern. **VOICE:** Flight call a harsh *kirrick;* alarm a shrill *krick.* **RANGE:** Nests in w. AK; casual to rare vagrant on both W. and E. Coasts; accidental in between. **HABITAT:** Mudflats, shores, tundra.

BLACK-TAILED GODWIT *Limosa limosa*   Casual vagrant
16½ in. (42 cm). This elegant Eurasian godwit resembles Hudsonian Godwit (white rump, white wing stripe, black tail), but bill is straighter. In spring/summer, has chestnut head and neck, black-and-white barred belly. Best field distinction in all plumages is *white* underwing linings in Black-tailed, *black* in Hudsonian. **VOICE:** Flight call a clear *reeka-reeka-reeka.* **RANGE:** Casual visitor to both AK and E. Coast. **HABITAT:** Large lakes with muddy shores.

"EURASIAN" WHIMBREL *Numenius phaeopus*   Vary rare vagrant
Two subspecies of Whimbrel from Eurasia occur as very rare visitors in N. America. Asian subspecies *variegatus* is a rare but regular migrant in w. AK; casual farther south along Pacific Coast. European subspecies *phaeopus* is a casual visitor along Atlantic Coast. Both differ from N. American Whimbrel by showing mostly *white rump* (mottled grayish in *variegatus*), white wedge up back, paler underwing. **VOICE:** Calls similar to N. American Whimbrel.

BRISTLE-THIGHED CURLEW *Numenius tahitiensis*   Rare, local, threatened
17½–18 in. (44–46 cm). Very similar to Whimbrel, but buffier to *tawnier*, back flecking darker, *tail and unbarred rump pale to rich orange*. Breast less streaked. Has unique bristlelike feathers extending from underparts near base of legs. Call very different. **VOICE:** Slurred *chi-u-it* (Inuit name) or *whee-oo-wheep;* suggests call of Black-bellied Plover but louder and slurred. Also a wolf whistle–like *whee-wheeo.* **RANGE:** Nests locally in w. AK; accidental vagrant farther south along Pacific Coast. Regular migrant and winter visitor to HI (p. 428). **HABITAT:** In summer, tundra; in winter, reefs, beaches, and fields.

ESKIMO CURLEW *Numenius borealis*   Almost certainly extinct
14 in. (36 cm). Last documented record in early 1960s and almost assuredly extinct. Much smaller than Whimbrel; bill shorter, thinner, only slightly curved. Linings of raised wing cinnamon-buff with unbarred primaries (unlike Little Curlew, Upland Sandpiper). Legs slate gray. **VOICE:** Call described as *tee-dee-dee* or *tee-dee* note suggestive of Common Tern. **HABITAT:** Open grasslands, coastal areas; in summer, tundra.

LITTLE CURLEW *Numenius minutus*   Accidental vagrant
12 in. (30 cm). The tiniest curlew. Bill *short and gently decurved.* Breast washed with buff, finely streaked. At rest, wingtips even with tail tip (extend beyond tail in Eskimo Curlew); note difference in *underwing* (pale buff, not cinnamon) and *flanks* (lightly barred, not heavy chevrons). Bill shape differs from Upland Sandpiper's. **RANGE:** Asian species; accidental along W. Coast.

RARE SHOREBIRDS

European
fall/winter

Alaskan
fall/winter

BAR-TAILED GODWIT

fall/
winter

juvenile

fall/winter

fall/winter

spring/
summer male

**BLACK-TAILED
GODWIT**

spring/
summer

**BRISTLE-
THIGHED
CURLEW**

"Eurasian"

WHIMBREL

**LITTLE
CURLEW**

underwing

ESKIMO CURLEW

underwing

RARE SHOREBIRDS

COMMON SANDPIPER *Actitis hypoleucos*   Rare vagrant

8 in. (20 cm). At all seasons resembles fall/winter Spotted Sandpiper (no spots). Best feature is *longer tail,* reaching only halfway to tail tip at rest; closer to tip in Spotted. Common has grayer legs, often more gray on breast. **VOICE:** In flight, *twee-see-see,* thinner than Spotted's call. **RANGE:** Rare but regular, mostly in spring, on Aleutians and Bering Sea islands; accidental in HI.

TEREK SANDPIPER *Xenus cinereus*   Casual vagrant

9 in. (23 cm). Note *upturned bill* and short *orange-yellow legs, jagged black stripe* along scapulars. Often bobs. In flight, wing has triangular *white trailing edge* at rear. **VOICE:** Fluty *dudududu* or sharp piping *twita-wit-wit-wit.* **RANGE:** Very rare in w. AK islands, accidental farther south and in HI.

LITTLE STINT *Calidris minuta*   Very rare vagrant

6 in. (15 cm). Slightly smaller than Semipalmated Sandpiper; bill finer. *Spring/summer:* Similar to some Red-necked Stints, but body less elongated, legs longer, and *dark breast markings washed with orange. Juvenile:* Like juvenile Semipalmated Sandpiper, but with longer wingtip projection, bold white V on mantle, black-centered and rufous-fringed wing coverts and tertials. **VOICE:** Sanderling-like *tit.* **RANGE:** Widespread casual visitor, mostly to coasts and to HI.

RED-NECKED STINT *Calidris ruficollis*   Rare visitor and breeder, local

6¼ in. (17 cm). Similar to other black-legged peeps but in spring/summer shows *bright rusty head and neck, bordered below by dark streaks. Juvenile:* Has long wingtip projection like Little Stint but plumper body, shorter legs; rusty-fringed upper scapulars contrast with brown-fringed wing coverts. Bill straight and fine at tip. **VOICE:** Short, clipped *chit,* or *chit chit,* suggesting Semipalmated Sandpiper. **RANGE:** Rare but regular migrant in w. AK, where very rare breeder; casual vagrant to CA and HI; accidental elsewhere in N. America.

GRAY-TAILED TATTLER *Tringa brevipes*   Rare vagrant, local

10 in. (25 cm). Very similar to Wandering Tattler; often best told by voice. *Spring/summer:* Compared with Wandering, upperparts paler, barring on underparts finer and less extensive; supercilium somewhat bolder. *Juvenile:* Gray-tailed has more extensive whitish spots and notches to scapulars, coverts, and tertials than Wandering, is slightly paler gray above (sometimes tinged brownish), and flanks paler (gray usually not extending below folded wings). **VOICE:** Up-slurred whistle, *too-weet?* or *tu-whip?,* with accent on second syllable. Beware Gray-tailed occasionally gives multinote call and Wandering occasionally gives two-note call, but note quality differs. **RANGE:** Asian species, rare but regular visitor to w. AK islands and HI; accidental vagrant elsewhere.

TEMMINCK'S STINT *Calidris temminckii*   Casual vagrant

6¼ in. (16 cm). A brownish gray stint (plainer than Least Sandpiper) with *irregular black spots* on scapulars. Has *elongated,* crouching look; *short dull yellow legs.* In flight, shows *whiter outer tail feathers* than other peeps and stints (but can be hard to discern). **VOICE:** In flight, a dry *trree,* often repeated in cricketlike trill. **RANGE:** Very rare visitor to w. AK islands, accidental vagrant farther south.

LONG-TOED STINT *Calidris subminuta*   Casual vagrant

6 in. (15 cm). Much like Least Sandpiper, but *brighter* above, with more erect stance, *longer legs* and *toes,* dark forehead. May suggest miniature Sharp-tailed Sandpiper. **VOICE:** Purring *prrp.* **RANGE:** Rare but regular migrant on w. AK islands; accidental farther south and in HI.

TEREK SANDPIPER

spring/ summer

COMMON SANDPIPER

juvenile

fall/winter Spotted Sandpiper (p. 138) for comparison

spring/ summer

Wandering Tattler (p. 130) for comparison

spring/ summer

LITTLE STINT

fall/winter

spring/ summer

spring/ summer

first summer

RED-NECKED STINT

GRAY-TAILED TATTLER

juvenile

juvenile

spring/ summer

TEMMINCK'S STINT

spring/ summer

LONG-TOED STINT

RARE SHOREBIRDS

SHARP-TAILED SANDPIPER *Calidris acuminata*   Rare to casual visitor
8½ in. (22 cm). Similar to Pectoral Sandpiper, but shows bolder whitish supercilium and brighter rusty crown. Most visitors to N. America are juveniles, which
have rich *orangey buff breast,* finely streaked on sides only, rather than across
breast as in Pectoral. Spring/summer adults have *dark chevrons* extending to
flanks. Crissum streaked. No plumage shows as sharp a demarcation between
white belly and streaked breast as in Pectoral. Smaller than Ruff, larger than
Long-toed Stint. **VOICE:** Trilled *prreeet* or *trrit-trrit,* sometimes twittered.
RANGE: Asian species. Regular fall migrant in w. AK and HI; rare in fall and
casual in spring along Pacific Coast; casual to accidental elsewhere. **HABITAT:**
Borders of wetlands, muddy shores, wet pastures; in summer, tundra.

GREAT KNOT *Calidris tenuirostris*   Very rare vagrant
10–11 in. (25–29 cm). An Asian species, similar to Red Knot but slightly larger
and chestier; bill longer and thinner at tip; legs duller, grayish green to olive.
Spring/summer: Breast conspicuously mottled black; upperpart feathers and
some wing coverts fringed bright rufous. *Winter/spring:* Similar to Red Knot but
upperparts indistinctly streaked; breast gray, usually with indistinct spots.
Juvenile: Breast pale buff with distinct brown triangular spots. **RANGE:** Very rare
visitor to w. AK; accidental vagrant along W. Coast and in East.

CURLEW SANDPIPER *Calidris ferruginea* (see also p. 152)   Very rare visitor
8½–8¾ in. (21–22 cm). A Eurasian species with slim downcurved bill, blackish
legs, and white rump in flight. *Spring/summer:* Male variably rich rufous red;
female duller with thin pale barring. *Fall/winter:* Resembles Dunlin, but slightly
longer legged, bolder pale supercilium; bill curved more evenly throughout
rather than drooping at tip; white rump. *Juvenile:* Buff edges on feathers of back
give a scaly look; breast washed with buff. Smaller than Red Knot and Stilt
Sandpiper, legs black, bill curves downward throughout its length. **VOICE:** Liquid *chirrip.* **RANGE:** Very rare migrant or vagrant along E. Coast; casual inland,
along W. Coast, and in HI. **HABITAT:** Marshy pools, mudflats; in summer, tundra.

RUFF *Calidris pugnax* (see also p. 152)   Very rare visitor
Male (Ruff) 12–13 in. (30–32 cm); female (known informally as Reeve) 9 in. (23
cm). *Spring/summer male:* Unique, with erectile *ruffs* and *ear tufts* that may be
black, brown, rufous, buff, white, or barred in various color combinations. Legs
greenish, yellow, or orange. *Spring/summer female:* Smaller than male; lacks
ruffs, breast *heavily blotched with dark. Fall/winter:* Rather plain, with short bill,
small head, thick neck. *Juvenile:* Rich buffy head and breast, very scaly on back.
In all plumages, note rather unique, small-headed, thicker-necked, and *erect
stance,* oval white patches on sides of tail in flight. **VOICE:** Often silent; flight call
a low *too-i* or *tu-whit.* **RANGE:** Breeds in Eurasia. Very rare but regular migrant
or vagrant along both coasts, in Great Lakes region, and in HI; casual vagrant
elsewhere inland. **HABITAT:** Mudflats, marshes, coastal pools, wet agricultural
fields; in summer, tundra.

COMMON SNIPE *Gallinago gallinago*   Rare, local visitor
10½ in. (27 cm). Compared with Wilson's Snipe, has paler underwing, bolder
white trailing edge to secondaries, weaker flank barring, slightly buffier overall
color, and lower-pitched winnowing in flight display. **RANGE:** Eurasian species.
Regular visitor to w. AK islands and probably HI; accidental vagrant in CA. **HABI-
TAT:** Similar to Wilson's Snipe.

RARE SHOREBIRDS

SHARP-TAILED SANDPIPER

juvenile

spring/summer

breeding dress of male variable

juvenile

GREAT KNOT

spring/summer

male

male

CURLEW SANDPIPER

juvenile

spring/summer male

juvenile female

fall/winter

juvenile male

RUFF

spring/summer female

COMMON SNIPE

BITTERNS, HERONS, and ALLIES Family Ardeidae

Medium to large wading birds with long legs and necks, spearlike bills. They hunt with neck erect and roost with head back on shoulders. In flight, neck is folded in an S; legs trail. Plumes develop in winter/spring that are flared when breeding. Sexes similar. Nest colonially in mangroves or large trees, often (but not always) near water. **FOOD:** Fish, frogs, crawfish, other aquatic life; mice, gophers, small birds, insects. **RANGE:** Worldwide except colder regions.

GREAT BLUE HERON *Ardea herodias*   Common

45–47 in. (115–120 cm). A lean gray bird that may stand 4 ft. (122 cm) tall. Long legs, long neck, daggerlike bill indicate a heron, and great size and blue-gray color mark it as this species. *Adult:* Crown white with long head, back, and breast plumes in winter through summer. *Juvenile and first-year:* duller, crown black or with limited white; plumes absent or shorter. White subspecies of s. FL known as "Great White" Heron (p. 164). Presumed intergrades with these ("Würdemann's Heron") in FL Keys have white head including plumes. **VOICE:** Deep harsh croaks: *frahnk, frahnk, frahnk.* **SIMILAR SPECIES:** Sandhill Crane, Reddish Egret. **HABITAT:** Marshes, swamps, shores, tidal flats, moist fields.

LITTLE BLUE HERON *Egretta caerulea*   Fairly common

24 in. (61 cm). A small, slender heron. *Adult:* Bluish slate with deep maroon-brown neck; legs dark, bill pale blue with dark tip. *First-year* (see p. 164): All white, often with *grayish wingtips* and sometimes blue tinge to crown. Legs *dull olive;* base of bill *pale blue-gray;* lores dull grayish or gray-green. Molting one-year-old birds (May–Sept.) are boldly pied white and dark (p. 165). **VOICE:** Loud, nasal *scaaah.* **SIMILAR SPECIES:** First-year Reddish Egret slightly larger overall and longer billed, with paler eye, brownish-gray head and neck, and pink-based black bill. Juvenile and first-year Little Blue like Snowy Egret except bill slightly thicker and grayer based, lores duller, and outer primary tips (if visible) dusky. **HABITAT:** Marshes, ponds, mudflats, swamps, rice fields. Rare vagrant well north and west of range, to W. Coast.

TRICOLORED HERON *Egretta tricolor*   Uncommon

26 in. (66 cm). A very slender, dark heron with contrasting *white belly* and white rump. *Long* slender bill. *Adult:* Mostly bluish above and on neck. White crown plumes and pale back plumes in spring/summer. *Juvenile:* Neck dull rusty brown, gradually mixing with blue during first year; wing coverts tipped rufous. **VOICE:** Series of drawn-out nasal quacks. **SIMILAR SPECIES:** Great Blue and Little Blue Herons. **HABITAT:** Marshes, swamps, shores. Rare to casual vagrant throughout interior N. America and to W. Coast.

REDDISH EGRET *Egretta rufescens*   Uncommon

30–31 in. (76–79 cm). Note pinkish, black-tipped bill of adult; habitat almost strictly coastal. *Adult:* Neck and back feathers shaggy. Pale eye. Two color morphs: (1) dark morph neutral gray, with bright rusty head and neck (first-year, not shown, duller grayish brown, with short or no plumes to neck, and with all-dark bill); (2) white morph completely white with blue-gray legs (see p. 165). When feeding, races about with spread wings. **VOICE:** Sometimes a harsh *kraaak!* **SIMILAR SPECIES:** Habitat and feeding behavior differ from other herons and egrets. Dark first-year can resemble adult Little Blue Heron, which shows purplish neck and bill with pale bluish base. White-morph Reddish Egret suggests Great or Snowy Egret, but bill pinkish-based with black tip, legs and feet blue-gray. **HABITAT:** Salt marshes, tidal flats, beaches. Rare visitor to the s. CA coast; accidental inland.

DARK HERONS AND EGRET

juvenile

herons' necks may stretch or be looped in when they are standing

herons fly with neck pulled in

"WÜRDEMANN'S" HERON (intergrade)

adult

adult

GREAT BLUE HERON (white subspecies on p. 165)

adult

juvenile

LITTLE BLUE HERON

(juvenile and first-year on p. 165)

adult

TRICOLORED HERON

adult

REDDISH EGRET

dark morph

Reddish Egret "dancing" while feeding

(white morph on p. 165)

GREAT EGRET *Ardea alba*   Common

38–39 in. (97–100 cm). A tall, stately, slender white heron with largely *yellow bill*. Legs and feet *black*. In winter through summer, *straight plumes* on back can extend beyond tail; lores greenish. When feeding, assumes an eager, forward-leaning pose, with neck extended. *First-year:* Similar but legs dusky greenish in juvenile; plumes absent or shorter. **VOICE:** Low, hoarse croak. Also *cuk, cuk, cuk.* **SIMILAR SPECIES:** Snowy Egret smaller and with all-black bill, yellow feet. Cattle Egret much smaller. **HABITAT:** Marshes, ponds, shores, mudflats, moist fields. Rare to casual vagrant well north of range and in interior West.

SNOWY EGRET *Egretta thula*   Common

24 in. (61 cm). Note the *"golden slippers."* A medium-sized heron, with slender black bill, yellow lores, *black legs*, and distinct *yellow feet. Recurved back plumes* and filamentous head plumes during winter through summer. When feeding, rushes about, shuffling its feet to stir up food. Adults in fall and first-year birds have yellowish or greenish on rear sides of legs; plumes absent or short. **VOICE:** Low croak; in colony, a bubbling *wulla-wulla-wulla.* **SIMILAR SPECIES:** Great Egret has larger yellow bill and black feet. Cattle Egret smaller, squatter, with yellow bill. White first-year Little Blue Heron has blue-gray base to thicker bill, grayer lores, dusky tips to primaries. **HABITAT:** Marshes, swamps, ponds, shores, tidal flats. Rare to casual vagrant well north of range.

LITTLE EGRET *Egretta garzetta* (not shown)   Casual vagrant

25 in. (64 cm). A vagrant from Eurasia to E. Coast, very similar to Snowy Egret, but slightly larger, larger billed, and with duller lores and feet. Develops two long head plumes in winter/spring. Young birds very difficult to distinguish. **VOICE AND HABITAT:** Similar to Snowy Egret.

LITTLE BLUE HERON *Egretta caerulea*   (adult on p. 162)

First-year: White with dusky wingtips, sometimes bluish tinge to crown. Base of bill blue-gray, lores greenish gray, legs dull olive. Less-active feeding style than Snowy Egret. Molting one-year-olds have contrasting gray-and-white feathering.

CATTLE EGRET *Bubulcus ibis*   Common

19–20 in. (48–51 cm). Smaller, squatter, and thicker necked than Snowy Egret. In spring and summer has variable (topically applied) *buff-orange* plumes on crown, breast, and back; fall/winter adult and first-year have little or no buff. Bill relatively short; bill and legs yellow (can be pinkish when nesting). *Juvenile and first-year:* May have yellow, greenish, or dusky legs; plumes absent or shorter, usually paler buff in spring. **VOICE:** Near breeding colony, a series of nasal grunts. **SIMILAR SPECIES:** Snowy Egret larger and more slender, has black bill and legs, contrasting yellow feet. See first-year Little Blue Heron. Great Egret much larger. **HABITAT:** Farms, marshes, fields, highway edges. Often associates with cattle. Rare to casual vagrant well north of range. Common resident in HI (see p. 432).

REDDISH EGRET *Egretta rufescens*   (dark morph on p. 162)

White morph: Note size, structure, feeding behavior, entirely blue-gray legs and feet. Bill blackish in juvenile, pink with black tip in adult. Strictly coastal.

"GREAT WHITE" HERON *Ardea herodias occidentalis*   Uncommon, local

47 in. (120 cm). Our largest white heron, found regularly only in s. FL. All white with yellow bill and dull horn-colored legs, the latter separating it from slightly smaller Great Egret, which has blackish legs. Currently regarded as a white subspecies (*occidentalis*, or possibly a morph) of Great Blue Heron, p. 162. **HABITAT:** Mangrove keys, salt bays, marsh banks, open mudflats.

WHITE HERONS AND EGRETS

GREAT EGRET

SNOWY EGRET

molting
one-year-
old

juvenile

**LITTLE BLUE
HERON**
(adult on p. 163)

**CATTLE
EGRET**

fall/winter

spring/
summer

**REDDISH
EGRET**

(dark morph
on p. 163)

white morph

**"GREAT WHITE"
HERON**

(see also
Great Blue
Heron on
p. 163)

BLACK-CROWNED NIGHT-HERON *Nycticorax nycticorax* Fairly common

25 in. (64 cm). This stocky, thick-billed, short-legged heron is usually hunched and inactive; flies to feed at dusk. *Adult: Black back and cap* contrast with pale gray or whitish underparts, two long white head plumes. Eyes red; legs yellowish or greenish (pinkish in high breeding condition). *Juvenile and first-year:* Brown, streaked and spotted with buff and white. Bill with greenish base; eyes small, reddish. Second-year has adultlike plumage but paler, washed brown. **VOICE:** Flat *quok!* or *quark!* Most often heard at dusk. **SIMILAR SPECIES:** Juvenile and first-year may be confused with American Bittern and similar-aged Yellow-crowned Night-Heron. **HABITAT:** Marshes, shores, marinas; roosts in trees. Common resident in HI (p. 432).

YELLOW-CROWNED NIGHT-HERON *Nyctanassa violacea* Uncommon

24 in. (61 cm). A chunky heron with longer neck and legs than Black-crowned. *Adult:* Gray overall; head black with buffy-white cheek patch and yellowish crown. *Juvenile and first-year:* Similar to Black-crowned Night-Heron, but grayer, underparts more finely streaked; back spotting smaller; wing coverts have pale edges. Bill thicker and lacks greenish-yellow base. Second-year grayer overall, has indistinct adultlike plumage. In flight, entire feet and some of lower legs extend beyond tail. **VOICE:** *Quark,* higher pitched than call of Black-crowned. **HABITAT:** Swamps, mangroves, bayous, marshes, streams. Rare to casual vagrant and breeder north and west of range to W. Coast.

GREEN HERON *Butorides virescens* Fairly common

17–18 in. (43–46 cm). A small dark heron that looks crowlike in flight (but flies with bowed wingbeats). When alarmed, stretches neck, elevates shaggy crest, and jerks tail. *Adult:* Comparatively *short* legs are *greenish yellow* or *orange* (when breeding). Back has blue-green gloss; neck deep chestnut. *Juvenile and first-year:* Streaked neck and breast, browner above. **VOICE:** Loud *skyow* or *skewk;* series of *kuck* notes. **HABITAT:** Lakes, ponds, marshes, streams. Rare in interior West.

LEAST BITTERN *Ixobrychus exilis* Uncommon, secretive

12–13 in. (31–33 cm). Very small, thin, furtive; straddles reeds. Note large *buff wing patch* (lacking in rails). Back black in adult male, rusty brown in female and juvenile. The dark reddish and blackish "Cory's" morph is extremely rare, seen most often around the Great Lakes. **VOICE:** Song a low, muted *coo-coo-coo;* also gives a raspy, rail-like *khak-khak-khak* series. **SIMILAR SPECIES:** Green Heron. **HABITAT:** Freshwater marshes, reedy ponds. Casual vagrant throughout interior West.

AMERICAN BITTERN *Botaurus lentiginosus* Uncommon

28 in. (71 cm). A stocky brown heron; size of a young night-heron but warmer brown with longer yellowish bill. In flight, *primaries and secondaries blackish to black* and bill held horizontal (slightly downward in night-herons). At rest or when approached, often stands rigid, bill pointing up. *Black stripe shows on sides of neck.* Ages similar. **VOICE:** "Pumping" sound, a low, deep, resonant *oong-ka´ choonk,* etc. Flushing call *kok-kok-kok.* **SIMILAR SPECIES:** First-year night-herons, Green Heron, and (much smaller) Least Bittern. **HABITAT:** Marshes, reedy lakes. Unlike night-herons, seldom sits in trees.

adult

BLACK-CROWNED NIGHT-HERON

juvenile

juvenile

adult

YELLOW-CROWNED NIGHT-HERON

typical

"Cory's"

LEAST BITTERN

juvenile

adult

GREEN HERON

AMERICAN BITTERN

LIMPKINS Family Aramidae

A monotypic family, related to rails and cranes, represented by one species. **FOOD:** Mostly large freshwater snails (mainly apple snails); a few insects, frogs. **RANGE:** Southeastern U.S., W. Indies, s. Mex. to Argentina.

LIMPKIN *Aramus guarauna*   Uncommon, local

26 in. (66 cm). A large, spotted wader, a bit larger than an ibis. Long legs and drooping bill give it an ibislike aspect, but no ibis is completely brown with bold white spots and streaks. Flight cranelike, with smart upward flaps. Ages and sexes similar. **VOICE:** Piercing, repeated wail, *kree-ow, kra-ow,* etc., especially at night and on cloudy days. **SIMILAR SPECIES:** First-year ibises, night-herons, American Bittern. **HABITAT:** Fresh swamps, marshes with large snails. Rare to accidental vagrant well north of range.

IBISES and SPOONBILLS Family Threskiornithidae

Ibises are long-legged, heronlike waders with slender, decurved bills. Spoonbills have spatulate bills. Both fly in Vs or lines and, unlike herons, fly with necks outstretched. **FOOD:** Small crustaceans, small fish, insects, etc. **RANGE:** Tropical and temperate regions.

WHITE-FACED IBIS *Plegadis chihi*   Fairly common

23–24 in. (58–62 cm). A long-legged wader with *long decurved bill.* Flies in lines with neck outstretched, alternately flapping and gliding. *Spring/summer adult:* Dark, with chestnut and bronzy sheen and maroon patch in wing. *White border* of feathers around face meets behind eye; variably red legs; pinkish to red facial skin; *red eye. Fall/winter adult:* similar but head and neck brown, streaked white; less white in face. *First-year:* Similar to fall/winter adult but lacks most of white around eye; body and legs duller; wings flat olive-green, without maroon. Eye of juvenile brown. **VOICE:** Deep gooselike quacking. **SIMILAR SPECIES:** Glossy Ibis has dark facial skin with thin cobalt blue borders, and without white feathers that meet behind eye; iris without red and legs with less or no red. Juveniles may be impossible to identify but by mid-fall iris and facial skin of White-faced turns red and pale stripes in facial skin of Glossy develop. Hybrids with White-faced known. **HABITAT:** Freshwater marshes, irrigated land. Casual vagrant well north of range and to E. Coast.

GLOSSY IBIS *Plegadis falcinellus*   Fairly common

23–24 in. (58–62 cm). Similar to White-faced Ibis, but adult has thin pale blue lines in dark loral skin; body a deeper glossy bronzy chestnut. Juveniles sometimes have white feathers in head or throat. First-year birds develop pale whitish lines in face by late summer, and retain dark facial skin and brown eye, while those of first-year White-faced turn reddish by mid-fall. **VOICE:** Guttural *ka-onk,* repeated; low *kruk, kruk.* **SIMILAR SPECIES:** See White-faced Ibis. **HABITAT:** Marshes, rice fields, swamps. Casual vagrant well north of range, inland, and to W. Coast.

WHITE IBIS *Eudocimus albus*   Common

24–25 in. (62–64 cm). *Adult:* White, with *restricted black in wingtips.* Note *red face,* long *decurved red bill.* Flies with neck outstretched; flocks fly in "roller-coasting" strings, flapping and gliding; may soar in circles. *Juvenile:* Dark brownish, with *white belly, white rump,* decurved *orangey pink bill.* Slowly develops white in plumage through first year; head and neck white by second spring. **VOICE:** Low and nasal *uuhhnn!* or *quaahh!* **SIMILAR SPECIES:** Wood Stork larger, with much more black in wing. First-year Glossy Ibis has uniformly dark appearance. **HABITAT:** Salt, brackish, and fresh marshes, rice fields, mangroves. Casual vagrant throughout East and to CA; accidental in interior West.

LIMPKIN AND IBISES

WHITE-FACED IBIS

facial comparison in breeding season

Glossy Ibis

LIMPKIN

GLOSSY IBIS

adult

first-year

WHITE IBIS

adult

juvenile

ROSEATE SPOONBILL *Platalea ajaja*   Uncommon

32 in. (81 cm). A *bright pink* wading bird with long, flat, spoonlike bill. When feeding, sweeps its bill from side to side. In flight, extends neck and often glides between series of wing strokes. *Adult: Shell pink,* with blood red "drip" of filamentous feathers on shoulders in spring through fall; tail orange. Crown and face naked, greenish gray. *Juvenile:* Spatulate bill smooth, yellowish; head feathered white; remainder of plumage whitish, slowly mixed with pale pink feathers through first year, brightest on underwing; outer primary brown. Crown and face become naked and full pink plumage and red ornamental feathering assumed in second and third years. **VOICE:** At nesting colony, a low grunting croak. **SIMILAR SPECIES:** American Flamingo. **HABITAT:** Coastal marshes, lagoons, mudflats, mangroves. Rare vagrant throughout East and to CO, AZ, and CA.

STORKS Family Ciconiidae

Large, long-legged, and heronlike, with very large, straight, recurved, or decurved bills. Some have naked heads. Sexes alike. Walk is sedate; flight deliberate, with neck and legs extended. **FOOD:** Frogs, crustaceans, lizards, rodents. **RANGE:** Southern U.S. to S. America; Africa, Eurasia, E. Indies, Australia.

WOOD STORK *Mycteria americana*   Uncommon

39–41 in. (100–105 cm). Very large; wingspan 5½ ft. (168 cm). *Adult:* White, with *dark naked head* and *much black in wing;* black tail. Bill long, thick, slightly decurved. *First-year:* Bill yellowish, head with downy white feathers slowly lost during first and second years. When feeding, keeps head down and walks on stiff legs. In flight, alternately flaps and glides. Often soars very high on thermals. **VOICE:** Hoarse croak; usually silent. **SIMILAR SPECIES:** In flight, American White Pelican, Whooping Crane. Jabiru *(Jabiru mycteria),* an accidental vagrant to TX, is a much larger stork; adult has bare black-and-red head and neck and entirely white wings. **HABITAT:** Marshes, ponds, lagoons, swamps. E. Coast populations threatened. Rare vagrant or visitor throughout East and to AZ, CA; accidental elsewhere in West.

FLAMINGOS Family Phoenicopteridae

Pinkish white to vermilion wading birds with extremely long neck and legs. Thick bill is bent sharply down and lined with numerous lamellae for straining food. **FOOD:** Small mollusks, crustaceans, blue-green algae, diatoms. **RANGE:** W. Indies, Yucatán, Galápagos, S. America, Africa, s. Eurasia, India.

AMERICAN FLAMINGO *Phoenicopterus ruber*   Rare vagrant

46–47 in. (115–118 cm). An extremely slim, rose pink wading bird as tall as or taller than a Great Blue Heron but much more slender. Note thick, sharply bent bill. Feeds with bill or head immersed. In flight, shows black in wings; extremely long neck is extended droopily in front, and long legs trail behind, giving impression the bird might as easily fly backward as forward. Pale, washed-out birds may be escapees from zoos, as color often fades under captive conditions. First- and second-year flamingos also much paler pink than wild adults; primary coverts and underwing coverts brownish; bill dull yellowish with indistinct dusky tip. **VOICE:** Gooselike calls, gabbling: *ar-honk,* etc. **SIMILAR SPECIES:** Roseate Spoonbill. Escapees of all five other flamingo species have been recorded in N. America; Chilean Flamingo *(P. chilensis),* most common in captivity, is paler pink and has more black on bill tip (includes angle). **RANGE:** Closest colonies in Bahamas, Cuba, and Yucatán Peninsula, Mex. Rare vagrant to FL bays; accidental elsewhere. **HABITAT:** Salt flats, saline lagoons.

VERY LARGE WADERS

adult

juvenile

ROSEATE SPOONBILL

Wood Stork

adult

first-year

White Ibis
(p. 168) for
comparison

**WOOD
STORK**

first-year

adult

adult

**AMERICAN
FLAMINGO**

CRANES Family Gruidae

Stately birds, more robust than herons, often with red facial skin. Note arching tufted feathering over rump. In flight, neck extended. Migrate in Vs or lines like geese. Large herons are sometimes wrongly referred to as cranes. **FOOD:** Omnivorous. **RANGE:** Nearly worldwide except Cen. and S. America and Oceania.

WHOOPING CRANE *Grus americana*　　　　Rare, very local, endangered
51–52 in. (130–132 cm); wingspan 7½ ft. (229 cm). The tallest N. American bird and one of the rarest. *Adult:* Large *white* crane with bare *red forehead and lower face.* Primaries *black. Juvenile:* Plumage washed with rust, especially on head, which is feathered; bill dusky. About three years required to develop full adult plumage and head condition. **VOICE:** Shrill, buglelike trumpeting, *ker-loo! ker-lee-oo!* **SIMILAR SPECIES:** Wood Stork has dark head, more black in wing. Egrets and swans lack black in wings. See also American White Pelican and Snow Goose. **HABITAT:** Prairies, fields and pastures, coastal marshes; in summer, muskeg. Casual migrant or vagrant in Mississippi Valley.

COMMON CRANE *Grus grus*　　　　　　　　Accidental vagrant
44–50 in. (112–127 cm). Eurasian. *Adult:* Note black neck, white cheek stripe. Feathers arching over rump are blacker than those of Sandhill Crane. *Juvenile:* Entirely gray with yellow bill; develops indistinct adultlike pattern in first year. This vagrant (probably migrating with Sandhill Cranes from Asia) has been recorded in midwestern to w. N. America, most frequently among flocks of Sandhill Cranes. Some escapees or presumed escapees have also occurred in e. N. America.

SANDHILL CRANE *Antigone canadensis*　　　Fairly common; scarce in East
36–48 in. (90–122 cm); wingspan 6–7 ft. (183–213 cm). Adult: Note *bare red crown,* bustlelike rear. A long-legged, long-necked, gray bird, often stained with rust in spring and summer. Juvenile browner, with feathered head, yellowish bill; about three years required to develop full adult plumage and head condition. In flight, neck extended and wings flap with an upward flick. **VOICE:** Rolling, bugled *garoo-a-a-a,* repeated. Younger birds also give a very different, cricketlike call. **SIMILAR SPECIES:** Great Blue Heron is sometimes wrongly called a crane. **HABITAT:** Prairies, fields, marshes, tundra. Smaller "Lesser" Sandhill Crane (subspecies *canadensis*) nests in tundra and winters primarily in West; larger "Greater" (subspecies *tabida*) nests in grasslands and bogs and winters across N. America, uncommonly to Midwest and as a scarce to casual vagrant to E. Coast north of FL. Populations of FL (subspecies *pratensis*) and MS (*pulla*) are resident, the latter endangered.

CRANES

storks, ibises, and cranes fly
with neck outstretched

adult

WHOOPING
CRANE

juvenile

adult

COMMON
CRANE

Sandhill
Crane

juvenile

adult

SANDHILL CRANE

COOTS, GALLINULES, and RAILS Family Rallidae

Rails are rather hen-shaped marsh birds, many of secretive habits and distinctive voices, more often heard than seen. Flight from marshes is brief and reluctant, with legs dangling, although they can also undertake remarkable long-distance migrations at night. Gallinules and coots are much easier to see; they swim and might be confused with small ducks or grebes. They spend most of their time swimming but may also feed on shores. Other than juveniles, ages and sexes generally alike or differ slightly. **FOOD:** Aquatic plants, seeds, insects, frogs, crustaceans, mollusks. **RANGE:** Nearly worldwide.

AMERICAN COOT *Fulica americana*   Uncommon to common

15–15½ in. (38–39 cm). *Adult:* A slaty, ducklike bird with blackish head and neck, slate gray body, *white bill*, and divided white patch under tail. No side striping. Its big feet are lobed ("scallops" on toes). *Juvenile and first-fall:* Paler, throat whiter, bill duller grayish, without shield. Downy chick has bushy *orange-red* feathers on head, a bald crown, and red bill. Gregarious. When swimming, pumps head back and forth. Taking off, it skitters; flight labored. **VOICE:** Grating *kuk-kuk-kuk-kuk; kakakakakaka;* etc.; also a measured *ka-ha, ha-ha;* various cackles, croaks. **SIMILAR SPECIES:** Juvenile Common Gallinule is browner above, has thin white stripe on flanks, and warmer-colored bill; more solitary. **HABITAT:** Ponds, lakes, marshes; in winter, also fields, park ponds, golf courses, lawns, salt bays.

COMMON GALLINULE *Gallinula galeata*   Uncommon

14 in. (36 cm). Also known as Common Moorhen. Note adult's *red bill with yellow tip, red forehead shield,* and white stripe on flanks. When walking, flicks white undertail coverts; while swimming, pumps head like a coot. *Juvenile and first-fall:* Duller, throat whiter, bill duller brownish, without shield. Downy chick with black feathers, a bald crown, and red bill. **VOICE:** Croaking *kr-r-ruk,* repeated; a froglike *kup;* complaining, henlike, *kek, kek, kek* (higher than coot's call). **SIMILAR SPECIES:** American Coot, juvenile and first-year Purple Gallinule. **HABITAT:** Freshwater marshes, reedy ponds. Casual to accidental vagrant in interior West.

PURPLE GALLINULE *Porphyrio martinica*   Uncommon

13 in. (33 cm). *Adult:* Head and underparts *deep violet-purple,* back bronzy green. Shield on forehead *pale blue;* bill red with yellow tip. Legs *yellow,* conspicuous in flight. *Juvenile and first-fall:* Buffy brown below, dark above tinged greenish; bill dark; sides unstriped; acquires mixed purple feathering in first year. **VOICE:** Henlike cackling, *kek, kek, kek;* also guttural notes, sharp reedy cries. **SIMILAR SPECIES:** Common Gallinule lacks greenish plumage, has white side-stripe in all plumages. Western Swamphen. **HABITAT:** Freshwater swamps, marshes, ponds. Swims, wades, and climbs bushes. Widespread vagrant north and west of range; accidental to CA and WA.

PURPLE SWAMPHEN *Porphyrio porphyria*   Fairly common, local

16–19 in. (40–48 cm). Introduced to se. FL (subspecies *poliocephalus,* sometimes split as Gray-headed Swamphen), where it's increasing in numbers and range despite control efforts. *Adult:* Purple and blue with turquoise wings, large fearsome red bill, red shield, and bright red legs and feet with dusky joints. *Juvenile and first-fall:* Plumage grayish; bill blackish. **VOICE:** Loud, sharp *ee-erk ee-erk.* **SIMILAR SPECIES:** Purple Gallinule is smaller and less blocky, has greener back, a pale blue shield, and yellow legs. **HABITAT:** Vegetated freshwater wetlands, including lakeshores, ponds, marshes, sloughs.

COOTS AND
GALLINULES

juvenile

coot chick

adult

lobed foot
of coot

adult

AMERICAN
COOT

gallinule
chick

juvenile

adult

COMMON
GALLINULE

adult

PURPLE
GALLINULE

juvenile

adult

adult

PURPLE
SWAMPHEN

VIRGINIA RAIL *Rallus limicola*   Fairly common

9½ in. (24 cm). A small rusty rail with gray cheeks, black bars on flanks, and long, slightly decurved, reddish bill with dark tip. Near size of meadowlark; only small rail with *long slender bill. Juvenile* (summer only): Shows much black; otherwise ages similar. **VOICE:** Descending grunt, *wuk-wuk-wuk-wuk,* etc.; also *kidick, kidick,* etc.; various "kicking" and grunting sounds. **SIMILAR SPECIES:** Sora has small stubby bill, unbarred undertail coverts. Clapper, Ridgway's, and King Rails much larger. **HABITAT:** Fresh and brackish marshes; in winter, also salt marshes.

KING RAIL *Rallus elegans*   Uncommon, secretive

15–16 in. (38–41 cm). A large rusty rail with long slender bill; twice the size of Virginia Rail, or about that of a small chicken. Similar to Ridgway's and brighter than Clapper Rail, but note rusty/chestnut cheeks and more contrasting black-and-white flanks, rustier overall with *bolder back pattern* (blacker feathers with buffier edges); prefers fresh marshes. Juvenile in summer (not shown) has black mottling, similar to juvenile Virginia Rail; otherwise ages similar. **VOICE:** Low, slow, grunting *bup-bup, bup-bup-bup,* etc., or evenly spaced *chuck-chuck-chuck* (deeper than Virginia Rail). **SIMILAR SPECIES:** Clapper and Ridgway's Rails. Virginia Rail half the size, has slaty gray cheeks. *Note:* Hybrids between Clapper and King occur. **HABITAT:** Fresh and brackish marshes, rice fields, ditches, swamps. In winter, also salt marshes. Rare to casual vagrant north and west of range.

CLAPPER RAIL *Rallus crepitans*   Fairly common

14–15 in. (35–38 cm). The large "marsh hen" of Atlantic and Gulf Coast marshes. Sometimes swims. Note henlike appearance; strong legs; long, slightly decurved bill; barred flanks; and white patch under short cocked tail, which it flicks nervously. Cheeks gray. Gulf Coast birds (subspecies *saturatus*) brighter than subspecies found along Atlantic Coast. Juveniles (summer only) are duller grayish with blackish mottled flanks; ages similar otherwise. **VOICE:** Clattering *kek-kek-kek-kek,* etc., or *cha-cha-cha,* etc. **SIMILAR SPECIES:** King Rail prefers fresh (sometimes brackish) marshes, has bolder pattern on back and flanks, rusty brown on wings. Its breast is brighter cinnamon, although note Clappers along Gulf Coast and in CA and Southwest have warmer tawny tones, approaching those of King Rail. Adult Clapper has grayer cheeks; juvenile is not as blackish on head and breast and has duller edging to secondaries. These two rails occasionally co-occur and hybridize in adjacent brackish marshes. **HABITAT:** Coastal salt marshes. Accidental vagrant inland.

RIDGWAY'S RAIL *Rallus obsoletus*   Uncommon, local, endangered

14½–15½ in. (37–39 cm). Recently split from Clapper Rail. Brighter overall than that species, with redder bill (especially when breeding). Appearance may be closer to King Rail, but back not as well marked, flank barring not as boldly black and white, bill redder. **VOICE:** Similar to Clapper Rail. **SIMILAR SPECIES:** Larger than Virginia Rail. Neither King nor Clapper Rail is found within the same range as Ridgway's Rail. **HABITAT:** Coastal and freshwater marshes. Populations of coastal CA (subspecies *obsoletus* and *levipes*) and Yuma, AZ *(yuma-nensis),* endangered. Accidental vagrant inland, away from range.

LONG-BILLED RAILS

juvenile

VIRGINIA RAIL

adult

KING RAIL

Atlantic
Coast

Limpkin
(p. 168) for
comparison

Gulf Coast
and West

**CLAPPER
RAIL**

chick

**RIDGWAY'S
RAIL**

adult

SORA *Porzana carolina* Fairly common

8½ in. (22 cm). Note *short yellow* bill. *Adult:* A small, plump, gray-brown rail with *black patch* on face and throat, more extensive in male than in female. Short, cocked tail reveals white or buff undertail coverts. *Juvenile and first-winter:* Lacks dark throat patch and is browner; acquires duller adult plumage by first spring. **VOICE:** Descending whinny, *whee-ee-ee-ee-ee-ee-e-e-e.* Also a plaintive whistled *keu-wee?* Clapping one's hands can cause startled birds to utter a sharp *keek.* **SIMILAR SPECIES:** Juvenile and first-winter Soras may be confused with smaller and rarer Yellow Rail, which has large white wing patches and blacker-centered feathers above. Virginia Rail has slender bill. **HABITAT:** Freshwater marshes; in migration, also wet meadows; in winter, also salt marshes.

YELLOW RAIL *Coturnicops noveboracensis* Scarce, secretive

7¼ in. (18 cm). Note *white wing patch* (in flight). A small buffy-and-black rail, suggesting a week-old chick. Bill very short, greenish or yellowish. Back dark, striped, barred, and checkered with buff, white, and black. *Mouselike; very difficult to see.* Ages similar. **VOICE:** Nocturnal ticking notes, often in long series: *tic-tic, tic-tic-tic, tic-tic, tic-tic-tic,* etc., in alternating groups of two and three. Compared to hitting two small stones together. **SIMILAR SPECIES:** Young Sora somewhat larger, buffier overall, lacks dark barring and checkering above, has thin pale trailing edge but no white patch in wing. **HABITAT:** Grassy marshes, wet meadows; winters mostly in salt marshes and grain fields. Scarce to casual migrant or vagrant throughout West.

BLACK RAIL *Laterallus jamaicensis* Scarce, local, secretive

6 in. (15 cm). A tiny blackish rail with small *black* bill; about the size of a young sparrow. Nape deep chestnut. *Very difficult to glimpse.* Full-grown birds of all ages similar. *Caution:* All young rails in downy plumage are black. **VOICE:** Male (mostly at night), *kiki-doo* or *kiki-krrr* (or *kitty go*). Also a growl. **HABITAT:** Salt marshes, freshwater marshes, grassy meadows. Rare to casual vagrant to e. CA and Midwest; accidental elsewhere away from range.

JACANAS Family Jacanidae

Jacanas are related to shorebirds but look like gallinules and walk like rails. Adults are dark with very long toes, perfect for walking over lily pads and other floating aquatic vegetation. Sexes alike. **FOOD:** Aquatic insects, seeds, and vegetation. **RANGE:** Pantropical.

NORTHERN JACANA *Jacana spinosa* Casual vagrant

9½ in. (24 cm). This vagrant has spectacularly long toes for walking on lily pads. *Adult:* Chestnut body with dark head. Yellow bill and forehead frontal shield. Striking yellow primaries and secondaries in flight. Holds wings over head when it lands. *Juvenile and first-winter:* Has white underparts, distinct line behind eye, slightly less yellow in wings; gradually gains incomplete adultlike body plumage by first spring. **VOICE:** Rapid series of high, nasal notes: *jeek-jeek-jeek-jeek.* **RANGE:** Casual visitor from Mex. to TX; accidental in AZ. **HABITAT:** Frequents ponds with emergent vegetation, especially lily pads.

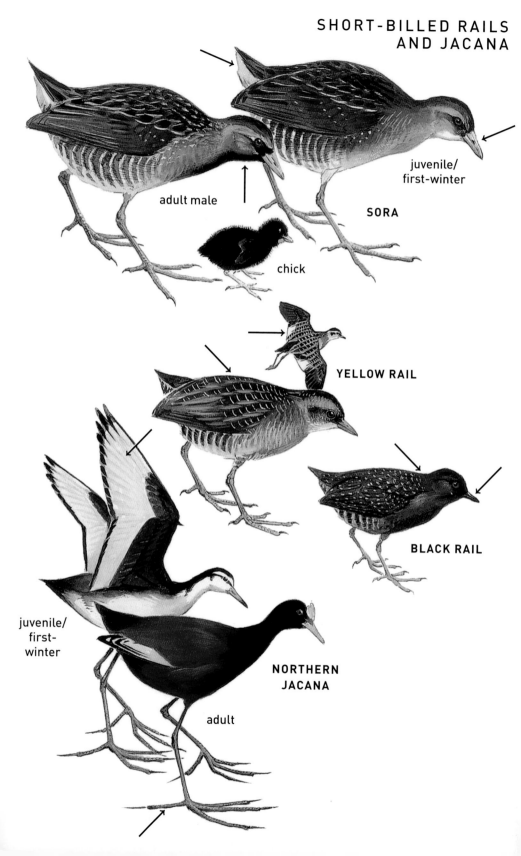

SHORT-BILLED RAILS AND JACANA

adult male

chick

juvenile/
first-winter

SORA

YELLOW RAIL

BLACK RAIL

juvenile/
first-
winter

**NORTHERN
JACANA**

adult

CURASSOWS and GUANS Family Cracidae

Tropical forest birds with long tails. Only one species reaches extreme s. U.S. Ages and sexes similar. **FOOD:** Insects, fruit, leaves, seeds. **RANGE:** New World Tropics.

PLAIN CHACHALACA *Ortalis vetula*　　　　Fairly common, local
22 in. (56 cm). A large olive-brown bird, shaped somewhat like a half-grown turkey with a small head. Long, rounded, pale-tipped tail, bare red throat. Difficult to observe away from feeding stations; best found in morning when calling raucously from treetops. **VOICE:** Alarm a harsh chickenlike cackle. Characteristic call a raucous three-syllabled *cha-ca-lac*, repeated in chorus from treetops, especially in morning and evening. **SIMILAR SPECIES:** Greater Roadrunner. **HABITAT:** Woodlands, tall brush, well-vegetated residential areas.

GALLINACEOUS BIRDS (TURKEYS, PHEASANTS, GROUSE, PARTRIDGES, and OLD WORLD QUAIL) Family Phasianidae

Often called "upland game birds." Turkeys are very large, with wattles and fanlike tail. Pheasants (introduced) have long pointed tail. Grouse are plump, chickenlike birds, without long tail. Partridges (of Old World origin) are intermediate in size between grouse and quail. Quail are the smallest. Ages generally similar, sexes usually differ. **FOOD:** Insects, seeds, buds, berries. **RANGE:** Nearly worldwide.

WILD TURKEY *Meleagris gallopavo*　　　　Fairly common
Male 46–47 in. (117–120 cm); female 36–37 in. (91–94 cm). A streamlined version of barnyard turkey, with dark (not white) plumage and rusty instead of white tail tips (southwestern birds have buff-white tail tips). *Adult male:* Head naked; bluish with red wattles, intensified in display. Tail erected like a fan in display. Bronzy iridescent body; barred primaries and secondaries; prominent "beard" on breast. *Female and first-year male:* Smaller, with smaller and duller head; less likely to have a beard. **VOICE:** "Gobbling" of male like domestic turkey's. Alarm *pit!* or *put-put!* Flock call *keow-keow*. Hen clucks to her chicks. **HABITAT:** Woods, mountain forests, wooded swamps, field edges, clearings. Reintroduced in many areas, and such birds are adapting well to being near people. Introduced and fairly common in HI (p. 436).

GUNNISON SAGE-GROUSE　　　　Scarce, very local, endangered
Centrocercus minimus
Male 21–22 in. (53–56 cm); female 18–19 in. (46–49 cm). Recently split from Greater Sage-Grouse, this species is found only in a very geographically restricted region of sw. CO and se. UT. Differs from Greater Sage-Grouse by its slightly smaller size, bushier "crest," and more distinct white barring on tail. Identification by range is most reliable.

GREATER SAGE-GROUSE *Centrocercus urophasianus*　　　　Uncommon
Male 27–28 in. (69–71 cm); female 22–23 in. (56–58 cm). A large grayish grouse of open sage country, almost as large as a small turkey; identified by its contrasting *black belly patch* and spikelike tail feathers. Male is considerably larger than female, has black throat, and, in communal dancing display, puffs out its white chest, exposing two yellow air sacs on neck, at same time erecting and spreading its pointed tail feathers in a spiky fan. **VOICE:** Flushing call *kuk kuk kuk*. In courtship display, male makes a popping sound. **SIMILAR SPECIES:** Gunnison Sage-Grouse, but these two resident species do not overlap in range. See female Ring-necked Pheasant. **HABITAT:** Sagebrush plains; also foothills and mountain slopes where sagebrush grows.

PLAIN CHACHALACA

WILD TURKEY

female

adult male

male display

male
Greater
display

female

male
display

**GUNNISON
SAGE-GROUSE**

**GREATER
SAGE-GROUSE**

RUFFED GROUSE *Bonasa umbellus*   Uncommon

17 in. (43 cm). Note short crest, bold flank bars, and fan-shaped tail with broad black band near tip. A large chickenlike bird of brushy woodlands, usually not seen until it flushes with a startling whir. Two color morphs occur: "rusty" with rufous tail and "gray" with gray tail. Rusty birds more common in southern parts of range (and in Pacific Northwest), gray birds more common northward. Female slightly smaller and duller than male, and usually has a broken black subterminal tail band. **VOICE:** Sound of drumming male suggests a distant motor starting up. Low muffled thumping starts slowly, accelerating into a whir: *Bup . . . bup . . . bup . . . bup . . . bup bup up r-rrrrr.* **SIMILAR SPECIES:** Sharp-tailed, Sooty, Dusky, and Spruce Grouse. **HABITAT:** Ground and understory of deciduous and mixed woodlands.

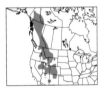

SPRUCE GROUSE *Falcipennis canadensis*   Scarce

16–17 in. (41–43 cm). Look for this tame, dark grouse in deep coniferous forests of North. *Male:* Sharply defined *black breast,* with some white spots or bars on sides and *chestnut band on tip of tail.* Erectile red comb above eye is visible at close range. "Franklin's Grouse" (*franklinii* subspecies group) of West lack chestnut tail tip and have larger white spots on uppertail coverts than "Northern" (*canadensis* group). *Female:* Dark rusty or grayish brown, thickly barred, and with black-and-white spotting below; tail short and dark. **VOICE:** Female call is an accelerating, then slowing, series of *wock* notes; also cluck notes. Wing flutter from male's courtship display may sound like distant rumble of thunder. **SIMILAR SPECIES:** Sooty and Dusky Grouse larger and grayer, lack bold black-and-white spotting below. **HABITAT:** Coniferous forests, jack pines, muskeg, blueberry patches.

DUSKY GROUSE *Dendragapus obscurus*   Uncommon

20 in. (51 cm). This is the more interior of the two species formerly lumped as "Blue Grouse." *Male:* In courtship display, eye combs may change from yellow to red. Neck sacs *purplish red* surrounded by broad ring of white feathers. *Female:* See Sooty Grouse. **VOICE:** Courting male gives a series of five to seven low, muffled booming or hooting notes, ventriloquial, usually from ground; lower pitched and softer than calls of male Sooty Grouse. **SIMILAR SPECIES:** Sooty Grouse darker overall; darker tail; male has yellowish neck sacs; both sexes have fewer and less distinct white spots; no range overlap. See Spruce Grouse. Female similar to Ruffed Grouse (see Sooty Grouse). **HABITAT:** In summer, all forest types, alpine meadow edges; may move to higher-elevation coniferous forests in winter.

SOOTY GROUSE *Dendragapus fuliginosus*   Uncommon

20 in. (51 cm). A large dark grouse with long neck and tail. Distinct gray band on tail tip. *Male:* In courtship display shows yellow to orange eye combs and inflates bright yellow neck sacs with narrow white border. *Female:* Gray-brown, mottled with blackish, belly paler than male's. **VOICE:** Courting male gives a series of five to seven low, muffled booming or hooting notes, ventriloquial, usually from perch in a tree; much louder than calls of Dusky Grouse. **SIMILAR SPECIES:** Dusky and Spruce Grouse. Females of both Sooty and Dusky Grouse may be confused with Ruffed Grouse, but Ruffed has slight crested look, bold flank bars, and lighter tail with *black band* near tip. **HABITAT:** In summer, all forest types, mountain meadow edges; may move to higher-elevation coniferous forests in winter.

GROUSE

RUFFED GROUSE

gray morph

male display

rusty morph

SPRUCE GROUSE

"Franklin's" male

"Northern" male

female

male display

female Dusky

male

male

male display

male display

SOOTY GROUSE

DUSKY GROUSE

SHARP-TAILED GROUSE *Tympanuchus phasianellus*   Uncommon

17 in. (43 cm). A pale, speckled-brown grouse of prairies and brushy draws. Note *short pointed tail,* which in display and flight shows *white* at sides. Slight crested look. Marked below by dark bars, spots, and chevrons. Displaying male has yellow eye combs and inflates *purplish* neck sacs; female slightly smaller and duller, has barred crown. **VOICE:** Cackling *cac-cac-cac,* etc. Courting note a single low *coo-oo,* accompanied by quill-rattling, foot-shuffling. **SIMILAR SPECIES:** Prairie-chickens have *rounded, dark* tail and are more barred, rather than spotted, below. Female Ring-necked Pheasant has *long pointed* tail. Ruffed Grouse has banded, *fan-shaped tail* and black neck ruff. **HABITAT:** Prairies, agricultural fields, forest edges, clearings, gullies, open burns and clear-cuts in coniferous and mixed forests.

GREATER PRAIRIE-CHICKEN *Tympanuchus cupido*   Uncommon, local

17 in. (43 cm). A henlike bird of prairies. Brown, heavily barred. Note *rounded dark tail* (black in male, barred in female). Courting males in communal "dance" inflate orange neck sacs, show off orangey yellow eye combs, and erect black hornlike neck feathers; female slightly smaller and duller, has less-elongated neck plumes and barred crown. **VOICE:** "Booming" male in dance makes a hollow *oo-loo-woo,* suggesting sound made by blowing across a bottle mouth. **SIMILAR SPECIES:** Lesser Prairie-Chicken. Sharp-tailed Grouse, slightly paler overall, has more spots or chevrons on underparts, and has more pointed, white-edged tail. Female Ring-necked Pheasant slightly larger, has long pointed tail. **HABITAT:** Native tallgrass prairie, now very localized; agricultural land. Populations of coastal TX (subspecies *attwateri*) endangered.

LESSER PRAIRIE-CHICKEN   Scarce, local, threatened
Tympanuchus pallidicinctus

16 in. (41 cm). A small, pale brown prairie-chicken; best identified by range. Male's neck sacs are dull *purplish* or *plum colored* (not yellow-orange as in Greater Prairie-Chicken). Breast barring usually paler and thinner than Greater's. **VOICE:** Male's courtship "booming" not as rolling or loud as Greater Prairie-Chicken's. Both sexes give clucking, cackling notes. **SIMILAR SPECIES:** Greater Prairie-Chicken, Sharp-tailed Grouse. **HABITAT:** Sandhill country (sage and bluestem grass, oak shrublands).

GROUSE

SHARP-TAILED GROUSE

female

male
display

GREATER
PRAIRIE-CHICKEN

female

male
display

LESSER
PRAIRIE-CHICKEN

female

male
display

PTARMIGANS

Hardy Arctic and alpine grouse with feathered feet. They molt three times a year; camouflaging themselves to match the seasons, they change from dark plumage in summer to white in winter; in spring, males are white with darker heads. During spring and fall molting periods they have a patchy look. Ages similar, sexes differ except in winter. A red comb above eye may be erected or concealed. **FOOD:** Buds, leaves, seeds.

WILLOW PTARMIGAN *Lagopus lagopus*   Fairly common

15 in. (39 cm). Willow and Rock Ptarmigans are fairly similar. In breeding season, Willows are variable, but most males are chestnut brown, redder than any plumage or subspecies of Rock Ptarmigan; females are a warm buffy brown that can overlap brown of Rock. White of wings retained all year and, in flight, contrast with summer body plumage. In winter, white overall with black tail, the latter retained year-round. There is much variation among sexes and between various molts; longest uppertail coverts in summer plumages are barred in females but not males. **VOICE:** Deep raucous calls. Male, a staccato crow, *kwow, kwow, tobacco, tobacco,* etc., or *go-back, go-back.* **SIMILAR SPECIES:** Rock Ptarmigan always has smaller and more slender bill that lacks strong curve on ridge shown by Willow. In winter, male Rock has *black lores between eye and bill,* lacking in both sexes of Willow. Habitats overlap, but Rock tends to prefer higher, more barren hills. See also White-tailed Ptarmigan. **HABITAT:** Tundra, willow scrub, muskeg; in winter, sheltered valleys at slightly lower altitudes.

ROCK PTARMIGAN *Lagopus muta*   Uncommon

14 in. (36 cm). Male during summer and fall is browner or grayer than Willow Ptarmigan, lacking rich chestnut around head and neck. Plumages vary geographically; some Rocks may be paler, grayer, or buffier than shown here, and subspecies *evermanni* of w. Aleutians can be blackish brown or tinged rufous. Females can be similar to female Willow Ptarmigan, but Rock has smaller bill. In winter, white male Rock has *black lores* between eyes and bill, reduced or absent in female, which may be told from female Willow at this time by Rock's smaller bill. **VOICE:** Croaks, growls, cackles; usually silent. **SIMILAR SPECIES:** Willow and White-tailed Ptarmigans. **HABITAT:** Tundra, above timberline in mountains (to lower levels in winter); also near sea level in bleak tundra of northern coasts.

WHITE-TAILED PTARMIGAN *Lagopus leucura*   Uncommon

12½–13 in. (31–33 cm). The only ptarmigan normally found south of Canada. Note *white tail,* particularly in flight. In summer, generally browner than other ptarmigan, with blacker sides in male and with white belly, wings, and tail. In winter, pure white except for black eyes and bill. Female similar to male in summer/fall plumages except for barred uppertail coverts. **VOICE:** Cackling notes, clucks, soft hoots. **SIMILAR SPECIES:** The other two ptarmigans have *black* tail in all plumages. **HABITAT:** Alpine tundra, including rocky outcrops and stunted willow thickets.

PTARMIGANS

WILLOW PTARMIGAN

winter

female

spring/
summer
male

spring
male

winter

spring/
summer
female

ROCK PTARMIGAN

males

winter

western Aleutians
male

winter

spring/
summer
female

spring/
summer
female

male

WHITE-TAILED PTARMIGAN

winter

spring/
summer
male

winter

early
spring
molting

spring/summer
female

spring/
summer
female

INTRODUCED GAME BIRDS

RING-NECKED PHEASANT *Phasianus colchicus*   Fairly common, introduced

Male 31–33 in. (79–84 cm); female 21–23 in. (53–59 cm). A large chickenlike bird introduced from Eurasia. Note long pointed tail. Runs swiftly; flight strong, takeoff noisy. *Male:* Highly colored and *iridescent,* with *scarlet wattles* on face and *white neck ring* (not always present). *Female:* Mottled brown, with *long pointed tail.* **VOICE:** Crowing male gives loud double squawk, *kork-kok,* followed by brief whir of wings. When flushed, harsh croaks. Roosting call a two-syllable *kutuck-kutuck,* etc. **SIMILAR SPECIES:** Female sage-grouse have black belly patch. Female Sharp-tailed Grouse and prairie-chickens have shorter tails, white (Sharp-tailed) or black (prairie-chickens) outer tail feathers, barred upperparts. **HABITAT:** Farms, fields, marsh edges, brush, grassy roadsides. Periodic local releases for hunting. Introduced and common in HI (p. 436).

GRAY PARTRIDGE *Perdix perdix*   Uncommon, introduced

12½–13 in. (32–34 cm). Introduced from Europe. A rotund gray-brown partridge, smaller than grouse but larger than quail; note short *rufous* tail, *rusty face,* chestnut bars on sides; male also has dark U-shaped splotch on belly; female slightly browner (less gray) above and with buffier lores and eye line. **VOICE:** Loud, hoarse *kar-wit, kar-wit.* **SIMILAR SPECIES:** Chukar (another introduced species of West, which also has rufous tail) prefers rockier habitat, has red bill and legs, black "necklace." **HABITAT:** Cultivated land, hedgerows, bushy pastures, meadows.

CHUKAR *Alectoris chukar*   Uncommon, introduced

13½–14 in. (34–36 cm). Introduced from Asia. Like a large quail; gray-brown with *bright red legs and bill;* light throat bordered by clean-cut black "necklace." Sides *boldly barred;* tail *rufous.* Sexes similar. **VOICE:** Series of raspy *chuck*s; a sharp *wheet-u.* **SIMILAR SPECIES:** Gray Partridge. Mountain Quail smaller and darker, with duller bill and legs. Red-legged Partridge (*Alectoris rufa*), an occasional escapee, is similar but has streaked breast. **HABITAT:** Rocky, grassy, or brushy slopes; arid mountains, canyons. Birds recently released for hunting may be found well out of range and habitat. Introduced and fairly common in HI (p. 434).

HIMALAYAN SNOWCOCK *Tetraogallus himalayensis*   Very local, exotic

28 in. (71 cm). An Asian species, introduced to Ruby Mts. of n. NV from ne. Pakistan. Large, gray-brown body; paler face and neck with rusty brown stripes. Shows white in wing in flight. Flies downslope in the morning to forage and walks upslope during the day. Sexes alike; subspecies in NV (*himalayensis*) has darker upperparts and sides than other subspecies. **VOICE:** Calls include cackles and clucks; display call a loud whistle. **SIMILAR SPECIES:** Chukar. **HABITAT:** Rugged alpine slopes.

INTRODUCED GAME BIRDS

RING-NECKED
PHEASANT

female

male

female

female

male

GRAY
PARTRIDGE

male

CHUKAR

Red-legged Partridge
for comparison

male

male

HIMALAYAN SNOWCOCK

NEW WORLD QUAIL Family Odontophoridae

Quail are smaller than grouse. Sexes can be alike or unlike. **FOOD:** Insects, seeds, buds, berries. **RANGE:** Nearly worldwide.

CALIFORNIA QUAIL *Callipepla californica*   Common

10 in. (25 cm). A small, plump, grayish, chickenlike bird, with a *short black plume* curving forward from crown. *Male:* Has *black-and-white face* and throat, *scaled belly pattern. Female:* Duller. **VOICE:** Three-syllable *qua-quergo,* or *chi-cago.* Also light clucking and sharp *pit* notes. Male on territory, a loud *kurr.* **SIMILAR SPECIES:** Gambel's Quail has rufous brown crown, different belly pattern; ranges barely overlap. **HABITAT:** Broken chaparral, woodland edges, coastal scrub, parks, estates, farms. Introduced and common in HI (p. 434).

GAMBEL'S QUAIL *Callipepla gambelii*   Common

10½–11 in. (26–28 cm). Replaces California Quail in most desert habitats. Similar to that species, but male Gambel's has *black patch* on light, *unscaled belly;* flanks and crown more russet. *Female:* Also *unscaled* on belly. **VOICE:** Loud *kaaaa;* also *ka-KAA-ka-ka* and sharp *ut, ut* notes. **HABITAT:** Variety of shrubby desert environments, including parks, suburbs. Uncommon exotic in HI (p. 434).

MOUNTAIN QUAIL *Oreortyx pictus*   Uncommon

11 in. (28 cm). A gray-and-brown quail of mountains and upland plateaus. *Male:* Distinguished from California Quail by long *straight* head plume and *chestnut* (not black) *throat.* Note chestnut-and-white side pattern. *Female:* Similar to male but with shorter plume, browner nape and upper back. **VOICE:** Mellow *wook?* or *to-wook?* repeated at intervals by male; loquacious *wew-wew-wew-wew* series. **HABITAT:** Open pine and mixed forests, brushy ravines, montane chaparral.

SCALED QUAIL *Callipepla squamata*   Fairly common

10 in. (25 cm). A pale grayish quail (sometimes called "Blue Quail") of arid country, with scaly markings on breast and back. *Male:* Note *short bushy white crest,* or "cotton top," a common nickname for this species. Runs; often reluctant to fly. *Female:* Has shorter crest than male, duller and finely streaked throat. **VOICE:** Guinea hen–like *che-kar* (also interpreted as *pay-cos*). **HABITAT:** Shrub-grasslands, brush, arid country.

NORTHERN BOBWHITE *Colinus virginianus*   Uncommon, declining

9½–10 in. (24–26 cm). A small, rotund fowl, near size of a meadowlark. Ruddy, barred and striped, with short dark tail. *Male:* Has conspicuous white throat and white eyebrow stripe; in female these are buff. Dark Mex. subspecies, "Masked" Bobwhite, with *black throat* and *rusty underparts,* endangered, was once found in s. AZ (subspecies *ridgwayi*), where it has been locally reintroduced. **VOICE:** Clearly whistled *Bob-white!* or *poor, Bob-whoit!* Covey call *ko-loi-kee?* answered by *whoil-kee!* **SIMILAR SPECIES:** No other N. American quail has white throat. Ruffed Grouse larger with fanlike tail. **HABITAT:** Farms, brushy open country, fencerows, roadsides, open woodlands.

MONTEZUMA QUAIL *Cyrtonyx montezumae*   Scarce, local

8½–9 in. (21–23 cm). A small round quail of Mexican mountains and canyons. *Male:* Note oddly striped *clown's face* (formerly known as "Harlequin Quail"), bushy crest on nape, and *spotted sides. Female:* Brown, with less obvious facial striping. Tame. **VOICE:** Male gives a descending whistle; a soft whinnying or quavering cry; ventriloquial. **HABITAT:** Grassy oak canyons, wooded mountain slopes with bunch grass.

QUAIL

CALIFORNIA QUAIL
female
male

GAMBEL'S QUAIL
female
male

MOUNTAIN QUAIL
female
male

SCALED QUAIL

NORTHERN BOBWHITE
female
"Masked" male
Northern male

MONTEZUMA QUAIL
male
female

NEW WORLD VULTURES Family Cathartidae

Blackish; often seen soaring high in wide circles. Their naked heads are relatively smaller than those of hawks and eagles. Vultures are often locally called "buzzards." Silent away from nest site. Ages vary in plumage and head features; sexes alike. **FOOD:** Carrion. **RANGE:** Southern Canada through S. America.

TURKEY VULTURE *Cathartes aura* (see also p. 198) Common

26–27 in. (66–69 cm); wingspan 6 ft. (183 cm). Nearly eagle-sized. From below, note dark color with *two-toned wings* (flight feathers paler). Soars with wings in dihedral (shallow V); rocks and tilts unsteadily. At close range, small, naked *red head* of adult is evident; juvenile has dark bill and grayish head with black mask and bristlelike feathers, head becoming purplish in first year and not fully naked and red until third year. **SIMILAR SPECIES:** Black Vulture; eagles and Zone-tailed Hawk, the latter of which "mimics" Turkey Vulture in flight profile, has larger, feathered head, shorter tail; eagles also soar with wings held in steady flat plane. **HABITAT:** Usually seen soaring in sky, on ground feeding, or perched on dead trees or posts, often sunning with wings outstretched. Ubiquitous through much of range.

BLACK VULTURE *Coragyps atratus* (see also p. 198) Common

25 in. (64 cm); wingspan less than 5 ft. (152 cm). This dark scavenger is readily identified by short, square tail that barely projects beyond rear edge of wings and by *whitish patch* toward wingtip. Legs longer and whiter than Turkey Vulture's; in flight, feet visible beyond tail. Note distinctive shallow and *quick flapping*, alternating with short glides. **SIMILAR SPECIES:** Turkey Vulture has longer, rounded tail; flapping is slower, less frequent; soars with noticeable dihedral. *Beware:* Juvenile and first-year Turkey Vultures have dark heads but show paler bills and structural and flight-style differences noted above. **HABITAT:** Similar to Turkey Vulture's but avoids higher mountains, prefers wetter lowland areas, sometimes scavenges in dumps. Widespread vagrant well north of breeding range; casual vagrant to CA.

CALIFORNIA CONDOR *Gymnogyps californianus* Rare, local, endangered

46–47 in. (117–120 cm); wingspan 8½–9½ ft. (259–290 cm). Was heading toward extinction; last wild birds captured in 1987. Captive breeding program successful, and some of these birds released to the wild in CA, AZ, and Baja CA. Much larger than Turkey Vulture and has much broader proportions and shorter tail. California Condor also has *flatter wing-plane* when soaring; does not rock or tilt. *Adult:* Extensive *white underwing linings* toward fore edge of wing. Head yellow-orange. *Juvenile and first-year:* Dusky-headed and lacks white underwing linings, size and shape diagnostic; takes up to six or more years to develop full adult plumage and head characters. **SIMILAR SPECIES:** Younger Golden and Bald Eagles have some white underwing, but this color is placed differently; size also quite smaller and overall shapes different, proportionally longer-winged. **HABITAT:** Mountains, grassy foothills, coastal bluffs, chaparral. Nests on mountain ledges or in large redwood trees.

VULTURES

adult

juvenile
Turkey

juvenile
Black

adult
BLACK VULTURE

**TURKEY
VULTURE**

fourth-/fifth-
year

juvenile

adult

CALIFORNIA CONDOR
adults

BIRDS of PREY

We tend to call all diurnal raptors with a hooked bill and hooked claws "birds of prey."
Actually, they fall into two quite separate families that recently have been shown to be
very distantly related:

1. The hawk group (Accipitridae)—kites, harriers, accipiters, buteos, and eagles
2. The falcon group (Falconidae)—falcons and caracaras. These are more closely
   related to parrots and songbirds than they are to the hawk group!

The many raptors can be sorted out by their basic shapes and flight styles. When not flapping, they may alternate between soaring, with wings fully extended and tail fanned, and
gliding, with wings slightly pulled back and tail folded. These two pages show some basic
silhouettes.

glide

full soar

BUTEOS are stocky, with broad wings and a wide, rounded tail.
They often soar and wheel high in the open sky.

glide

full soar

ACCIPITERS have a small head, short rounded wings, and a longish tail.
They typically fly with several rapid beats and a short glide.

HARRIERS are slim, with long, slim, round-tipped wings and a long tail.
They fly in open country and glide low, with a vulturelike dihedral.

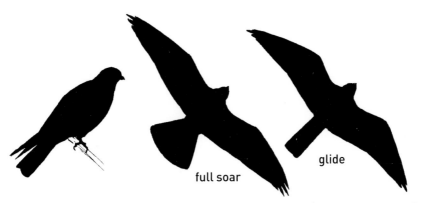

KITES (except for Snail Kite and Hook-billed Kite) are falcon-shaped,
but unlike falcons, they are buoyant gliders, not power fliers.

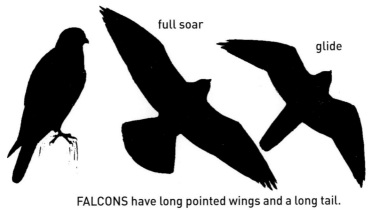

FALCONS have long pointed wings and a long tail.
Their wing strokes are strong and rapid.

OSPREYS Family Pandionidae

A monotypic family comprising a single bird of prey that forages above water for fish. Sexes alike. **FOOD:** Fish. **RANGE:** All continents except Antarctica.

OSPREY *Pandion haliaetus* (see also p. 198)   Fairly common
23–24½ in. (58–62 cm); wingspan to 6 ft. (183 cm). Large. Our only raptor that actively plunges into water feet-first for fish. *Adult:* Blackish brown above, *white below;* head largely white, suggesting Bald Eagle, but with *broad black mask through eyes.* Flies with distinctive gull-like kink or crook in wings, showing black "wrist" patch to underwing. *Juvenile:* Upperpart feathers fringed whitish or buff, forming scaly pattern. **VOICE:** Series of sharp, annoyed whistles: *cheep, cheep* or *yewk, yewk,* etc. Near nest, a frenzied *cheereek!* **SIMILAR SPECIES:** Large gulls. First-year Bald Eagle may have dusky "mask." Rough-legged Hawk is similar and occasionally hovers over marshes, but it usually has dark belly patch. **HABITAT:** Rivers, lakes, marshes, coasts.

HAWKS, KITES, EAGLES, and ALLIES
Family Accipitridae

Diurnal birds of prey, with hooked bills and powerful talons. Though formerly persecuted by many, they are very important to the health of ecosystems. **RANGE:** Almost worldwide.

EAGLES

Distinguished from buteos, to which they are related, by their greater size and broad wings. Powerful bills are nearly as long as head. **FOOD:** Bald Eagle, fish, injured waterfowl, carrion; Golden Eagle eats chiefly rabbits, large rodents, snakes, game birds.

BALD EAGLE   Uncommon, locally common
Haliaeetus leucocephalus (see also p. 198)
31–37 in. (79–94 cm); wingspan 7–8 ft. (213–244 cm). National bird of U.S. *Adult:* Huge size and dark plumage, except *white head* and *white tail.* Bill yellow, massive. Wings held flat when soaring. *Juvenile and first-year:* Mottled dark overall; in second and third year develops variable amounts of whitish in lower underparts, underwing, flight feathers, and tail; by fourth and fifth year can be adultlike or may have white head with darkish patch through eye, reminiscent of Osprey. **VOICE:** Harsh, high-pitched cackle, *kleek-kik-ik-ik-ik,* or lower *kak-kak-kak.* **SIMILAR SPECIES:** Golden Eagle, Turkey Vulture. **HABITAT:** Coasts, rivers, large lakes; in migration and winter, also mountains, open country.

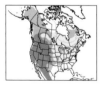

GOLDEN EAGLE *Aquila chrysaetos* (see also p. 198)   Uncommon
30–40 in. (76–102 cm); wingspan 7 ft. (213 cm). This majestic eagle glides and soars flat-winged with occasional shallow wingbeats. *Adult:* Uniformly dark below, or with slight paling at base of obscurely banded tail. On hindneck, a *wash of buffy gold. Juvenile and first-year:* In flight, shows *white flash in wings* at base of primaries, and *white tail base with broad dark tip.* Reaches adult plumage (without white in tail) by third or fourth year. **VOICE:** Seldom heard, a yelping bark, *kya;* also whistled notes. **SIMILAR SPECIES:** Younger Bald Eagles have larger heads and develop *extensive blotchy white in underwing linings* and lower underparts; tail may be mottled with white at base but is not cleanly banded. Dark-morph buteos are smaller, with more-rounded wings and different patterns of whitish in flight feathers. **HABITAT:** Open mountains, foothills, plains, deserts, open country.

OSPREY AND EAGLES

hovering

OSPREY

adult

BALD EAGLE

juvenile

overhead flight
patterns on p. 199

adult

adult

GOLDEN EAGLE

Golden Eagle
juvenile

OSPREY, EAGLES, and VULTURES from Below

OSPREY *Pandion haliaetus*   p. 196
White body and coverts; black wrist patch; crooked wing.

BALD EAGLE *Haliaeetus leucocephalus*   p. 196
Adult: White head and tail.
Juvenile: Some white in underwing linings; develops more white on belly and elsewhere in second year.

GOLDEN EAGLE *Aquila chrysaetos*   p. 196
Adult: Almost uniformly dark; underwing linings dark.
Juvenile: White patch at base of primaries and tail; no white on body.

TURKEY VULTURE *Cathartes aura*   p. 192
Mostly brownish black. Two-toned wings held in distinct dihedral. Small head, red in adult, blackish to dark pinkish purple in first- and second-years. Longish tail. Tips and teeters in flight.

BLACK VULTURE *Coragyps atratus*   p. 192
Blackish overall. Silver patch in outer primaries. Wings held flat or in very slight dihedral. Rapid, shallow wingbeats. Stubby tail. Gray head.

Where the Bald Eagle, Turkey Vulture, and Osprey all are found, they can be separated at a great distance by their manner of soaring: the Bald Eagle with flat wings; the Turkey Vulture with a dihedral; the Osprey often with a gull-like kink or crook in its wings.

Turkey Vulture (p. 192)

Black Vulture (p. 192)

VULTURES, OSPREY, AND EAGLES
From Below

OSPREY

BALD EAGLE
adult

BALD EAGLE
juvenile

GOLDEN EAGLE
adult

GOLDEN EAGLE
juvenile

KITES

Graceful birds of prey of southern distribution. Somewhat falconlike, with pointed wings. Ages and sexes can be similar or differ. **FOOD:** Large insects, reptiles, rodents. Snail Kite and Hook-billed Kite specialize in snails.

SWALLOW-TAILED KITE *Elanoides forficatus*   Uncommon

22–23 in. (55–58 cm). A sleek, elegant, black-and-white kite that flies with incomparable grace. Note blue-black upperparts, clean white head and underparts, and long, mobile, deeply forked tail. Ages and sexes similar. **VOICE:** Shrill, keen *ee-ee-ee* or *pee-pee-pee.* **HABITAT:** Wooded river swamps and pine lands, where it feeds mainly on snakes. Widespread spring vagrant north of range in East. Casual vagrant in West; accidental to CA.

MISSISSIPPI KITE *Ictinia mississippiensis* (see also p. 210)   Fairly common

14–14½ in. (36–37 cm). Falcon-shaped, graceful, and gray. Gregarious; spends much time soaring. *Adult:* Dark above, lighter below; head *pale gray;* tail and underwing blackish. No other falconlike bird has *black unbarred tail.* Whitish secondaries visible from above. *Juvenile:* Heavily streaked on rusty underparts; assumes adultlike plumage by first spring except retains rusty-mottled underwing. **VOICE:** Usually silent; near nest, a two-syllable *phee-phew.* **SIMILAR SPECIES:** Male Northern Harrier. Falcons. **HABITAT:** Nests in riparian woodlands, residential areas, groves, shelterbelts. Vagrant in East north of range and in West; casual to CA.

WHITE-TAILED KITE *Elanus leucurus* (see also p. 210)   Uncommon

15½–16 in. (39–41 cm). This whitish kite is very buoyant in flight, with pointed wings and *long white tail* that is slightly notched. Soars and glides like a small gull; *often hovers* and drops to ground with wings up. *Adult:* Pale gray above, with white head (male whiter than female), underparts, and tail. *Large black patch* on fore edge of upperwing is obvious on perched birds. From below, shows oval black patch at carpal joint ("wrist") of underwing. *Juvenile:* Like adult, but has rusty mottling to crown, back, and breast, and narrow dark band near tip of pale grayish tail; assumes adultlike body plumage in first fall. **VOICE:** Whistled *kew kew kew,* abrupt or drawn out. **HABITAT:** Open groves, river valleys, marshes, grasslands, roadsides. May form communal roosts at night in fall and winter seasons. Widespread vagrant north of range.

SNAIL KITE *Rostrhamus sociabilis*   Scarce, local

17 in. (43 cm). Suggests Northern Harrier at a distance, but with broader wings and without gliding, tilting flight; flies more floppily on cupped wings, head down, searching for snails. *Adult male:* All slaty black except for broad white band across base of tail; legs, bill, and face red. *Female and juvenile male:* Heavily streaked on buffy body; white stripe over eye; white band across black tail. Male develops adult plumage by third year. **VOICE:** Cackling *kor-ee-ee-a, kor-ee-ee-a.* **HABITAT:** Freshwater marshes and canals with apple snails (*Pomacea* spp.). FL populations (subspecies *plumbeus*) endangered.

HOOK-BILLED KITE *Chondrohierax uncinatus*   Rare, local

16½–17½ in. (42–45 cm). Bill has long, hooked tip. Legs yellow. Plumage varies from blackish (rare) or grayish in males to rufous brown in females to much paler below in juveniles. Adults have horizontally barred underparts. Note paddle-shaped wings. **VOICE:** Repeated *kik-kik-kik-kik* recalling Northern Flicker. **HABITAT:** Subtropical woodlands. Spends most of its time in the woods, soaring only briefly when traveling.

additional overhead flight patterns on p. 211

SWALLOW-TAILED KITE

adult

juvenile

MISSISSIPPI KITE

adult

juvenile

juvenile

adult

juvenile

adult

juvenile

WHITE-TAILED KITE

black-morph juvenile

adult male

female

black-morph adult

typical

SNAIL KITE

adult male

typical

HOOK-BILLED KITE

adult female

ACCIPITERS

Long-tailed woodland raptors with short, rounded wings, adapted for hunting among trees. Typical flight mixes quick beats and a glide. Adult males have bluer upperparts than adult females; females larger. Size distinguishes N. American species within each sex but not always reliably in the field. **FOOD:** Chiefly birds, some small mammals. Sharp-shinned and Cooper's often seen hunting birds at backyard feeders.

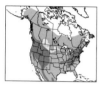

SHARP-SHINNED HAWK *Accipiter striatus* (see also p. 220)   Fairly common
10–14 in. (25–36 cm). A small, slim woodland hawk, with slim *square-tipped tail* and *short, rounded wings. Adult male:* Dark bluish back, *rusty-barred* breast, red eye; adult female browner and with yellower eye. *Juvenile and first-year:* Dark brown above, *thickly streaked* with rusty brown on underparts; yellow eye. **VOICE:** Like Cooper's Hawk, but shriller; a high *kik, kik, kik* given near nest. **SIMILAR SPECIES:** Cooper's larger, with *larger head* (protruding farther forward past wings in flight), *rounded* tail with broader white tip, thicker legs; male Cooper's and female Sharp-shinned can be close in size, especially in w. N. America. Adult Cooper's has more defined cap. First-year Cooper's *tawnier* on head and has whiter, more *finely streaked* breast. **HABITAT:** Breeds in extensive forests; in migration and winter, open woodlands, wood edges, residential areas.

COOPER'S HAWK *Accipiter cooperii* (see also p. 220)   Fairly common
14–20 in. (36–51 cm). Very similar to Sharp-shinned Hawk but larger, particularly female. See Sharp-shinned Hawk. **VOICE:** About nest, a rapid *kek, kek, kek;* suggests a flicker. Also a sapsucker-like mewing. **SIMILAR SPECIES:** Sharp-shinned Hawk, Northern Goshawk. **HABITAT:** Like Sharp-shinned but prefers drier and more open areas.

NORTHERN GOSHAWK *Accipiter gentilis* (see also p. 220)   Scarce
21–26 in. (53–66 cm). Larger, broader-winged, broader-tailed, more buteo-like than Cooper's Hawk. *Adult:* Crown and cheek blackish; *broad white stripe over eye.* Underparts *pale gray, finely barred;* back, bluer in male and grayer in female, is paler than in Cooper's or Sharp-shinned Hawk. *Juvenile and first-year:* Buffier overall than young Cooper's with bolder eyebrow, more extensive streaking below, and wavy, irregular tail banding. **VOICE:** *Kak, kak, kak* or *kuk, kuk, kuk,* heavier than Cooper's, given near nest. **SIMILAR SPECIES:** Cooper's Hawk. A soaring goshawk may be initially misidentified as a Red-shouldered Hawk or other buteo. **HABITAT:** Coniferous and mixed forests, especially in mountains; forest edges; winters also in wooded lowlands. Periodic irruptions in fall and winter farther to south.

HARRIERS

Slim raptors with long wings and tail. Flight low, languid, gliding, with wings held in shallow V (dihedral). Sexes not alike. They hunt in open country.

NORTHERN HARRIER *Circus hudsonius* (see also p. 210)   Fairly common
18–21 in. (46–54 cm). A slim, long-winged, long-tailed raptor of open country. When hunting, it glides and flies buoyantly and unsteadily low over ground, with wings held slightly above horizontal. Flaps steadily when migrating. In all plumages, distinct *white rump patch* distinguishes Northern Harrier from most other N. American raptors; see juvenile and first-year Gray Hawk and note Cooper's Hawks can flare up white flank patches when courting. *Adult male:* Pale gray, whitish beneath, wingtips black as if "dipped in ink." *Adult female:* Brown to grayish brown, streaked below. *Juvenile and first-year:* Russet to warm buff below, with fewer or no streaks. **VOICE:** Weak, nasal whistle, *pee, pee, pee.* **SIMILAR SPECIES:** Short-eared Owl. **HABITAT:** Marshes, fields, prairies.

juvenile

accipiters have small heads, short rounded wings, long tails

adult male

SHARP-SHINNED HAWK

additional overhead flight patterns on p. 211

adult

juvenile

COOPER'S HAWK

adult male

adult

juvenile

adult male

NORTHERN GOSHAWK

adult

juvenile

NORTHERN HARRIER

adult male

adult female

BUTEOS and BUTEO-LIKE HAWKS

Large, thickset hawks, with broad wings and wide, rounded tails. Many buteos habitually soar high in wide circles. Much variation; sexes similar, females slightly larger. Young birds usually streaked below. Dark morphs often occur. **FOOD:** Small mammals, sometimes small birds, reptiles, grasshoppers. **RANGE:** Widespread in New and Old Worlds.

GRAY HAWK *Buteo plagiatus* (see also p. 210)   Uncommon, local
17 in. (43 cm); wingspan 3 ft. (91 cm). A small buteo. *Adult:* Distinguished by its buteo-like proportions, gray back, *thickly barred gray* breast, white rump band, and *banded* tail (similar to Broad-winged Hawk's). *Juvenile and first-year:* Narrowly barred tail, striped buffy breast, bold face pattern, *white U-shaped bar* across rump. **VOICE:** Drawn-out whistles, *ka-lee-oh* or *kleeeeoo.* **SIMILAR SPECIES:** First-year Broad-winged Hawk has weaker face pattern, lacks white U on rump, has shorter tail, more pointed wings. **HABITAT:** Streamside and subtropical woodlands. Accidental vagrant to CA.

WHITE-TAILED HAWK   Uncommon, local
Geranoaetus albicaudatus (see also p. 210)
21–23 in. (53–58 cm); wingspan 4 ft. (122 cm). Large buteo-like hawk, with long pointed wings. Flies with marked dihedral. *Adult:* White underparts contrasting with dark flight feathers; white tail with black band, shoulders rusty red. *Juvenile and first-year:* Narrower wings and longer tail than adult. Blackish below with white breast patch. Pale U across upper tail. May have dark belly patch like Red-tailed Hawk but note blacker wing lining. Tail pale gray with weak barring. *Second-year:* Intermediate between juvenile and adult. **VOICE:** Nasal note followed by high-pitched series of doubled notes: *aaraahh kee-REEK, kee-REEK kee-REEK.* **SIMILAR SPECIES:** Juvenile and first-year Red-tailed Hawk. Adult Swainson's Hawk smaller, has dark chest. **HABITAT:** Coastal prairies, brushlands.

HARRIS'S HAWK *Parabuteo unicinctus* (see also p. 214)   Fairly common
20–21 in. (50–53 cm); wingspan 3½ ft. (107 cm). A blackish-brown, buteo-like hawk, with flashing *white rump* and *white band* at tip of tail. Often hunts cooperatively in small groups. *Adult:* Chestnut areas on thighs, shoulders, and underwing; *rusty shoulders;* conspicuous *white* at base of tail. *Juvenile and first-year:* Underparts streaked pale. **VOICE:** Low-pitched, harsh *raaaah!* **SIMILAR SPECIES:** Dark morphs of Ferruginous and Red-tailed Hawks larger, lack bold rusty patches and white tail base. **HABITAT:** Mesquite, cactus deserts. Rare breeder and vagrant north of range.

ZONE-TAILED HAWK *Buteo albonotatus* (see also p. 214)   Uncommon
20 in. (51 cm); wingspan 4 ft. (122 cm). Dull *black,* with more *slender* wings than most other buteos. Often mistaken for Turkey Vulture because of up-tilted wings — but Zone-tailed has larger feathered head, square-tipped tail, barred underwing, yellow cere and legs. *Adult: White tail bands* (pale gray on topside). *Juvenile and first-year:* Narrower tail bands, *small white spots* on breast. **VOICE:** Nasal, drawn-out *keeeeah.* **SIMILAR SPECIES:** Turkey Vulture, Common Black Hawk, other dark-morph buteos. **HABITAT:** Riparian woodlands, mountains, canyons. Vagrant north of range in West; accidental in East.

COMMON BLACK HAWK *Buteogallus anthracinus* (see also p. 214)   Scarce, local
21 in. (53 cm); wingspan 4 ft. (122 cm). A buteo-like hawk with chunky shape, exceptionally wide wings, and *long* yellow legs. *Adult:* All black with broad white *band* crossing middle of short tail. In flight, whitish spot shows at base of primaries. *Juvenile and first-year:* Dark-backed with heavily striped *buffy* head and underparts; tail white with five or six wavy dark bands. **VOICE:** Series of loud whistles. **SIMILAR SPECIES:** Zone-tailed Hawk. **HABITAT:** Wooded river and stream bottoms. Casual vagrant to CA and elsewhere in West north of range.

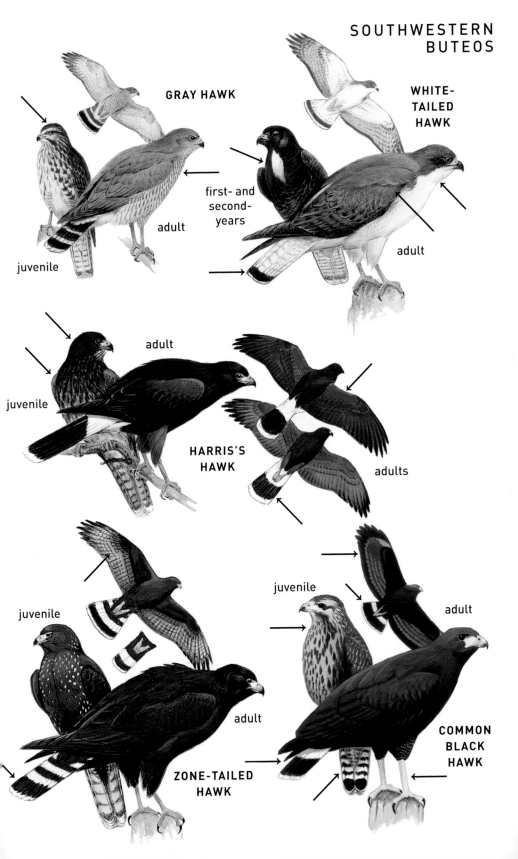

SOUTHWESTERN
BUTEOS

GRAY HAWK

WHITE-
TAILED
HAWK

first- and
second-
years

adult

juvenile

adult

adult

juvenile

HARRIS'S
HAWK

adults

juvenile

juvenile

adult

adult

ZONE-TAILED
HAWK

COMMON
BLACK
HAWK

ROUGH-LEGGED HAWK *Buteo lagopus* (see also pp. 212 and 214)   Uncommon

21–22 in. (53–55 cm). This hawk of open country often *hovers on beating wings*, more so than other buteos, and has smaller bill and feet. Legs feathered. Somewhat longer, narrower wings and tail than other buteos except Ferruginous Hawk. Many birds have *solid or blotched dark belly* and *black patch* at "wrist" (carpal joint) of underwing. Some adult males have dark bib but lack blackish belly band. Tail *white,* with *broad black band or bands* toward tip. White flash on upperwing. Juvenile and first-year similar but tail with less-distinct band. Dark morph may lack extensive white on tail, but broad terminal band and extensive white on underwing are good field marks. **VOICE:** High-pitched squeal, mostly near nest site. **SIMILAR SPECIES:** Red-tailed Hawk, Northern Harrier, dark-morph Ferruginous Hawk. **HABITAT:** Nests on tundra escarpments along Arctic coasts; in winter, open fields, plains, marshes.

RED-SHOULDERED HAWK *Buteo lineatus* (see also p. 212)   Fairly common

16–20 in. (40–50 cm). In flight, note *translucent patch* or "window" at base of primaries, longish tail. *Adult:* Heavy black-and-white bands on wings and tail, dark *rufous shoulders* (not always easy to see) and underwing linings, rufous red underparts. *Juvenile and first-year:* Variably streaked and/or barred below; recognized by proportions, tail bands, and, in flight, wing "windows." Western Red-shouldereds (subspecies *elegans*) have brighter underparts and shoulders, are paler-headed, with bolder black-and-white wings; do not soar as much as eastern birds. FL birds (subspecies *extimus*) smaller and paler; can have whitish heads. **VOICE:** Two-syllable scream, *kee-yer* (dropping inflection), repeated in series. **SIMILAR SPECIES:** Light-morph Broad-winged Hawk has paler underwing linings, more pointed wing, broader bands on tail, lacks wing "windows." Juvenile Cooper's Hawk can be similar in flight but has longer tail. See also Red-tailed Hawk. **HABITAT:** Woodlands in valleys, canyons, along rivers, swamp edges, residential areas. Both subspecies are vagrants to interior West.

BROAD-WINGED HAWK *Buteo platypterus* (see also pp. 212 and 214)   Common

15–16 in. (38–41 cm). A small, chunky buteo, often seen migrating in fall in spiraling flocks called "kettles." *Pale-morph adult:* Note tail banding, with one obvious thick white band often visible from below (Red-shouldered has multiple bands). Underwing linings whitish, the edge trimmed with black. *Juvenile and first-year:* Heavily streaked along sides of neck, breast, and belly; chest often unmarked. Terminal tail band twice as wide and distinct as other bands. Scarce dark morph, which breeds primarily in Prairie Provinces, similar to dark Short-tailed Hawk but browner (not as black); tail pattern as in light-morph Broad-winged; secondaries paler and less barred underneath. **VOICE:** High-pitched, shrill, two-part downward *pwe-eeeeee.* **SIMILAR SPECIES:** Juvenile/first-year Red-shouldered Hawk can be similar to like-aged Broad-winged but has heavier streaking on breast, wingtips with bold pale "window." See also juvenile Gray and Short-tailed Hawks, accipiters. **HABITAT:** Woods, groves. Rare vagrant to W. Coast.

SHORT-TAILED HAWK *Buteo brachyurus* (see also p. 214)   Uncommon, local

15–16 in. (38–41 cm). A small black or black-and-white buteo. Dark morph has blackish brown body and black underwing linings; light-morph adult blackish above, white below, dark cheeks, *two-toned* underwing pattern, white underwing linings. *Light-morph juvenile and first-year:* Similar to juvenile Broad-winged but less streaked below; secondaries darker underneath, with more-distinct barring. **VOICE:** Descending, high-pitched scream: *kleeear!* **SIMILAR SPECIES:** Broad-winged Hawk in flight has slimmer wings, whiter flight feathers below; often perches in open, unlike Short-tailed. See also Swainson's Hawk. **HABITAT:** Pines, woodland edges, cypress swamps, mangroves.

BUTEOS

additional overhead
flight patterns on
pp. 213 and 215

dark
morph

light-morph
adults

**ROUGH-LEGGED
HAWK**

ale FL
bspecies

adult

juvenile

Eastern

Western

RED-SHOULDERED HAWK

juvenile

adult

dark
morph

**BROAD-WINGED
HAWK**

adult

juvenile

dark
morph

light-
morph
ivenile

dark-morph
adult

light-morph
adult

light-morph
adult

dark-morph
adult

SHORT-TAILED HAWK

RED-TAILED HAWK *Buteo jamaicensis* (see also pp. 212 and 214)   Common

19–22 in. (48–56 cm). The common conspicuous hawk of roadsides and wood-land edges. When soaring, adult has diagnostic *rufous* on topside of tail, paler reddish below. On light-morph birds, note mottled *white patches* on scapulars; *dark patagial bar* on fore edge of wing from below is also rather diagnostic of Red-tailed. Otherwise body plumage quite variable. *Juvenile and first-year:* Tail brownish with narrow, dark banding. Underparts typically "zoned" (light breast, dark *belly band*), although some paler birds of sw. TX (subspecies *fuertesi*) can lack belly band. Dark-morph birds variably dark brown to blackish; red tail of adults diagnostic; broad wing shape and tail pattern help identify juvenile and first-year birds. On Great Plains, whitish "Krider's" morph has whitish tail that may be tinged with pale rufous. Western Red-tailed Hawks show much varia-tion, with rufous- and dark-morph birds more common. Dark-morph "Har-lan's" Red-tailed Hawk (subspecies *harlani*), an uncommon hawk breeding in AK and wintering to CA and TX, is sootier and tail is usually dirty white, with *longitudinal* mottling and freckling of gray, black, sometimes with red, merging into dark subterminal band. **VOICE:** Asthmatic squeal, *keeer-r-r* (slurring down-ward). **SIMILAR SPECIES:** Rough-legged, Ferruginous, Swainson's, Red-shoul-dered, and Broad-winged Hawks. **HABITAT:** Open country, woodlands, prairie groves, mountains, plains, roadsides.

SWAINSON'S HAWK *Buteo swainsoni* (see also pp. 212 and 214)   Common

19–21 in. (48–53 cm). A buteo of the plains, quite variable in body plumage. Slimmer than Red-tailed Hawk, with narrower, more pointed wings at tips. When gliding, holds wings slightly above horizontal. When perched, *wingtips extend to tail tip.* In light and intermediate morphs, *pale underwing linings contrast with dark flight feathers* from below. *Adult:* Light morph has dark breastband and often a dark-hooded look; tail gray-brown above, often pale toward base. Dark- and rufous-morph birds best identified by shape, shaded flight feathers, and tail pattern. *Juvenile and first-year:* Light morph variably streaked below, usually more heavily marked on breast than belly; forehead usually pale; white band across rump; often best identified by shape and wing pattern. **VOICE:** Shrill, plaintive whistle, *kreeeeeeer.* **SIMILAR SPECIES:** Swainson's wing shape distinctive for a buteo. Lacks white scapular patches and dark patagial marks of bulkier Red-tailed. In TX, see White-tailed Hawk. **HABITAT:** Plains, grasslands, agricultural land, open hills, sparse trees. Casual vagrant to E. Coast.

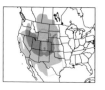

FERRUGINOUS HAWK *Buteo regalis* (see also pp. 210 and 214)   Uncommon

23–24 in. (58–61 cm). A large buteo of w. states. Note large bill, long gape line, *long tapered wings* with *pale panel* on upper surface of primaries, *mostly white tail.* *Adult:* Rufous above, especially shoulder, mostly whitish head and breast, rufous wash on tail, rufous thighs form *dark V* on birds from below. Dark morphs are dark rufous to brown with whitish flight feathers and whitish tail. *Juvenile and first-year:* Similar to adult but duller, with fewer rufous tones; tail with indistinct bars or marks. **SIMILAR SPECIES:** Red-tailed Hawk and dark-morph Rough-legged Hawk. Perched dark-morph Ferruginous Hawk can resemble an eagle but is smaller, has paler tail. **HABITAT:** Plains, grasslands, agricultural fields. Casual vagrant east of range accidentally to E. Coast.

BUTEOS

rufous adult

Western juvenile

Eastern juvenile

dark adult

Western adult

Eastern adult

RED-TAILED HAWK

rider's juvenile

"Harlan's" adult

"Harlan's" adult

"Harlan's" adult

dark morph

juvenile

adult

light morph

light morph

adult

SWAINSON'S HAWK

light morph

light morph

adult

dark morph

FERRUGINOUS HAWK

KITES, PALE BUTEOS, and HARRIER from Below

Accipiters (bird hawks) have short rounded wings and a long tail. They fly with several rapid beats and a short glide. They are better adapted to hunting in the woodlands than most other hawks. Females are larger than males. Juveniles (not shown) have a streaked breast.

FERRUGINOUS HAWK *Buteo regalis* (light morph)   **p. 208**
Whitish underparts, with dark V formed by reddish thighs in adult. Wings and tail long for a buteo. A bird of western plains and open range.

GRAY HAWK *Buteo plagiatus*   **p. 204**
Stocky. Broadly banded tail (suggestive of Broad-winged Hawk); adults have gray-barred underparts. Uncommon resident of Rio Grande Valley and se. AZ.

WHITE-TAILED HAWK *Geranoaetus albicaudatus*   **p. 204**
Adult: Whitish underparts, gray head. White tail with black band near tip. Soars with marked dihedral. Resident of coastal prairie of TX.

COOPER'S HAWK *Accipiter cooperii*   **p. 202**
Underparts rusty (adult). Tail rounded and tipped with broad white terminal band. Note head and neck projecting noticeably beyond leading edge of wing.

NORTHERN GOSHAWK *Accipiter gentilis*   **p. 202**
Adult with bold facial pattern, underbody heavily barred with pale gray. Tail and wings broad.

SHARP-SHINNED HAWK *Accipiter striatus*   **p. 202**
Small. When folded, tail square or notched, with narrow pale tip. Fanned tail slightly rounded. Note small head and short neck barely projecting beyond wing.

NORTHERN HARRIER *Circus hudsonius*   **p. 202**
Male: Whitish wings with black tips and dark trailing edge. Gray hood.
Female: Brown, heavily streaked; note long, slim wings and tail.
Juvenile and first-year (not shown): Warmer brown than adult female, unstreaked body, dark head. From above, all plumages have characteristic white rump.

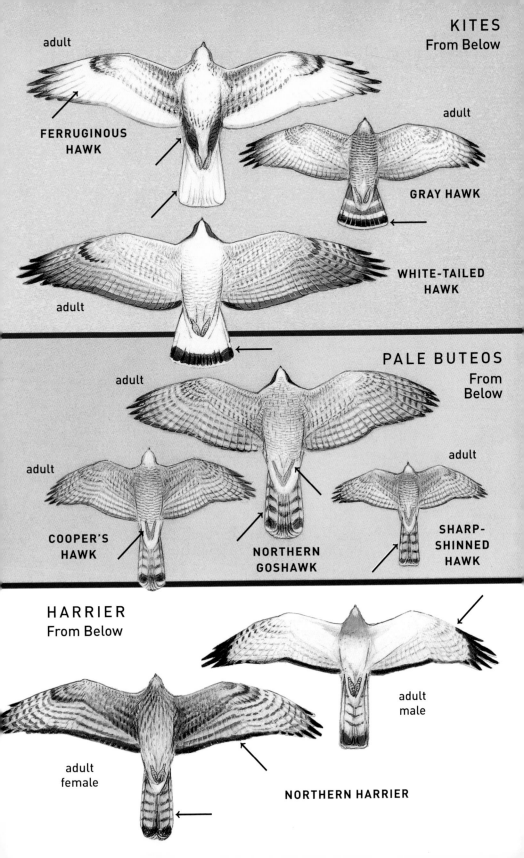

KITES
From Below

adult

FERRUGINOUS HAWK

adult

GRAY HAWK

adult

WHITE-TAILED HAWK

PALE BUTEOS
From Below

adult

adult

adult

COOPER'S HAWK

NORTHERN GOSHAWK

SHARP-SHINNED HAWK

HARRIER
From Below

adult male

adult female

NORTHERN HARRIER

PALE BUTEOS from Below

RED-TAILED HAWK *Buteo jamaicensis* (light morph)   **p. 208**
Reddish tail and dark patagial bar at fore edge of wing are best mark from below. *Adult:* Light chest, streaked belly (often forming belly band); tail plain with little or no banding.
Juvenile and first-year: Streaked below, tail without red and with light banding.

SWAINSON'S HAWK *Buteo swainsoni* (light morph)   **p. 208**
Adult: Dark breast-band. Long, pointed, two-toned wings.
Juvenile and first-year: Similar, but has streaks on underbody.

RED-SHOULDERED HAWK *Buteo lineatus*   **p. 206**
Adult: Tail strongly banded (white bands narrower than black ones). Body and underwing coverts barred or mottled reddish.
Juvenile and first-year: Chest and belly heavily streaked brown. Both first-year and adult have light crescent "window" on outer wings, longish tail.

BROAD-WINGED HAWK *Buteo platypterus* (light morph)   **p. 206**
Smaller and chunkier than Red-shouldered with shorter tail, more pointed wings. *Adult:* Widely banded tail (white bands wider); underwing pale with dark rear margin and tip.
Juvenile and first-year: Body usually streaked, tail narrowly banded, the outermost dark band widest and most distinct.

ROUGH-LEGGED HAWK *Buteo lagopus* (light morph)   **p. 206**
Note black primary covert patch at "wrist" contrasting with white primaries and secondaries. Broad, blackish band ("cummerbund") across belly (blacker and more solid than in Red-tailed) is distinctive. Tail light, with broad, dark subterminal band.

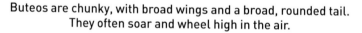

Buteos are chunky, with broad wings and a broad, rounded tail.
They often soar and wheel high in the air.

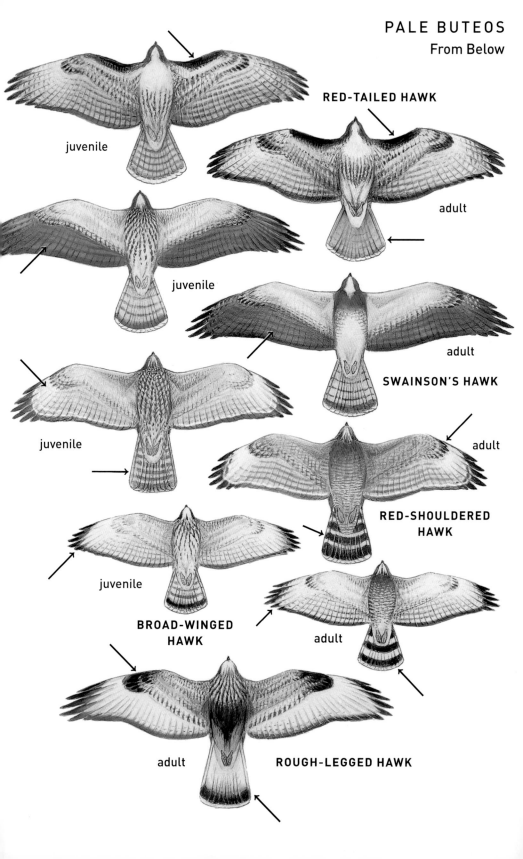

PALE BUTEOS
From Below

RED-TAILED HAWK

juvenile

adult

juvenile

adult

SWAINSON'S HAWK

juvenile

adult

RED-SHOULDERED
HAWK

juvenile

BROAD-WINGED
HAWK

adult

adult

ROUGH-LEGGED HAWK

DARK BIRDS of PREY from Below

CRESTED CARACARA *Caracara cheriway*   **p. 216**
Whitish chest, black belly, large pale patches in primaries, white tail with black band. Elongated neck, stiff-winged flight.

ROUGH-LEGGED HAWK *Buteo lagopus* (dark morph)   **p. 206**
Dark body and underwing linings; whitish flight feathers; tail light from below, with one broad, black terminal band in female; additional bands in male.

FERRUGINOUS HAWK *Buteo regalis* (dark morph)   **p. 208**
Similar to dark-morph Rough-legged Hawk, but tail whitish, without dark banding. Note also white wrist marks, or "commas."

SWAINSON'S HAWK *Buteo swainsoni* (dark morph)   **p. 208**
In dark morph, pointed wings are usually dark throughout, including flight feathers; tail narrowly banded, whitish undertail coverts. Rufous morph may be rustier, with lighter rufous underwing linings.

RED-TAILED HAWK *Buteo jamaicensis* (dark morph)   **p. 208**
Typical chunky shape of Red-tailed; tail reddish, brighter above than below; variable. Dark patagial bar on leading edge of wing obscured.

"HARLAN'S" RED-TAILED HAWK *Buteo jamaicensis harlani* **p. 208**
Similar to dark-morph Red-tailed Hawk. Breast mottled white; tail tends to be mottled with gray and whitish and with dusky subterminal band, usually lacks obvious red; primary tips barred dark and light.

BROAD-WINGED HAWK *Buteo platypterus* (dark morph)   **p. 206**
Typical small size and broad-winged shape. Tail pattern and flight feathers as in light morph, but body and underwing linings dark brownish to brownish black. Note whiter flight feathers than Short-tailed.

ZONE-TAILED HAWK *Buteo albonotatus* (first-year)   **p. 204**
Slim and longish, two-toned wings (suggesting Turkey Vulture) with barred flight feathers. Several white bands on slim tail (only one visible on folded tail). Yellow legs. Wings held at slight dihedral.

SHORT-TAILED HAWK *Buteo brachyurus* (dark morph)   **p. 206**
Jet-black body and underwing linings. Lightly banded tail; flight feathers more shaded and often more distinctly barred than in dark Broad-winged.

COMMON BLACK HAWK *Buteogallus anthracinus*   **p. 204**
Very broad black wings; faint light patches near wingtips. Short, broad tail with broad white band at midtail and very broad black subterminal band. Whereas Zone-tailed Hawk seems to mimic Turkey Vulture, a deceptive ploy when it is hunting, chunkier Common Black Hawk may be compared to Black Vulture.

HARRIS'S HAWK *Parabuteo unicinctus*   **p. 204**
Chocolate brown body, chestnut underwing linings. Very broad white band at base of black tail, narrow white terminal band. Flies more buoyantly than buteos.

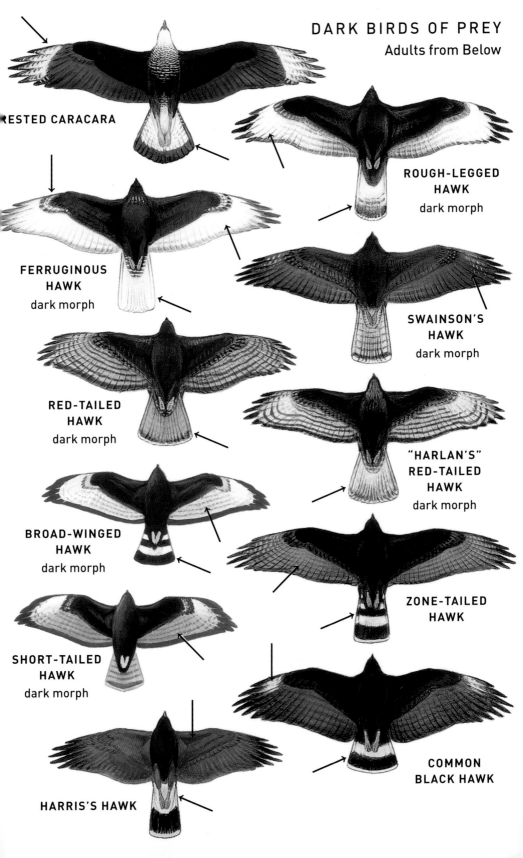

DARK BIRDS OF PREY
Adults from Below

CRESTED CARACARA

ROUGH-LEGGED
HAWK
dark morph

FERRUGINOUS
HAWK
dark morph

SWAINSON'S
HAWK
dark morph

RED-TAILED
HAWK
dark morph

"HARLAN'S"
RED-TAILED
HAWK
dark morph

BROAD-WINGED
HAWK
dark morph

ZONE-TAILED
HAWK

SHORT-TAILED
HAWK
dark morph

COMMON
BLACK HAWK

HARRIS'S HAWK

CARACARAS and FALCONS Family Falconidae

Caracaras are large, long-legged birds of prey, some with naked faces. Sexes alike. **FOOD:** Our one U.S. species feeds mostly on carrion. **RANGE:** Southern U.S. to Tierra del Fuego, Falklands. Falcons are streamlined birds of prey with pointed wings, longish tail; recently found to be more closely related to parrots than to other diurnal raptors. Ages and sexes similar or vary in different combinations. **FOOD:** Birds, rodents, reptiles, insects. **RANGE:** Almost worldwide.

CRESTED CARACARA *Caracara cheriway* (see also p. 214)   Uncommon, local
23 in. (58 cm). A large, long-legged, big-headed, long-necked bird of prey, often seen feeding on carrion or roadkill with vultures. *Adult: Black crest* and *red face* distinctive. In flight, underbody presents alternating areas of light and dark: white chest, black belly, and whitish, dark-tipped tail. Note combination of *pale wing patches, pale chest, and pale tail panel,* giving impression of "white at all four corners." *Juvenile and first-year:* Browner, streaked on breast; second-year intermediate. Sexes similar. **VOICE:** Weird, guttural series of croaks and rattles. **HABITAT:** Prairies, rangeland, deserts. Population in FL (subspecies *auduboni*) threatened. Casual vagrant well north of range.

GYRFALCON *Falco rusticolus* (see also p. 220)   Scarce
20–25 in. (51–64 cm). A very large Arctic falcon, larger and more robust and buteo-like than Peregrine Falcon; tail broader and longer. On perched birds, wingtips do not reach near tail tip. Wingbeats slower. Thinner mustache. Occur as brown, gray, and white color morphs. Juvenile and first-year birds duller and more prone to wander south. Sexes similar. **VOICE:** Harsh *kak-kak-kak* series. **SIMILAR SPECIES:** Peregrine Falcon smaller, slimmer, with dark hood and broad black mustache, and shorter and more-tapered tail. Prairie Falcon slimmer, pale brown, wingtips fall closer to tail tip. See also Northern Goshawk. **HABITAT:** Arctic barrens, seacoasts, open mountains; in winter, open country, coastlines. Vagrant south of normal winter range.

PRAIRIE FALCON *Falco mexicanus* (see also p. 220)   Uncommon
16–19 in. (41–50 cm). Like a sandy-colored Peregrine Falcon, with *white eyebrow stripe* and *narrower mustache*. In flight from below, shows *blackish patches* in axillars ("wingpits") and inner coverts. Ages and sexes similar. **VOICE:** Generally silent. Harsh *kak-kak-kak* around nest. **SIMILAR SPECIES:** Juvenile Peregrine has darker brown back and face pattern, different underwing pattern. Female Prairie Merlin *(richardsonii)* same color above but much smaller, lacks dark underwing patch. **HABITAT:** Open country, from alpine tundra to grasslands, prairies, agricultural land, deserts, marshes. Vagrant east of range, accidentally to E. Coast.

PEREGRINE FALCON *Falco peregrinus* (see also p. 220)   Fairly common
16–20 in. (41–51 cm). A robust, medium-large falcon with pointed wings, narrow tail, and quick, powerful wingbeats. Note *wide black mustache.* Size and strong face pattern indicate this species. *Adult:* In widespread "N. American" subspecies *(anatum),* upperparts slaty blue, breast washed rose, barred and spotted black below breast. *Juvenile and first-year:* Brown, heavily streaked below. Northwestern "Peale's" (subspecies *pealei*), breeding off s. AK and BC, is larger, adults more heavily marked on breast, juveniles much *darker* (blackish in some). Smaller "Tundra" Peregrine (subspecies *tundrius*), which migrates through the U.S., is slimmer, adult is paler, and juvenile has pale crown. **VOICE:** A rapid *kek kek kek kek.* At eyrie, a repeated *we'chew.* **SIMILAR SPECIES:** Merlin, Gyrfalcon. **HABITAT:** Nests on cliffs and ledges; open country, from mountains to coasts. Established as a reintroduced breeder (on building ledges and bridges) in many major cities. Regular migrant and winter visitor to small numbers in HI (p. 440).

CARACARA AND LARGE FALCONS

juvenile

CRESTED CARACARA

adults

gray morph

brown morph

GYRFALCON

white morph

gray morph

brown morph

PRAIRIE FALCON

Tundra juvenile

Pacific ("Peale's") juvenile

Tundra adult

Pacific ("Peale's") adult

PEREGRINE FALCON

North American adults

AMERICAN KESTREL *Falco sparverius* (see also p. 220)   Fairly common

9½–10½ in. (24–27 cm). A small and delicate falcon. No other N. American *small* hawk has *rufous back or tail*. Male has blue-gray wings. Both sexes have black-and-white face with double mustache. *Hovers* for prey on rapidly beating wings. Sits fairly erect, occasionally lifting tail. Ages similar. **VOICE:** Rapid, high *klee klee klee* or *killy killy killy*. **SIMILAR SPECIES:** Merlin (which only rarely perches on wires) lacks rufous and is more compact in shape, flies much quicker. Sharp-shinned Hawk has rounded wings, gray or brown back and tail. Neither species hovers. **HABITAT:** Open country, farmland, wood edges, residential areas, dead trees, wires, roadsides.

MERLIN *Falco columbarius* (see also p. 220)   Uncommon

11–12 in. (28–31 cm). A small and compact falcon; suggests a miniature Peregrine Falcon, but with less distinct mustache. *Adult male:* In most common N. American subspecies (*columbarius,* "Taiga" Merlin), upperparts darkish blue-gray, tail *gray* with broad black bands, underparts streaked reddish brown. *Female, juvenile, and first-year:* Dark brown above, with banded tail; boldly streaked below. "Prairie" subspecies *(richardsonii)* paler gray or brown (color of a Prairie Falcon), lacks or has indistinct mustache. Coastal Northwestern "Black" subspecies *(suckleyi),* very dark, lacks light eyebrow stripe. **VOICE:** High, rapid *kee-kee-kee-kee.* **SIMILAR SPECIES:** Sharp-shinned Hawk has rounded (not pointed) wings. See American Kestrel, Peregrine and Prairie Falcons. **HABITAT:** Open woods, cliffs, grasslands, tundra; in migration and winter, also open country, marshes, beaches, locally in cities and neighborhoods.

EURASIAN KESTREL *Falco tinnunculus*   Accidental vagrant

13½–14 in. (34–36 cm). Similar to American Kestrel, but slightly larger. *Adult male:* Duskier mustache on grayish head, spotted upperparts and wing coverts; gray tail ending in black subterminal band and white tip. *Female and juvenile:* Rusty brown crown, upperparts, and secondaries; duskier primaries; buff white underparts, strongly barred on breast and boldly spotted in lines on belly. **RANGE:** Eurasian species. Accidental vagrant to e. N. America (Atlantic Canada south to FL) and along W. Coast from w. AK to CA.

EURASIAN HOBBY *Falco subbuteo*   Casual vagrant

12½–13 in. (31–33 cm). Most aerial of the falcons; sickle-shaped wings and short tail produce a swiftlike outline. Flight dashing, with rapid, clipped wing-beats; when patrolling, action slower, more rowing, recalling Peregrine Falcon; never hovers. *Adult:* Distinctly patterned, with dark slate mustache, cap, and upperparts contrasting with cream throat, heavily streaked underparts, chestnut thighs and vent, and darkly barred underwing. *Juvenile and first-year:* Lacks chestnut areas. **SIMILAR SPECIES:** Peregrine Falcon. **RANGE:** Eurasian species. Casual vagrant to w. AK; accidental elsewhere.

APLOMADO FALCON *Falco femoralis* (see also p. 220)   Rare, local

15–16½ in. (38–42 cm). A medium-sized falcon, a little smaller than Peregrine Falcon. *Long wings and tail.* Note *dark underwing* and *black belly,* contrasting with white or pale cinnamon breast. Thighs and undertail coverts orange-brown. **VOICE:** High-pitched whistled scream: *klee-klee-klee-klee!* **SIMILAR SPECIES:** Peregrine Falcon. **RANGE:** Formerly a very rare visitor from Mex., but population in U.S. considered endangered and enhanced by reintroduction program in s. TX and s. NM. **HABITAT:** Arid brushy deserts and grasslands, yucca flats.

SMALL FALCONS

AMERICAN KESTREL

female

male

female

male

"Taiga" juvenile female

"Taiga" male

"Pacific" (Black) male

"Prairie" male

MERLIN

RARE FALCONS

EURASIAN KESTREL

EURASIAN HOBBY

juvenile

male

adult

female

adult male

APLOMADO FALCON

ACCIPITERS and FALCONS from Below

Kites (except Snail Kite and Hook-billed Kite) are falcon-shaped but, unlike falcons, are buoyant gliders, not power fliers. All are southern.

WHITE-TAILED KITE *Elanus leucurus*   p. 200
Adult: White body; whitish tail; dark underside to primaries, black mark at primary coverts.

MISSISSIPPI KITE *Ictinia mississippiensis*   p. 200
Falcon-shaped. *Adult:* Pale gray head, black tail, dark gray and blackish wings, gray body.
Juvenile: Streaked breast; banded square-tipped or notched tail. First-spring and summer are adultlike but with underwing mottled brownish.

Falcons have long, pointed wings and a relatively long tail.
Wing strokes are typically rapid and continuous.

PEREGRINE FALCON *Falco peregrinus*   p. 216
Falcon shape; large; bold face pattern; longer wings than Merlin or Kestrel.

AMERICAN KESTREL *Falco sparverius*   p. 218
Small; banded rufous tail. Paler underwing and less heavily marked underparts than Merlin.

MERLIN *Falco columbarius*   p. 218
Small; heavily marked underparts and dark underwing; heavily banded tail.

GYRFALCON *Falco rusticolus*   p. 216
Larger than Peregrine Falcon; without that bird's contrasting facial pattern, and with broader wings and tail. Varies in color from brown to gray to white.

APLOMADO FALCON *Falco femoralis*   p. 218
Black belly band or vest, light chest, orange undertail. Tail barred with black.

PRAIRIE FALCON *Falco mexicanus*   p. 216
Size of Peregrine Falcon. *Dark axillars* ("wingpits") and inner coverts.

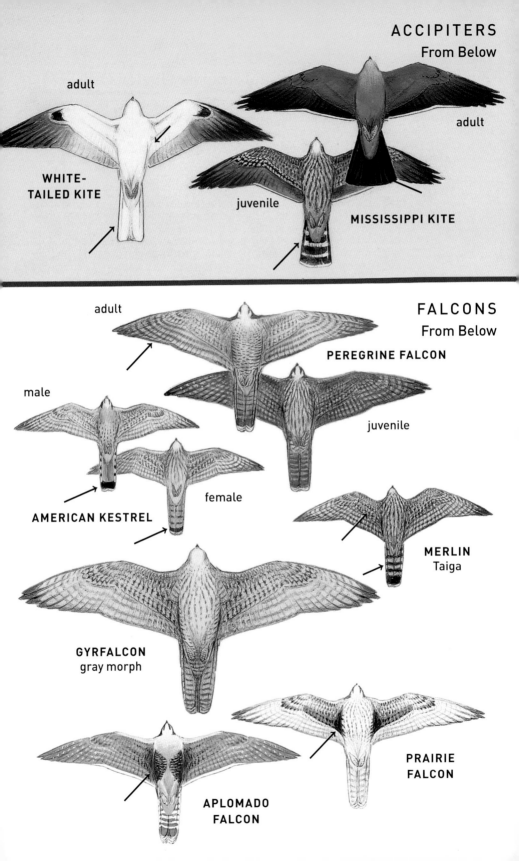

ACCIPITERS
From Below

adult

WHITE-
TAILED KITE

juvenile

adult

MISSISSIPPI KITE

FALCONS
From Below

adult

PEREGRINE FALCON

male

juvenile

AMERICAN KESTREL

female

MERLIN
Taiga

GYRFALCON
gray morph

PRAIRIE
FALCON

APLOMADO
FALCON

OWLS
Families Tytonidae (Barn Owls) and Strigidae (Typical Owls)

Chiefly nocturnal birds of prey, with large heads and flattened faces forming facial disks; large, forward-facing eyes; hooked bill and claws; usually feathered feet (outer toe reversible). Flight noiseless, mothlike. Some species have "horns," or ear tufts. Ages and sexes largely similar; females larger than males. **FOOD**: Rodents, birds, reptiles, fish, large insects. **RANGE**: Nearly worldwide.

BARN OWL *Tyto alba*   Uncommon

16 in. (41 cm). A long-legged, pale, monkey-faced owl. *White heart-shaped face and dark eyes;* no ear tufts. Distinguished in flight as an owl by large head and quiet, mothlike flight; as this species by unstreaked whitish, buff, or pale cinnamon underparts (ghostly at night) and warm tawny-brown back. **VOICE**: Shrill, rasping hiss or screech: *kschh* or *shiiish.* **SIMILAR SPECIES**: Short-eared Owl streaked, has darker face and underparts, *yellow eyes.* **HABITAT**: Open country, groves, farms, barns, towns, cliffs, marshes.

SHORT-EARED OWL *Asio flammeus*   Uncommon

15 in. (38 cm). An owl of open country; often foraging at dawn and dusk or during cloudy days. Sometimes tussles with Northern Harrier, with which it shares habitats and prey resources. Streaked, tawny brown color and diagnostic, irregular flopping flight identify it. Large buffy wing patches show in flight, along with black carpal ("wrist") marks and pale trailing edge to secondaries. *Dark facial disk* emphasizes yellow eyes. Females average darker than males. **VOICE**: Emphatic, sneezy bark: *kee-yow!, wow!,* or *waow!* **SIMILAR SPECIES**: Long-eared Owl similar in flight, but with jerkier wing action, more-orange eyes, darker feathering without white trailing edge to secondaries. **HABITAT**: Grasslands, fresh and salt marshes, dunes, tundra. Roosts on ground, rarely in trees. Winter range and numbers vary from year to year. Indigenous resident in HI (p. 438).

LONG-EARED OWL *Asio otus*   Uncommon

15 in. (38 cm). A slender, crow-sized owl with long ear tufts. Usually seen "frozen" close to trunk of a tree. Much smaller and slimmer than Great Horned Owl; underparts streaked *lengthwise,* not barred crosswise. Ears *closer together, erectile;* much black around eyes. **VOICE**: One or two long *hooos*; usually silent. Also a catlike whine and doglike bark. **SIMILAR SPECIES**: Short-eared Owl in flight. See Great Horned Owl. **HABITAT**: Coniferous and deciduous woodlands, desert groves. Often roosts in groups in fall and winter. Hunts over open country.

GREAT HORNED OWL *Bubo virginianus*   Common

21–22 in. (54–56 cm). A *very large* owl with ear tufts, or "horns." Heavily *barred* beneath; conspicuous *white throat bib.* In flight, as large as our larger hawks; looks neckless, large-headed, broad-winged. Varies geographically and individually from very dark to rather pale. Often active just before dark. **VOICE**: Male usually utters five or six resonant hoots: *hoo hu-hu-hu, hoo! hoo!* Female's hoots slightly higher pitched than male's, one note less. Young birds make catlike screams, especially when begging in late summer and fall. **SIMILAR SPECIES**: Long-eared Owl smaller (crow-sized in flight), with lengthwise streaking rather than crosswise barring beneath; ears closer together; lacks white bib. **HABITAT**: Forests, woodlots, deserts, residential areas, open country.

OWLS

BARN OWL

female
(male is whiter below)

SHORT-EARED OWL

female

male

female

fly on awkward stiff wings, often at dusk

LONG-EARED OWL

flies like Short-eared but not as often seen at dusk

typical

subarctic

GREAT HORNED OWL

SPOTTED OWL *Strix occidentalis*

Scarce

17½–18 in. (45–46 cm). A large, dark-brown forest owl with puffy round head. Large *dark eyes* and *heavily spotted chest and barred belly* identify this bird, which in northern parts of range is being displaced by Barred Owl; populations here (subspecies *caurina*) and in the sw. U.S. (*lucida*) are considered threatened. **VOICE:** High-pitched hoots, like barking of a small dog; usually in groups of three (*hoo, hoo-hoo*) or four (*hoo, who-who-whooo*). Also a longer series of rapid hoots in crescendo; female gives a rising whistle. **SIMILAR SPECIES:** See Barred Owl. **HABITAT:** In North, mature old-growth coniferous and mixed coniferous forests; in South, more varied habitats, including conifers, mixed woods, wooded canyons.

BARRED OWL *Strix varia*

Fairly common

20–21 in. (51–53 cm). A large, brown, puffy-headed woodland owl with large, moist *brown eyes*. Barred *across* chest and streaked *lengthwise* on belly; this combination separates it from Spotted Owl. **VOICE:** Usually eight accented hoots, in two groups of four: *hoohoo-hoohoo, hoohoohooHOOaaw*. Sometimes rendered as *who cooks for you, who cooks for you-all*. The *aaw* at end is characteristic and sometimes uttered singly or as *hoo-aww*. **SIMILAR SPECIES:** Other large owls, except Barn and Spotted, have ear tufts and/or yellow eyes. **HABITAT:** Woodlands, wooded river bottoms, wooded swamps. Recent colonizer in West; increasing in CA.

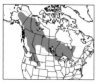

GREAT GRAY OWL *Strix nebulosa*

Scarce

26–28 in. (67–73 cm). Our largest N. American owl; very tame. Plumage soft, dusky gray, heavily striped *lengthwise* on underparts. Round-headed, without ear tufts; large, *strongly lined facial disk* dwarfs *yellow eyes*. Note *black chin spot* bordered by two broad *white mustaches*. Tail long for an owl. An irruptive species. Invades well to the south one year, then may be rare for several years. **VOICE:** Deep *whoo-hoo-hoo*. Also deep single *whoo*s. **SIMILAR SPECIES:** Barred and Spotted Owls much smaller, browner. **HABITAT:** Coniferous forests, adjacent meadows, bogs. Often hunts by day, particularly in winter.

SNOWY OWL *Bubo scandiacus*

Scarce

22–24 in. (56–61 cm). An irruptive, large, mostly *white*, Arctic, day-flying owl. Round head, *yellow eyes*. Variably flecked or barred with black to dusky, adult males less so than females and young birds. **VOICE:** Usually silent. Flight call when breeding a loud, repeated *krow-ow*; also a repeated *rick*. **SIMILAR SPECIES:** Barn Owl whitish on underparts only; much smaller and has dark eyes. Many downy young owls are whitish. See Gyrfalcon (white morph). **HABITAT:** Prairies, fields, marshes, beaches; in summer, Arctic tundra. Perches on dunes, posts, haystacks, ground in open country, sometimes buildings. Has cyclic winter irruptions southward into U.S., with vagrants as far as cen. CA, HI, TX, FL, and Bermuda.

SPOTTED
OWL

Barred

BARRED
OWL

Spotted

first-year
female

GREAT GRAY OWL

SNOWY OWL
adult
male

WESTERN SCREECH-OWL *Megascops kennicottii* Fairly common

8½ in. (22 cm). A widespread small owl with conspicuous ear tufts. Yellow eyes. Usually *gray* overall, but n. Great Basin population has two color morphs, *gray* and *brown*. Birds in northwestern humid regions are *usually* darker brown; those in arid regions paler, grayer. Bill dark with pale tip. **VOICE:** Series of hollow whistles on one pitch, running into a tremolo (rhythm of a small ball bouncing to a standstill). **SIMILAR SPECIES:** Eastern Screech-Owl has paler bill but best told by voice and ranges, which barely overlap. See Whiskered Screech-Owl. Flammulated Owl smaller, plumage darker and tinged rusty, has dark eyes. **HABITAT:** Wooded canyons, oak groves, shade trees, well-vegetated residential areas, pinyon-juniper and cactus woodlands.

WHISKERED SCREECH-OWL *Megascops trichopsis* Uncommon, local

7¼–7½ in. (18–19 cm). Very similar to Western Screech-Owl. Has large white spots on scapulars, coarser black spots on underparts, longer facial bristles, *yellow-green bill, smaller legs and feet*. Readily identified by voice. **VOICE:** *Boo-boo, booboo-boo-boo, booboo-boo-boo,* etc.; arrangement of this "code" may vary. At times a repeated, four-syllable *chooyoo-coo-cooo,* vaguely suggestive of White-winged Dove. **SIMILAR SPECIES:** Western Screech-Owl. **HABITAT:** Canyons, pine-oak woods, sycamores; typically at higher elevation than Western Screech-Owl.

FLAMMULATED OWL *Psiloscops flammeolus* Uncommon

6–7 in. (15–18 cm). Smaller than a screech-owl and less conspicuous. *Our only small owl north of AZ with dark eyes.* Dark, largely gray, with *tawny scapulars* and inconspicuous ear tufts. Southern birds rustier. **VOICE:** Mellow *hoot* (also *hoo-hoot* or *hu-hu, hoot*), low in pitch for so small an owl; repeated steadily at intervals of two or three seconds. Ventriloquial. **SIMILAR SPECIES:** Screech-owls. **HABITAT:** Open pine and fir forests in mountains and canyons. Migratory habits poorly known; accidental vagrant along Gulf Coast.

EASTERN SCREECH-OWL *Megascops asio* Common

8½ in. (22 cm). The only small eastern owl with ear tufts. Two color morphs: red and gray. No other owl is bright foxy red. Juvenile fluffy and may lack conspicuous ear tufts. **VOICE:** Mournful whinny or wail; tremulous, *descending* in pitch. Sometimes a series of notes on one pitch. **SIMILAR SPECIES:** Like Western Screech-Owl, but separated by voice and, usually, range. Bill paler (greenish, versus gray-black in Western). Also differs in having bright *red* morph. **HABITAT:** Deciduous woodlands, shade trees.

BURROWING OWL *Athene cunicularia* Uncommon

9½ in. (24 cm). A medium-small owl of open country, often seen by day standing erect on ground or low perches near nesting or wintering burrows, culverts, or drain-pipe entrances. Note *long legs*. Barred and spotted, with white chin stripe, round head. Bobs and bows when agitated. **VOICE:** Rapid, chattering *quick-quick-quick*. At night, a mellow *co-hoo,* higher than Mourning Dove's *coo*. Also a Barn Owl–like screech. Juvenile in burrow rattles like rattlesnake to deter predators. **HABITAT:** Open grasslands, unplowed prairies, farmland, airfields, golf courses. Widespread vagrant throughout East north of FL.

SMALL OWLS

Northwest

WESTERN
SCREECH-
OWL

Great Basin

gray
morph

FLAMMULATED
OWL

dark
morph

WHISKERED
SCREECH-
OWL

gray
morph

EASTERN
SCREECH-OWL

BURROWING
OWL

red morph

NORTHERN HAWK OWL *Surnia ulula*　　　　　　　　　　　Scarce

16 in. (41 cm). A medium-sized, slender, day-flying owl, with *long, rounded tail* and *barred underparts*. Often *perches at tip of tree* and jerks tail like a kestrel. **VOICE:** Falconlike chattering *kikikiki,* and kestrel-like *illy-illy-illy-illy.* Also a harsh scream. **HABITAT:** Open coniferous forests, birch scrub, tamarack bogs, muskeg, field edges. Sporadically appears well south of normal range.

NORTHERN SAW-WHET OWL *Aegolius acadicus*　　　　　Uncommon

8 in. (20 cm). A very tame little owl at daytime roosts; smaller than a screech-owl, without ear tufts. Underparts have blotchy, reddish brown streaks. Bill black. Forehead streaked white. *Juvenile:* Chocolate brown in summer, with conspicuous white eyebrows; belly *tawny ocher.* **VOICE:** Song a mellow, whistled note repeated in endless succession, often 100 to 130 times per minute: *too, too, too, too,* etc. Longer and faster than in Northern Pygmy-Owl, which is also more apt to vary tempo. Also raspy, squirrel-like yelps. **SIMILAR SPECIES:** Boreal Owl. **HABITAT:** Coniferous and mixed woods, swamps.

BOREAL OWL *Aegolius funereus*　　　　　　　　　　　　Scarce

10 in. (25 cm). A small, flat-headed, earless owl of northern and high-elevation coniferous forests. Tame. Similar to Northern Saw-whet Owl, but a bit larger; facial disk pale grayish white, *framed with black;* bill pale horn color or *yellowish;* forehead *thickly spotted* with white. *Juvenile:* Similar to juvenile Northern Saw-whet, but duskier; eyebrows grayish; belly obscurely blotched. **VOICE:** An accelerating series of hoots, similar to a winnowing snipe; call includes a raspy *skew.* **SIMILAR SPECIES:** Northern Saw-whet Owl. **HABITAT:** Spruce, fir, and lodgepole-pine forests; muskeg. Sporadically appears well south of normal range, in East.

NORTHERN PYGMY-OWL *Glaucidium gnoma*　　　　　Uncommon

6¾–7 in. (17–18 cm). *Black patches* on each side of hindneck suggest "eyes on back of the head." A very small, earless owl; warm or gray brown, with *sharply streaked underparts* and *rather long tail barred with white.* Frequently heard calling in daytime, particularly early and late. Often mobbed by birds. Tail often held at perky angle. **VOICE:** Single mellow whistle, *hoo,* repeated in well-spaced series, once every two or three seconds. Also a rolling series, ending with two or three deliberate notes: *too-too too-too-too-too-too-too-took-took-took.* Birds in se. AZ mountain canyons double the *hoos.* **SIMILAR SPECIES:** Ferruginous Pygmy-Owl, Northern Saw-whet Owl. **HABITAT:** Open coniferous and mixed woods, wooded canyons.

FERRUGINOUS PYGMY-OWL *Glaucidium brasilianum*　　Scarce

6½–6¾ in. (16–17 cm). Hunts and calls by day, particularly early and late. Often mobbed by birds. Streaking on breast *brownish* rather than black; crown has fine pale streaks (not dots). Tail *rusty, barred with black.* **VOICE:** *Chook* or *puip;* sometimes repeated monotonously two or three times per second. **SIMILAR SPECIES:** Northern Pygmy-Owl (note habitat). **HABITAT:** In s. TX, mesquite and subtropical woods; in s. AZ, saguaro desert.

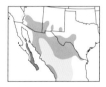

ELF OWL *Micrathene whitneyi*　　　　　　　　　　　　Uncommon

5¾ in. (15 cm). A tiny, short-tailed, earless owl. Underparts softly striped rusty; eyebrows white. Favors woodpecker holes in saguaros, telephone poles, or trees. Found at night by call. **VOICE:** Rapid, high-pitched *whi-whi-whi-whi-whi-whi* or *chewk-chewk-chewk-chewk,* etc., puppylike, with chattering in middle of series. **SIMILAR SPECIES:** Western Screech-Owl. **HABITAT:** Saguaro and mesquite woodlands and deserts, wooded canyons.

SMALL OWLS

NORTHERN
HAWK OWL

juvenile

NORTHERN
SAW-WHET
OWL

adult

FERRUGINOUS
PYGMY-OWL

note "eye pattern"
on nape

BOREAL
OWL

ELF
OWL

gray
morph

typical

NORTHERN
PYGMY-OWL

GOATSUCKERS (NIGHTJARS) Family Caprimulgidae

Nocturnal birds with ample tails, large eyes, tiny bills, large bristled gapes, and very short legs. By day, they rest on limbs or on ground, camouflaged by their "dead-leaf" patterns. Ages similar; sexes can differ in wing and tail patterns. Most species best detected and identified at night by voice. **FOOD:** Nocturnal insects. **RANGE:** Nearly worldwide in temperate and tropical land regions.

COMMON NIGHTHAWK *Chordeiles minor* Uncommon to fairly common

9½ in. (24 cm). A slim-winged, gray-brown bird, often seen high in air; flies with easy strokes, changing gear to quicker erratic strokes. Prefers dusk, but may be abroad at midday. Note *broad white bar* across pointed wing. Barred white-and-gray undertail coverts. Male has white bar across notched tail, whiter throat, and larger white bars in wings than female. At rest, *tertials extend well past white wing patch* and wingtips extend to or beyond tail tip; in flight, white bars occur about halfway out primaries. Darker eastern and northwestern subspecies shown; interior western subspecies are paler and/or tawnier, more similar in color to Lesser. **VOICE:** Nasal *peer* or *pee-ik*. In aerial display, male dives, then zooms up sharply with sudden deep whir of wings. **SIMILAR SPECIES:** Antillean Nighthawk regular in FL Keys; best distinguished by voice. Lesser Nighthawk's white on wing closer to tip of primaries, wings more bluntly tipped; most are buffier and less barred than most Commons. **HABITAT:** Open country from mountains to lowlands; open pine woods; sagebrush; often seen in air over cities, towns. Also over ponds. Sits on ground, posts, rails, roofs, limbs.

ANTILLEAN NIGHTHAWK *Chordeiles gundlachii* Scarce, local

8–8½ in. (20–22 cm). This W. Indian species is a regular late-spring and summer visitor to FL Keys and Dry Tortugas. Somewhat tawnier and smaller than Common Nighthawk, but readily distinguished from it only by call. **VOICE:** Katy-did-like *killy-kadick* or *pity-pit-pit.* **SIMILAR SPECIES:** Common and Lesser Nighthawks. **HABITAT:** Open fields, suburban areas.

LESSER NIGHTHAWK *Chordeiles acutipennis* Fairly common

8½–9 in. (21–23 cm). Slightly smaller than Common Nighthawk; white bar (*buffy* in female) *closer to tip of wing;* at rest, this bar even with or slightly beyond tips of tertials. More extensive brown spotting on inner primaries. Undertail coverts browner, less sharply barred. Readily identified by odd calls. Does not power-dive. **VOICE:** Low *chuck chuck* and soft purring or whinnying sound, much like trilling of a toad. **SIMILAR SPECIES:** Common Nighthawk. **HABITAT:** Lowlands; arid scrub, dry grasslands, farm fields, deserts, dirt roads. Also seen in air over ponds. Sits on branches and ground. Casual vagrant to Southeast; accidental well north of range.

COMMON PAURAQUE *Nyctidromus albicollis* Uncommon, local

11 in. (28 cm). Larger than Whip-poor-will. Dark brown, with long, round wings and tail. Flight floppy with deep wingbeats. Note *broad white band* across pointed wing of male; bar in female buffy. Extensive *white in middle tail feathers* on each side form obvious double stripe in males; more confined to feather tips in females. At rest, note *pale-edged scapulars.* Recognized by its call. **VOICE:** A hoarse slurred whistle: *purr-WEE-eeerr.* **SIMILAR SPECIES:** Other nightjars. Tail pattern and habits differ from nighthawks. **HABITAT:** Dense brushy woodlands, farmlands.

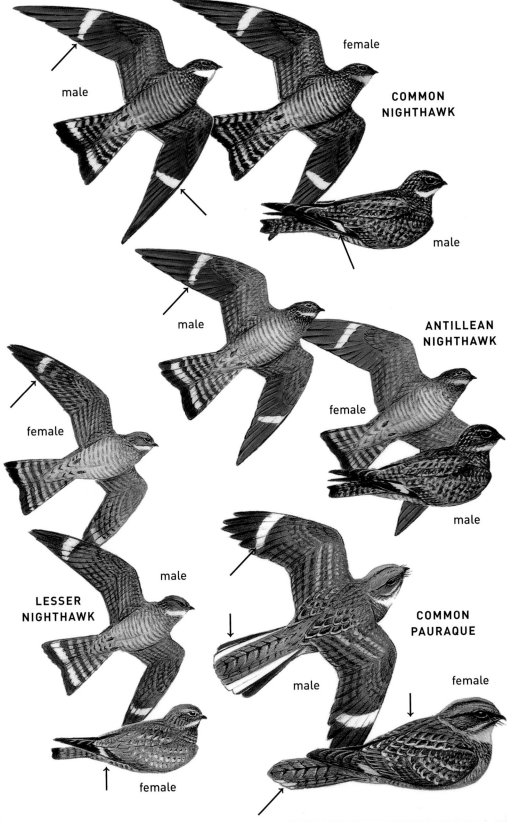

NIGHTHAWKS

male

female

COMMON
NIGHTHAWK

male

male

ANTILLEAN
NIGHTHAWK

female

female

male

LESSER
NIGHTHAWK

male

male

COMMON
PAURAQUE

female

female

female

BUFF-COLLARED NIGHTJAR *Antrostomus ridgwayi*   Rare, local

8¾–9 in. (22–23 cm). Similar to Mexican Whip-poor-will but with *buff or tawny collar* across hindneck. Outer tail feathers with distinct white tips in male but not in female. Best told by calls. **VOICE:** Staccato, cricketlike notes, terminating with longer, strongly accented phrase, *cuk-cuk-cuk-cuk-cuk-cuk-cuk-cukacheea.* **SIMILAR SPECIES:** Common Poorwill, Mexican Whip-poor-will. **RANGE:** Annual spring and summer visitor to se. AZ. **HABITAT:** Rocky slopes and washes near mesquite or junipers. Accidental vagrant to CA.

COMMON POORWILL *Phalaenoptilus nuttallii*   Uncommon

7½–7¾ in. (19–20 cm). Best known by its night cry in arid hills. Appears smaller than a nighthawk, has shorter, more rounded wings *(no white bar)*, and the short and rounded tail has *white corners;* these are slightly buffier in female, but sexes otherwise very similar in plumage. Short wings and tail give it a *compact look* at rest. **VOICE:** At night, a loud, repeated *poor-will* or *poor-jill.* **SIMILAR SPECIES:** Mexican Whip-poor-will. **HABITAT:** Dry or rocky hills, including open pine forests, sagebrush, juniper, and chaparral; roadsides.

MEXICAN WHIP-POOR-WILL *Antrostomus arizonae*   Uncommon

9¾–10 in. (25–26 cm). Recently split from Eastern Whip-poor-will. Slightly larger, central tail feathers buffier, not contrasting with back, extent of white in male's tail is reduced. **VOICE:** Similar to Eastern Whip-poor-will's but *much burrier in quality.* **SIMILAR SPECIES:** Eastern Whip-poor-will, Common Poorwill. **HABITAT:** Drier second-growth montane woodlands, especially oak and pine.

EASTERN WHIP-POOR-WILL *Antrostomus vociferus*   Uncommon

9½–9¾ in. (24–25 cm). A voice in the night woods, this species is more often heard than seen. When flushed by day, flits away on rounded wings, like a large brown moth. Male has large *white tail patches;* in female these are smaller and buffy. At rest, tail extends beyond wings, unlike nighthawk's. Note *black throat* and *broad black crown stripe.* **VOICE:** At night, a rolling, tiresomely repeated *WHIP poor-WEEL,* or *purple-rib,* etc. **SIMILAR SPECIES:** Mexican Whip-poor-will, Chuck-will's-widow. **HABITAT:** Deciduous forests, drier second-growth woodlands. Accidental vagrant to CA.

CHUCK-WILL'S-WIDOW *Antrostomus carolinensis*   Uncommon

12 in. (30 cm). Similar to Eastern Whip-poor-will but larger and with flat, bull-headed appearance, much browner, with *brown* (not blackish) throat and *streaked crown;* white areas in tail of adult male restricted. Tail of first-year males and females have buff tips instead of white. **VOICE:** Call a four-syllable *chuck-will-widow* (less vigorous than effort of Eastern Whip-poor-will); *chuck* often very low and difficult to hear. **SIMILAR SPECIES:** Eastern Whip-poor-will, Common Poorwill. **HABITAT:** Pine and mixed forests, river woodlands, groves. Accidental vagrant to CA.

GOATSUCKERS

BUFF-COLLARED
NIGHTJAR

male

COMMON
POORWILL

male

female

MEXICAN
WHIP-POOR-
WILL

male

female

female

male

adult
male

CHUCK-WILL'S-
WIDOW

female

EASTERN WHIP-
POOR-WILL

first-year male
and female

PIGEONS and DOVES Family Columbidae

Plump, fast-flying birds with small heads and low, cooing voices. Some have fanlike tails (such as Rock Pigeon) and others have pointed tails (such as Mourning Dove). Ages and sexes mostly similar; juveniles are scaled above. **FOOD:** Seeds, waste grain, fruit, insects. **RANGE:** Nearly worldwide. Passenger Pigeon *(Ectopistes migratorius)*, p. 237, formerly abundant throughout e. N. America, became extinct in 1914.

BAND-TAILED PIGEON *Patagioenas fasciata*   Fairly common

14½–15 in. (37–38 cm). Heavily built; prefers woodland habitats and often alights in trees. Note *broad pale band* across end of tail; *white band* on nape. Feet *yellow.* Bill *yellow* with *dark tip.* **VOICE:** Hollow owl-like *oo-whoo* or *whoo-oo-whoo,* repeated. **SIMILAR SPECIES:** Rock Pigeon. **HABITAT:** Oak canyons, foothills, chaparral, mountain forests; also some residential areas, parks. Often flies high over trees in flocks. Vagrant to East, accidentally to E. Coast.

RED-BILLED PIGEON *Patagioenas flavirostris*   Scarce, local

14–14½ in. (36–37 cm). A large all-dark pigeon (in good light deep maroon), including underbelly. Bill red with yellowish tip. Shy, mostly arboreal. Recent decline in numbers. **VOICE:** *Whoo, whoo, whooooooo.* **SIMILAR SPECIES:** Rock Pigeon. **HABITAT:** Riparian woodlands with tall trees and brush.

WHITE-CROWNED PIGEON *Patagioenas leucocephala*   Uncommon, local

13½ in. (34 cm). A stocky, shy pigeon completely dark except for immaculate white crown. **VOICE:** Low, owl-like *wof, wof, wo, co-woo.* **SIMILAR SPECIES:** Rock Pigeon. **HABITAT:** Mangrove keys, thickets, hardwood hammocks. Perches on power lines, treetops.

AFRICAN COLLARED-DOVE *Streptopelia roseogrisea*   Exotic

12 in. (30 cm). Escaped cage bird, also known as Ringed Turtle-Dove *(S. risoria),* has declined with arrival of Eurasian. Paler than Eurasian, especially underside of flight feathers. Voice a two-syllable cooing rather than three as in Eurasian. Paler (leucistic?) Eurasian Collared-Doves complicate identification.

EURASIAN COLLARED-DOVE *Streptopelia decaocto*   Common

12½–13 in. (32–33 cm). Recent colonizer of N. America from Eurasia via the Caribbean; has rapidly increased throughout our area. Slightly chunkier than Mourning Dove, *paler beige,* and with *square-cut tail.* Note *narrow black ring on hindneck.* **VOICE:** *Three*-noted *coo-COOO-cup.* **SIMILAR SPECIES:** African Collared-Dove. White-winged Dove smaller, white in wing obvious. **HABITAT:** Towns, field edges, cultivated land.

SPOTTED DOVE *Streptopelia chinensis*   Uncommon, local, exotic

12 in. (30–31 cm). Introduced from Asia. Note *broad collar of black and white spots* on hindneck. Larger than Mourning Dove; tail with white corners. *Juvenile:* Upperparts scaled; lacks collar. **VOICE:** *Coo-who-coo;* resembles cooing of White-winged Dove. **SIMILAR SPECIES:** Mourning Dove. Introduced populations in s. CA, now much reduced but common in HI (p. 438). **HABITAT:** Residential areas, parks.

ROCK PIGEON (ROCK DOVE, DOMESTIC PIGEON)   Common, introduced
Columba livia

12½ in. (32 cm). Typical birds are silvery gray with iridescent purple and green head and breast, *whitish rump, two black wing bars,* and broad, dark tail band. Domestic stock or feral birds may have many color variants. **VOICE:** Soft, gurgling *coo-roo-coo.* **SIMILAR SPECIES:** Band-tailed Pigeon. **HABITAT:** Cities, farms, cliffs, bridges. Introduced and common in HI (p. 438).

PIGEONS
AND DOVES

BAND-TAILED
PIGEON

RED-BILLED
PIGEON

AFRICAN
COLLARED-
DOVE

WHITE-
CROWNED
PIGEON

EURASIAN
COLLARED-
DOVE

plumages
variable

ROCK
PIGEON

SPOTTED
DOVE

typical form

WHITE-WINGED DOVE *Zenaida asiatica*   Common

11½–12 in. (29–30 cm). A dove of desert, readily known by *white wing patches, large when bird is in flight, narrow when at rest.* Otherwise similar to Mourning Dove, but tail *rounded* and tipped with broad white corners, bill slightly longer, eye orangey red. **VOICE:** Harsh cooing, *ooo-uh-CUCK oo (who cooks for you?).* Sounds vaguely like crowing of a young rooster. **SIMILAR SPECIES:** Mourning Dove, Eurasian Collared-Dove. **HABITAT:** Open areas: river woods, mesquite, saguaros, desert oases, groves, towns, feeders. Widespread vagrant north of range.

MOURNING DOVE *Zenaida macroura*   Common

12 in. (30–31 cm). The common widespread wild dove. Brown; smaller and slimmer than Rock Pigeon and Eurasian Collared-Dove. Note *pointed tail* with large white spots. Male with slightly bluer crown and rosier breast than female; juvenile scaled above. **VOICE:** Hollow, mournful *coah, cooo, coo, cooo.* At a distance, only the three *coo*s are audible. **SIMILAR SPECIES:** White-winged Dove. **HABITAT:** Farms, towns, open woods, fields, scrub, roadsides, grasslands, feeders. Introduced and uncommon in HI (p. 438).

WHITE-TIPPED DOVE *Leptotila verreauxi*   Uncommon, local

11½ in. (29 cm). Large stocky dove with broad, dark wings. Short tail has *white corners.* Body pale, underwings cinnamon. **VOICE:** Long, drawn-out, hollow *who — whoooooooooo.* **SIMILAR SPECIES:** White-winged and Mourning Doves. **HABITAT:** Often seen walking in shadows of brushy tangles or dense woods; flies furtively away.

RUDDY GROUND DOVE *Columbina talpacoti*   Rare

6½–6¾ in. (16–17 cm). This rare but regular visitor (and very rare breeder) from Mex. is similar to Common Ground Dove but is slightly larger, longer tailed, and longer billed; has *dark, grayish base* to bill, *lacks all scaliness,* and has dark underwing lining (rufous in Common Ground Dove). *Male:* Washed rufous, crown pale blue. *Female and juvenile:* Plain brown and gray; *blackish spots or streaks on wing coverts extend to scapulars.* **VOICE:** Cooing similar to Common Ground Dove's, but faster and more repetitive: *pity-you pity-you pity you.* **SIMILAR SPECIES:** Inca Dove, Common Ground Dove. **HABITAT:** Farms, livestock pens, fields, brushy areas. Often found with Inca Dove and Common Ground Dove.

COMMON GROUND DOVE *Columbina passerina*   Uncommon

6¼–6½ in. (15–16 cm). A very small dove. Note *stubby black tail,* scaly breast, pinkish or orangey base of bill. Rounded wings flash *rufous* in flight; *bronzy* spots on wing coverts; underwing coverts rufous. Feet yellow or pink. *Male:* Body tinged pinkish. *Female:* Browner; scapulars lack marks found on female Ruddy. **VOICE:** Soft, monotonously repeated *woo-oo, woo-oo,* etc. May sound monosyllabic — *wooo,* with rising inflection. **SIMILAR SPECIES:** Inca Dove, Ruddy Ground Dove. **HABITAT:** Farms, orchards, brushy areas, roadsides. Casual vagrant north of range.

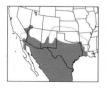

INCA DOVE *Columbina inca*   Fairly common

8¼–8½ in. (21–22 cm). A very small, slim dove with *scaly* look. *Rufous* in primaries (as in ground doves), but has *longer tail* with *white sides and corners,* noticeable in flight. **VOICE:** Monotonous *coo-hoo* or *no-hope.* **SIMILAR SPECIES:** Common Ground Dove has short tail without obvious white, lacks scaling on back. **HABITAT:** Towns, parks, farms.

DOVES

WHITE-WINGED DOVE

PASSENGER PIGEON
extinct 1914

MOURNING DOVE

male

female

WHITE-TIPPED DOVE

male

RUDDY GROUND DOVE

female

COMMON GROUND DOVE

male

female

INCA DOVE

CUCKOOS, ROADRUNNERS, and ANIS
Family Cuculidae

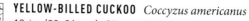

Slender, long-tailed birds; feet zygodactyl (two toes forward, two backward). Sexes alike. **FOOD:** Cuckoos eat caterpillars, other insects; roadrunners eat reptiles, rodents, large insects, small birds; anis eat seeds, fruit. **RANGE:** Warm and temperate regions of world; some cuckoos (but not ours) are parasitic.

YELLOW-BILLED CUCKOO *Coccyzus americanus*   Fairly common

12 in. (30–31 cm). Slim and sinuous with brown back and white underparts. *Rufous* in wings, *large white* spots at tips of dark undertail feathers, *yellow* lower mandible on slightly curved bill, and dusky orbital ring; juvenile and first-fall birds have less-distinct tail spots and yellowish orbital rings. **VOICE:** Song a distinctive, rapid, throaty *ka-ka-ka-ka-ka-ka-ka-ka-ka-ka-ka-ka-kow-kow-kowlp-kowlp — kowlp — kowlp* (slowing toward end). Often heard during hot afternoons. **SIMILAR SPECIES:** Black-billed Cuckoo. **HABITAT:** Riparian woodlands, particularly cottonwoods in West, where populations are threatened; vagrant north of range in West.

MANGROVE CUCKOO *Coccyzus minor*   Uncommon, local

12 in. (30–31 cm). Adult and first-fall birds similar to Yellow-billed Cuckoo (both found in s. FL), but belly creamy buff; no rufous in wing. Note black ear patch. **VOICE:** Accelerating series of guttural notes, almost like grunts: *unh unh unh unh unh unh aanngg aanngg*. Final two notes longer. **SIMILAR SPECIES:** Other cuckoos, especially Yellow-billed. **HABITAT:** Mangroves, hardwood forests. Casual vagrant along Gulf Coast.

BLACK-BILLED CUCKOO *Coccyzus erythropthalmus*   Uncommon

11½–12 in. (29–30 cm). *Adult:* Similar to Yellow-billed Cuckoo, but *bill dark gray to blackish;* adult has narrow *red orbital ring. No rufous in wing;* undertail spots small. *Juvenile and first-fall:* Has greenish to yellowish orbital ring and often small amount of rufous in wing; thus more like Yellow-billed Cuckoo, but has *all-dark bill.* **VOICE:** Fast, rhythmic *cucucu, cucucu, cucucu,* etc. The grouped rhythm (three or four) is typical, but often employs irregular cadences. May sing at night. **HABITAT:** Wood edges, groves, thickets. Accidental vagrant to W. Coast.

GROOVE-BILLED ANI *Crotophaga sulcirostris*   Uncommon, local

13–13½ in. (33–34 cm). A coal black, grackle-sized bird with long loose-jointed tail, short wings, and large bill with high curved ridge and noticeable angle to lower mandible (giving it puffinlike profile), with distinct bill grooves or ridges, more prominent in older adults. Flight weak; alternately flaps and sails. Often moves in groups. **VOICE:** Repeated *whee-o* or *tee-ho,* first note slurring up. **SIMILAR SPECIES:** Grackles, Smooth-billed Ani. **HABITAT:** Thickets, open woodlands. Widespread vagrant north of range.

SMOOTH-BILLED ANI *Crotophaga ani*   Casual vagrant

14–14½ in. (35–37 cm). Similar to Groove-billed Ani but larger, *bill with higher ridge* and lacking grooves. **VOICE:** Whining whistle. Querulous *que-lick.* **HABITAT:** Brushy edges, thickets. Recently extirpated as breeding species in FL and now a vagrant from Caribbean.

GREATER ROADRUNNER *Geococcyx californianus*   Fairly common

22–23 in. (56–58 cm). Roadrunners are peculiar cuckoos that run on ground. A large, slender, streaked bird, with long, white-edged tail; shaggy crest; long legs. White crescent on wing (visible when spread). **VOICE:** Six to eight low, dovelike *coos,* descending in pitch. **SIMILAR SPECIES:** Thrashers are much smaller. **HABITAT:** Deserts, open country with scattered cover, chaparral, brush.

CUCKOOS, ETC.

YELLOW-BILLED
CUCKOO

adults

adult

BLACK-
BILLED
CUCKOO

first-
fall

MANGROVE
CUCKOO

adult

GROOVE-
BILLED
ANI

SMOOTH-
BILLED ANI

GREATER
ROADRUNNER

PARAKEETS and PARROTS Family Psittacidae

Noisy and gaudily colored. Compact, short-necked birds with stout, hooked bills. Parakeets smaller, with long, pointed tail. Feet zygodactyl (two toes fore, two aft). **RANGE:** Worldwide in Tropics and Subtropics. Several additional species, shown on p. 242, have not yet become established; most are found in s. FL, CA, TX, and HI. Carolina Parakeet *(Conuropsis carolinensis)* formerly occurred throughout the e. U.S. north to NY and west to CO; became extinct around 1918.

MONK PARAKEET *Myiopsitta monachus*   Locally fairly common, exotic
11 in. (28 cm). Native to Argentina. Pale gray face and chest, buff band across belly. Established in spots from CT to FL and west to IL and TX. Massive stick nest with several compartments. Raucous calls. Comes to feeders.

GREEN PARAKEET *Psittacara holochlorus*   Locally fairly common, exotic
10–12 in. (25–30 cm). Long pointed tails readily separate parakeets from parrots. Relatively large, is green above, yellow-green below. **VOICE:** Sharp, squeaky notes, shrill noisy chatter. **RANGE AND HABITAT:** Tropical ne. Mex. to s. Nicaragua. Exotic population in Miami. Resident populations established in residential areas of s. Rio Grande Valley, TX, may include natural strays from Mex.

NANDAY PARAKEET *Aratinga nenday*   Locally fairly common, exotic
12 in. (30 cm). Native to S. America; locally established on western coast of FL and in n. Los Angeles, CA. Also known as "Black-hooded" Parakeet, in reference to its diagnostic black face and crown. Long tail, remiges black below; undertail black; uppertail green, tipped blue. Loud, shrill ternlike calls.

WHITE-WINGED PARAKEET *Brotogeris versicolurus*   Locally uncommon, exotic

YELLOW-CHEVRONED PARAKEET   Locally fairly common, exotic
Brotogeris chiriri
9 in. (23 cm). Native to S. America, these two similar *Brotogeris* parakeets are locally established in Miami and Los Angeles areas. Green; note yellow primary coverts, white secondaries in White-winged Parakeet. White-winged formerly more common; this species has since been replaced and greatly outnumbered by Yellow-chevroned Parakeets, especially in southern CA.

RED-CROWNED PARROT *Amazona viridigenalis*   Locally fairly common, exotic
12 in. (30 cm). Large, with red crown (reduced in first-year), blue nape, red wing panels. **VOICE:** Loud, familiar, raucous notes and squeals of Amazon parrots. **RANGE AND HABITAT:** Native to ne. Mex. Exotic populations in s. CA, s. FL, Honolulu (p. 440), and s. TX; the latter may include natural strays from Mex.

THICK-BILLED PARROT *Rhynchopsitta pachyrhyncha*   Rare, local, endangered
16–17 in. (40–43 cm). Large, primarily green with red forehead, eyebrow, and bend of wing; underwing patterned with black and yellow bars, green and red wing lining. Long tail separates it from Amazon parrots. **VOICE:** Loud, laughinglike *ca-ca-ca-ca* calls. **RANGE AND HABITAT:** Native to n. Mex.; formerly wandered to AZ. Reintroduction programs unsuccessful but possible strays reported.

ROSY-FACED LOVEBIRD *Agapornis roseicollis*   Locally established, exotic
6–6½ in. (15–16 cm). A small, short-tailed parakeet, adult male with distinctive peach-colored to red face, green body, and blue rump. Female and first-year male greener. Found in large tight flocks. **VOICE:** High-pitched, twittering *cheep* calls. **RANGE AND HABITAT:** Native to Africa; established locally in Phoenix area and on Maui (p. 440). Escapees sometimes observed elsewhere.

PARAKEETS
AND PARROTS
Established

MONK
PARAKEET

GREEN
PARAKEET

WHITE-
WINGED
PARAKEET

YELLOW-
CHEVRONED
PARAKEET

BLACK-
HOODED
PARAKEET

adult
male

RED-CROWNED
PARROT

THICK-BILLED
PARROT
adult

ROSY-FACED
LOVEBIRD

ROSE-RINGED PARAKEET *Psittacula krameri* Unestablished exotic

(Africa, India) 16 in. (41 cm). Small populations in FL and Los Angeles; larger population in Bakersfield, CA. Introduced and common in HI (p. 440).

RED-MASKED PARAKEET *Psittacara erythrogenys* Unestablished exotic

(S. America) 12½–13½ in. (30–34 cm). Moderate populations in California cities; smaller populations in s. FL. Established on Oahu and Hawaii I. (p. 440).

MITRED PARAKEET *Psittacara mitratus* Unestablished exotic

(S. America) 15 in. (38 cm). Moderate populations in Los Angeles area and s. FL; found occasionally elsewhere in N. America and on Maui (p. 440).

BUDGERIGAR *Melopsittacus undulatus* Unestablished exotic

(Australia) 7 in. (18 cm). May also be blue, yellow, or white. Populations formerly established in FL; now extirpated. Escapees found in many areas.

LILAC-CROWNED PARROT *Amazona finschi* Unestablished exotic

(Mex.) 12½–13½ in. (30–34 cm). Moderate populations in Los Angeles and San Diego; smaller populations in Miami and s. TX.

YELLOW-HEADED PARROT *Amazona oratrix* Unestablished exotic

(Mex. and Belize) 14–15 in. (36–38 cm). Escapees found in several areas; small populations found locally in Los Angeles region, also in s. FL and s. TX.

KINGFISHERS Family Alcedinidae

Chiefly solitary birds with large heads, long pointed bills, and small syndactyl feet (two toes partially joined). Most are fish eaters, perching above water or hovering and plunging headfirst. **FOOD:** Mainly fish; some species eat insects, lizards. **RANGE:** Almost worldwide.

GREEN KINGFISHER *Chloroceryle americana* Uncommon, local

8½–8¾ in. (22 cm). Kingfisher shape, small size; flight buzzy, direct. Upperparts deep green with white spots; collar and underparts white, sides spotted. *Adult male:* Has *rusty* breast-band. *Adult female:* Has one or two greenish bands. (The reverse is true in Belted Kingfisher.) *First-year:* Birds of both sexes have mixed rufous and green feathers in breast. **VOICE:** Sharp clicking, *tick tick tick;* also a sharp squeak. **SIMILAR SPECIES:** Larger and much larger-billed Amazon Kingfisher (*C. amazona*) of Mex. accidental in TX. **HABITAT:** Small rivers and streams with clear water. Accidental vagrant north of range.

RINGED KINGFISHER *Megaceryle torquata* Uncommon, local

16 in. (41 cm). Larger than Belted Kingfisher; bill very large. *Male:* Has entirely chestnut breast and belly (ages similar). *Adult female:* Has broad blue-gray band across breast, separated from chestnut belly by narrow white line (chest mixed with rufous feathers in first-year female). **VOICE:** Rusty *cla-ack* or *wa-ak* or rolling rattle after a loud *chack*. **SIMILAR SPECIES:** Belted Kingfisher. **HABITAT:** Slow rivers (particularly the Rio Grande in our area), marshes.

BELTED KINGFISHER *Megaceryle alcyon* Fairly common

13 in. (33 cm). Our common widespread kingfisher, this big-headed and big-billed fisher hovers on rapidly beating wings in readiness for the plunge, or flies with uneven wingbeats, rattling as it goes: the Belted Kingfisher is easily recognized. *Adult male:* Blue-gray above, with ragged bushy crest and broad gray chest-band. *Adult female:* Has an additional rusty breast-band. *First-year:* Similar in both sexes except blue chest-band mottled with rusty feathers. **VOICE:** Distinctive, loud dry rattle. **SIMILAR SPECIES:** Ringed Kingfisher in TX. **HABITAT:** Streams, lakes, bays, coasts; nests in banks, perches on wires.

PARAKEETS AND PARROTS
Exotics

ROSE-RINGED PARAKEET

RED-MASKED PARAKEET

MITRED PARAKEET

BUDGERIGAR

LILAC-CROWNED PARROT

YELLOW-HEADED PARROT

Unestablished Exotics

KINGFISHERS

GREEN KINGFISHER

adult male

adult female

hovering

RINGED KINGFISHER

first-year female

male entirely chestnut below

BELTED KINGFISHER

adult male

plunging

WOODPECKERS Family Picidae

Chisel-billed, wood-boring birds with strong zygodactyl feet (usually two toes front, two rear), remarkably long tongues, and stiff spiny tails that act as props for climbing. Flight usually undulating. **FOOD:** Tree-boring insects and grubs; some species eat ants, flying insects, berries, acorns. **RANGE:** Most wooded parts of world; absent in Australian region, Madagascar.

RED-HEADED WOODPECKER *Melanerpes erythrocephalus*   Uncommon

9¼ in. (24 cm). *Adult:* A black-backed woodpecker with *entirely red* head (other woodpeckers may have patch of red). Back *solid black,* rump white. Large, square *white patches* conspicuous on wing, including when sitting on a tree. Sexes similar. *Juvenile:* Dusky-headed; wing patches mottled with dark through first year. **VOICE:** Loud *queer* or *queeah.* **SIMILAR SPECIES:** Red-bellied Woodpecker has only partially red head. **HABITAT:** Groves, farm country, shade trees in towns, large scattered trees. Casual vagrant in West, accidentally to CA.

LEWIS'S WOODPECKER *Melanerpes lewis*   Uncommon

10¾–11 in. (27–28 cm). A large, dark woodpecker with *crowlike flight,* flycatching habits. *Adult:* Has extensive *pinkish red belly, wide gray collar,* and dark red face patch. Sexes similar. *Juvenile:* Duller. **VOICE:** Usually silent. Occasionally a harsh *churr* or *chee-ur.* **SIMILAR SPECIES:** Red-headed and Acorn Woodpeckers, American Crow. **HABITAT:** Open, burned, or logged forests, usually of ponderosa pine or oak, river groves, oak savanna. Casual vagrant east of range, accidentally to E. Coast.

ACORN WOODPECKER *Melanerpes formicivorus*   Common

9 in. (23 cm). Social, usually found in clans. A black-backed woodpecker with conspicuous white rump, *white wing patches* in flight, and whitish eyes. Note *clownish black, white, and red head pattern,* female with an extra black band on crown. Ages similar. Stores acorns in holes drilled in bark and wooden building sides. **VOICE:** *Whack-up, whack-up, whack-up,* or *ja-cob, ja-cob.* **HABITAT:** Oak woods, mixed oak-pine forests, foothills. Casual vagrant north and east of range.

RED-BELLIED WOODPECKER *Melanerpes carolinus*   Common

9¼ in. (24 cm). *Adult:* A *zebra-backed* woodpecker with *red cap, white rump.* Red covers both crown and nape in male, *only nape in female.* *Juvenile:* Also zebra-backed, but has brown head, devoid of red. **VOICE:** Call *kwirr, churr,* or *chaw;* also *chiv, chiv* and a muffled flickerlike series. **SIMILAR SPECIES:** Golden-fronted and Red-headed Woodpeckers. **HABITAT:** Woodlands, groves, orchards, towns, feeders. Casual vagrant west of range.

GILA WOODPECKER *Melanerpes uropygialis*   Fairly common

9¼ in. (24 cm). A zebra-backed woodpecker; in flight, shows *white wing patch.* Head and underparts gray-brown; male but not female has *red cap.* **VOICE:** Rolling *churr* and a sharp *pit* or *yip.* **SIMILAR SPECIES:** Ladder-backed Woodpecker, found in same habitats, blackish with striped face, lacks white wing patch. See also female Williamson's Sapsucker. **HABITAT:** Desert washes, saguaros, riparian woodlands, towns.

GOLDEN-FRONTED WOODPECKER *Melanerpes aurifrons*   Common

9½ in. (25 cm). A zebra-backed woodpecker with light underparts and white rump. Has white wing patch in flight. *Male:* Note *multicolored head* (yellow near bill, poppy red on crown, orange nape). *Female:* Lacks red crown patch (juvenile has tan head and nape, lacking color). **VOICE:** Tremulous *churrrr;* flickerlike *kek-kek-kek-kek.* **SIMILAR SPECIES:** Note aberrant Red-bellied Woodpecker can have yellow lores. **HABITAT:** Mesquite, woodlands, groves.

WOODPECKERS

juvenile

adult

RED-HEADED WOODPECKER

LEWIS'S WOODPECKER

juvenile

adult

male

female

ACORN WOODPECKER

male

female

RED-BELLIED WOODPECKER

male

female

GILA WOODPECKER

male

female

GOLDEN-FRONTED WOODPECKER

NORTHERN FLICKER *Colaptes auratus*   Common

12–12½ in. (30–32 cm). Conspicuous *white rump* in flight, *barred brown back,* and *black patch* across chest mark this bird as a flicker. Unlike other woodpeckers, often hops awkwardly on ground, feeding on ants. Two basic subspecies groups: "Yellow-shafted" Flicker, of the North and East, has *golden yellow* underwings and tail. *Red crescent* on nape; *gray crown; tan-brown cheeks;* male has *black* mustache. "Red-shafted" Flicker of the West has *salmon red* underwing and undertail. Both sexes lack red crescent on nape; have *brownish crown* and *gray cheeks;* male has *red* mustache. Intergrades are fairly common in western edge of plains, and less commonly in winter, throughout West. **VOICE:** Loud *wick wick wick wick wick,* etc. Also a loud *klee-yer* and a squeaky *flick-a, flick-a,* etc. (See also Pileated Woodpecker.) **SIMILAR SPECIES:** Gilded Flicker. **HABITAT:** Open forests, woodlots, towns.

GILDED FLICKER *Colaptes chrysoides*   Uncommon, local

11–11½ in. (28–29 cm). Wing and tail linings *yellow,* crown mustard brown, male has *red* mustache. Black breast patch slightly thicker, dark barring on back slightly narrower than in Yellow-shafted Flicker. **VOICE:** Same as Northern Flicker's, but slightly higher pitched. **HABITAT:** Cactus deserts, riparian woodland corridors; some overlap in range (but rarely habitat) with Northern Flicker.

WILLIAMSON'S SAPSUCKER *Sphyrapicus thyroideus*   Uncommon

9 in. (23 cm). Characteristic sapsucker white wing patches. *Male:* Black with white rump. Note white facial stripes, *red throat, yellow belly. Female:* Very different looking: a brownish *zebra-backed* woodpecker with white rump, *barred sides, brown head,* yellow belly. **VOICE:** Nasal *cheeer.* Drum is several rapid thumps followed by three or four slow, accented thumps. **SIMILAR SPECIES:** Gila Woodpecker lacks barred sides and yellow belly, and does not overlap in habitat. **HABITAT:** High-elevation coniferous forests; in winter, to lower elevations, and occasionally in other types of trees. Casual vagrant east of range.

RED-BREASTED SAPSUCKER *Sphyrapicus ruber*   Uncommon

8½ in. (22 cm). Sapsuckers drill orderly rows of small holes in trees for sap and the insects it attracts. Note longish sapsucker wing patch. Red-breasted has *entirely red head and breast.* Sexes similar. *Juvenile:* Head and body mottled brown in summer. Northern Red-breasteds are more color-saturated, with blacker back, redder face than birds from CA. Hybridizes regularly with Red-naped Sapsucker. **VOICE:** Nasal mewing note, *cheerrrr;* drum in this, Yellow-bellied, and Red-breasted Sapsuckers is several rapid thumps followed by several slow, rhythmic thumps. **SIMILAR SPECIES:** Hybrid Red-naped × Red-breasted Sapsuckers usually have more black and white on face (although southern Red-breasteds can be similar) and mix of black and red on breast. **HABITAT:** Coniferous and mixed woods, groves, fruit trees.

RED-NAPED SAPSUCKER *Sphyrapicus nuchalis*   Fairly common

8½ in. (22 cm). Very similar to Yellow-bellied but note *red nape.* Black frame around throat *broken* toward rear. Female has white chin. Hybridizes with Red-breasted Sapsucker. **VOICE:** Similar to Red-breasted Sapsucker. **SIMILAR SPECIES:** Yellow-bellied Sapsucker. **HABITAT:** Coniferous, mixed, and deciduous woodlands; in summer, particularly aspen groves. Casual vagrant to Gulf Coast.

YELLOW-BELLIED SAPSUCKER *Sphyrapicus varius*   Fairly common

8½ in. (22 cm). *Adult:* Note sapsucker wing stripe, red forehead. Male has all-red throat, female white. *Juvenile:* Unlike other sapsuckers, retains brown plumage through winter. **VOICE:** Similar to Red-breasted Sapsucker. **SIMILAR SPECIES:** Red-naped Sapsucker. **HABITAT:** Coniferous, mixed, and deciduous woods, shade trees. Scarce vagrant to W. Coast.

WOODPECKERS
Flickers and Sapsuckers

"Red-shafted" female

"Red-shafted" male

"Yellow-shafted" male

NORTHERN FLICKER

female

"Red-shafted"

males

"Yellow-shafted"

Gilded Flicker

GILDED FLICKER

"Red-shafted" male

juvenile male

WILLIAMSON'S SAPSUCKER

male

southern

northern

juvenile

RED-BREASTED SAPSUCKER

male

female

female

male

juvenile

RED-NAPED SAPSUCKER

male

female

YELLOW-BELLIED SAPSUCKER

NUTTALL'S WOODPECKER *Dryobates nuttallii* Fairly common

7½ in. (19 cm). The black-and-white zebra-backed woodpecker found away from arid habitats *in far West.* Male has red crown. Juvenile *Dryobates* and *Picoides* woodpeckers have sparse red flecking to crown in both sexes (more red in males). **VOICE:** Descending rattle, sharper than in Downy. Call a low *pa-tick,* lower and raspier than in Ladder-backed Woodpecker. **SIMILAR SPECIES:** Ladder-backed Woodpecker inhabits more arid country; range barely overlaps (hybrids are known); has thicker white stripes on face and back. See Downy Woodpecker. **HABITAT:** Oak woodlands; recently expanding to other habitats.

LADDER-BACKED WOODPECKER *Dryobates scalaris* Fairly common

7¼ in. (18 cm). The black-and-white zebra-backed woodpecker found in more arid country *east of Sierra Nevada.* Male has red crown. **VOICE:** Rattling series, *chikikikikikikikikik,* diminishing. Call a sharp *pick* or *chik* (like Downy Woodpecker). **SIMILAR SPECIES:** Nuttall's Woodpecker. **HABITAT:** Deserts, canyons, pinyon-juniper, riparian woodlands, arid brush.

HAIRY WOODPECKER *Dryobates villosus* Fairly common

9–9¼ in. (23–24 cm). Note *white* back and *large* bill. Downy and Hairy Woodpeckers are almost identical in pattern, checkered and spotted with black and white; male has small red patch on back of head, female does not. Hairy is like an exaggerated Downy, especially its bill. *Juvenile:* May have red to yellowish crown patch, more extensive in male. **VOICE:** Kingfisher-like rattle, quicker than that of Downy. Call a sharp *peek!* (Downy says *pick.*) **SIMILAR SPECIES:** Downy Woodpecker. American Three-toed Woodpecker has some barring on back and barred sides. **HABITAT:** Coniferous forests, deciduous woods, shade trees, suet feeders.

DOWNY WOODPECKER *Dryobates pubescens* Common

6½–6¾ in. (17 cm). Note *white back* and *small bill.* This industrious bird is like a small edition of Hairy Woodpecker. Outer tail feathers spotted, red nape patch of male in unbroken square. Coloration and amount of white spotting in wings varies regionally in both Downy and Hairy. **VOICE:** Rapid whinny of notes, descending in pitch. Call a flat *pick,* not as sharp as Hairy's *peek!* **SIMILAR SPECIES:** Hairy Woodpecker larger, has larger bill and clean white outer tail feathers. Ladder-backed Woodpecker has similar call. **HABITAT:** Woods, riparian thickets, residential areas, suet feeders, even corn and cattail stems.

AMERICAN THREE-TOED WOODPECKER *Picoides dorsalis* Scarce

8½–8¾ in. (22 cm). Males of this and the next species are our only woodpeckers that have three toes and, normally, a *yellow cap* (note some juvenile Hairys have sparse yellow in crown). Both have *barred sides.* This species is distinguished by irregular white patch on back (Rockies) or *bars* (farther north). Female lacks yellow cap and can suggest Downy or Hairy Woodpecker, but note *barred sides.* **VOICE:** A level-pitched whinny and a flat *pyik.* **SIMILAR SPECIES:** Black-backed Woodpecker, Hairy Woodpecker. **HABITAT:** Coniferous forests, particularly in burned areas and where deadwood is present. Casual vagrant south of range in East.

BLACK-BACKED WOODPECKER *Picoides arcticus* Scarce

9½ in. (24 cm). Note combination of *solid black back* and *barred sides.* Male has *yellow cap.* This and preceding species inhabit boreal and montane forests; their presence can be detected by patches of bark scaled from dead conifers. **VOICE:** Low flat *kuk* or *puk* and a short buzzy call. **SIMILAR SPECIES:** American Three-toed and Hairy Woodpeckers. **HABITAT:** Coniferous forests, particularly in burned areas and where deadwood is present.

WOODPECKERS

male

male

female

NUTTALL'S WOODPECKER

LADDER-BACKED WOODPECKER

female

eastern male

western and southwestern male

Rockies male

female

northwestern male

Rockies and eastern male

female

DOWNY WOODPECKER

HAIRY WOODPECKER

female

Rockies male

northern male

AMERICAN THREE-TOED WOODPECKER

male

female

BLACK-BACKED WOODPECKER

ARIZONA WOODPECKER *Dryobates arizonae* Uncommon, local

7½ in. (19 cm). A *brown-backed* woodpecker with *white-striped face;* spotted and barred below. Male has red nape patch. The only U.S. woodpecker with *solid brown* back. **VOICE:** Sharp *spik;* a hoarse whinny. Fairly similar to Hairy Woodpecker's calls. **SIMILAR SPECIES:** Ladder-backed, Downy, and Hairy Woodpeckers. **HABITAT:** Canyon woodlands of oak, juniper, and pine-oak.

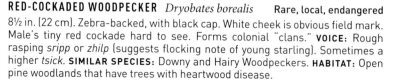

RED-COCKADED WOODPECKER *Dryobates borealis* Rare, local, endangered

8½ in. (22 cm). Zebra-backed, with black cap. White cheek is obvious field mark. Male's tiny red cockade hard to see. Forms colonial "clans." **VOICE:** Rough rasping *sripp* or *zhilp* (suggests flocking note of young starling). Sometimes a higher *tsick.* **SIMILAR SPECIES:** Downy and Hairy Woodpeckers. **HABITAT:** Open pine woodlands that have trees with heartwood disease.

WHITE-HEADED WOODPECKER *Dryobates albolarvatus* Uncommon

9¼ in. (23 cm). Our only woodpecker with *white head.* Male (but not female) has red patch on nape; otherwise black overall, with large white patch in primaries. No white on rump (as in Acorn Woodpecker). **VOICE:** Sharp, doubled *ki-dik,* sometimes rapidly repeated, *chick-ik-ik-ik;* also a rattle similar to Downy Woodpecker's. **SIMILAR SPECIES:** Downy and Hairy Woodpecker calls are *single, not double,* notes. **HABITAT:** Mountain pine forests, particularly ponderosa, Jeffrey, and sugar pines.

PILEATED WOODPECKER *Dryocopus pileatus* Uncommon

16½–17 in. (42–44 cm). A spectacular, *crow-sized* woodpecker, black with flaming red *crest.* Female has blackish forehead, lacks red on mustache. Great size, sweeping wingbeats, and flashing white underwing coverts identify Pileated in flight. Large foraging pits in dead or dying trees—large *oval* or *oblong* holes—indicate its presence. **VOICE:** Call resembles that of a flicker, but louder, deeper, irregular: *kik-kik-kikkik-kik-kik,* etc. Also a more ringing, double-note call that may rise or fall slightly in pitch and volume. **SIMILAR SPECIES:** Ivory-billed Woodpecker (probably extinct). **HABITAT:** Coniferous, mixed, and hardwood forests with large mature trees; woodlots.

IVORY-BILLED WOODPECKER Almost certainly extinct
Campephilus principalis

19–19½ in. (40–50 cm). Separated from Pileated Woodpecker by its slightly larger size, longer wings, ivory white bill, large white upperwing patch in secondaries, visible at rest, and all-white underwing pattern with black line through it. Female has black crest. **VOICE:** A single loud tooting note constantly uttered as bird forages—a sharp nasal *kent* suggesting to some a big nuthatch. Drum is a quick double knock, unique among N. American woodpeckers. **SIMILAR SPECIES:** Pileated Woodpecker. **RANGE:** Throughout the Southeast. Reports persist, but the last documented sightings of this conspicuous species were in the 1940s. **HABITAT:** Bottomland hardwood forests, wooded bayous and swamps.

WOODPECKERS

male

male

(female lacks red "cockade")

female

RED-COCKADED WOODPECKER

ARIZONA WOODPECKER

PILEATED WOODPECKER

female

male

female

male

WHITE-HEADED WOODPECKER

Pileated below

IVORY-BILLED WOODPECKER

below

male

above

TROGONS Family Trogonidae

Solitary forest birds with short necks, stubby bills, long tails, and very small feet. Erect when perched. May remain motionless for long periods, then explode in a flutter when plucking berries. **FOOD:** Small fruit, insects. **RANGE:** Mainly tropical parts of world.

EARED QUETZAL *Euptilotis neoxenus* — Very rare

13½–14 in. (35–36 cm). Compared to Elegant Trogon, note *black* bill, *lack of white breast-band*, and mostly *white* underside of blue tail. **VOICE:** High-pitched, rising squeal; series of whistled notes. **RANGE AND HABITAT:** Very rare visitor from Mex. to mountains and canyons in se. AZ, accidental to cen. AZ.

ELEGANT TROGON *Trogon elegans* — Uncommon, local

12–12½ in. (31–32 cm). *Adult male:* Note *geranium red belly, white breast-band,* yellow bill, and *finely barred underside of tail* (coppery above). *Female:* Brown head with *white mark* on cheek. First-year male mottled red and green. **VOICE:** Series of low, coarse notes: *kowm kowm kowm kowm kowm kowm* or *koa, koa, koa,* etc. **HABITAT:** Mountain forests, pine-oak and sycamore canyons.

SWIFTS Family Apodidae

Swallowlike in habits, but structurally distinct, with shorter forewing, and feet with all four toes pointing forward. Flight very rapid, "twinkling," and sailing; narrow wings often stiffly bowed. Ages and sexes similar. **FOOD:** Flying insects. **RANGE:** Nearly worldwide.

VAUX'S SWIFT *Chaetura vauxi* — Uncommon

4¾ in. (12 cm). A small swift, with rapid wingbeats; glides with wings bowed in a crescent; small size, dingy underparts. **VOICE:** High-pitched, rapid ticking or chippering notes, often run into an insectlike trill. **SIMILAR SPECIES:** Chimney Swift is slightly larger and longer winged, has darker throat and rump, and louder chippering call. **HABITAT:** Open sky over woodlands, lakes, and rivers; can roost in chimneys during migration. Casual to scarce vagrant to East, particularly Gulf Coast.

CHIMNEY SWIFT *Chaetura pelagica* — Common

5¼ in. (13 cm). Like a cigar with wings. A dark swift with long, slightly curved, stiff wings and stubby tail. **VOICE:** Loud, rapid ticking or twittering notes. **SIMILAR SPECIES:** In West, see Vaux's and Black Swifts. Also see swallows. **HABITAT:** Open sky, especially over cities, towns; nests and roosts in chimneys (originally in large hollow trees and cliff crevices). Casual vagrant to W. Coast.

BLACK SWIFT *Cypseloides niger* — Uncommon, local

7¼ in. (18 cm). A large *blackish* swift with noticeable notched tail (sometimes fanned), deeper in adult male. At close range, a touch of white on forehead. Slower wingbeats than in other U.S. swifts. **VOICE:** Sharp *plik-plik-plik-plik-plik,* etc., at nest site. **SIMILAR SPECIES:** Vaux's and Chimney Swifts much smaller, Vaux's with paler throat. **HABITAT:** Favors mountain country, coastal cliffs; nests on sea cliffs and behind waterfalls. Accidental in East.

WHITE-THROATED SWIFT *Aeronautes saxatalis* — Uncommon

6½ in. (17 cm). Separated from other N. American swifts by its contrasting *black-and-white pattern,* long slim tail. **VOICE:** Shrill, excited *jejejejeje,* in descending scale, similar to Canyon Wren song. **SIMILAR SPECIES:** Other swifts and swallows. **HABITAT:** Breeds mainly in dry mountains, canyons, cliffs; locally on sea cliffs and man-made structures. Casual vagrant to Gulf Coast.

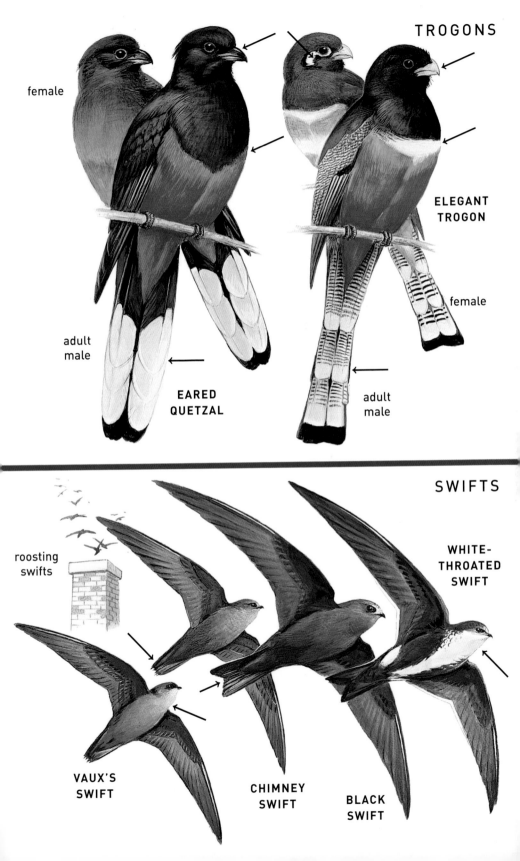

TROGONS

female

adult male

EARED QUETZAL

ELEGANT TROGON

female

adult male

SWIFTS

roosting swifts

WHITE-THROATED SWIFT

VAUX'S SWIFT

CHIMNEY SWIFT

BLACK SWIFT

HUMMINGBIRDS Family Trochilidae

The smallest of the world's birds, with needlelike bills for sipping nectar. Adult males of most species with jewel-like, iridescent gorget throat and sometimes crown feathers; in poor light feathers can appear dark. Hummingbirds hover when feeding and can fly backward; their wingbeats are so rapid that they appear as a blur. Pugnacious. Vocal differences can be important identification aids. **FOOD:** Nectar (red flowers favored), small insects, spiders. **RANGE:** W. Hemisphere; majority in Tropics.

RUBY-THROATED HUMMINGBIRD *Archilochus colubris*   Fairly common

3¾ in. (10 cm). *Adult male: Fiery red throat,* iridescent green back, forked tail. *Female:* Lacks red throat; tail blunt, with white spots. *First-fall male:* Like female but tail slightly forked, a few scattered ruby feathers molt during fall. *The only widespread species in East;* several other hummers may turn up as strays, especially in se. states in fall and winter. **VOICE:** Male's wings hum in courtship display. Chase calls high, squeaky. Other call a soft *chew.* **SIMILAR SPECIES:** Male Broad-tailed Hummingbird lacks forked tail, typically makes wing-trill sound. Female and first-fall male similar to Black-chinned Hummingbird but have *brighter green crown and back,* shorter bill; *outermost primary is narrower and straighter at tip,* more club-shaped in Black-chinned. See also Anna's and Costa's Hummingbirds. **HABITAT:** Flowers, gardens, wood edges, over streams. Casual vagrant to W. Coast.

COSTA'S HUMMINGBIRD *Calypte costae*   Uncommon

3½ in. (9 cm). *Adult male:* Note *purple* or *amethyst* throat and crown. Feathers of gorget *project* markedly rearward at sides and can be flared during courtship or disputes. *Female and first-fall male:* Similar to other hummingbirds but whiter, especially on throat. The inner six primaries of *Calypte* are the same width as the outer primaries, whereas those of *Archilochus* are thinner. **VOICE:** Series of pipping notes. Male in display, a rising *zing.* **SIMILAR SPECIES:** Females and first-fall males very similar to those of Black-chinned Hummingbird, but duller green above, shorter bill and tail, inner primaries broader, *voices differ.* Female Anna's Hummingbird slightly larger, mottled, gray and green on sides. **HABITAT:** Deserts, coastal sage scrub, chaparral, arid hillsides, feeders. Casual vagrant to E. and Gulf Coasts.

BLACK-CHINNED HUMMINGBIRD *Archilochus alexandri*   Fairly common

3¾ in. (10 cm). *Adult male:* Note *black throat* and conspicuous white collar; iridescent blue-violet of lower throat shows only in certain lights. *Female and first-fall male:* Similar to these plumages in Ruby-throated Hummingbird but crown often grayish, back duller, bill longer. **VOICE:** Like Ruby-throated. **SIMILAR SPECIES:** Ruby-throated, Costa's, and Anna's Hummingbirds. *Caution:* Throats of other adult male hummers may look black until they catch light. **HABITAT:** Riparian woodlands, wooded canyons, semiarid country, chaparral, suburbs, feeders. Rare vagrant to E. and Gulf Coasts.

ANNA'S HUMMINGBIRD *Calypte anna*   Common

4 in. (10 cm). *Adult male:* The only U.S. hummer with rose *red crown;* throat also rose red. *Female and first-summer male:* Slightly larger than other hummers, grayer below, with green sides and more heavily spotted throat than female Costa's or Black-chinned Hummingbird; adult female has small, red, central throat patch. First-fall male gains mottled red throat and crown. The only hummingbird commonly found along Pacific Coast in winter. **VOICE:** Feeding call *chick.* Chase call a raspy chatter. Song from perch squeaking, grating notes, and when diving in its aerial display male makes *sharp popping sound* (with tail) at bottom of arc. **SIMILAR SPECIES:** Black-chinned and Costa's Hummingbirds. Vocal differences important. **HABITAT:** Gardens, parks, feeders, chaparral, open woods. Casual vagrant to E. and Gulf Coasts.

adult male

adult male

RUBY-
THROATED
HUMMINGBIRD

sphinx moths resemble
hummingbirds

female and
first-fall male

adult
male

adult
male

female and
first-fall
male

female and
first-fall male

COSTA'S
HUMMINGBIRD

BLACK-CHINNED
HUMMINGBIRD

adult
male

adult
female

ANNA'S
HUMMINGBIRD

BROAD-TAILED HUMMINGBIRD *Selasphorus platycercus*   Fairly common

4 in. (10 cm). Tail long, the central feathers broad relative to other hummers in our area. *Adult male:* Crown and back green; throat bright *rose red,* greenish on sides. *Female and first-fall male:* Slightly larger and larger-tailed than female Black-chinned Hummingbird; sides tinged with buff; touch of rufous at basal corners of tail. Male known by *shrill trilling* sound of wings (*except when in molt, on winter grounds*). **VOICE:** A variety of vocal sounds. *Chi-chewee chi-chewee* often given in flight. Call a sharp *chit!* **SIMILAR SPECIES:** Female and first-fall male Calliope Hummingbirds smaller, with smaller bill; at rest *wingtips extend beyond short, square-cut tail.* Female and first-fall male Rufous Hummingbirds have smaller tail, usually richer rufous on sides and more rufous in tail. Male Ruby-throated Hummingbird smaller with forked tail. **HABITAT:** Mountains and canyons; common at feeders. Casual vagrant to E. and Gulf Coasts.

RUFOUS HUMMINGBIRD *Selasphorus rufus*   Common

3¾ in. (9–10 cm). *Adult male:* No other N. American hummingbird has bright *rufous or red-brown upperparts,* sometimes mottled green but rufous predominates; throat flaming orange-red. Aerial display is a closed ellipse, slowing on return climb. *Female and first-fall male:* Green-backed; dull *rufous on sides and at base of outer tail feathers* (visible when tail fully spread). Adult females and first-fall birds show iridescent orange-red feathers on throat. **VOICE:** Aggressive flight call a buzzy *zap* followed by sputtering notes, or *zeee chippity chippity.* Male's wings make high trill in flight. **SIMILAR SPECIES:** Allen's, Calliope, and Broad-tailed Hummingbirds. **HABITAT:** Wooded or brushy areas, parks, gardens, feeders; in southbound migration, also mountain meadows. Scarce vagrant to E. and Gulf Coasts.

ALLEN'S HUMMINGBIRD *Selasphorus sasin*   Fairly common

3¾ in. (9–10 cm). *Adult male:* Like Rufous Hummingbird (*rufous* sides, rump, tail, and cheeks; fiery throat), but back *green,* sometimes mottled orange but green predominates. *Female and first-fall male:* Very difficult to distinguish in field from those of Rufous, especially in Mar.–May and July–Aug. when both species co-occur in CA; Allen's has narrower rectrices, and these can sometimes be used with experience to separate birds of known age and sex to species. **VOICE:** Flight call similar to that of Rufous. Aerial display of male unlike that of Rufous. Starts "pendulum display" in a shallow arc and after several swoops goes into steep climb and swoops back, with an air-splitting *vrrrip.* **SIMILAR SPECIES:** Rufous Hummingbird. See also female Broad-tailed and Calliope Hummingbirds. **HABITAT:** Scrubby or brushy slopes, riparian areas, parks, gardens, feeders. Accidental vagrant to E. and Gulf Coasts.

CALLIOPE HUMMINGBIRD *Selasphorus calliope*   Uncommon

3¼ in. (8 cm). The smallest hummer found in U.S. and Canada. *Adult male:* Throat with purple-red rays on white background (may be folded like a dark inverted V on white throat); the only U.S. hummingbird with this effect. *Female and first-fall male:* Similar to female Broad-tailed and Rufous Hummingbirds (which have buffy sides, some rufous at base of tail), but Calliope has a *shorter wedge-shaped tail (wingtips extend beyond tail at rest),* slightly smaller, and shorter billed; rust on sides paler, face pattern has dark and pale spots in front of eye, weak pale line over base of bill. **VOICE:** High-pitched chips and buzzes in series. **HABITAT:** Mountains and canyons, feeders; in migration, also foothills and occasionally lowlands. Casual vagrant to E. and Gulf Coasts.

adult male

female and first-fall male

BROAD-TAILED HUMMINGBIRD

RUFOUS HUMMINGBIRD

adult male

female and first-fall male

adult male

ALLEN'S HUMMINGBIRD

adult male

female and first-fall male

CALLIOPE HUMMINGBIRD

BROAD-BILLED HUMMINGBIRD *Cynanthus latirostris*   Uncommon, local

4 in. (10 cm). *Adult male:* Dark green above and below, with *blue throat* (bird may look all black at a distance or in poor light). Bill *reddish* with black tip. Tail notched and *bluish black*, often flicked when hovering. *Female:* Identified by combination of *dull orange-red base to bill* (often restricted to lower mandible), *dark tail*, and *unmarked, pearly gray* throat; thin white line behind eye. *First-year male:* Femalelike as juvenile but mottled male coloration increases through year. **VOICE:** Distinctive rough, dry chattering, like that of Ruby-crowned Kinglet, diagnostic among hummingbirds in our area. **SIMILAR SPECIES:** White-eared Hummingbird. **HABITAT:** Desert canyons, mountain slopes, riparian woodlands, agaves, mesquite, feeders. Casual vagrant to CA, and to E. and Gulf Coasts.

VIOLET-CROWNED HUMMINGBIRD *Amazilia violiceps*   Scarce, local

4½ in. (11 cm). A medium-sized hummer with *immaculate white underparts, including throat;* bill *red with dark tip. Crown violet-blue* in adult, *dull greenish blue* in first-year birds; sexes similar although adult males average brighter crowns. No iridescent gorget on male. **VOICE:** Aggressive call a series of squeaky notes. Call note *chak.* **SIMILAR SPECIES:** Costa's Hummingbird white below but smaller, bill without red. **HABITAT:** Riparian woodlands, lower canyons, sycamores, agaves, feeders. Accidental vagrant to CA.

WHITE-EARED HUMMINGBIRD *Hylocharis leucotis*   Rare, local

3¾ in. (10 cm). A rare but regular summer visitor to s. AZ mountains. *Adult male:* Bill short, orangey red, with black tip; *broad white stripe behind eye.* Underparts dark greenish, throat blue and green, crown purple. *Female:* Orangey red bill, bold white stripe behind eye. Note small *green spots* on throat. *First-year male:* Femalelike but gradually acquires blue-green in breast, purple crown. **VOICE:** Makes a variety of thin *chips*, sometimes in rapid series. **SIMILAR SPECIES:** Female Broad-billed Hummingbird often mistaken for rarer White-eared (reddish-based bill and pronounced white eye stripe), but note *vocal differences* and Broad-billed's slightly longer bill, slightly shorter white eyebrow, more forked tail, and evenly gray throat and underparts. **HABITAT:** Montane pine-oak woods near streams; feeders.

BLUE-THROATED MOUNTAIN-GEM *Lampornis clemenciae*   Uncommon, local

5 in. (13 cm). Formerly known as Blue-throated Hummingbird. Note large tail with *large white patches. Male:* A very large hummingbird, with black and white stripes about eye and *blue throat;* big black tail with large white patches at corners. First-year male has duller and more-restricted blue in throat. *Female:* Large, with *evenly gray* throat and underparts, white marks on face, and tail with *large white corners,* as in male. **VOICE:** Call a distinctive squeaking *seek.* **SIMILAR SPECIES:** Rivoli's Hummingbird, Plain-capped Starthroat. **HABITAT:** Near wooded streams in mountain canyons; feeders. Casual vagrant north of range.

RIVOLI'S HUMMINGBIRD *Eugenes fulgens*   Uncommon

5¼ in. (13 cm). Recently split from Magnificent Hummingbird. *Adult male:* A very large hummingbird with *blackish belly, bright green throat,* and *purple crown.* Can look all black at a distance. Sometimes the bird briefly glides on set wings. *Female:* Large; greenish above, washed with greenish or dusky below. First-year male is femalelike but mottled male coloration increases through year. **VOICE:** Call a thin, sharp *chip;* distinctive. **SIMILAR SPECIES:** Female told from female Blue-throated Mountain-gem by voice, more mottled underparts, short eye stripe, and tail with greenish and more obscure pale corners. **HABITAT:** Mountain glades, pine-oak woods, canyons, feeders. Casual vagrant north of range; accidental to CA, Gulf Coast.

WHITE-EARED
HUMMINGBIRD

male

female

adult
male

BROAD-BILLED
HUMMINGBIRD

female

VIOLET-CROWNED
HUMMINGBIRD

female

adult
male

male

adult
male

female

female

BLUE-THROATED
MOUNTAIN-GEM

RIVOLI'S
HUMMINGBIRD

MEXICAN VIOLETEAR *Colibri thalassinus*   Casual vagrant
4¾ in. (12 cm). Recently split from Green Violetear. Stray from Mex., most records in summer from TX but records throughout U.S. A large, dark hummingbird. Sexes mostly similar. Green with violet ear patch, bluish tail. Bill long and slightly decurved. **VOICE:** Song and call a series of dry *chips*. **SIMILAR SPECIES:** Broad-billed and Rivoli's Hummingbirds. **RANGE AND HABITAT:** Mountains, canyons; in U.S., almost always seen at feeders.

GREEN-BREASTED MANGO *Anthracothorax prevostii*   Casual vagrant
4¾ in. (12 cm). Stray from Mex. and the Caribbean, primarily to s. TX but also as far afield as NC and WI. Almost always at feeders. Large, with long downcurved bill. *Adult male:* Dark emerald green above with velvety black throat edged in emerald. Center of belly deep blue-green. Tail purple. *Female:* Paler green back, light underparts with irregular dark stripe from throat to belly. Dusky tail. *First-year male:* Accounts for most sightings north of border; similar to female, but lacks stripe on chin; gradually obtains dark green body feathering. **VOICE:** Call a high-pitched *tzat*. Song a metallic series of two-part notes. **SIMILAR SPECIES:** Other all-dark hummingbirds.

BUFF-BELLIED HUMMINGBIRD *Amazilia yucatanensis*   Uncommon, local
4¼ in. (11 cm). Note combination of buff underparts, rufous tail, and green throat. Bill orange-red with dark tip. Ages and sexes similar. **VOICE:** Call a surprisingly loud *smak smak smak*. Aggressive flight call an unmusical buzz: *chr chr chr chr chr*. **SIMILAR SPECIES:** Extremely rare Berylline Hummingbird similar in appearance but wings with more rufous; does not overlap in range within our area. **HABITAT:** Open woodlands, gardens, feeders. Casual vagrant to Gulf Coast states.

BERYLLINE HUMMINGBIRD *Amazilia beryllina*   Rare
4¼ in. (11 cm). Mexican species; rare visitor and casual breeder in se. AZ. *Male:* Glittering green on underparts; *deep rich rufous* in *wings*, rump, and tail. Bill partly red. *Female:* Duller; throat and belly mottled gray. **VOICE:** All vocal sounds very scratchy and buzzy. **SIMILAR SPECIES:** Buff-bellied Hummingbird. **HABITAT:** Oak-clad mountain canyons, often at feeders.

LUCIFER HUMMINGBIRD *Calothorax lucifer*   Scarce, local
3½ in. (9 cm). A small hummingbird. Note pronounced *decurved bill*. *Adult male:* Purple throat, rusty or buffy sides. *No* purple on crown (as in Costa's Hummingbird); tail *deeply forked*, often folded. *Female:* Decurved bill, underparts extensively buff, rufous at base of outer tail feathers; older birds sometimes have purple in throat. First-year male is like female but tail shallowly forked, gradually acquires purple in throat. **VOICE:** Series of dry twitters. Male in courtship display makes "playing-card shuffle" sound. **SIMILAR SPECIES:** Black-chinned Hummingbird's long bill may also have slight curve. **HABITAT:** Arid slopes, agaves, feeders. Accidental vagrant to Gulf Coast.

PLAIN-CAPPED STARTHROAT *Heliomaster constantii*   Casual vagrant
5 in. (13 cm). Mexican species, casual visitor at lower elevations in s. AZ. Sexes similar. A large, *long-billed* hummer, adult with red throat, *white facial stripes, white rump. Juvenile:* Throat gray, gradually acquires red throat feathers through first year. Often hawks insects. **VOICE:** Variety of strong *chips* given singly or in series. **SIMILAR SPECIES:** Blue-throated Mountain-gem, Rivoli's and Anna's Hummingbirds. **HABITAT:** Creek beds, dry washes, often at feeders.

male

MEXICAN
VIOLETEAR

adult
male

female

GREEN-
BREASTED
MANGO

BUFF-BELLIED
HUMMINGBIRD

female

male

BERYLLINE
HUMMINGBIRD

adult
male

female

tail may
fold in a
spikelike
point

LUCIFER
HUMMINGBIRD

adult

PLAIN-CAPPED
STARTHROAT

PASSERINES Order Passeriformes

Passerines, also known as "perching birds" or "songbirds," comprise the rest of the species in this book. They are distinguished by having one toe back and three forward, ideal for perching.

TYRANT FLYCATCHERS Family Tyrannidae

New World or Tyrant flycatchers make up the largest family of birds in the world, with approximately 425 known species. Many can be difficult to identify. Most species perch quietly, sitting upright on exposed branches, from which they sally forth to snap up insects. Bill flattened, with bristles at base. Ages and sexes similar in most but not all species. **FOOD:** Mainly flying insects. Some species also eat fruit in winter. **RANGE:** New World.

OLIVE-SIDED FLYCATCHER *Contopus cooperi*   Uncommon

7½ in. (19 cm). A stout, large-headed flycatcher; often perches on dead snags at tops of trees. Note large bill and *dark chest patches* separated by narrow strip of white (like unbuttoned vest). A *cottony tuft* may poke from behind wing. **VOICE:** Call a two- or three-note *pip-pip-pip.* Song a spirited whistle, *I SAY there* or *Quick three beers!,* middle note highest, last one sliding. **SIMILAR SPECIES:** Wood-pewees, Greater Pewee. **HABITAT:** Coniferous forests, bogs, burns.

GREATER PEWEE *Contopus pertinax*   Uncommon, local

7¾ in. (20 cm). Resembles Olive-sided Flycatcher, but more obvious crest, breast more uniformly gray with *no white stripe* down center. *Lower mandible brighter and more extensively orangey.* **VOICE:** Thin, plaintive whistle, *ho-say, ma-re-ah.* Call *pip-pip.* **SIMILAR SPECIES:** Olive-sided Flycatcher. **HABITAT:** High in trees of pine and pine-oak forests, canyons. Casual to s. CA.

WESTERN WOOD-PEWEE *Contopus sordidulus*   Fairly common

6¼ in. (16 cm). A dusky, medium-small flycatcher with two narrow wing bars but *no eye-ring.* Often appears "vested" below (with "top button buttoned"). Black bill usually has small amount of pale at base of lower mandible. **VOICE:** Nasal *peeeer* (less commonly, *pee-yee*), more guttural (less clear) than in Eastern Wood-Pewee. **SIMILAR SPECIES:** Eastern Wood-Pewee. Olive-sided Flycatcher larger, more strongly "vested," different voice. Distinguished from *Empidonax* flycatchers by lack of any tail flicking, longer primaries, and calls; most *Empidonax* also have eye-rings. **HABITAT:** Pine-oak forests, open conifers, canyon and riparian woodlands. Prefers mid-canopy. Casual vagrant to E. Coast.

EASTERN WOOD-PEWEE *Contopus virens*   Fairly common

6¼ in. (16 cm). Note *two narrow wing bars, no eye-ring,* and variably pale orangish lower mandible. *Slightly larger* than *Empidonax* flycatchers, but with no eye-ring; wings extend farther down tail; *does not flick tail.* Very similar to Western Wood-Pewee, but slightly greener or paler gray above and clearer below (vest "not buttoned"); best distinguished by voice, range. **VOICE:** Sweet plaintive whistle, *pee-a-wee,* slurring down then up (less commonly, *pee-ur*), and a *chip.* **SIMILAR SPECIES:** Western Wood-Pewee. Eastern Phoebe lacks wing bars. **HABITAT:** Woodlands, groves. Mid-canopy. Casual vagrant to W. Coast.

NORTHERN BEARDLESS-TYRANNULET
Camptostoma imberbe   Uncommon, local

4¼ in. (11 cm). A very small, nondescript flycatcher suggesting a kinglet or Verdin. Grayish olive, *slight crest, dull wing bars.* **VOICE:** Thin *peeee-yuk.* A gentle, descending *ee, ee, ee, ee, ee.* **SIMILAR SPECIES:** *Empidonax* flycatchers are larger and larger-headed. **HABITAT:** Lowland woods, mesquite, stream thickets, lower canyons. Builds a globular nest with entrance on side.

FLYCATCHERS

OLIVE-SIDED
FLYCATCHER

GREATER
PEWEE

WESTERN
WOOD-PEWEE

EASTERN
WOOD-PEWEE

NORTHERN
BEARDLESS-TYRANNULET

EMPIDONAX FLYCATCHERS

Flycatchers of this genus display light eye-ring and two pale wing bars. Species are difficult to separate, especially cross-continental vagrants. When breeding, they can be identified by habitat, songs, and calls. Distinguishing characters of silent birds, including migrants, include size, shape, and color of bill, shape and boldness of eye-ring, color of wings and wing-feather edging, primary projection, tail length, and direction of tail wag.

ACADIAN FLYCATCHER *Empidonax virescens*   Fairly common

5¾ in. (15 cm). A large and elongated *greenish Empidonax* with *pale* underparts, thin eye-ring, and thin, *long* bill with yellow lower mandible. First years in fall (p. 268): brighter, yellower below. **VOICE:** "Song" a sharp explosive *pit-see!* or *wee-see!* (sharp upward inflection); also a sharp *peet*. **SIMILAR SPECIES:** Other eastern *Empidonax*. Whitish chin and throat can be used to separate Acadian from Yellow-bellied Flycatcher. **HABITAT:** Shady deciduous forests, ravines, swampy woods, beech and hemlock groves. Accidental vagrant to AZ.

YELLOW-BELLIED FLYCATCHER *Empidonax flaviventris*   Uncommon

5½ in. (14 cm). *Breeding adult:* Back green, rounded yellowish eye-ring, dusky breast-band, wings blackish with bold whitish edging. First-years in fall (p. 268) much yellower below, including *chin and throat*. **VOICE:** Song a simple, spiritless *chi-lek;* also a rising *chu-wee;* call an explosive *peeyup,* distinct among *Empidonax*. **SIMILAR SPECIES:** Among other eastern *Empidonax,* only Acadian is so green above but Acadian has *white* throat and *paler,* less olive-washed breast. Cordilleran and Pacific-slope Flycatchers very similar but slightly browner, with peaked head; *teardrop-shaped eye-ring;* duller wings and wing-feather edging. **HABITAT:** In summer, boreal forests, muskeg, bogs. Casual vagrant to W. Coast.

LEAST FLYCATCHER *Empidonax minimus*   Fairly common

5¼ in. (13 cm). A small *Empidonax,* plumage variable but usually *grayish* above and *pale* below with *bold white eye-ring,* medium-short wingtip projection, and short, wide-based bill. Whitish wing bars on mostly blackish wing. First years in fall (p. 268) fresher, greener and yellower. Actively flicks tail. **VOICE:** Song an emphatic, sharply snapped *che-bek!* Call a sharp, dry *whit.* **SIMILAR SPECIES:** Willow and Alder Flycatchers are browner above with bigger bill, longer wingtips, and weaker eye-ring. Hammond's and Dusky Flycatchers have darker throat and underparts, duller wings. Hammond's also has *thinner, darker bill,* more teardrop-shaped eye-ring, and longer wingtips. **HABITAT:** Deciduous and mixed woodlands, poplars, aspens. Rare vagrant to W. Coast.

WILLOW FLYCATCHER *Empidonax traillii*   Fairly common

5¾ in. (15 cm). Alder and Willow Flycatchers are nearly identical in appearance, a bit larger, longer billed, and often browner than Least Flycatcher. They may be separated from each other mainly by voice and breeding habitat. Willow averages paler and browner (less olive) and has grayer head than Alder, has a slightly weaker or no eye-ring, and duller wing-feather edging on average. **VOICE:** Song a sneezy *fitz-bew,* unlike the *fee-BE-o* of Alder. Call a soft *whit.* **HABITAT:** Bushes, willow thickets, etc.; often in drier situations (brushy fields, upland copses, etc.) than Alder, but can be found in close proximity where ranges overlap. Subspecies of Southwest *(estimus)* endangered.

ALDER FLYCATCHER *Empidonax alnorum*   Fairly common

5¾ in. (15 cm). The northern counterpart of Willow Flycatcher, with which it was formerly lumped as "Traill's Flycatcher." Greener, smaller-billed, and with brighter wing-feather edging than Willow but best distinguished by voice. **VOICE:** Song an accented *fee-BE-o* or *rree-BE-o.* Call *kep* or *pit,* sharper than in Willow. **HABITAT:** Willows, alders, brushy swamps, swales. Usually in moister areas than Willow. Casual vagrant to W. Coast.

Adults on Breeding Grounds

pit-see!

EMPIDONAX FLYCATCHERS

Empidonax flycatchers are often best identified by voice. Breeding habitat is also a helpful clue.

chi-lek

deciduous woods, especially beech trees; wooded swamps; s. and cen. U.S.

coniferous woods, bogs; Canada, n. edge of U.S.

ACADIAN FLYCATCHER

greener than Least, Alder, or Willow

LEAST FLYCATCHER

che-BEK or *chebek*

YELLOW-BELLIED FLYCATCHER

throat and breast washed with yellow

farms, orchards, groves, open woods; n. U.S. and Canada

grayest of eastern species

fitz-bew

fee-bee´-o

wet and dry thickets, brushy pastures, old orchards, willows; mostly in U.S.

WILLOW FLYCATCHER

alder swamps, wet thickets, usually near water; n. U.S., Canada

ALDER FLYCATCHER

BUFF-BREASTED FLYCATCHER *Empidonax fulvifrons*   Scarce, local

5 in. (13 cm). Easily distinguished from the other *Empidonax* by its small size and *rich buffy breast*. **VOICE:** Accented *chee-lik*. Call a dry *pit* or *whit*. **SIMILAR SPECIES:** Northern Beardless-Tyrannulet. **HABITAT:** High-elevation canyons, open pine forests. Accidental vagrant to CA.

PACIFIC-SLOPE FLYCATCHER *Empidonax difficilis*   Common

5½ in. (14 cm). This species and Cordilleran Flycatcher formerly considered conspecific, as "Western Flycatcher." Silent birds impossible to tell apart with certainty. Voice and range are best identification clues. Pacific-slope Flycatcher slightly less colorful than Cordilleran but much overlap. Both species have greenish to olive upperparts and *yellowish* underparts, *including throat*. First years in fall (p. 268) duller olive above, dingier below. Other western *Empidonax* may have wash of yellow, especially in fall, but their throats are gray or whitish and they are less green above. Eye-ring of Pacific-slope and Cordilleran is *tear-drop-shaped and broken above*. **VOICE:** Song of both a thin, squeaky *pit-PEET SWEEE*; variable. Call a thin upslurred *tsueet*. **SIMILAR SPECIES:** Cordilleran and Yellow-bellied Flycatchers. **HABITAT:** Riparian, mixed, or coniferous woodlands. This or Cordilleran casual vagrant to East, accidental to E. Coast.

CORDILLERAN FLYCATCHER *Empidonax occidentalis*   Uncommon

5½ in. (14 cm). This species and Pacific-slope Flycatcher were split and are not possible to tell apart, except by range and voice. **VOICE:** Song similar to that of Pacific-slope; variable. Call a two-noted *soo-seet*. **SIMILAR SPECIES:** Pacific-slope and Yellow-bellied Flycatchers. **HABITAT:** Riparian, mixed, or coniferous woodlands; shaded canyons, often with rock walls.

HAMMOND'S FLYCATCHER *Empidonax hammondii*   Fairly common

5½ in. (14 cm). Both Hammond's and Dusky Flycatchers breed in coniferous and mixed woods, with Hammond's preferring a more closed canopy. Hammond's has more *teardrop-shaped eye-ring*; slightly *shorter and thinner bill* (almost kingletlike); is more prone to flick wings; has slightly shorter tail and longer wings. In late summer and fall it molts *before* migrating, after which both age groups (p. 268) more greenish above and yellowish below with grayer throat. **VOICE:** Song typically three-parted and similar to that of Dusky Flycatcher but slightly lower pitched. Abrupt *tse-beek*. Call a sharp, thin *peep* or *peek*. **SIMILAR SPECIES:** Dusky Flycatcher. Least Flycatcher has blacker wings with brighter edging, wider and thicker bill, shorter wingtips, and lacks pale edges to tail. **HABITAT:** Woodlands with coniferous component; in migration through lowlands, other trees, thickets. Rare vagrant to East, casual to E. Coast.

DUSKY FLYCATCHER *Empidonax oberholseri*   Uncommon

5¾ in. (15 cm). Very similar to Hammond's Flycatcher; see that account for differences. First years in fall (p. 268) greener, yellower. **VOICE:** Three-part song ends in a high *preet*. Call a dry *whit*. **SIMILAR SPECIES:** Least, Hammond's, and Gray Flycatchers. **HABITAT:** Breeds in open pine forests, montane chaparral with scattering of trees, brushy meadow and stream edges. Casual vagrant to East, accidental to E. Coast.

GRAY FLYCATCHER *Empidonax wrightii*   Uncommon

6 in. (15 cm). Similar to Dusky and Hammond's Flycatchers, but in spring and summer paler and grayer overall; bill larger, and lower mandible mostly pinkish with a distinct black tip. In fall and early winter (p. 268), trace of yellow below, olive above, more similar to Dusky Flycatcher. Has habit of *first wagging tail downward* like a phoebe, then bringing it back up (all other *Empidonax* flick tail upward); best noted immediately after bird lands. **VOICE:** Two-syllable *chewip* or *cheh-we*. Call a dry *whit*. **SIMILAR SPECIES:** Other western *Empidonax*. **HABITAT:** Dry pine forests with sagebrush, pinyon-juniper; in winter, willows, mesquite. Often drops to ground to grab prey. Casual vagrant to East, accidental to E. Coast.

WESTERN *EMPIDONAX* FLYCATCHERS

Adults on Breeding Grounds

Empidonax flycatchers are often best identified by voice. Breeding habitat is also a helpful clue.

BUFF-BREASTED FLYCATCHER
oak-pine canyons; AZ, NM

PACIFIC-SLOPE FLYCATCHER and CORDILLERAN FLYCATCHER
moist woods, groves, shady canyons; generally not separable except by range

cheeLIK *CHEWW*

zvREET

pit-PEET *swEEE*

PIT-ik

PRI-drt *PRRDT*

chVREE

SEE-pik

HAMMOND'S FLYCATCHER
closed-canopy coniferous forests

chwEEP *CHI-wik*

DUSKY FLYCATCHER
montane chaparral, open coniferous woodlands

GRAY FLYCATCHER
sagebrush, pinyon-juniper

FIRST-FALL *EMPIDONAX* FLYCATCHERS

First-fall *Empidonax* flycatchers differ from worn breeding adults of the same species, averaging brighter, having buffier wing bars, and showing more orange to the lower mandible. Vagrants of most species can occur across N. America, making identification of first-fall migrants challenging; vagrants often occur later in fall than normal migrants.

ACADIAN FLYCATCHER
Fairly common in East, accidental vagrant in West
Empidonax virescens (see also p. 264)
5¾ in. (15 cm). Note long wings, tail, and bill; white chin.

YELLOW-BELLIED FLYCATCHER
Uncommon in East, casual vagrant in West
Empidonax flaviventris (see also p. 264)
5½ in. (14 cm). Difficult to separate from "Western" Flycatchers; back brighter green; wings blacker with brighter edging and distinct black bar below lower wing bar; eye ring rounded; olive-streaked breast-band usually present.

"WESTERN" FLYCATCHERS
Common in West, casual vagrant in East
Empidonax difficilis/occidentalis (see also p. 266)
5½ in. (14 cm). Vagrant Pacific-slope and Cordilleran flycatchers largely if not entirely inseparable. Compared to Yellow-bellied note wings browner with duller edging and less-defined bar below lower wing bar; eye-ring almond shaped, tail averages longer.

ALDER FLYCATCHER
Fairly common in East, casual vagrant in West
Empidonax alnorum (see also p. 264)
5¾ in. (15 cm). Head and upperparts greener (less olive, grayish, or brownish) than in Willow Flycatchers; wing-feather edging brighter; bill smaller.

WILLOW FLYCATCHER
Uncommon (West) to fairly common (East)
Empidonax traillii (see also p. 264)
5¾ in. (15 cm). See Alder Flycatcher. Eastern Willows (subspecies *traillii* and *campestris*, casual in West) are greener and can be more difficult to separate.

LEAST FLYCATCHER
Fairly common in East, rare vagrant in West
Empidonax minimus (see also p. 264)
First-fall birds variable, generally grayish, sometimes tinged olive above and washed lemon below. Bill more triangular, broader based, and deeper from sides than in Hammond's and Dusky; wings blackish with bolder lemon edging; outer edges of tail can be pale but not whitish. Wingtip projection intermediate but not as long as in Hammond's.

GRAY FLYCATCHER
Uncommon in West, accidental vagrant in East
Empidonax wrightii (see also p. 266)
Plumage pale grayish, although note first-fall birds can be tinged olive above and yellow below. Bill long with distinct black tip; wags tail down.

DUSKY FLYCATCHER
Uncommon in West, accidental vagrant in East
Empidonax oberholseri (see also p. 266)
Grayish, washed olive when fresh; underparts tinged yellow; wing projection shortish. Bill longer and pale loral spot often more prominent than in Least or Hammond's. Wings duller and tail longer than in Least.

HAMMOND'S FLYCATCHER
Fairly common in West, casual vagrant in East
Empidonax hammondii (see also p. 266)
Bill very small, almost warblerlike; thinner from sides than in Least. Wing projection long. Fresh fall birds can be grayish to bright greenish above and yellow below. Outer edges of tail whitish; wings usually duller than in Least.

FIRST-FALL *EMPIDONAX* FLYCATCHERS

YELLOW-BELLIED
FLYCATCHER

"WESTERN"
FLYCATCHER

ACADIAN
FLYCATCHER

ALDER
FLYCATCHER

WILLOW
FLYCATCHER

LEAST
FLYCATCHER

GRAY
FLYCATCHER

DUSKY
FLYCATCHER

HAMMOND'S
FLYCATCHER

MISCELLANEOUS FLYCATCHERS

BLACK PHOEBE *Sayornis nigricans* **Common**
6¾–7 in. (17–18 cm). Our only *black-breasted* flycatcher; belly white. Has typical phoebe tail-bobbing habit. *Juvenile:* Wing bars cinnamon-buff. **VOICE:** Thin, strident *fi-bee, fi-bee,* rising then dropping; also a sharp slurred *chip*. **SIMILAR SPECIES:** Eastern Phoebe, juncos (which are ground-loving birds). **HABITAT:** Streams, walled canyons, farmyards, towns, parks; usually near water. Vagrant well north of range.

EASTERN PHOEBE *Sayornis phoebe* **Fairly common**
7 in. (18 cm). Note *downward tail-bobbing.* A grayish, medium-sized flycatcher *without eye-ring or strong wing bars* (thin buff wing bars on juvenile); small, *all-dark bill* and dark head; yellowish belly in fall. **VOICE:** Song a well-enunciated *phoe-be* or *fi-bree* (second note alternately higher or lower). Call a sharp *chip*. **SIMILAR SPECIES:** Eastern Wood-Pewee and smaller *Empidonax* flycatchers have conspicuous wing bars; bills partly yellowish or horn colored on lower mandible. All *Empidonax* except Gray Flycatcher flick tail *upward.* **HABITAT:** Streamsides, bridges, farms, roadsides, towns. Rare vagrant in fall and winter to W. Coast.

SAY'S PHOEBE *Sayornis saya* **Fairly common**
7½ in. (19 cm). A midsized, pale brownish flycatcher with contrasty black tail and *orange-buff belly.* **VOICE:** Plaintive, down-slurred *pweer* or *pee-ee.* **SIMILAR SPECIES:** Ash-throated and Dusky-capped Flycatchers, Eastern Phoebe. **HABITAT:** Open country, dry scrub, canyons, ranches. Rare vagrant to E. Coast.

VERMILION FLYCATCHER *Pyrocephalus rubinus* **Uncommon**
6 in. (15 cm). *Adult male:* Crown (often raised in slight bushy crest) and underparts *flaming vermilion;* upperparts brown and tail blackish. *First-year male:* Femalelike but lower belly washed pinkish, variably gains red mottling throughout body feathering during first year. *Female:* Breast whitish, narrowly streaked; belly washed with pinkish to salmon (adult) or pale lemon (first-year). **VOICE:** *P-p-pit-zee* or *pit-a-zee.* **SIMILAR SPECIES:** Female told from Say's Phoebe by shorter tail, pale supercilium, dusky streaks on breast. **HABITAT:** Moist areas in arid country, such as streams, ponds, pastures, golf courses, ranches. Vagrant well north and east of range, casually to se. coast.

GREAT KISKADEE *Pitangus sulphuratus* **Fairly common, local**
9¾ in. (25 cm). A large, *big-headed* flycatcher, like Belted Kingfisher in actions, even catching small fish. Note *striking head pattern,* rufous wings and tail, *yellow underparts and crown.* **VOICE:** Loud *kiss-ka-dee;* also a loud *reea.* Often heard before it is seen. **SIMILAR SPECIES:** Tropical and Couch's Kingbirds, which share this kiskadee's limited range. **HABITAT:** Woodlands and brushy edges, usually near water. Accidental vagrant north of range to FL.

SULPHUR-BELLIED FLYCATCHER *Myiodynastes luteiventris* **Uncommon, local**
8½ in. (22 cm). A large flycatcher with *bright rufous tail* and dark patch through eye; underparts *pale yellowish, with black streaks.* No other U.S. flycatcher is streaked *above and below.* **VOICE:** High, penetrating *kee-ZEE ick! kee-ZEE ick!* (like squeezing a bathroom rubber duckie). **HABITAT:** Midelevation canyons, often with sycamores. Accidental vagrant north of range.

FLYCATCHERS

BLACK
PHOEBE

EASTERN
PHOEBE

SAY'S
PHOEBE

adult
male

first-year
female

adult
female

VERMILION
FLYCATCHER

first-
year
male

GREAT
KISKADEE

SULPHUR-BELLIED
FLYCATCHER

MYIARCHUS FLYCATCHERS

BROWN-CRESTED FLYCATCHER *Myiarchus tyrannulus*   Uncommon

8¾ in. (22 cm). Similar to Ash-throated Flycatcher, but larger, with noticeably larger bill. Underparts brighter yellow. Tail rusty, a bit less so than in Ash-throated. Voice important. **VOICE:** Sharp *whit* and rolling, throaty *purreeer.* Voice much more vigorous and raucous than Ash-throated's. **SIMILAR SPECIES:** Great Crested Flycatcher. **HABITAT:** In Southwest, sycamore-dominated canyons, cottonwood groves, saguaros. In TX, woodlands and well-vegetated residential areas. Accidental vagrant north of range.

GREAT CRESTED FLYCATCHER *Myiarchus crinitus*   Fairly common

8½–8¾ in. (21–22 cm). A kingbird-sized flycatcher with cinnamon wings and tail, dark olive back, *mouse gray breast,* and bright yellow belly. Often erects bushy crest. Note *strongly contrasting tertial pattern* and pink-based bill. **VOICE:** Loud whistled *wheeep!* Also a rolling *prrrrreet!* **SIMILAR SPECIES:** Brown-crested and Ash-throated Flycatchers have dark lower mandibles, paler gray breasts, paler yellow bellies, and duller wings with less contrasting tertials. Vocal differences important. **HABITAT:** Woodlands, groves. Very rare vagrant to W. Coast.

DUSKY-CAPPED FLYCATCHER *Myiarchus tuberculifer*   Uncommon, local

7 in. (18 cm). Similar to Ash-throated Flycatcher, but slightly smaller overall with proportionately larger bill; cap and throat darker, belly brighter yellow, and *almost no rusty* in tail. **VOICE:** Distinctive, mournful, down-slurred whistle, *pweeeur.* **HABITAT:** Pine-oak and deciduous canyons. Rare winter vagrant north along Pacific Coast.

LA SAGRA'S FLYCATCHER *Myiarchus sagrae*   Casual vagrant

7¼–7½ in. (19 cm). Very rare visitor to FL from W. Indies. Similar to Ash-throated Flycatcher, but smaller, darker above, has only a *hint of yellow on belly. Tail brownish, not rufous.* Short primaries. Often "droopy" posture. **VOICE:** High, rapid double *wick-wick.* **SIMILAR SPECIES:** Great Crested and Ash-throated Flycatchers. **HABITAT:** Shrubby coastal woods.

ASH-THROATED FLYCATCHER *Myiarchus cinerascens*   Fairly common

8–8¼ in. (20–21 cm). A medium-sized flycatcher, smaller than a kingbird, grayish brown above with two pale wing bars, *whitish* throat, *pale gray breast, pale yellowish belly,* and *rufous tail.* Head slightly bushy. Except for prairie and Southwest border areas, this is normally the only flycatcher in West with rusty tail. **VOICE:** *Prrt* (likened to a police whistle); also a rolling *chi-queer* or *prit-wheer.* **SIMILAR SPECIES:** Great Crested, Brown-crested, and Dusky-capped Flycatchers; Say's Phoebe. **HABITAT:** Semiarid country, deserts, brush, mesquite, pinyon-juniper, chaparral, open woods. Very rare vagrant to E. Coast.

BROWN-CRESTED
FLYCATCHER

MYIARCHUS FLYCATCHERS
Most have extensively
rusty tails

GREAT
CRESTED
FLYCATCHER

DUSKY-CAPPED
FLYCATCHER

ASH-THROATED
FLYCATCHER

LA SAGRA'S
FLYCATCHER

KINGBIRDS

WESTERN KINGBIRD *Tyrannus verticalis*   Common

8¾ in. (22 cm). The most widespread kingbird in West. Note *pale gray head and breast,* white throat, *yellowish belly,* smaller bill. Western's *black tail* has *narrow white edges.* **VOICE:** Shrill, bickering calls; a sharp *kip* or *whit-ker-whit;* dawn song *pit-PEE-tu-whee.* **SIMILAR SPECIES:** Cassin's, Couch's, and Tropical Kingbirds. **HABITAT:** Farms, shelterbelts, semiopen country, roadsides, fences, wires. Rare vagrant to E. Coast.

EASTERN KINGBIRD *Tyrannus tyrannus*   Common

8½ in. (22 cm). Lack of yellow underparts and the *white band* across tail tip marks Eastern Kingbird. Red crown mark is concealed and rarely seen. Often seems to fly quiveringly on tips of wings. Harasses crows, hawks. **VOICE:** Rapid sputter of high, bickering electric-shock notes: *dzee-dzee-dzee,* etc., and *kit-kit-kitter-kitter,* etc. Also a nasal *dzeep.* **SIMILAR SPECIES:** Thick-billed and Gray Kingbirds. **HABITAT:** Wood edges, river groves, farms, shelterbelts, roadsides, fences, wires. Rare vagrant to W. Coast.

CASSIN'S KINGBIRD *Tyrannus vociferans*   Uncommon to fairly common

9 in. (23 cm). Like Western Kingbird, but *darker head and chest contrast with whitish chin and upper throat,* darker olive-gray back; *no distinct white sides* on dark brown (not truly black) tail, which may be *lightly tipped with gray-buff.* Wing coverts often edged pale gray. **VOICE:** Low, nasal *queer, chi-queer,* or *chi-beer;* also an excited *ki-ki-ki-dear, ki-dear, ki-dear.* **SIMILAR SPECIES:** Some worn Western Kingbirds may lack white sides on tail, but head, breast, and back *paler, lack contrasty pale chin* and pale edges to wing coverts, and have *different call.* In much of interior, Cassin's prefers higher elevations. **HABITAT:** Semiopen country, pine-oak mountains, pinyon-juniper; in winter, ranch groves, eucalyptus, olive orchards. Accidental vagrant to E. Coast.

THICK-BILLED KINGBIRD *Tyrannus crassirostris*   Scarce, local

9½ in. (24 cm). A large kingbird with *oversized bill;* differs from similar kingbirds in having extensive *dark cap.* Entirely dark tail. *Adult:* Upperparts *brownish,* underparts *whitish* with pale yellow wash on belly. *Fall adult and first-fall:* May be washed quite yellow below, first-fall with cinnamon wing-feather edging. **VOICE:** Quick, shrill *brrr-zee* or *kut'r-eet.* **SIMILAR SPECIES:** Bright, fresh fall birds told from Tropical Kingbird by bill size, dark head. **HABITAT:** Riparian woodlands, particularly sycamores. Casual winter vagrant to s. CA.

TROPICAL KINGBIRD *Tyrannus melancholicus*   Uncommon, local

9¼ in. (23 cm). Nearly identical to Couch's Kingbird. Both species similar to Western and Cassin's Kingbirds, but, in Tropical, the birds that reach our area usually have *bill much larger and longer,* tail *notched* and *brownish;* bright yellow on underparts *includes breast.* **VOICE:** Repeated twittery *kip-kip-kip* calls. **SIMILAR SPECIES:** Couch's Kingbird. **HABITAT:** Groves along streams and ponds, open areas with scattered trees, phone wires. Scarce fall vagrant well north along Pacific Coast; accidental elsewhere north and east of N. American range.

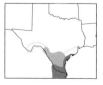

COUCH'S KINGBIRD *Tyrannus couchii*   Fairly common, local

9¼ in. (23 cm). Very similar to Tropical Kingbird and best distinguished by voice. Couch's usually has shorter and smaller bill than Tropicals that reach our area, and brighter green back. **VOICE:** Nasal *queer* or *beeer* (suggests Common Pauraque). Also a sharp *kip.* **SIMILAR SPECIES:** Tropical Kingbird. **HABITAT:** Open wooded and brushy areas with large trees; most common in native habitat. Accidental vagrant to CA and E. Coast.

KINGBIRDS

WESTERN KINGBIRD

EASTERN KINGBIRD

CASSIN'S KINGBIRD

THICK-BILLED KINGBIRD

fall

TROPICAL KINGBIRD

COUCH'S KINGBIRD

Tropical

FORK-TAILED FLYCATCHER *Tyrannus savana* **Very rare vagrant**
14½–16 in. (37–41 cm). Vagrant from Tropics. Told from Scissor-tailed Fly-catcher by *black cap,* white flanks and underwing. Black tail not rigid in flight. *First-year:* Much shorter tail; might be confused with Eastern Kingbird but note paler gray back. **VOICE:** Mechanical-sounding *tik-tik-tik.* **SIMILAR SPECIES:** Scissor-tailed Flycatcher. **RANGE:** Normal range from Mex. to S. America. Vagrant to U.S. and Canada; records widespread but predominantly in the East and in summer through fall. **HABITAT:** Open fields, pastures with scattered trees, wires.

SCISSOR-TAILED FLYCATCHER *Tyrannus forficatus* **Common**
13–15 in. (33–38 cm). A beautiful bird, pale pearly gray, adult male with *extremely long, scissorlike tail* that is usually folded. Flanks orange-buff, under-wing linings salmon pink. *Female and first-year male:* Shorter tail and duller sides may suggest Western Kingbird. Hybrids are known. **VOICE:** Harsh *keck* or *kew;* a repeated *ka-leep;* also shrill, kingbirdlike bickerings and stutterings. **SIMILAR SPECIES:** Western Kingbird, Fork-tailed Flycatcher. **HABITAT:** Semi-open country, ranches, farms, roadsides, fences, wires. Widespread vagrant throughout U.S., casually to W. and E. Coasts.

GRAY KINGBIRD *Tyrannus dominicensis* **Fairly common, local**
9 in. (23 cm). Resembles Eastern Kingbird, but larger and much paler. Conspic-uously *notched* tail has no white band. *Very large bill* gives large-headed look. Dark ear patch. **VOICE:** Rolling *pi-teer-rrry* or *pe-cheer-ry.* **SIMILAR SPECIES:** Eastern Kingbird. **HABITAT:** Roadsides, wires, mangroves, edges. Vagrant in spring and summer north of range along E. Coast; accidental elsewhere in N. America.

ROSE-THROATED BECARD *Pachyramphus aglaiae* **Rare, local**
7¼ in. (18 cm). Big-headed and thick-billed. *Adult male:* Dark gray above, pale to dusky below, with *blackish cap and cheeks* and lovely *rose-colored throat* (lacking or reduced in some males). *Female:* Brown above, with *dark cap* and *light buffy collar* around nape. Underparts strong buff. *First-year male:* Like female but with rose feathers in throat, grayish feathers in back. **VOICE:** Thin, slurred whis-tle, *seeoo.* **SIMILAR SPECIES:** Kingbirds, Say's Phoebe. **HABITAT:** Riparian wood-lands, particularly cottonwoods and sycamores.

FLYCATCHERS

FORK-TAILED
FLYCATCHER

adult

SCISSOR-TAILED
FLYCATCHER

adult
male

first-year
female

adult

ROSE-THROATED
BECARD

GRAY
KINGBIRD

female

adult
male

SWALLOWS and MARTINS Family Hirundinidae

Slim, streamlined form and graceful flight characterize swallows and martins. Pointed wings; short bill with very wide gape; tiny feet. **FOOD:** Mostly flying insects. **RANGE:** Worldwide except for polar regions, remote islands.

TREE SWALLOW *Tachycineta bicolor*   Common

5¾ in. (15 cm). *Adult:* Male *steely blue,* tinged green above; *white below.* Female varies from slightly duller than male to largely brown. *Juvenile:* Dusky gray-brown back and smudgy band across breast. Tree Swallows have distinctly notched tail; glide in circles, ending glide with quick flaps and a short climb. **VOICE:** Rich *cheet* or *chi-veet;* a liquid twitter, *weet, trit, weet,* etc. **SIMILAR SPECIES:** Violet-green Swallow smaller, has white or light brown above eye, obvious white patches on sides of rump, male green and purple above. Northern Rough-winged Swallow has dingier throat, different flight style, and Bank Swallow is smaller, browner, and has bolder dark breast-band than juvenile Tree. All N. American swallows also have different calls. **HABITAT:** Open country near water, marshes, meadows, streams, lakes, wires. Fall premigratory flocks roost in reeds. Nests in holes, in trees and birdhouses.

BANK SWALLOW *Riparia riparia*   Fairly common

5 in. (12 cm). *Our smallest swallow. Brown-backed with slightly darker wings and paler rump.* Note distinct *dark breast-band* in all plumages. White of throat *curls up behind ear. Wingbeats rapid and shallow.* Ages and sexes similar. **VOICE:** Dry, trilled chitter or rattle, *brrt* or *trr-tri-tri.* **SIMILAR SPECIES:** Northern Rough-winged Swallow and juvenile Tree Swallow. When perched in mixed-species flocks, Bank's smaller size stands out. **HABITAT:** Near water; fields, marshes, lakes. Nests colonially in dirt and sandbanks.

NORTHERN ROUGH-WINGED SWALLOW   Fairly common
Stelgidopteryx serripennis

5¼ in. (12 cm). *Adult: Brown-backed;* does not have paler rump that Bank Swallow does; *throat and upper breast brownish to dusky;* no breast-band. Flight more languid; wings pulled back at end of stroke. Juvenile has cinnamon-rusty wing bars. **VOICE:** Call a low, liquid *trrit,* lower and less grating than Bank Swallow's. **SIMILAR SPECIES:** Bank Swallow and juvenile Tree Swallow. **HABITAT:** Near streams, lakes, rivers, coasts. Nests in banks, pipes, and crevices, but not colonially as Bank Swallow does.

VIOLET-GREEN SWALLOW *Tachycineta thalassina*   Fairly common

5¼ in. (13 cm). Note *white patches that almost meet* over base of tail. *Adult male:* Dark and shiny above; glossed with beautiful *green on back and purple on rump and uppertail;* clear white below. *White of face partially encircles eye.* Female and first-winter male are duller above, white above eye tinged grayish or brownish; juveniles are brown above, with little or no green. **VOICE:** A twitter; a thin *ch-lip* or *chew-chit;* rapid *chit-chit-chit wheet, wheet.* **SIMILAR SPECIES:** Tree Swallow lacks pale feathering above eye, has bluer back, lacks white patches on sides of rump; slightly larger size and longer wings. See also White-throated Swift. **HABITAT:** Widespread but more often in mountains than other swallows. Nests in holes in trees, sometimes in birdhouses, in open coniferous woods, canyons, towns. Casual vagrant in the East, accidentally to the coast.

SWALLOWS

nests in tree holes or nest boxes

adult male

TREE SWALLOW

juvenile

some can show an indistinct brown breast band

Bank Swallow colony

BANK SWALLOW

NORTHERN ROUGH-WINGED SWALLOW

VIOLET-GREEN SWALLOW

adult male

Violet-green

Cliff (p. 280)

Barn (p. 280)

Purple Martin (p. 280)

Northern Rough-winged

Tree

Bank

Swallows on a wire

PURPLE MARTIN
Progne subis   Fairly common in East, uncommon and local in West

8 in. (20 cm). The largest N. American swallow. *Adult male:* Uniformly blue-black *above and below;* no other swallow is dark-bellied. *Female and first-fall male:* Light-bellied; throat and breast grayish, often with faint gray collar; first-spring male with some dark mottling. Glides in circles, alternating quick flaps and glides; often spreads tail. **VOICE:** Throaty and rich *tchew-wew,* etc., or *pew, pew.* Song gurgling, ending in a succession of rich, low guttural notes. **SIMILAR SPECIES:** Tree and Violet-green Swallows, much smaller than female Purple Martin, are cleaner white below. In flight, male martin might be confused with European Starling as wing shape somewhat similar. **HABITAT:** Towns, farms, open or semiopen country, often near water. In East, nests exclusively in human-supplied martin houses. In West, uses cavities in trees (such as syca-mores and ponderosa pines), posts, and, in s. AZ, saguaros; rarely martin houses.

CAVE SWALLOW   *Petrochelidon fulva*   Uncommon

5½ in. (14 cm). *Adult:* Similar to Cliff Swallow (rusty rump, square-cut tail), but face colors reversed: *throat and cheeks buffy* (not dark), forehead *dark chestnut* (not pale, although Cliff Swallows in Southwest have chestnut forehead). *Buff color sets off dark mask and cap.* Juvenile is brown overall, including pale brown to whitish throat and breast. **VOICE:** Clear, sweet *weet* or *cheweet;* a loud, accented *chu, chu.* **SIMILAR SPECIES:** Cliff Swallow; Cave has buffier throat and face, more deeply colored rump, different call; juvenile has paler throat. **HABITAT:** Open country. Cuplike nest placed in caves, culverts, and under bridges; nests colonially. Rare but increasing vagrant in East north to Great Lakes and e. Canada in late fall; casual to accidental vagrant to s. CA.

CLIFF SWALLOW   Common in West, uncommon in East
Petrochelidon pyrrhonota

5½ in. (14 cm). *Adult:* Note *rusty,* orange, or *buffy rump,* steely blue upperparts, pale hind collar. From below, appears square-tailed, with red face and dark throat patch. Glides in a long ellipse, ending each glide with a roller coaster–like climb. Juvenile is dusky above with muted head pattern; breast buff; throat mixed with some dark. **VOICE:** *Zayrp;* a low *chur.* Alarm call *keer!* Song consists of creaking notes and guttural gratings; harsher than Barn and Cave Swallows' songs. **SIMILAR SPECIES:** Barn and Cave Swallows. **HABITAT:** Open to semiopen land, farms, cliffs, lakes. Nests colonially on cliffs, barn sides, under eaves and bridges; rarely on trees. Builds mud jug, or gourdlike, nest. Barn and Cave Swallows build cuplike open nest; and Barn Swallows often but not always nest *inside* the barn.

BARN SWALLOW   *Hirundo rustica*   Common

6¾ in. (17 cm). Our only swallow that is truly *swallow-tailed;* also the only one with *white tail spots. Adult:* Blue-black above; cinnamon-buff below, with darker throat; male brighter and has longer tail than female. *Juvenile and first-fall:* Duller overall and paler, more whitish below. Flight direct, close to ground; wingtips pulled back at end of stroke; not much gliding. **VOICE:** Soft *vit* or *kvik-kvik, vit-vit.* Also *szee-szah* or *szee.* Anxiety call a harsh, irritated *ee-tee* or *keet.* Song a long, musical twitter interspersed with guttural notes. **SIMILAR SPE-CIES:** Other N. American swallows have notched (not deeply forked) tail. Cliff Swallow is colonial, building mud jugs under eaves or cliffs; orange to buff rump separates this and Cave Swallow. **HABITAT:** Open or semiopen land; farms, fields, marshes, lakes; often perches on wires; usually near habitation. Builds *cuplike nest inside* barns or under eaves, not in tight colonies like Cliff Swallow.

SWALLOWS

martin house

adult male

PURPLE MARTIN

female and first-year male

adult

CAVE SWALLOW

adult

Southwest

CLIFF SWALLOW

juglike nests under eaves or on cliffs; colonial

nests on beams inside barns

adult male

female

BARN SWALLOW

LEAF WARBLERS Family Phylloscopidae

Large family of similar, small green birds resembling some wood-warblers in size, habits, and habitats. Have short outer primaries, lacking in wood-warblers. **RANGE:** Eurasia and Africa; one species breeds in AK.

DUSKY WARBLER *Phylloscopus fuscatus* Very rare vagrant

5¼ in. (13 cm). A small, plain Old World warbler; *brown above, no wing bars.* Whitish below, with *buffy eyebrow,* flanks, and undertail coverts. **VOICE:** Call a hard *tik* or *tik-tik.* **SIMILAR SPECIES:** Arctic Warbler. **RANGE:** Asian species; vagrant to AK and CA, mostly in fall. **HABITAT:** Thick, scrubby cover.

ARCTIC WARBLER *Phylloscopus borealis* Uncommon, local

5 in. (13 cm). A small, greenish, Old World warbler; bill and legs slightly thicker than in wood-warblers. Dull greenish above, whitish below; light eyebrow; *narrow whitish wing bar* and sometimes short upper bar; pale or dusky legs. Fresh birds in fall are brighter green above, yellowish below. Sexes similar. **VOICE:** Song a monotonous series of buzzy notes; call a buzzy *tsik* or *dzrit.* **SIMILAR SPECIES:** Orange-crowned and Tennessee Warblers have different bill shapes, lack prominent wing bars and short outer primary, have different calls. Recently split Kamchatka Leaf Warbler *(P. examinandus),* a casual vagrant to AK and possibly nw. Canada and CA, averages slightly greener by age and a slightly longer outer primary; perhaps best identified by call notes, a drier and faster *trrt* or *trr-trrt.* **HABITAT:** Willow and alder scrub. Arctic Warbler possibly an accidental vagrant to nw. Canada, CA.

OLD WORLD FLYCATCHERS Family Muscicapidae

Large and varied, primarily Old World family. Delicate sparrow-sized birds, often flicking wings and wagging tails near ground level. **FOOD:** Insects, fruit. **RANGE:** Throughout Eurasia and Africa; two species breed in Arctic N. America.

BLUETHROAT *Luscinia svecica* Scarce, local

5½ in. (14 cm). A small, sprightly bird; often cocks tail. Skulking, except for singing male. When tail slightly spread, shows *chestnut base.* Distinct pale supercilium. *Male:* Blue throat (mottled buff in fall/winter plumage) with *reddish patches. Female:* Whitish throat with *dark necklace.* **VOICE:** Call a sharp *tac* and soft *wheet;* often a cricketlike note. Song composed of repetitious notes, musical and varied. **SIMILAR SPECIES:** Siberian Rubythroat. **HABITAT:** Dwarf willows and alders, thick brush. Accidental vagrant to CA.

SIBERIAN RUBYTHROAT *Calliope calliope* Very rare vagrant

6 in. (15 cm). Brown above; white eyebrow and whiskers. *Male: Ruby red throat,* gray breast. *Female:* White throat, light brown sides. **VOICE:** Series of chattering notes. Call a sharp *chak.* **SIMILAR SPECIES:** Bluethroat. **RANGE:** Asian species; vagrant to w. AK. **HABITAT:** Thickets.

NORTHERN WHEATEAR *Oenanthe oenanthe* Uncommon, local

5¾ in. (15 cm). A small, dapper bird of Arctic barrens, particularly rocky areas and roadsides, fanning its tail and bobbing. Note *white rump and sides of tail.* Black on tail forms *broad inverted T. Spring/summer male:* Pale gray back, black wings, and *black ear patch. Female and fall/winter male:* Variably buffier, with brown back, reduced black in face. **VOICE:** Call a hard *chak-chak* or *chack-weet, weet-chack.* **SIMILAR SPECIES:** Mountain Bluebird and Horned Lark lack distinct rump and tail pattern. **HABITAT:** Open, stony areas; in summer, rocky tundra. Very rare vagrant south of breeding range in East; casual vagrant to CA.

ALASKA AND ARCTIC NESTERS AND VAGRANTS

ARCTIC WARBLER

DUSKY WARBLER

adult male

female

BLUETHROAT

female

male

SIBERIAN RUBYTHROAT

fall/winter

spring/ summer male

NORTHERN WHEATEAR

ACCENTORS Family Prunellidae

Eurasian family, appear thrushlike but are more closely related to pipits. Only one species occurs as a vagrant in N. America. **FOOD:** Insects, seeds, fruit. **RANGE:** Palearctic.

SIBERIAN ACCENTOR *Prunella montanella*   Very rare vagrant

5½ in. (14 cm). *Dark cheeks; bright ocher-buff eyebrow; bright ocher-buff throat and underparts;* plum brown upperparts. Sides streaked; bill *warblerlike.* Ages and sexes alike. **VOICE:** Call a thin, high-pitched *sree* given in series. **RANGE:** Very rare fall visitor to w. AK islands; accidental elsewhere in AK, nw. Canada, and nw. U.S., usually in winter at feeders. **HABITAT:** Thickets, feeders.

THRUSHES Family Turdidae

Large-eyed, slender-billed, usually strong-legged songbirds. Many species are brown-backed with spotted breasts; bluebirds, solitaires, and robins have speckle-breasted young. Thrushes are often fine singers, making up for their generally drab plumages. **FOOD:** Insects, worms, snails, berries, fruit. **RANGE:** Nearly worldwide.

EASTERN BLUEBIRD *Sialia sialis*   Fairly common

7 in. (18 cm). A blue bird with *rusty red breast;* appears round-shouldered when perched. Female duller than male, with pale rusty throat, breast, and flanks; *white* belly. *Juvenile:* Mottled grayish with blue wings and tail. **VOICE:** Call a musical *chur-wi.* Song three or four gurgling notes. **SIMILAR SPECIES:** Western Bluebird, but *throat rusty,* vent *whiter,* back without rust. Fresh female Mountain Bluebirds may be warm buff below but flanks gray, wings longer. **HABITAT:** Open country with scattered trees; farms, roadsides. Often nests in bluebird boxes.

WESTERN BLUEBIRD *Sialia mexicana*   Fairly common

7 in. (18 cm). *Male:* Head, wings, and tail *blue;* breast and back *rusty red. Throat blue. Female:* Paler, duller, with *grayish* throat and belly. Juvenile is similar to juvenile Eastern Bluebird; almost always accompanied by parents. **VOICE:** Short *pew* or *mew.* Also a hard, chattering note. **SIMILAR SPECIES:** Eastern and Mountain Bluebirds. **HABITAT:** Open pine forests, oak savannas, farms; in winter, semiopen fields and terrain of varied habitats. Nests in cavities, including bird boxes.

MOUNTAIN BLUEBIRD *Sialia currucoides*   Fairly common

7¼–7½ in. (18–19 cm). *Adult male: Turquoise blue,* paler below; belly whitish. No rusty; first-year male duller blue with some gray-brown. *Female:* Dull brownish gray, with touch of pale blue on rump, tail, and wings. In fresh fall plumage female can show pale rusty breast and sides, more similar to female Western Bluebird, but lacking rusty flanks. **VOICE:** Low *chur* or *vhew.* Song a short, subdued warble. **SIMILAR SPECIES:** Has straighter posture than female Western and Eastern Bluebirds, with longer wings and slightly longer bill and tail. **HABITAT:** Open country with some trees; in winter, also treeless terrain. Often nests in bluebird boxes. Usually found in flocks or small groups in winter. Very rare vagrant to East, accidentally to coast.

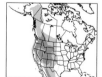

TOWNSEND'S SOLITAIRE *Myadestes townsendi*   Uncommon

8½ in. (22 cm). A slim gray bird with *white eye-ring, white sides on tail,* and *buffy wing patches. Juvenile:* Dark overall with light spots and scaly belly. **VOICE:** Song a rich warbling. Call a high-pitched *eek,* like a squeaky bicycle wheel. **SIMILAR SPECIES:** Plumage patterns might suggest Northern Mockingbird, but note eye-ring, darker breast, buff wing patches. **HABITAT:** Variety of coniferous forests almost to tree line, rocky cliffs; in winter, particularly fond of junipers, also chaparral, open woods. Nests on ground. Very rare vagrant to East, accidentally to coast.

ACCENTOR, BLUEBIRDS,
AND SOLITAIRE

SIBERIAN
ACCENTOR

male

female

WESTERN
BLUEBIRD

juvenile

EASTERN
BLUEBIRD

male

female

adult
male

MOUNTAIN
BLUEBIRD

juvenile

TOWNSEND'S
SOLITAIRE

VEERY *Catharus fuscescens*   Fairly common

7 in. (18 cm). *Catharus* thrushes are all brownish to reddish above, spotted below, and can be difficult to separate; ages are similar (except juvenile plumage, briefly held, is spotted above) and sexes alike. In Veery, note *uniform rusty brown cast* above and pale grayish flanks (often looking whitish). No strong eyering (may have thin, incomplete whitish ring) on grayish face. This is the *Catharus* with least spotting on breast (spots often indistinct). **VOICE:** Song liquid, breezy, ethereal, wheeling downward: *vee-ur, vee-ur, veer, veer.* Call a downslurred *phew* or *view.* **SIMILAR SPECIES:** Out-of-range vagrants can be confused with russet-backed subspecies of Swainson's Thrush (Pacific Coast states), but latter has distinct buffy eye-ring or spectacles, more spotting on breast, browner sides and flanks, and different vocalizations. Also Bicknell's Thrush. **HABITAT:** Moist deciduous woods, willow and alder thickets along streams and meadows in pine forests. Casual vagrant to CA coast.

SWAINSON'S THRUSH *Catharus ustulatus*   Fairly common

7 in. (18 cm). This thrush is marked by its conspicuous *buffy eye-ring* or *spectacles*, buff on cheeks and upper breast, and tail the same color as the back. Interior and eastern subspecies (*swainsoni* group) are dull *olivey brown* above; subspecies in Pacific Coast region (*ustulatus* group) warmer brown, sometimes approaching *russet.* **VOICE:** Song is breezy, flutelike phrases, each phrase sliding *upward.* Call a liquid *whit* or *foot.* Migrants at night (in sky) give a short whistled *quee.* **SIMILAR SPECIES:** Gray-cheeked Thrush has thin, often *incomplete* grayish eye-ring on *grayish face.* Hermit Thrush may have indistinct eye-ring, but is smaller, more upright in posture, and has *contrasty rufous tail, little or no buff* on breast, more-distinct and blackish breast spotting; regularly *flicks wings and raises tail,* and vocalizations differ. See Veery. **HABITAT:** Moist spruce and fir forests, riparian woodlands; in migration, other woods. Often skulks in thick vegetation.

BICKNELL'S THRUSH *Catharus bicknelli*   Scarce, local

6½–6¾ in. (17 cm). Slightly smaller than Gray-cheeked Thrush, upperparts *warmer brown, tail dull chestnut,* breast *washed buff,* lower mandible usually more than half yellow (usually less than half in Gray-cheeked). Legs more dusky than toes (uniform pale in Gray-cheeked). **VOICE:** Melodic flutelike rolling from high to low to high, *whee-toolee-weee,* rising at close (falling in Gray-cheeked). **SIMILAR SPECIES:** Gray-cheeked and Hermit Thrushes. **HABITAT:** Breeds in stunted mountain fir forests of Northeast to shoreline in Maritimes. In migration, forests.

GRAY-CHEEKED THRUSH *Catharus minimus*   Uncommon

7–7¼ in. (17–18 cm). A dull, "cold-colored," *gray-brown,* furtive thrush, distinguished from Swainson's by its *grayish* cheeks and *grayish,* less conspicuous, often broken eye-ring. *Little or no buff on breast.* **VOICE:** Song thin and nasal, downward, suggesting Veery's: *whee-wheeoo-titi-wheew.* Call a downward *pheu.* **SIMILAR SPECIES:** Other thrushes. **HABITAT:** Boreal forests, tundra willow and alder scrub; in migration, other woodlands. Casual vagrant to CA.

HERMIT THRUSH *Catharus guttatus*   Fairly common

6¾ in. (17 cm). A smallish spot-breasted brown thrush with *rufous* tail. When perched, it has habit of *flicking wings* and of *cocking tail and dropping it slowly.* Different subspecies groups vary in exact color of back and flanks, eastern and Pacific coastal birds generally being warmer, interior western birds grayer. **VOICE:** Call a low *chuck;* also a scolding *tuk-tuk-tuk* and a rising, whiny *pay.* Song clear, ethereal, flutelike; three or four phrases at *different pitches,* each with a *long introductory note.* **SIMILAR SPECIES:** Swainson's and Gray-cheeked Thrushes. **HABITAT:** Coniferous or mixed woods; in winter, woods, thickets, chaparral, parks, gardens.

SPOTTED
THRUSHES

VEERY

SWAINSON'S
THRUSH

East and
interior West

Pacific
Coast

BICKNELL'S
THRUSH

GRAY-CHEEKED
THRUSH

tail-lifting

interior
West

HERMIT
THRUSH

Pacific Coast
and East

AMERICAN ROBIN *Turdus migratorius* Common

10 in. (25 cm). A very familiar bird; often seen on lawns, with an erect stance, giving short runs then pauses. Recognized by dark gray back and brick red breast. Dark stripes on white throat. Subspecies vary in plumage brightness (West Coast birds are paler than shown here), but within subspecies adult males have head and tail blacker and underparts solid deep reddish; these colors are duller in females, and first-year birds of each sex are slightly duller than adults. *Juvenile:* Has dark-speckled, pale rusty breast. **VOICE:** Song a clear caroling; short phrases, rising and falling, often prolonged. Calls *tyeep* and *tut-tut-tut.* **SIMILAR SPECIES:** Varied Thrush; Clay-colored Thrush and Rufous-backed Robin (both rare). **HABITAT:** Wide variety of habitats, including towns, parks, lawns, farmland, shade trees, many types of forests and woodlands; in winter, often found in berry-producing trees. Eyebrowed Thrush (*T. obscurus*, not shown), a rare vagrant to AK and CA, is robinlike but slimmer and with distinct white or buff eyebrow.

VARIED THRUSH *Ixoreus naevius* Uncommon

9½ in. (24 cm). Similar to American Robin, but with *orangish eye stripe, orange wing bars,* and *orange bar on underwing* visible in flight. *Male:* Blue-gray above, with wide *black breast-band. Female:* Duller gray above, with *gray breast-band.* First-year birds within each sex are duller than adults. *Juvenile:* Dull brown; breast-band imperfect or speckled. **VOICE:** Song a long, eerie, quavering, whistled note, followed, after a pause, by one on a lower or higher pitch. Call a quivering low-pitched *zzzew* or *zzzeee,* and a liquid *chup.* **SIMILAR SPECIES:** Orangey wing bars and eye stripe, and a breast-band, distinguish it from a robin, with which it only rarely mingles. **HABITAT:** Thick, wet coniferous and mixed forests; in winter, also other moist, dense woods, ravines, thickets, roadsides at dawn. Widespread rare to casual winter vagrant to East, accidentally to coast, often detected at feeders.

WOOD THRUSH *Hylocichla mustelina* Fairly common

7¾ in. (20 cm). *Rusty-headed.* Smaller than a robin; plumper than *Catharus* thrushes, distinguished by deepening rufous about head, *streaked gray cheeks,* white eye-ring, and *rounder, bolder,* more numerous *breast spots.* Ages similar (briefly held juvenile plumage with pale spots on back) and sexes alike. **VOICE:** Song a pleasing series of notes with rounder phrases than other thrushes. Listen for flutelike *ee-o-lay.* Occasional guttural notes are distinctive. Call a rapid *pip-pip-pip-pip.* **SIMILAR SPECIES:** Other *Catharus* thrushes, juvenile American Robin. **HABITAT:** Mainly deciduous woodlands, cool moist glades; commonly detected by distinctive song. Casual vagrant to W. Coast.

male

female

juvenile

AMERICAN ROBIN

adult
male

female

juvenile

**VARIED
THRUSH**

juvenile

WOOD THRUSH

FIELDFARE *Turdus pilaris* Very rare vagrant

10 in. (25 cm). Robinlike in size and posture, with heavily marked tawny breast. *Back rusty, contrasting with gray head and rump, dark tail.* Female and first-year birds average duller than male and adult. **VOICE:** Harsh, chattering *tchak-tchak-tchak* and a quiet *see.* Song a rapid mix of feeble squeaking, chuckling notes, often given in flight. **SIMILAR SPECIES:** Juvenile American Robin, Redwing (vagrant, smaller in size), other spot-breasted thrushes. **RANGE:** Eurasian species; most N. American records from Northeast to northern Midwest in winter; also AK, BC in West. **HABITAT:** Open country, fields, hedgerows, residential areas.

REDWING *Turdus iliacus* Very rare vagrant

8¼ in. (21 cm). Named for its rust-colored underwing linings (most visible in flight). Broad *pale eyebrow, heavily streaked below.* Bill two-toned, black at tip, yellow at base. Ages and sexes alike. **VOICE:** Flight call a thin, high, reedy *seeeh.* **SIMILAR SPECIES:** Fieldfare (vagrant) and juvenile American Robin both much larger. **RANGE:** Eurasian species; most N. American records from Northeast in winter; also, in West, to AK, BC, and WA. **HABITAT:** Semiopen country and young woodlands.

RUFOUS-BACKED ROBIN *Turdus rufopalliatus* Rare visitor

9¼ in. (24 cm). This rare Mexican winter visitor is like a pale American Robin (extensive cinnamon underparts; grayish head, wings, and tail), but with orangier tinge below, *rufous back,* and *no white around eye.* More heavily streaked throat. *Orangier bill.* Female and first-year male duller. A timid skulker. **VOICE:** Call a soft whistled *teeww.* Song a mellow series of warbles, each repeated two or more times. **SIMILAR SPECIES:** American Robin. **RANGE AND HABITAT:** Most records from AZ, but casual vagrants also recorded west to CA, north to UT, and east to s. TX. Woods and thickets, often near water.

CLAY-COLORED THRUSH *Turdus grayi* Scarce, local

9 in. (23 cm). Scarce resident of southernmost TX. Warm brown above, dull tan on chest, paling to light tawny buff on belly. Throat streaked with light brown, not black. Ages and sexes similar. **VOICE:** Lower-pitched, simpler version of American Robin's song. **SIMILAR SPECIES:** *Catharus* thrushes (which are smaller and less like American Robin). **HABITAT:** Tropical woodlands and well-vegetated residential areas.

AZTEC THRUSH *Ridgwayia pinicola* Casual visitor

9¼ in. (24 cm). Resembles Varied Thrush but with *dark hood,* white belly, white rump. Wings strikingly *patched with white. Male:* Blackish on head, breast, and back. *Female:* Brownish. First-year birds duller within each sex. Often sits still for long periods. **VOICE:** Nasal, wheezy *wheeeah.* Usually silent. **SIMILAR SPECIES:** Northern Mockingbird, juvenile Spotted Towhee. **RANGE AND HABITAT:** Casual late-summer visitor from Mex. to se. AZ and w. TX. Mixed montane woodlands, especially pine-oak forests. Can be furtive in dense vegetation.

RARE THRUSHES

FIELDFARE

REDWING

RUFOUS-BACKED
ROBIN

male

CLAY-COLORED
ROBIN

male

female

AZTEC
THRUSH

MOCKINGBIRDS and THRASHERS Family Mimidae

Excellent songsters; some mimic other birds. Strong-legged; usually longer tailed than true thrushes, bill usually longer and more decurved. Ages and sexes similar. **FOOD:** Insects, fruit. **RANGE:** New World.

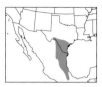

LONG-BILLED THRASHER *Toxostoma longirostre* Uncommon, local

11½ in. (29 cm). *Duller brown* above than Brown Thrasher, breast stripes *blacker, cheeks grayer;* bill longer, slightly more curved, and all dark. **VOICE:** Song similar to Brown Thrasher's, but more jumbled. Call a harsh *tchuk.* **SIMILAR SPECIES:** Brown Thrasher. **HABITAT:** Brush, mesquite. Casual vagrant to NM, CO.

BROWN THRASHER *Toxostoma rufum* Fairly common

11½ in. (29 cm). Slimmer but longer tailed than a robin; *bright rufous* above, *heavily streaked* below. Note *wing bars,* slightly curved bill, long tail, and yellow eyes. **VOICE:** Song a succession of deliberate notes and phrases resembling Gray Catbird's song, but each phrase usually *in pairs.* Call a harsh *chack!* **SIMILAR SPECIES:** The various brown thrushes have shorter tails, lack wing bars, are spotted (not striped) below, and have brown (not yellow) eyes. In s. TX see Long-billed Thrasher. **HABITAT:** Thickets, brush. Very rare vagrant to W. Coast.

SAGE THRASHER *Oreoscoptes montanus* Uncommon

8½ in. (22 cm). Smaller than other thrashers. Gray-backed, with heavily streaked breast, white wing bars, and *white tail corners.* Eyes pale yellow, duller in juvenile and first-fall. Small size, shorter tail, *shorter bill,* and *striped breast* distinguish it from other western thrashers (but see Bendire's Thrasher). Streaking may be muted in worn plumage in late summer. **VOICE:** Song is clear, ecstatic warbled phrases, sometimes repeated in thrasher fashion; more often continuous, suggestive of Black-headed Grosbeak. Call a blackbirdlike *chuck.* **SIMILAR SPECIES:** Cactus Wren, Bendire's Thrasher. **HABITAT:** Sagebrush, mesas; in winter, also deserts. Rare vagrant to East, accidentally to coast.

GRAY CATBIRD *Dumetella carolinensis* Common

8¾ in. (23 cm). Slate gray; slim. Note *black cap. Chestnut undertail coverts* (may not be noticeable). Flips tail jauntily. **VOICE:** Catlike mewing; distinctive. Also a grating *tcheck-tcheck.* Song is disjointed notes and phrases; not repetitious, compared with other mimids. **HABITAT:** Riparian undergrowth, brush. More often heard than seen. Rare vagrant to W. Coast.

BAHAMA MOCKINGBIRD *Mimus gundlachii* Rare vagrant

11 in. (28 cm). Chunkier than Northern Mockingbird and overall browner with *less white in tail* and *no white in wings.* Dark streaks on flanks, belly, and neck give this species a thrasherlike appearance. **VOICE:** Song simpler than Northern's, with two-syllable phrases. Call a sharp *tchak,* like Northern's but harsher. **RANGE:** Rare but near-annual vagrant from Caribbean to s. FL, especially Dry Tortugas, Keys. **HABITAT:** A skulker in deep brushy cover.

NORTHERN MOCKINGBIRD *Mimus polyglottos* Common

10 in. (25 cm). A familiar and conspicuous species. Gray; slimmer, longer tailed than a robin. Note *large white patches* on wings and tail, prominent in flight. **VOICE:** Song a varied, prolonged succession of notes and phrases, may be repeated up to a half dozen times before changing; frequently mimics other species. Often heard at night. Call a loud *tchack;* also *chair.* **SIMILAR SPECIES:** Shrikes have dark facial masks. Juvenile mockingbird might be similar to Sage Thrasher but latter shows streaks rather than spots below and lacks white in wings. See Bahama Mockingbird. **HABITAT:** Towns, parks, gardens, farms, roadsides, thickets. Introduced and uncommon in HI (p. 444).

THRASHERS AND
MOCKINGBIRDS

LONG-BILLED
THRASHER

BROWN
THRASHER

SAGE
THRASHER

BAHAMA
MOCKINGBIRD

GRAY
CATBIRD

NORTHERN
MOCKINGBIRD

juvenile

wing-flashing

CALIFORNIA THRASHER *Toxostoma redivivum*   Fairly common

12 in. (31 cm). A large, brownish thrasher, with *pale cinnamon belly and undertail coverts;* tail long; bill long and *sickle-shaped.* Eyes dark brown. The only thrasher of this type in CA west of deserts (except locally where LeConte's Thrasher overlaps). **VOICE:** Call a dry *chak,* also a sharp *g-leek.* Song a long, sustained series of notes and phrases, some musical, some harsh. Phrases may be *repeated* once or twice, but not several times as in Northern Mockingbird, and also more leisurely. **SIMILAR SPECIES:** Crissal Thrasher very similar but has deeper chestnut undertail coverts; ranges do not overlap. **HABITAT:** Chaparral, coastal sage scrub, thickets, parks, gardens.

CRISSAL THRASHER *Toxostoma crissale*   Uncommon

11½ in. (29 cm). A *rather dark* thrasher of desert habitats, with long, *deeply curved bill.* Note dark *chestnut undertail coverts* (or "crissum"), darker than in other thrashers. No breast spots. Eyes dull yellowish. **VOICE:** Song sweeter and less spasmodic than in other thrashers. Call *pichoory* or *chideary,* repeated two or three times. **SIMILAR SPECIES:** California Thrasher does not overlap in range. **HABITAT:** Dense brush along desert streams, mesquite thickets, willows, locally at higher elevations in manzanita, scrub oak.

LECONTE'S THRASHER *Toxostoma lecontei*   Uncommon to scarce

11 in. (28 cm). A *very pale* thrasher of driest deserts. Has contrastingly *darker tail.* Salmon-rust undertail coverts. Dark eyes stand out on plain face. Rather shy. Runs long distances on ground. **VOICE:** Song (Jan.–Apr.) similar to songs of most other thrashers. Call *ti-reep,* rising on second syllable. **SIMILAR SPECIES:** Crissal and California Thrashers much darker overall. **HABITAT:** Desert flats with sparse bushes, mostly saltbush *(Atriplex)* or creosote bush.

CURVE-BILLED THRASHER *Toxostoma curvirostre*   Fairly common

11 in. (28 cm). This, the most common desert thrasher, can be told from others that have *well-curved* bill by *mottled breast,* less distinct in subspecies *palmeri* of AZ than in subspecies *oberholseri* of TX and NM. Some individuals have narrow white wing bars. Eyes pale orange. Juvenile shows yellower eyes, somewhat straighter bill. **VOICE:** Call a sharp, liquid *whit-wheet!* (like a whistle to attract attention). Song a musical series of notes and phrases, almost grosbeaklike in quality but faster. Not much repetition. **SIMILAR SPECIES:** Bendire's Thrasher has *shorter, straighter bill, with slight paling at base,* is slightly browner overall, breast spots more triangular (except when worn), different call. **HABITAT:** Deserts, arid brush, lower canyons, ranch yards. Vagrant north and east of range.

BENDIRE'S THRASHER *Toxostoma bendirei*   Uncommon, local

9¾ in. (25 cm). Of the various drab, longer-billed desert thrashers, this one may be known by its *shorter, more robinlike bill* (lower mandible quite straight) with paler (horn-colored or pale gray) base. Breast lightly spotted. Eyes usually *yellow.* **VOICE:** Song a *continuous,* clear, double-note warble, not broken into phrases. Call a soft *tirup.* **SIMILAR SPECIES:** Juvenile Curve-billed may have a bill as short as Bendire's, and yellow eyes, but plumage fluffy and fresh versus worn in adult Bendire's. Bendire's may be confused with worn Sage Thrasher but this species' bill is much shorter and straighter, back usually darker and wing bars more distinct, even in worn plumage. **HABITAT:** Deserts, yuccas, dry brushy farmland. Accidental vagrant to north of range.

THRASHERS

CALIFORNIA
THRASHER

CRISSAL
THRASHER

LECONTE'S
THRASHER

CURVE-
BILLED
THRASHER

AZ

TX and
NM

BENDIRE'S
THRASHER

DIPPERS Family Cinclidae

Plump, stub-tailed; wrenlike. Dippers dive and swim underwater, where they walk on bottom. **FOOD:** Aquatic invertebrates, small fish. **RANGE:** Eurasia, American mountains.

AMERICAN DIPPER *Cinclus mexicanus*   Uncommon

7½ in. (19 cm). A chunky, *slate-colored* bird of rushing mountain streams. *Tail stubby.* Legs pale, *eyelids white.* Note bobbing motions, slaty color, flashing eyelid. *Juvenile:* Has paler underparts and bill. **VOICE:** Call a sharp, buzzy *zeet,* heard above rushing water. Song clear and ringing, mockingbird-like but higher, more wrenlike. **HABITAT:** Fast-flowing streams in mountains and canyons; more rarely pond edges. Nests under bridges, behind waterfalls. Some birds move to lower elevations in winter.

WAXWINGS Family Bombycillidae

Pointed crest may be raised or lowered. Waxy red tips on secondaries in adult and some first-year individuals; male has more waxy tips and blacker throat than female. Gregarious. **FOOD:** Berries, insects. **RANGE:** N. Hemisphere.

BOHEMIAN WAXWING *Bombycilla garrulus*   Uncommon, irregular

8¼ in. (21 cm). Similar to Cedar Waxwing but larger and grayer, with *no yellow on belly;* wings with strong white or *white and yellow* markings, warmer brown to face. Note *deep rusty* undertail coverts (white in Cedar Waxwing). Juvenile larger, grayer than juvenile Cedar. Often travels in large nomadic flocks. Shape in flight starlinglike. **VOICE:** *Zrreee,* rougher than thin note of Cedar Waxwing. **HABITAT:** In summer, boreal forests, muskeg; in winter, widespread in search of berries, often in towns with fruiting trees. Irruptive; vagrants occur well south of range in some years.

CEDAR WAXWING *Bombycilla cedrorum*   Common

7¼ in. (18 cm). Note *yellow band* at tip of tail. A sleek, crested, brown bird, larger than House Sparrow. *Juvenile:* Grayish olive-brown, with blurry streaks below. Gregarious when not breeding, flying and feeding in compact flocks, usually on berries. **VOICE:** High, thin lisp or *zeee;* sometimes slightly trilled; rather constantly given while feeding and in flight. **SIMILAR SPECIES:** Differs from Bohemian Waxwing in having yellow on belly, white (not rusty) undertail coverts, fewer markings on wings. Juvenile smaller, browns more olive (less grayish). Not as starlinglike in flight. **HABITAT:** Open woodlands, streamside willows and alders, orchards; in winter, widespread, including towns, fruiting trees and bushes; nomadic.

SILKY-FLYCATCHERS Family Ptiliogonatidae

Slim, crested, waxwinglike birds. **FOOD:** Berries, insects. **RANGE:** Southwestern U.S. to Panama.

PHAINOPEPLA *Phainopepla nitens*   Uncommon

7¾ in. (20 cm). Both sexes are sleek, crested, with red eye. *Adult male: Glossy black* with conspicuous *white wing patches* in flight. *Female: Dark gray;* wing patches paler than male's. First-year male is gray-mottled black. Eats berries but also catches insects. **VOICE:** Call a soft, rising *wurp* and harsher *churrrr.* Song a weak, casual warble, wheezy and disconnected. **SIMILAR SPECIES:** Cedar Waxwing browner, has yellow tail band, lacks pale wing patches. Northern Mockingbird lacks crest and has much white in tail. **HABITAT:** Desert scrub, mesquite, oak foothills, pepper trees; fond of mistletoe berries. Casual vagrant to East, accidentally to coast.

DIPPER, WAXWINGS, AND PHAINOPEPLA

adult

juvenile

AMERICAN DIPPER

CEDAR WAXWING

juvenile

BOHEMIAN WAXWING

PHAINOPEPLA

adult male

female

JAYS, CROWS, and ALLIES Family Corvidae

Large perching birds with strong, longish bill, nostrils covered by forward-pointing bristles. Jays are often blue. Crows and ravens are large and black. Magpies are black and white, with long tails. Sexes alike. First-year birds of most species resemble adults. **FOOD:** Almost anything edible. **RANGE:** Worldwide except s. S. America, Antarctica, Oceana.

FLORIDA SCRUB-JAY *Aphelocoma coerulescens*   Uncommon, local, threatened
11–11¼ in. (29 cm). Look for this *crestless* jay in FL in stretches of oak scrub. Similar to California Scrub-Jay but smaller, paler. **VOICE:** Rough, rasping *kwesh . . . kwesh.* Also a low, rasping *zhreek* or *zhrink.* **SIMILAR SPECIES:** Blue Jay has crest and bold white spotting on wings and tail. **HABITAT:** Mainly scrub, low oaks.

CALIFORNIA SCRUB-JAY *Aphelocoma californica*   Common
11–11¼ in. (29 cm). *Crestless* with blue head, wings, and tail, *brownish back,* white throat with *necklace.* **VOICE:** Rough, rasping *kwesh . . . kwesh.* Also a harsh *shreck-shreck-shreck-shreck.* **SIMILAR SPECIES:** Woodhouse's Scrub-Jay does not overlap in range. **HABITAT:** Oaks, pine-oak, oak-chaparral of foothills, riparian woodlands, residential areas, parks. A noisy familiar bird in CA.

ISLAND SCRUB-JAY *Aphelocoma insularis* (not shown)   Very local
12½–13 in. (31–33 cm). Found only on Santa Cruz I. off coast of s. CA, most restricted range of any species in N. America. **VOICE:** Same as California Scrub-Jay. **SIMILAR SPECIES:** Similar to California Scrub-Jay (no range overlap) but slightly longer and larger billed; deeper blue, darker cheek. **HABITAT:** Woodlands and scrubby habitat.

WOODHOUSE'S SCRUB-JAY *Aphelocoma woodhouseii*   Common
11–11¼ in. (29 cm). Similar to California Scrub-Jay (from which it was recently split) but duller. **VOICE:** Similar to California Scrub-Jay. **SIMILAR SPECIES:** Mexican Jay. **HABITAT:** Riparian and oak woodlands, pinyon-juniper, residential areas, parks.

MEXICAN JAY *Aphelocoma wollweberi*   Fairly common, local
11½ in. (29 cm). A blue crestless jay of the Southwest. Resembles Woodhouse's Scrub-Jay, but *more uniform;* back and breast grayer. *No strong contrast* between throat and breast. Also *lacks narrow whitish line over eye.* In AZ, juvenile has partly yellow bill. **VOICE:** Rough, querulous *wink? wink?* or *zhenk?* **SIMILAR SPECIES:** Woodhouse's Scrub-Jay. **HABITAT:** Pine-oak and oak-juniper woodlands.

BLUE JAY *Cyanocitta cristata*   Common
11 in. (28 cm). A showy, noisy, infamous, *crested jay;* larger than a robin. Bold *white spots on wings and tail;* whitish and dull gray underparts; *black necklace.* **VOICE:** Harsh slurring *jeeah* or *jay;* a musical *queedle, queedle;* many other notes. Mimics calls of Red-shouldered and Red-tailed Hawks. **SIMILAR SPECIES:** Florida Scrub-Jay, Steller's Jay. **HABITAT:** Woodlands, suburban gardens, groves, towns, feeders. Casual vagrant to W. Coast.

STELLER'S JAY *Cyanocitta stelleri*   Common
11½ in. (29 cm). Foreparts *blackish;* rear parts (wings, tail, belly) *deep blue.* Some interior birds have white eyebrow. **VOICE:** Loud *shook-shook-shook* or *shack-shack-shack* or *wheck-wek-wek-wek-wek* or *kwesh kwesh kwesh;* harsh *jjaairr* and many other notes. Frequently mimics hawks. **SIMILAR SPECIES:** Other "blue jays" have white below. **HABITAT:** Montane coniferous and pine-oak forests; also some residential areas, feeders; in winter, lowlands. Rare vagrant or visitor east of range.

TAMAULIPAS
CROW

FISH CROW

NORTHWESTERN
CROW

AMERICAN
CROW

American Crow

Fish Crow

Tamaulipas
Crow

CHICKADEES and TITMICE Family Paridae

Small, plump, small-billed birds. Acrobatic when feeding. Ages and sexes similar. Often found in mixed-species flocks with other parids, kinglets, warblers, etc. **FOOD:** Seeds, acorn mast, suet, sunflower seeds. **RANGE:** Widespread in N. America, Eurasia, Africa.

CAROLINA CHICKADEE *Poecile carolinensis*   Common

4¾ in. (12 cm). Very similar to Black-capped Chickadee and best distinguished by range and voice. **VOICE:** "Chickadee" call of this species is higher pitched and more rapid than that of Black-capped. Whistled song is a four-syllable *fee-bee, fee-bay.* **SIMILAR SPECIES:** Black-capped Chickadee is slightly larger with cleaner white cheek patch, more prominent white edging in wing coverts, and pinker sides and flanks. Hybrids are known. In some winters, Black-cappeds penetrate southward into range of Carolina. **HABITAT:** Mixed and deciduous woods; willow thickets, shade trees, residential areas, feeders.

BLACK-CAPPED CHICKADEE *Poecile atricapillus*   Common

5–5¼ in. (12–13 cm). Small, familiar acrobat; note *solid black cap,* pink sides, white in wing. **VOICE:** Clearly enunciated *chick-a-dee-dee-dee.* Song a clear whistle, *fee-bee-ee* or *fee-bee,* first note higher. **SIMILAR SPECIES:** Carolina Chickadee. **HABITAT:** Woods; riparian thickets, shade trees, residential areas, feeders. Somewhat irruptive in winter, especially in East.

CHESTNUT-BACKED CHICKADEE *Poecile rufescens*   Fairly common

4¾ in. (12 cm). The cap, bib, and white cheeks indicate a chickadee; the *chestnut back and rump,* this species. Sides *chestnut* (or *gray* in race found along coast of cen. CA). **VOICE:** Hoarser and more rapid than Black-capped Chickadee: *sick-a-see-see.* No whistled song. **HABITAT:** Moist coniferous forests, oaks, willows, shade trees, parks.

MOUNTAIN CHICKADEE *Poecile gambeli*   Fairly common

5¼ in. (13 cm). Similar to Black-capped Chickadee, but black of cap interrupted by *white line over eye.* **VOICE:** Song a clear whistled *fee-ee-bee-bee* (first note higher) or *tsick-a-zee-zee-zee,* huskier than Black-capped's, and a rolling *deedleedleoo.* **SIMILAR SPECIES:** Other chickadees, Black-crested Titmouse. **HABITAT:** Mountain forests, conifers; irregularly moves to lower elevations in winter. Casual vagrant east of range and to W. Coast.

GRAY-HEADED CHICKADEE *Poecile cinctus*   Rare, local

5½ in. (14 cm). This subarctic chickadee can be separated from Boreal Chickadee by its *grayer cap* and *more extensive white cheek.* **VOICE:** Peevish *dee-deer* or *chee-ee.* **HABITAT:** Spruce forests, particularly at border with streamside willow and alder thickets and cottonwoods.

MEXICAN CHICKADEE *Poecile sclateri*   Uncommon, local

5 in. (13 cm). Similar to Black-capped Chickadee, but *black of throat more extensive,* spreading across upper breast. Note *dark gray sides.* Lacks whitish supercilium of Mountain Chickadee. The only chickadee in its local U.S. range. **VOICE:** Nasal and husky for a chickadee: a low *dzay-dzeee.* **HABITAT:** Montane coniferous forests; sometimes moves to lower canyons in winter.

BOREAL CHICKADEE *Poecile hudsonicus*   Uncommon

5½ in. (14 cm). Note dull *brown cap,* rich brown to pinkish brown flanks, extensively *grayish cheeks.* **VOICE:** Wheezy *chick-che-day-day;* notes slower, more raspy and drawling than those of Black-capped Chickadee. **SIMILAR SPECIES:** Gray-headed Chickadee. **HABITAT:** Coniferous forests, evergreen plantations; occasionally erupts south of normal range in winter.

CHICKADEES

BLACK-CAPPED
CHICKADEE

CAROLINA
CHICKADEE

CHESTNUT-BACKED
CHICKADEE

Rockies

cen. CA
coast

MOUNTAIN
CHICKADEE

MEXICAN
CHICKADEE

GRAY-HEADED
CHICKADEE

BOREAL
CHICKADEE

BLACK-CRESTED TITMOUSE *Baeolophus atricristatus* Fairly common

6¼ in. (16 cm). Birds bearing the name "titmouse" are our only small, gray-backed birds with pointed crest. Black-crested is a small gray bird with *black crown and crest.* Forehead and underparts pale, sides rusty. Juveniles, found only in spring/summer and usually with their parents, have mostly gray crest. **VOICE:** Chickadee-like calls. Song a whistled *peter peter peter peter* or *hear hear hear hear.* Varied. **SIMILAR SPECIES:** Tufted Titmouse has plain gray crest and black forehead. Bridled Titmouse has harlequin face pattern. **HABITAT:** Woodlands, canyons, towns, feeders.

TUFTED TITMOUSE *Baeolophus bicolor* Common

6¼ in. (16 cm). A small, gray, *mouse-colored bird with tufted crest. Flanks rusty buff.* Plain face, large black eyes. Very inquisitive and loudly vocal; tend to be the leaders of bird flocks including migrant warblers. **VOICE:** Clear whistled chant: *peter, peter, peter* or *here, here, here, here.* Calls similar to those of chickadees, but more drawling, nasal, wheezy, and complaining. **SIMILAR SPECIES:** Other titmice, chickadees. **HABITAT:** Woodlands, shade trees, groves, residential areas, feeders.

OAK TITMOUSE *Baeolophus inornatus* Fairly common

5¾ in. (15 cm). This is the sole titmouse west of Sierra Nevada. Very like Juniper Titmouse (formerly considered subspecies of one species, "Plain Titmouse") but slightly browner. **VOICE:** Call a scratchy *sissi-chee.* Song a whistled *weety weety* or *tee-wit tee-wit tee-wit;* highly variable but huskier than Chestnut-backed Chickadee. **SIMILAR SPECIES:** Other titmice, but separated by range. **HABITAT:** Oak and oak-pine woods; locally in riparian woodlands, shade trees, residential areas.

JUNIPER TITMOUSE *Baeolophus ridgwayi* Uncommon

5¾ in. (15 cm). Very similar to Oak Titmouse, although Juniper is slightly grayer. **VOICE:** Call more rapid than Oak's, *si-dee-dee-dee-dee.* **SIMILAR SPECIES:** Juvenile Black-crested Titmice with gray crests, especially at Big Bend and Edwards Plateau areas of TX, where Juniper Titmice do not occur. **HABITAT:** Pinyon-juniper and oak-juniper woodlands.

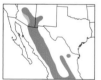

BRIDLED TITMOUSE *Baeolophus wollweberi* Fairly common

5¼ in. (13 cm). Crest and black-and-white *"bridled"* face identify this small gray titmouse of Southwest. **VOICE:** Similar to other titmice and chickadees, but higher and faster. Song a repeated two-syllable phrase. **SIMILAR SPECIES:** Black-crested Titmouse. Mountain Chickadee has a different face pattern, lacks crest. **HABITAT:** Oak, pine-oak, and sycamore canyons, riparian woodlands, feeders.

TUFTED
TITMOUSE

BLACK-
CRESTED
TITMOUSE

JUNIPER
TITMOUSE

OAK
TITMOUSE

BRIDLED
TITMOUSE

Mountain Chickadee
(p. 306)
for comparison

NUTHATCHES Family Sittidae

Small, stubby tree climbers with strong, woodpecker-like bills and strong feet. Short, square-cut tails are not braced like those of woodpeckers during climbing. Nuthatches habitually go down trees headfirst. Ages and sexes similar or differ slightly. **FOOD:** Bark insects, seeds, nuts; attracted to feeders by suet, sunflower seeds. **RANGE:** Most of N. Hemisphere.

WHITE-BREASTED NUTHATCH *Sitta carolinensis*　　　　Common

5¾ in. (15 cm). This widespread and familiar nuthatch is known by its *black cap* (gray in female) and beady black eye on white face. Undertail coverts chestnut. **VOICE:** Song a rapid series of low, nasal, whistled notes on one pitch: *whi, whi, whi, whi, whi, whi* or *who, who, who,* etc. Notes of birds in interior West higher pitched and given in rapid series. Call a distinctive nasal *yank, yank, yank;* also a nasal *tootoo.* **SIMILAR SPECIES:** Red-breasted Nuthatch. **HABITAT:** Forests, woodlots, groves, river woods, shade trees; visits feeders; slightly less common in the West, where found primarily in oaks.

RED-BREASTED NUTHATCH *Sitta canadensis*　　　　Common

4½ in. (11 cm). A small nuthatch with *broad black line* through eye and white line above it. Crown black in male, gray in female; underparts washed rusty in male, paler in female. First-year birds of each sex duller than adults, crown blackish rather than black in male and duller gray in female. **VOICE:** Call higher, more nasal than White-breasted Nuthatch, a distinctive *ank* or *enk,* sounding like a baby nuthatch or tiny tin horn. **SIMILAR SPECIES:** Pygmy and Brown-headed Nuthatches have gray-brown or brown crowns, lack white superciliums, have very different calls. **HABITAT:** Coniferous forests; in winter, also other trees, feeders. Irruptive, sometimes moving well south of range in winter.

PYGMY NUTHATCH *Sitta pygmaea*　　　　Fairly common

4¼ in. (11 cm). A very small, pine-loving nuthatch, with *gray-brown cap coming down to eye* and a whitish spot on nape. Usually roams about in flocks. Ages and sexes similar. **VOICE:** High, piping *peep-peep* or *pit-pi-dit-pi-dit.* Also a high *ki-dee;* incessant, becoming an excited chatter when flocks are on the move. Often heard before it is seen. **SIMILAR SPECIES:** Brown-headed Nuthatch does not overlap in range. Red-breasted Nuthatch. **HABITAT:** Favors ponderosa, Jeffrey, and Monterey pines, Douglas-fir.

BROWN-HEADED NUTHATCH *Sitta pusilla*　　　　Uncommon

4½ in. (11 cm). A small nuthatch of southeastern pinelands. Smaller than White-breasted Nuthatch, with brown cap coming down to eye and a usually pale or whitish spot on nape. Travels in groups. Ages and sexes similar. **VOICE:** Sounds like a toy rubber duck: a high, rapid *kit-kit-kit;* also a squeaky piping *ki-day* or *ki-dee-dee,* constantly repeated, sometimes becoming an excited twitter or chatter. **SIMILAR SPECIES:** Other nuthatches, Brown Creeper. **HABITAT:** Open pine woods.

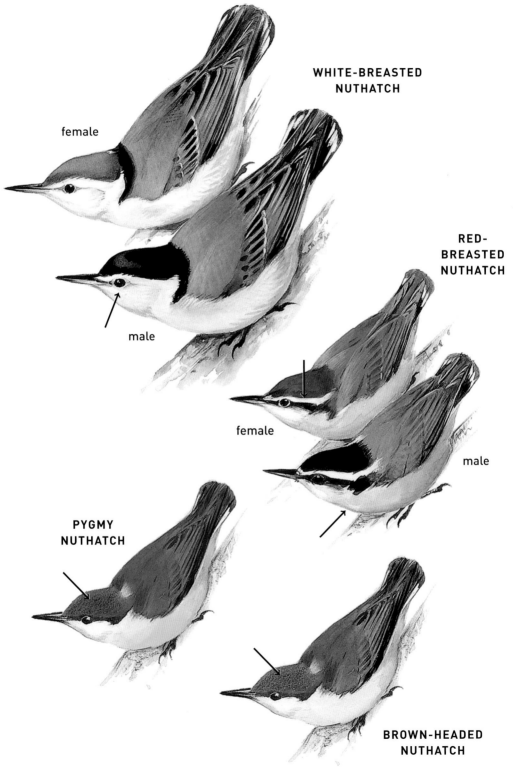

NUTHATCHES

WHITE-BREASTED
NUTHATCH

female

male

RED-
BREASTED
NUTHATCH

female

male

PYGMY
NUTHATCH

BROWN-HEADED
NUTHATCH

TREE CREEPERS Family Certhiidae

Small, slim, stiff-tailed birds that creep up and around tree trunks and branches for bark insects. Ages and sexes alike. **RANGE:** Cooler parts of N. Hemisphere.

BROWN CREEPER *Certhia americana*   Uncommon

5¼ in. (13 cm). A small, slim, camouflaged tree climber. Brown above, whitish below, with *slender decurved bill* and *stiff tail,* which is used as a brace during climbing. **VOICE:** Call a single high, thin *seee.* Song a high, thin, sibilant *see-ti-wee-tu-wee* or *trees, trees, trees, see the trees.* **HABITAT:** Coniferous and mixed woodlands; in fall and winter, also in deciduous woods, groves, shade trees.

LONG-TAILED TITS Family Aegithalidae

Very small birds with long tail. Found in flocks (except when breeding), often with other small birds. **FOOD:** Insects. **RANGE:** Primarily Asia with single species each in Europe and N. America.

BUSHTIT *Psaltriparus minimus*   Common

4½ in. (11 cm). A very small, plain bird that, except briefly during nesting season, moves from bush to tree in *straggling flocks,* conversing in twittering notes. Nondescript; gray and brown; stubby bill, longish tail. Adult male and juvenile have dark eyes, female yellow eyes; juvenile male of "Black-eared Bushtit" (subspecies *dimorphicus*) of s. NM and w. TX has black or black-marked cheeks. Builds large spherical nest. **VOICE:** *Tsits* and *clenks* given constantly as flocks move. **SIMILAR SPECIES:** Verdin. **HABITAT:** Oak scrub, chaparral, mixed woods, pinyon-juniper, parks, residential areas.

PENDULINE TITS Family Remizidae

Small, active, primarily desert birds with short, rounded tails and tiny pointed bills. Often heard before seen. Found singly or in pairs, not flocks. Roost in large spherical nests. **FOOD:** Insects, fruit, berries. **RANGE:** Asia, Africa, single species in N. America.

VERDIN *Auriparus flaviceps*   Fairly common

4½ in. (11 cm). Tiny. *Adult:* Gray, with *yellowish head, rufous bend of wing.* Sexes similar. *Juvenile:* Plain gray. **VOICE:** Insistent *see-lip.* Rapid chipping. Song a whistled *tsee see-see.* **SIMILAR SPECIES:** Bushtit longer tailed; bill thicker; habitats seldom overlap. See also Lucy's Warbler, Northern Beardless-Tyrannulet. **HABITAT:** Brushy desert and semiarid lowlands, mesquite.

PARROTBILLS, WRENTITS, and ALLIES
Family Paradoxornithidae

Small, long-tailed denizens of brushy cover. This Old World family is represented in N. America by just one species. **FOOD:** Insects, fruit. **RANGE:** Temperate Asia.

WRENTIT *Chamaea fasciata*   Fairly common

6½ in. (17 cm). Heard far more often than seen. Note *long,* rounded, slightly cocked tail and obscurely streaked breast. *Eye distinctly pale.* Bill short. Behavior wrenlike; rarely flies more than 30 feet. Ages and sexes alike. **VOICE:** Song of staccato ringing notes on one pitch; starting deliberately, running into a trill — like a bouncing ball. Female gives slower, double-noted version. Call a soft *prr.* **SIMILAR SPECIES:** Wrens have shorter tails. **HABITAT:** Chaparral, coastal sage scrub, brush, parks, garden shrubs.

CREEPER, BUSHTIT,
VERDIN, AND WRENTIT

BROWN
CREEPER

Pacific
Coast

interior

BUSHTIT

females have
yellow eyes

juvenile male
"Black-eared"

adult

VERDIN

juvenile

WRENTIT

northern

southern

WRENS Family Troglodytidae

Mostly small, energetic brown birds; stumpy, with slim, slightly curved bill; tail often cocked. Songs are complex and often pleasing, making up for the drab plumage. Often nests in dark nooks and crannies or elaborately built nests, including birdhouses in some species. Ages and sexes alike. **FOOD:** Insects, spiders. **RANGE:** Throughout Americas; one species in Eurasia.

HOUSE WREN *Troglodytes aedon*   Common
4½–4¾ in. (11–12 cm). A small, energetic, gray-brown wren with long tail, light eye-ring, and no strong eyebrow stripe. A familiar songster in residential areas and on farms, especially in the East. **VOICE:** Stuttering, gurgling song rises in a musical burst, then falls at end; calls a rolled *prrrrr* and harsh *cheh, cheh*. **SIMILAR SPECIES:** Winter and Pacific Wrens. **HABITAT:** Open woods, thickets, towns, gardens; often nests in bird boxes.

WINTER WREN *Troglodytes hiemalis*   Uncommon
4 in. (10 cm). A very small, round wren, told from House Wren by its smaller size, *much stubbier tail*, stronger eyebrow, and *dark, heavily barred belly.* Often bobs body and flicks wings; mouselike, staying close to ground. **VOICE:** Song a rapid succession of high tinkling warbles, trills. Call a soft, two-syllable *chemp-chemp* (suggests Song Sparrow); also a rapid chatter that may be given more frequently than similar calls of Pacific Wren. **SIMILAR SPECIES:** House Wren. May be quite difficult to separate from Pacific Wren in West where both may co-occur on migration or in winter. **HABITAT:** Dense, shaded woodlands under-brush, fallen trees. Casual winter vagrant to W. Coast.

PACIFIC WREN *Troglodytes pacificus*   Fairly common
4 in. (10 cm). Recently split from Winter Wren. Slightly darker and warmer than Winter Wren, with less distinct barring to wings and tail, but best identified by voice. **VOICE:** Song similar to Winter Wren but with fewer trailing segments. Call a harder *timp-timp* (suggests Wilson's Warbler). **SIMILAR SPECIES:** House Wren, Winter Wren. **HABITAT:** Dense, shaded canyons; ferns; streambeds; in summer, coniferous forests. Nests in deep wooded canyons, often under mossy tree roots over streams.

BEWICK'S WREN *Thryomanes bewickii*   Common in West, scarce in East
5¼ in. (13 cm). Note longish tail with *white corners* and bold *white eyebrow stripe.* Most are mouse brown above but coloration varies from grayish to reddish brown. **VOICE:** Variable. Typical song suggests Song Sparrow's, but thinner, starting on two or three high notes, dropping, ending in a trill; calls sharp *vit, vit* and buzzy *dzzzzzt*. **SIMILAR SPECIES:** Redder birds can be similar to Carolina Wrens but note tail length, slimmer body, often flips tail. Habitats of Marsh and Bewick's Wrens do not overlap. **HABITAT:** Thickets, underbrush, gardens; in West, also coastal chaparral, sagebrush.

CAROLINA WREN *Thryothorus ludovicianus*   Common
5½ in. (14 cm). A large familiar wren, near size of a sparrow. *Warm rusty brown* above, variably buff below; conspicuous *white eyebrow stripe.* Often travels in pairs, near ground, skulking over and under logs and brush for insects. **VOICE:** Two- or three-syllable chant: *tea-kettle, tea-kettle, tea kettle,* or *chirpity, chirpity, chirpity, chirp.* Chips and churrs. **SIMILAR SPECIES:** Bewick's and Marsh Wrens. **HABITAT:** Tangles, undergrowth, woods, gardens. Sometimes nests in bird boxes. Casual vagrant west of range.

WRENS

WINTER
WREN

HOUSE
WREN

PACIFIC
WREN

BEWICK'S
WREN

CAROLINA
WREN

SEDGE WREN *Cistothorus platensis* Uncommon, secretive

4½ in. (11 cm). Stubbier than Marsh Wren; buffier, with *buffy* undertail coverts, *barred wings*, and *finely streaked* crown. **VOICE:** Song a dry staccato chattering: *chap chap chap chap chap chap chap chapper-rrrrr.* Call a single or double warblerlike *chap.* **SIMILAR SPECIES:** House Wren, Marsh Wren. **HABITAT:** Grassy and sedgy marshes and meadows. Casual vagrant to W. Coast.

MARSH WREN *Cistothorus palustris* Fairly common

5 in. (13 cm). *White stripes on back* and white eyebrow stripe identify this marsh dweller. Note larger size, unstreaked dark crown, more distinct back stripes, and whiter sides of breast than Sedge Wren. Coloration and distinctness of pattern varies geographically. **VOICE:** Song reedy, gurgling, *cut-cut-turrrrrrrrr-ur,* often ending in rattle; can sing at night. Call a low *tsuck-tsuck.* **SIMILAR SPECIES:** Sedge Wren. **HABITAT:** Fresh and brackish cattail, tule, and bulrush marshes; in winter, also salt marshes.

CANYON WREN *Catherpes mexicanus* Fairly common

5¾–6 in. (15 cm). Note *white bib.* Rusty, with dark rufous brown belly contrasting with white breast and throat. Long, slightly decurved bill. Often climbs vertically on rocks, exploring cracks and crevices. **VOICE:** Gushing cadence of clear, curved notes tripping down scale; *te-you, te-you, tew tew.* Or *tee tee tee tee tew tew tew tew.* Call a shrill *beet.* **SIMILAR SPECIES:** Rock and Bewick's Wrens. **HABITAT:** Drier habitats: cliffs, canyons, rockslides, stone buildings. Casual vagrant east of range.

ROCK WREN *Salpinctes obsoletus* Fairly common

6 in. (15 cm). A gray western wren with *finely streaked breast,* rusty rump, and *buffy terminal tail band.* Frequently bobs. Skulks around on talus slopes and in similar rocky habitats; nests in holes or crevices. **VOICE:** Song consists of thrasherlike phrases and buzzy trills, repeated at lazy intervals; can be heard at distance in open rocky habitats. Also a loud call, *ti-keer.* **SIMILAR SPECIES:** Canyon Wren. **HABITAT:** Rocky slopes, canyons, rubble. Rare vagrant to East, accidentally to coast.

CACTUS WREN *Campylorhynchus brunneicapillus* Fairly common

8½ in. (22 cm). A very large wren of arid country. Distinguished from other N. American wrens by *much larger size and heavy spotting,* which in adults gathers into *a cluster on upper breast.* White supercilium, chestnut cap. Spotted outer tail feathers. Males may build and defend several nests of thorny sticks. **VOICE:** Monotonous *chu-chu-chu-chu* or *chug-chug-chug-chug,* on one pitch, gaining speed. **SIMILAR SPECIES:** Sage Thrasher. **HABITAT:** Arid areas of cactus, mesquite, yucca.

WRENS

SEDGE
WREN

MARSH
WREN

CANYON
WREN

ROCK WREN

juvenile

CACTUS
WREN

adult

KINGLETS Family Regulidae

Tiny active birds with small slender bills, short tails, bright red crowns in males. In fall and winter seasons, often found in mixed-species flocks with chickadees, warblers, nuthatches, and creepers. Ages alike, sexes differ. **FOOD:** Insects, larvae. **RANGE:** Eurasia, N. America.

RUBY-CROWNED KINGLET *Regulus calendula*   Common

4¼ in. (11 cm). Tiny, olive-gray, smaller than warblers, *flicks wings constantly.* Note broken white eye-ring, bold wing bars bordered behind by *black "highlight bar."* Male has *scarlet crown patch* (usually concealed; stands out when crest erect in excitement); female lacks red. **VOICE:** *Husky ji-dit.* Song is three or four high notes, several lower notes, and a chant, *tee tee tee-tew tew tew—ti-didee, ti-didee, ti-didee.* **SIMILAR SPECIES:** Golden-crowned Kinglet, Orange-crowned Warbler. See Hutton's Vireo. **HABITAT:** In summer, coniferous forests; in migration and winter, variety of other woodlands, residential areas.

GOLDEN-CROWNED KINGLET *Regulus satrapa*   Fairly common

4 in. (10 cm). Tiny olive-gray bird, smaller than warblers. Note *boldly striped face,* wing bars. Flicks wings, though less emphatically than Ruby-crowned Kinglet. Male has red in crown. **VOICE:** High, wiry *see-see-see.* Song a series of high thin notes, ascending, then dropping into a little chatter. **SIMILAR SPECIES:** Ruby-crowned Kinglet. **HABITAT:** Conifers; in winter, sometimes other trees.

GNATCATCHERS Family Polioptilidae

Active birds with slender bills and long mobile tails. **FOOD:** Insects. **RANGE:** Americas.

BLUE-GRAY GNATCATCHER *Polioptila caerulea*   Fairly common

4½ in. (11 cm). Tiny, slim, blue-gray above, whitish below, with *narrow white eye-ring. Long tail* is *mostly white underneath* and often flipped about and cocked. Adults and males average brighter than first-year birds and females; male acquires black line above eye in spring/summer. **VOICE:** Call a thin, peevish *zpee;* often doubled, *zpee-zee.* Song a thin, squeaky, wheezy, bubbly series of notes, easily overlooked. **SIMILAR SPECIES:** Other gnatcatchers. **HABITAT:** Dry, open scrub in West; swampier woods in East; brushy habitats in winter.

BLACK-CAPPED GNATCATCHER *Polioptila nigriceps*   Rare, local

4¼ in. (11 cm). This visitor to se. AZ is a very local breeder there. Note *largely white undertail* (largely black in Black-tailed Gnatcatcher) and *long bill.* Spring/summer male has *black cap;* winter male with black mark above eye; female lacks black in head, has browner wash to back and wings than Blue-gray Gnatcatcher. **VOICE:** Rough *meeeer.* **SIMILAR SPECIES:** Blue-gray Gnatcatcher. **HABITAT:** Brushy washes and streamside habitat in desert.

BLACK-TAILED GNATCATCHER *Polioptila melanura*   Uncommon

4½ in. (11 cm). Similar to Blue-gray Gnatcatcher, but spring/summer male has *black cap,* winter male has black mark above eye; both sexes have darker underparts, underside of tail *largely black.* **VOICE:** Call a thin harsh *chee,* repeated two or three times; soft *chip-chip-chip* series. **SIMILAR SPECIES:** California Gnatcatcher. **HABITAT:** Desert brush, ravines, dry washes, mesquite.

CALIFORNIA GNATCATCHER *Polioptila californica*   Scarce, local

4½ in. (11 cm). No range overlap with Black-tailed Gnatcatcher. Dull *gray below,* tinged buff-brown on wings and flanks, less white on undertail than Black-tailed Gnatcatcher. **VOICE:** Kittenlike *meew,* rising, then falling; harsher *jih-jih-jih.* **SIMILAR SPECIES:** Blue-gray Gnatcatcher. **HABITAT:** Restricted to coastal sage scrub. CA populations endangered.

KINGLETS AND GNATCATCHERS

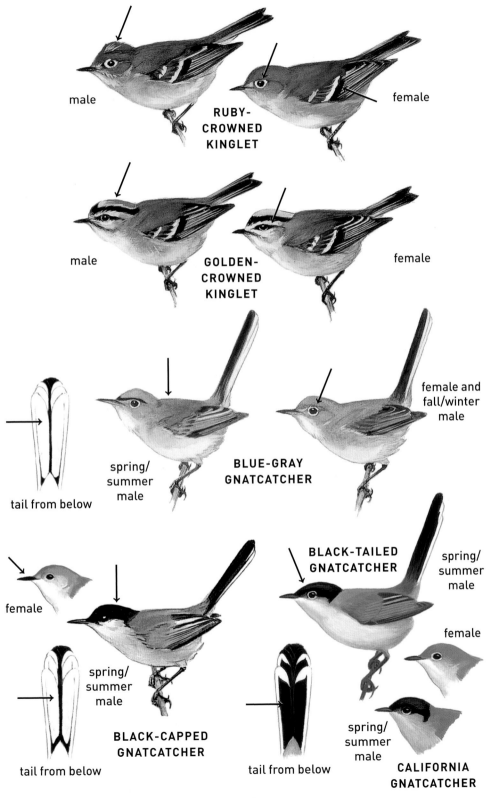

male

female

RUBY-CROWNED KINGLET

male

GOLDEN-CROWNED KINGLET

female

female and fall/winter male

spring/summer male

BLUE-GRAY GNATCATCHER

tail from below

female

spring/summer male

BLACK-TAILED GNATCATCHER

spring/summer male

female

spring/summer male

tail from below

BLACK-CAPPED GNATCATCHER

tail from below

CALIFORNIA GNATCATCHER

SHRIKES Family Laniidae

Rather fierce songbirds with hook-tipped bills. Shrikes perch watchfully on bush tops, treetops, wires; often impale prey on thorns, barbed wire. **FOOD:** Insects, lizards, small rodents, small birds. **RANGE:** Widespread in Old World; two species breed in N. America.

NORTHERN SHRIKE *Lanius borealis*   Scarce

10–10¼ in. (25–26 cm). An irregular winter visitor south of Canadian border; sometimes well south of normal range. Similar to Loggerhead Shrike, but larger, note *narrower dark mask, faintly barred* breast, and longer, more hooked bill with *pale base. Juvenile:* Brown, with weak mask and extensive *fine barring* below; becomes mottled gray in first year. **VOICE:** Song a disjointed, thrasherlike succession of harsh and musical notes. Call *shek-shek;* a grating *jaaeg.* **SIMILAR SPECIES:** Loggerhead Shrike, Northern Mockingbird. **HABITAT:** Semiopen country with lookout posts; in summer, taiga, muskeg, tundra.

LOGGERHEAD SHRIKE *Lanius ludovicianus*   Uncommon to rare

9 in. (23 cm). Big head, slim tail; gray, black, and white, with *black mask, short hooked bill.* Sits quietly on wires or bush tops; flies low with flickering shallow flight showing white patches in wings, then swoops up to perch. *Juvenile:* Has faint barring below *briefly in late summer.* **VOICE:** Song consists of harsh, deliberate notes and phrases, repeated 3 to 20 times; *queedle, queedle,* over and over, or *tsurp-see, tsurp-see.* Call *shack shack* or *jeeer jeeer.* **SIMILAR SPECIES:** Northern Shrike. Northern Mockingbird lacks dark mask and hooked bill. **HABITAT:** Semiopen country with lookout posts: wires, fences, trees, shrubs. Populations on San Clemente I., CA (subspecies *mearnsi*), endangered.

VIREOS Family Vireonidae

Small olive- or gray-backed birds, much like wood-warblers, usually less active. Bill slightly thicker, with more curved ridge and small hook to tip. May be divided into those with eye-rings, those with spectacles, and those with eye lines. Ages and sexes usually similar. **FOOD:** Mostly insects, also fruit in winter. **RANGE:** Canada to Argentina.

BELL'S VIREO *Vireo bellii*   Uncommon

4¾ in. (12 cm). Small, nondescript. Usually stays concealed in dense cover. Thin, pale, broken eye-ring and loral stripe. One or two weak wing bars. Endangered, Southwestern "Least Bell's Vireo" (subspecies *pusillus*) is grayer, flips tail like gnatcatcher; eastern birds are brighter, pump tail like Palm Warbler. **VOICE:** Husky phrases at short intervals: *cheedle cheedle chee? cheedle cheedle chew!* **SIMILAR SPECIES:** Warbling Vireo, first-fall White-eyed Vireo, Gray Vireo. **HABITAT:** Willows, streamsides, hedgerows, mesquite. Casual vagrant to W. and E. Coasts.

BLACK-CAPPED VIREO *Vireo atricapilla*   Scarce, local, endangered

4½ in. (11 cm). Small and sprightly; cap *glossy black* in adult male, slate gray in first-fall male and female, mottled in first-spring male. Note wing bars, white spectacles, *red* eyes. **VOICE:** Song hurried phrases. Call a harsh *chit-ah.* **SIMILAR SPECIES:** Blue-headed and Cassin's Vireos. **HABITAT:** Oak scrub, brushy hills, rocky canyons. Often hard to see. Accidental vagrant west and north of range.

WHITE-EYED VIREO *Vireo griseus*   Fairly common

5 in. (13 cm). Distinctive combination of *yellow spectacles, whitish throat.* Also note wing bars, yellowish sides, white eye (dark through first fall). Somewhat skulking. **VOICE:** Song a sharp *CHICK-a-per-weeoo-CHICK;* variable, usually starts and ends with *chick.* **SIMILAR SPECIES:** Bell's Vireo. **HABITAT:** Wood edges, brush, brambles, dense undergrowth. Very rare vagrant to W. Coast.

SHRIKES

adult

juvenile

NORTHERN
SHRIKE

LOGGERHEAD
SHRIKE

VIREOS

Southwest

BELL'S VIREO

East

adult
male

female

BLACK-CAPPED VIREO

adult

first-
fall

WHITE-EYED VIREO

GRAY VIREO *Vireo vicinior*　　　　　　　　　Scarce

5½ in. (14 cm). This plain, gray-backed vireo of arid mountains has *complete, narrow, white eye-ring* and only *one faint wing bar.* Though drab, it has a feisty character, flipping tail like a gnatcatcher. **VOICE:** Song similar to Plumbeous Vireo's, but sweeter, more rapid, in regular series. **SIMILAR SPECIES:** Plumbeous Vireo stockier, has shorter tail that is not flipped, bold spectacles rather than just eye-ring, and two, thicker wing bars. See Bell's Vireo. **HABITAT:** Pinyon-juniper woodlands, brushy slopes, chamise-dominated chaparral, scrub oak.

HUTTON'S VIREO *Vireo huttoni*　　　　　　Fairly common

5 in. (13 cm). A chunky olive-brown vireo with bold wing bars. Note *incomplete eye-ring,* broken *above,* and large light loral spot. **VOICE:** Buzzy, rising *zu-weep* or falling *zee-ur,* oft-repeated; a hoarse, deliberate *day dee dee.* **SIMILAR SPECIES:** Ruby-crowned Kinglet very similar in plumage but smaller with skinny black legs, smaller bill, quicker movements, black "highlight bar" below lower wing bar. **HABITAT:** Woodlands, parks, particularly with oaks.

BLUE-HEADED VIREO *Vireo solitarius*　　　Fairly common

5¼ in. (14 cm). The northern/eastern representative of the spectacled "Solitary Vireo" complex. Note *sharply demarcated* blue-gray cap, *bright white* spectacles and throat, *bright green* back, yellowish wash to side. **VOICE:** Song of burry phrases with deliberate pauses between; sweet and high pitched: *wee-ay, chweeo, chuweep* (slower than Red-eyed Vireo with fewer notes per phrase). All three species also give a whiny chatter. **SIMILAR SPECIES:** Cassin's Vireo. **HABITAT:** Coniferous, mixed, and deciduous woods. Rare vagrant to W. Coast.

CASSIN'S VIREO *Vireo cassinii*　　　　　　　Uncommon

5¼ in. (14 cm). The Pacific Northwest representative of the "Solitary Vireo" complex. Greener back and more yellowish sides than Plumbeous. Duller overall with less contrasting face pattern than Blue-headed. Bill averages smaller. **VOICE:** Song of slurred phrases with deliberate pauses between. Blue-headed Vireo's phrases sweeter. Cassin's and Plumbeous Vireos have burrier phrases than Blue-headed, a slurred *wee-ay, chweeo, chuweep.* **SIMILAR SPECIES:** Some dull first-year female Blue-headeds can be difficult to separate from bright adult male Cassin's, and some dull Cassin's can approach bright Plumbeous. See also Gray and Bell's Vireos. **HABITAT:** Coniferous, mixed, and deciduous woods. Casual vagrant east of range.

PLUMBEOUS VIREO *Vireo plumbeus*　　　　　Uncommon

5½ in. (15 cm). The Rocky Mt./Great Basin representative of the "Solitary Vireo" complex. Although their nesting ranges barely overlap, all three species may occur together on migration and winter grounds. Plumbeous is mostly gray above, whitish below, with grayish to sides of breast and variable wash of gray or yellow on flanks. **VOICE:** Song similar to Cassin's but Plumbeous is slowest, burriest. **SIMILAR SPECIES:** Blue-headed and Cassin's Vireos. Some dull Cassin's are difficult to separate from Plumbeous. See also Gray Vireo. **HABITAT:** Coniferous, mixed, and deciduous woods.

YELLOW-THROATED VIREO *Vireo flavifrons*　　Fairly common

5½ in. (14 cm). Bright yellow throat, yellow spectacles, and white wing bars. Olive back contrasts with gray rump. **VOICE:** Song similar to Blue-headed Vireo's, but lower pitched with *burry quality;* swings back and forth with phrases that sound like *ee-yay, three-eight.* **SIMILAR SPECIES:** Pine Warbler has some dusky streaks below, white tail spots, smaller bill. **HABITAT:** Deciduous woodlands, shade trees, particularly oaks. Rare vagrant to W. Coast.

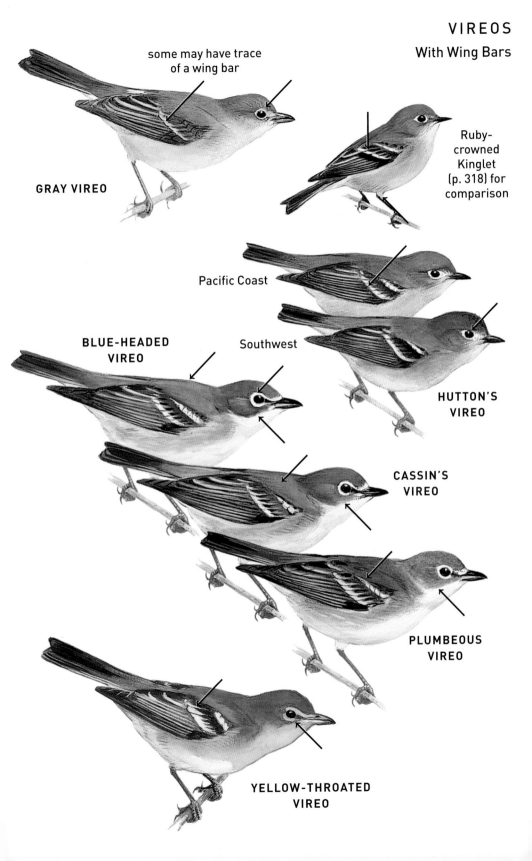

VIREOS
With Wing Bars

some may have trace
of a wing bar

GRAY VIREO

Ruby-
crowned
Kinglet
(p. 318) for
comparison

Pacific Coast

BLUE-HEADED
VIREO

Southwest

HUTTON'S
VIREO

CASSIN'S
VIREO

PLUMBEOUS
VIREO

YELLOW-THROATED
VIREO

YELLOW-GREEN VIREO *Vireo flavoviridis* Very rare, local

6–6¼ in. (15–16 cm). This tropical species is very similar to Red-eyed Vireo, but has *strong yellow tones* on sides, flanks, and undertail coverts; back *yellower* green; head stripes *less distinct;* bill slightly *longer* and paler. **SIMILAR SPECIES:** Note first-fall Red-eyed Vireos may have yellow on flanks and undertail coverts. **VOICE:** Song slower than Red-eyed's, suggestive of House Sparrow. **RANGE:** Rare summer resident in lower Rio Grande Valley, TX. Casual farther north in TX and in s. AZ; very rare (and increasing) fall vagrant to coastal CA. **HABITAT:** Deciduous woods.

RED-EYED VIREO *Vireo olivaceus* Common

6 in. (15 cm). Note *gray cap* contrasting with olive back, and strong, *black-bordered white eyebrow stripe (supercilium)*. Red iris may not be obvious at a distance and is brown in first-fall birds of this, Yellow-green, and Black-whiskered Vireos. **VOICE:** Song is abrupt, robinlike phrases, monotonous. Call a nasal, whining *chway.* **SIMILAR SPECIES:** Warbling Vireo slightly smaller, duller and less contrasty above, with pale lores, arching supercilium, and dark brown eyes. See Yellow-green and Black-whiskered Vireos, both scarce and local. **HABITAT:** Deciduous woodlands, shade trees, groves. Very rare vagrant to W. Coast.

BLACK-WHISKERED VIREO *Vireo altiloquus* Uncommon, local

6¼ in. (16 cm). Narrow dark whisker on each side of throat. Otherwise similar to Red-eyed Vireo, but duller overall, particularly head pattern, and more brownish olive above, with slightly longer bill. **VOICE:** Song slightly slower than Red-eyed's. **HABITAT:** Mangroves, subtropical hardwoods. Casual vagrant to n. Gulf Coast states.

WARBLING VIREO *Vireo gilvus* Fairly common

5½ in. (14 cm). One of the widespread vireos that lack wing bars. In this *very plain* species, note *whitish breast, pale lores,* and *lack of black borders* on eyebrow stripe that also arches slightly above dark eye. Back tinged dull greenish. First-fall and western birds have more yellow on sides. **VOICE:** Song distinctive: a languid warble, unlike broken phrases of other vireos; suggests Purple Finch's song, but less spirited, with burry undertone. Call a wheezy querulous *twee* and short *vit.* **SIMILAR SPECIES:** Philadelphia Vireo smaller billed and "cuter" faced; yellowish on throat and breast, as bright in middle as on sides, has slate gray line through lores. Red-eyed Vireo larger, greener above, and has bolder eyebrow stripe. **HABITAT:** Deciduous and mixed woods, aspen groves, cottonwoods, riparian woodlands, shade trees.

PHILADELPHIA VIREO *Vireo philadelphicus* Uncommon

5¼ in. (13 cm). This smallish vireo has a face pattern reminiscent of Warbling Vireo, but with more distinct dark eye line (including lores) imparting "cuter" look, slightly greener back, and single faint wing bar. Underparts pale and vary from a small wash of pale yellow on lower throat and upper breast in duller adults to more extensive yellow in bright first-fall birds (see p. 350). **VOICE:** Song very similar to Red-eyed Vireo's; higher, slower. Call, a quick, husky *niff-niff-niff-niff.* **SIMILAR SPECIES:** Bright Warbling Vireo in fall tinged green above and has yellow on sides, but that yellow is *dull or lacking in center of breast and throat;* also *lacks Philadelphia's dark line through lores.* Different song. Tennessee Warbler slightly smaller, has finer bill, clear white (not yellow) undertail coverts, blackish rather than blue-gray legs. **HABITAT:** Second-growth woodlands, poplars, willows, alders. Very rare vagrant to W. Coast.

YELLOW-GREEN VIREO

RED-EYED VIREO

adult

first-fall

BLACK-WHISKERED VIREO

adult

first-fall

adult

WARBLING VIREO

spring/ summer

Tennessee Warbler (p. 328) for comparison

fall/ winter

first-fall female

PHILADELPHIA VIREO

spring/summer male

OLIVE WARBLER Family Peucedramidae

Single species. Closely resembles a wood-warbler but now placed in its own family. Longer winged than wood-warblers, tail deeply notched; short, tenth outer primary present. **FOOD:** Insects. **RANGE:** Pine and oak forests in mts. of AZ and NM to Nicaragua.

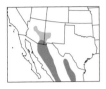

OLIVE WARBLER *Peucedramus taeniatus*　　　　Uncommon, local

5¼ in. (13 cm). All plumages have *deeply notched tail* and bold wing bars with *white patch at base of primaries. Adult male:* Note *orange-brown head and chest* and *black ear patch. Female:* Duller crown tinged olive, breast yellowish. Ear patch dusky. *First-year male:* Like female, but orange-brown mottling often present in crown and breast. **VOICE:** Song a ringing *peter peter peter peter,* variable. Call a rich *kew.* **SIMILAR SPECIES:** Hermit Warbler. **HABITAT:** Pine and fir forests of high mountains. Forages high in trees.

WOOD-WARBLERS Family Parulidae

Popular, active, brightly colored birds, with thin bills. Ages and sexes usually differ. **FOOD:** Mainly insects, though also eat fruit in fall and winter. **RANGE:** N. America to n. Argentina.

BACHMAN'S WARBLER *Vermivora bachmanii*　　Almost certainly extinct

4¾ in. (12 cm). Bill thin and *downcurved. Male:* Face and underparts yellow; bib and crown black. *Female:* Forehead yellow; crown and cheek grayish; eye-ring yellow. **VOICE:** Song a rapid series of flat mechanical buzzes rendered on one pitch: *bzz-bzz-bzz-bzz-bzz-bzz-bzz-bzz.* **SIMILAR SPECIES:** Female might recall female Yellow and Nashville Warblers. **RANGE:** Former resident of Southeast; likely extinct. **HABITAT:** Swampy areas, canebrakes.

GOLDEN-WINGED WARBLER *Vermivora chrysoptera*　　Uncommon

4¾ in. (12 cm). Gray above, white below. *Male:* Unique with combination of *yellow wing patch* and *black throat.* Note yellow forecrown, black *ear patch,* whitish underparts. *Female:* Ear and throat patches grayer. First-year birds average duller than adults within each sex. **VOICE:** Song a buzzy note followed by one to three on a lower pitch: *bee-bz-bz-bz.* Call like Blue-winged's. **SIMILAR SPECIES:** See "Brewster's," "Lawrence's," and Blue-winged Warblers. **HABITAT:** Open woodlands, swampy edges, brushy clearings, undergrowth. Declining in many northeastern and southern areas. Very rare vagrant to W. Coast.

"BREWSTER'S" AND "LAWRENCE'S" WARBLERS　　　　Scarce

Golden-winged and Blue-winged Warblers hybridize where their ranges overlap, producing two basic types, "Brewster's" and "Lawrence's" Warblers. Brewster's typically shows whitish underparts; some can have white or yellow wing bars and some are tinged yellow below. Lawrence's is typically bright yellow below, but with black head pattern of Golden-winged. Back-crosses, females, and first-year males can show mixed and duller plumage combin-ations. **VOICE:** May sing like either parent. **HABITAT:** Same as Blue-winged and Golden-winged Warblers. Accidental vagrants to W. Coast.

BLUE-WINGED WARBLER *Vermivora cyanoptera*　　Fairly common

4¾ in. (12 cm). Note narrow *black line through eye.* Face and underparts yellow; wings have *two white bars.* Female averages duller than male, especially in crown, and first-year birds average duller than adults within each sex. **VOICE:** Song a buzzy *beeee-bzzz,* as if inhaled and exhaled. Call a sharp *tsik.* **SIMILAR SPECIES:** "Brewster's," "Lawrence's," Prothonotary, Golden-winged, and Yellow Warblers. **HABITAT:** Field edges, undergrowth, bushy edges, woodland openings. Very rare vagrant to W. Coast.

WARBLERS

female

adult
male

OLIVE
WARBLER

female

male

BACHMAN'S
WARBLER

female

GOLDEN-
WINGED
WARBLER

male

male

"BREWSTER'S"
WARBLER

male

"LAWRENCE'S"
WARBLER

male

BLUE-WINGED
WARBLER

TENNESSEE WARBLER *Leiothlypis peregrina*   **Fairly common**

4¾ in. (12 cm). Note short tail, *bold eyebrow, white undertail coverts. Spring/ summer male: Pale bluish gray head contrasting with greenish back.* Female and first-fall male: Washed with greenish on head, yellow on breast; often showing a trace of a single wing bar. First-fall females duller (p. 350). **VOICE:** Song staccato, three-part: *ticka ticka ticka ticka, swit swit, chew-chew-chew-chew-chew.* Call a sweet *chip.* **SIMILAR SPECIES:** Arctic Warbler, Orange-crowned Warbler. Vireos larger and thicker billed. **HABITAT:** Deciduous and mixed forests; in migration, a variety of woodlands. Rare vagrant to W. Coast.

ORANGE-CROWNED WARBLER   **Common in West, uncommon in East**
Leiothlypis celata

5 in. (13 cm). Generally drab *olive green* with *yellow undertail coverts* and *blurry breast streaking.* Subspecies vary in brightness: eastern *(celata)* and Great Basin birds *(orestera)* gray-headed, Pacific coastal birds *(lutescens)* brighter yellow-green. Within each subspecies, adult males brighter than first-year males and females, with first-year females dullest (see p. 350). Orange crown-patch largest in males but seldom visible. **VOICE:** Song a colorless trill, becoming weaker toward end. Call a sharp *stik.* **SIMILAR SPECIES:** Fall/winter Tennessee Warbler brighter green, with white undertail coverts, shorter tail. **HABITAT:** Open woodlands, brushy clearings, willows, chaparral, parks, gardens.

COLIMA WARBLER *Leiothlypis crissalis*   **Scarce, local**

5¾ in. (15 cm). Found in Chisos Mts. in w. TX. Drab, with *yellow rump* and under-tail coverts. Larger than Virginia's Warbler; sides *brownish;* lacks yellow on breast. **VOICE:** Song a trill, like Chipping Sparrow, but more musical and ending in two lower notes. **SIMILAR SPECIES:** Lucy's and Virginia's Warblers. **HABITAT:** Oak-pine canyons.

NASHVILLE WARBLER *Leiothlypis ruficapilla*   **Uncommon**

4¾ in. (12 cm). Note *white eye-ring* in combination with *yellow throat. Head gray,* contrasting with olive-green back. No wing bars. Underparts bright yellow with white vest. Adults and males brighter than first-year birds and females. Regularly bobs tail. **VOICE:** Song two-part: *seebit, seebit, seebit, seebit, titititi* (ends like Chipping Sparrow's song). Call a sharp *pink.* **SIMILAR SPECIES:** Connecticut Warbler is larger, behaves very differently, and has grayish or brownish throat. Some dull first-year female Nashvilles (see p. 350) can look almost as dull as Virginia's, but always have *yellow on throat.* **HABITAT:** Open mixed woods with undergrowth, forest edges, bogs; in migration, also brushy areas.

VIRGINIA'S WARBLER *Leiothlypis virginiae*   **Uncommon**

4¾ in. (12 cm). *Male:* A slim *gray* warbler with *yellowish rump* and *bright yellow undertail coverts, white eye-ring,* rufous patch in crown (usually concealed), and touch of yellow on breast. Flicks or jerks tail. *Female and first-year male:* Duller. First-year female can lack yellow on breast, but always has *contrasting yellow undertail coverts.* **VOICE:** Song loose, colorless notes on nearly the same pitch: *chlip-chlip-chlip-chlip-chlip-wick-wick.* Call a sharp *pink,* like Nashville and Lucy's Warblers' calls. **SIMILAR SPECIES:** Nashville and Lucy's Warblers. **HABITAT:** Oak canyons, brushy slopes, pinyon-juniper. Casual vagrant to East, accidentally to coast.

LUCY'S WARBLER *Leiothlypis luciae*   **Uncommon**

4¼ in. (11 cm). A small desert warbler; known by its *chestnut rump patch.* Dull white eye-ring, small patch of chestnut on crown (difficult to see). Ages and sexes similar though females slightly duller. **VOICE:** High *weeta weeta weeta che che che che,* on two pitches. Call a sharp *pink,* like Virginia's Warbler. **SIMILAR SPECIES:** Virginia's and Colima (rare) Warblers. **HABITAT:** Mesquite along desert streams and washes; willows, cottonwoods. Casual vagrant to East.

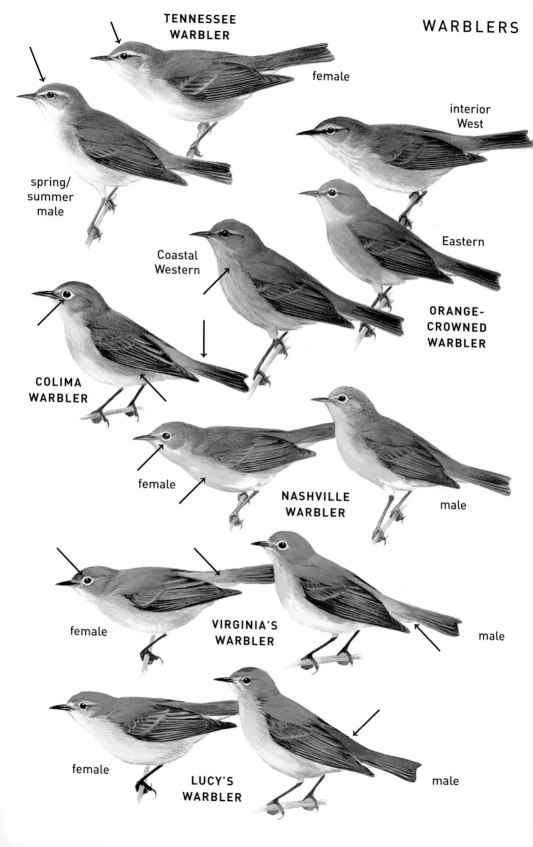

TENNESSEE
WARBLER

WARBLERS

female

interior
West

spring/
summer
male

ORANGE-
CROWNED
WARBLER

Coastal
Western

Eastern

COLIMA
WARBLER

female

NASHVILLE
WARBLER

male

female

VIRGINIA'S
WARBLER

male

female

LUCY'S
WARBLER

male

NORTHERN PARULA *Setophaga americana*

4½ in. (11 cm). A small, short-tailed warbler, *bluish above,* with yellow throat and breast and two white wing bars. Suffused *greenish patch* on back. Distinct *broken white eye-ring.* Varies from bright adult male with *dark breast-band* to first-year female that lacks breast-band, has greenish wash on head (see p. 348). **VOICE:** Song a buzzy trill that climbs the scale and trips over the top: *zeeeeeeeeee-up.* Also *zh-zh-zh-zheeeeee.* **SIMILAR SPECIES:** Tropical Parula of s. TX has dark face mask, no eye-ring. **HABITAT:** Breeds mainly in humid woods where lichen or Spanish moss hangs from trees (occasionally where neither is found). Scarce vagrant to and rare breeder in CA.

TROPICAL PARULA *Setophaga pitiayumi*

Rare, local

4½ in. (11 cm). Similar in size and habits to Northern Parula, but limited in our area to s. TX, near Rio Grande. Dark head and *black face, lacks white eye-ring.* Two bold white wing bars. Lacks distinct color bands across chest of adult male Northern Parula. Adult and male slightly brighter than first-year birds and female. **VOICE:** Like Northern Parula's. **SIMILAR SPECIES:** Northern Parula. **HABITAT:** Oaks, dry forests. Accidental vagrant to AZ, CA.

YELLOW WARBLER *Setophaga petechia*

Common

5 in. (13 cm). No other warbler is so extensively yellow and the only warbler with *yellow tail spots* (other warblers have white tail spots or none); all ages/sexes also have yellow edgings to wing and tail. Male has *rusty breast streaks* (in females and first-fall male these are faint or lacking). Note dark beady eye. First-fall female lacks breast streaks; some individuals may be quite dull, with noticeable eye-ring and brighter yellow restricted to lower vent and undertail coverts (see p. 348). **VOICE:** Song a bright cheerful *tsee-tsee-tsee-tsee-titi-wee* or *weet weet weet weet tsee-tsee wew.* Variable. Call a soft, rich *chip.* **SIMILAR SPECIES:** Wilson's Warblers and brighter Orange-crowned Warblers are longer tailed, lack yellow tail spots. Note vocal differences. **HABITAT:** Riparian woodlands and understory, swamp edges, particularly alders and willows; also parks, gardens.

CHESTNUT-SIDED WARBLER *Setophaga pensylvanica*

Fairly common

5 in. (13 cm). Usually holds tail cocked up at an angle. *Spring/summer:* Identified by combination of *yellow crown, chestnut sides.* Males brighter than females in spring. In fall, chestnut in sides lacking or reduced, upperparts plainer lime greenish with narrow white eye-ring and *two pale yellow* wing bars (p. 348). **VOICE:** Song similar to Yellow Warbler's: *see see see see Miss BEECHer* or *please please pleased to MEETcha,* last note dropping. Call a rich *chip,* like Yellow Warbler's. **HABITAT:** Undergrowth, overgrown field edges, small trees. Rare vagrant to W. Coast.

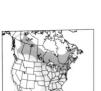

MAGNOLIA WARBLER *Setophaga magnolia*

Fairly common

5 in. (13 cm). A distinctive "black-and-yellow" warbler. *Spring/summer male:* Upperparts blackish, with large white patches on wings and tail; underparts yellow, with heavy black stripes. *Female and fall/winter male:* Duller. First-fall female has weak stripes on sides and thin, weak grayish band across upper breast, but tail pattern distinctive (p. 348). In all ages and sexes, black tail crossed midway by *broad white band* (from beneath, tail is white with broad black tip). **VOICE:** Song suggests Yellow Warbler's but is shorter: *weeta weeta weetsee* (last note rising); or a Hooded Warbler–like *weeta weeta wit-chew.* Call an odd nasal note. **SIMILAR SPECIES:** Yellow-rumped and Black-throated Green Warblers. **HABITAT:** Low conifers; in migration, a variety of woodlands. Rare vagrant to W. Coast.

WARBLERS

female

male

NORTHERN PARULA

TROPICAL PARULA

male

spring/ summer female

YELLOW WARBLER

spring/ summer male

spring/ summer female

CHESTNUT-SIDED WARBLER

spring/ summer male

spring/ summer female

MAGNOLIA WARBLER

spring/ summer male

CAPE MAY WARBLER *Setophaga tigrina* Uncommon

5 in. (13 cm). *Spring/summer male:* Note *chestnut* cheeks. Yellow below, striped with black; rump yellow, crown black. *Female and fall/winter male:* Lacks chestnut cheeks; duller, breast often whitish, streaked. Note dull *patch of yellow behind ear, yellowish rump,* and *one wing bar bolder than the other.* First-fall female (p. 348) distinctly *gray,* can lack yellow. **VOICE:** Song a very high, thin *seet seet seet seet.* May be confused with song of Bay-breasted or Black-and-white Warbler. **SIMILAR SPECIES:** Dull fall/winter females may be confused with Yellow-rumped Warbler but are plainer; have small pale patch behind ear; duller, greenish-yellow rump; and shorter tail. **HABITAT:** Spruce forests, often searches out isolated spruce and fir trees in migration, also broadleaf trees. Populations fluctuate with those of spruce budworms, its preferred food in summer. Very rare vagrant to W. Coast.

BLACK-THROATED BLUE WARBLER *Setophaga caerulescens* Fairly common

5¼ in. (13 cm). *Male:* Clean-cut; upperparts *deep blue;* throat and sides *black,* belly white; wing with large white spot at base of primaries. First-year male similar but slightly duller, wing edging greener. *Female:* Olive-backed, with light line over eye and smaller *white wing spot.* First-year female (p. 350) may lack this white spot but note *dark cheek.* **VOICE:** Song a husky, lazy *zur, zur, zur, zreee* or *beer, beer, bree* (ending higher). Call a hard *thip,* similar to call of Dark-eyed Junco. **HABITAT:** Understory of deciduous and mixed woodlands. Very rare vagrant to W. Coast.

YELLOW-RUMPED WARBLER *Setophaga coronata* Common

5½ in. (14 cm). Includes "Audubon's" *(auduboni)* and "Myrtle" *(coronata)* Warblers, two subspecies groups formerly considered separate species. Note bright *yellow rump* in all subspecies, ages, and sexes. *Spring/summer male:* Blue-gray above; heavy black breast patch (like an inverted U); crown and side patches yellow. Audubon's (breeds in w. U.S., sw. Canada) differs from Myrtle (breeds in AK, much of Canada, e. U.S.) in having *yellow throat* (which does not extend back below cheek, as white does in Myrtle), larger white wing patches, no white supercilium, plainer face. *Spring/summer female:* Similar but duller overall. *Fall/winter* (see also p. 348): More brownish above; whitish below; throat often lacks yellow in first-fall Audubon's; *rump yellow.* **VOICE:** Variable song, juncolike but two-part, rising or dropping in pitch, *seet-seet-seet-seet-seet, trrrrrrrr.* Call a loud *check* or *chip* (Myrtle) or more nasal *tchenp* (Audubon's). **SIMILAR SPECIES:** Cape May and Magnolia Warblers. **HABITAT:** Coniferous forests. In migration and winter, varied; open woods, coastal bushes, brush, thickets, parks, gardens, upper beaches.

BLACK-THROATED GRAY WARBLER *Setophaga nigrescens* Fairly common

5 in. (13 cm). *Spring/summer and adult male:* Gray above, with black throat, cheek, and crown separated by white. *Small yellow spot in lores.* Female: Slaty crown and cheek; dusky or light throat; loral spot duller yellow. *First-fall:* Male like adult female but throat mottled black; female duller, may be tinged brownish above; cheeks dull gray; loral spot pale. **VOICE:** Song a buzzy chant, "full of Zs," *zeedle zeedle zeedle ZEETche* (next-to-last or last note higher). Call a dull *tup.* **SIMILAR SPECIES:** Suggests Black-and-white Warbler, but lacks white stripes on back and crown, does not crawl around on branches and limbs. **HABITAT:** Nests in oaks, pinyon-juniper, mixed woods. Casual vagrant to E. Coast.

WARBLERS

spring/
summer
male

spring/
summer
female

CAPE MAY WARBLER

female

BLACK-THROATED BLUE WARBLER

male

first-fall

spring/summer male

"Myrtle" Warbler

YELLOW-RUMPED WARBLER

spring/summer female

BLACK-THROATED GRAY WARBLER

spring/
summer male

spring/
summer
male

"Audubon's" Warbler

female and
fall/winter
male

first-fall male

female

GOLDEN-CHEEKED WARBLER

Scarce, local, endangered

Setophaga chrysoparia

5¼ in. (14 cm). Breeds in Ashe juniper hills of Edwards Plateau, TX. *Spring/summer and adult male:* Similar to Black-throated Green Warbler, but with *black back* and blacker line through eye. *Female and first-fall male:* Similar to female Black-throated Green, but back darker olive with dusky streaks, belly snowy white (lacking tinge of yellow on flanks). **VOICE:** Song a hurried *tweeah, tweeah, tweesy* or *bzzzz, laysee, daysee.* Call a flat *tip* or *tup.* **SIMILAR SPECIES:** Black-throated Green, Hermit, and Townsend's Warblers. **HABITAT:** Junipers, oaks; also streamside trees. Accidental vagrant to CA.

HERMIT WARBLER *Setophaga occidentalis*

Uncommon

5 in. (13 cm). *Spring/summer and adult male:* Note bright *yellow face* set off by black throat and nape and gray back. *Female and first-fall male:* Black of throat much reduced or wanting, but plain-looking yellow face, gray back, and *unstreaked* underparts identify it. **VOICE:** Song three high lisping notes followed by two abrupt lower ones: *seedle, seedle, seedle, CHUP CHUP.* Call a flat *tip* (like Townsend's Warbler's). **SIMILAR SPECIES:** Black-throated Green Warbler. Townsend's Warbler has dark cheeks, olive back, extensive yellow below. Hybrid Townsend's × Hermit Warblers occur regularly and can have various combinations of parent species' characters. **HABITAT:** Coniferous forests; in migration, coniferous and deciduous woods. Accidental vagrant to E. Coast.

TOWNSEND'S WARBLER *Setophaga townsendi*

Fairly common

5 in. (13 cm). *Spring/summer and adult male:* Easily distinguished by *black-and-yellow pattern of head,* with *blackish cheek patch; underparts yellow;* and heavily striped sides. *Adult female and first-fall male:* Throat largely yellow, with no or mottled black; *well-defined dark cheek patch, bordered by yellow* as in male. *First-fall female:* Duller, with grayish cheeks. **VOICE:** Song like Black-throated Gray Warbler's but higher: *dzeer dzeer dzeer tseetsee* or *weazy, weazy, seesee.* Call a soft, flat *tip.* **SIMILAR SPECIES:** See Hermit Warbler. Black-throated Green Warbler, dull Blackburnian Warblers. **HABITAT:** Tall conifers, cool fir forests; in migration and winter, also oaks, riparian woodlands, parks, gardens. Casual vagrant to E. Coast.

BLACK-THROATED GREEN WARBLER *Setophaga virens*

Fairly common

5 in. (13 cm). *Spring/summer and adult male:* Bright *yellow face* is framed by black throat and olive-green crown. *Female and first-fall male:* Yellow face; much less black on throat; unmarked olive green back, black mottling on sides of upper breast. *First-fall female:* Dullest (see also p. 348). All birds have small yellow spot near vent. **VOICE:** Lisping, weezy or buzzy *zoo zee zoo zoo zee* or *zee zee zee zee zoo zee.* Call a flat *tip* or *tup.* **SIMILAR SPECIES:** Townsend's Warbler has darker cheek, darker above, yellow on lower breast. Hermit Warbler has yellow on crown, lacks eye stripe; back gray; no black stripes on sides. Golden-cheeked Warbler has black line through eye. **HABITAT:** Mainly coniferous or mixed woods; in migration, variety of woodlands. Very rare vagrant to W. Coast.

BLACKBURNIAN WARBLER *Setophaga fusca*

Fairly common

5 in. (13 cm). The "fire throat." *Spring/summer and adult male:* Black and white, with *flame orange* on head and throat. *Female and first-fall male:* Paler orange on throat; dark cheek patch. First-fall female (p. 348) dullest with yellow throat. Note head stripes, *pale back stripes.* **VOICE:** Song *zip zip zip titi tseeeeee,* ending on a very high, up-slurred note (inaudible to some ears). Also a two-part *teetsa teetsa teetsa teetsa zizizizizi,* more like Nashville Warbler. Call a rich *chip.* **SIMILAR SPECIES:** Dull Townsend's Warbler yellower in head, back greener. See also Yellow-throated and Cerulean Warblers. **HABITAT:** Woodlands; in summer, conifers. Rare vagrant to W. Coast.

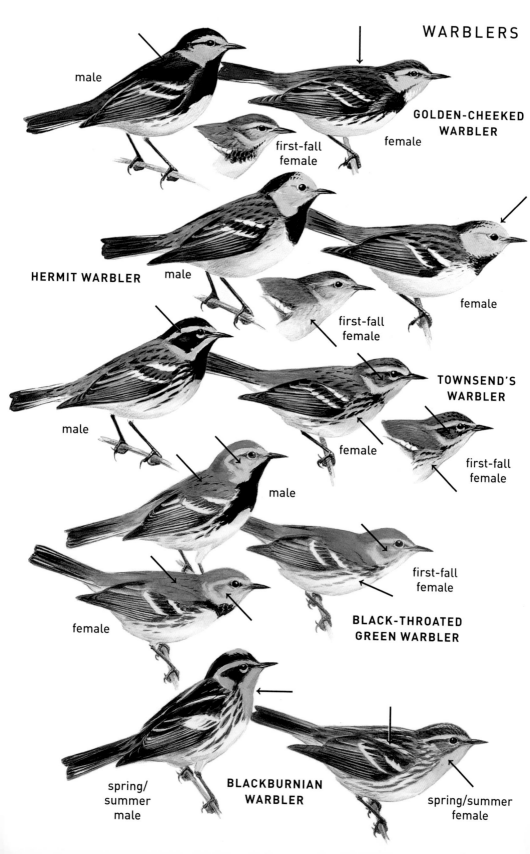

WARBLERS

male

first-fall
female

female

GOLDEN-CHEEKED
WARBLER

HERMIT WARBLER

male

first-fall
female

female

male

male

female

TOWNSEND'S
WARBLER

first-fall
female

male

first-fall
female

female

BLACK-THROATED
GREEN WARBLER

spring/
summer
male

BLACKBURNIAN
WARBLER

spring/summer
female

PINE WARBLER *Setophaga pinus*   Common

5½ in. (14 cm). All plumages have dark cheeks, blurry streaking at breast-sides, unstreaked back, white tail spots, and dark feet. *Adult male:* Yellow-breasted, with olive-green back, *white wing bars.* Adult female and first-year male duller; brownish olive above. *First-fall female:* Often obscure, can lack yellow (see also p. 348). **VOICE:** Song a trill on one pitch, like Chipping Sparrow's song, but more musical, slower. Call a sweet *chip.* **SIMILAR SPECIES:** Fall/winter Blackpoll and Bay-breasted Warblers have more black streaking in back, less prominent dark cheeks. **HABITAT:** Pine woods. In winter sometimes in fields with bluebirds. Very rare vagrant and winter visitor to W. Coast.

PRAIRIE WARBLER *Setophaga discolor*   Fairly common

4¾ in. (12 cm). This warbler *bobs its tail* (as does Palm Warbler); underparts yellow with black stripes *confined to sides; two black face marks,* one through eye, one below. At close range, chestnut marks may be seen on back of male (reduced in female). First-fall birds (p. 348) duller, especially female. **VOICE:** Song a thin *zee zee zee zee zee zee zee zee,* ascending the chromatic scale. Call a sharp *tschip.* **SIMILAR SPECIES:** Pine, Palm, and Yellow Warblers. **HABITAT:** Brushy pastures, low pines, mangroves. Very rare vagrant to W. Coast.

PALM WARBLER *Setophaga palmarum*   Common

5¼ in. (14 cm). Note constant *bobbing* of tail. Both sexes brownish or olive above; yellowish or dirty white below, narrowly streaked; *bright yellow undertail* coverts, white spots in tail corners. In spring/summer has *chestnut cap;* ages and sexes rather similar. Two subspecies: Eastern breeders have more yellow below and on eyebrow; western breeders duller (p. 348), may have yellow restricted to undertail coverts in fall. **VOICE:** Song weak, repetitious notes: *zhe-zhe-zhe-zhe-zhe-zhe.* Call a distinctive sharp *tsup.* **SIMILAR SPECIES:** Yellow-rumped and Prairie Warblers. **HABITAT:** In summer, wooded borders of muskeg, bogs. In migration and winter, bushes, weedy fields. A ground-loving warbler. Scarce vagrant and winter visitor to W. Coast.

YELLOW-THROATED WARBLER *Setophaga dominica*   Fairly common

5½ in. (14 cm). A gray-backed warbler with *yellow throat. Black eye mask,* white wing bars, black stripes on sides. Ages and sexes similar; first-fall female slightly duller. Creeps about branches of trees. "Sutton's" Warbler is a very rare hybrid of Yellow-throated Warbler and Northern Parula. **VOICE:** Song a series of clear slurred notes dropping slightly in pitch: *tee-ew, tew, tew, tew, tew, tew wi* (last note rising). Call a rich *chip.* **SIMILAR SPECIES:** Grace's and female Black-burnian Warblers. **HABITAT:** Open woodlands, especially sycamores, live oaks, pines. In winter, palms. Very rare vagrant to W. Coast.

KIRTLAND'S WARBLER *Setophaga kirtlandii*   Rare, local, endangered

5¾ in. (15 cm). Bluish gray above, *streaked with black;* yellow below, with black spots or streaks confined to sides. *Male:* Has *blackish mask. Female:* Duller, lacks mask; first-fall female browner. Persistently wags tail. **VOICE:** Song, loud and low-pitched, three or four low staccato notes, followed by rapid ringing notes on higher pitch, which end abruptly. **SIMILAR SPECIES:** Yellow-rumped, Yellow-throated, and Magnolia Warblers. **HABITAT:** Groves of young jack pines 5 to 18 ft. high with ground cover of berries and fern.

GRACE'S WARBLER *Setophaga graciae*   Uncommon

5 in. (13 cm). *Gray-backed, with yellow throat and upper breast,* two wing bars, *yellowish eyebrow stripe,* dark streaks on sides. Ages and sexes rather similar. **VOICE:** *Cheedle cheedle che che che che* (ends in a trill). Call a soft, sweet *chip.* **SIMILAR SPECIES:** Yellow-rumped ("Audubon's") Warbler. Yellow-throated Warbler has white patch behind ear, blacker facial pattern. **HABITAT:** Pine-oak forests of canyons and mountains. Very rare vagrant to CA.

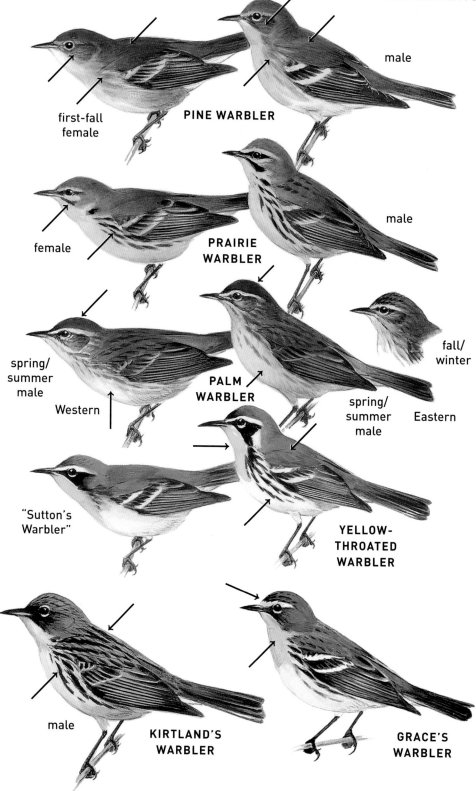

first-fall
female

PINE WARBLER

male

female

PRAIRIE
WARBLER

male

spring/
summer
male

Western

PALM
WARBLER

spring/
summer
male

fall/
winter

Eastern

"Sutton's
Warbler"

YELLOW-
THROATED
WARBLER

male

KIRTLAND'S
WARBLER

GRACE'S
WARBLER

BAY-BREASTED WARBLER *Setophaga castanea* Uncommon

5½ in. (14 cm). *Spring/summer male:* Dark looking, with *chestnut throat, upper breast,* and sides. Note *buff patch* on neck. *Spring/summer female:* Paler, with whitish throat. *Fall/winter* (see also p. 348): Olive green above; two white wing bars; pale buff to chestnut flanks, dark feet. **VOICE:** High, sibilant *tees teesi teesi;* resembles song of Black-and-white Warbler, but thinner, shorter, more on one pitch. Call a sharp *chip,* like Blackpoll Warbler's. **SIMILAR SPECIES:** See fall/winter Blackpoll and Pine Warblers. **HABITAT:** Woodlands; in summer, conifers. Very rare vagrant to W. Coast.

BLACKPOLL WARBLER *Setophaga striata* Common

5½ in. (14 cm). *Spring/summer male:* A striped gray warbler with *black cap, white cheeks, distinct pale legs. Spring/summer female: Greenish gray above,* whitish below, *streaked. Fall/winter* (see also p. 348): Olive above, greenish yellow below, *faintly streaked* on back and on breast; two wing bars; *whitish undertail coverts;* usually *bright yellow legs* (or at least *feet*). **VOICE:** Song a thin, mechanical, very high-pitched *zi-zi-zi-zi-zi-zi-zi-zi-zi* on one pitch, becoming stronger, then diminishing. Call a sharp *chip.* **SIMILAR SPECIES:** Black-and-white Warbler has white stripe through crown and on back, different behavior. Fall/winter Bay-breasted Warbler has buff wash on flanks and undertail coverts and dark feet. See also Pine Warbler. **HABITAT:** Conifers; in migration, broadleaf trees. Rare vagrant to W. Coast.

BLACK-AND-WHITE WARBLER *Mniotilta varia* Common

5¼ in. (13 cm). *Creeping along trunks* and branches of trees, this warbler is *striped lengthwise with black and white* and has striped crown, white stripes on back. *Spring/summer and adult male:* Black throat partly or mostly lost in winter. *Female and first-fall male:* Paler cheeks, fainter streaks below, and buffy wash on flanks. **VOICE:** Song a thin *weesee weesee weesee weesee;* suggests one of American Redstart's songs, but higher pitched and longer; sometimes can drop in pitch midway. Call a sharp *chip.* **SIMILAR SPECIES:** Blackpoll and Black-throated Gray Warblers. **HABITAT:** Woods. Rare vagrant and winter visitor to W. Coast.

CERULEAN WARBLER *Setophaga cerulea* Uncommon

4¾ in. (12 cm). A small, short-tailed warbler, often high up in large trees. *Spring/summer and adult male: Blue* above, white below. Note *narrow black band* across chest. *Adult female:* Dull blue (mostly restricted to crown and rump) and *olive green above,* whitish below; two white wing bars, *broad whitish eyebrow. First-fall:* Male like a dull female; washed with pale yellow on breast; female green with white wing bars, can lack blue. **VOICE:** Buzzy notes on same pitch, followed by longer note on a higher pitch: *zray zray z-z-z zeeeee.* Call a rich, slurred *chip.* **SIMILAR SPECIES:** First-fall female can suggest Tennessee Warbler, but latter lacks bold white wing bars; also fall/winter Blackpoll Warbler, but smaller, greener above, whitish below, with more conspicuous eyebrow. Dull female Blackburnian Warbler has darker streaked back pattern. **HABITAT:** High in deciduous forests, especially in river valleys and ridges. Accidental vagrant to W. Coast.

AMERICAN REDSTART *Setophaga ruticilla* Common

5¼ in. (13 cm). Butterfly-like; actively flitting, with drooping wings and spread tail. *Adult male:* Black; *bright orange patches* on wings and tail. *Female:* Gray-olive above; *yellow flash patches* on wings and tail. *First-year male:* Like female, but tinged with orange on chest patches, acquires black splotches on face in spring. **VOICE:** Songs (often alternated) *zee zee zee zee zwee* (last note higher), *tsee tsee tsee tsee tsee-o* (last syllable dropping), and *teetsa teetsa teetsa teetsa teet* (notes paired). Call a slurred, rich *chip.* **HABITAT:** Second-growth woods, riparian woodlands. Scarce vagrant to W. Coast.

WARBLERS

fall/winter

BAY-BREASTED WARBLER

spring/summer male

spring/ summer female

spring/ summer male

fall/winter

BLACKPOLL WARBLER

spring/ summer female

female and first-fall male

adult and spring male

BLACK-AND-WHITE WARBLER

adult and spring male

adult male

female

CERULEAN WARBLER

first-year male

female

AMERICAN REDSTART

SWAINSON'S WARBLER *Limnothlypis swainsonii* Uncommon

5½ in. (14 cm). A plain brown skulker, difficult to see. Long bill. Olive-brown above and buffy white below, with *brown crown* and *light eyebrow stripe.* Ages and sexes similar. **VOICE:** Song suggests Louisiana Waterthrush's, but shorter (five notes: two slurred notes, two lower notes, and a higher note): *wee-wee-chip-poor-will.* Call a sharp, loud *chip.* **SIMILAR SPECIES:** Ovenbird, Worm-eating Warbler, waterthrushes. **HABITAT:** Cane thickets, swamps, stream bottoms, thick woodland brush; locally in rhododendron-hemlock tangles in Appalachians. Accidental vagrant to AZ.

WORM-EATING WARBLER *Helmitheros vermivorum* Uncommon

5¼ in. (13 cm). An unobtrusive forager of wooded slopes and thick understory. Often probes dead-leaf clusters. *Dull olive,* with *black stripes on buffy head.* Breast *rich buff.* Ages and sexes similar. **VOICE:** Song a series of thin dry notes; resembles trill or rattle of Chipping Sparrow, but thinner, more rapid, and insectlike. Call a flat *chip,* also a distinctive *zeet-zeet* in flight. **SIMILAR SPECIES:** Ovenbird, Swainson's Warbler, waterthrushes. **HABITAT:** Wooded hillsides, undergrowth, ravines. Very rare vagrant and winter visitor to W. Coast.

OVENBIRD *Seiurus aurocapilla* Common

6 in. (15 cm). When breeding, less often seen than heard. When seen, usually walking on leafy floor of woods. Suggests a small thrush, but *striped* rather than spotted beneath. *Orangish patch on crown bordered by blackish stripes. White eye-ring.* Ages and sexes similar. **VOICE:** Song an emphatic *TEACHer, TEACHer, TEACHer,* etc., in crescendo. In some areas, monosyllabic *TEACH, TEACH, TEACH,* etc. Call a loud, sharp *tshuk.* **SIMILAR SPECIES:** Waterthrushes. See also spotted thrushes (p. 286). **HABITAT:** Near or on ground in leafy and pine-oak woods; in migration, also thickets. Rare vagrant to W. Coast.

NORTHERN WATERTHRUSH *Parkesia noveboracensis* Common

5¾ in. (15 cm). Suggests a small thrush. *Walks* along water's edge and *teeters* like a Spotted Sandpiper. Brown-backed, often tinged olive, with *striped* underparts, strong eyebrow stripe; both eyebrow and underparts vary from whitish to pale yellow. *Throat striped.* Ages and sexes similar. **VOICE:** Call a sharp *chink.* Song a vigorous, rapid *twit twit twit sweet sweet sweet chew chew chew* (chews drop in pitch). **SIMILAR SPECIES:** Louisiana Waterthrush, Ovenbird. **HABITAT:** Swamps, bogs, wet woods with standing water, streamsides, pond shores; in migration, also marsh edges, puddles, mangroves. Rare vagrant and winter visitor to W. Coast.

LOUISIANA WATERTHRUSH *Parkesia motacilla* Uncommon

6 in. (15 cm). Similar to Northern Waterthrush, but underparts *white on breast, pinkish buff on flanks and undertail coverts.* Bill slightly larger. *Eyebrow stripe pure white and flares noticeably behind eye.* Throat usually *lacks stripes.* Legs pinkish. Ages and sexes similar. **VOICE:** Song musical and ringing; three clear slurred whistles, followed by a jumble of twittering notes dropping in pitch. **SIMILAR SPECIES:** Some fall/winter Northern Waterthrushes (particularly of western subspecies, *P. n. notabilis*) have whitish eyebrow stripe. Northern has small spots or stripes on throat and *even-toned* (yellow to off-white) underparts, without buff flanks as in Louisiana. Song of Swainson's Warbler somewhat similar. **HABITAT:** Streams, brooks, ravines, wooded swamps. Bobs when walking, more exaggerated than in Northern. Casual vagrant and winter visitor to W. Coast.

SWAINSON'S
WARBLER

WORM-EATING
WARBLER

OVENBIRD

fresh fall

NORTHERN
WATERTHRUSH

worn
spring

LOUISIANA
WATERTHRUSH

PROTHONOTARY WARBLER *Protonotaria citrea*   Fairly common

5½ in. (14 cm). A golden bird of wooded swamps. *Male:* Entire head and breast deep *yellow to orangey.* Wings blue-gray *with no bars. Female:* Duller, fewer white spots in tail. First-year birds are duller within each sex (p. 350). **VOICE:** Song *zweet zweet zweet zweet zweet zweet,* on one pitch. Call a loud *seep.* **SIMILAR SPECIES:** Yellow and Blue-winged Warblers. **HABITAT:** Wooded swamps, backwaters, river edges. Very rare vagrant to W. Coast.

KENTUCKY WARBLER *Geothlypis formosa*   Uncommon

5¼ in. (13 cm). Note *broad black sideburns* extending down from eye and *yellow spectacles.* Female and first-year male duller but retain distinctive mask pattern. **VOICE:** Song a rapid rolling chant, *tory-tory-tory-tory* or *churry-churry-churry-churry,* suggestive of Carolina Wren, but less musical (two-syllable rather than three-syllable phrases); heard about ten times more often than seen. Call a rich, low *tup.* **SIMILAR SPECIES:** Common Yellowthroat lacks spectacles. See also Hooded Warbler. **HABITAT:** Woodland undergrowth, swamps. Very rare vagrant to W. Coast.

CONNECTICUT WARBLER *Oporornis agilis*   Uncommon

5¾–6 in. (15 cm). Shy and skulking. Similar to MacGillivray's and Mourning Warblers, but slightly larger and plumper; note *walking behavior* — on limbs and ground — and *complete white eye-ring, long undertail coverts* reaching almost to tail tip. *Spring/summer and adult:* Hood gray in male, gray-brown in female. *First-fall:* Duller, with brownish hood, paler throat (see also p. 350). **VOICE:** Repetitious *chip-chup-ee, chip-chup-ee, chip-chup-ee, chip* or *sugar-tweet, sugar-tweet, sugar-tweet.* **SIMILAR SPECIES:** First-fall Mourning Warbler has broken eye-ring (rarely looking complete); yellow throat. Also, Mourning is faster and twitchier, hops rather than walks. Nashville Warbler also has eye-ring, but is smaller, has yellow throat, and actively feeds in trees. See also MacGillivray's Warbler. **HABITAT:** Poplar bluffs, muskeg, mixed woods; in migration, undergrowth. Feeds mostly on ground. Very rare vagrant to W. Coast.

MOURNING WARBLER *Geothlypis philadelphia*   Uncommon

5¼ in. (13 cm). Shy and skulking. Olive above, yellow below, with slate-gray hood encircling head and neck. *Spring/summer and adult male:* Has irregular black bib. *Female and first-fall male:* May have thin eye-ring that is barely broken, typically not thicker eye-arcs of MacGillivray's Warbler. Some spring/summer females and all first-fall birds (see p. 350) have yellow throats, in some extending through middle breast, in others separated by thin band. Yellow undertail coverts of medium length between Connecticut and MacGillivray's Warblers. **VOICE:** Song *chirry, chirry, chorry, chorry* (*chorry* lower). Considerable variation. Call a hard, buzzy, wrenlike *chack.* **SIMILAR SPECIES:** MacGillivray's and Connecticut Warblers. **HABITAT:** Thickets, undergrowth. Rare vagrant to W. Coast.

MACGILLIVRAY'S WARBLER *Geothlypis tolmiei*   Uncommon

5¼ in. (13 cm). *Spring/summer and adult male:* Olive above, yellow below, with *slate gray hood* (blackish lores and upper breast) completely encircling head and neck. Thick, *partial white eye-ring is broken fore and aft,* forming crescents. *Female:* Similar, but hood paler, washed out on throat. *First-fall:* Like female but duller; throat buff. **VOICE:** Song a rolling *chiddle-chiddle-chiddle, turtle-turtle,* last notes dropping; or *sweeter-sweeter-sweeter, sugar-sugar.* Call a low, hard *chik,* given often. **SIMILAR SPECIES:** First-fall birds told from those of Mourning Warbler by buff to *grayish white* throat, without yellow. Orange-crowned Warbler has grayish head, olive-yellow body, and pale, broken eye-ring; but is smaller, has a sharper bill, and feeds more actively, higher up in bushes and trees. See also voice. **HABITAT:** Low dense undergrowth; shady thickets. Casual vagrant to E. Coast.

WARBLERS

PROTHONOTARY
WARBLER

female

male

KENTUCKY
WARBLER

spring/summer
male

CONNECTICUT
WARBLER

first-fall
female

Nashville Warbler
(p. 328) for
comparison

spring/
summer
female

MOURNING
WARBLER

spring/
summer male

spring/
summer
female

first-fall
female

spring/
summer male

first-fall
female

spring/
summer
female

MACGILLIVRAY'S
WARBLER

GRAY-CROWNED YELLOWTHROAT *Geothlypis poliocephala* Very rare visitor

5½ in. (14 cm). Male has partial mask *not extending to forehead or cheeks; gray crown*. Both sexes have *thick bill* with *pale lower mandible*; broken white eye-ring. First-year birds duller than adults of each sex. **VOICE:** Burbling warble. Call *chlee-dee*. **SIMILAR SPECIES:** Common Yellowthroat slightly smaller and smaller billed, has different vocalizations. **RANGE:** Very rare visitor from Mex. to s. TX, where it formerly bred. **HABITAT:** Reeds and weedy vegetation near water.

COMMON YELLOWTHROAT *Geothlypis trichas* Common

5 in. (13 cm). Wrenlike. *Spring/summer and adult male:* Distinctive *black mask,* yellow throat and upper breast; first-fall male has reduced and duller dusky mask. *Female:* Olive-brown, with rich yellow throat (can be buff in first-fall; p. 350), duller below, but brighter yellow undertail coverts; lacks black mask. **VOICE:** Bright rapid chant, *witchity-witchity-witchity-witch;* sometimes *witchy-witchy-witchy-witch.* Call a husky *tchep.* **SIMILAR SPECIES:** Female distinguished from first-fall and female Mourning and MacGillivray's Warblers by whitish belly, smaller size. **HABITAT:** Swamps, marshes, wet thickets, woodland edges.

WILSON'S WARBLER *Cardellina pusilla* Common in West, uncommon in East

4¾ in. (12 cm). *Male:* Golden yellow with *round black cap. Female:* Has smaller or no cap, located closer to forecrown. First-year birds have smaller caps than adults, sex for sex (often lacking in females; p. 350), and eastern birds have smaller caps than western birds within each age and sex group. Otherwise, back is olive, underparts yellow, supercilium indistinct yellow, *lores yellow,* tinged olive in East, orange on Pacific Coast. Constantly moving and flitting about. **VOICE:** Song a thin, rapid little chatter, dropping in pitch at end: *chi chi chi chi chi chet chet.* Call a flat *timp.* **SIMILAR SPECIES:** Female Hooded Warbler has white spots in tail, dark lores. Yellow Warbler has yellow spots in shorter tail, yellow edging in wings. See also Orange-crowned Warbler. Note vocal differences. **HABITAT:** Thickets and trees along streams, moist tangles, low shrubs, willows, alders.

HOODED WARBLER *Setophaga citrina* Fairly common

5¼ in. (13 cm). *Male: Black hood* or cowl encircles yellow face and forehead; ages similar. *Female:* Has variable amount of black in head, from a partial hood to none in most first-year females (p. 350); yellow face is usually distinctively outlined, and note *white tail spots.* **VOICE:** Song a loud whistled *weeta wee-tee-o.* Also other arrangements; slurred *tee-o* is a clue. Call a sharp *chink,* like water-thrushes. **SIMILAR SPECIES:** Female Wilson's Warblers without black cap lack tail spots and any suggestion of Hooded's face pattern. **HABITAT:** Wooded undergrowth, laurels, wooded swamps. Rare vagrant to W. Coast.

CANADA WARBLER *Cardellina canadensis* Uncommon

5¼ in. (13 cm). The "necklaced warbler." *Spring/summer and adult male:* Solid *gray above;* bright yellow below, with *necklace of short black stripes;* white vent; first-year male duller, more femalelike. *Female:* Similar but necklace fainter, upperparts may be washed with brownish; first-fall female (p. 350) may have only hint of necklace. All have *spectacles of white eye-ring and yellow loral stripe.* No white in wings or tail. **VOICE:** Song a staccato burst, irregularly arranged. *Chip, chupety swee-ditchety.* Call *tchip.* **SIMILAR SPECIES:** Magnolia, Yellow-throated, and Grace's Warblers. **HABITAT:** Forest undergrowth, shady thickets. Very rare vagrant to W. Coast.

WARBLERS

GRAY-CROWNED
YELLOWTHROAT

COMMON
YELLOWTHROAT

female

male

male

female

WILSON'S
WARBLER

females

increasing black
in forehead from
East to West

male

HOODED
WARBLER

female

male

CANADA
WARBLER

female

male

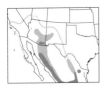

PAINTED REDSTART *Myioborus pictus* Uncommon

5¾ in. (15 cm). Beautiful; postures with half-spread wings and tail, showing off *large white patches*. Black head and upperparts; *large bright red patch* on lower breast and belly. White crescent under eye. *Juvenile:* Lacks red; otherwise ages and sexes similar. **VOICE:** Song a repetitious *weeta weeta weeta wee* or *weeta weeta chilp chilp chilp*. Call *clee-ip*, suggesting a siskin, not warbler. **SIMILAR SPECIES:** Red-faced Warbler, American Redstart. **HABITAT:** Pine-oak canyons and mountains; comes to sugar-water feeders. Rare vagrant north of range and to coastal cen. CA.

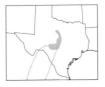

RED-FACED WARBLER *Cardellina rubrifrons* Uncommon, local

5½ in. (14 cm). The only U.S. warbler with *bright red face and throat*. Has gray back, black patch on head, and white nape and rump. Female and first-year birds only slightly duller than adult male. **VOICE:** Clear, sweet song, similar to Yellow Warbler. Call a sharp *chip* or *chup*. **SIMILAR SPECIES:** Painted Redstart overlaps in range and habitat. **HABITAT:** Open fir and pine-oak forests in upper canyons, mountains. Casual vagrant north to coastal cen. CA.

GOLDEN-CROWNED WARBLER *Basileuterus culicivorus* Casual vagrant

5 in. (13 cm). Yellow crown and gray eyebrow stripe bordered by black. Broken eye-ring. Dusky yellow below, drab olive above. Ages and sexes similar. **VOICE:** Song a series of slurred whistles. Call a short, sharp *tuk*. **SIMILAR SPECIES:** Common Yellowthroat, Orange-crowned Warbler. **RANGE:** Casual stray from Mex. to s. TX, NM, and e. CO. **HABITAT:** Dense woodland understory.

RUFOUS-CAPPED WARBLER *Basileuterus rufifrons* Very rare visitor

5 in. (13 cm). *Rufous cap and cheek* separated by white eyebrow stripe. Throat and upper breast bright yellow, upperparts olive. Long, spindly tail often held cocked up at angle. Ages and sexes similar. **VOICE:** Accelerating series of whistled, musical chips and warbles. Call *tick*. **SIMILAR SPECIES:** Common Yellowthroat. **RANGE:** Very rare visitor from Mex. to s. AZ (where it has bred) and TX. **HABITAT:** Thick brush, oak woodlands near water.

YELLOW-BREASTED CHAT Family Icteriidae

Traditionally placed with wood-warblers, the Yellow-breasted Chat was recently afforded its own family, Icteriidae (as opposed to Icteridae for blackbirds), because of its larger body and bill size and other factors.

YELLOW-BREASTED CHAT *Icteria virens* Uncommon

7½ in. (19 cm). Larger than our warblers, with *heavy bill* and *long tail*. Note white spectacles, *bright yellow* throat and breast. No wing bars. Habitat and voice suggest a thrasher or mockingbird. **VOICE:** Repeated whistles, alternating with harsh notes and soft *caws*. Suggests Northern Mockingbird, but repertoire more limited; much longer pauses between phrases. Single notes: *whoit, kook, zhairr*, etc. Often sings in short, awkward courtship display flight. **SIMILAR SPECIES:** Common Yellowthroat (much smaller). **HABITAT:** Brushy tangles, briars, stream thickets, where it skulks.

WARBLERS

juvenile

adult

PAINTED
REDSTART

RED-FACED
WARBLER

RUFOUS-
CAPPED
WARBLER

GOLDEN-
CROWNED
WARBLER

YELLOW-
BREASTED
CHAT

male

Common Yellowthroat
(p. 344)
for comparison

FALL WARBLERS

Most of these have streaks or wing bars.

RUBY-CROWNED KINGLET *Regulus calendula* p. 318
(Not a warbler.) Smaller than warblers; wing-flicking behavior.

CHESTNUT-SIDED WARBLER *Setophaga pensylvanica* p. 330
First-fall: Green above, grayish white below; eye-ring; tail cocked at angle. Sexes overlap in plumage.

PINE WARBLER *Setophaga pinus* p. 336
First-fall birds differ from Blackpoll and Bay-breasted Warblers in heavier bill, unstreaked back, darker cheeks. Also note dark legs and feet, white undertail coverts. First-fall female can lack yellow.

BAY-BREASTED WARBLER *Setophaga castanea* p. 338
Note dark legs and feet, buff flanks and undertail coverts, unstreaked breast. First-fall males can have some richer bay to flanks. Ages and sexes similar in fall in this and Blackpoll Warbler.

BLACKPOLL WARBLER *Setophaga striata* p. 338
Very similar to Bay-breasted Warbler, but note streaked back and breast, white (not buff or off-white) undertail coverts; yellowish legs and feet.

NORTHERN PARULA *Setophaga americana* p. 330
First-fall: Small and short-tailed. Bluish head, broken eye-ring, and yellow throat; wing bars. Female lacks marks on breast.

MAGNOLIA WARBLER *Setophaga magnolia* p. 330
First-fall: Broad white band midtail, yellow rump, faint gray band across breast, side streaking. Sexes similar in first fall, though male has more white in tail.

PRAIRIE WARBLER *Setophaga discolor* p. 336
First-fall: Jaw stripe, side streaks. Bobs tail. Female duller than male.

YELLOW WARBLER *Setophaga petechia* p. 330
Yellow edging to wings and tail. Beady dark eye. Some first-fall females are very drab but yellow in tail unique to this species.

BLACKBURNIAN WARBLER *Setophaga fusca* p. 334
First-fall: Yellow or yellow-orange throat, dark cheek, broad supercilium, dark brown to blackish back with pale stripes. Obvious wing bars, the upper one often short, triangular, and conspicuous.

BLACK-THROATED GREEN WARBLER *Setophaga virens* p. 334
First-fall: Olive cheek framed by black on sides, plain greenish back.

PALM WARBLER *Setophaga palmarum* p. 336
Brownish back, yellowish undertail coverts. Bobs tail.

YELLOW-RUMPED WARBLER *Setophaga coronata* p. 332
First-fall: Bright yellow rump, streaked back; brownish above. Flightier behavior than most wood-warblers; hawks insects; eats berries in winter.

CAPE MAY WARBLER *Setophaga tigrina* p. 332
First-fall: Streaked breast, greenish yellow rump. Female grayer than dull Yellow-rumped.

RUBY-CROWNED KINGLET

female

not a warbler

CHESTNUT-SIDED WARBLER

first-fall

SELECTED FALL WARBLERS

With Streaks or Wing Bars

fall male

PINE WARBLER

first-fall

BAY-BREASTED WARBLER

BLACKPOLL WARBLER

first-fall

PINE WARBLER

first-fall female

NORTHERN PARULA

first-fall

MAGNOLIA WARBLER

first-fall male

PRAIRIE WARBLER

YELLOW WARBLER

first-fall female

first-fall male

first-fall

BLACKBURNIAN WARBLER

first-fall female

BLACK-THROATED GREEN WARBLER

PALM WARBLER
western first-fall

first-fall female

YELLOW-RUMPED WARBLER
"Audubon's" (plainer face)

first-fall female

CAPE MAY WARBLER

FALL WARBLERS

Most of these lack streaks or wing bars.

ORANGE-CROWNED WARBLER *Leiothlypis celata*   p. 328
First-year: Dingy breast with faint dusky streaks, yellow undertail coverts, faint eye line. First-fall birds of eastern and interior western subspecies (*celata* and *orestera*) greenish drab and have grayer head; those of western subspecies (*lutescens*) have olive or yellowish heads.

TENNESSEE WARBLER *Leiothlypis peregrina*   p. 328
First-fall: Similar to Orange-crowned Warbler but has white undertail coverts; more conspicuous eyebrow stripe; greener above; paler underparts, with no hint of streaks; trace of a pale yellowish wing bar; shorter tail. Note also needle-thin bill.

PHILADELPHIA VIREO *Vireo philadelphicus*   p. 324
(Not a warbler.) "Vireo" song and actions. Note also thicker vireo bill. Compare with female Tennessee Warbler.

HOODED WARBLER *Setophaga citrina*   p. 344
First-year female: Yellow eyebrow stripe, mostly yellow face highlighted, dark lores, bold white tail spots. (First-fall male resembles adult male.)

WILSON'S WARBLER *Cardellina pusilla*   p. 344
First-year: Smaller and slimmer than Hooded Warbler with yellow lores, mostly olive cheeks, slimmer tail with no white. First-fall male has partial black cap; many first-fall females lack black.

BLACK-THROATED BLUE WARBLER *Setophaga caerulescens*   p. 332
Female: Dark cheek, white wing spot. In some first-fall females this white spot is obscured and these may suggest Tennessee Warbler, but note dark cheek and duller (browner olive) back. (First-fall male resembles adult male.)

CONNECTICUT WARBLER *Oporornis agilis*   p. 342
First-fall: Large size. Plump. Brownish hood; complete, bold, eye-ring. Walks.

MOURNING WARBLER *Geothlypis philadelphia*   p. 342
First-fall female: Suggestion of hood; broken eye-ring. Brighter yellow below than Connecticut Warbler, including throat, contrary to grayish white throat of MacGillivray's Warbler.

NASHVILLE WARBLER *Leiothlypis ruficapilla*   p. 328
First-fall: Yellowish (male) to buff (female) throat; sides of breast and undertail coverts tinged yellow, dull in females; eye-ring white to dingy pale; crown and nape grayish. Short tail, which it can bob.

COMMON YELLOWTHROAT *Geothlypis trichas*   p. 344
First-fall female: Yellowish to buff throat, dull yellow breast and undertail coverts; brownish sides; white belly. Large bill and behavior help separate this from similar dull warblers.

PROTHONOTARY WARBLER *Protonotaria citrea*   p. 342
First-year: Dull golden head heavily tinged greenish on crown in first-year females; dark eye stands out on plain face. Gray wings, white undertail, long bill.

CANADA WARBLER *Cardellina canadensis*   p. 344
First-fall: Lores yellow, eye-ring white. Grayish to brownish gray above, yellow below, trace of necklace (nearly absent on duller females).

SELECTED FALL WARBLERS
Without Streaks or Wing Bars

western

eastern

first-fall

ORANGE-CROWNED WARBLER

first-fall female

TENNESSEE WARBLER

PHILADELPHIA VIREO
not a warbler

first-fall female East and interior West

first-fall female

HOODED WARBLER

WILSON'S WARBLER

first-fall female

adult female

BLACK-THROATED BLUE WARBLER

first-fall

CONNECTICUT WARBLER

first-fall female

MOURNING WARBLER

first-fall female

NASHVILLE WARBLER

first-fall female

COMMON YELLOWTHROAT

first-fall female

PROTHONOTARY WARBLER

first-fall female

CANADA WARBLER

PIPITS and WAGTAILS Family Motacillidae

Pipits are streaked brown ground birds with white outer tail feathers, long hind claws, and thin bills; they walk instead of hopping and most wag their tails. Wagtails are widespread in the Old World, with two species breeding eastward into AK. Constantly wag long tails; undulate in flight. **FOOD:** Insects, seeds. **RANGE:** Nearly worldwide.

AMERICAN PIPIT *Anthus rubescens* Fairly common

6½ in. (17 cm). A *slim-billed, sparrowlike* bird of open country. *Bobs tail* as it *walks.* Underparts buffy or off-whitish with streaks; *outer tail feathers white;* legs blackish to dusky pinkish. Spring/summer birds grayer above, pinker and less streaked below; fall/winter birds washed olive and buff. Ages and sexes alike. Asian subspecies *(japonicus)* rare but regular in w. AK and casual vagrant farther south, grayer above, more boldly streaked below, legs pinkish. **VOICE:** Call a distinctive, thin *jeet* or *jee-eet.* In aerial song flight, *chwee chwee chwee chwee chwee chwee chwee.* **SIMILAR SPECIES:** Red-throated and Sprague's Pipits. Savannah and Vesper Sparrows have thicker bills, do not wag tails. **HABITAT:** Fields, short-grass habitats, shores; in summer, alpine tundra.

SPRAGUE'S PIPIT *Anthus spragueii* Uncommon, secretive

6½ in. (17 cm). A furtive species, often hard to see well. Note *pinkish legs.* Buffy below, with *striped back* and white outer tail feathers. *Plain buffy face with beady dark eye.* Ages and sexes alike. More solitary than American Pipit. When flushed, often towers high, then drops like a rock back to ground. Does *not* wag tail. **VOICE:** Sings high in air; a sweet, thin, descending *shiing-a-ring-a-ring-a-ring-a.* When flushed, often gives a distinctive *squeet* or *squeet-squeet* call. **SIMILAR SPECIES:** American Pipit differs in facial pattern and voice, has darker legs, wags tail. See juvenile Horned Lark. **HABITAT:** Short- to medium-grass prairies and fields. Very rare winterer to CA and vagrant east of range.

RED-THROATED PIPIT *Anthus cervinus* Rare, local

6 in. (15 cm). Rare Pacific Coast visitor, almost exclusively in fall south of AK. Also in spring in w. AK, where a few nest. *Adult:* Spring/summer male has *pinkish red face and breast;* less extensive in female. In fall/winter, *heavily streaked below; bold striping on back,* pinkish legs. **VOICE:** Call a distinctive, high, thin *speeee* or *speeuh* and a hoarse *tzeez.* **SIMILAR SPECIES:** American Pipit lacks pale back stripes, is less heavily marked below; different call, darker legs. **HABITAT:** In summer, hillside tundra; in migration, same as American Pipit, sometimes with more cover. Rare vagrant along Pacific Coast in migration, often found with American Pipits.

WHITE WAGTAIL *Motacilla alba* Rare, local

7¼ in. (18 cm). Note bold head pattern, gray back, and white wing patches. "Black-backed" Wagtail (subspecies *lugens*) has *black back* and *white chin* in spring/summer plumage (dark gray back in fall/winter), *more white in wings.* Male more boldly marked than female, and first-fall birds duller than adults, sex by sex. **VOICE:** Call a lively *tchizzik,* also an abrupt *tchik.* **SIMILAR SPECIES:** Duller first-fall Eastern Yellow Wagtails are off-white below, but have less white in face and wings; shorter tail; different call. **HABITAT:** Tundra, open country, shorelines. Casual vagrant along Pacific Coast and accidental in the East.

EASTERN YELLOW WAGTAIL *Motacilla tschutschensis* Uncommon, local

6½ in. (17 cm). A species that breeds in AK and northeasternmost Asia. *Adult:* Variably grayish to brownish above, *yellow below;* male brighter than female. *First-fall:* Dull whitish below, some tinged yellow; throat outlined in dark. **VOICE:** Call a buzzy *tsoueep.* Song *tsip-tsip-tsipsi.* **SIMILAR SPECIES:** White Wagtail. **HABITAT:** Willow scrub on tundra, marshy country, shorelines. Casual vagrant along Pacific Coast.

PIPITS AND WAGTAILS

fall/winter

spring/summer

Asian

AMERICAN PIPIT

North American

American and Red-throated pipits wag their tails

SPRAGUE'S PIPIT

Sprague's overhead

towering flight

spring/summer female

fall/winter

RED-THROATED PIPIT

spring/summer male

WHITE WAGTAIL

spring/summer male

fall/winter

first-fall female

EASTERN YELLOW WAGTAIL

spring/summer male

"Black-backed"

spring/summer male

LARKS Family Alaudidae

Brown terrestrial birds with long hind claws. Often joined by longspurs and Snow Buntings during fall and winter. Larks often sing in high display flights. **FOOD:** Seeds, insects. **RANGE:** Mainly Old World.

HORNED LARK *Eremophila alpestris*   Uncommon to common

7–7¼ in. (18–19 cm). Male: Note head pattern. Larger than a sparrow, with *black mustache,* two small *black "horns"* (not always noticeable), and black breast splotch. *Walks* on short legs. From below, white with *black* tail. Upperparts vary geographically, from paler to darker. *Female:* Similar but duller. *Juvenile:* Very different, *streaked below.* **VOICE:** Song tinkling, irregular, high-pitched, often prolonged; from ground or in air. Call a clear *tsee-titi.* **SIMILAR SPECIES:** Juvenile can be misidentified as Sprague's Pipit, longspurs, or sparrows. **HABITAT:** Prairies, short-grass and dirt fields, airports, shores, tundra. Populations of w. WA–OR (subspecies *strigata*) threatened.

EURASIAN SKYLARK *Alauda arvensis*   Scarce, local, introduced and vagrant

7¼ in. (19 cm). Slightly larger than a sparrow with short *crest;* brown, back and breast streaked; *trailing edge of wing and sides of tail white.* Ages and sexes similar. **VOICE:** Call a clear, liquid *chir-r-up.* Song, in hovering flight, musical, with a long sustain. **SIMILAR SPECIES:** Juvenile Horned Lark, pipits. **RANGE:** Introduced birds from Europe are resident on s. Vancouver I., BC, and in HI (p. 444). Casual vagrants from Asia reach w. AK islands, the Pacific Northwest Coast, QC (once), and HI. **HABITAT:** Open country, fields, airports.

LONGSPURS and SNOW BUNTINGS Family Calcariidae

Recently split from Old World Emberizidae, this family now consists of six species, all of which occur in our area. Legs are short such that birds appear to feed on their bellies. Longspurs are birds of open country; in fall/winter season, often found in flocks with pipits and larks. **FOOD:** Seeds, insects on breeding grounds.

SNOW BUNTING *Plectrophenax nivalis*   Uncommon

6¾ in. (17 cm). Snow Buntings often swirl over snowy fields or dunes in flocks. Note extensive amount of white. In fall and winter, individuals look quite brown, but note flashing *white wing patches* in flight. From below, Snow Bunting is almost entirely white. *Spring/summer male:* Black back contrasting with white head and underparts; bill black. Females and first-fall birds duller, less white, bill dull yellowish brown; all ages and sexes become whiter in spring due to plumage wear (not molt). **VOICE:** Call a sharp, whistled *teer* or *tew;* also a rough, purring *brrt,* both similar to Lapland Longspur's calls. Song a musical *ti-ti-chu-ree,* repeated. **SIMILAR SPECIES:** McKay's Bunting. Leucistic juncos, House Sparrows, etc., sometimes mistaken for Snow Buntings. **HABITAT:** Prairies, fields, dunes, shores. In summer, tundra. Vagrant well south of normal winter range, including to HI.

MCKAY'S BUNTING *Plectrophenax hyperboreus*   Scarce, local

7 in. (18 cm). A specialty of w. AK, breeding regularly only on St. Matthew and Hall Is. *Spring/summer male:* Almost pure white, except for ends of primaries and scapulars and near tips of central tail feathers. *Spring/summer female:* Has some dark on back. *Fall/winter:* Light touches of warm, tan-brown above, but less than in Snow Bunting; wings and tail have more white. Hybridizes with Snow Bunting. **VOICE:** Song of male suggests American Goldfinch. **SIMILAR SPECIES:** Spring/summer Snow Bunting has *darker back* while winter Snow Bunting is browner with more dark in tail, rump, and back. **HABITAT:** Tundra, barrens, shores; in fall/winter mixes with Snow Buntings. Vagrant to WA.

LARKS AND BUNTINGS

overhead

towering flight

juvenile

prairie

adult

EURASIAN SKYLARK

northern

HORNED LARK

winter female

SNOW BUNTING

Snow Bunting summer male

winter male

winter

summer male

summer female

winter male

summer   Snow Bunting male

MCKAY'S BUNTING

McKay's Bunting male

LAPLAND LONGSPUR *Calcarius lapponicus* Uncommon to fairly common

6¼ in. (16 cm). The most widespread N. American longspur. *Spring/summer male:* Black face outlined with white is distinctive. Rusty collar. *Fall/winter male:* Sparse black streaks on sides, dull rusty nape, and smudge across breast help identify it. *Female:* Resembles fall/winter male, first-year duller. In all fall/winter plumages note *dark frame to rear cheek, rufous-brown edging to wing coverts,* tail pattern. **VOICE:** In flight, a dry rattle, also a musical *teew;* when perched, a soft *pee-dle.* Song in display flight is vigorous, musical. **SIMILAR SPECIES:** Smith's Longspur has similar tail pattern but buffier below; note face pattern, white checks in wings. Other longspurs have more white in tail. **HABITAT:** In summer, tundra; in winter, open fields, short-grass prairies, shores.

CHESTNUT-COLLARED LONGSPUR *Calcarius ornatus* Uncommon

6 in. (15 cm). *Spring/summer male:* Solid *black* below, except on throat and lower belly; nape *chestnut. Fall/winter male:* Colors muted by brown feather edging. *Female:* Very plain; best field marks are tail pattern (dark triangle on white tail), dark bill, and flight call. **VOICE:** Song short, feeble, but musical; suggests Western Meadowlark. Call a finchlike or turnstonelike *ji-jiv* or *kittle-kittle,* unique among longspurs. **SIMILAR SPECIES:** McCown's Longspur. **HABITAT:** Plains, native-grass prairies; generally prefers some cover. Winter flocks may disappear in grass until flushed. Rare vagrant to W. Coast and casual vagrant to E. Coast.

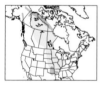

MCCOWN'S LONGSPUR *Rhynchophanes mccownii* Uncommon, local

6 in. (15 cm). *Spring/summer male:* Crown and patch on breast black, tail largely white. Hindneck *gray* (brown or chestnut in other longspurs). *Female and fall/winter male:* Rather plain; note tail pattern (inverted T of black on white) and *swollen-looking, pinkish, fleshy bill.* Some birds are especially *plain looking,* reminiscent of female House Sparrow. **VOICE:** Song in display flight is clear, sweet warbles, suggestive of Lark Bunting. Call a dry rattle, softer than Lapland Longspur's. Also a soft *pink.* **SIMILAR SPECIES:** Female Chestnut-collared Longspur is darker, usually more heavily marked below, has slightly smaller and darker (not pinkish) bill, different call. **HABITAT:** Plains, prairies, short-grass and dirt fields. Very rare to casual vagrant to CA and Midwest.

SMITH'S LONGSPUR *Calcarius pictus* Scarce, local

6¼ in. (16 cm). This secretive longspur prefers enough grassy cover to disappear. It is *warm buff on entire underparts.* Tail edged with white, as in Vesper Sparrow and Lapland Longspur. *Spring/summer male:* Deep buff; ear patch with *white* spot, strikingly outlined by *black triangle. Female and fall/winter:* Less distinctive; *buffy breast* lightly streaked; small pale spot on side of neck; most have white patch in wing coverts (absent or obscure in some females). **VOICE:** Rattling or clicking notes in flight (likened to winding a cheap watch). Song sweet, warblerlike, terminating in *WEchew.* Does not sing in flight. **SIMILAR SPECIES:** Lapland and Chestnut-collared Longspurs, Vesper Sparrow, Sprague's Pipit. **HABITAT:** Prairies, fields, airports; in summer, tundra with scattered bushes. Casual vagrant to W. and E. Coasts.

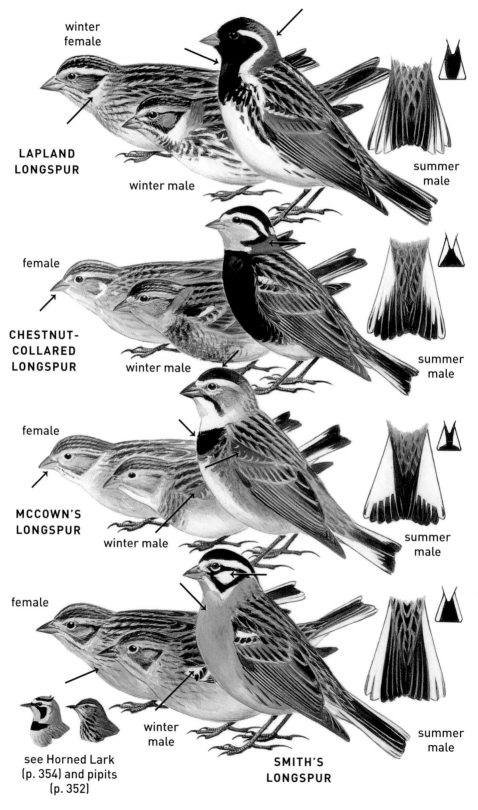

LAPLAND LONGSPUR

winter female

winter male

summer male

CHESTNUT-COLLARED LONGSPUR

female

winter male

summer male

MCCOWN'S LONGSPUR

female

winter male

summer male

SMITH'S LONGSPUR

female

winter male

summer male

see Horned Lark (p. 354) and pipits (p. 352)

SPINDALISES Family Spindalidae

A family of four Caribbean species formerly considered part of the tanagers (Thraupidae). Ages and sexes differ. Found in forests. **FOOD:** Primarily fruit.

WESTERN SPINDALIS *Spindalis zena*   Very rare vagrant

6¾ in. (17 cm). *Male:* Bold black-and-white head stripes and shoulder patch stand out. Body burnt orange, back color varies from black to green. *Female:* Plain gray-brown, sometimes with yellow wash to breast; note size, thick tanager-like bill, and pale patch at base of primaries. **VOICE:** Series of thin high notes, *tzee-tzee-tzee,* often with buzzy phrase toward end. **SIMILAR SPECIES:** Female Brown-headed Cowbird, other tanagers. **RANGE:** Rare visitor to s. FL from W. Indies. **HABITAT:** Brushy woodlands, fruit trees.

TROPICAL TANAGERS Family Thraupidae

A large, diverse, and colorful family of Neotropical birds. N. American tanagers have been recently moved to Cardinalidae (p. 392). **FOOD:** Nectar, insects. **RANGE:** New World tropical areas.

BANANAQUIT *Coereba flaveola*   Very rare vagrant

4½ in. (11 cm). A small, short-tailed bird with decurved bill and bold white supercilium. *Adult:* Note bold plumage pattern, white check in wings. Sexes similar. Juvenile (not shown) paler overall, supercilium indistinct. **VOICE:** Explosive series of buzzy notes and sneezy squeaks. **RANGE:** Rare visitor to s. FL from W. Indies. **HABITAT:** Open brushy areas, nectar- and fruit-bearing trees.

MORELET'S SEEDEATER *Sporophila morelleti*   Rare, local

4½ in. (11 cm). Formerly known as White-collared Seedeater. Tiny, with stubby bill. *Adult male:* Dark cap, incomplete light collar, white wing spot; duller in fall/winter. *Female:* Buffy with eye-ring, wing bars. First-year male variably intermediate. **VOICE:** High, then low *sweet, sweet, sweet, cheer, cheer, cheer.* Call a high *wink.* **HABITAT:** Tall, thick stands of grass and other similar deep cover.

NORTH AMERICAN TOWHEES, SPARROWS, and JUNCOS Family Passerellidae

Formerly lumped with Old World buntings, this family now consists of our familiar sparrows and allies. Juveniles are more heavily streaked; otherwise, ages and sexes similar in most species. **FOOD:** Seeds, insects, fruit. **RANGE:** Throughout the Americas.

OLIVE SPARROW *Arremonops rufivirgatus*   Uncommon, local

6¼ in. (16 cm). Olive above, gray below, with two dull brown stripes on crown (sexes similar). Juvenile plainer and streaked. **VOICE:** Song composed of dry notes on one pitch going into Chipping Sparrow–like rattle; reminiscent of Field Sparrow. Call a sharp *chip* like Orange-crowned Warbler; also a hissing trill. **HABITAT:** Bushy thickets.

GREEN-TAILED TOWHEE *Pipilo chlorurus*   Uncommon to fairly common

7¼ in. (18 cm). A slender towhee, known by its *rufous cap,* conspicuous *white throat,* black mustache, gray chest, and plain *olive green upperparts,* brightest on wings and tail (sexes similar). Juvenile has plainer head pattern, streaks on breast. **VOICE:** Call a catlike mewing note. Song variable; opening with sweet notes, followed by burry notes: *weet-churr-cheeeeee-churr.* **HABITAT:** Brushy montane slopes, pine woods, meadows, sage, chaparral; in winter, also brushy and riparian woods. Rare winter vagrant to W. Coast and casual to Midwest.

MISCELLANEOUS PASSERINES

male

female

WESTERN SPINDALIS

female

MORELET'S SEEDEATER

adult

adult male

BANANAQUIT

GREEN-TAILED TOWHEE

OLIVE SPARROW

EASTERN TOWHEE *Pipilo erythrophthalmus* **Fairly common**

8 in. (20–21 cm). Smaller and more slender than a robin; rummages among leaf litter. Readily recognized by rufous sides. *Male:* Head and upperparts black; sides rufous rust, belly white. Flashes white patches at base of primaries and on tail corners. Eye usually red (but white in birds of s. Atlantic Coast and FL). *Female:* Similar, but brown where male is black. *Juvenile:* Streaked below like a large sparrow, but with diagnostic towhee wing and tail patterns. **VOICE:** Song *drink-your-tea,* last syllable higher, wavering. Call a loud *chewink!* Southern white-eyed subspecies *(alleni)* gives a more slurred *shrink* or *zree;* song *cheet cheet cheeeeee.* **SIMILAR SPECIES:** Spotted Towhee. **HABITAT:** Open woods, undergrowth, brushy edges, hedgerows, feeders. Casual vagrant to Plains states.

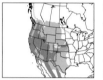

SPOTTED TOWHEE *Pipilo maculatus* **Common**

8 in. (20–21 cm). The western counterpart to Eastern Towhee, this species is also readily recognized by *rufous sides. Male:* Head and chest black; sides rufous red, belly white, *back heavily spotted with white* (amount varying geographically, subspecies of the Pacific Northwest having the least amount of spotting). Flashes *white patches* in tail corners. Eye fiery red. *Female:* Similar, but black replaced by dusky grayish black to brownish black — also varying geographically. *Juvenile:* Streaked below, like a large sparrow, but with flash pattern in tail; duller and browner iris. **VOICE:** Song a drawn-out, buzzy *chweeeeee.* Sometimes *chup chup chup zeeeeeeee;* variable. Call a catlike *gu-eeee?* or (Southwest mountains) rising and falling *chreeeer.* **SIMILAR SPECIES:** Eastern Towhee overlaps slightly on Great Plains in winter; lacks white spotting on back, has white patch at base of primaries; female is dark chocolate brown. **HABITAT:** Open woods, undergrowth, chaparral, brushy edges, gardens. Casual vagrant to Midwest and Gulf Coast.

CANYON TOWHEE *Melozone fusca* **Uncommon**

8¾ in. (22 cm). Slightly paler and grayer than California Towhee, with rufous crown, faint dusky necklace, and dark spot on breast (sexes similar). Juvenile rather heavily streaked. **VOICE:** Call an odd *shed-lp* or *kedlp.* Song an accelerating string of call notes. Very different from California Towhee. **SIMILAR SPECIES:** Abert's Towhee overlaps in range. **HABITAT:** Brushy areas in canyons and deserts, residential areas, feeders.

CALIFORNIA TOWHEE *Melozone crissalis* **Common**

9 in. (23 cm). A common, dull brown, ground-loving bird, with moderately long, dark tail; suggests a very plain, slim, overgrown sparrow. Note pale *rusty undertail coverts* and streaked buffy or rusty throat. Juvenile indistinctly streaked on breast, has cinnamon wing bars. **VOICE:** Call a metallic *chink.* Song a rapid *chink-chink-ink-ink-ink-ink-ink-ink* on one pitch; often ends in trill. **SIMILAR SPECIES:** Canyon and Abert's Towhees (but ranges of these do not overlap with California). California Thrasher larger, with long, slim, curved bill. **HABITAT:** Brushy areas, chaparral, coastal sage scrub, canyons, gardens. Populations of Inyo Co., CA (subspecies *eremophila*), threatened.

ABERT'S TOWHEE *Melozone aberti* **Uncommon**

9½ in. (24 cm). A desert species, similar to California Towhee, but note *blackish facial patch embracing base of bill.* Entire underparts buffy brown, sometimes appearing washed with cinnamon or pinkish buff; rustier on undertail coverts. Juvenile indistinctly streaked overall, as in other towhees, but has a dark face. **VOICE:** Call a sharp *peek* and high squeal. Song a rapid series of high *peek* and lower *tuk* notes. **SIMILAR SPECIES:** Canyon Towhee lacks black face, has streaks bordering pale throat. **HABITAT:** Riparian scrub, desert brush, mesquite, parks.

TOWHEES

male white-eyed variant

female

juvenile

EASTERN TOWHEE

male

male

juvenile

SPOTTED TOWHEE

female

CANYON TOWHEE

CALIFORNIA TOWHEE

ABERT'S TOWHEE

RUFOUS-WINGED SPARROW *Peucaea carpalis*   Scarce, local

5¾ in. (15 cm). An AZ specialty. Suggests Chipping Sparrow, but plumper bod-ied, tail not notched. *Double black "whiskers,"* rufous eye line, gray stripe through rufous crown. *Rufous shoulder* not easily seen. Juvenile has streaked breast. **VOICE:** Song one or two sweet introductory notes and a rapid series of musical chips on one pitch. **SIMILAR SPECIES:** Rufous-crowned and Field Spar-rows. **HABITAT:** Desert grasslands, thorn brush, desert hackberry, mesquite.

RUFOUS-CROWNED SPARROW *Aimophila ruficeps*   Uncommon

6 in. (15 cm). A dark sparrow with plain dusky breast, rufous cap, dark line behind eye, and rounded tail. Note *black whiskers* bordering throat and *distinct circular whitish eye-ring.* Juvenile has streaked breast. Seen singly or in pairs. **VOICE:** Song stuttering, gurgling, suggesting a thin, weak House Wren song. Call *dear, dear, dear.* **SIMILAR SPECIES:** Rufous-winged and Chipping Sparrows paler, more slender, smaller billed, lack or have less-distinct whiskers. **HABI-TAT:** Grassy or rocky slopes with sparse low bushes; open pine-oak woods.

BOTTERI'S SPARROW *Peucaea botterii*   Uncommon, local

6 in. (15 cm). Nondescript. Buffy breast, plain brown tail lacking white corners. Juvenile has sparse streaks on breast. *Best identified by voice.* Bill slightly curved on upper edge. **VOICE:** Song a constant tinkling and "pitting," sometimes running into a dry trill on same pitch. Very unlike song of Cassin's Sparrow. **SIMILAR SPECIES:** Cassin's Sparrow, breeding in same habitat, is very similar, but usually grayer, has faint dusky streaks on flanks, small white corners to tail, straighter upper edge to bill; upperparts often look patterned, as opposed to more streaked in Botteri's. **HABITAT:** Desert grasslands and bunch grass (particularly sacaton grass).

CASSIN'S SPARROW *Peucaea cassinii*   Fairly common

6 in. (15 cm). A large, drab sparrow of open arid country; underparts dingy with-out markings, or with faint streaking on flanks. Upperparts appear patterned, with anchor-shaped markings on individual feathers. Individuals can be either more rufous or grayer than shown. *Pale or whitish corners* on *rounded,* gray-brown tail. Juvenile has dark breast streaking. *Song a good clue.* **VOICE:** Song one or two short notes, a high sweet trill, and two lower notes: *ti ti tseeeeeee tay tay.* Often "skylarks" in air, giving trill at climax; Botteri's Sparrow does not sky-lark. Cassin's also flicks wings and tail in flight. **SIMILAR SPECIES:** Botteri's Sparrow. Savannah Sparrow has yellow lore spots and is smaller, streakier overall, and shorter tailed than Cassin's. **HABITAT:** Desert grasslands and semiarid prairies, bushes. Casual to accidental vagrant to n. CA coast and n. Midwest.

BACHMAN'S SPARROW *Peucaea aestivalis*   Scarce

6 in. (15 cm). Restricted primarily to open pine woods with grass and palmetto scrub of Southeast, this shy sparrow flushes reluctantly, then drops back into cover. A large sparrow, with long, rounded tail. Striped with reddish brown above, washed with dingy buff across plain breast, with gray bill. Juvenile has streaked breast. **VOICE:** Song variable; usually a clear liquid whistle followed by loose trill or warble on a different pitch, e.g., *seeeee, slip slip slip slip slip.* **SIMI-LAR SPECIES:** Field Sparrow smaller, with pink bill. Grasshopper Sparrow lives in meadows, has light crown stripe and short tail. Juvenile Bachman's can sug-gest Lincoln's Sparrow, which would not be in the same range in summer and has smaller bill and bolder streaks to breast. See also Cassin's Sparrow, vagrants of which might casually be found in Bachman's range. **HABITAT:** Open pine or oak woods, palmetto scrub. Casual vagrant north of range.

RUFOUS-WINGED
SPARROW

RUFOUS-
CROWNED
SPARROW

BOTTERI'S
SPARROW

CASSIN'S
SPARROW

BACHMAN'S
SPARROW

LARK SPARROW *Chondestes grammacus* Fairly common

6½ in. (17 cm). *Adult:* Note *black tail with white corners;* also dark *central breast spot* on clean whitish underparts, and *quail-like head pattern,* with *chestnut ear patch* and striped crown. *Juvenile:* Head pattern duller, a few dusky streaks on breast. **VOICE:** Clear notes and trills with pauses between, characterized by buzzing and churring passages. Call a sharp *tsip.* **SIMILAR SPECIES:** Vesper Sparrow. **HABITAT:** Open country with bushes, trees; pastures, farms, roadsides. Rare vagrant to E. Coast.

BELL'S SPARROW *Artemisiospiza belli* Uncommon

6–6¼ in. (15–16 cm). *Adult:* Generally darker and browner than Sagebrush Sparrow, with less streaking on back and heavier black whiskers. *Juvenile:* Brown and streaked but usually has bold eye-ring of adult. **VOICE:** Similar to Sagebrush Sparrow but higher pitched, less musical. **SIMILAR SPECIES:** Bell's from eastern part of range most similar to Sagebrush and can overlap on winter grounds. **HABITAT:** Dry brushy foothills, chaparral. Subspecies *clementeae* of San Clemente Is., CA, threatened.

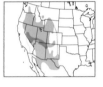

SAGEBRUSH SPARROW *Artemisiospiza nevadensis* Uncommon

6–6¼ in. (15–16 cm). Formerly conspecific with Bell's Sparrow (as "Sage Sparrow"). A gray sparrow of arid brush. Note combination of *single breast spot* and dark *"whiskers" on sides of throat. Adult:* White eye-ring, touch of whitish over eye. *Gray head contrasts with browner back and wing,* generally more so than in Bell's. Long tail often *flicked and waved* about. *Often runs on ground, with tail held high.* **VOICE:** Song four to seven musical notes, *tsit-tsoo-tseee-tsay* or *tsit, tsit, tsi you, tee a-tee;* recalls Western Meadowlark. Twittering call. **SIMILAR SPECIES:** Bell's Sparrow. See juvenile Black-throated Sparrow. **HABITAT:** Sage and saltbush flats; in winter, also creosote bush. Casual vagrant to Plains states.

BLACK-THROATED SPARROW *Amphispiza bilineata* Fairly common

5½ in. (14 cm). *Adult:* Note face pattern. A pretty, gray, desert sparrow, with *white face stripes* and *jet-black throat and chest.* White corners to *distinct black tail.* Sexes alike. *Juvenile:* Seen into fall; *lacks* black throat but has similar head pattern; breast weakly streaked. **VOICE:** Song a sweet *cheet cheet cheeeeeeee* (two short, clear opening notes and a fine trill); calls are light tinkling notes. **SIMILAR SPECIES:** Juvenile recalls juvenile Sagebrush Sparrow but has a supercilium and contrastingly black tail. **HABITAT:** Arid brush, creosote-bush and cactus deserts, juniper hillsides. Rare to casual vagrant to Northwest coast and East, largely first-fall birds.

FIVE-STRIPED SPARROW *Amphispiza quinquestriata* Very rare, local

6 in. (15 cm). A rare Mexican sparrow. *Dusky,* with *five white stripes* on head (white supercilium, subauricular streak, and throat), black whiskers, and single black spot on dark gray breast. **VOICE:** High-pitched, watery phrases, each note repeated several times, like a thrasher. Call a sharp *tchak!* **SIMILAR SPECIES:** Black-throated and Sagebrush Sparrows. **HABITAT:** Dense shrubs on dry canyon slopes, rocky arid hillsides.

BLACK-CHINNED SPARROW *Spizella atrogularis* Uncommon

5¾ in. (15 cm). A small, slim, somewhat juncolike sparrow (but with no white in tail); has streaked brown back, *head and underparts medium gray,* small *pinkish bill. Spring/summer male:* Bill encircled by bold *black chin* and lores. *Female and fall/winter male:* Most lack black face. Juvenile has indistinct streaks on head and breast. **VOICE:** Song a sweet series of notes on about same pitch, or descending slightly; starts with several high, thin, clear notes and ends in rough trill, *sweet, sweet, sweet, weet-trrrrrrr.* **SIMILAR SPECIES:** Black-throated Sparrow, juncos. **HABITAT:** Brushy mountain slopes, open chaparral, juniper; winters on rocky, brushy canyon slopes, usually in flocks. Casual vagrant north of range.

first-year

adult

LARK SPARROW

**SAGEBRUSH
SPARROW**

juvenile

**BELL'S
SPARROW**

adult

adult

adult

**BLACK-
THROATED
SPARROW**

**FIVE-STRIPED
SPARROW**

adult

juvenile

**BLACK-CHINNED
SPARROW**

spring/
summer
male

fall/winter
female

AMERICAN TREE SPARROW *Spizelloides arborea*   Fairly common

6¼ in. (16 cm). Note *dark "stickpin" on breast*, and *red-brown cap. Bill dark above, yellow below;* white wing bars; rufous wash on flanks. Ages and sexes rather similar (juvenile is streaked). **VOICE:** Song sweet, variable, opening on one or two high, clear notes. Call *tseet;* feeding call a musical *teelwit.* **SIMILAR SPECIES:** Field and Chipping Sparrows. **HABITAT:** Arctic and taiga scrub, willow thickets; in winter, brushy roadsides, weedy edges, cattail marshes, feeders. Casual vagrant well south of winter range.

CHIPPING SPARROW *Spizella passerina*   Common

5½ in. (14 cm). *Spring/summer:* A small, slim, long-tailed, plain-breasted sparrow with bright *rufous cap, black eye line, white eyebrow. Fall/winter:* Duller; note *dark eyeline, dirty grayish breast, gray rump. Juvenile:* Has fine streaks on breast, rump not as gray; this plumage may be held through fall migration. **VOICE:** Song a dry chipping rattle on one pitch. Call a thin *tseet.* **SIMILAR SPECIES:** Clay-colored, Brewer's, Rufous-winged, and Swamp Sparrows. **HABITAT:** Open woods, especially pine, oak; orchards, farms, towns, lawns, feeders. Often forms flocks in fall and winter.

FIELD SPARROW *Spizella pusilla*   Fairly common

5¾ in. (15 cm). A small, slim, rusty-capped sparrow. Note small *pink bill,* white eye-ring, plain buffy breast; rusty upperparts, and weak face striping. *Juvenile:* Has finely streaked breast; plumage not held long. **VOICE:** Song a distinctive accelerating trill, *psew-psew-psew-see-see-see-see* (ascending, descending, or on one pitch). Call *tseew.* **SIMILAR SPECIES:** American Tree, Chipping, and Brewer's Sparrows. **HABITAT:** Overgrown fields, pastures, brush, feeders. Casual vagrant to W. Coast.

CLAY-COLORED SPARROW *Spizella pallida*   Fairly common

5½ in. (14 cm). Paler and buffier than fall/winter Chipping Sparrow, with *paler lores, more sharply outlined face pattern,* more contrasting grayer nape, *browner rump,* whiter underparts; eye-ring rather indistinct, broken. Juvenile streaked below (held only briefly on breeding grounds). **VOICE:** Insectlike; three or four low, flat buzzes: *bzzz, bzzz, bzzz.* Call a thin *tseet,* like Chipping's but higher. **SIMILAR SPECIES:** Brewer's Sparrow. **HABITAT:** Scrub, brushy prairies, jack pines, weedy areas. Scarce vagrant or migrant to W. and E. Coasts.

BREWER'S SPARROW *Spizella breweri*   Fairly common

5½ in. (14 cm). A small, slim, pale, *nondescript* sparrow of sagebrush and desert scrub. Resembles dull Chipping and Clay-colored Sparrows. Note pale lores, brownish rump, distinct full whitish *eye-ring,* and *lack of white central crown stripe.* "Timberline" subspecies *(taverneri)* has slightly bolder plumage; nests near tree line in n. Canadian Rockies and e. AK. Juvenile on breeding grounds streaked below. **VOICE:** Song long, musical buzzy trills on different pitches; canarylike. Call a thin *tsee.* **SIMILAR SPECIES:** Dull Chipping Sparrows redder on back, lacks eye-ring, has gray rump. Dull Clay-colored Sparrows buffier, head pattern and pale crown stripe usually more distinct. *Caution:* Very dull Clay-coloreds can closely resemble Brewer's, but note especially weaker eye-ring on these. **HABITAT:** Nests in sagebrush, saltbush; winters in brushy plains and deserts, weedy fields. "Timberline" Sparrow nests near tree line, mostly in stunted willow. Casual vagrant to Midwest, accidental to E. Coast.

SPARROWS

AMERICAN
TREE
SPARROW

fall/
winter

spring/
summer

juvenile

CHIPPING SPARROW

FIELD
SPARROW

juvenile

adult

CLAY-COLORED
SPARROW

spring/
summer

fall/
winter

BREWER'S
SPARROW

SAVANNAH SPARROW *Passerculus sandwichensis*   Common

5½–5¾ in. (14–15 cm). This streaked, open-country sparrow suggests a small, short-tailed Song Sparrow, but it usually has *yellowish on front of eyebrow, whitish stripe through crown,* and pinker legs. Ages and sexes similar. Note especially the *short,* notched tail, with palish but not bright white outer feathers. "Large-billed" Savannah Sparrow (subspecies *rostratus*), a scarce post-breeding visitor to dry, sandy s. CA habitats, is pale with a larger, paler bill. "Belding's" Savannah Sparrow *(beldingi)* is one of several very dark subspecies that are permanent residents in coastal salt marshes of s.-cen. CA. The "Ipswich" subspecies *(princeps),* which breeds on Sable I., NS, and winters along Atlantic Coast beaches, is paler overall and slightly larger than other eastern subspecies. **VOICE:** Song a lisping, buzzy *tsit-tsit-tsit, tseeee-tsaaay* (last note lower). Call a short *tseep* or light *tsu.* **SIMILAR SPECIES:** Song Sparrow's tail longer, rounded. See also Vesper Sparrow. Savannah's song similar to Grasshopper Sparrow's except for lower last note. **HABITAT:** Open fields, farms, meadows, salt marshes, prairies, dunes.

GRASSHOPPER SPARROW *Ammodramus savannarum*   Uncommon

5 in. (13 cm). A small, compact-bodied sparrow, with large and flat head and short and sharp tail, found in taller grasslands. Flight feeble. *Adult:* Crown with pale median stripe; *yellow lores; whitish eye-ring,* purplish-edged upperpart feathers; note relatively *unstriped buffy breast.* Endangered resident FL subspecies *(floridanus)* darker and browner above, paler below, larger billed. *Juvenile:* Less colorful, has dusky streaks on breast (found on migration). **VOICE:** Distinctive, very thin, dry, insectlike *pi-tup zeeeeeeeeeeee.* **SIMILAR SPECIES:** LeConte's Sparrow slimmer, longer tailed, smaller billed; adult with orangier eyebrow; juvenile buffier, plainer faced. See Savannah Sparrow, female Bobolink. **HABITAT:** Grasslands, hay fields, pastures, prairies.

HENSLOW'S SPARROW *Centronyx henslowii*   Scarce, local

5 in. (13 cm). A secretive sparrow best located by its odd song. Short-tailed and flat-headed, with large pale bill. *Adult:* Has fine stripes across breast. Olive-colored head, double mustache stripes, spots behind "ear," and reddish wings. *Juvenile:* Back and underparts dull olive and without breast streaking (breeding grounds only). **VOICE:** Song a hiccuping *tsi-lick.* May sing on quiet, windless nights. **SIMILAR SPECIES:** Juvenile Henslow's Sparrow (without breast streaks) might resemble adult Grasshopper Sparrow, whereas juvenile Grasshopper has breast streaks but lacks Henslow's olive and russet tones. **HABITAT:** Breeding habitat very specific: partially overgrown fields with dead or dried vegetation and dense leaf litter; has adapted to hay fields. Winters in dense cover in southern pine forests. Casual vagrant to the Plains states, accidental to CO.

BAIRD'S SPARROW *Centronyx bairdii*   Scarce, local

5½ in. (14 cm). An elusive, skulking prairie sparrow. *Adult:* Light breast crossed by *narrow band* of fine black streaks. Head ocher-buff, streaked. Key mark is broad *ocher* median crown stripe. *Double mustache stripes.* Flat head. Hard to see well except when singing. Juvenile (which can be found on migration) has a scaly pattern above. **VOICE:** Song begins with two or three high musical *zips,* ends with trill on lower pitch; more musical than Savannah Sparrow. **SIMILAR SPECIES:** Savannah Sparrow has smaller bill, more extensively streaked below, lacks dark marks at rear of auriculars and double mustache stripes. See Henslow's Sparrow (ranges do not overlap). **HABITAT:** Native prairies, scattered bushes used as song perches. Accidental vagrant to the W. Coast and East.

STREAK-BREASTED GRASS SPARROWS

"Belding's"

typical

"Large-billed"

SAVANNAH
SPARROW

"Ipswich"

adult

juvenile

GRASSHOPPER
SPARROW

HENSLOW'S
SPARROW

juvenile

adult

BAIRD'S
SPARROW

VESPER SPARROW *Pooecetes gramineus* Uncommon

6¼ in. (16 cm). *White outer tail feathers* are conspicuous when bird flies. Otherwise suggests slightly largish Savannah Sparrow or grayish Song Sparrow, but has prominent *whitish eye-ring, chestnut* bend of wing *(sometimes difficult to see).* Note white malar stripe and lack of central crown stripe. **VOICE:** Song similar to Song Sparrow's but throatier; usually begins with two clear minor notes, followed by two higher ones. Call a brief *tseet.* **SIMILAR SPECIES:** Savannah Sparrow lacks bright white outer tail feathers and distinct eye-ring. Other sparrowlike field birds with white tail-sides or corners include pipits, longspurs, and Lark Sparrow. **HABITAT:** Meadows and prairies with scattered trees or bushes (such as sage), roadsides, farm fields.

NELSON'S SPARROW *Ammospiza nelsoni* Uncommon

5 in. (13 cm). A shy marshland skulker with three widely separated breeding populations. Note bright *orange on face,* completely surrounding gray ear patch. *Breast warm buff with faint blurry streaks,* stronger streaks on flanks. Gray central crown and *unmarked gray nape.* Back sharply striped with white. Ages and sexes similar. Birds of New England and Maritimes grayer with less-distinct stripes. Juvenile similar but washed orange-buff. **VOICE:** Song a buzzy, two-part *shleeee-tup.* **SIMILAR SPECIES:** Saltmarsh Sparrow has heavier breast streaking and orange on breast, if present, is *paler* than orange on face (breast and face equally bright in Nelson's); juveniles paler, less orangish. LeConte's Sparrow has white median crown stripe, purplish chestnut streaks on nape. **HABITAT:** In summer, prairie and coastal marshes, muskeg; in winter, coastal marshes. Very rare winter visitor to CA salt marshes; casual inland migrant or vagrant in interior West and East.

SALTMARSH SPARROW *Ammospiza caudacuta* Uncommon

5¼ in. (13 cm). A short-tailed, often shy sparrow of coastal marshes. Note deep ocher yellow or orange of face, which completely surrounds gray ear patch. Distinct streaks on mostly whitish or light buff breast, flat-headed appearance. Juvenile similar but washed pale buff. **VOICE:** Song a weak varied jumble of buzzy hisses and clicks; not distinctly two-part like Nelson's. **SIMILAR SPECIES:** Nelson's and LeConte's Sparrows. Juvenile Seaside Sparrow on same breeding grounds grayer, loral area yellowish. Savannah Sparrow smaller, smaller headed, shorter notched tail. **HABITAT:** Coastal salt marshes.

LECONTE'S SPARROW *Ammospiza leconteii* Uncommon

5 in. (13 cm). A skulking sharp-tailed sparrow of prairie marshes, boggy fields. Note *bright orange* eyebrow and buffy breast (with streaks *confined to sides*), *purplish-chestnut streaks on nape,* white median crown stripe, strong stripes on back. Juvenile, which can be found on migration, is buffier overall and has a streaked breast. **VOICE:** Song consists of two extremely thin, grasshopper-like hisses. **SIMILAR SPECIES:** Nelson's Sparrow. Adult and juvenile Grasshopper Sparrow. **HABITAT:** Grassy marshes, tallgrass fields, weedy hay fields. Casual vagrant to W. and E. Coasts.

SEASIDE SPARROW *Ammospiza maritima* Fairly common

6 in. (15 cm). A dark, *gray* sparrow of salt marshes. *Adult:* Short *yellow area above lores.* Whitish throat and white above dark malar. *Juvenile:* Similar but duller, browner. Shares marshes with Nelson's and Saltmarsh Sparrows along Atlantic Coast. "Cape Sable" Seaside Sparrow (subspecies *mirabilis*) is an endangered subspecies confined to s. FL (the only Seaside Sparrow breeding there); more greenish than typical birds with *much heavier breast streaking.* **VOICE:** Song *cutcut ZHE-eeeeeeee;* much stronger than Saltmarsh Sparrow. Call *chack.* **HABITAT:** Salt marshes.

PRAIRIE AND MARSH SPARROWS

VESPER SPARROW

SALTMARSH SPARROW

NELSON'S SPARROW

coastal

interior

LECONTE'S SPARROW

juvenile

adult

SEASIDE SPARROW

"Cape Sable"

FOX SPARROW *Passerella iliaca*   Fairly common in West, uncommon in East

7 in. (18 cm). A large, plump sparrow; most subspecies have *rusty rump and tail.* Action towheelike, kicking dead leaves and other ground litter. *Breast heavily streaked* with triangular spots, often clustering in a large blotch on the upper breast. Ages and sexes similar. Fox Sparrows vary, with subspecies roughly divided into four groups: (1) "Red" subspecies (subspecies group *iliaca*): bright rusty with rusty back stripes (breeds in northern and eastern regions); (2) "Sooty" subspecies *(unalaschcensis):* dusky or sooty head, back (unstreaked), and upper breast variably tinged reddish (Pacific Northwest coast); (3) "Slate-colored" subspecies *(schistacea):* gray-headed and gray-backed (unstreaked), yellowish-based bill (Rockies, Great Basin); and (4) "Thick-billed" subspecies *(megarhyncha):* similar to Slate-colored but large-billed (s. Cascades, CA mountains). In fall and winter, these types intermingle in the West. **VOICE:** Song brilliant and musical; a varied arrangement of short clear notes and sliding whistles. Call varies by type, a sharp *chink* (Thick-billed group) to flatter *chup* or *chick.* **SIMILAR SPECIES:** Song Sparrows in AK. **HABITAT:** Wooded undergrowth, brush, feeders.

SONG SPARROW *Melospiza melodia*   Common

5¾–6½ in. (15–17 cm). This common, mid-sized sparrow has a *long rounded tail* and *heavy breast streaks* that merge into a *large central spot.* Broad grayish eyebrow. Juvenile is more finely streaked, often lacks central spot. Song Sparrows vary widely, as shown on the plate, with many recognized subspecies. **VOICE:** Song a variable series of notes, some musical, some buzzy; usually starts with three or four bright repetitious notes, *sweet sweet sweet,* etc., and ends in lower buzzy trill. Call a low, nasal *tchep.* **SIMILAR SPECIES:** Savannah Sparrow paler and has yellowish over eye; tail shorter, notched; legs brighter pink. See Lincoln's and Swamp Sparrows. AK birds large, like Fox Sparrow, but not as red; bill smaller, with less-curved culmen. **HABITAT:** Thickets, brush, marshes, roadsides, gardens, feeders.

LINCOLN'S SPARROW   Fairly common in West, uncommon in East
Melospiza lincolnii

5¾ in. (15 cm). Skulking; prefers to be near cover. Adult and juvenile similar to Song Sparrow, but smaller and trimmer, side of face grayer, sharp breast streaks *much finer* and overlaid on *creamy buff* breast; also has narrow whitish eye-ring and buffy mustache. **VOICE:** Song sweet and gurgling; suggests both House Wren and Purple Finch; starts with low passages, rises abruptly, drops. Calls a hard *tik* and buzzy *zzzeeet.* **SIMILAR SPECIES:** First-year Swamp Sparrow has duller breast, with blurry streaks and rustier wing. Juvenile Swamp, Song, and Lincoln's Sparrows very similar: check differences in breast streaking, malar stripe, bill size and shape. **HABITAT:** Willow and alder thickets, mountain meadows, muskeg, brushy bogs; in winter, wet fields, brush, thickets, sometimes feeders.

SWAMP SPARROW *Melospiza georgiana*   Fairly common

5¾ in. (15 cm). A plump, dark, *rusty-winged* sparrow with *broad black back striping.* Adult male: White throat, rusty cap, blue-gray neck and breast. Female and first-year: Variably average duller; *blackish or dark rust crown, olive-gray neck and breast;* dim flank streaking. Juvenile is heavily streaked. **VOICE:** Song a trill, similar to Chipping Sparrow's but slower, sweeter, and stronger. Call a hard *cheep,* similar to Black or Eastern Phoebe's. **SIMILAR SPECIES:** Song Sparrow slightly larger, larger billed, longer tailed, has *heavier breast streaks,* lacks tawny flanks. Lincoln's Sparrow has buff breast with fine sharp streaks, finer bill. **HABITAT:** Nests in freshwater marshes with bushes, cattails, sedges, willows; winters in fresh and salt marshes, pond edges, weedy ditches. Rare migrant in West and scarce winter visitor to CA.

STREAKED
SPARROWS

"Red" (North and East)

"Slate-colored" (Rockies)

"Thick-billed" (CA)

incl. breeding ranges for subspecies

"Sooty" (Northwest coast)

FOX SPARROW

AK

Southwest

SONG SPARROW

East

(typical)

SWAMP SPARROW

LINCOLN'S SPARROW

first-year female

adult

WHITE-THROATED SPARROW
Zonotrichia albicollis

Common in East, uncommon in West

6¾ in. (17 cm). *Spring/summer:* A gray-breasted sparrow with distinct white throat and yellow lores. Bill grayish. Polymorphic, with head stripes varying in shades of black, brown, and tan; some adults have bold black-and-white head stripes, others duller brown and tan. Tan morph may be moderately streaked on breast; throat duller. Ages and sexes similar although first-fall birds and females average duller than adults and males within each morph. **VOICE:** Song several clear pensive whistles often rendered *old sam peabody peabody peabody.* Call a hard *chink;* also a thin, slurred *tseet.* **SIMILAR SPECIES:** White-crowned Sparrow. **HABITAT:** Thickets, brush, undergrowth of coniferous and mixed woodlands. Regularly visits feeders, preferring to stay on ground. Rare migrant in interior West; uncommon winter visitor to CA.

WHITE-CROWNED SPARROW
Zonotrichia leucophrys

Common in West, uncommon in East

7 in. (18 cm). This species comprises multiple subspecies, which exhibit whitish or black lores and/or tawny or yellowish bills. *Adult:* Clear breast, crown *striped with black and white. First-fall/winter:* Head stripes dark red-brown and light buff. **VOICE:** Song one or more clear, plaintive whistles, often *chew-chee-tzip-tzip-tzip tseew* but variable, many local dialects. Call a sharp *pink.* **SIMILAR SPECIES:** White-throated Sparrow has well-defined white throat, yellow spot before eye, grayish bill. First-fall/winter Golden-crowned Sparrow slightly larger, has *duskier bill and underparts,* more muted head pattern, usually with *dull yellowish forehead.* **HABITAT:** Brush, forest edges, thickets, chaparral; in winter, also farms, desert washes, gardens, parks, feeders.

GOLDEN-CROWNED SPARROW *Zonotrichia atricapilla*

Fairly common

7¼ in. (18 cm). *Spring/summer:* Has *yellow central crown stripe,* bordered broadly with black. Dusky bill. *Fall/winter first-year:* May look like large female House Sparrow but usually with dull yellow suffusion on forehead; fall/winter adult similar but with blacker head stripes. **VOICE:** Song three to five high whistled notes of plaintive minor quality, *oh-dear-me.* Sometimes a faint trill. Call a sharp *tsew.* **SIMILAR SPECIES:** White-crowned Sparrow. **HABITAT:** Boreal and subalpine scrub, willow thickets, stunted spruces; in winter, similar to that of White-crowned (with which it is often found in mixed flocks), but Golden-crowned favors denser shrubs. Widespread vagrant and winter visitor to East, largely at feeders; casual to E. Coast.

HARRIS'S SPARROW *Zonotrichia querula*

Uncommon

7½ in. (19 cm). Large; almost size of Fox Sparrow. *Adult:* Black crown, face, and bib encircling pink bill (sexes similar). *First-fall/winter:* Has *white on throat,* less black on crown, buffy brown on rest of head; blotched and streaked on breast. Plumage varies. **VOICE:** Song has quavering quality of other *Zonotrichia* sparrows: one to three clear whistles, *peee* to *peee-pee-pee* on same pitch. Alarm call *wink.* **HABITAT:** Stunted boreal forests; in winter, brush, hedgerows, open woods. May mix with White-crowned Sparrows in winter. Casual to very rare vagrant to W. and E. Coasts.

SPARROWS

tan-striped morph

dull

WHITE-THROATED SPARROW

white-striped morph

Eastern and Western mountain first-fall/ winter

Western interior and coastal

WHITE-CROWNED SPARROW

adult

first-fall/ winter

GOLDEN-CROWNED SPARROW

adult

spring/ summer

HARRIS'S SPARROW

first-fall/ winter

DARK-EYED JUNCO *Junco hyemalis*   Common

6–6½ in. (15–16 cm). This familiar songbird is characterized by a variably darker-hooded appearance and *white outer tail feathers* that flash conspicuously in flight. Bill and belly white to whitish. Adult male has dark hood; first-year male and adult female slightly less so, and first-year female is drabbest. *Juvenile:* Finely streaked on head and breast; identified from other juvenile sparrows by white outer tail feathers. This species has formerly been divided into up to four full species in N. America but they are now lumped as one highly complex species. Intergrades are known. Treated separately, the main subspecies groups are as follows.

"Oregon" Junco (*oreganus* subspecies group) is the widespread subspecies in the West. Male has *rusty brown back* with *blackish hood* and *buffy, brownish, or rusty sides* (side color variable). Female duller, but note contrast between paler gray hood and brown back, convex shape to lower border of hood.

"Pink-sided" Junco (*mearnsi* group) breeds in the n. Prairie region and Great Basin, winters to south and west (rarely to W. and E. Coasts). Male has a gray hood, pink flanks, and black lores; female duller.

"Gray-headed" Junco (*caniceps* group) occurs in Great Basin and s. Rockies. Rufous patch on back of otherwise pale to medium gray plumage, with *gray sides* and *gray head, dark lores.* Breeders in Southwest have bicolored bill.

"Slate-colored" Junco (*hyemalis* group) is most northern and eastern subspecies, wintering mainly east of Rockies, sparingly westward. A gray junco with *gray back* and sides, white belly. Female and first-year duller gray tinged brownish on back. The more uniform coloration, lacking rusty areas, is distinctive. Some particularly brownish young birds may be confused with Oregon Junco but usually have gray rather than brown or buff sides.

"White-winged" Junco (*aikeni* group) breeds in Black Hills region. A large, dark junco (resembling Slate-colored) with gray back; usually has *two whitish wing bars* and exhibits considerably more white in tail (four outer feathers on each side). Some female White-winged Juncos and some Slate-colored Juncos can have thin, weak, or broken wing bars, so caution is warranted.

VOICE: Song a loose trill, suggestive of Chipping Sparrow but more musical. Call a light *smack;* also clicking or twittering notes. **HABITAT:** Coniferous and mixed woods. In fall/winter season, open woods, undergrowth, roadsides, brush, parks, gardens, feeders; usually in flocks. In West, multiple subspecies can commingle.

YELLOW-EYED JUNCO *Junco phaeonotus*   Uncommon, local

6¼ in. (16 cm). Our only junco with *yellow eyes,* which give it a somewhat fierce look. Otherwise like "Gray-headed" Junco except slightly darker head contrasts with whiter throat; rufous on back *extends onto wing.* Ages and sexes vary but not as much as in Dark-eyed Juncos. Walks rather than hops. **VOICE:** Song musical, more complicated than Dark-eyed's, three-part: *chip chip chip, wheedle wheedle, che che che che che.* **HABITAT:** Coniferous forests, pine-oak woods; in winter, some come down to slightly lower elevations in canyons, including to feeders.

JUNCOS

DARK-EYED JUNCO

adult female

adult male

"Oregon" West

juvenile

adult male

"Pink-sided" N. Great Basin

N. Great Basin adult male

adult male

"Gray-headed" S. Great Basin

"Slate-colored" East

adult female

adult male East

adult male

"White-winged" Black Hills region

adult male

adult male

YELLOW-EYED JUNCO

OLD WORLD BUNTINGS Family Emberizidae

Recently split from New World sparrows and longspurs, which they resemble outwardly. **FOOD:** Seeds, insects on breeding grounds. **RANGE:** Eurasia and Africa.

RUSTIC BUNTING *Emberiza rustica*   Scarce vagrant

5¾–6 in. (16 cm). Note *rusty upperparts and breast-band; dark cheek outlined in white.* Head slightly crested, bill pink. *Spring/summer male:* Black head markings. Female and winter males duller, browner, with dark spot in brown cheek patch. **VOICE:** Call a loud distinctive *tick.* **SIMILAR SPECIES:** Little Bunting (*E. pusilla;* not shown), a similar Asian vagrant, is less rusty, more sparrowlike. **RANGE:** Regular Asian stray to w. AK Is.; casual south along Pacific Coast.

OLD WORLD SPARROWS Family Passeridae

Differ from our native sparrows by having a more curved bill culmen (ridge). The widespread House Sparrow is well known. **FOOD:** Mainly insects, seeds. **RANGE:** Old World.

HOUSE SPARROW *Passer domesticus*   Common, introduced

6¼ in. (16 cm). Introduced from Europe in 1840. Familiar to many people. *Male: Black throat, white cheeks, chestnut nape. Female and juvenile:* Lack black throat, have dingy breast, and dull eye stripe *behind eye only;* note *single bold wing bar.* City birds often sootier than clean country birds. **VOICE:** Hoarse *chirp* and *shillip* notes, also a rising *sweep.* Song a series of such notes. **SIMILAR SPECIES:** Female Dickcissel, buntings, sparrows, Eurasian Tree Sparrow. **HABITAT:** Cities, towns, farms, feeders. Also introduced and common in HI (p. 448).

EURASIAN TREE SPARROW *Passer montanus*   Uncommon, local, introduced

6 in. (15 cm). Both sexes resemble male House Sparrow, but black throat patch smaller. Note *black ear spot;* crown brown. **VOICE:** A metallic *chik* or *chup,* a repeated *chit-tchup.* In flight, a hard *tek, tek.* **SIMILAR SPECIES:** House Sparrow. **RANGE:** Introduced around St. Louis in 1870; some northward expansion since. **HABITAT:** Farmland, weedy patches, locally in residential areas, feeders.

WEAVERS Family Ploceidae

Old World family including weavers and bishops. Escaped captives established very locally in s. CA and possibly elsewhere. **FOOD:** Seeds, insects. **RANGE:** Native to Old World.

NORTHERN RED BISHOP *Euplectes franciscanus*   Uncommon, local, exotic

4¼ in. (10 cm). Sometimes still referred to as "Orange Weaver." Native to Africa; introduced in CA (semi-established in Los Angeles area), Puerto Rico, and Bermuda. Short tail, large head and bill. *Spring/summer male:* Bright reddish body; black face, bill, belly. *Female and fall/winter male:* Similar to Grasshopper Sparrow, but with larger, *paler bill, short tail.*

ESTRILDID FINCHES Family Estrildidae

Old World family represented in N. America by escaped cage birds, including Scaly-breasted Munia. A number of species introduced and established in HI (p. 446).

SCALY-BREASTED MUNIA *Lonchura punctulata*   Fairly common, local, exotic

4½ in. (11 cm). Known by several names, including "Nutmeg Mannikin." A small, dark finch, native to se. Asia but introduced to CA and s. FL, as well as HI. Now established in s. CA. *Adult:* Dark, large dark bill, brown *belly checked with white.* Sexes similar. *Juvenile:* Pale brown overall, bill dark.

MISCELLANEOUS SEED-EATING BIRDS

RUSTIC BUNTING

spring/
summer
male

**HOUSE
SPARROW**

male

female

**EURASIAN
TREE
SPARROW**

spring/
summer
male

female

**NORTHERN
RED BISHOP**

juvenile

adult

**SCALY-
BREASTED
MUNIA**

FINCHES and ALLIES Family Fringillidae

Plump, small to medium-small birds with seed-cracking bills; relatively short, notched tails; often undulating flight. Sexes usually differ. More arboreal than sparrows. **FOOD:** Seeds, small fruit. **RANGE:** Worldwide, including Hawaiian Honeycreepers (see p. 450).

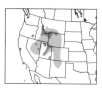

BLACK ROSY-FINCH *Leucosticte atrata*　　　　Uncommon, local

6–6¼ in. (16 cm). Differs from other rosy-finches by male's blackish body color, feathering sometimes edged in gray. Female grayer; the only truly grayish rosy-finch; first-year female duller, has less black in face. **VOICE:** High chirping notes, suggestive of House Sparrow. **SIMILAR SPECIES:** Other rosy-finches. **HABITAT:** Similar to other rosy-finches. Casual winter vagrant to s. CA, AZ.

BROWN-CAPPED ROSY-FINCH *Leucosticte australis*　　Uncommon, local

6–6¼ in. (16 cm). The plainest rosy-finch. Like Gray-crowned, but male has more restricted gray on head, darker crown. Female much drabber than male. **VOICE:** As in Black Rosy-Finch. **SIMILAR SPECIES:** Other rosy-finches. **HABITAT:** Similar to other rosy-finches.

GRAY-CROWNED ROSY-FINCH *Leucosticte tephrocotis*　　Uncommon

6–8 in. (16–20 cm). Sparrow-sized birds of high snowfields and tundra; rosy-finches walk rather than hop. *Male: Dark brown,* with *pinkish wash* on belly, wings, and rump. *Light gray patch* on back of head. Montane western subspecies (*tephrocotis* group) brown cheeked, those of coastal AK to WA (*littoralis* group QY) gray cheeked. Females are duller; gray patch reduced or almost wanting. **VOICE:** As in Black Rosy-Finch. **SIMILAR SPECIES:** Other rosy-finches. **HABITAT:** Rocky summits, alpine cirques and snowfields; also rocky islands (off AK); winters in open country at mid- and lower elevations, regular at feeders in mountain towns. Casual winter vagrant east of range; accidental to Midwest.

WHITE-WINGED CROSSBILL *Loxia leucoptera*　　Uncommon, irregular

6½ in. (17 cm). Note *crossed mandibles, bold white wing bars,* and white tertial tips in all plumages. *Adult male:* Dull *rose pink.* Female and first-year male olive-gray, with yellowish rump (see Red Crossbill). *Juvenile:* Heavily streaked. **VOICE:** Calls a liquid *peet* and a dry *chif-chif.* Song a succession of loud trills on different pitches. **SIMILAR SPECIES:** Red Crossbill has no or thin and weak pale wing bars and tertial edging. **HABITAT:** Spruce and fir forests, hemlocks; very rarely at feeders. Irruptive winter visitor south of normal range.

RED CROSSBILL *Loxia curvirostra*　　　　Uncommon, irregular

5¾–7 in. (14–17 cm). Note *crossed mandibles* and *plain wings.* Usually found in flocks. *Adult male: Dull red,* brighter on rump. Second-year male often washed orange. *Female and first-year:* Dull olive-gray to mustard-yellow; yellowish on rump. *Juvenile:* Streaked above and below, suggesting a large Pine Siskin, but note bill. **VOICE:** Call a hard *jip-jip* or *kip-kip-kip* (in some populations, *kwit-kwit* or *kewp-kewp*). Song consists of finchlike warbled passages, *jip-jip-jip-jeeaa-jeeaa;* trills, *chips.* **SIMILAR SPECIES:** White-winged and Cassia Crossbills. **HABITAT:** Variety of conifers; rarely at feeders. Erratic and irruptive wanderings throughout range, especially in winter.

CASSIA CROSSBILL *Loxia sinesciuris*　　　Fairly common, Local

6–7 in. (15–17 cm). Recently split from Red Crossbill. Resident to South Hills and Albion Mts., ID. Similar to Red Crossbill but bill much larger because of larger cones, resulting from the absence of squirrels, within isolated range. **VOICE:** Call a more liquid and slightly deeper *quip-quip-quip,* more emphatic than Red Crossbills in area. **SIMILAR SPECIES:** Best separated from Red Crossbill by bill size, calls. **HABITAT:** Lodgepole pine forest.

ROSY-FINCHES AND CROSSBILLS

female

male

BLACK ROSY-FINCH

first-
year
female

**BROWN-CAPPED
ROSY-FINCH**

"Hepburn's"

Gray-crowned
Rosy-Finch

Pribilofs
male

male

male

**GRAY-CROWNED
ROSY-FINCH**

juvenile

adult
male

**WHITE-WINGED
CROSSBILL**

adult
male

**RED
CROSSBILL**

**CASSIA
CROSSBILL**

adult
female

adult
male

juvenile

COMMON REDPOLL *Acanthis flammea* Uncommon, irregular

5¼ in. (13 cm). Small finch; note *bright red forehead* and *black chin. Adult male:* Has noticeable *pink breast. Adult female and first-year male:* Usually show a pink tinge; first-year female lacks pink. Often found in flocks. **VOICE:** Song a trill, followed by the rattling *chet-chet-chet*, the latter also given in flight. **SIMILAR SPECIES:** Hoary Redpoll, Pine Siskin. **HABITAT:** Birches, tundra scrub. In winter, weeds, brush, thistle feeders. Irruptive winter visitor south of normal range.

HOARY REDPOLL *Acanthis hornemanni* Rare, irregular

5¼–5½ in. (13–14 cm). Can be found in winter flocks of Common Redpolls. Look for a "frostier" bird, with whiter rump containing *little or no streaking; bill stubbier;* streaks on flanks and undertail coverts reduced. Adult males whitest; females and first-year birds duller, can overlap with adult male Commons, and can be *very difficult to identify.* **VOICE:** As in Common Redpoll. **SIMILAR SPECIES:** Common Redpoll, Pine Siskin. **HABITAT:** Birches, tundra scrub. In winter, weeds, brush, feeders. Irruptive in winter, though not as much as Common.

HOUSE FINCH *Haemorhous mexicanus* Common

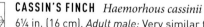

5¾–6 in. (14–15 cm). Slimmer than Purple and Cassin's Finches; tail longer, square-tipped. *Male:* Breast, forehead, stripe over eye, and rump vary from *red to orange to dull mustard yellow* (diet related). Note *dark streaks* on sides and belly. *Female:* Streaked brown; told from Purple Finch by paler brown overall, slimmer body, longer tail, smaller head and bill; *plainer face;* undertail coverts usually streaked. **VOICE:** Song bright, loose, and disjointed finchlike notes; often ends in nasal *wheer.* Call a nasal, finchlike *chirp.* **SIMILAR SPECIES:** Purple and Cassin's Finches. **HABITAT:** Cities, suburbs, farms, feeders; prefers drier habitats. Introduced and common in HI (p. 458).

PURPLE FINCH *Haemorhous purpureus* Uncommon

6 in. (15 cm). *Adult male:* Like a sparrow dipped in raspberry juice. Dull rose red, brightest on head, chest, and rump. Sides and flanks unstreaked. *Female and first-year male:* Heavily streaked, brown to olive-brown; undertail coverts usually lack streaks. **VOICE:** Song a fast lively warble recalling Warbling Vireo but bubblier; call a dull, flat, metallic *pik* or *tick.* **SIMILAR SPECIES:** Cassin's and House Finches. See female Rose-breasted Grosbeak. **HABITAT:** Woods, groves, riparian thickets, suburbs, feeders.

CASSIN'S FINCH *Haemorhous cassinii* Fairly common

6¼ in. (16 cm). *Adult male:* Very similar to Purple Finch, but red of breast paler, more scarlet; *red crown patch contrasts abruptly* with brown of nape; bill has straighter ridge. *Female and first-year male:* Whiter underparts, sharper streaking above and below, streaked undertail coverts, pale eye-ring, and bill shape distinguish it from Purple Finch. **VOICE:** Song flutier and more varied than Purple's. Call a musical *chidiup.* **HABITAT:** Conifers in mountains; some move to lower elevations in winter. Casual to very rare winter vagrant to W. Coast and Plains states.

PINE GROSBEAK *Pinicola enucleator* Scarce, irregular

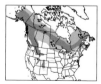

8¾–9 in. (23 cm). A large, plump, tame finch with dark, stubby bill, longish tail, dark wings with two white wing bars. Flight undulating. *Adult male:* Dull *rose red.* Female and first-fall/winter male: Gray; head and rump tinged with dull mustard yellow; first-spring/summer male can molt in scattered red feathers. **VOICE:** Song rich, rapid warbling: *richy-rich-chew-twee-chur-chur.* Call a musical *chee-vli* in West; *pe-pew-pew* in East. **SIMILAR SPECIES:** Crossbills, Purple Finch. **HABITAT:** Conifers, particularly lodgepole pines, larches; in winter, also crabapples and other fruiting trees, ashes. Irruptive winter visitor south of normal range in East (much more rarely so in West).

RED FINCHES, ETC.

COMMON
REDPOLL

orange
variant

female

male

male

female

HOUSE FINCH

adult
male

HOARY
REDPOLL

male

female

PURPLE
FINCH

female

adult
male

CASSIN'S
FINCH

adult
male

female

PINE GROSBEAK

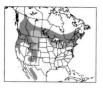

EVENING GROSBEAK *Coccothraustes vespertinus* Uncommon, irregular

8 in. (20 cm). Size of a starling. A *chunky, short-tailed* finch with *very large, pale, conical bill* (sometimes tinged greenish). *Male:* Deep yellow, with darker head, *yellow eyebrow,* and black-and-white wings. *Female:* Silver gray, with yellow sides of neck, patterned black-and-white wings and tail; suggests an over-grown female American Goldfinch. Gregarious. In flight, overall shape and *large white wing patches* identify this species. **VOICE:** Song is repeated short trills. Calls distinctive, ringing, finchlike *clee-ip* and a high, clear *thew.* **SIMILAR SPE-CIES:** American Goldfinch (much smaller), female crossbills. **HABITAT:** Conifer-ous and mixed forests; in winter, box elders, fruiting shrubs, feeders. Shows decadal irruptive tendencies to winter south of normal range.

AMERICAN GOLDFINCH *Spinus tristis* Common

5 in. (13 cm). Goldfinches are distinguished from other small, olive-yellow birds (such as warblers) by their short, conical bill and behavior. *Spring/summer male:* Bright *yellow with black forehead and wings;* tail also black; bill pale. *Spring/summer female:* Dull yellow-olive; darker above, with brownish-black wings and conspicuous wing bars. *Fall/winter:* Both sexes much like spring/summer female, but bill dark; wings blacker in males. **VOICE:** Song clear, light, canary-like. Call, in undulating flight, each dip is punctuated by *ti-DEE-di-di* or *per-chik-o-ree* or *po-ta-to-chip.* **SIMILAR SPECIES:** Lesser and Lawrence's Gold-finches, Pine Siskin. **HABITAT:** Patches of thistles and weeds, dandelions on lawns, sweetgum balls, roadsides, open woods, edges; in winter, also feeders, where often in flocks.

LESSER GOLDFINCH *Spinus psaltria* Fairly common

4½ in. (11 cm). *Male:* A very small finch with *black cap* and yellow underparts; white on wings. Males of subspecies *psaltria* (s. Rockies) have *black* back; males of western subspecies *hesperophilus* have *greenish* back. Some birds have mot-tled back. *Female:* Similar to fall/winter American Goldfinch, but usually yel-lower below, has *less contrasting wing bars,* yellowish (not white) *undertail coverts,* and *dark rump.* Calls differ. First-year female plain, dull greenish over-all. **VOICE:** Sweet, plaintive, whiny notes, *tee-yee* (rising) and *tee-yer* (dropping). Song more phrased than American Goldfinch's. **SIMILAR SPECIES:** American Goldfinch. **HABITAT:** Dry brushy and weedy country, open woods, wooded streams, towns, parks, gardens, feeders. Casual vagrant east of range, acci-dentally to E. Coast.

LAWRENCE'S GOLDFINCH *Spinus lawrencei* Uncommon, irregular

4¾ in. (12 cm). Known in all plumages by *large amount of yellow in wings. Male:* Has bold *black face* (including chin). *Female:* Plain and gray. **VOICE:** Song similar to Lesser Goldfinch's, but with high tinkling notes. Call distinctive, thin *tink-oo,* syllables emphasized equally. **SIMILAR SPECIES:** Other goldfinches. **HABITAT:** Oak-pine and riparian woodland edges, chaparral, ranch yards, parks; often found near water such as stream pools, stock tanks, dripping faucets. Casual north and east of range, accidentally to TX.

PINE SISKIN *Spinus pinus* Fairly common, irregular

5 in. (13 cm). Size of a goldfinch. A small, dark, *heavily streaked* finch with deeply notched tail, sharply pointed bill. *Yellow bases to wings and tail* (more prominent in male; less evident in female). Often first detected by voice, flying over. **VOICE:** Call a loud finchy *jjeee-ip;* also a light *tit-i-tit;* a buzzy *shreeeee.* Song suggests goldfinch, but coarser, wheezy. **SIMILAR SPECIES:** Fall/winter American Gold-finch lacks streaks. Female House Finch much larger, has stubbier bill. Com-mon Redpoll has red forehead. All lack yellow in wings and tail. **HABITAT:** Conifers, mixed woods, alders, sweetgum balls, weedy areas, feeders.

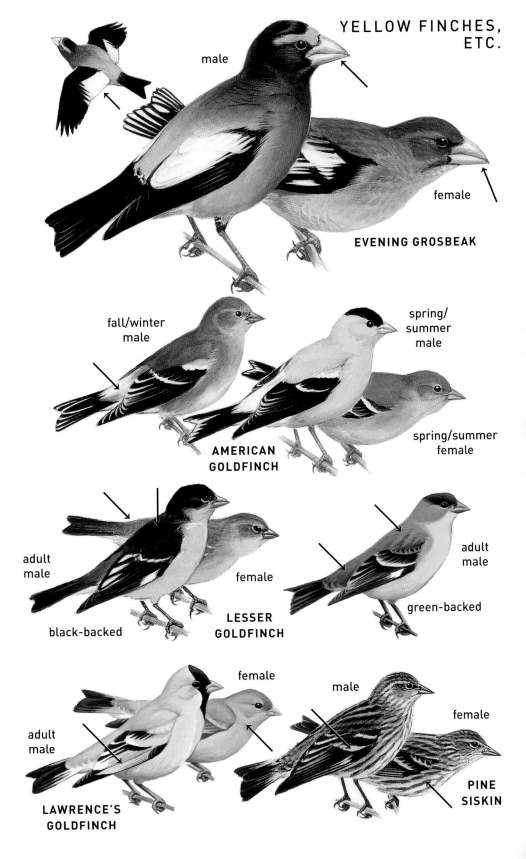

YELLOW FINCHES, ETC.

male

female

EVENING GROSBEAK

fall/winter male

spring/ summer male

spring/summer female

AMERICAN GOLDFINCH

adult male

female

black-backed

LESSER GOLDFINCH

adult male

green-backed

female

male

female

adult male

LAWRENCE'S GOLDFINCH

PINE SISKIN

EUROPEAN GOLDFINCH *Carduelis carduelis*　　　　Scarce, exotic

5½ in. (14 cm). Occasional reports, mostly at feeders. Assumed to be escaped captive birds. Note red face, yellow wing patches.

BRAMBLING *Fringilla montifringilla*　　　　Rare vagrant

6¼ in. (16 cm). *Tawny* or *orangey buff* breast and shoulders, *whitish rump distinctive in flight. Spring/summer male:* Black head and back. *Female and fall/winter:* Gray cheek bordered by dark, flanks streaked or spotted. **VOICE:** Call a whiny *zweee;* in flight, a distinctive nasal, hollow *eck.* **RANGE:** Eurasian species; regular on w. AK islands, casual but widespread records elsewhere in N. America.

NORTH AMERICAN TANAGERS, CARDINALS, BUNTINGS, and ALLIES Family Cardinalidae

Medium-sized songbirds with heavy, fruit-eating or seed-crushing bills. Now includes the N. American tanagers, as well as the crested cardinals, heavy-billed grosbeaks, smaller Passerina buntings, and the Dickcissel. **FOOD:** Seeds, fruit, insects. **RANGE:** New World.

ROSE-BREASTED GROSBEAK *Pheucticus ludovicianus*　　　　Fairly common

8 in. (20 cm). *Adult male:* Black and white, with large triangle of rose red on breast and thick pale bill. In flight, pattern of black and white flashes across upperparts. Underwing linings rose pink. Plumage fringed brown in fall/winter. *Female:* Streaked, like a large sparrow or female Purple Finch; recognized by large, pink, grosbeak bill, broad white wing bars, striped crown, and broad white eyebrow stripe. Underwing linings yellow. First-year male like female in first-fall but has pink underwing lining; attains partial adult plumage by first spring/summer. **VOICE:** Song consists of rising and falling passages; resembles American Robin's song, but more melodic. Call a squeaky, metallic *kick* or *eek.* **SIMILAR SPECIES:** Purple Finch. Female and first-fall male differs from Black-headed Grosbeak in having *heavier streaks* to paler breast, paler bill; underwing pink in male. Beware some intermediates and hybrids also occur that can be difficult to identify. **HABITAT:** Deciduous woods, orchards, groves, thickets, sometimes at feeders in spring. Scarce vagrant to W. Coast.

BLACK-HEADED GROSBEAK *Pheucticus melanocephalus*　　　　Fairly common

8¼ in. (21 cm). A stocky bird, larger than a sparrow, with outsized bill. *Adult male:* Black head; breast, collar, and rump *dull orange-brown;* bold black-and-white wing and tail as in Rose-breasted Grosbeak. In fall/winter, head striped with brown. *Female and first-fall male:* Largely brown, with sparrowlike streaks above; head strongly patterned with light stripes and dark ear patch. Breast *washed with yellow-buff, ocher-buff, or butterscotch;* dark streaks on sides *fine,* nearly absent across middle of chest. Underwing linings yellow in all ages/sexes. *Maxilla dark.* First-spring/summer male adultlike but head variably mottled buff and wings brown rather than black. **VOICE:** Similar to Rose-breasted Grosbeak. Call a flat *ik* or *eek.* **SIMILAR SPECIES:** Female and first-fall male Rose-breasted Grosbeak. Occasionally hybridizes with Rose-breasted where ranges come into contact. **HABITAT:** Deciduous and riparian woods; rarely at feeders in winter. Rare vagrant to E. Coast.

YELLOW GROSBEAK *Pheucticus chrysopeplus*　　　　Casual vagrant

9¼ in. (24 cm). Slightly larger than Black-headed Grosbeak. *Adult male:* Golden yellow and black, goldfinchlike except for large, blackish grosbeak bill. *Female and first-year male:* Duller, with streaked back and crown. **VOICE:** Rich, whistly warble, similar to Rose-breasted Grosbeak: *cheer-reah, churr-weoh.* **SIMILAR SPECIES:** Evening Grosbeak lacks extensive yellow head; has different wing pattern. **RANGE:** Mexican species, casual visitor to sw. states. **HABITAT:** Deciduous woods, often near water. Escapees occasionally occur in CA and elsewhere.

EURASIAN FINCHES AND GROSBEAKS

EUROPEAN GOLDFINCH

BRAMBLING

fall/ winter male

female

spring/ summer male

adult male

ROSE- BREASTED GROSBEAK

female

female

BLACK-HEADED GROSBEAK

adult male

YELLOW GROSBEAK

female

adult male

CRIMSON-COLLARED GROSBEAK *Rhodothraupis celaeno*   Casual vagrant

8½ in. (22 cm). *Adult male:* A blackish grosbeak with *dark red collar and underparts* encircling throat and chest. Red underparts often spotted or blotched with black. *Female and first-fall male:* Similar but *dark olive* replaces red. First-spring male acquires red on nape and breast. **VOICE:** Song similar to Black-headed Grosbeak; a hoarse, bouncy warble, ending in up-slurred note: *zwee!* **SIMILAR SPECIES:** Female tanagers and orioles. **RANGE:** Mexican species, casual visitor (mostly in winter) to s. TX. **HABITAT:** Brushy woods, second growth.

NORTHERN CARDINAL *Cardinalis cardinalis*   Common

8¾ in. (22 cm). *Male:* An *all-red* bird with pointed *crest* and black patch at base of heavy, *triangular reddish bill. Female:* Brown tinged pinkish buff, with some red on wings and tail. *Crest, dark face,* and *heavy reddish orange bill* distinctive. *Juvenile:* Similar to female, but with blackish bill. **VOICE:** Song is clear, slurred whistles, repeated. Several variations: *what-cheer cheer cheer,* etc.; *whoit whoit whoit* or *birdy birdy birdy,* etc.; usually two-part. Call a short, sharp *tik*. **SIMILAR SPECIES:** Pyrrhuloxia. Male Summer and Hepatic Tanagers lack cardinal's crest and black face. **HABITAT:** Woodland edges, thickets, deserts, towns, gardens, feeders. Wanders casually well north and west of range. Introduced and fairly common in HI (p. 448).

PYRRHULOXIA *Cardinalis sinuatus*   Fairly common

8¾ in. (22 cm). *Male:* A slender, gray and red bird, with *long, spiky crest* and *pale yellowish,* stubby, almost parrotlike bill (strongly curved upper mandible). *Female:* Has gray back, buff breast, and touch of red in wings. Always note spiky crest and *stubby yellow bill*. **VOICE:** Song a clear *quink quink quink quink quink,* on one pitch; also a slurred, whistled *what-cheer, what-cheer,* etc., usually not two-part like Northern Cardinal's song. **SIMILAR SPECIES:** Best told from Northern Cardinal by bill color and shape, also by grayer color overall, spikier crest, lack of black mask in female, red face and throat in male. **HABITAT:** Mesquite, thorn scrub, deserts, feeders. Casual vagrant west and north of range.

BLUE GROSBEAK *Passerina caerulea*   Uncommon

6¾ in. (17 cm). *Adult male:* Deep *dull blue,* with thick bill, *two broad rusty or chestnut wing bars.* Often *flips or twitches tail.* Head mottled brown in fresh fall/winter plumage. *Female and first-fall/winter male:* About size of Brown-headed Cowbird; warm or tawny brown, slightly lighter below, with two *rusty buff wing bars;* rump or tail may be tinged with blue. First-year male begins acquiring mottled blue plumage on winter grounds and by first spring/summer is a variable mixture of brown and blue, as in Indigo Bunting. **VOICE:** Warbling song, phrases rising and falling; suggests Purple or House Finch, but slower, more guttural. Call a sharp *chink,* in flight a flat *bzzzt.* **SIMILAR SPECIES:** Female and first-year male Indigo Bunting usually paler (less tawny) brown, show weaker wing bars, and are much smaller and smaller billed. **HABITAT:** Thickets, hedgerows, riparian undergrowth, brushy hillsides, weedy ditches. Casual vagrant well north of range.

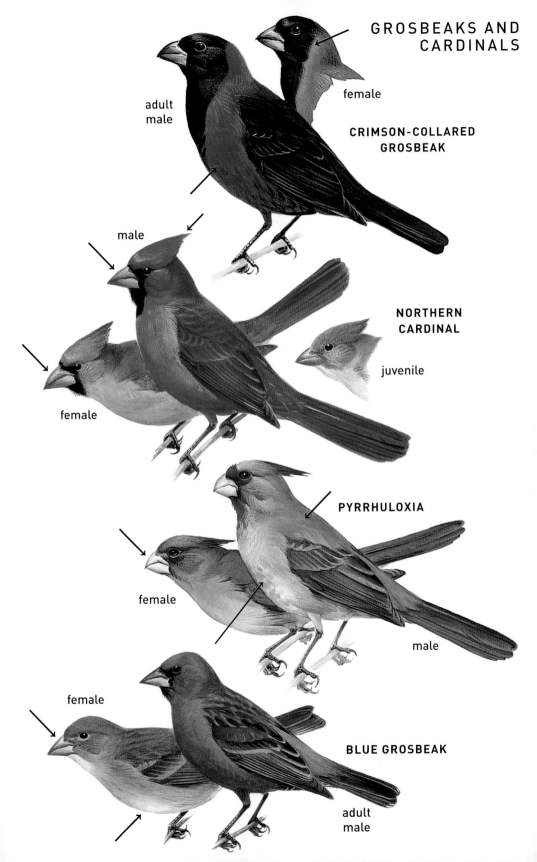

GROSBEAKS AND CARDINALS

adult
male

female

**CRIMSON-COLLARED
GROSBEAK**

male

**NORTHERN
CARDINAL**

juvenile

female

PYRRHULOXIA

female

male

female

BLUE GROSBEAK

adult
male

INDIGO BUNTING   *Passerina cyanea*   Common

5½ in. (14 cm). *Adult spring/summer male:* A small songbird, *rich deep blue all over.* *First-spring/summer male:* Blue is duller and variably mottled brown. Fall/winter adult male brown, like female, but usually with some blue in wings and tail. *Female and first-fall/winter male:* Medium brown to olive-brown; breast slightly paler with faint *blurry* streaks; paler wing bars indistinct. **VOICE:** Song lively, high, and strident; measured phrases, usually paired: *sweet-sweet, chew-chew,* etc. Call a sharp, thin *spit* and a dry *buzz* (in flight). **SIMILAR SPECIES:** Blue Grosbeak much larger and has rusty wing bars. Female and juvenile Lazuli Bunting have slightly grayer brown upperparts; more distinct, whitish wing bars; and unstreaked and warmer-colored breast (except for juveniles, whose streaks are finer and sharper than Indigo's broader and blurrier streaks). Occasionally hybridizes with Lazuli Bunting where ranges overlap. **HABITAT:** Overgrown brushy fields, riparian thickets, bushy wood edges. Scarce vagrant and casual as breeder to W. Coast.

BLUE BUNTING   *Cyanocompsa parellina*   Casual vagrant

5½ in. (14 cm). *Adult male:* Deep blue-black; brighter blue on crown, shoulders, and rump. *Female and first-fall/winter male:* Richer brown than female Indigo Bunting; no bars or streaks; *bill blacker.* **VOICE:** Song a high and sweet jumble of warbled phrases. Call a metallic *chink!* **SIMILAR SPECIES:** Indigo Bunting, Blue Grosbeak. **RANGE:** Mexican visitor, casual to s. TX, mostly in winter. **HABITAT:** Brushy woods with dense cover.

LAZULI BUNTING   *Passerina amoena*   Fairly common

5½ in. (14 cm). *Adult male:* A bright turquoise blue songbird with burnt orangey breast and white belly, suggesting a bluebird, but with *two white wing bars.* Fall/winter adult and first-spring/summer males have brownish tips to feathers, muting some of the blue. *Female and first-fall/winter male:* Unstreaked plain brown back and two pale wing bars (stronger than in female Indigo Bunting); breast, washed deep buff, is typically unstreaked except in juvenile, which may retain fine, sharp streaks into fall. **VOICE:** Song similar to Indigo Bunting's, but faster. Calls similar. **SIMILAR SPECIES:** Female Indigo Bunting. **HABITAT:** Open brush, grassy hillsides with scattered oaks, riparian shrubs, chaparral, weedy fields and ditches. Casual vagrant to E. Coast, often in winter at feeders.

PAINTED BUNTING   *Passerina ciris*   Uncommon

5½ in. (14 cm). The most gaudily colored N. American songbird. Size of a goldfinch. *Adult male:* A patchwork of *blue-violet* on head, *green* on back, *red* on rump and underparts, red orbital ring. *Female and first-year male:* Electric green *above,* paling to lemon-yellow below; *no other small finch is so green.* Juvenile is grayer above with only tinge of green, duller gray to buff below. **VOICE:** Song a wiry warble; suggests Warbling Vireo. Call a sharp *chip.* **HABITAT:** Riparian undergrowth, brushy hedgerows, woodland edges, weedy fields. Widespread vagrant west and north of range, sometimes at feeders although beware cage bird escapees.

VARIED BUNTING   *Passerina versicolor*   Scarce, local

5½ in. (14 cm). *Adult male:* Plum purple body (looks black at a distance). Crown, face, and rump blue, with *bright red patch on nape. Female and first-year male:* Gray-brown with lighter underparts. *No strong wing bars, breast streaks, or distinctive marks of any kind.* Bill smaller and ridge more curved than other buntings. **VOICE:** Song thin, bright, more distinctly phrased, less warbled than Painted Bunting's; notes not as paired as Lazuli Bunting's. **SIMILAR SPECIES:** Female Indigo Bunting more olive-brown, with hint of blurry breast streaks. Female Lazuli with noticeable wing bars. **HABITAT:** Riparian thickets, mesquite and other scrub in washes and lower canyons. Accidental vagrant to CA.

BUNTINGS

adult male

first-spring/
summer male

female

**INDIGO
BUNTING**

female

adult
male

BLUE BUNTING

adult male

female

LAZULI BUNTING

female

adult male

adult male

VARIED BUNTING

adult male

female

PAINTED BUNTING

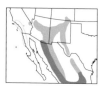

HEPATIC TANAGER *Piranga flava* — Uncommon, local

8 in. (20 cm). Male tanagers in our area are brightly colored with red; females and first-fall males are greenish and yellow. The rather stout bills are notched. *Adult male:* Darker than Summer Tanager; orange-red, *brightest on crown and throat*, with *dark ear patch, dark bill, grayish flanks. Female and first-year male:* Dull yellowish and gray, but shares male's pattern with dusky gray bill, cheeks, and flanks; yellow on throat may be tinged orange. First-year male becomes mixed red and yellow by spring. **VOICE:** Song very similar to Black-headed Grosbeak's. Call a single *chuck.* **SIMILAR SPECIES:** Summer Tanager. **HABITAT:** Open mountain and canyon woodlands with oaks, pines; occasionally to lowlands in winter. Casual vagrant west and north of range; accidental to IL, LA.

SUMMER TANAGER *Piranga rubra* — Fairly common

7¾ in. (20 cm). *Adult male:* Rose red all over, with *pale* bill. *Female and first-winter male:* Olive above, *mustard yellow* below; pale bill. First-spring/summer males patched with red, yellow, and green; some adult females have orangey throat and undertail coverts. **VOICE:** Call a staccato *pi-tuk* or *pik-i-tuk-i-tuk.* Song robinlike phrases, richer and less nasal than Western Tanager's. **SIMILAR SPECIES:** Female Scarlet Tanager is more yellow-green in color and has darker wings, whiter underwing lining, and smaller, duskier bill. Hepatic Tanager has darker bill, grayish cheek, grayish flanks; brightest on crown and throat. **HABITAT:** Riparian woodlands, oaks. Rare to casual vagrant well north of range.

SCARLET TANAGER *Piranga olivacea* — Fairly common

7 in. (18 cm). *Spring/summer male:* Flaming scarlet, with *jet-black* wings and tail. *Female and fall/winter male:* Greenish olive above, variably *yellowish* below; *dark brownish to black wings;* normally no wing bars, but young birds may have single faint bar. **VOICE:** Song four or five short phrases, robinlike but hoarse (suggesting a robin with a sore throat): *hurry-worry-flurry-blurry.* Call distinctive *chip-burr.* **SIMILAR SPECIES:** Summer and Western Tanagers. **HABITAT:** Deciduous and mixed forests, shade trees, especially oaks. Often stays high in trees. Very rare vagrant to W. Coast.

WESTERN TANAGER *Piranga ludoviciana* — Fairly common

7¼ in. (18 cm). Our only tanager with *strong wing bars. Adult male:* Yellow with black back, wings, and tail, two wing bars, and *reddish head.* Red is much reduced in fall and winter. *Female and first-fall/winter male:* Variably yellow below, with white belly but yellow undertail coverts; dull olive above, dull grayish "saddle" may be apparent on back, white wing bars thinner than adult male's. **VOICE:** Song is short phrases; similar to American Robin's in form, but less sustained, hoarser. Calls a dry *pr-tee* or *pri-ti-tic* and breathy *whee?* **SIMILAR SPECIES:** Resembles female orioles, but tail shorter, bill stouter. Worn birds in late summer may have very faint wing bars and might be confused with other tanagers. **HABITAT:** Nests in open coniferous or mixed forests; widespread in migration; a few winter in coastal CA.

FLAME-COLORED TANAGER *Piranga bidentata* — Very rare vagrant

7¼ in. (18 cm). *Adult male:* Fire red with *streaked back, dark ear patch,* two white wing bars, and white tips on tertials. Dark tail tipped at corners with white. *Female and first-fall/winter male:* Look like female Western Tanager, but note *streaked back, dark cheek patch,* pale tips on tertials and tail, and dark bill; hybrids known. **VOICE:** Husky and burry series of phrases, like a slowed-down Western Tanager. **RANGE:** Casual spring and summer visitor from Mex. to mountains of se. AZ; accidental to TX. **HABITAT:** Pine-oak forests.

TANAGERS

HEPATIC TANAGER

female

adult male

first-year male

adult male

SUMMER TANAGER

female

first-spring male

molting (winter grounds)

female

fall/winter male

spring/summer male

SCARLET TANAGER

orange variant spring male

adult male

female

FLAME-COLORED TANAGER

female

female

spring/summer male

WESTERN TANAGER

first-fall/winter male

DICKCISSEL *Spiza americana*   Fairly common

6¼ in. (16 cm). A grassland and farmland bird; migrants often travel in large flocks. Sings from fenceposts and wires. *Adult male:* Suggests a miniature meadowlark (black bib, yellow chest). Has chestnut shoulder patch. In fall, bib obscure. *Female and first-year male:* Much like female House Sparrow, but with bolder stripe over eye (often tinged yellowish), touch of yellow on breast, and blue-gray bill. Dullest first-year females can lack yellow. **VOICE:** Song a staccato *dick-ciss-ciss-ciss* or *chup-chup-klip-klip-klip.* Call a short, hard buzz, often given in flight. **SIMILAR SPECIES:** Female House Sparrow has duller underparts, lacks whitish throat. **HABITAT:** Alfalfa and other fields, meadows, prairies, weedy patches. Casual to scarce vagrant to W. and E. Coasts.

LARK BUNTING   Fairly common
Calamospiza melanocorys (Family Passerellidae)

7 in. (18 cm). A plump, short-tailed prairie sparrow. Gregarious in fall/winter season. Note rather *heavy, blue-gray bill. Spring/summer male: Black,* with *large white wing patches. Female and fall/winter males:* Brown, streaked; *whitish* or *buffy white wing patches* and *tail corners.* In fall/winter adult males can retain some black on face, wings, and belly; otherwise, ages and sexes similar. **VOICE:** Song, given in display flight, composed of cardinal-like slurs, unmusical chatlike *chug*s, piping whistles and trills; each note repeated three to eleven times. Call a flat, mellow *heew.* **SIMILAR SPECIES:** Spring/summer male Bobolink has yellow nape patch and white rump. Beware leucistic blackbirds with odd patches of white in wings. **HABITAT:** Plains, prairies; in winter, also weedy desert lowlands and farm fields. Widespread vagrant north of range and to W. and E. Coasts.

BLACKBIRDS and ORIOLES Family Icteridae

Varied color patterns; sharp bills. Some black and iridescent; orioles are highly colored. Sexes are usually unlike and, in most blackbirds and orioles, males are noticeably larger than females. **FOOD:** Insects, fruit, seeds, waste grain, small aquatic life. **RANGE:** New World; most species occur in Tropics.

EASTERN MEADOWLARK *Sturnella magna*   Uncommon to fairly common

9½ in. (24 cm). In grassy country, a chunky, brown, starling-shaped bird. Warm, reddish brown above, with blacker crown. When bird perches on a post, chest shows bright yellow crossed by black V; flanks buffier. Ages and sexes are similar. When flushed, meadowlarks show conspicuous white sides on short tail. Several shallow, snappy wingbeats alternate with short glides, like a Spotted Sandpiper. Walking, it flicks tail open and shut. Southwestern U.S. "Lilian's" Meadowlark *(lilianae)* paler overall with more white in tail. **VOICE:** Song composed of two clear, slurred whistles, musical and pulled out, *tee-yah, tee-yair* (last note slurred and descending). Call a rasping or buzzy *dzrrt;* also a guttural chatter. **SIMILAR SPECIES:** Western Meadowlark, Dickcissel. **HABITAT:** Open fields and pastures, meadows, prairies, marsh edges; Lilian's Meadowlark partial to grasslands. Accidental vagrant to CA.

WESTERN MEADOWLARK *Sturnella neglecta*   Fairly common

9½ in. (24 cm). Nearly identical to Eastern Meadowlark, but paler above and on flanks; yellow of throat invades farther into malar area behind bill. Crown stripes paler, more streaked with buff; in the Southwest, "Lilian's" Eastern Meadowlarks are just as pale as Westerns but have much more white in the tail. Best identified by vocalizations. **VOICE:** Song variable; seven to ten flutelike notes, gurgling and double-noted, unlike clear whistles of Eastern Meadowlark. Calls *chupp* or *chuck* and a dry rattle. Occasionally gives *dzzrt* call like Eastern. **SIMILAR SPECIES:** Eastern Meadowlark. **HABITAT:** Grasslands, cultivated fields and pastures, meadows, prairies, marshes. Scarce winter visitor to Southeast coast; casual vagrant to Northeast. Introduced and fairly common on Kauai (p. 458).

female

adult
male

fall/
winter

DICKCISSEL

Bobolink
(p. 396) for
comparison

female and fall/
winter male

spring/
summer
male

LARK BUNTING

**WESTERN
MEADOWLARK**

**EASTERN
MEADOWLARK**

BOBOLINK *Dolichonyx oryzivorus*   Fairly common

7 in. (18 cm). *Spring/summer male:* Our only songbird that is *solid black below and partially white above.* Has buff-yellow nape. Returning migrants in spring have extensive brownish tips to dark feathering. *Female and fall/winter male:* A bit larger than House Sparrow; rich buff-yellow, with dark striping on crown and back. Bill more like a sparrow's than a blackbird's. Note pointed tail feathers. VOICE: Song, in hovering flight and quivering descent, ecstatic and bubbling: starts with low, reedy notes and rollicks upward. Flight call a clear *ink*, often heard overhead in migration. SIMILAR SPECIES: Male Lark Bunting has white confined to wings. Female Red-winged Blackbird heavily striped below; longer bill, less buff-yellow overall. Grasshopper Sparrow much smaller. HABITAT: Hayfields, moist meadows, marsh edges. Scarce to rare vagrant or migrant to Southwest and W. Coast.

YELLOW-HEADED BLACKBIRD   Fairly common
Xanthocephalus xanthocephalus

9–9¾ in. (23–25 cm). Gregarious. *Adult male:* A robin-sized blackbird, with *yellow or orange-yellow head and breast;* in flight, shows *white wing patch. Female and first-year male:* Smaller (female) and browner; most of yellow confined to throat and chest; lower breast streaked with white; white wing patch restricted or lacking. VOICE: Song consists of low, hoarse rasping notes produced with much effort; suggests rusty hinges. Call a low *kruck* or *kack.* HABITAT: Nests in freshwater marshes. Forages in farm fields, open country, feedlots. Often associates with other blackbirds in mixed flocks in fall and winter. Rare to casual vagrant to n. Pacific Coast and E. Coast.

RED-WINGED BLACKBIRD *Agelaius phoeniceus*   Common

8½–8¾ in. (22 cm). *Adult male:* Black, with *bright red or orange-red, yellow-margined epaulets* (wing-covert patches), most conspicuous in breeding display. Much of the time red is concealed and only yellowish or off-whitish margin shows. "Bicolored" subspecies *(californicus)* in cen. CA lacks yellow margin. *First-year male:* Sooty brown, mottled (like larger version of female), but with dull red wing-covert patch. *Female:* Brownish, with sharply pointed bill, "blackbird" appearance, and *well-defined dark streaking* below; adult females may have pinkish or dull red tinge to throat or shoulder. Gregarious, traveling and roosting in flocks during fall/winter season. VOICE: Calls a loud *check* and a high, slurred *tee-err.* Song a liquid, gurgling *konk-la-ree* or *o-ka-lay.* SIMILAR SPECIES: Other blackbird species, especially Tricolored Blackbird. HABITAT: Breeds in marshes, brushy swamps, fields, pastures; forages also in cultivated land, feedlots, towns, feeders, etc.

TRICOLORED BLACKBIRD *Agelaius tricolor*   Uncommon, local

8½–8¾ in. (22 cm). Bill longer and proportionally thinner than in Red-winged Blackbird; body averages slimmer, tail longer. *Adult male:* Similar to Red-winged Blackbird, but shoulder patch darker red, with conspicuous *white margin.* Overall plumage slightly glossier. *Female:* Darker than most subspecies of Red-winged, particularly on belly, and never has pinkish on throat, but can be difficult to identify. See voice. Highly gregarious; nests in dense colonies often numbering in the hundreds or thousands, whereas Red-winged is territorial. In fall/winter season, may segregate by sex. VOICE: More nasal than Red-winged: *on-ke-kaangh.* A nasal *kemp.* SIMILAR SPECIES: Red-winged Blackbird. HABITAT: Traditionally nested almost exclusively in cattail or tule marshes; more recently has also switched to blackberry patches, willows, and other scrubby habitats as marshes have been converted. In winter, forages in fields, farms, feedlots, park lawns.

ICTERIDS
(BLACKBIRDS, ETC.)

female

BOBOLINK

fall/winter

spring/
summer
male

adult
male

YELLOW-HEADED
BLACKBIRD

female

red epaulets
hidden

female

adult
male

RED-WINGED
BLACKBIRD

first-year male
Red-winged
Blackbird

"Bicolored"
adult male
(CA)

Tricolored
Blackbird
adult male

female

TRICOLORED
BLACKBIRD

RUSTY BLACKBIRD *Euphagus carolinus* Uncommon

9 in. (23 cm). Feathers fringed rusty only in fall and winter. *Spring/summer male:* A medium-sized black bird with pale yellow eye. Black head may show faint *greenish* gloss (not purplish). *Spring/summer female:* Slate colored, with *light eye.* *Fall/winter:* Feathers variably *fringed rusty,* creating *overall rusty appearance, buffy eyebrow, narrow dark patch through eye.* **VOICE:** Call *chack.* "Song" a split *creak,* like a rusty hinge: *kush-a-lee,* alternating with *ksh-lay.* **SIMILAR SPECIES:** Brewer's Blackbird; Common Grackle much larger, bill much stronger. **HABITAT:** River groves, wooded swamps, muskeg, pond edges; in winter, also muddy fields, with other blackbirds. Very rare vagrant to W. Coast.

BREWER'S BLACKBIRD *Euphagus cyanocephalus* Common

9 in. (23 cm). A familiar blackbird in w. N. America. *Male:* All black, with whitish eye; in good light, *purplish* reflections may be seen on head and neck, with some greenish reflections on body. *Fresh first-fall male:* Can be fringed olive-brown. *Female:* Brownish gray, usually with *dark* eye. **VOICE:** Song a harsh, wheezy, creaking *ksh-eee.* Call *chack.* **SIMILAR SPECIES:** Spring/summer male Rusty Blackbird flatter black with dull *greenish* head reflections (can be hard to see); bill slightly longer. Female Rusty has *light* eye. Beware first-fall male Brewer's can be fairly heavily fringed, like Rusty, but fringe color muddier brown, not rusty. **HABITAT:** Fields, mountain meadows, prairies, farms, feedlots, towns, parks, lawns, shopping malls, parking lots. Rare to casual winter visitor or vagrant to E. Coast.

BROWN-HEADED COWBIRD *Molothrus ater* Common

7½ in. (19 cm). A rather small blackbird with short, sparrowlike bill. *Male:* Black with *brown head (may appear all black in poor light).* *Female:* Gray-brown with lighter throat; note short *finchlike bill.* *Juvenile:* Paler than female. Buffy gray, with soft breast streaking and pale scaling above. *Molting first-fall male:* Splotched tan and black. A nest parasite (never builds its own nest), juveniles are often seen being fed by smaller warblers, sparrows, and other birds. Cowbirds look smaller than blackbirds in mixed feeding flocks, and feed on ground with tails lifted high. **VOICE:** Flight call *weee-titi.* Song a bubbly and creaky *glug-glug-gleeee.* Call *chuck.* **SIMILAR SPECIES:** Female told from female Brewer's and Rusty Blackbirds by its *stubby bill* and smaller size. Juvenile cowbirds can be misidentified as sparrows or other non-blackbirds. **HABITAT:** In nesting season, forests and woodlands; also farms, fields, feedlots, roadsides, towns, parks, lawns, feeders.

BRONZED COWBIRD *Molothrus aeneus* Fairly common

8½–8¾ in. (21–22 cm). *Male:* Slightly larger and more *bull-headed* than Brown-headed Cowbird. Does *not* have brown head. Bill longer. *Red eye* can be seen at close range. In breeding season, raises conspicuous *ruff* on nape. *Female:* Smaller nape ruff; dark brown to sooty overall, darker than female Brown-headed; eye reddish. Juvenile like large-billed juvenile Brown-headed. **VOICE:** High-pitched mechanical creakings. Male's display very animated. **SIMILAR SPECIES:** Other cowbirds. **HABITAT:** Cropland, brush, semiopen country, feedlots. Rare vagrant along Gulf Coast.

SHINY COWBIRD *Molothrus bonariensis* Scarce, local

7½ in. (19 cm). *Male:* Same size as Brown-headed Cowbird, but black with overall violet gloss, thin pointed bill. *Female:* Warm brown, slightly thinner, blacker bill compared with Brown-headed's. **VOICE:** Series of liquid burbles, ending in thin whistled note. **SIMILAR SPECIES:** Other cowbirds. **RANGE:** An invader to s. FL since 1985, with scattered vagrant records, formerly from as far north as NB and west to OK; has since declined in the U.S. and Canada. **HABITAT:** Agricultural areas, disturbed habitats, suburban lawns.

ICTERIDS (BLACKBIRDS, ETC.)

RUSTY BLACKBIRD

spring/summer female

spring/summer male

fall/winter male

BREWER'S BLACKBIRD

female

first-fall/winter male

male

male

BROWN-HEADED COWBIRD

female

molting first-fall male

juvenile

male

male

female

BRONZED COWBIRD

SHINY COWBIRD

COMMON GRACKLE *Quiscalus quiscula* Common

12½ in. (32 cm). *Male:* A large, *iridescent,* yellow-eyed blackbird, larger than a robin, with long, *keel-shaped tail.* In good light, iridescent purple-blue on head. "Bronzed" Grackle (subspecies *versicolor*) of New England and west of Appalachians deep bronze on back and belly; "Purple" Grackle (*quiscula* and *stonei*) of se. U.S. has glossy purple head and greener tinge to back. *Female:* Smaller and somewhat duller, with less wedge-shaped tail. Juveniles of both sexes are dull sooty brown with dark eyes. VOICE: Call *chuck* or *chack.* "Song" a split rasping note, *zhreep zhrap,* etc. SIMILAR SPECIES: Boat-tailed and Great-tailed Grackles, Rusty and Brewer's Blackbirds. HABITAT: Cropland, towns, parks, feeders, groves; swampy woods; often nests in conifers. Very rare vagrant to W. Coast.

BOAT-TAILED GRACKLE *Quiscalus major* Fairly common, local

Male 16½ in. (42 cm); female 14½ in. (37 cm). *Male:* A very large blackbird; larger than Common Grackle, with longer, more ample tail. More rounded head than other grackles. Males of Atlantic Coast north of FL (subspecies *torreyi*) have bright yellow eyes; those of Gulf region and FL (subspecies *major* and *westoni,* respectively) have brown to dull yellow eyes. *Female:* Smaller than male; much browner than female Common Grackle and with pale brownish breast. Juvenile of both sexes is paler than female, with more distinct supercilium. VOICE: Harsh *check check check;* harsh whistles and clucks. SIMILAR SPECIES: Common Grackle shorter tailed, not often found in same coastal habitats. From LA westward, see Great-tailed Grackle. HABITAT: Largely resident near salt water along coasts, marshes; more widespread habitats in FL. Casual vagrant along Atlantic Coast north of range.

GREAT-TAILED GRACKLE *Quiscalus mexicanus* Common

Male 18 in. (46 cm); female 15 in. (38 cm). Like several other blackbirds, often found in large flocks, including while roosting, when they are quite noisy. *Male:* A very large, purple-glossed blackbird, distinctly larger than Common and Boat-tailed Grackles and with longer, more ample tail. *Female:* Smaller than male; dark gray-brown above, warm brown below. Adults of both sexes have yellow eyes. Juveniles of both sexes have dark eyes and are indistinctly streaked below. VOICE: Harsh *check check check;* also a high *kee-kee-kee-kee.* Shrill, discordant notes, whistles, and clucks. A rapid, upward-slurring *ma-ree.* SIMILAR SPECIES: Common Grackle much smaller, tail not nearly as keel shaped; female blacker. Boat-tailed Grackle slightly smaller, with dark eyes (where ranges overlap), rounder crown (male), and slightly shorter, more rounded tail. HABITAT: Groves, farms, feedlots, towns, city parks, parking lots. Casual vagrant well north and east of range.

male

COMMON GRACKLE

male

"Purple"

female

male Atlantic Coast

"Bronzed"

female

FL and Gulf Coast

male

BOAT-TAILED GRACKLE

male

female

GREAT-TAILED GRACKLE

ORCHARD ORIOLE *Icterus spurius*   Fairly common

7–7¼ in. (18 cm). A small, short- and straight-billed oriole. Often flicks tail sideways. *Adult male:* All dark; rump and underparts *deep chestnut. Female and juvenile:* Olive or greenish gray above, yellowish below; two white wing bars. *First-year male:* Develops black bib down to chest in fall and winter (usually in Tropics, after departing U.S.). **VOICE:** Song a fast-moving outburst interspersed with piping whistles and guttural notes. Suggests Purple or House Finch. A strident slurred *wheeer!* at or near end is distinctive. Call a soft *chuck.* **SIMILAR SPECIES:** Baltimore Oriole slightly larger and more orange. Female Scarlet and Summer Tanagers lack wing bars, have different bill shape. Female and first-year male Orchard and Hooded Orioles difficult to separate but note Hooded's thinner-based and more curved bill, longer tail, weaker wing bars, and quite different calls. Beware especially juvenile Hooded Orioles with developing bill and tail lengths; these only rarely overlap in range with Orchard Orioles in summer. **HABITAT:** Wood edges, orchards, shade trees; more likely than other orioles to be seen in brushy areas. Rare vagrant and winter visitor to W. Coast.

BALTIMORE ORIOLE *Icterus galbula*   Fairly common

8¼–8½ in. (21–22 cm). *Adult male:* Flame orange and black, with solid black head, tail boldly patterned, black with orange sides. *Adult female:* Olive-brown above, burnt orange-yellow below; two white wing bars; a variable amount of black on head, often suggesting hood of male; orange tail. *First-fall/winter:* Duller, with grayer back and limited to some orange on underparts. Both sexes variably develop adultlike pattern over first winter and spring. **VOICE:** Song rich, piping whistles: *hew-hee-hee-hew-hee-hew-hew,* etc. Call a low, whistled *hewli.* Chatter call not as rough as Bullock's. **SIMILAR SPECIES:** Female Orchard Oriole smaller and yellow-green, less orange. Dull first-fall Baltimore much like female Bullock's, but latter has more distinct dark eye line and yellowish supercilium, plainer gray back lacking dark mottling, whiter flanks contrasting more with yellowish undertail coverts. **HABITAT:** Open deciduous woods, elms, shade trees. Very rare vagrant to W. Coast.

BULLOCK'S ORIOLE *Icterus bullockii*   Fairly common

8¼–8½ in. (21–22 cm). *Adult male:* Note *orange cheeks* and *dark eye line, large white wing patches,* and *black-tipped tail. Female and juvenile:* Dark eye line, yellowish supercilium, plain gray back, *whitish belly.* First-year male is similar to female, but orange feathering brighter and develops black throat during first fall and winter. **VOICE:** Phrase of doubled musical whistles and rattles: *jet-jet whichy-whichy ju-ju tthat-tthat,* etc. Calls include a rough chatter and low *churp.* **SIMILAR SPECIES:** Baltimore Oriole; also Hooded and Orchard Orioles; Bullock's and Baltimore can hybridize where ranges meet. **HABITAT:** Deciduous and riparian woods, oaks, shade trees, ranch yards; small numbers winter in flowering trees of coastal CA. Casual vagrant to East, accidentally to coast.

SPOT-BREASTED ORIOLE *Icterus pectoralis*   Uncommon, local

9¼–9½ in. (24 cm). A large, robin-sized oriole. *Adult male:* Note *orange crown,* black bib, and black spots on sides of breast. Much white in wing, including bases to primaries, but no wing bar. Female and first-year male similar to adult male but duller, often yellower. **VOICE:** Song a long, melodic series of whistles, slower than other orioles. **SIMILAR SPECIES:** Baltimore Oriole smaller, white wing-covert bar; most have black in crown. **HABITAT:** Flowering trees, residential areas.

adult
male

ORCHARD
ORIOLE

first-year
male

juvenile and
female

adult
male

BALTIMORE
ORIOLE

adult
female

juvenile and
first-fall/winter

adult male

BULLOCK'S
ORIOLE

juvenile and
female

SPOT-BREASTED
ORIOLE

adult male
female similar but duller

HOODED ORIOLE *Icterus cucullatus* Fairly common

7½–8 in. (19–20 cm). *Adult male:* Orange and black, with black throat and *orange crown.* In winter, back scaled yellow or orange. *Female:* Similar to female Bullock's Oriole, but bill longer, slightly curved; more extensively greenish yellow below; back olive-gray; head and tail more yellowish. Call very different. *First-year male:* Like female, with slightly shorter bill (much like female Orchard Oriole), develops black throat during first winter. **VOICE:** Song consists of rambling, grating notes and piping whistles: *chut chut chut whew whew;* opening notes throaty. Call a distinctive, up-slurred, whistled *eek* or *wheenk.* **SIMILAR SPECIES:** Orchard and Scott's Orioles. **HABITAT:** Open woods, shade trees, towns, gardens, palms. Casual vagrant well north of range.

ALTAMIRA ORIOLE *Icterus gularis* Uncommon, local

10 in. (25 cm). *Adult:* Similar to male Hooded Oriole but larger, with thicker bill. Upperwing bar yellow or orange, not white. Sexes similar. First-year yellower, with less pure black. **VOICE:** Song disjointed whistled notes. A harsh "fuss" note. **SIMILAR SPECIES:** Other orange orioles. **HABITAT:** Scrubby woodlands, often near water. Its name, in Spanish, means "look high," and species is often found in treetops.

STREAK-BACKED ORIOLE *Icterus pustulatus* Very rare vagrant

8¼ in. (21 cm). This Mexican oriole has a *streaked back,* much white in wing. Otherwise resembles Hooded Oriole or perhaps first-year male Bullock's Oriole. *Adult male:* Basically yellow-orange, head much deeper orange. Female, first-year birds, and juveniles are duller, but streaking still obvious; juvenile lacks black on throat. **VOICE:** Rich warble, similar to Baltimore or Bullock's Oriole. **SIMILAR SPECIES:** Adult male Hooded Oriole in winter has scaled or scalloped black back pattern, not streaked, and bill not as thick at base. **RANGE:** Very rare visitor from Mex., mostly in fall and winter, to AZ; casual west to CA and east to TX. **HABITAT:** Arid scrub, woodland edges.

AUDUBON'S ORIOLE *Icterus graduacauda* Uncommon, local

9½ in. (24 cm). *Adult:* A yellow oriole with black wings, head, and tail. Yellowish back distinctive. Other male orioles have black back. Sexes similar. First-year duller, head mixed yellowish and black, tail green or mixed green and black. Juvenile lacks black in head. **VOICE:** Disjointed notes suggesting a child learning to whistle. **SIMILAR SPECIES:** Scott's Oriole. Green Jay at a distance can appear yellow with a black head. **HABITAT:** Riparian woods.

SCOTT'S ORIOLE *Icterus parisorum* Uncommon

8¾–9 in. (22–23 cm). *Adult male:* Solid black head and back and *lemon yellow* underparts distinguish this oriole. *Female:* More greenish yellow below and more olive-gray and streaked above than other female orioles. *Juvenile and first-year:* Both sexes lack black at first but variably develop blackish in throats (female) and/or heads (male) by spring. **VOICE:** Song composed of rich fluty whistles; suggests Western Meadowlark. Call a harsh *chuck.* **SIMILAR SPECIES:** Female Hooded and Bullock's Orioles. **HABITAT:** Dry woods and scrub in desert mountains, yucca forests, Joshua trees, pinyon-juniper, sugar-water feeders. Also eucalyptus and date palms in winter. Casual vagrant well north and east of range.

first-year male

adult male

juvenile and female

HOODED ORIOLE

adult

ALTAMIRA ORIOLE

adult male

STREAK-BACKED ORIOLE

AUDUBON'S ORIOLE

adult

female

first-fall

adult male

SCOTT'S ORIOLE

STARLINGS Family Sturnidae

A large and varied family; some blackbirdlike. Sharp-billed, usually short-tailed. Gregarious and adaptable. **FOOD:** Insects, seeds, berries. **RANGE:** Widespread in Old World. Introduced in New World.

EUROPEAN STARLING *Sturnus vulgaris*   Common, introduced

8½ in. (22 cm). Introduced from Europe in 1890. A gregarious, garrulous species; shape of a meadowlark with *short tail* and *sharply pointed bill.* In flight, has *triangular wings;* flies swiftly and directly. *Spring/summer:* Plumage iridescent, bill *yellow,* blue-based in male, pink-based in female. *Fall/winter: Heavily speckled with white,* bill dark. Males have longer head and neck plumes than females, and adults have longer plumes than first-year birds, sex for sex; otherwise ages and sexes similar in plumage following juvenile. *Juvenile:* Dusky gray-brown, a bit like a female cowbird, but stockier, tail shorter, bill longer. **VOICE:** Harsh, wheezy *tseeeer;* a whistled *whooee.* Also clear whistles, clicks, chuckles; often mimics other birds. **SIMILAR SPECIES:** Cedar and Bohemian Waxwings, in flight. Mynas. **HABITAT:** Cities, suburbs, parks, feeders, farms, livestock pens, open groves, fields. Competes for nesting holes with several native cavity-nesting species, with negative impact.

COMMON HILL MYNA *Gracula religiosa*   Unestablished exotic

10½ in. (27 cm). *Glossy black* body, orange bill, yellow face wattles and legs. *White wing patches* stand out in flight. Ages (including juvenile) and sexes similar. **VOICE:** Squawks, buzzes, whistles; excellent mimic. **SIMILAR SPECIES:** European Starling, Common Myna. **RANGE:** Exotic from Asia, formerly established in s. FL; escapees occasionally still encountered here and elsewhere. **HABITAT:** Lush suburban neighborhoods and parks.

COMMON MYNA *Acridotheres tristis*   Common, local, exotic

10 in. (25 cm). A *brown-bodied* relative of European Starling, with black head and *white undertail.* Bill, face, and legs bright yellow. Ages (including juvenile) and sexes similar. **VOICE:** Starlinglike gurgles, squeaks, and cackles. **SIMILAR SPECIES:** European Starling, Common Hill Myna. **RANGE:** Introduced from s. Asia. Widespread and increasing in s. and cen. FL. Also introduced and abundant in HI (p. 458). **HABITAT:** Urban and suburban habitats. Often occurs in noisy flocks.

BULBULS Family Pycnonotidae

Native to Africa, Asia, Australia, and some Pacific Is. One species introduced in FL and CA. Slender songbirds with curved bills; many have crests. Found largely in forested habitats but have adapted to towns and residential areas. Often noisy, with disjointed nasal or flutelike notes. Ages and sexes largely similar. **FOOD:** Insects, fruit.

RED-WHISKERED BULBUL *Pycnonotus jocosus*   Uncommon, local, exotic

7 in. (18 cm). Note black crest, red cheek patch, black half-collar, and red undertail coverts; juvenile similar but with duller head pattern. **VOICE:** Noisy chattering. **SIMILAR SPECIES:** Phainopepla, waxwings. **RANGE:** This native of se. Asia was established locally in s. Miami, FL, and the Los Angeles area, CA, in the early 1960s. Breeding populations in these areas still occur and have become established. Also introduced on Oahu, HI (p. 458). **HABITAT:** Large trees and thick vegetation in suburban neighborhoods.

STARLING, MYNAS, AND BULBUL

spring/summer

fall/winter

juvenile

EUROPEAN STARLING

COMMON HILL MYNA

COMMON MYNA

adult

RED-WHISKERED BULBUL

BIRDS OF
HAWAII

RESIDENT HAWAIIAN WATERFOWL

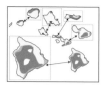

HAWAIIAN GOOSE *Branta sandvicensis*　　　Uncommon, endangered
23–27 in. (58–69 cm). A distinctive small goose found primarily in upland areas away from water. Face, cap, and throat black; *neck buff with distinct dark fur-rows;* black ring around base of neck; body brownish, irregularly barred dark. Bill and legs black; feet with reduced toe webbing. Ages and sexes similar. **VOICE:** High-pitched, whiny *ee-ehh* and small squeaks, often double-noted, giv-ing rise to popular Hawaiian name, "Néné." **SIMILAR SPECIES:** Cackling Goose and Brant, both rare in HI, similar in size but Hawaiian Goose lacks dark body plumage of Brant and black neck and white cheek patch of Cackling Goose. **HABITAT:** Open upland pastures and lava flows (Hawaii I. and Maui) and lowland fields (Kauai, Molokai). Individuals disperse after breeding season; occasionally found in coastal areas; rarely flies between islands.

HAWAIIAN DUCK *Anas wyvilliana*　　　Locally uncommon, endangered
18–19 in. (45–48 cm). Like a small version of Mallard, to which it is closely related; plumage of both sexes resembles female Mallard, but darker with more distinct dark chevrons; *tail and bill darker,* speculum greenish blue, legs duller orange. *Male:* Bill tinged yellowish, crown often with dark green tinge in adults. *Female:* Bill dark with orange tip, speculum duller. Hybridizes fairly extensively with feral Mallards, resulting in a mixture of characters; conserva-tion efforts ongoing to restore genetic purity of Hawaiian Ducks. Known as "Koloa" in Hawaiian. **VOICE:** Calls of male and female similar to those of Mal-lard but softer, given less frequently. **SIMILAR SPECIES:** Mallard. Laysan Duck, but ranges do not overlap. **HABITAT:** Marshes, ponds, wooded streams (espe-cially on Kauai).

LAYSAN DUCK *Anas laysanensis*　　　Very local, endangered
17–18 in. (43–45 cm). A small duck (formerly called "Laysan Teal") resembling a dark female Mallard but with variable conspicuous *white patch around eye.* Speculum dark green with broad white tips, bill dark, legs bright orange. Sexes similar except adult male can have dark green tinge to crown and head and averages larger eye patch and brighter speculum; bill tinged dark yellowish in male, dark orange in female. **VOICE:** Similar to calls of Mallard but softer, given less frequently. **SIMILAR SPECIES:** Mallard much larger and lacks eye patch. See Hawaiian Duck. **HABITAT:** Central brackish lagoon (Laysan I.). Recently introduced to man-made wetlands on Midway and Kure Atolls.

MALLARD *Anas platyrhynchos*　　　Uncommon exotic and rare vagrant
See also p. 26. Introduced to the Hawaiian Is. during the 1800s; feral populations now thrive on most se. Hawaiian Is. Found in various levels of domestication in parks, wetlands, and refuges. Hybridizes extensively with Hawaiian Duck; control efforts have reduced populations of pure Mallards and hybrids. Also a rare vagrant to the nw. Hawaiian Is., presumably from continental populations; wild birds likely occur undetected in se. Hawaiian Is. as well.

MUSCOVY DUCK *Cairina moschata*　　　Local, exotic
See p. 24. Domesticated flocks of white morphs occur in parks, neighborhoods.

RESIDENT HAWAIIAN
WATERFOWL

HAWAIIAN GOOSE
(NÉNÉ)

HAWAIIAN
DUCK

female

male

LAYSAN DUCK
male

hybrid male Laysan Duck
with Mallard

female

MALLARD

male

domestic
variation

MUSCOVY DUCK

REGULAR MIGRATORY WATERFOWL in HAWAII

Most migratory N. American and Asian swans, geese, ducks, and mergansers have occurred in HI as regularly wintering, casual-to-scarce vagrant, or accidental species.

CACKLING GOOSE *Branta hutchinsii* — Scarce
See p. 18. Annual in small numbers, some remaining for years. Smallest subspecies *minima* ("Ridgway's") and subspecies *leucopareia* ("Aleutian") most commonly observed. A flock of feral Canada Geese (p. 18) occurs in Hilo, Hawaii I.; otherwise Canada Goose accidental in se. Hawaiian Is.

BRANT *Branta bernicla* — Scarce
See p. 18. One to five "Black Brants" (subspecies *nigricans*) annually in se. Hawaiian Is., in wetlands, coastal areas, occasionally on ocean.

NORTHERN PINTAIL *Anas acuta* — Fairly common
See p. 26. The most common migratory waterfowl throughout Hawaiian Is. Formerly very common, with flocks of more than 1,000 recorded; more recently groups of up to 40 (occasionally more than 100) found in lakes and wetlands.

NORTHERN SHOVELER *Spatula clypeata* — Fairly common
See p. 28. Found throughout Hawaiian Is. Formerly more common, with flocks of up to 300 recorded; more recently up to 30 found in lakes and wetlands.

AMERICAN WIGEON *Mareca americana* — Uncommon
See p. 24. Usually found with pintails and shovelers in small numbers (fewer than ten). Gadwall (p. 26) very rare in HI.

EURASIAN WIGEON *Mareca penelope* — Scarce
See p. 24. Often with American Wigeon. Rare in se. Hawaiian Is. (up to two per year) but more regular in nw. Hawaiian Is., where American is rare.

BLUE-WINGED TEAL *Spatula discors* — Scarce
See p. 28. Found occasionally in marshes and ponds. Has bred on Hawaii I.

GREEN-WINGED TEAL *Anas crecca* — Uncommon
See p. 28. Groups of up to a dozen found in Hawaiian Is. with other migratory ducks. "American" subspecies regular in se. Hawaiian Is. "Eurasian" subspecies (p. 28) regular in nw. Hawaiian Is.

LESSER SCAUP *Aythya affinis* — Fairly common
See p. 36. Flocks of up to 40 on lakes, reservoirs, and ponds. Greater Scaup (p. 36), Tufted Duck (p. 50), and other *Aythya* ducks very rare among Lesser Scaup and Ring-necked Ducks in Hawaiian Is.

RING-NECKED DUCK *Aythya collaris* — Uncommon
See p. 36. Up to a dozen can be found, usually among Lesser Scaup.

BUFFLEHEAD *Bucephala albeola* — Scarce
See p. 38. Found occasionally on ponds, lakes, rivers; usually female-plumaged birds.

PIED-BILLED GREBE *Podilymbus podiceps* — Scarce
See p. 58. Found occasionally in lakes and rivers. Has bred on Hawaii I. Most other N. American grebe species (p. 58) have occurred in HI accidentally.

"Aleutian"

CACKLING GOOSE

"Ridgway's"

REGULAR MIGRATORY WATERFOWL

adult

"BLACK" BRANT

first-year

NORTHERN PINTAIL

female

male

female

male

NORTHERN SHOVELER

AMERICAN WIGEON

male

female

female

male

EURASIAN WIGEON

BLUE-WINGED TEAL

female

GREEN-WINGED TEAL

male

American

female

female

LESSER SCAUP

male

female

male

RING-NECKED DUCK

female

male

BUFFLEHEAD

female

spring/ summer adult

fall/winter adult

PIED-BILLED GREBE

ALBATROSSES and LARGE PETRELS in HAWAII

SHORT-TAILED ALBATROSS *Phoebastria albatrus*   Rare, endangered
See p. 78. Prospective breeding and courting birds occur regularly in very small numbers in nw. Hawaiian Is. (present late Oct. through June). Single pair has recently bred on Midway Atoll and others attempted breeding on Kure.

LAYSAN ALBATROSS *Phoebastria immutabilis*   Fairly common
See p. 78. Breeds abundantly in nw. Hawaiian Is. and on Kauai and Oahu (present late Oct. through July; absent Aug. through mid-Oct.). Uncommon at sea in HI waters except near breeding sites. Hybrids with Black-footed Albatross occur where both species breed.

BLACK-FOOTED ALBATROSS *Phoebastria nigripes*   Uncommon
See p. 78. Breeds commonly in nw. Hawaiian Is. (present late Oct. through July; absent Aug. through mid-Oct.). Uncommon at sea off se. Hawaiian Is.

HAWAIIAN PETREL *Pterodroma sandwichensis*   Uncommon, endangered
17–18 in. (43–46 cm). Blackish to brownish upperparts with slightly darker M-pattern; *black hoodlike cap* with broad *white patch around bill;* broad dark diagonal *underwing carpal bars.* Breeding endemic to se. Hawaiian Is.; ranges at sea throughout ne. Pacific to N. American coast (see p. 70). Arrives and departs colonies at night. Uncommon in waters off colonies; most frequently observed from shore near sunset off e. Kauai in Apr.–Sept. **VOICE:** Primary vocalization above colonies at night *ooo-aah-ooo,* begetting Hawaiian name "U'au"; also shorter, low-pitched and high-pitched calls at nests. **SIMILAR SPECIES:** Juan Fernandez Petrel, White-necked Petrel. **HABITAT:** Breeds colonially in dry high-elevation habitats.

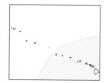

JUAN FERNANDEZ PETREL *Pterodroma externa*   Uncommon
17–18 in. (43–46 cm). Similar in size and shape to Hawaiian Petrel but bill larger, less dark to head, white to partially white uppertail coverts, *almost completely white underwing,* without or with very narrow and indistinct carpal bars. White-necked Petrel similar but nape usually whiter; back paler and grayer than upperwings; underwing carpal mark thicker and longer; uppertail coverts with little or no white. **RANGE:** Breeds in Juan Fernandez Is. off Chile, ranges widely into tropical and subtropical Pacific. Scarce in se. Hawaiian waters, primarily in summer/fall; can be observed from shore from north tip of Hawaii I. in Aug.–Nov. Accidental vagrant to AZ.

WHITE-NECKED PETREL *Pterodroma cervicalis*   Uncommon
17–18 in. (43–46 cm). Similar in size and shape to Hawaiian and Juan Fernandez Petrels. Distinguished by broad white nape collar (beware Juan Fernandez can have narrow collar); *gray back contrasts with blackish upperwing;* underwing carpal bar narrower than in Hawaiian, broader and longer than in Juan Fernandez. **RANGE:** Breeds in Kermadec Is. off New Zealand, ranges widely into tropical and subtropical Pacific. Uncommon in HI waters, year-round but most often in late fall and winter. Accidental vagrant to w. Mex.

LAYSAN
ALBATROSS

SHORT-TAILED
ALBATROSS

BLACK-
FOOTED
ALBATROSS

HAWAIIAN
PETREL

JUAN
FERNANDEZ
PETREL

WHITE-
NECKED
PETREL

SHEARWATERS and SMALL PETRELS in HAWAII

BLACK-WINGED PETREL *Pterodroma nigripennis*   Fairly common

10–11 in. (25–29 cm). Medium-small petrel, *pale gray crown and upperparts* with moderately distinct M pattern and *bold black underwing carpal bar.* Bill fairly stout. When worn, upperwing can become very dark, obscuring M pattern. **SIMILAR SPECIES:** Bonin, Cook's, Stejneger's (*P. longirostris;* not shown), and Mottled Petrels. **RANGE:** Open ocean; breeds on islands north of New Zealand; found regularly year-round in HI waters.

MOTTLED PETREL *Pterodroma inexpectata*   Scarce to uncommon

See p. 70. Scarce to uncommon passage migrant through HI waters during short windows in Mar.–Apr. and Oct.–Nov. Similar to Black-winged Petrel but dark belly patch (occasionally extending to head) usually obvious.

COOK'S PETREL *Pterodroma cookii*   Scarce

See p. 70. Scarce passage migrant through HI waters in spring and fall. Stejneger's Petrel (*P. longirostris;* not shown), very rare migrant through HI waters (and casual off CA), has similar underwing pattern but has dusky to black crown.

BONIN PETREL *Pterodroma hypoleuca*   Common, local

11–12 in. (29–31 cm). Medium-small petrel; dark grayish brown head pattern and upperparts, unique pattern to underwing with broad and distinct, dark carpal bar and an *extensive black patch* to under-primaries. Legs pinkish with black toes. Abundant breeder in nw. Hawaiian Is. (primarily Oct.–Apr.) but absent in se. Hawaiian waters. **VOICE:** Raspy descending *keeekekh* calls at colonies; can create a nighttime din. **SIMILAR SPECIES:** Underwing pattern darker than on other pale-bodied petrels. Hawaiian Petrel (rarely overlaps in range) also larger. **HABITAT:** Breeds in sandy burrows on atolls; uncommonly seen at sea.

WEDGE-TAILED SHEARWATER *Ardenna pacifica*   Common

16–18 in. (41–46 cm). Breeds throughout Hawaiian Is.; most common tubenose offshore. A lanky shearwater with long, *thin grayish bill,* tipped dark; *pale fringes to upperpart feathers;* long wedge-shaped tail. Legs and feet pinkish. Light morph most common in HI, variable plumage like that of Pink-footed Shearwater (p. 76; accidental in HI) but with thinner and grayer bill, longer tail, floppier flight. Dark morph scarce to uncommon in s. HI waters, all dark, with larger and more buoyant flight than Sooty Shearwater, dark underwing; bill grayer and thinner than in Flesh-footed Shearwater (p. 76). **VOICE:** Haunting, drawn-out "moaning" call *oooooo-ahhh* given by courting adults at breeding sites. Squeaky begging calls given by chicks. **SIMILAR SPECIES:** Sooty Shearwater (uncommon in HI), Short-tailed (p. 76) and Flesh-footed Shearwaters (rare in HI); Newell's Shearwater is smaller, shorter-tailed, more contrasting in plumage, and has faster stiff-winged flight. **HABITAT:** Breeds in sandy coastal areas, offshore islets. Casual vagrant to CA.

NEWELL'S SHEARWATER *Puffinus newelli*   Uncommon, endangered

13–14 in. (33–36 cm). Contrasting *black-and-white* pattern and rapid shallow wingbeats. Similar to Manx Shearwater (p. 74; unrecorded in HI) blacker, tail longer, *distal half of undertail coverts dark,* sides of rump with white patches. **VOICE:** A raspy bray, *heecha-heecha-heecha* given over colonies at night. **SIMILAR SPECIES:** Wedge-tailed Shearwater. **HABITAT:** Breeds in steep mid- to high-elevation fern tangles and scrubby forests. Uncommon in se. Hawaiian waters; can be observed near sunset off e. Kauai in Apr.–Sept. Accidental in CA.

BULLER'S SHEARWATER *Ardenna bulleri*   Scarce

See p. 76. Scarce passage migrant through HI waters in spring and late fall.

BLACK-BELLIED PLOVER

juveniles

fall/winter

PACIFIC GOLDEN-PLOVER

fall/winter

juvenile

spring/summer

fall/winter

spring/summer

SEMIPALMATED PLOVER

fall/winter

spring/summer

WANDERING TATTLER

spring/summer

juvenile

fall/winter

fall/winter

spring/summer

RUDDY TURNSTONE

spring/summer

North American

Eurasian

SANDERLING

WHIMBREL

BRISTLE-THIGHED CURLEW

LESS-COMMON MIGRATORY SHOREBIRDS
to HAWAII

LESSER YELLOWLEGS *Tringa flavipes*   Scarce

See p. 142. Scarce fall migrant to HI, rarer in winter and spring. Greater Yellowlegs (p. 142), Wilson's Phalarope (p. 144), and most other *Tringa*-like shorebirds (pp. 154 and 158) are accidental to rare vagrants to HI.

BAR-TAILED GODWIT *Limosa lapponica*   Scarce

See p. 156. Asian subspecies *(baueri)* a scarce but regular migrant, more common in the nw. Hawaiian Is. Occasionally winters, regularly on Laysan I. All three other godwit species (pp. 128 and 156) are accidental vagrants in HI.

LONG-BILLED DOWITCHER *Limnodromus scolopaceus*   Uncommon

See p. 140. Regular winter visitor in small numbers (flocks of 30 or more occasional), in wetlands of se. Hawaiian Is.; scarce in NW Is. Short-billed Dowitcher (p. 140) is a very rare in HI; most reports turn out to be Long-billeds.

WILSON'S SNIPE *Gallinago delicata*   Uncommon

See p. 140. Small numbers winter annually throughout Hawaiian Is., though often difficult to find. Common Snipe (p. 160) has also been recorded as a casual vagrant, but Wilson's more prevalent, at least in the se. Hawaiian Is. Pin-tailed Snipe (*G. stenura*; not shown) accidental in nw. Hawaiian Is.

DUNLIN *Calidris alpina*   Scarce

See p. 132. Small numbers winter throughout Hawaiian Is., occasionally in groups of up to ten. Palearctic subspecies *(sakhalina)*, with shorter bill than N. American subspecies *(pacifica)*, occasionally recorded but latter more regular.

WESTERN SANDPIPER *Calidris mauri*   Rare

See p. 134. One or two found in se. Hawaiian Is. during most winters; rare vagrant to nw. Hawaiian Is. Semipalmated Sandpiper (p. 134), White-rumped Sandpiper (p. 136), and Red-necked and Little Stints (p. 158) are accidental to casual vagrants to HI.

LEAST SANDPIPER *Calidris minutilla*   Scarce

See p. 134. One to a few found in se. Hawaiian Is. during most winters; unconfirmed in nw. Hawaiian Is., where Long-toed Stint (p. 158) is accidental.

PECTORAL SANDPIPER *Calidris melanotos*   Scarce to uncommon

See p. 136. Annual irregular fall migrant throughout HI, occasionally in flocks of dozens, exceptionally over 100. Found throughout Hawaiian Is. Scarce in spring and winter. Baird's Sandpiper (p. 136) and Buff-breasted Sandpiper (p. 138) are very rare vagrants to HI.

SHARP-TAILED SANDPIPER *Calidris acuminata*   Scarce to uncommon

See p. 160. Status similar to Pectoral Sandpiper (more than 100 occasionally encountered), but more common in nw. Hawaiian Is. than Pectoral.

RUFF *Calidris pugnax*   Scarce

See p. 160. Somewhat irregular migrant or vagrant throughout Hawaiian Is.; has declined in recent years. About half of recorded migrants remain to overwinter.

RED PHALAROPE *Phalaropus fulicarius*   Uncommon

See p. 144. Regular in migration and winter in surrounding pelagic waters; sometimes in multiples. Rarely seen ashore. Wilson's and Red-necked Phalaropes (p. 144) are rare vagrants, the latter mostly on Laysan I.

LESS-COMMON MIGRATORY SHOREBIRDS

LESSER YELLOWLEGS

BAR-TAILED GODWIT

fall/winter

juvenile

LONG-BILLED DOWITCHER

juvenile

fall/winter

WILSON'S SNIPE

DUNLIN

fall/winter

fall/winter

juvenile

WESTERN SANDPIPER

fall/winter

juvenile

LEAST SANDPIPER

juvenile

juvenile

spring/summer and adult

PECTORAL SANDPIPER

juvenile

fall/winter

RUFF

juvenile male

spring/summer female

SHARP-TAILED SANDPIPER

RED PHALAROPE

RESIDENT WETLAND BIRDS in HAWAII

BLACK-NECKED STILT *Himantopus mexicanus* Fairly common
See also p. 126. "Hawaiian Stilt" (subspecies *knudseni*) breeds commonly throughout coastal wetlands of se. Hawaiian Is.; vagrant to nw. Hawaiian Is. Darker on head and neck than N. American stilts. Known as "A'eo" in Hawaiian. **VOICE:** Sharp yipping: *kyip, kyip, kyip,* a distinctive loud sound in HI coastal wetlands. Black-winged Stilt (*H. himantopus;* not shown) of Asia an accidental vagrant to nw. Hawaiian Is. Hawaiian populations endangered.

CATTLE EGRET *Bubulcus ibis* Common, introduced and vagrant
See also p. 164. Common throughout lowland agricultural areas, parks, and roadsides of se. Hawaiian Is. and scarce migrant to nw. Hawaiian Is.; has bred on Midway. European and American subspecies (*B. i. ibis*) introduced to Hawaii in the 1960s but vagrants undoubtedly also arrived since then, including Asian subspecies (*B. i. coromandus*) recorded in nw. Hawaiian Is. Cattle Egrets in HI often stained with red dirt. Snowy and Great Egrets (p. 164), accidental vagrants to HI, are larger, longer necked, have different bill and/or leg colors.

BLACK-CROWNED NIGHT-HERON *Nycticorax nycticorax* Fairly common
See also p. 166. Indigenous to HI. Fairly common in lowland marshes, estuaries, marinas, and aquafarms throughout se. Hawaiian Is.; most common on Kauai and Oahu. Occasionally found in higher-elevation forested streams. Predates tern chicks on offshore islets. The only indigenous Hawaiian waterbird that is not an endemic subspecies; known as "Auku'u" in Hawaiian. Great Blue Heron (p. 162) and Green Heron (p. 166) are rare vagrants to HI.

WHITE-FACED IBIS *Plegadis chihi* Scarce
See p. 168. Scarce in HI but flocks of up to 11 birds have been recorded and, once having arrived, they often stay for years. Found in wetlands throughout se. Hawaiian Is.

HAWAIIAN COOT *Fulica alai* Fairly common, endangered
14–15½ in. (36–39 cm). *Adult:* Very similar to American Coot (p. 174), which has no confirmed records in HI; adult has either a white shield that is more extensive than in American or a brighter red-topped shield than in American. Juveniles and first-year birds more similar to American Coot, with developing small dark red shields. Known as "Alae kea" in Hawaiian. **VOICE:** Similar to American Coot's. **SIMILAR SPECIES:** Common (Hawaiian) Gallinule. **HABITAT:** Coastal wetlands throughout se. Hawaiian Is., occasionally in upland ponds. Migrates between islands and has been recorded as a rare vagrant throughout nw. Hawaiian Is.

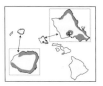

COMMON GALLINULE *Gallinula galeata* Fairly common, local
See also p. 174. "Hawaiian Gallinule" (subspecies *sandvicensis*), which is endangered, is very similar to N. American Common Gallinule. Found locally in freshwater wetlands of Kauai and Oahu; formerly on Molokai, Maui, and Hawaii I. Known as "Alae ula" in Hawaiian.

RESIDENT WETLAND BIRDS

HAWAIIAN STILT

male

CATTLE EGRET

nonbreeding

breeding

WHITE-FACED IBIS

adult

juvenile

adult

BLACK-CROWNED NIGHT-HERON

HAWAIIAN COOT

white-shielded adult

red-shielded adult

juvenile/first-year

some with small dark red shields

chick

adult

juvenile

adult

COMMON GALLINULE

chick

INTRODUCED GAME BIRDS in HAWAII

CHUKAR *Alectoris chukar*   Locally fairly common, introduced

See p. 188. Found fairly commonly at higher elevations of the six largest se. Hawaiian Is.; most common on Maui and Hawaii Is.

GRAY FRANCOLIN *Francolinus pondicerianus*   Locally common, introduced

11–13 in. (28–33 cm). Francolins are medium-sized, ground-dwelling game birds found primarily in cen. Asia; Gray Francolin was introduced to HI from India in 1958–1962. Drab, grayish brown, with *buff to tawny forehead and throat;* reddish back; pink to orangish legs. Sexes similar. **VOICE:** Loud, ringing *dee-luku-dee-luku* repeated up to many times. Can be similar to calls of Common Myna but more regular. **SIMILAR SPECIES:** Chukar more boldly marked with red bill. Female Black Francolin has rufous patch on nape, otherwise lacks tawny in face and reddish in upperparts. **HABITAT:** Confined to drier coastal and lowland areas; brushy regions, resorts, golf courses.

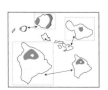

BLACK FRANCOLIN *Francolinus francolinus*   Locally fairly common, introduced

12–14 in. (30–36 cm). Introduced to HI from India or Nepal in 1959–1962. *Male:* Striking game bird with *black head and underparts,* chestnut neck, white *cheek patch* and spots to sides, and bright orange legs. *Female:* Brown with dark eye line though *pale face, rufous patch on hind neck,* dull orange legs. **VOICE:** Distinctive, insectlike *dzee-dee-dee—dee-de-dit.* **SIMILAR SPECIES:** For female, see Gray Francolin, Erckel's Francolin. **HABITAT:** Lowland and mid-elevation drier grasslands, brushy fields. Skulking; can be difficult to see except when male perches to sing.

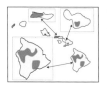

JAPANESE QUAIL *Coturnix japonica*   Locally scarce to uncommon, introduced

7–8 in. (18–20 cm). Introduced to HI from Japan in 1921 and 1929–1930. By far the smallest game bird in HI; *resembles a small buffy Northern Bobwhite* but patterns often difficult to observe on this elusive species. Male slightly brighter than female and with more striking head pattern. **VOICE:** A subtle but distinctive (once learned), raspy ascending two-note or three-note *pratch-wheeth* or *pratch-a-wirth.* Call may be best way to detect this species. **SIMILAR SPECIES:** Smaller than California Quail; posture lower to ground and more skulking. **HABITAT:** Grasslands and edges to fields, both lower and higher elevations. Has declined in HI during late twentieth century; now uncommon on Kauai (and possibly Niihau), rare or extirpated on other islands.

CALIFORNIA QUAIL *Callipepla californica*   Locally uncommon, introduced

See p. 190. Common at low and high elevations of Molokai, Maui, and Hawaii Is. Rare on Kauai; absent from Oahu and Lanai.

GAMBEL'S QUAIL *Callipepla gambelii*   Locally uncommon, introduced

See p. 190. Uncommon to fairly common on Lanai and Kahoolawe Is.

SMALL INTRODUCED
GAME BIRDS

GRAY
FRANCOLIN

CHUKAR

BLACK
FRANCOLIN

female

female

male

male

JAPANESE
QUAIL

GAMBEL'S
QUAIL

female

female

CALIFORNIA
QUAIL

male

male

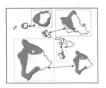

ERCKEL'S FRANCOLIN *Pternistis erckelii*   Locally fairly common, introduced

14–16 in. (36–41 cm). Introduced to HI from Africa in 1957–1966. A large, dumpy game bird; primarily *gray with rufous crown and streaks* to upperparts and underparts. Bill strong and hooked, legs yellow. Sexes alike. **VOICE:** Ducklike quacking sounds; can repeat these notes as explosive descending cackle. **SIMILAR SPECIES:** Larger than other francolins in HI; found at higher elevations. Female Ring-necked Pheasant has longer tail, brown crown, not as boldly streaked. **HABITAT:** Mid- to higher- (occasionally lower-) elevation grasslands and scrubby forests on drier sides of islands; sometimes sits in trees; common on Hawaii I., less common elsewhere.

KALIJ PHEASANT *Lophura leucomelanos*   Uncommon, introduced

Male 24–29 in. (65–73 cm); female 21–23 in. (53-58 cm). Introduced to Hawaii I. in 1962, probably from Nepal. A relatively small pheasant. *Male:* Glossy *black and silver* plumage. Long spiky crest and *arched tail,* bare red face. *Female:* Brown with white scaling and shorter *crest and arched tail.* **VOICE:** Subtle clucks and squeals, given primarily in courtship or with chicks. **SIMILAR SPECIES:** Female darker and smaller than female Ring-necked Pheasant, has crest; longer tailed than female Red Junglefowl or domestic chickens. **HABITAT:** Mid- to higher-elevation forests. Becoming established in nw. Oahu and recently observed in upland Maui.

RING-NECKED PHEASANT *Phasianus colchicus*   Fairly common, introduced

See p. 188. Found fairly commonly in open areas of six larger se. Hawaiian Is.

INDIAN PEAFOWL *Pavo cristatus*   Locally uncommon, introduced

Male 75–90 in. (190–229 cm); female 35–40 in. (90–102 cm). Introduced to HI from unknown sources as early as 1860. Large, pheasantlike bird, often domesticated for aesthetic purposes but wild populations have become established in remote areas of the four larger se. Hawaiian Is. and Niihau. *Male:* Familiar "peacock" with bright *iridescent blue body,* barred back and wings, and *long green train* (uppertail coverts) with blue "eyespots." *Female:* Smaller and browner than male, *greenish head and neck, white belly.* **VOICE:** Loud, whiny, repeated *carauww;* can be heard over great distances. **SIMILAR SPECIES:** Much larger than Ring-necked Pheasant and walks upright. See female Wild Turkey. **HABITAT:** Wild populations found in dry lowland and mid-elevation forested areas; semi-domesticated birds also encountered in park and suburban settings.

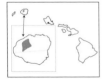

WILD TURKEY *Meleagris gallopavo*   Fairly common, introduced

See also p. 180. Found fairly commonly in open woodlands of most se. Hawaiian Is.

RED JUNGLEFOWL *Gallus gallus*   Locally fairly common, introduced

Male 24–29 in. (60–73 cm); female 16–18 in. (41-46 cm). The ancestral chicken, Red Junglefowls were introduced by Polynesian settlers to HI as early as 1,500 years ago. Original junglefowl populations have been extirpated or diluted by more-recent strains throughout most of se. Hawaiian Is., but wild strains persist in upland areas of Kauai. *Male:* Colorful *orange and glossy purplish* with long glossy dark green uppertail coverts and red head combs. *Female:* Smaller, variably brown, *short blackish tail.* **VOICE:** Familiar *cock-a-doodle-doo* given by male, various repeated *cluck*s by female, and *cheep*s by chick. **SIMILAR SPECIES:** Ring-necked Pheasant, female Kalij Pheasant. **HABITAT:** Upland forests and open areas; frequents field and forest edges in Kokee State Park. Domesticated strains frequently encountered elsewhere in HI.

LARGE INTRODUCED GAME BIRDS

ERCKEL'S FRANCOLIN

female

male

KALIJ PHEASANT

female

male

INDIAN PEAFOWL

male

RING-NECKED PHEASANT

male

female

female

male

RED JUNGLEFOWL

female

male

WILD TURKEY

female

male display

HAWK, OWL, SANDGROUSE, and DOVES in HAWAII

HAWAIIAN HAWK *Buteo solitarius*　　　Uncommon, endangered

16–18 in. (41–46 cm). Endemic to Hawaii I. Similar to Broad-winged Hawk (p. 206) in size. *Pale-morph adult:* Primarily buff (fading to whitish), often with thin dark mask; wings mostly dark above, tail pale with indistinct gray bars. *Juvenile and first-year:* Has dark hood and streaking on sides of breast. *Dark morph:* Largely or entirely dark brown to dark rufous. **VOICE:** Raspy repeated *kee-oo kee-oo kee-oo* begetting Hawaiian name "I'o." Begging chicks give high-pitched screams. **SIMILAR SPECIES:** See Short-eared Owl. **HABITAT:** Forests, open fields, lava flow areas; virtually all elevations and habitats on Hawaii I.

SHORT-EARED OWL *Asio flammeus*　　　Uncommon

See also p. 222. Endemic subspecies *(sandwichenisis)* uncommon throughout se. Hawaiian Is. over agricultural fields, wetlands. Known locally as "Pueo." Averages smaller and darker than continental subspecies, sex for sex. Has different wing shape and flight than Hawaiian Hawk, dark commas to underwings.

CHESTNUT-BELLIED SANDGROUSE　　　Locally uncommon, introduced
Pterocles exustus

11–13 in. (28–33 cm). Sandgrouse are native to cen. Asia; Chestnut-bellied introduced to Hawaii I. from India in 1961–1962. A distinctively shaped, stream-lined bird with small head and long pointed tail. *Male: Sandy colored with pale tawny face* and neck and dark chestnut abdomen (often difficult to see in field). *Female:* Similar to male but *heavily barred* above and below. **VOICE:** Low-pitched gobbling notes. **HABITAT:** Dry ranchlands; most frequently encountered near dawn and dusk along highway south of Waimea.

SPOTTED DOVE *Streptopelia chinensis*　　　Common, introduced

See also p. 234. Introduced to HI from China prior to 1855. Found commonly on all se. Hawaiian Is., primarily in lowlands. Larger size, *broad collar of black and white spots* on hindneck separates it from Mourning Dove. Juvenile lacks collar. **VOICE:** *Coo-whooo-coo*, the second note guttural. **SIMILAR SPECIES:** Mourning Dove. Courting Spotted Doves can be mistaken for falcons or small hawks. **HABITAT:** Agricultural fields, residential areas, parks, open forests.

MOURNING DOVE *Zenaida macroura*　　　Uncommon, introduced

See p. 236. Uncommon in lowlands and mid-elevation open areas of se. Hawaiian Is., most regularly found on Hawaii I. and Maui.

ROCK PIGEON (ROCK DOVE, DOMESTIC PIGEON)　　　Common, introduced
Columba livia

See also p. 234. Common throughout all se. Hawaiian Is., in agricultural areas, towns, cities; abundant in Honolulu. Plumages variable with many "typical" birds as well as white, blackish, and reddish variants. See White Tern, which can be mistaken for white Rock Pigeon in Honolulu.

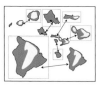

ZEBRA DOVE *Geopelia striata*　　　Common, introduced

8–9½ in. (20–24 cm). Introduced to HI from se. Asia in the 1920s. Has become one of the most abundant species in lowlands throughout se. Hawaiian Is. Resembles Inca Dove (p. 236) in size and shape but head and throat have pale bluish gray, *underparts have distinct black barring.* Cere and eye-ring bright pale blue. **VOICE:** Sharp, flutelike *pi-too-pi-poo-poo-poo-poo*, a very familiar sound in HI. **SIMILAR SPECIES:** Spotted Dove is much larger. **HABITAT:** Residential and cultivated areas, parks, city streets; underfoot at outdoor eateries.

HAWK, OWL, SANDGROUSE, AND DOVES

HAWAIIAN HAWK

dark-morph adult

juvenile

dark morph

light-morph adult

SHORT-EARED OWL

fly on awkward stiff wings, often at dusk

CHESTNUT-BELLIED SANDGROUSE

female

female

male

SPOTTED DOVE

male

MOURNING DOVE

plumages variable

ROCK PIGEON

typical form

ZEBRA DOVE

SWIFT, FALCON, PARROTS, and CROW in HAWAII

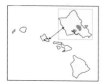

MARIANA SWIFTLET *Aerodramus bartschi* **Very local, introduced, endangered**
4–5 in. (10–12 cm). Introduced to Oahu from Guam in 1962 to control mosquitoes; population size 100–200 birds. Most similar to Vaux's Swift (p. 252). **VOICE:** Twittery clicking notes. **RANGE AND HABITAT:** Sparsely distributed over forested southwestern slopes of the Koolau Mts. north of Honolulu, cen. Oahu. Nests in water-project tunnel in upper Halawa Valley.

PEREGRINE FALCON *Falco peregrinus* **Uncommon**
See also p. 216. Annual in HI in small numbers. Tundra subspecies *(tundrius)* most common during migration; small numbers Asian and N. American subspecies can overwinter. Seen over coasts and wetlands; also at sea in Hawaiian waters. Smaller Merlin (p. 218) casual in winter in HI.

RED-CROWNED PARROT **Locally established, introduced**
Amazona viridigenalis
See also p. 240. Population established from escaped cage birds on Oahu beginning in late 1960s. Found primarily in vicinity of Pearl City, where flocks of up to 60 can be seen flying to roosts at sunset; overall population of 150–200 birds estimated. The only short-tailed parrot established in HI.

RED-MASKED PARAKEET **Locally established, introduced**
Psittacara erythrogenys
12–14 in. (30–35 cm). Escapees in 1980s have now established small populations in e. Oahu and w. Hawaii I. Long-tailed parakeet; primarily green with red bend of underwing and *extensive red patch on crown and around face.* Juvenile entirely green; mottled first-year birds can be confused with other species. **VOICE:** Medium-pitched, laughing, parakeet-like cackles. **SIMILAR SPECIES:** Mitred Parakeet (p. 242) found along the n. Maui coast and occasionally elsewhere in HI has less red in head as adult and lacks red to forepart of underwing. **HABITAT:** Large fruiting trees, residential areas, coastal habitats; forested slopes of Hawaii I.

ROSY-FACED LOVEBIRD *Agapornis roseicollis* **Locally established, introduced**
See also p. 240. Recently established in c. Maui, primarily around and upslope from Kihei.

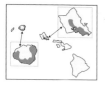

ROSE-RINGED PARAKEET *Psittacula krameri* **Common, introduced**
See also p. 242. A large, long-tailed, and conspicuous parakeet. Populations established on Kauai beginning in the 1960s and Oahu in the 1970s. Now abundant in drier lowlands of s. Kauai (where an agricultural pest) and eastern portions of Honolulu. Seen in large flocks going to roost at sunset.

HAWAIIAN CROW *Corvus hawaiiensis* **Extirpated from wild, endangered**
12–14 in. (47–51 cm). Formerly an endemic resident on Hawaii I., primarily at mid-elevations on western slopes. Captive population exist for future propagation if habitat can be created and predators controlled. A large-billed, ravenlike corvid, slightly browner than N. American ravens and crows. **VOICE:** Variety of sounds: *wree-o-wreep, kwak,* upslurred *kaaak,* etc. **SIMILAR SPECIES:** The only large *blackish bird* in HI. One record of Common Raven (p. 302) in nw. Hawaiian Is. **HABITAT:** Forested slopes with fruiting trees.

SWIFT, FALCON, PARROTS, AND CROW

MARIANA SWIFTLET

PEREGRINE FALCON

juvenile

adults

RED-MASKED PARAKEET

RED-CROWNED PARROT

ROSY-FACED LOVEBIRD

ROSE-RINGED PARAKEET

HAWAIIAN CROW

ENDEMIC HAWAIIAN MONARCHS, SOLITAIRES, and *ACROCEPHALUS* WARBLER

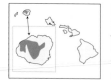

KAUAI ELEPAIO *Chasiempis sclateri*   Fairly common, local

5½–6½ in. (14–16 cm). Formerly part of one species *(Elepaio)*. Elepaios are small, variably plumaged, and active birds, *frequently flicking wings and cocking tails.* Kauai Elepaio is plainest of three species. *Adult:* gray above, white rump and throat, cinnamon breast, *wings dark with bold white wing bars and spots* (sexes similar in Kauai Elepaio). In all three elepaio species, juveniles are dull brown with buff spotting and yellow base to lower mandible and first-years are similar but without buff spots (sexes similar); second-years have plumage variably intermediate between first-year and adult of each sex. **VOICE:** Elepaios give distinctive, often repeated, raspy or whistled, three- to five-note *el-e-PAI-o*; also short squeaks and chatters. Kauai Elepaio has shorter (often three-note) song with less emphasis on any note. **SIMILAR SPECIES:** Juvenile Puaiohi larger, less active. **HABITAT:** Wet, dense, native forest of Alakai Plateau; less common in drier lower-elevation forests.

OAHU ELEPAIO *Chasiempis ibidis*   Scarce, local, endangered

5½–6½ in. (14–16 cm). Populations fragmented and declining. *Adult male:* Browner above than Kauai Elepaio and with variably extensive *black in face and throat;* adult female similar but with less black. **VOICE:** See Kauai Elepaio. Oahu Elepaio's song is longer (often five notes) with emphasis on second and fourth notes. **SIMILAR SPECIES:** Hwamei much larger. **HABITAT:** Native and non-native forests, primarily in mid-elevation valleys.

HAWAII ELEPAIO *Chasiempis sandwichensis*   Fairly common

5½–7 in. (14–18 cm). *Adults:* Similar to Oahu Elepaio but *ruddier;* average *increasing amounts of white in head,* from wetter eastern slopes to drier western slopes to mesic high-elevation areas; male has more black in throat than female. Variably intermediate juvenile, first-year, and second-year plumages. **VOICE:** See Kauai Elepaio. Hawaii Elepaio often gives classic four-note *el-e-PAI-o* song. **SIMILAR SPECIES:** Juvenile Omao larger, less active, lacks white. **HABITAT:** Mid- to high-elevation native forests, more common in wetter slopes than in drier and mesic habitats.

OMAO *Myadestes obscurus*   Fairly common

6½–7½ in. (17–19 cm). Endemic to Hawaii I. Very similar Amaui *(M. woahensis)* of Oahu, Olomau *(M. lanaiensis)* of Molokai and Lanai, and Kamao *(M. myadestinus)* of Kauai last recorded in 1825, 1980, and 1987, respectively. *Adult:* A plump, short-tailed, dark brown-and-gray thrush with buff wing stripe in flight. Juvenile similar but with pale spotting (see Puaiohi). **VOICE:** Jumbled thrushlike song: *wheech-eech-chup-chup-weechy-chup.* Also dry rattle, "police whistle," mew, and other short notes. **SIMILAR SPECIES:** Hawaii Elepaio smaller; Hwamei redder with distinct eye markings. **HABITAT:** High-elevation wet forests and mesic scrub.

PUAIOHI *Myadestes palmeri*   Uncommon, local, endangered

6–7 in. (16–18 cm). The remaining thrush on Kauai. *Adult:* Smaller then Omao with *distinct whitish eye-ring.* *Juvenile:* Similar to adult but with buff spotting above, mottling below, pale tips to wing coverts. **VOICE:** Tremulous, flutelike *jeer-jure-weet;* call a dry buzzy *jjjent.* **HABITAT:** Wet native-forest gulches.

MILLERBIRD *Acrocephalus familiaris*   Local, endangered

4½–5 in. (11–12 cm). Endemic to nw. Hawaiian Is. Recently reintroduced from Nihoa to Laysan after extirpated from latter in 1923. Small, *plain brown* bird (ages and sexes alike). **VOICE:** A variable series of notes recalling song of Marsh Wren (p. 316). Also a dry *jat.* **HABITAT:** Low-lying scrub.

KAUAI ELEPAIO
first-year
adult

OAHU ELEPAIO
adult male
juvenile
second-year male

adult female wet side
second-year female wet side
first-year
adult female high elevation

adult male wet side
adult male dry side
HAWAII ELEPAIO

OMAO
adult

PUAIOHI
juvenile

MILLERBIRD

adult

INTRODUCED PASSERINES in HAWAII

NORTHERN MOCKINGBIRD *Mimus polyglottos*   Uncommon, introduced
See p. 292. Introduced to HI in 1928. Found in dry habitats of all se. Hawaiian Is.; accidental in nw. Hawaiian Is. **SIMILAR SPECIES:** See Common Myna.

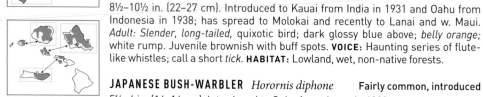

WHITE-RUMPED SHAMA *Copsychus malabaricus*   Fairly common, introduced
8½–10½ in. (22–27 cm). Introduced to Kauai from India in 1931 and Oahu from Indonesia in 1938; has spread to Molokai and recently to Lanai and w. Maui. *Adult: Slender, long-tailed,* quixotic bird; dark glossy blue above; *belly orange;* white rump. Juvenile brownish with buff spots. **VOICE:** Haunting series of flute-like whistles; call a short *tick.* **HABITAT:** Lowland, wet, non-native forests.

JAPANESE BUSH-WARBLER *Horornis diphone*   Fairly common, introduced
5½–6 in. (14–16 cm). Introduced to Oahu from Japan in 1929; spread to other se. Hawaiian Is. Much more often heard than seen. Small, brownish; *pale supercilium and dark eye line* (ages and sexes similar). **VOICE:** Distinctive haunting *hooohweeeo,* carries across slopes and valleys. **HABITAT:** Mid- to high-elevation scrub, often on ridges; in winter to dense lower-elevation habitats.

JAPANESE WHITE-EYE *Zosterops japonicus*   Common, introduced
4½ in. (11–12 cm). Introduced to HI from Japan in 1929–1937; rapidly spread throughout all se. Hawaiian Is.; accidental vagrant to nw. Hawaiian Is. Small, active, *bright green above,* yellow throat and breast, white below; *bold white eye-ring* (ages and sexes similar). Often in small groups. **VOICE:** Series of high-pitched *jeet* notes, variable in pitch. **SIMILAR SPECIES:** Greenish Hawaiian finches duller, not as white ventrally, lack white eye-ring. **HABITAT:** All habitats from lowland residential areas to high-elevation native forests and alpine scrub.

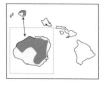

GREATER NECKLACED LAUGHINGTHRUSH   Uncommon, introduced
Ianthocincla pectoralis
11–13 in. (28–34 cm). Introduced to Kauai from Asia in 1919. A large jaylike babbler, primarily *brownish olive above,* white below, with black-and-white cheeks and *blackish blue patch to side of neck* (ages and sexes similar). Usually travels in loose flocks. **VOICE:** Song a series of loud pure whistles; *wheet* contact calls. **HABITAT:** Moist lowland woods of ne. Kauai; scarce on Alakai Plateau.

HWAMEI *Garrulax canorus*   Uncommon to fairly common, introduced
8–10 in. (21–25 cm). Introduced from China in 1890s–1920s to Oahu, Kauai, Maui, and Hawaii I.; now scarce on Oahu. Reddish brown with distinct *pale blue eye patch and line* (ages and sexes similar). **VOICE:** Song recalls strident, jeering Northern Mockingbird. Heard more than seen. **HABITAT:** Moist forests.

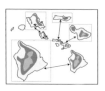

RED-BILLED LEIOTHRIX *Leiothrix lutea*   Uncommon to common, introduced
5½–6 in. (14–15 cm). A popular cage bird, introduced to the six larger se. Hawaiian Is. in 1918–1929; subsequently extirpated from Kauai. Medium-small, grayish and greenish with *yellow throat* and wing edging, *bright red bill,* and notched tail (ages and sexes similar). Frequently travels in groups. **VOICE:** Pleasing series of whistles, similar to Hwamei but less jeering. **HABITAT:** Mid- to upper-elevation forests; can disperse upslope in late summer to highest peaks.

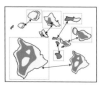

EURASIAN SKYLARK   Uncommon to common, introduced and vagrant
Alauda arvensis
See p. 354. Introduced to HI in 1870; currently scarce on Kauai and uncommon on Oahu. Also an accidental vagrant from Asia to nw. Hawaiian Is. Found in open habitats, most commonly mid- to high-elevation pastures.

NORTHERN
MOCKINGBIRD

Kauai
adult

wing-
flashing

juvenile

WHITE-
RUMPED
SHAMA

Oahu adult

JAPANESE
BUSH-
WARBLER

JAPANESE
WHITE-EYE

GREATER
NECKLACED
LAUGHINGTHRUSH

HWAMEI

RED-BILLED
LEIOTHRIX

EURASIAN
SKYLARK

INTRODUCED ESTRILDIDAE FINCHES in HAWAII

Estrildid finches are popular, small-bodied, active cage birds originally from Africa and Asia. In HI, most found in tight flocks of dozens, to thousands. Ages and/or sexes similar unless noted.

LAVENDER WAXBILL *Estrilda caerulescens*   Scarce to uncommon, introduced
4–4½ in. (10–11 cm). Introduced or escaped in Oahu and Hawaii I. in 1965; now scarce on Oahu. *Pale lavender-gray* with thin black mask and *dark red bill, vent, and tail*. Found singly or in small groups. **VOICE:** Two- to three-note *tsee-tsee-tseer*. **HABITAT:** Dry residential areas, scrub.

ORANGE-CHEEKED WAXBILL *Estrilda melpoda*   Uncommon, exotic
4 in. (10 cm). Introduced or escaped in Maui in 1989, where population is declining. *Adult:* Plain (unbarred) gray and brown plumage with *round orange cheek patch*, red bill, *red rump*, and *black tail*. Juvenile browner with pale cheek patch. **VOICE:** Rapid series of cheeps. **SIMILAR SPECIES:** Common Waxbill barred, lacks red rump. **HABITAT:** Dry residential areas and scrub.

COMMON WAXBILL *Estrilda astrild*   Common, introduced
4-5 in. (10–12 cm). Introduced or escaped in Oahu in 1973; spread and rapidly expanding on Kauai, Maui, Hawaii I., and Molokai. *Adult:* Gray crown, white throat, red bill, *elongated red mask*; body brownish, *finely barred black*. Juvenile brown with dull red eye patch. **VOICE:** Raspy *jee-jeh-jeya*; calls drier than Orange-cheeked Waxbill's. **HABITAT:** Grassy fields; move according to grass-seed production.

RED AVADAVAT *Amandava amandava*   Fairly common, introduced
3½–4 in. (9–10 cm). Introduced or escaped in Oahu in early 1900s; since spread to Kauai, Maui, and Hawaii I. *Adult male:* Primarily *dark red with white spots*; black wings and tail. *Adult female:* Primarily *gray with white spots*; red bill and rump stand out. Juvenile brown with dark bill, buff wing bars. **VOICE:** High-pitched *cheets*. **HABITAT:** Grassy fields, responding to grass-seed production.

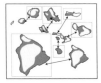

JAVA SPARROW *Lonchura oryzivora*   Fairly common, introduced
5½–6½ in. (14–17 cm). Introduced or escaped on Oahu in 1960s; spread to other se. Hawaiian Is. *Adult: Black head with white face patch*; back and breast gray; belly pinkish; *large red bill*. *Juvenile:* Browner, bill dull red. **VOICE:** Melodic jumbled *pseeps* and whistled *pseews*; call a dry *chep*. **SIMILAR SPECIES:** Juvenile Chestnut Munia. **HABITAT:** Residential areas, bird feeders.

AFRICAN SILVERBILL *Euodice cantans*   Fairly common, introduced
4–5 in. (10–12 cm). Introduced or escaped on Hawaii I. in 1960s; spread to other se. Hawaiian Is. Pale brown head, *white underparts*, dark brown wings and tail, *silver bill*. **VOICE:** Gives distinctive metallic *pit* notes in flight. **HABITAT:** Scrublands, more common in dry areas.

SCALY-BREASTED MUNIA *Lonchura punctulata*   Common, introduced
See p. 378. Introduced to Oahu in 1866; had spread to other se. Hawaiian Is. by 1900. Found in grassy fields, cemeteries, lawns, and forest edges up to medium-high elevations.

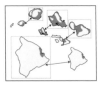

CHESTNUT MUNIA *Lonchura atricapilla*   Fairly common, introduced
4½–5 in. (11–12 cm). Introduced or escaped on Oahu in 1959; spread or escaped on most other se. Hawaiian Is. (recently to Hawaii I.). *Adult:* Chestnut body, black head, large silver bill. *Juvenile:* Brown with *gray bill*. **VOICE:** Nondescript *tips* and *cheps*. **SIMILAR SPECIES:** Juvenile Scaly-breasted Munia has blacker bill. **HABITAT:** Grassy and weedy fields, farms, cemeteries, residential areas.

INTRODUCED ESTRILDIDAE FINCHES

LAVENDER WAXBILL

adult

ORANGE-CHEEKED WAXBILL

COMMON WAXBILL

adult

RED AVADAVAT

adult male

adult female

juvenile

AFRICAN SILVERBILL

adult

JAVA SPARROW

juvenile

SCALY-BREASTED MUNIA

adult male

juvenile

CHESTNUT MUNIA

adult

INTRODUCED OLD WORLD SPARROW, CARDINALS, and TANAGERS in HAWAII

HOUSE SPARROW *Passer domesticus*
Common, introduced

See p. 378. Introduced to HI in 1866–1871. Found in urban, pastoral, and some rural habitats throughout se. Hawaiian Is. but most commonly in downtown area of cities and large towns.

NORTHERN CARDINAL *Cardinalis cardinalis*
Fairly common, introduced

See p. 388. Introduced to HI in 1929. A familiar bird of lowland and occasionally higher-elevation forests. Found commonly in suburban and scrubby habitats throughout se. Hawaiian Is.; accidental vagrant to Nihoa, nw. Hawaiian Is.

RED-CRESTED CARDINAL *Paroaria coronata*
Common, introduced

7–8 in. (18–20 cm). This and the following three species are in the tanager family, Thraupidae, and reside in S. America. Red-crested Cardinal introduced to Oahu in 1928 and spread to Niihau, Kauai, Molokai, Lanai, and Maui; vagrant to Hawaii I. *Adult:* Gray and white with *noticeably crested red head* extending to center breast in triangular point. *Juvenile:* Similar but head brown. A tame and confiding species in HI. **VOICE:** Pure melodious two-note whistles in vireo-like phrases. Call a short ascending *waenk*. **SIMILAR SPECIES:** Yellow-billed Cardinal. **HABITAT:** Open parks, coastal strands, and residential areas; restricted to low-lands.

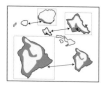

YELLOW-BILLED CARDINAL *Paroaria capitata*
Common, introduced

6–7 in. (16–18 cm). Introduced to Hawaii I. probably in 1960s. Replaces Red-crested Cardinal on this island. *Adult:* Dark gray and white with dark red head and black throat extending to center breast; *bill orange-yellow. Juvenile:* Similar but head brown. **VOICE:** Double-noted *whee-cheer* frequently repeated; call a harsh *craark*. **SIMILAR SPECIES:** Red-crested Cardinal has noticeable crest, red (rather than black) point extending to breast. **HABITAT:** Scrubby forest along coastal strands, beach parks.

SAFFRON FINCH *Sicalis flaveola*
Uncommon to common, introduced

5½–6½ in. (14–16 cm). Introduced or escaped on Oahu and Hawaii I. in 1965 and Kauai in 2004. *Adult male: Bright lemon yellow* and greenish with *orange wash to forecrown and throat. Juvenile:* Largely brownish with dark streaking to back and yellow wash to nape and breast; *faint malar streak and supercilium.* Adult female similar to juvenile but brighter. Occasionally found in flocks of hundreds on Hawaii I., fairly common on Oahu, and uncommon on Kauai. **VOICE:** Song a series of clear, high-pitched *seep-seeup-tsee-tseep*, etc., continuing for several minutes or more. Single or double-noted calls similar. **SIMILAR SPECIES:** Yellow-fronted Canary similar to juvenile Saffron Finch but has much more distinct dark malar streak and pale supercilium. **HABITAT:** Lowland residential areas, coastal strands, city and beach parks.

YELLOW-FACED GRASSQUIT *Tiaris olivaceus*
Scarce, exotic

3½–4½ in. (9–11 cm). Introduced or escaped on Oahu by 1974. *Adult male:* Largely olive and gray with distinct *yellow supercilium and throat and black fore-crown, face, and breast. Juvenile and female:* Pale grayish olive with *pale yellow lores,* and *pale crescent above and below eye.* **VOICE:** Very rapid and high-pitched trill, *ti-ti-ti-ti-ti-ti*, recalls Chipping Sparrow but higher pitched. **HABITAT:** Weedy or grassy fields. Only sporadically observed, singly or in pairs.

INTRODUCED OLD WORLD SPARROW, CARDINALS, AND TRUE TANAGERS

HOUSE SPARROW

female

male

NORTHERN CARDINAL

female

male

RED-CRESTED CARDINAL

adult

juvenile

YELLOW-BILLED CARDINAL

adult

juvenile

SAFFRON FINCH

adult

juvenile

YELLOW-FACED GRASSQUIT

female

adult male

ENDEMIC, LARGE-BILLED, and REDDISH HAWAIIAN FINCHES

Hawaiian finches, subfamily Drepanidinae, form a large diverse group of the family Fringillidae (p. 380) that became established in the Hawaiian Is. 3 to 7 million years ago and has since shown spectacular adaptive radiation in bill forms.

LAYSAN AND NIHOA FINCHES
Local, endangered

Telespiza cantans and *T. ultima*

6–7½ in. (15–19 cm). Endemics to nw. Hawaiian Is. *Adult male: Yellow head and underparts,* gray and green back, thick bill. *Adult female:* Duller, variable. *Juvenile: Streaked* brown. Nihoa Finch (not shown) smaller, bill stubbier. **VOICE:** Tinkling songs and calls. **HABITAT:** Laysan: scrub, beaches; Nihoa: rocks.

PALILA   *Loxioides bailleui*
Uncommon, endangered

6–7½ in. (16–19 cm). Endemic to Hawaii I. *Adult:* Bright *yellow head and breast;* gray back, black wings edged yellow; *black parrotlike bill.* Female slightly duller, juvenile more so. **VOICE:** Finchlike phrases, including *pa-li-la* or *pa-li-la-la.* **HABITAT:** Dry forest; feeds on green seedpods.

MAUI PARROTBILL   *Pseudonestor xanthophrys*
Scarce, local, endangered

5–6 in. (13–15 cm). Endemic to e. Maui. *Adult male:* Olive above, yellow *supercilium,* face, throat, underparts; *parrotlike bill with overhanging upper mandible. First-year female:* Duller olive above, lacks yellow. Adult female, first-year male intermediate. **VOICE:** Descending melodic notes recalling Canyon Wren (p. 316). Call a strident *chet,* also a melodic *see-uw.* **HABITAT:** Wet upland forest.

AKOHEKOHE   *Palmeria dolei*
Uncommon, local, endangered

6½–7 in. (16–18 cm). Formerly known as "Crested Honeycreeper." *Adult: Blackish* starlinglike bird, white crest; *orange eye patch and nape* (sexes similar). *Juvenile:* Duller, reduced crest. **VOICE:** Variable noises; shrieks, whistled *schweep* or *ki-pur-kipur,* guttural *ako-he-ko-he,* etc. **HABITAT:** Wet upland forest.

IIWI   *Drepanis coccinea*
Uncommon to fairly common

5½–6 in. (14–16 cm). Iconic Hawaiian finch, absent or rare on Molokai, Lanai, and Oahu; uncommon to fairly common on Kauai, Maui, and Hawaii Is. *Adult:* Scarlet with black wings and tail; *decurved bill, bright orange-red* (sexes alike). *Juvenile:* Greenish black wings; *decurved pinkish bill;* molting birds mottled *green and red.* **VOICE:** Distinctive *cheree, che-choo, jaaa, cho-chee,* etc., with "rusty gate" quality; calls a nasal *chee-ree* or *chee-air,* or sharp whistled *pee-er.* **SIMILAR SPECIES:** Apapane. **HABITAT:** Upland forest; flowers, berries.

APAPANE   *Himatione sanguinea*
Fairly common to common

4½–5½ in. (12–14 cm). The most common Hawaiian finch; similar Laysan Honeycreeper (*H. fraithii*) extinct since 1923. *Adult: Dark red;* brighter face; black wings and tail; *white vent;* curved black bill (sexes alike). *Juvenile:* Pale brown. **VOICE:** Jumbled, generally descending *kee-chew-rich-choo-choo-jit-choo-chi-chi-chi.* Short *cheet* flight calls. **SIMILAR SPECIES:** Iiwi has a red bill, white-edged tertials, lacks white vent. **HABITAT:** Upland native forest; flowering Ohia trees.

HAWAII AKEPA   *Loxops coccineus*
Uncommon, local, endangered

4–5 in. (11–13 cm). Endemic to Hawaii I. Small. *Adult male:* Bright *orange* with dusky wings and tail; bill small, *siskinlike, pale,* slightly crossed. *Adult female:* Grayish and olive with yellow-orange breast. *First-year:* Dull olive. *Second-year male:* Yellowish or duller orange than adult male. **VOICE:** High, tinkling *tseedle-lee-tseedle-lee,* etc. Calls of same quality: *tsee, tsee-wee, tsee-tle-tsee,* etc. **HABITAT:** Upland forest; forages in leaf crowns.

ENDEMIC, LARGE-BILLED, AND REDDISH HAWAIIAN FINCHES

LAYSAN FINCH

Nihoa Finch is similar (see text)

juvenile

adult female

adult male

PALILA

first-year female

MAUI PARROTBILL

adult male

AKOHEKOHE

juvenile

adult

adult

IIWI

juvenile

molting first-year

adult

juvenile

molting first-year

APAPANE

first-year

second-year male

female

adult male

HAWAII AKEPA

ENDEMIC GREEN-AND-YELLOW FINCHES
on KAUAI and OAHU

AKIKIKI *Oreomystis bairdi*　　　　　　Scarce, local, endangered

5–5½ in. (12–14 cm). Formerly "Kauai Creeper." Endemic to Kauai. *Adult:* Plain, *grayish olive above, whitish below; short decurved pink bill. First-year:* Has *white spectacles.* Creeps nuthatchlike on larger branches. **VOICE:** Wood-warblerlike *we-see-se-see-we-see,* sometimes rising. Call *tseet* or *tse-wee.* **HABITAT:** Wet, native forest.

ANIANIAU *Magumma parva*　　　　　　　　Uncommon, local

4–4½ in. (10–11 cm). Endemic to Kauai; declining. Small. *Adult male:* Uniformly *bright yellow; short curved beak. Female and first-year male:* Slightly duller. **VOICE:** Similar to Akikiki but more melodic. **SIMILAR SPECIES:** Akekee and Kauai Amakihi have black lores. **HABITAT:** Wet, native forest; flowering trees and shrubs.

AKEKEE *Loxops caeruleirostris*　　　　　　Scarce, local, endangered

4–5 in. (10–12 cm). Formerly "Kauai Akepa"; Oahu Akepa *(L. wolstenholmei)* and Maui Akepa *(L. ochraceous)* last recorded in 1893 and ca. 1980, respectively. Endemic to Kauai. *Adult male:* Olive above with *yellow rump,* underparts yellow; *black face mask.* Bill sharp, pale bluish. Female and first-year male slightly duller. **VOICE:** Song slightly more monotone than Akikiki's, often dropping: *tsee-tsee-tsee-tsu-tsu-tsee.* **SIMILAR SPECIES:** Anianiau and Kauai Amakihi have curved bills, lack yellow in rumps. **HABITAT:** Wet, native forest; feeds in canopy.

KAUAI AMAKIHI *Chlorodrepanis stejnegeri*　　　Fairly common, local

4–5 in. (11–12 cm). Endemic to Kauai. *Adult male:* Somewhat bright olive and yellow; *small black face mask.* Bill large and decurved. Female and first-year duller. **VOICE:** A rapid trill on plane or slightly descending *tse-tse-tse-tse-tsip-tsip* or *tseewe-tsewe-tsewe.* Calls nasal finchlike *churee* or *chewip,* or gnat-catcher-like *cheaaah.* **SIMILAR SPECIES:** Anianiau, Akekee. **HABITAT:** Upland native forest; flowers.

OAHU AMAKIHI *Chlorodrepanis flava*　　　　　　Fairly common

4–4½ in. (11–12 cm). Endemic to Oahu. *Adult male:* Similar to Kauai Amakihi but bill smaller; indistinct malar streak sometimes present. *Adult female:* Olive-gray above, pale greenish below; indistinct pale yellow to whitish wing bars. *Juvenile:* Grayer than female, more-distinct wing bars. **VOICE:** As in Kauai Amakihi. **SIMILAR SPECIES:** Japanese White-eye. **HABITAT:** Native and non-native forests, arboretums; flowering trees and shrubs. Moves to lower elevations in winter.

ENDEMIC GREEN-AND-YELLOW FINCHES
Kauai and Oahu

adult

juvenile

AKIKIKI

first-year
female

adult
male

ANIANIAU

AKEKEE

adult male

adult
male

**KAUAI
AMAKIHI**

juvenile

molting
first-year

OAHU AMAKIHI

ENDEMIC GREEN-AND-YELLOW FINCHES on MOLOKAI, MAUI, and HAWAII IS.

AKIAPOLAAU *Hemignathus wilsoni*   Uncommon, local, endangered
5–6 in. (13–15 cm). Endemic to Hawaii I. *Adult male:* Yellow; black lores; *upper mandible long and curved, lower mandible short and chisel-like. First-year female:* Duller; underparts olive. Adult female and first-year male intermediate, some with green bodies and bright yellow throats. **VOICE:** Distinctive, melodic series of 10–12 notes, *which-chu-chwee-chu,* often ending with two- to three-note *chwee-chwee.* Common call a pure *chuwee.* **SIMILAR SPECIES:** *Beware:* Hawaii Amakihis with deformed upper mandibles are not infrequent. **HABITAT:** Wet upland forest (formerly dry high-elevation forest). The similar but extinct Oahu Nukupuu (*H. lucidus;* not shown) and Kauai Nukupuu (*H. hanapepe;* not shown) were last collected in 1838–1841 and 1899, respectively.

HAWAII AMAKIHI *Chlorodrepanis virens*   Uncommon to common
4–4½ in. (11–12 cm). Common on Maui and Hawaii I.; uncommon on Molokai; extirpated from Lanai. *Adult male:* Similar to Kauai Amakihi but bill smaller. *Adult female:* Duller, less yellow. *Juvenile:* Dull greenish with indistinct wing bars. Females on Maui and Molokai (subspecies *wilsoni*) grayer. **VOICE:** As in Kauai Amakihi. **SIMILAR SPECIES:** Japanese White-eye. Maui Alauahio lacks mask, has straighter bill. Hawaii Creeper more olive; mask broader; bill slightly straighter, forages on branches. **HABITAT:** Wet to dry native forests; flowering trees and shrubs, where primarily a nectar feeder. Can be found in non-native, low-elevation forests in winter. Larger, extinct, Greater Amakihi *(Viridonia sagittirostris)* last collected on Hawaii I. in 1902.

MAUI ALAUAHIO *Paroreomyza montana*   Fairly common
4–4½ in. (11–12 cm). Formerly "Maui Creeper" although only occasionally creeps. Found on Maui; extirpated from Lanai. Plump. *Adult male:* Rather bright olive above and yellow below; bill fairly straight, pale. *First-year female:* Much duller, olive above, grayish below. Adult female and first-year male intermediate. Often in family groups. **VOICE:** Melodic, repeated *cheep-pur wee-da,* more musical than amakihi. Call a distinctive short *chep.* **SIMILAR SPECIES:** Hawaii Amakihi. **HABITAT:** High-elevation wet native and non-native forests. Forages primarily in leaves, on branches.

HAWAII CREEPER *Loxops mana*   Uncommon, endangered
4½–5 in. (11–13 cm). Endemic to Hawaii I. Olive above with gray-washed crown; dull, pale greenish to brownish below; small *squarish black mask;* bill *thin, sharp, slightly decurved* (sexes similar). *Juvenile and first-year:* Grayer, reduced or no blackish mask, pale supercilium. Often creeps horizontally along branches. **VOICE:** Quiet trill: *che-che-che-she-she,* often slightly descending. Call slightly nasal *cheit* or *cheerit.* **SIMILAR SPECIES:** Hawaii Amakihi. **HABITAT:** High-elevation native forests.

ENDEMIC GREEN-AND-YELLOW FINCHES
Molokai, Maui, and Hawaii Island

AKIAPOLAAU

first-year female

adult male

HAWAII AMAKIHI

juvenile

adult female

adult male

MAUI ALAUAHIO

first-year female

adult male

adult

juvenile/ first-year

HAWAII CREEPER

EXTINCT HAWAIIAN BIRDS

Thirty-three endemic Hawaiian species and an additional three subspecies are now extinct. Many other species went extinct in Hawaii before specimens were collected and are now known only from fossils. This represents the greatest loss of avian diversity in the world. Here we show a cross-section of extinct taxa.

LAYSAN RAIL *Zapornia palmeri*
A flightless species formerly on Laysan I. (last seen 1923) and introduced to Midway Atoll (last seen in 1944). Hawaiian Rail (*Z. sandwichensis*) was a forest species last collected in 1884. Many similar species in the fossil record of HI.

BISHOP'S OO *Moho bishopi*
Formerly on Molokai (last seen 1903–1904). The similar Oahu Oo (*M. apicalis*), Hawaii Oo (*M. nobilis*), and Kauai Oo (*M. braccatus*) were last recorded in 1837, 1902, and 1987, respectively.

KIOEA *Chaetoptila angustipluma*
Part of family Mohoidae, along with the oos. Little-known species from Hawaii I.; last collected about 1859.

KAKAWAHIE *Paroreomyza flammea*
Dark reddish alauahio last seen in 1963. Oahu Alauahio (*P. maculata*) was last collected on that island in 1968.

POO-ULI *Melamprosops phaeosoma*
Unique Hawaiian finch discovered on Maui in 1973. Presumably the last individual died in captivity in 2004.

KONA GROSBEAK *Chloridops kona*
Formerly found in dry high-elevation forests of Hawaii I., where its bill was used to crack seeds, producing clicking sounds. This species, the Greater Koa-Finch (*Rhodacanthis palmeri*), and the Lesser Koa-Finch (*R. flaviceps*) were last collected in dry upland forests of Hawaii I. in 1891–1896.

BLACK MAMO *Drepanis funerea*
This black relative of the Iiwi was found only in dense, ridge-line scrub forests of Molokai, where it was last collected in 1907. The Hawaii Mamo (*D. pacifica*) of Hawaii I. (last collected in 1898) had a bright yellow rump, vent, and bend of wing, thus a Hawaiian finch rather like the oos in plumage.

ULU-AI-HAWANE *Ciridops anna*
Only five specimens of this elegant Hawaiian finch were collected from Hawaii I., the last in 1892. It fed on the flower nectar or insects in native palm tree species.

OU *Psittirostra psittacea*
Formerly very common in lowland forests but last recorded on Oahu (in 1893), Maui (1901), Molokai (1907), Lanai (1931), Hawaii I. (1986), and Kauai (1989).

LANAI HOOKBILL *Dysmorodrepanis munroi*
Known from only one specimen, collected on Lanai in 1913, an adult of unknown sex. Thus, plumage variation by age and sex unknown.

KAUAI AKIALOA *Akialoa stejnegeri*
Spectacularly long-billed Hawaiian finch, last recorded on the Alakai Plateau in 1969. The similar Oahu Akialoa (*A. ellisiana*) of Oahu, Maui-nui Akialoa (*A. lanaiensis*) of Lanai, and Lesser Akialoa (*A. obscura*) of Hawaii I. were last seen in 1892, 1894, and 1903, respectively.

EXTINCT HAWAIIAN BIRDS

LAYSAN RAIL

BISHOP'S OO

adult

KIOEA

adult

adult male

KAKAWAHIE

POO-ULI

KONA GROSBEAK

BLACK MAMO

LANAI HOOKBILL

adult male

OU

adult male

ULU-AI-HAWANE

KAUAI AKIALOA

adult male

INTRODUCED FINCHES, MEADOWLARK, MYNA, and BULBULS in HAWAII

HOUSE FINCH *Haemorhous mexicanus*　　　Common, introduced

See p. 382. Introduced to HI in 1859. Found in dry, open, rural, and suburban habitats throughout se. Hawaiian Is.; casual vagrant to nw. Hawaiian Is. as far as Midway. Yellow-headed variants found more regularly in HI than in N. America.

YELLOW-FRONTED CANARY *Crithagra mozambica*　　　Common, introduced

4½–5 in. (11–13 cm). This African Fringillid finch was introduced or escaped on Oahu in 1964 and Hawaii I. in 1966. Head gray and yellow with dark lores and malar stripe creating *distinctly patterned face;* back olive; wings and tail dark; *rump and underparts bright yellow* (ages and sexes similar). **VOICE:** Song a series of high-pitched *tsees* and warbles. Call *tsee-lee.* **SIMILAR SPECIES:** Juvenile Saffron Finch. **HABITAT:** Open parks, residential areas; restricted to lowlands.

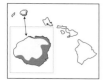

ISLAND CANARY *Serinus canaria*　　　Local, exotic

5–5½ in. (12–14 cm). Native to the Canary and Azores Is., this popular cage bird was introduced to Midway Atoll in 1909, where it has become common, especially after rats were eradicated in 1997. The cage-bird variant predominates: *entirely pale yellow* or with bleached whitish wings and tail; juveniles and some adults have variable brown-streaked patches of original native stock. **VOICE:** Melodic tinkling *tsee-tsee-tseew-tseew-tsip-tsip-tsip,* a unique sound on Midway. **HABITAT:** Ironwood trees; residential areas; open sandy fields.

WESTERN MEADOWLARK *Sturnella neglecta*　　　Fairly common, introduced

See p. 394. Introduced from N. America to Kauai in 1928. Found in pastures and open fields throughout lowlands; may be declining.

COMMON MYNA *Acridotheres tristis*　　　Common, introduced

See also p. 406. Introduced from Asia to Oahu in 1866 and had spread to all other se. Hawaiian Is. by the 1880s and to Midway in the 1970s. Found abundantly and conspicuously in urban and rural lowland habitats of Hawaii, less commonly to high-elevation pastures and forests. Gregarious; sometimes found in large flocks. White patches in wings characteristic (although see Northern Mockingbird).

RED-VENTED BULBUL *Pycnonotus cafer*　　　Common, introduced

8–9 in. (20–23 cm). A cage-bird species from India that escaped on Oahu in 1966 and is now abundant there; occasionally reported from other islands. *Black head with prominent crest;* gray body; *white rump;* red vent (ages and sexes similar). **VOICE:** A husky, guttural *chwee-juu-wur,* repeated sporadically as song. **SIMILAR SPECIES:** Red-whiskered Bulbul is slightly smaller; has a patterned white, black, and red face; and lacks a white rump. **HABITAT:** Residential areas, parks, scrub. Restricted to lowlands.

RED-WHISKERED BULBUL *Pycnonotus jocosus*　　　Fairly common, introduced

See also p. 406. Asian cage-bird species escaped on Oahu in 1965 and is now fairly common although, unlike Red-vented Bulbul, found more commonly on mid-elevation slopes, in residential areas and parks that include large trees. **SIMILAR SPECIES:** Red-vented Bulbul.

INTRODUCED FINCHES, MEADOWLARK, MYNA, AND BULBULS

orange variant
male

female

**HOUSE
FINCH**

male

**YELLOW-FRONTED
CANARY**

**ISLAND
CANARY**

**WESTERN
MEADOWLARK**

**COMMON
MYNA**

**RED-
WHISKERED
BULBUL**

**RED-VENTED
BULBUL**

LIFE LIST

PHOTO
CREDITS

INDEX

LIFE LIST

The following pages contain the American Birding Association's Checklist as of September 2019 (also available online at http://listing.aba.org/aba-check list/). The ABA Checklist "includes ABA-area breeding species, regular visitors, and casual and accidental species from other regions that are believed to have strayed here without direct human aid, and well-established introduced species that are now part of our avifauna."

Scientific names are not given below but can be found on the ABA Checklist. Note that the sequence here does not follow that of the plates in this book, which have been arranged as much for ease of identification as in accordance with our understanding of current (and frequently changing) phylogenetic sequence. (Note that the birds of Hawaii are in their own section.)

DUCKS, GEESE, AND SWANS (ANATIDAE)

_____ Black-bellied Whistling-Duck

_____ Fulvous Whistling-Duck

_____ Emperor Goose

_____ Snow Goose

_____ Ross's Goose

_____ Graylag Goose

_____ Greater White-fronted Goose

_____ Lesser White-fronted Goose

_____ Taiga Bean-Goose

_____ Tundra Bean-Goose

_____ Pink-footed Goose

_____ Brant

_____ Barnacle Goose

_____ Cackling Goose

_____ Canada Goose

_____ Hawaiian Goose

_____ Mute Swan

_____ Trumpeter Swan

_____ Tundra Swan

_____ Whooper Swan

_____ Egyptian Goose

_____ Common Shelduck

_____ Muscovy Duck

_____ Wood Duck

_____ Baikal Teal

_____ Garganey

_____ Blue-winged Teal

_____ Cinnamon Teal

_____ Northern Shoveler

_____ Gadwall

_____ Falcated Duck

_____ Eurasian Wigeon

_____ American Wigeon

_____ Laysan Duck

_____ Hawaiian Duck

_____ Eastern Spot-billed Duck

_____ Mallard

_____ American Black Duck

_____ Mottled Duck

_____ White-cheeked Pintail

_____ Northern Pintail

_____ Green-winged Teal

_____ Canvasback

_____ Redhead

_____ Common Pochard

_____ Ring-necked Duck

_____ Tufted Duck

_____ Greater Scaup

_____ Lesser Scaup

_____ Steller's Eider

_____ Spectacled Eider

_____ King Eider

_____ Common Eider

_____ Harlequin Duck

_____ Labrador Duck (extinct)

_____ Surf Scoter

_____ White-winged Scoter

_____ Stejnegner's Scoter

_____ Common Scoter

_____ Black Scoter

_____ Long-tailed Duck

_____ Bufflehead

_____ Common Goldeneye

_____ Barrow's Goldeneye

_____ Smew

_____ Hooded Merganser

_____ Common Merganser

_____ Red-breasted Merganser

_____ Masked Duck

_____ Ruddy Duck

CURASSOWS AND GUANS (CRACIDAE)

_____ Plain Chachalaca

NEW WORLD QUAIL (ODONTOPHORIDAE)

_____ Mountain Quail

_____ Northern Bobwhite

_____ Scaled Quail

_____ California Quail

_____ Gambel's Quail

_____ Montezuma Quail

PARTRIDGES, GROUSE, TURKEYS, AND OLD WORLD QUAIL (PHASIANIDAE)

_____ Chukar

_____ Gray Francolin

_____ Black Francolin

_____ Erckel's Francolin

_____ Himalayan Snowcock

_____ Gray Partridge

_____ Red Junglefowl

_____ Kalij Pheasant

_____ Ring-necked Pheasant

_____ Indian Peafowl

_____ Ruffed Grouse

_____ Greater Sage-Grouse

_____ Gunnison Sage-Grouse

_____ Spruce Grouse

_____ Willow Ptarmigan

_____ Rock Ptarmigan

_____ White-tailed Ptarmigan

_____ Dusky Grouse

_____ Sooty Grouse

_____ Sharp-tailed Grouse

_____ Greater Prairie-Chicken

_____ Lesser Prairie-Chicken

_____ Wild Turkey

FLAMINGOS (PHOENICOPTERIDAE)

_____ American Flamingo

GREBES (PODICIPEDIDAE)

_____ Least Grebe

_____ Pied-billed Grebe

_____ Horned Grebe

_____ Red-necked Grebe

_____ Eared Grebe

_____ Western Grebe

_____ Clark's Grebe

SANDGROUSES (PTEROCLIDAE)

_____ Chestnut-bellied Sandgrouse

PIGEONS AND DOVES (COLUMBIDAE)

_____ Rock Pigeon

_____ Scaly-naped Pigeon

_____ White-crowned Pigeon

_____ Red-billed Pigeon

_____ Band-tailed Pigeon

_____ Oriental Turtle-Dove

_____ European Turtle-Dove

_____ Eurasian Collared-Dove

_____ Spotted Dove

_____ Zebra Dove

_____ Passenger Pigeon (extinct)

_____ Inca Dove

_____ Common Ground Dove

_____ Ruddy Ground Dove

_____ Ruddy Quail-Dove

_____ Key West Quail-Dove

_____ White-tipped Dove

_____ White-winged Dove

_____ Zenaida Dove

_____ Mourning Dove

CUCKOOS, ROADRUNNERS, AND ANIS (CUCULIDAE)

_____ Smooth-billed Ani

_____ Groove-billed Ani

_____ Greater Roadrunner

_____ Common Cuckoo

_____ Dark-billed Cuckoo

_____ Oriental Cuckoo

_____ Yellow-billed Cuckoo

_____ Mangrove Cuckoo

_____ Black-billed Cuckoo

GOATSUCKERS (CAPRIMULGIDAE)

_____ Lesser Nighthawk

_____ Common Nighthawk

_____ Antillean Nighthawk

_____ Common Pauraque

_____ Common Poorwill

_____ Chuck-will's-widow

_____ Buff-collared Nightjar

_____ Eastern Whip-poor-will

_____ Mexican Whip-poor-will

_____ Gray Nightjar

SWIFTS (APODIDAE)

_____ Black Swift

_____ White-collared Swift

_____ Chimney Swift

_____ Vaux's Swift

_____ White-throated Needletail

_____ Mariana Swiftlet

_____ Common Swift

_____ Fork-tailed Swift

_____ White-throated Swift

_____ Antillean Palm-Swift

HUMMINGBIRDS (TROCHILIDAE)

_____ Mexican Violetear

_____ Green-breasted Mango

_____ Rivoli's Hummingbird

_____ Plain-capped Starthroat

_____ Amethyst-throated Mountain-gem

_____ Blue-throated Mountain-gem

_____ Lucifer Hummingbird

_____ Ruby-throated Hummingbird

_____ Black-chinned Hummingbird

_____ Bahama Woodstar

_____ Anna's Hummingbird

_____ Costa's Hummingbird

_____ Bumblebee Hummingbird

_____ Broad-tailed Hummingbird

_____ Rufous Hummingbird

_____ Allen's Hummingbird

_____ Calliope Hummingbird

_____ Broad-billed Hummingbird

_____ Berylline Hummingbird

_____ Buff-bellied Hummingbird

_____ Cinnamon Hummingbird

_____ Violet-crowned Hummingbird

_____ White-eared Hummingbird

_____ Xantus's Hummingbird

RAILS, GALLINULES, AND COOTS (RALLIDAE)

_____ Yellow Rail

_____ Black Rail

_____ Corn Crake

_____ Ridgway's Rail

_____ Clapper Rail

_____ King Rail

_____ Virginia Rail

_____ Rufous-necked Wood-Rail

_____ Sora

_____ Laysan Rail (extinct)

_____ Hawaiian Rail (extinct)

_____ Paint-billed Crake

_____ Spotted Rail

_____ Purple Gallinule

_____ Western Swamphen

_____ Common Gallinule

_____ Common Moorhen

_____ Eurasian Coot

_____ Hawaiian Coot

_____ American Coot

SUNGREBES (HELIORNITHIDAE)

_____ Sungrebe

LIMPKINS (ARAMIDAE)

_____ Limpkin

CRANES (GRUIDAE)

_____ Sandhill Crane

_____ Common Crane

_____ Whooping Crane

THICK-KNEES (BURHINIDAE)

_____ Double-striped Thick-knee

STILTS AND AVOCETS (RECURVIROSTRIDAE)

_____ Black-winged Stilt

_____ Black-necked Stilt

_____ American Avocet

OYSTERCATCHERS (HAEMATOPODIDAE)

_____ Eurasian Oystercatcher

_____ American Oystercatcher

_____ Black Oystercatcher

LAPWINGS AND PLOVERS (CHARADRIIDAE)

_____ Northern Lapwing

_____ Black-bellied Plover

_____ European Golden-Plover

_____ American Golden-Plover

_____ Pacific Golden-Plover

_____ Eurasian Dotterel

_____ Killdeer

_____ Common Ringed Plover

_____ Semipalmated Plover

_____ Piping Plover

_____ Little Ringed Plover

_____ Lesser Sand-Plover

_____ Greater Sand-Plover

_____ Wilson's Plover

_____ Collared Plover

_____ Mountain Plover

_____ Snowy Plover

JACANAS (JACANIDAE)

_____ Northern Jacana

SANDPIPERS, PHALAROPES, AND ALLIES (SCOLOPACIDAE)

_____ Upland Sandpiper

_____ Bristle-thighed Curlew

_____ Whimbrel

_____ Little Curlew

_____ Eskimo Curlew	_____ White-rumped Sandpiper
_____ Long-billed Curlew	_____ Buff-breasted Sandpiper
_____ Far Eastern Curlew	_____ Pectoral Sandpiper
_____ Slender-billed Curlew	_____ Semipalmated Sandpiper
_____ Eurasian Curlew	_____ Western Sandpiper
_____ Bar-tailed Godwit	_____ Short-billed Dowitcher
_____ Black-tailed Godwit	_____ Long-billed Dowitcher
_____ Hudsonian Godwit	_____ Jack Snipe
_____ Marbled Godwit	_____ Eurasian Woodcock
_____ Ruddy Turnstone	_____ American Woodcock
_____ Black Turnstone	_____ Solitary Snipe
_____ Great Knot	_____ Pin-tailed Snipe
_____ Red Knot	_____ Common Snipe
_____ Surfbird	_____ Wilson's Snipe
_____ Ruff	_____ Terek Sandpiper
_____ Broad-billed Sandpiper	_____ Common Sandpiper
_____ Sharp-tailed Sandpiper	_____ Spotted Sandpiper
_____ Stilt Sandpiper	_____ Green Sandpiper
_____ Curlew Sandpiper	_____ Solitary Sandpiper
_____ Temminck's Stint	_____ Gray-tailed Tattler
_____ Long-toed Stint	_____ Wandering Tattler
_____ Spoon-billed Sandpiper	_____ Lesser Yellowlegs
_____ Red-necked Stint	_____ Willet
_____ Sanderling	_____ Spotted Redshank
_____ Dunlin	_____ Common Greenshank
_____ Rock Sandpiper	_____ Greater Yellowlegs
_____ Purple Sandpiper	_____ Common Redshank
_____ Baird's Sandpiper	_____ Wood Sandpiper
_____ Little Stint	_____ Marsh Sandpiper
_____ Least Sandpiper	_____ Wilson's Phalarope

_____ Red-necked Phalarope

_____ Red Phalarope

PRATINCOLES (GLAREOLIDAE)

_____ Oriental Pratincole

SKUAS AND JAEGERS (STERCORARIIDAE)

_____ Great Skua

_____ South Polar Skua

_____ Pomarine Jaeger

_____ Parasitic Jaeger

_____ Long-tailed Jaeger

AUKS, MURRES, AND PUFFINS (ALCIDAE)

_____ Dovekie

_____ Common Murre

_____ Thick-billed Murre

_____ Razorbill

_____ Great Auk (extinct)

_____ Black Guillemot

_____ Pigeon Guillemot

_____ Long-billed Murrelet

_____ Marbled Murrelet

_____ Kittlitz's Murrelet

_____ Scripps's Murrelet

_____ Guadalupe Murrelet

_____ Craveri's Murrelet

_____ Ancient Murrelet

_____ Cassin's Auklet

_____ Parakeet Auklet

_____ Least Auklet

_____ Whiskered Auklet

_____ Crested Auklet

_____ Rhinoceros Auklet

_____ Atlantic Puffin

_____ Horned Puffin

_____ Tufted Puffin

GULLS, TERNS, AND SKIMMERS (LARIDAE)

_____ Swallow-tailed Gull

_____ Black-legged Kittiwake

_____ Red-legged Kittiwake

_____ Ivory Gull

_____ Sabine's Gull

_____ Bonaparte's Gull

_____ Gray-hooded Gull

_____ Black-headed Gull

_____ Little Gull

_____ Ross's Gull

_____ Laughing Gull

_____ Franklin's Gull

_____ Belcher's Gull

_____ Black-tailed Gull

_____ Heermann's Gull

_____ Mew Gull

_____ Ring-billed Gull

_____ Western Gull

_____ Yellow-footed Gull

_____ California Gull

_____ Herring Gull

_____ Yellow-legged Gull

_____ Iceland Gull

_____ Lesser Black-backed Gull

_____ Slaty-backed Gull

_____ Glaucous-winged Gull

_____ Glaucous Gull

_____ Great Black-backed Gull

_____ Kelp Gull

_____ Brown Noddy

_____ Black Noddy

_____ Blue-gray Noddy

_____ White Tern

_____ Sooty Tern

_____ Gray-backed Tern

_____ Bridled Tern

_____ Aleutian Tern

_____ Little Tern

_____ Least Tern

_____ Large-billed Tern

_____ Gull-billed Tern

_____ Caspian Tern

_____ Black Tern

_____ White-winged Tern

_____ Whiskered Tern

_____ Roseate Tern

_____ Common Tern

_____ Arctic Tern

_____ Forster's Tern

_____ Royal Tern

_____ Great Crested Tern

_____ Sandwich Tern

_____ Elegant Tern

_____ Black Skimmer

TROPICBIRDS (PHAETHONTIDAE)

_____ White-tailed Tropicbird

_____ Red-billed Tropicbird

_____ Red-tailed Tropicbird

LOONS (GAVIIDAE)

_____ Red-throated Loon

_____ Arctic Loon

_____ Pacific Loon

_____ Common Loon

_____ Yellow-billed Loon

ALBATROSSES (DIOMEDEIDAE)

_____ Yellow-nosed Albatross

_____ White-capped Albatross

_____ Chatham Albatross

_____ Salvin's Albatross

_____ Black-browed Albatross

_____ Light-mantled Albatross

_____ Wandering Albatross

_____ Laysan Albatross

_____ Black-footed Albatross

_____ Short-tailed Albatross

SOUTHERN STORM-PETRELS (OCEANITIDAE)

_____ Wilson's Storm-Petrel

_____ White-faced Storm-Petrel

_____ Black-bellied Storm-Petrel

NORTHERN STORM-PETRELS (HYDROBATIDAE)

_____ European Storm-Petrel

_____ Fork-tailed Storm-Petrel

_____ Ringed Storm-Petrel

_____ Swinhoe's Storm-Petrel

_____ Leach's Storm-Petrel

_____ Townsend's Storm-Petrel

_____ Ashy Storm-Petrel

_____ Band-rumped Storm-Petrel

_____ Wedge-rumped Storm-Petrel

_____ Black Storm-Petrel

_____ Tristram's Storm-Petrel

_____ Least Storm-Petrel

SHEARWATERS AND PETRELS (PROCELLARIIDAE)

_____ Northern Fulmar

_____ Grey-faced Petrel

_____ Providence Petrel

_____ Kermadec Petrel

_____ Trindade Petrel

_____ Herald Petrel

_____ Murphy's Petrel

_____ Mottled Petrel

_____ Bermuda Petrel

_____ Black-capped Petrel

_____ Juan Fernandez Petrel

_____ Hawaiian Petrel

_____ White-necked Petrel

_____ Bonin Petrel

_____ Black-winged Petrel

_____ Fea's Petrel

_____ Zino's Petrel

_____ Cook's Petrel

_____ Stejneger's Petrel

_____ Tahiti Petrel

_____ Bulwer's Petrel

_____ Jouanin's Petrel

_____ White-chinned Petrel

_____ Parkinson's Petrel

_____ Streaked Shearwater

_____ Cory's Shearwater

_____ Cape Verde Shearwater

_____ Wedge-tailed Shearwater

_____ Buller's Shearwater

_____ Short-tailed Shearwater

_____ Sooty Shearwater

_____ Great Shearwater

_____ Pink-footed Shearwater

_____ Flesh-footed Shearwater

_____ Christmas Shearwater

_____ Manx Shearwater

_____ Newell's Shearwater

_____ Bryan's Shearwater

_____ Black-vented Shearwater

_____ Audubon's Shearwater

_____ Barolo Shearwater

STORKS (CICONIIDAE)

_____ Jabiru

_____ Wood Stork

FRIGATEBIRDS (FREGATIDAE)

_____ Lesser Frigatebird

_____ Magnificent Frigatebird

_____ Great Frigatebird

BOOBIES AND GANNETS (SULIDAE)

———— Masked Booby

———— Nazca Booby

———— Blue-footed Booby

———— Brown Booby

———— Red-footed Booby

———— Northern Gannet

CORMORANTS (PHALACROCORACIDAE)

———— Brandt's Cormorant

———— Neotropic Cormorant

———— Double-crested Cormorant

———— Great Cormorant

———— Red-faced Cormorant

———— Pelagic Cormorant

DARTERS (ANHINGIDAE)

———— Anhinga

PELICANS (PELECANIDAE)

———— American White Pelican

———— Brown Pelican

BITTERNS, HERONS, AND ALLIES (ARDEIDAE)

———— American Bittern

———— Yellow Bittern

———— Least Bittern

———— Bare-throated Tiger-Heron

———— Great Blue Heron

———— Gray Heron

———— Great Egret

———— Intermediate Egret

———— Chinese Egret

———— Little Egret

———— Western Reef-Heron

———— Snowy Egret

———— Little Blue Heron

———— Tricolored Heron

———— Reddish Egret

———— Cattle Egret

———— Chinese Pond-Heron

———— Green Heron

———— Black-crowned Night-Heron

———— Yellow-crowned Night-Heron

IBISES AND SPOONBILLS (THRESKIORNITHIDAE)

———— White Ibis

———— Scarlet Ibis

———— Glossy Ibis

———— White-faced Ibis

———— Roseate Spoonbill

NEW WORLD VULTURES (CATHARTIDAE)

———— Black Vulture

———— Turkey Vulture

———— California Condor

OSPREYS (PANDIONIDAE)

———— Osprey

HAWKS, KITES, EAGLES, AND ALLIES (ACCIPITRIDAE)

———— White-tailed Kite

———— Hook-billed Kite

———— Swallow-tailed Kite

_____ Golden Eagle

_____ Double-toothed Kite

_____ Northern Harrier

_____ Chinese Sparrowhawk

_____ Sharp-shinned Hawk

_____ Cooper's Hawk

_____ Northern Goshawk

_____ Black Kite

_____ Bald Eagle

_____ White-tailed Eagle

_____ Steller's Sea-Eagle

_____ Mississippi Kite

_____ Crane Hawk

_____ Snail Kite

_____ Common Black Hawk

_____ Great Black Hawk

_____ Roadside Hawk

_____ Harris's Hawk

_____ White-tailed Hawk

_____ Gray Hawk

_____ Red-shouldered Hawk

_____ Broad-winged Hawk

_____ Hawaiian Hawk

_____ Short-tailed Hawk

_____ Swainson's Hawk

_____ Zone-tailed Hawk

_____ Red-tailed Hawk

_____ Rough-legged Hawk

_____ Ferruginous Hawk

_____ Long-legged Buzzard

BARN OWLS (TYTONIDAE)

_____ Barn Owl

TYPICAL OWLS (STRIGIDAE)

_____ Oriental Scops-Owl

_____ Flammulated Owl

_____ Western Screech-Owl

_____ Eastern Screech-Owl

_____ Whiskered Screech-Owl

_____ Great Horned Owl

_____ Snowy Owl

_____ Northern Hawk Owl

_____ Northern Pygmy-Owl

_____ Ferruginous Pygmy-Owl

_____ Elf Owl

_____ Burrowing Owl

_____ Mottled Owl

_____ Spotted Owl

_____ Barred Owl

_____ Great Gray Owl

_____ Long-eared Owl

_____ Stygian Owl

_____ Short-eared Owl

_____ Boreal Owl

_____ Northern Saw-whet Owl

_____ Northern Boobook

TROGONS (TROGONIDAE)

_____ Elegant Trogon

_____ Eared Quetzal

HOOPOES (UPUPIDAE)

_____ Eurasian Hoopoe

KINGFISHERS (ALCEDINIDAE)

_____ Ringed Kingfisher

_____ Belted Kingfisher

_____ Amazon Kingfisher

_____ Green Kingfisher

WOODPECKERS AND ALLIES (PICIDAE)

_____ Eurasian Wryneck

_____ Lewis's Woodpecker

_____ Red-headed Woodpecker

_____ Acorn Woodpecker

_____ Gila Woodpecker

_____ Golden-fronted Woodpecker

_____ Red-bellied Woodpecker

_____ Williamson's Sapsucker

_____ Yellow-bellied Sapsucker

_____ Red-naped Sapsucker

_____ Red-breasted Sapsucker

_____ American Three-toed Woodpecker

_____ Black-backed Woodpecker

_____ Great Spotted Woodpecker

_____ Downy Woodpecker

_____ Nuttall's Woodpecker

_____ Ladder-backed Woodpecker

_____ Red-cockaded Woodpecker

_____ Hairy Woodpecker

_____ White-headed Woodpecker

_____ Arizona Woodpecker

_____ Northern Flicker

_____ Gilded Flicker

_____ Pileated Woodpecker

_____ Ivory-billed Woodpecker (extinct)

CARACARAS AND FALCONS (FALCONIDAE)

_____ Collared Forest-Falcon

_____ Crested Caracara

_____ Eurasian Kestrel

_____ American Kestrel

_____ Red-footed Falcon

_____ Merlin

_____ Eurasian Hobby

_____ Aplomado Falcon

_____ Gyrfalcon

_____ Peregrine Falcon

_____ Prairie Falcon

PARAKEETS, MACAWS, AND PARROTS (PSITTACIDAE)

_____ Monk Parakeet

_____ Carolina Parakeet (extinct)

_____ Nanday Parakeet

_____ Green Parakeet

_____ Thick-billed Parrot

_____ White-winged Parakeet

_____ Yellow-chevroned Parakeet

_____ Red-crowned Parrot

LORIES, LOVEBIRDS, AND AUSTRALASIAN PARROTS (PSITTACULIDAE)

_____ Rose-ringed Parakeet

_____ Rosy-faced Lovebird

BECARDS, TITYRAS, AND ALLIES (TITYRIDAE)

_____ Masked Tityra

_____ Gray-collared Becard

_____ Rose-throated Becard

TYRANT FLYCATCHERS (TYRANNIDAE)

_____ Northern Beardless-Tyrannulet

_____ Greenish Elaenia

_____ White-crested Elaenia

_____ Dusky-capped Flycatcher

_____ Ash-throated Flycatcher

_____ Nutting's Flycatcher

_____ Great Crested Flycatcher

_____ Brown-crested Flycatcher

_____ La Sagra's Flycatcher

_____ Great Kiskadee

_____ Social Flycatcher

_____ Sulphur-bellied Flycatcher

_____ Piratic Flycatcher

_____ Variegated Flycatcher

_____ Crowned Slaty Flycatcher

_____ Tropical Kingbird

_____ Couch's Kingbird

_____ Cassin's Kingbird

_____ Thick-billed Kingbird

_____ Western Kingbird

_____ Eastern Kingbird

_____ Gray Kingbird

_____ Loggerhead Kingbird

_____ Scissor-tailed Flycatcher

_____ Fork-tailed Flycatcher

_____ Tufted Flycatcher

_____ Olive-sided Flycatcher

_____ Greater Pewee

_____ Western Wood-Pewee

_____ Eastern Wood-Pewee

_____ Cuban Pewee

_____ Yellow-bellied Flycatcher

_____ Acadian Flycatcher

_____ Alder Flycatcher

_____ Willow Flycatcher

_____ Least Flycatcher

_____ Hammond's Flycatcher

_____ Gray Flycatcher

_____ Dusky Flycatcher

_____ Pine Flycatcher

_____ Pacific-slope Flycatcher

_____ Cordilleran Flycatcher

_____ Buff-breasted Flycatcher

_____ Black Phoebe

_____ Eastern Phoebe

_____ Say's Phoebe

_____ Vermilion Flycatcher

SHRIKES (LANIIDAE)

_____ Red-backed Shrike

_____ Brown Shrike

_____ Loggerhead Shrike

_____ Northern Shrike

VIREOS (VIREONIDAE)

_____ Black-capped Vireo

_____ White-eyed Vireo

_____ Thick-billed Vireo

_____ Cuban Vireo

_____ Bell's Vireo

_____ Gray Vireo

_____ Hutton's Vireo

_____ Yellow-throated Vireo

_____ Cassin's Vireo

_____ Blue-headed Vireo

_____ Plumbeous Vireo

_____ Philadelphia Vireo

_____ Warbling Vireo

_____ Red-eyed Vireo

_____ Yellow-green Vireo

_____ Black-whiskered Vireo

_____ Yucatan Vireo

JAYS AND CROWS (CORVIDAE)

_____ Canada Jay

_____ Brown Jay

_____ Green Jay

_____ Pinyon Jay

_____ Steller's Jay

_____ Blue Jay

_____ Florida Scrub-Jay

_____ Island Scrub-Jay

_____ California Scrub-Jay

_____ Woodhouse's Scrub-Jay

_____ Mexican Jay

_____ Clark's Nutcracker

_____ Black-billed Magpie

_____ Yellow-billed Magpie

_____ Eurasian Jackdaw

_____ American Crow

_____ Northwestern Crow

_____ Tamaulipas Crow

_____ Fish Crow

_____ Hawaiian Crow

_____ Chihuahuan Raven

_____ Common Raven

MONARCH FLYCATCHERS (MONARCHIDAE)

_____ Kauai Elepaio

_____ Oahu Elepaio

_____ Hawaii Elepaio

LARKS (ALAUDIDAE)

_____ Eurasian Skylark

_____ Horned Lark

SWALLOWS (HIRUNDINIDAE)

_____ Bank Swallow

_____ Tree Swallow

_____ Bahama Swallow

_____ Violet-green Swallow

_____ Mangrove Swallow

_____ Northern Rough-winged Swallow

_____ Brown-chested Martin

_____ Purple Martin

_____ Cuban Martin

_____ Gray-breasted Martin

_____ Southern Martin

_____ Barn Swallow

_____ Common House-Martin

_____ Cliff Swallow

_____ Cave Swallow

CHICKADEES AND TITMICE (PARIDAE)

_____ Carolina Chickadee

_____ Black-capped Chickadee

_____ Mountain Chickadee

_____ Mexican Chickadee

_____ Chestnut-backed Chickadee

_____ Boreal Chickadee

_____ Gray-headed Chickadee

_____ Bridled Titmouse

_____ Oak Titmouse

_____ Juniper Titmouse

_____ Tufted Titmouse

_____ Black-crested Titmouse

VERDIN (REMIZIDAE)

_____ Verdin

BUSHTITS (AEGITHALIDAE)

_____ Bushtit

NUTHATCHES (SITTIDAE)

_____ Red-breasted Nuthatch

_____ White-breasted Nuthatch

_____ Pygmy Nuthatch

_____ Brown-headed Nuthatch

CREEPERS (CERTHIIDAE)

_____ Brown Creeper

WRENS (TROGLODYTIDAE)

_____ Rock Wren

_____ Canyon Wren

_____ House Wren

_____ Pacific Wren

_____ Winter Wren

_____ Sedge Wren

_____ Marsh Wren

_____ Carolina Wren

_____ Bewick's Wren

_____ Cactus Wren

_____ Sinaloa Wren

GNATCATCHERS AND GNATWRENS (POLIOPTILIDAE)

_____ Blue-gray Gnatcatcher

_____ California Gnatcatcher

_____ Black-tailed Gnatcatcher

_____ Black-capped Gnatcatcher

DIPPERS (CINCLIDAE)

_____ American Dipper

BULBULS (PYCNONOTIDAE)

_____ Red-vented Bulbul

_____ Red-whiskered Bulbul

KINGLETS (REGULIDAE)

_____ Golden-crowned Kinglet

_____ Ruby-crowned Kinglet

BUSH-WARBLERS (CETTIIDAE)

_____ Japanese Bush-Warbler

LEAF WARBLERS (PHYLLOSCOPIDAE)

_____ Willow Warbler

_____ Common Chiffchaff

_____ Wood-Warbler

_____ Dusky Warbler

_____ Golden-crowned Sparrow

_____ Harris's Sparrow

_____ White-throated Sparrow

_____ Sagebrush Sparrow

_____ Bell's Sparrow

_____ Vesper Sparrow

_____ LeConte's Sparrow

_____ Seaside Sparrow

_____ Nelson's Sparrow

_____ Saltmarsh Sparrow

_____ Baird's Sparrow

_____ Henslow's Sparrow

_____ Savannah Sparrow

_____ Song Sparrow

_____ Lincoln's Sparrow

_____ Swamp Sparrow

_____ Canyon Towhee

_____ Abert's Towhee

_____ California Towhee

_____ Rufous-crowned Sparrow

_____ Green-tailed Towhee

_____ Spotted Towhee

_____ Eastern Towhee

SPINDALISES (SPINDALIDAE)

_____ Western Spindalis

YELLOW-BREASTED CHATS (ICTERIIDAE)

_____ Yellow-breasted Chat

BLACKBIRDS (ICTERIDAE)

_____ Yellow-headed Blackbird

_____ Bobolink

_____ Eastern Meadowlark

_____ Western Meadowlark

_____ Black-vented Oriole

_____ Orchard Oriole

_____ Hooded Oriole

_____ Streak-backed Oriole

_____ Bullock's Oriole

_____ Spot-breasted Oriole

_____ Altamira Oriole

_____ Audubon's Oriole

_____ Baltimore Oriole

_____ Black-backed Oriole

_____ Scott's Oriole

_____ Red-winged Blackbird

_____ Tricolored Blackbird

_____ Tawny-shouldered Blackbird

_____ Shiny Cowbird

_____ Bronzed Cowbird

_____ Brown-headed Cowbird

_____ Rusty Blackbird

_____ Brewer's Blackbird

_____ Common Grackle

_____ Boat-tailed Grackle

_____ Great-tailed Grackle

WOOD-WARBLERS (PARULIDAE)

_____ Ovenbird

_____ Worm-eating Warbler

_____ Louisiana Waterthrush

_____ Northern Waterthrush

_____ Bachman's Warbler

_____ Golden-winged Warbler

_____ Blue-winged Warbler

_____ Black-and-white Warbler

_____ Prothonotary Warbler

_____ Swainson's Warbler

_____ Crescent-chested Warbler

_____ Tennessee Warbler

_____ Orange-crowned Warbler

_____ Colima Warbler

_____ Lucy's Warbler

_____ Nashville Warbler

_____ Virginia's Warbler

_____ Connecticut Warbler

_____ Gray-crowned Yellowthroat

_____ MacGillivray's Warbler

_____ Mourning Warbler

_____ Kentucky Warbler

_____ Common Yellowthroat

_____ Hooded Warbler

_____ American Redstart

_____ Kirtland's Warbler

_____ Cape May Warbler

_____ Cerulean Warbler

_____ Northern Parula

_____ Tropical Parula

_____ Magnolia Warbler

_____ Bay-breasted Warbler

_____ Blackburnian Warbler

_____ Yellow Warbler

_____ Chestnut-sided Warbler

_____ Blackpoll Warbler

_____ Black-throated Blue Warbler

_____ Palm Warbler

_____ Pine Warbler

_____ Yellow-rumped Warbler

_____ Yellow-throated Warbler

_____ Prairie Warbler

_____ Grace's Warbler

_____ Black-throated Gray Warbler

_____ Townsend's Warbler

_____ Hermit Warbler

_____ Golden-cheeked Warbler

_____ Black-throated Green Warbler

_____ Fan-tailed Warbler

_____ Rufous-capped Warbler

_____ Golden-crowned Warbler

_____ Canada Warbler

_____ Wilson's Warbler

_____ Red-faced Warbler

_____ Painted Redstart

_____ Slate-throated Redstart

CARDINALS, PIRANGA TANAGERS AND ALLIES (CARDINALIDAE)

_____ Hepatic Tanager

_____ Summer Tanager

_____ Scarlet Tanager

_____ Western Tanager

_____ Flame-colored Tanager

_____ Crimson-collared Grosbeak

_____ Northern Cardinal

_____ Pyrrhuloxia

_____ Yellow Grosbeak

_____ Rose-breasted Grosbeak

_____ Black-headed Grosbeak

_____ Blue Bunting

_____ Blue Grosbeak

_____ Lazuli Bunting

_____ Indigo Bunting

_____ Varied Bunting

_____ Painted Bunting

_____ Dickcissel

TANAGERS AND ALLIES (THRAUPIDAE)

_____ Red-crested Cardinal

_____ Yellow-billed Cardinal

_____ Saffron Finch

_____ Red-legged Honeycreeper

_____ Bananaquit

_____ Yellow-faced Grassquit

_____ Black-faced Grassquit

_____ Morelet's Seedeater

PHOTO CREDITS

Jeffrey A. Gordon
Page 484, Blue Grosbeak

Brian E. Small
Pages ii–iii, Horned Grebe
Page vi, Yellow-headed Blackbird
Page vii, Sandhill Crane
Page ix, Belted Kingfisher
Page xii, Steller's Jay

Page 1, Snowy Owl
Pages 14–15, Bald Eagle
Pages 460–461, Red-breasted
  Merganser
Page 462, Killdeer
Page 485, Anna's Hummingbird

Jack Jeffrey
Page i, Iiwi
Pages 408–409, Akiapolaau

INDEX

SHORE SILHOUETTES

1 Forster's Tern
2 Black Tern
3 Herring Gull
4 Cormorant
5 Loon
6 Great Blue Heron
7 Mallard
8 Pied-billed Grebe
9 Marbled Godwit
10 Greater Yellowlegs
11 Dowitcher
12 Clapper Rail
13 Whimbrel
14 Black-bellied Plover
15 Turnstone
16 Night-Heron
17 Phalarope
18 Least Sandpiper
19 Semipalmated Plover
20 Sanderling
21 Spotted Sandpiper
22 Killdeer
23 Coot
24 Green-backed Heron